ISBN 978-0-267-00248-1
PIBN 10805573

THE

ATHOLIC WORLD.

A

MONTHLY MAGAZINE

OF

GENERAL LITERATURE AND SCIENCE.

VOL. XIV.

OCTOBER, 1871, TO MARCH, 1872.

NEW YORK:

THE CATHOLIC PUBLICATION HOUSE,

9 Warren Street.

1872.

Cc

JOHN ROSS & COMPANY,
PRINTERS AND STEREOTYPERS,
27 ROSE ST., NEW YORK.

CONTENTS.

POETRY.

NEW PUBLICATIONS.

can be opposed and Christianity defended only on Catholic ground; and so far as Dr. McCosh really does either, he must assume our ground and serve in our ranks, or at any rate be on our side; and it would be churlish in us to reject or underrate his services because in certain other matters he is against us, or is not enrolled in our ranks.

It is certain that in these lectures, which show marks of much hard mental labor, the author has said many good things, and used some good arguments; but having truth only in a mutilated form, and only his private judgment to oppose to the private judgment of Positivists, he has been unable to give a full and conclusive refutation of positivism. As a Protestant trained in Protestant schools, he has no clear, well-defined catholic principles to which he can refer the particular truths he advances, and the special arguments he urges for their unity and support. His book lacks unity, lacks the mental grasp that comprehends in its unity and universality the whole subject, under all its various aspects, or in its principle, on which it depends, and which explains and justifies it. His book is a book of particulars, of details, of general conclusions drawn from particular facts and statements, like all Protestant books. This is not so much the fault of the author perhaps as of his Protestantism, which, since it rejects catholicity and has nothing universal, is essentially illogical, and can deal only in particulars or with individual things. The contents of the book are referred to no general principle, and the particular conclusions drawn are of little value, because isolated, each standing by itself instead of being reduced to its principle and co-ordinated under its law. The author lacks the conception of unity and universality; he

has particulars, but no unive
variety, but no identity—multi
but no unity, except in words.
is a great defect, and rend
work inconclusive as an arg
and exceedingly tedious to th
er as well as the reviewer.
defect runs all through the a
philosophy. In his *Intuitions*
Mind, there is no unity of
tion, but a variety of isolated
tions—no intuition of princip
the universal, but simply intel
apprehension of supersensible
culars, as in *The Human Inte*
Prof. Porter, who is a far able
than Dr. McCosh.

We are utterly unable to a
these lectures, reduce their d
ances to a universal principle,
if accepted, is decisive of the
controversy they attempt to
or if rejected proves the whole
less. Then we complain of t
thor for the indignity he offers to
tianity by suffering the Positiv
put it on the defensive, and
tempting to prove it against p
ism. Christianity is in poss
and is not called upon to
her right till strong reasons a
duced for ousting her. Conseq
it is for those who would ou
to prove their case, to make
their cause. The Christian c
versialist at this late day do
begin with an apology or d
of Christianity, but attacks tho
assail her, and puts them o
defence. It is for the scienti
Positivists, who oppose the Ch
religion, to prove their positiv
science. It is enough for the
tian to show that the positivi
alleged science is not itself p
or, if proven, that it proves n
against Christ and his church
McCosh seems to have some
cion of this, and occasional
tempts to put positivism on

[illegible], but he does it without laying down the principle which justifies it; and in doing it he renders it useless, by immediately running away after some pet speculation of his own, which gives his opponent ample opportunity to resume the offensive.

Dr. McCosh, also, more than half agrees with the Positivists, and concedes that the religious society, as such, has no right to judge of the [illegible] of the conclusions of the [illegible] on religion. "All this [illegible]," he says, pp. 5, 6, "that religious [illegible] religious men are not to be allowed to decide for us the [illegible] of science. Conceive an [illegible] Council at Rome, or [illegible] of Divines at Westminster, [illegible] Episcopal Convocation at [illegible] a Congregational Council [illegible], or a Methodist [illegible] in Connecticut (why not [illegible]?) taking upon it to decide against the discoveries of [illegible] Newton, or the grand doctrine [illegible] in our day of the conservation of force and the correlation of all the physical forces, on the ground of their being favorable or unfavorable to religion!" This concedes to the Positivists that science is independent of religion, and that religion is to be accepted or rejected as it does or does not accord with science, and wholly overlooks the fact that religion is the first science, and that nothing can be true, scientifically or otherwise, that is contrary or unfavorable to religion. Religion is the word of God, and every religious man says with the inspired apostle, "Let God be true, and every man a liar."

Dr. McCosh, of course, cannot say this, for, having no infallible authority to define what is or is not religious truth or the word of God, he is obliged to place religion in the category of opinions which may or may not be true, and therefore to deny it as the law for all intelligences. Supposing God has appointed an authority, infallible through his gracious assistance, to teach all men and nations his religion, or the truth he has revealed, and the law he commands all to obey, this authority must be competent to decide whether any alleged scientific discoveries are or are not favorable to religion, and must necessarily have the right to decide prior to all scientific investigation. If this authority decides that this or that theory is unfavorable to religion, we as religious men must pronounce it false, and refuse to entertain it. Dr. McCosh, as a Presbyterian or Protestant, would have no right to say so, but the Catholic would have the right, and it is his duty to say so; because religion is absolutely true, and the supreme law for reason as well as for conscience, and what is or is not religion, the authority unerringly decides for him. Nothing that is not in accordance with the teachings of religion can be true in science any more than in religion itself, though many things may be true that are not in accordance with the opinions and theories held by religious men.

The moment the Christian allows that the authority is not catholic; that it is limited and covers only one part of truth; and that there is by its side another and an independent authority, another and independent order of truth, he ceases to be able to meet successfully the Positivists; for truth is one, and can never be in opposition to truth—that is, in opposition to itself. Religion, we concede, does not teach the sciences, or the various facts with which they are constructed, but it does judge and pronounce authoritatively on the inferences or conclusions scientific men draw from these facts, or the ex-

planations they give of them, and to decide whether they are or are not consistent with her own teachings. If they are inconsistent with the revealed word, or with what that word implies, she pronounces them false; and, if warranted by the alleged facts, she pronounces the alleged facts themselves to be misinterpreted, misapprehended, misstated, or to be no facts. Her authority is higher than any reasonings of men, than the authority even of the senses, if it comes to that, for nothing is or can be more certain than that religion is true. We cannot as Catholics, as Christians, make the concession to the Positivists the Presbyterian doctor does, that their science is an authority independent of religion, and not amenable to it.

Dr. McCosh, we think, is unwise, in a controversy with Positivists, in separating natural theology, as he calls it, from revealed theology. The two are only parts of one whole, and, in point of fact, although distinguishable, have never existed separately at any epoch of history. The existence of God, the immateriality of the soul, and the liberty of man or free-will, are provable with certainty by reason, and are therefore truths of philosophy, but they were not discovered by unassisted reason or the unassisted exercise of our natural powers before they were taught to our first parents by the Creator himself, and have never been held as simple natural truths, unconnected with supernatural instruction or some reminiscences of such instruction. Natural theology, or philosophy, and revealed theology form one indissoluble whole, and Christianity includes both in their unity and catholicity. In defending Christianity against positivism, which denies both, we should defend both as a whole; because the natural is incomplete and

unable of itself alone to
the demands of reason, w
never sufficient for itself; a
truths necessary to complete
to solve the objections to
ing and providence of God
obtainable by reason alone
out the light of revelation. W
assert and prove miracles as
but the objections of Positi
them cannot be scientifically
ed till we have proved that th
their law in the supernatural
The inferences we draw from
cles will not be appreciated or
ed by men who deny the sup
ral and reduce God to nature.

The author in reality has
thod, but he begins by attemp
prove the being of God, th
existence of mind in man, a
reality of knowledge, and fin
the second part, that the life of
was the life of a real personag
proves the reality of his religion
offers only one argument to
that God is, and that is th
known argument from design,
he bases on the principle that
effect has its cause. He do
develop this argument, whic
been so fully done by Paley a
Bridgewater Treatises, but sim
serts its sufficiency. There ar
of design in adapting one th
another throughout the u
which can be only the effect
action of an intelligent d
Giving this argument all p
force, it does not carry the au
his conclusion beyond Plato o
totle, neither of whom was p
a theist. Plato and Aristotle b
lieved in an intelligent mind
universe, operating on an etern
created matter, forming all
from pre-existing materials, a
ranging them in an artistic
The argument from design c
no farther, and this is all that i

by Paley's illustration of the watch, which would be no illustration at all to a mind that had no intuition or conception of a designer. Neither Plato nor Aristotle had any conception of a creator or supermundane God. Whether the intelligent mind has created all things from nothing, or has only formed and disposed all things from pre-existing matter, as the soul of the world, *anima mundi*, is what can never be determined by any induction from the alleged marks of design discoverable in the universe.

We therefore hold, and have always held, that this famous argument, the only one the Baconian philosophy admits, however valuable it may be in proving or illustrating the attributes or perfections of God, when God is once known to exist, is inconclusive when relied on alone to prove that God is, or is that by which the mind first obtains the idea. It may serve as a corroborative argument, but of itself alone it cannot originate the idea in the mind, or carry one beyond an intelligent soul of the world, or the pantheism of Plato and Aristotle, and of all Gentile philosophy, except the school of Leucippus and Democritus, followed as to physics by Epicurus — unless we must also except the sceptics, Pyrrho and Sextus Empiricus. We think, therefore, the author has damaged the cause of Christianity, instead of serving it, by risking it on a single argument, by no means conclusive to the purpose. A weak and inadequate defence is worse than no defence at all.

The principle that every effect has a cause, on which the author bases his argument, is no doubt true; but we must know that the fact is an *effect* before we can infer from it that it has or has had a cause. Cause and effect are correlative terms, which connote one another; but this is no proof that this or that fact is an *effect;* and we cannot pronounce it an effect unless we know that it has begun to exist; nor even then, unless we have the intuition of cause; and no intuition even of a particular cause suffices, unless we have intuition of a universal cause. It is not so simple a thing, then, to pronounce a given fact an *effect*, and to conclude that there is between it and something else, the relation of cause and effect. It is precisely this relation that Hume, Kant, Thomas Browne, Sir William Hamilton, Dr. Mansel, Auguste Comte, John Stuart Mill, Huxley, Herbert Spencer, and all the so-called Positivists deny or relegate to the region of the unknowable. Dr. McCosh does not refute them, by assuming and arguing from the principle; he simply begs the question.

Now, we venture to tell our learned and philosophic author that his whole argument for natural theology falls to the ground before a mind that has no intuition of the relation of cause and effect, that is not previously furnished with the knowledge of design and of a designing cause. Hence, from the alleged marks of design and adaptation of means to ends, it is impossible to infer a designer. When the watch was presented for the first time to the untutored savage, he looked upon it as a living thing, not as a piece of artificial mechanism constructed by a watchmaker. He must know that it is a piece of artificial mechanism before he can conclude man has made it. There falls under our observation no more perfect adaptation of means to ends than the octagonal cell of the bee. Does the bee work by design in constructing it? Does the beaver work by design, by intelligent design, in building its dam and constructing

its house? It is generally held that the bee as well as the beaver works by instinct, or by a law of its nature, as does the swallow in building its nest. This proves that a designer cannot be inferred from the simple facts observed in nature, as the Positivists maintain. This is the condemnation of the so-called inductive philosophy. The induction, to be valid, must be by virtue of a principle already held by the mind, intuitively or otherwise, and therefore can never of itself supply or give its principle, or by itself alone obtain its principle. God is not an induction from the facts observed in nature; and the Positivists have shown, demonstrated so much, and have therefore shown that observation and induction alone can give no principle, and, therefore, end in nescience—the termination of the so-called *philosophie positive*.

Dr. McCosh is not wholly insensible to this conclusion, and seeks to escape it by proving that there is a mind in man endowed with the capacity of knowing things as they are. But if the existence of the mind needs to be proved, with what can we prove it? By consciousness, the author answers; but that is a sheer paralogism, for consciousness is simply an act of the mind, and presupposes it. God can no more be an induction from the facts of consciousness than from the facts of nature. In either case, the God induced is a generalization; in the one case, the generalization of nature, and, in the other, the generalization of consciousness. The former usually goes by the name of atheism, the latter by the name of egoism.

Dr. McCosh very properly rejects Hamilton's and Mansel's doctrine of the pure relativity of all knowledge, and Herbert Spencer's doctrine that all knowledge is restricted to the knowledge of phenomena or ances, though conceding that ances are unthinkable withoı lity beyond them, but that th‹ beyond them, and which apj them, is itself unknowable; ar tains truly that we know thing selves, both sensibles and sı sibles. We know them, he cc by intuition, or a direct loo: or beholding them by the siı tellectual force of our minc this we are not so certain, fo not ourselves know by intuiti salt is bitter and sugar swe we think the doctor knows themselves only in so far as cepts their essence or substan confounds the thing with its ties, or its accidents, as say the men, in which case he makes preciable advance on Mr.] Spencer. I know the appe and the sensible properties of but I do not know its essence stance. Has the Presbyteria tor, who seems to have a holy of Catholicity, invented a phil for the express purpose of c ing with apparent reason th tery of transubstantiation, by it conflict with the positive te: of the senses and the humaı lect?

But let that pass. The iı the doctor recognizes is er intuition, and intuition of pa or individual things, not of ples, causes, relations. And fi knowledge of those individual he holds that man rises by gı zation and abstraction—that is tion—from one degree of kno to another, till he finally att the knowledge of God distinc the world, and clothes him wi nite perfections. Yet the goc tor claims to be a philosoph‹ enjoys a high reputation as None of these individual thin

all of them together, are God, or [illegible] him; does, then, from them, [illegible] you know them, rise scientifically to him? and what by abstraction and generalization is that to which the mind attains? Only this generalization or abstraction, which as a creation of the mind is a nullity. He, like Hamilton, in this [illegible] make philosophy end in nescience.

We, of course, hold that we apprehend and know things themselves, not phenomena merely, and as they are, not as they are not—that is, in their real relations, not to us only, but in the objective world. But to know things as they are, in their real objective relations, or to know them at all, demands intuition of them, in their contingency or in their character of creatures or effects—that is to say, as existences, not as independent, self-existent beings, which they are not. And this is not possible without the intuition of the necessary, of real being, on which they depend and from which they are derived. When I say a thing is an effect, I say it has been caused, and therefore, in order to say it, I must have intuition of cause; and if I say of a thing that it is a particular cause, I deny that it is a universal cause, which I could not do without the intuition of universal cause. So when I say of a thing it is contingent, I simply deny it to be necessary being, and I could not deny a thing to be necessary being if I had no intuition of necessary being. If the author means by abstracting and generalizing our knowledge of things or individual existence, distinguishing this ideal intuition, or the intuition of real necessary and universal being—what philosophers sometimes call necessary ideas—from the intuition of things or contingent existences, along with which it is presented in thought, and as the necessary condition of our apprehending them, and by reflection and contemplation ascertaining that this ideal, necessary and universal, is really God, though not intuitively known to be God, we do not object to the assertion that we rise from our knowledge of things to the knowledge of God himself. What we deny is that God can be concluded from the intuition or apprehension of things. We rise to him from the ideal intuition, or intuition of the real and necessary, which enters the mind with the intuition of the things, and without which we never do or could have intuition of them, any more than they could exist without the creative act of real and necessary being creating them from nothing and sustaining them in existence; but it needs to be disengaged by a mental process from the empirical intuition with which it is presented.

This ideal intuition is not immediate and direct intuition of God, as the pseudo-ontologists contend, and which the church has condemned; but is intuition under the form of necessary, universal, eternal, and immutable ideas—of that which the mind, by reasoning, reflection, and contemplation, proves really is God. What misleads the author and so many others who use the argument he uses, is that the intuition of real and necessary being, and the intuition of contingencies, are given both in the same thought, the one along with the other, and most minds fail to distinguish them—which is done, according to St. Thomas, by the *intellectus agens*, in distinction from the passive or receptive intellect—and hence they suppose that they conclude the ideal intuition from the empirical intuition. This is decidedly the case with Dr. McCosh. The learned doctor admits intuitions, but only intuitions of individual existen-

ces—what we call empirical intuitions —whether causes or effects, not intuition of the ideal; and hence his argument for the existence of God proves nothing, for the universal is not derivable from the particular, the necessary from the contingent, nor being from existences. Had he recognized that along with, as its necessary condition, the intuition of the particular there always is the intuition of the universal, etc., he would have placed theology against positivism on an impregnable foundation. The necessary ideas, the universal, the eternal, the immutable, the necessary, connoted in all our thoughts, cannot be simply abstractions, for abstractions have no existence *a parte rei*, and are formed by the mind operating on the concrete object of empirical intuition. As these ideas are objects of intuition, they are real; and if real, they are either being or existences. But no existences are or can be necessary, universal, eternal, immutable, for they depend to be on another, as is implied in the very word existence, from *ex-stare*. Then they must be being, and identifiable in the one universal, eternal, real, and necessary being, and distinguishable from existences or things, as the creator from his creatures, the actor from the act.

We have said that the ideal intuition is not intuition of God, but of that which is God; we say now that the ideal intuition is not formally intuition of *ens* or being, as erroneously supposed by some to be maintained by Gioberti and Dr. Brownson, but of that which is *ens*. The process of demonstrating that God is consists in identifying, by reflection and reasoning, the necessary ideas or ideal intuition with real, necessary, universal, eternal, and immutable being, and real and necessary being in which they are all identified with God. This process is demonst not intuition. When I say, syllogism, the conclusion follo cessarily from the premises, I intuition of the necessary, could not say it; but I have tuition of the fact that the ne is being, far less that it is God is known only by reflection an soning, disengaging the ideal the empirical. The idea m real, or there could be no intui it, but if real, it must be being; if it must be real and necessary and real and necessary being i So of all the other necessary As the intuition is of both th or necessary and the conting its principle, and in their real re it gives the principles of a co demonstration of the being o as creator, and of the unive the effect of his creative act therefore of the complete refu of pantheism. The vice o McCosh's argument is that i ceeds on the denial of ideal tion, and the assumption that God, is obtainable by general and abstraction from the indi things given in empirical int It is not obtained by reflection them, but from the ideal int never separable from the empi

This process of proving tha is may be called the ideal cess, or the argument from u sal and necessary ideas intu given. It is not *a priori*, b the ideal is held by int nor is it an argument from ideas, as Descartes held; nor— really objective, and present mind—is it an argument fro primitive beliefs or constituent ciples of human nature, as Dr and the Scottish school maint and which is only another fo the Cartesian doctrine of ideas; or an argument drawn

our own *fonds*, as Leibnitz imagined, or from the *a priori* cognitions or necessary forms of the intellect, as Kant held, and which is only the doctrine of the Scottish school of Reid and Stewart differently stated; but from principles or data really presented in intuition, and along with the empirical intuition of things. It places, therefore, the being of God on as firm a basis and renders it as certain to the understanding as our own existence, or as any fact whatever of which the human mind has cognizance; indeed, renders it absolutely certain and undeniable. But while we say this, and while we maintain that the ideal intuition is given along with the empirical intuition, with which our author confounds it, and from which philosophy or natural theology disengages it, we by no means believe that the race is indebted to this ideal or metaphysical process—which is too difficult not only for the Positivists, but for their great opponent, Dr. McCosh—for the origin of their belief in God. All ages and nations, even the most barbarous and savage tribes, have some sort of belief in God, some religious notions which imply his existence; and, hovering above the various Eastern and Western mythologies, we find the belief in one God or the divine unity, though neglected or rejected for the worship of inferior gods or demons, or the elements—that is, the worship of creatures, which is idolatry, since worshipped as God. The ignorant savage, but a grade above the beasts, has never risen to the conception of God or of the Great Spirit from the contemplation of nature, nor has he attained to religious conceptions by a law of his nature or by instinct, as the bee constructs its cell or the

It is very true, nothing more true than that "the heavens show forth the glory of God, and the firmament declareth the work of his hands," but to him only who has the idea of God or already believes that he is. Nothing more true than God can be traced in all his works, or that "the invisible things of him, even his eternal power and divinity, are clearly seen from the creation of the world, being understood by the things that are made," but only by those who have already learned that he is, are intent on answering the question, *Quid est Deus?* not the question, *An sit Deus?* Hence we so far agree with the traditionalist, not indeed that the existence of God cannot be proved by reason prior to faith, but that, as a fact, God revealed himself to man before his expulsion from the garden; and the belief, clear and distinct or dim and confused, in the divine being, universally diffused among all races and conditions of men, originated in revelation and is due to the tradition, pure or impure, in its integrity or mutilated and corrupted, of the primitive revelation made by God himself to man. In this way the fact of the universality of the belief in some form is a valid argument for the truth of the belief, and we thus obtain a historical argument to corroborate the already conclusive ideal or metaphysical argument, the principles of which we have given.

We bear willing testimony to the good-will and laudable intention of our author, but we cannot regard him as able, with his mutilated theology and his imperfect and rather superficial philosophy—though less superficial than the philosophy generally in vogue among British and American Protestants—to carry on a successful war against the Positivists. We are almost tempted to say to him:

> Non tali auxilio nec defensoribus istis
> Tempus eget.

He is too near of kin to the Positiv-

ists themselves, and adopts too many of their principles and conclusions, to be able to battle effectively against them. No doubt he urges much that is true against them, but his arguments, as far as effective, are inconsistent with his position as a Protestant, and are borrowed from Catholicity, or from what he has retained from Catholic instruction and Catholic tradition, not from his Protestantism. Having no authority but his own private interpretation of the Scriptures to define what is or is not Christianity, he knows not how much or how little he must defend against the Positivists, or how much or how little he is free to concede to them. He practically concedes to them the Creator. He defends God as the efficient cause, indeed, but not as Creator, producing all things by his word from nothing. He would seem to hold it enough to defend him as the organizer and disposer of materials already furnished to his hand. God does not seem to him to be his own *causa materialis.* He works on a pre-existing matter. He constructs, the author concedes, the existing worlds out of "star-dust," or disintegrated stars, without telling us who made the stars that have dissolved and turned to dust, and without bearing in mind, or without knowing, that Christianity teaches us that "in the beginning God *created* the heavens and the earth," and therefore could not have formed them out of "star-dust" or any other material.

The Protestant divine accepts and defends Darwin's theory of the origin of species by "natural selection," though he does not believe that it applies universally, or that man has been developed from the ape or the tadpole. He denies that Huxley's protoplasm can be developed from protein, or life from dead matter; maintains that all life proceeds from a living organism, that the plant can spring only from a seed, and the animal only from a living cell or germ; and yet concedes that some of the lower forms of organic life may spring or may have sprung from spontaneous generation, and even goes so far as to tell us that some of the most eminent of the fathers held or conceded as much. What becomes, then, of the assertion that life cannot be evolved from dead matter? He would seem to hold or to concede that man lived, for an indefinite time, a purely animal life, before the Almighty breathed into his nostrils and he became a spiritual man, and quotes to prove it St. Paul's assertion that "not first that which is spiritual, but that which is animal; afterwards that which is spiritual" (1 Cor. xv. 46). He seems, in fact, ready to concede any and everything except the intelligent Mind recognized by Plato and Aristotle, that has arranged all things according to a preconceived plan, and throughout the whole adapted means to ends. He insists on efficient causes and final causes, but hardly on God as the *causa causarum* or as the *causa finalis* of all particular final causes.

Throughout, as we have already remarked, there is a want of unity and universality in his philosophy, as there necessarily must be in his Protestant theology, and a sad lack of logical consistency and order, or co-ordination. His world is a chaos, as is and must be the Protestant world. Herbert Spencer undertakes to explain the universe without God, or, what is the same thing, with an absolutely unknowable God, which is of course an impossibility; but he has a far profounder intellect and a far more logical mind than Dr. McCosh. He is heaven-wide from the truth, yet nearer to it than his Presbyterian critic. His logic is good;

being granted, his
ough absurd, can-
His error lies in his
if you correct them,
ne. He will correct
arrive at just conclu-
her assistance. But
one who, however
talk about them,
his doctrines to their
es, or reasons from
is a genuine Protes-
be refuted in refuting
hich vary with the exi-
gument, and are real-
at all, but must be
; and when you have
wice three are six, you
ove that three times
.

man—and he is, per-
average of Presbyte-
the last man in the
pt the refutation of
Protestant can do it.
vowed Positivists we
ard Protestant Chris-
nsignificant a matter
It is too vague and
uncertain and indefi-
stantial and intangi-
natic and illogical, to
ast respect from them.
glance that it is too
gion and too much to
It cannot, with its
s and its whole deni-
nent before an intel-
who has a scientific
The Positivist rejects
ourse, but he respects
logical system, con-
elf, coherent in all its
him there is no *via*
it and positivism. If
ositivist, he says open-
Catholic, by no means
which he looks upon
hing nor another; and
t, could we cease to be

a Catholic, we should be a Positivist, for to a logical mind there is no medium between the church and atheism. The middle systems, as Protestantism, Rationalism, Deism, etc., are divided against themselves, and cannot stand, any more than a house divided against itself. Their denials vitiate their affirmations and their affirmations vitiate their denials. They are all too much or too little.

The Positivists reject for what they call the scientific age both theology and metaphysics. They believe in the progress of the race, and indeed in all races, as does Dr. McCosh. They distinguish in the history of the human race or of human progress three epochs or stages—first, the theological; second, the metaphysical; and third, the scientific. Theology and metaphysics each in its epoch were true and good, and served the progress of man and society. They have now passed away, and the race is now entering the scientific age, which is the final stage, though not to last for ever; for when the field of science is exhausted, and all it yields is harvested, the race will expire, and the world come to an end, as having no more work to do. It will be seen there is here a remarkable difference between the real Positivists, or believers in Auguste Comte, and our author and his Protestant brethren. The Positivists never calumniate the past, but seek to appreciate its services to humanity, to acknowledge the good it did, and to bury it with honor, as the children of the New Dispensation did the Old, when it had lived its day. One of the finest appreciations from the point of view of humanity of the services of the mediæval monks we have ever read is from the pen of M. E. Littré, the chief of the French Positivists, and one of the most learned men of France. It said not all a Catholic would say, but

scarcely a word that could grate on a Catholic ear. Dr. McCosh also believes in progress, in the progress of our species, and, for aught we know, in the progress of all species and genera, and that we outgrow the past; but he takes pleasure only in calumniating it, and like a bad son curses the mother that bore him. Because he has outgrown his nurse, he contends the nurse was of no use in his childhood, was a great injury, and it would have been much better to leave him to himself, to toddle about at will, and toddle into the fire or the cistern, as he saw proper.

Now, we think, if one believes in the progress of the species or the perfectibility of man by development or by natural agencies, the Positivist doctrine is much the most reasonable as well as far the most amiable. Its effect, too, is far better. We—we speak personally—owed much to the doctrine, which we borrowed not from Comte, but from Comte's master, Saint-Simon, the influence of which, under the grace of God, disposed us to return to the old church. It softened the animosity, the bitter hatred, toward the past which we had inherited from our Protestant education, and enabled us to study it with calm and gentle feelings, even with gratitude and respect, and disposed us to view it with impartiality and to appreciate it with justice. Studying the past, and especially the old church which we had complacently supposed the race had outgrown as the man has outgrown the bib and tucker of his childhood, in this new and better mood, we soon discovered that there was much more in the past than we had ever dreamed of, and that it was abundantly able to teach us much more than we or any of our Protestant contemporaries supposed; and we were not long in beginning to doubt if we had really outgrown it, nor ... convinced that, instead of ... it, we had fallen below ... old church, the central ... the world, was as needful to ... as in the beginning; and that, ... parison with the full noond... which beamed from her divi... tenance, the light in which ... hitherto walked, or stumbled, ... was but a fading twilight, ... night darkness.

Of course we differ far mo... positivism than does Dr. M... but we can as Catholics bet... criminate than he what is tr... just in them, and better und... and refute their errors or fal... ciples, because we have the ... truth to oppose to them, not ... certain fragments or disfigured ... of truth. It is only Catholi... can really set right the class ... Dr. McCosh wars against. Pro... cannot do it. When Theodor... er published his *Discourse of ... pertaining to Religion*, we had ... we speak personally again—ou... the Protestantism in which ... been trained. We set about ... him, and we saw at once we ... not do it on Protestant grounds, ... planted ourselves on Catholic ... as far as we then knew it, a... refutation was a total failure ... so far as we opposed to the *D...* the principles of the Catholic C... Dr. McCosh has tried his h... the volume before us against ... dore Parker and the Free R... ists, and with no success save ... as he abandons his Protestanti... quietly appropriates the arg... of Catholics, to which he has n... right than he has to his nei... horse. It was hardly gener... the learned doctor, while usin... arguments—and they were th... arguments that availed him ar... —to turn upon Catholics an...

[illegible] "ignorance and superstition." [illegible] people might dis- [illegible] whence he drew the [illegible] of wisdom and truth he [illegible],—

[illegible] Dr. McCosh's [illegible] of presenting a [illegible] of positivism, but we had already taken up from time to time the false principles, the errors and untenable theories and hypotheses, which his lectures treat, and refuted them, so far as they are hostile to Christianity, far more effectively, in our judgment, than he has done or could do. He may be more deeply versed in the errors and absurd hypotheses of the false scientists of the day, who are laboring to explain and account for the universe without creation and Providence, than we are; but we have not found in his volume anything of any value which we have not ourselves already said, and said too, perhaps, in a style more easily understood than his, and in better English than he ordinarily uses. Our readers could learn nothing of positivism from him, and just as little of the principles and reasonings that Christianity is able to oppose to it. He writes as a man who measures the known by what he himself knows, and is now and then out in his measurement.

Dr. McCosh, also, adopts rather too depreciatory a tone in speaking of our countrymen, especially considering that he has but just come among us, and knows us at best only imperfectly. We own it was no striking indication of American intelligence and judgment the importation of him to preside over one of the best Protestant American institutions of learning and science; but men often loom up larger at a distance than they are when seen close by, and there is no country in which bubble reputations from abroad more speedily collapse than our own. The doctor will find, when he has lived longer among us, and becomes better acquainted with us, that if England is nearer Germany, German speculations are known to Americans and appreciated by them at least as soon as they are by Englishmen or Scotsmen. Kant, Fichte, Schelling, Hegel, were known to American scholars before there was much knowledge of them in England or Scotland. The English and Scotch are now just becoming acquainted with and are carried away by theories and speculations in philosophy which had been examined here, and exploded more than thirty years ago by Americans. The doctor underrates the scholarship and intelligence even of his American Presbyterian friends, and there are scholars, men of thought, of science, general intelligence, in the country many degrees above Presbyterians, respectable as they are. Presbyterians are not by any means the whole American people, nor the most advanced portion of them. They are really behind the Congregationalists, to say nothing of "the ignorant and superstitious" Catholics, whose scholars are in science and learning, philosophy, theology, especially in the history of the church, it is no boast to say, superior to either, and know and understand better the movements of the age, intellectual, moral, social, and political theories, crotchets, and tendencies of the present, than any other class of American citizens. It takes more than a Dr. McCosh, although for a time a professor in Belfast, Ireland, to teach them more than they already know.

We pass over the second part of the lectures, devoted to Apologetics, as of no importance. One needs to know what Christianity is, and to have clearly in his mind the entire Christian plan, before one can suc-

cessfully defend it against the class of persons the author calls Positivists. This is more than the author knows, or as a Protestant can know. His Christianity is an indefinite, vague, variable, and uncertain opinion, and he has no conception at all of the Christian plan, or what St. Paul calls "the new creation." No doubt the miracles are provable by simple historical testimony by and to one who knows nothing of the Christian plan, or of its supernatural character; but to the unbelievers of our time it is necessary to set forth, in its unity and catholicity, the Christian *schema*, if we may be allowed the term, and to show that miracles themselves have their reason or law in the divine plan or decree, and are no more anomalies, in relation to that plan or decree, or *ex parte Dei*, than are earthquakes and volcanoes. It is only in this way we can satisfy the demand for order and regularity. The unbeliever may not be able to resist the testimony which proves the miracle a fact, but till we show him that in a miracle the natural laws are not violated, or that nature does not go out of her course, as he imagines, we cannot satisfy him that he can yield to the miracle without surrendering his natural reason, and the law and order of the universe.

Now, this the Protestant cannot do; and though he might adduce the historical evidences of Christianity satisfactory to a simpler age, or to minds, though steeped in error, yet retaining from tradition a full belief in the reality of a supernatural order, he cannot as a Protestant do it to minds that deny that there is or can be anything above nature, and that refuse utterly to admit the supernatural order, which the miracles manifest, or that reject miracles, not because the testimony is insufficient, but because they cannot be a without admitting the realit supernatural. The prejudice the supernatural must be r as the preliminary work, and be done only by presenting tianity as a whole in its u catholicity, and showing that, ing to it, the supernatural o tian order enters into the decree of God, and is nece complete what is initial in mos, or to perfect the natur and to enable it to fulfil the for which it exists, or realize tiny or final cause, in whic beatitude or supreme goo done, the prejudice against pernatural is removed, mira seen to be in the order, not of nature, as Carlyle pretend the order of the supernatu demanding only ordinary h testimony to be proved, and quently Hume's famous a against miracles, refuted by testant that has protested a shown to have no force.

Now, this requires a p knowledge of Christianity, not attainable by private ju from the Scriptures, or outsid infallible authority of the chu which the revelation of G revealed word, is deposited guardian and interpreter. M indeed, admits some treatise by Protestants into his colle works he has published un title of *Evangelical Demon* which are not without the but are valuable only on points, and on those only so fa rest on Catholic principles Catholic arguments. Christi ing supernatural, a revelatio supernatural, it, of course, w dressed to natural reason, ca determined or defined by nat son, and can be determined

THE HOUSE OF YORKE.

CHAPTER XIV.

BREAKING THE ICE.

SHORTLY after Mr. Rowan's baptism, a miniature avalanche of letters reached the Yorke family. Mrs. Rowan-Williams wrote to Edith, in a very scrawly hand, in lines that sloped down, in a depressing manner, toward the southeastern corner of the page: "Do come and make me a visit, now that Dick is at home. You have no idea how handsome, and good, and smart he is. Mr. Williams thinks the world of him; and as to Ellen—well, it wouldn't become me to say what I think. But it's of no use for her to try. Now, do come. This is the twentieth time I have asked you. We will go everywhere, see all that is worth seeing, and you shall be waited on like a lady, as you are.

"So the old clay bank has slipped down again, and the bushes have tumbled into the mud, and the men have piled their lumber over the ashes of my poor home. O Edith! my heart is buried under those boards. Thank you, dear, for going to see it for me."

Dick wrote: "Which is Mohammed, and which is the mountain? I must see you, and if you cannot come here, I shall go to Seaton, though that would not be easy for me to do now. Besides, I want you to see your namesake. I have not long to stay, for the ship is about ready to start, and we take our cargo in at New York. It would be almost like a soldier deserting his army on the eve of battle for me to go away now. Do come if you can. It seems to me that you must wish to."

This young man, we may remark, has got quite beyond the model letter-writer and the practice of penmanship. He writes quite in his own way, and is a very creditable writer, too. He has also a fair education, and can converse more intelligently on most subjects of general interest than many a young man for whom education has done its best. When Dick Rowan spoke, he said something, and one never heard from his lips inanities, meanness, nor malice. Neither did he say much of such things, even in condemnation. He looked on them with a sort of wonder, a flitting expression of disgust, then forgot all about them. His time had been too much occupied, his mind too busy for trifling. He had studied constantly and methodically, and the little library in his cabin on board ship was a treasury of science, art, and *belles-lettres*. So far as it went, it was the library of a man of cultivated mind. His life, too, had educated him, and been a perpetual commentary on, or illustration or refutation of, his books. The phenomena of the sea he had studied not merely as a sailor, but as a student of natural history. Whatever culture can be derived from the intelligent visiting of foreign countries, without going into society there, that he had. He had not spent his time about wharves, and ships, and sailors' boarding-houses. Aside from his own tastes, he never forgot that he was aspiring toward a girl who, if she should visit these lands, would walk in palaces. Therefore, what-

have written the most dreadful things of me."

The Yorkes were highly amused by this letter. "You see, Edith, she is a dragon," her uncle said. "You will have to carry yourself very gingerly."

"I am not sure that is the best way to keep the peace with her," Mrs. Yorke remarked. "It would do with some, but she grows more overbearing with indulgence. If she were touched by sweetness and submission, it would be different. I have thought of late years that such persons are benefited by a firm resistance."

Clara also wrote: "Let mamma come with Edith, and stay at my house, of course. It is really a shame that she has never visited me in the city yet. Come right away, and we will all go back to Seaton together. You should come for poor Carl's sake, to cheer him up a little, if for nothing else, for he must lead a miserable life with that awful old woman. You would not have believed he could be so patient. Indeed, he would have left long ago, if it had not been for the hope of bringing you all back here again. If he were the only one in question, he would not stay a day."

Miss Mills also wrote in the same strain, and the result of it all was that the invitations were accepted. with a difference. "I will stop at Miss Clinton's, since you think it better," Edith said to her aunt. "But I must see a good deal of the Rowans."

"Certainly, dear," Mrs. Yorke replied. "But say as little as possible of the Rowans to Miss Clinton. It will only make her disagreeable. Hester will be happy to see the young man and his mother, and since he is a Catholic, I should think that Alice might be civil to him."

Her invitation accepted, M
ton began to look at the d
"Are you sure that the gi
very green, Carl," she asl
detest country manners."

"Oh! she is very green
was the reply.

Carl sat looking out into
den, unconscious that his co
was observing him curiously

"Are you in love with th
she asked after a moment.

Bold and hardened as
she started and shrank at th
he gave her. No words co
been more haughty and rep

"Well," she said pettish
need not look daggers at n
question is not to your likin
are not obliged to answer it

He looked out the windo
and said nothing. "She sh
to keep her claws off
thought.

No one but himself knew
price Carl Yorke was payin
expected inheritance. Th
less irritation and annoya
enforced giving up of his
and those literary labors wh
seemed to him his vocation,
constant confinement, were
more than he could bear.
thought supported him, and
that he should some day b
restore his family to their lo
and to pursue those plans
own which their reverses ha
rupted.

He was also, not quite
sciously, gaining somethin
than gold. He was seeing
deformity of selfishness, and
loveliness of that wit whos
power is to wound. In as
bitter questions, What is this
living for? what good does
do the world? echo had
the same questions in his ow
What are you living for

good does the world derive from your being in it? What in him and in others had been vices or faults, veiled with a certain decorum so as to look almost like virtues, in this woman's character were stripped of the veil, and showed in all their native hatefulness. Here, too, were free-thinking and atheism *au naturel*, without the crown on their brows, the lustre he had fancied their faces radiated, and without their airy grace. He saw a scoffer, and it was as though he saw a devil. He had not the consolation of thinking her really worse than himself, for he could not shut his eyes to the fact that the difference between them had been in manner, not in essence. He had shown more good taste and delicacy, that was all.

"After all," he thought, as he sat there that day, looking out the window, "however it may be with men, women need religion. I would not trust a woman without it. I will not retract my saying that religion is a strait-jacket, and intended only for those who cannot stand straight without it, but I begin to think that we are all of us partial lunatics."

"I have heard say that parlor was a place to parle in," remarked Miss Clinton presently.

"The orioles are building in this tree," Carl said, quite as though nothing unpleasant had happened.

She tossed her head. What did she care about orioles?

"How blood will show, both good and bad," she said with the air of one who has just discovered a great truth. "Wealth, associates, travel, occupations, education, neither will efface the signature. The original stamp remains in spite of circumstances."

At the beginning, Carl scented battle, but he assumed an air of great thoughtfulness. "You are quite right," he said. "That great *parvenu*, Adam, and that still more frightfully new person, his wife, have left an indelible stain upon their progeny. We can see it to this day, faintly in some, more strongly marked in others. And, on the other hand, that prince of the *ancien régime*, Lucifer—"

"Nonsense!" interrupted Miss Clinton. "I was going to say, if you can stop your most disagreeable and disrespectful mocking—I was going to say that you have some of the Bohemian lounging ways of your father, though you never saw him, and though you have been under the training of Charles Yorke since your babyhood."

"Do you think I have my father's ways?" Carl asked, with an air of delight. "How glad I am! No one else ever told me so, and I was afraid I might be all Arnold. My mother is, of course, an angelic lady; but some of her family have had traits which—really—well, I should a little rather not inherit. And so you think me like my father? Thank you!"

"The Arnolds and the Clintons, sir, are families from whom you may be proud to inherit anything!" the old lady cried, beating the table with her fan. "They were among the *élite* of Boston and New York when this country was a British province. We had colonial governors and judges, sir, when your father's people were painting signs and door-steps. It is rather late in the day, young man, for you to have to be told what my descent is!"

She stopped, choking with anger.

The young man seemed to be much interested in this recital. "Indeed!" he said, "this is very delightful to know, and it makes such a difference! Though I had always understood that your descent had been very—precipitous!"

Miss Clinton glared at him, unable to utter a word, and seemed only just able to restrain herself from throwing her snuff-box at him.

He rose wearily, and went out of the room, having half a mind to run away altogether.

But ah! who met him at the door, bringing sunshine and peace in her fair face, holding out two dear little hands, and scattering with a word all his annoyance?

"Dear Carl," Edith said, "are you really glad to see me—really glad?"

"How could you imagine such a thing?" he replied.

"Then I will go back to Seaton again. Good-by!"

She took a step toward the street-door, only a step, both her hands being strongly held.

"You forget, then, silvern speech and golden silence," the young man said.

"No," she replied. "But solid silver is better than airy gold. If people say kind things to you, then you are sure, and have something to remember; but looks fade, and you can think that you mistake, or mistook. Oh! I like silence, Carl, but it must be a silence that follows after speech. That is the sole golden silence."

"I am glad to see your face and hear your voice once more, Edith," he said seriously. "I have many a time longed for both."

"Dear Carl!" she exclaimed. "But what is that I hear? Is it a parrot?"

Carl laughed. "Hush! It is Miss Clinton. She is calling out to know who has come. We will go in and see her."

Miss Clinton had one pleasant expression, and that was a smile, when she was so delighted by something out of herself as to forget herself. This smile brightened her face as she watched the young couple approach her, hand in hand. She leaned back in her chair, and contemplated Edith, without thinking of returning her greeting.

"I'm sure that is a golden silence," Carl said, laughing. "But what do you think of her, aunt? She likes to have people speak first, and look afterward."

"You are welcome, dear!" the old lady said softly, and extended her hand, but without leaning forward. To take it, therefore, Edith had to come very near, and was drawn gently down to the footstool by Miss Clinton's chair.

The old lady took off the girl's hat, and dropped it on to the carpet, then studied her face with delight. She loosened one of the braids of hair wound around her head, and held it out to a sunbeam to see the sparkle of it. She pushed it back from the face. "Did you ever see such ears?" she said to Carl. "They are rose-leaves! There must be a large pearl hung in each. She drew her finger along the smooth curve of the brows. "A great artist and physiognomist once told me that such brows show a fine nature. Broken brows, he said, indicate eccentricities of character, brows bent toward the nose a tyrannical disposition, heavy brows reserve and silence, but this long, smooth brow versatility and grace. Read Lavater if you want to know all about eyebrows." She took the cheek, now glowing with blushes, in the hollow of her hand, and held the eyelids down to admire the lashes. "They make the eyes look three shades darker than they really are. But what color are the eyes? They are no color. Did you ever see a shaded forest spring, Carl? These eyes are as limpid."

"Oh! please don't!" the girl begged, trying to hide her face.

"My dear, I shall call you Eugénie, and shall adore you," Miss Clinton continued. "I hope they have not told you horrible stories about me, or that, if they have, you will not believe them. People are fond of saying that I am sharp, but I quote Victor Hugo to them, '*La rose de Bengale, pour être sans épines, est une rose sans parfum.*' A character without any sharpness would be like … without salt. Temper … When any person is represented to me as of a very mild … position, never getting angry, I always say, Keep that person out of my sight! Yes, I shall call you Eugénie. I dislike the Edith on account of old Mrs. Yorke. She and I always quarrelled, dear. We were what some one has called 'intimate enemies.' But I don't mean to quarrel with her grand-daughter. You have your father's eyes and hair, Eugénie, but your mother's features. I hope you have not her disposition. She was too positive, and, besides, she ran away with another woman's beau."

Edith drew back, and stood up, turning to Carl.

"There! she is angry the first thing," the old lady cried. "No danger of anybody's thinking her *sans épines*. Take her down to get some …

"Dick Rowan is here," Edith said, as the two went down-stairs; "and he is a Catholic; and he has a new ship which he has named for …

There was no reply. They were passing through the shady entry, and, if the young man frowned at the … was, the frown was not seen.

"Aunt Amy has gone to Hester's," Edith went on. "She got over the journey nicely, and wants to see you very soon. She will send Hester up to see me presently. I am too tired to go out to-day, would you believe it? You see, travel was so new to me that I could not sleep. I stayed on deck as long as I could, then I listened all night. It seemed so strange to be on the water, out of sight of land."

Later, while the young traveller was resting in the chamber assigned her, a visitor entered gently, unannounced. "I thought I might come, dear," Miss Mills said.

Edith raised herself, and eagerly held out her arms. The lady embraced her tenderly, then dropped, rather than sat down, in a chair by the bed. She looked with a strange mingling of feelings on this child of her lost lover. When she recognized the tint of his hair and eyes in Edith's, she bent toward her with yearning love; but then appeared some trait of the mother—a turn of the head, a smile unconsciously proud, an exquisitely fine outline of feature; and, at sight of it, that wounded heart shrank back as from a deadly enemy. The interview was friendly, and even tender, and engagements were made for future meetings; but the lady was glad to get away. The sight of Robert Yorke's child had wakened all the sleeping past, and for a time the years that had intervened since her parting with him faded like a mist. Since that day, more than one power, at first pride, later religion, had strengthened her, had raised up new hopes and new joys; but they were not the sweet human hopes and joys that every man and woman looks naturally for; they were those born of struggle and self-denial. She had lived truly and nobly, but she was human; and to-day her humanity rose, and swept over her like a flood.

Miss Mills locked herself into her

room, and for once gave herself up to regret. It was no ordinary affection which she mourned. It had entered her heart silently, and been welcomed like an angel visitant; it had been held sacred. She had watched it with awe and delight as it grew, that strange, beautiful, terrible power! How complex it had become, entering into every feeling, every interest! How it had changed and given a new meaning to life, and a new idea and comprehension of herself!

Then, when it had got to seem that she alone was not a complete being, but only about to become perfect—then destruction came.

> "Jove strikes the Titans down,
> Not when they set about their mountain-piling,
> But when another rock would crown their work."

If the foundation merely of an edifice be overthrown, there is hope that it may be rebuilt; but destruction overtaking when the topmost height is almost attained is destruction indeed.

In the evening a knock was heard at the chamber door, which she had all day refused to open, a note was pushed under the door, and a servant waited outside for her to read it. She rose wearily, lighted the gas, and glanced over the lines. "I am sorry you have headache, sorry for you and for me. Edith is talking with Mr. Rowan, and I am, consequently, *de trop*. There is no one I care to see to-night but you. Send me word if you are better."

"Tell him to wait," she ordered, and, hastily dressing for a walk, went down. The front parlor was not lighted, but she saw him sitting by a window there. "Come out!" she said. "I wanted to go to the chapel, and you are just in time."

Scarcely a word was spoken as they went through the streets together. They entered the chapel, and turned aside into a shady corner. Carl sat, and his companion, too exha
kneel, sat beside him. In
near by, a choir was singing t
beautiful of hymns—

> "Jesus, lover of my soul."

"Alice," Carl whispered,
enough to break one's heart

Her tears broke forth afres
Carl, it is enough to heal
already broken." She liste
looking toward the altar,
over and over,

> "Other refuge have I none.

The solitude and quiet wer
ing to both—the sense of
presence more than soothin
who had faith in it.

They had not been there lo
a gentleman came up the ai
a firm, but light step, passed
out noticing them, and kne
just before them. Carl sat a
at him in astonishment. Th
Rowan should outwardly a
licly conform to the chu
Edith's sake, was not surpri
that he should come private
chapel to pray was inex
Could it be that a brave, man
like this could sincerely belie

Utterly unconscious of obs
the sailor knelt there motionl
his face hidden in his han
when Carl's companion whis
him, and they both went o
figure had not stirred.

Edith Yorke's friend b
once to show her what was
in the city; but, as often
what they considered wortl
disappointed the neophyte, a
they passed without notice sh
fain have paused to look at.
perienced persons who ha
much usually overestimate t
nitude of the wonders they h
seen. What young travelle
ing for the first time a city, ev
its houses as palatial, its st

monuments as grand, as

hing looks so much smaller shabby," Edith confessed o Dick Rowan. "Trees are finer than any pictures it I have seen, and faces ınd smile are more beau- ny painted ones. Only res of Italian scenes de- Now, Dick, please do not when I tell you that I to stop and look at the ers and their monkeys, in at the shop windows. , you know, for that would l and Hester and Miss ıed of me."

ılt of this confidence was d to attract as little atten- sible, these two friends set side, and went on long gether. They paid not ntion to the finer sights, into all sorts of byways. d in at shop windows, at ells and jewels, and more hopkeeper was smilingly display his best wares at ady's shy request, though forehand that she did not uy. They watched the ers and their monkeys to s' content; they amused with the gamins, and held versations with them; they ntiful to street-beggars. chins were astonished by candy that seemed to de- heaven on their heads, weeping outcasts were ll their griefs, and listened der sympathy, tears per- into one pair of eyes that ıem. Sometimes a wretch- , walking with downcast h the street, felt something hand and leave a bit of re, and looked up to see a entleman just passing, and one sweet face glance momentarily back with a smile at once arch and pitying. "Shall I ruin you, Dick?" Edith asks gleefully. "I have ruined myself; but that didn't take long. My poor little money is all gone. Are you very rich?"

"Oh! immensely!" Dick replies. "I have chests of gold. Give away as much as you wish to."

One blind man gone astray long remembered how a soft hand took one of his, and a firm hand the other, and his two guides led him home, inquiring into his misfortune by the way, and commiserating him more tenderly than brother or sister ever had.

"It is so sad to have all the beautiful world shut out," said the sweet voice out of the dark. "But one might, I think, see heavenly things the more plainly."

The poor man never lost himself afterward, but he looked blindly, and listened to hear once more those two voices, and to feel the clasp of those two hands, one soft as charity, the other strong as faith. And since they never came to him again, to his imprisoned soul it seemed as though heavenly visitants had led him, and spoken sacred words for him to remember. These two young creatures, out of the happy world of the rich and prosperous, were not afraid of soiling their hands or their clothes, and did not look on the poor as they did on the paving-stones.

"O Dick!" Edith said in one of those walks, "I do not wonder that the Lord could not stay in heaven when he saw the misery of earth, and knew that there was no comfort even in another world for it. What a trial it must have been for him to sit above there, and hear all the cries of pain that went up, and see all the weeping faces that were raised. Why, Dick, it seems to me that if I could see and

know at once all the suffering there is to-day in this one city, it would kill me. I wish we could do something besides play, as we do. Perhaps we ought to work all our lives for the wretched, you and I; who can tell?"

"Yes!" the young man replied slowly, and was silent a moment, thinking. "That idea comes into my mind sometimes," he added. "I always fancy that the poor and the wicked look at me in an asking way, differently from what they do to others, as if they expected me to do something for them. It may be only because they see how I look at them. I never see one but I think, How should I feel if that were my father or my mother? But I don't know what great work I could do. My life seems mapped out."

Sometimes their expeditions were merrier. They went to the Back Bay lands, then not filled in, and stood so close to the railroad tracks that the passing trains blew in their faces. "I like strength and force," Edith said; "and I like the wind in my face. It would be pleasant to ride in a car with an open front, and the engine on behind. Does it not seem like that in a ship at sea, Dick?"

"Better than that," he answered, his eyes brightening. "For at sea you have a clear track, and can fly on without stopping or turning out for anything."

"Now, let's go and see that large building," the girl said. "Isn't it fine to go about in this way? You are Haroun-al-Raschid, and I am anybody, and we are exploring our capital. We are, perhaps, invisible. Stop a minute. There are fishes in this ditch. I am going to catch one with a crooked pin."

They looked at the large building, Chickering's piano-forte factory, and Dick described foreign buildings to his companion, and described so vividly and so simply that the structures seemed to rise before her. He was remarkably gifted in this respect. His clear eyes took in the general effect, and caught here and there a salient point to give it character and sharpness, and his descriptions were never blurred by superfluous words, or by imagination, which often destroys the outlines of tangible things by its perceptions of their intangible meaning.

One morning they went to Mass to receive communion together. The morning was lovely, the spring green all freshness, the birds singing, the sun stealing goldenly through a faint mist. Edith rose happy, and everything added to her happiness. It was delightful to have some one to go to Mass with. It only now occurred to her that she had been lonely in her religion.

"I hope that I shall make a good communion," she said to herself, as she began to dress. "What should I do? Let me think! If I had a house of my own, rather a poor little place, and some one I loved and honored were coming to visit me, I should first make my house clean. Then I should adorn it all I could, and p pare a little feast. I have no servan I will say, and must do everythin myself. I am rather glad of that, for I can show my good-will so. will not mind getting on my knees t scrub out the darkest corners. Bu I must let in light to see where t cleanse. Come, Holy Spirit! enlighten my soul, and let no darkness remain where a sin can hide itself Then comes my confession; but wha poor things confessions are! I wish I could say, I accuse myself of having broken all the ten commandments of God, and the six commandmen of the church, and of having committed the seven deadly sins, and every sin that could be committed,

and each a thousand times over. Then I should be sure to get them all in. But Father Rasle says that, if our dispositions are good, the sins we forget, or do not understand, are included and forgiven with those we confess. As when a woman sweeps her room, she sweeps out, perhaps, some things she does not see. Well, say that my house is clean, what have I to adorn it with?" She paused with the brush half-drawn through her hair, and the first sunbeams, shining in her face, shone on gathering tears. She recollected herself, and went on with her dressing. "Such a bare reception! Nothing to offer! How about faith, hope, and charity? I believe everything, I could believe a thousand times more; but even the devils believe, Father Rasle says. I don't know whether I hope in the right way. Hope is a hard virtue to manage. Do I love him? Yes! Even though I do wrong, still I love him. It is no sign that you do not love a person, even if you do things to vex him. What good work can I do to-day? I will read Miss Clinton to sleep, and let Bird go out. That will be something, because I would rather go out myself. And I will ask Miss Clinton if I may read a paper to her. That will be awfully hard, for she will stare at me, and then laugh in that way that makes me want to run out of the room. And I will—yes—no—will I? Yes, I will try to kiss her, if I possibly can. She would be pleased; but I shouldn't be. Those will be like little daisies at the doorstep when he comes in. But my house is bare yet. If only I had some pain to offer!"

Her eyes chanced to fall on a coil of picture-cord, and the sight of it gave her a new and startling thought. She paused a moment, then, rising, pulled her curtains close, opened the door to assure herself that there was no one in the corridor outside, then shut the door and locked it. This done, she looped and knotted the cord into a discipline—ah! not in vain had she once asked Father Rasle what that was. Her hands trembled with eagerness while she fastened the five lashes together. Then, with one glowing upward glance, she knelt, and brought the discipline, with the full force of her arm, round across her shoulders. A faint cry followed the first blow, and the blood rushed crimson over her face and neck. "O Lord! I did not mean to cry out!" she whispered, and listened, and struck again, and yet again. "One for each of the five wounds, one for each of the times he prayed in the garden." She paused, and dropped forward with her face on the floor, writhing in silent pain. "Now, one for each station of the way of the cross." Tears ran down her cheeks, but her strong young arm and heart did not falter. "Now, a decade of the rosary."

Sobbing, half-fainting, she rose after a while, and hid the precious pencil, with which she had painted a picture for the wall of her little reception-room.

"I must put on something extra, so that the blood shall not show through my dress," she said; but, looking to wipe away the blood, behold! not a drop was there, but only long welts of red and white crossing her fair shoulders.

Edith hid her face, with a *feeling* of utter humiliation and grief. She had been agonizing under the blows which had produced only a few marks, and yet fancying that she imitated him whose flesh had been torn by the lash, and whose blood had flowed in streams. "I can do nothing, nothing! I am silly and presumptuous," were the thoughts

with which she finished her preparation to go out.

But, trivial as her penance had been, it brought humility, and a deeper sense of the sufferings of our Lord.

A servant who was washing the steps as Edith went out, smiled gratefully to the pleasant greeting of the young lady, and looked after her as she went down the street. The servants, all Catholics, were very proud and fond of this young Catholic in their Protestant household.

"Since I cannot do anything," Edith pursued, as she walked on toward the church, "I will ask the Blessed Virgin and St. Joseph to come first, and be in my house when the Lord shall enter. He will be pleased to find them there. Then, when the time comes, I will go and meet him at the door; but how dreadfully ashamed I shall be! I shall not dare to look up, but I shall say, 'Welcome, Lord!' and kneel down, and kiss his feet. Then, if there is anything more to be done, he will do it, for I can do nothing. How odd it is that I should feel so ashamed at having him come to me, and yet should want him to come! I wouldn't put it off for anything."

Dick was waiting inside the chapel-door for her. He pointed her to a confessional, then took his place near the altar. When it came time for communion, they knelt side by side, but retired again to different seats.

How long Edith knelt there she did not know. She had covered her face with her hands, shutting out the sight of all about her, and her soul had entered a new scene. There was a simple, small room, bare save for two vague, luminous presences, one at either side, lighting the place. There was an open door, with vines swinging about it, and a half-seen picture of verdure, and deep blue heavens outside. Up through that pure, intense color stretched two lines of motionless winged forms, as if they bowed at either side of a path down which one had come. Within the door, under the vines, stood the Lord, and she was prostrate on the floor, with her arms clasped around, and her lips pressed to, his feet. She did not look up, and he did not speak nor stir, but his smile shone down through all her being. Let it last so for ever!

The tinkling of a bell awoke her as from a sound sleep—a flicker, as of flames in the wind, moved those heavenly lines of receding faces, and Edith lifted her head, and recollected where she was, seeming to be suddenly transported back there from a distance. The priest was carrying the host away from the altar of the chapel up to the church. He held the sacred burden clasped closely to his breast, and bent his head slightly toward it. He looked at it as he walked, yet chose his steps with care. He wrapped around it the golden veil, of which the fringe glistened like fire as he moved. No mother could carry a sleeping infant more tenderly.

Edith stretched out her hands, with a momentary feeling of bereavement, for the Lord was going away. "Oh! take my heart with thee!" she prayed.

The lights disappeared, the sound of the bell grew fainter up the stairs, and ceased. She sighed, then smiled again, and became aware of Dick sitting at the furthest end of the bench, and waiting for her. They went out by separate aisles, and met at the door.

"I would like to have followed up into the church, and waited till he was at rest again, and seen where

they lay him," Edith said after a while.

Dick smiled quietly, and said nothing. He was looking quite pale, but bright. She made no comment on his looks, thinking that the communion was the cause of his emotion.

They went to the public gardens before going home. It was very lovely there. The mists of the morning had slowly gathered themselves into detached clouds, and they scarcely moved, the air was so still. The trees and the many pink flowers about glistened with dew.

Edith began to love her quietude, and grow merry, but with an angelic merriment. "Do you think that the Lord came down to the garden only at evening?" she asked. "I think he came at early morning, unless he stayed all night—morning is so beautiful! How alive everything is! You can almost see eyes in the flowers. See the swans on the water. They float like clouds in the sky. Fancy a pink swan in a large blue lake, throwing up sprays as white as snow over his bosom! Do you think that the earth was any more beautiful when it was first made? Is it not lovely now?"

There was no answer in words, but the young man's eyes, glancing about, were eloquent, and his smile was one of peaceful delight.

"Come," the girl said, "let's play that this is really the Garden of Eden, and that you and I are just taking our first walk in it, wondering over everything. Let us look at ourselves in the water, and see if we are as beautiful as all the rest."

He smiled at the childish fancy, took the hand she offered him, and went with her over the water. The swans passed by, and sent ripples over their mirror, but it was clear enough to give back the image of a sweet oval face with bright eyes and lips, and of another face more richly tinted, peach-colored with sun and wind, with eyes that sparkled, and white teeth that laughed through a chestnut beard.

"Adam," said the woman, "thou art more stately than the palm, and thine eyes have beams like the sun. Let us praise the Creator who hath formed thee in his own image!"

Dick's hand and voice trembled, his face grew red in the water, then grew pale. "Eve," he said, "thou art whiter and more graceful than the swan, and, while thou art speaking, the birds listen. I praise him who has given thee to me to be mine alone and for ever—my mate in this world and in the next."

Speaking, his light clasp grew tight on her hand.

The face and throat that had shown swan-white in the water grew rose-red, then disappeared as Edith started back.

"How could I look forward to anything else, Edith?" the young man exclaimed desperately. "I have never dreamed of any other life. I have worked, and studied, and hoped for you. What! will you turn away from me now, for the first time? God have mercy on me!"

She did not utter a word at first. She was too much confounded. It was to her as though the friend she had so long known had been suddenly snatched from her side, and a stranger like, and yet unlike, him put in his place. This man with the pallid face and trembling voice was not Dick Rowan. She wanted to get away from him. But after a step or two she turned back again.

"Who would have thought it?" she said, looking at him anxiously, as though half hoping that the whole was a jest.

"Who would have thought any-

thing else?" he replied, taking courage

She turned away again, but he walked on beside her. It was too late to withdraw. Having spoken, he must say all.

"I think you were the only person who did not see what I lived for," he said.

"But it is nonsense!" she exclaimed.

"We have always known each other. We are like brother and sister. Is it only strangers who marry?" he asked.

"Marry! Fie! I never thought of such a thing!" she said angrily.

"Won't you please think of it now, Edith?" he asked, in a voice so gentle and controlled that it recalled her own self-possession. "This has been the great thought of my life. It made me ambitious, for your sake. I am a Catholic, thank God! and a sincere one, but it was love of you that led me to study and think on that subject. When my life hangs in the balance, I am sure you will at least stop to think, dear."

She looked at him, but he did not return her glance. His eyes were fixed on the ground, and it really seemed as though his life did hang in the balance.

"I'd like to stop and talk about it a little while, Dick," she said. "Sit here. Now, be reasonable, and I will not be cross again. Forgive me! I was so surprised, you know; for I have been studying all my life, and never thought about this. Now, it seems to me, Dick, that I shall never want to be married to any one whatever. I shall live with Aunt Amy, and, when she is dead, I will go into a convent. or, if I should have money, will do something for the poor, perhaps. If you want to have me with you, some time I can go on a voyage in your ship, and you can always come to see me when you come home. Won't that do?"

He smiled faintly.

"Oh! thank you!" she said, greatly relieved.

"Has any one else ever spoken to you in this way, Edith?" he asked, looking at her searchingly.

"Oh! no," she answered with decision. "I am not at all engaged, or anything like it. No one ever cared anything about me. And I hope you are satisfied now, Dick. It it is very well for people to marry who are afraid of losing each other; but we can live close by when we grow old, or perhaps in the same house."

"I have disturbed and troubled you, Edith," the young man said after awhile, "but I could not help it. There must be a beginning to everything, and I had to make a beginning of this. I don't expect you to treat it seriously now, but I want you to think of it. It seemed right that I should speak, or some one else might speak while I am gone, and take you away from me."

"But I should never think of having any one else, if you want me," she replied with perfect conviction. "I may not ever marry at all, but, if I do, you will have the first chance."

Dick Rowan's whole face caught fire. "Why, darling!" he exclaimed joyfully, "do you mean that?"

She was astonished and pleased at the effect of her words. "Truly," she answered. "You know very little of me if you do not know that I have always considered myself to belong more to you than to any one else."

They had now reached Miss Clinton's door, and there they parted without more words.

But Edith's indecision was of shorter duration than either she or her friend had anticipated. The subject

was so foreign to her thoughts that at first she had comprehended nothing, and had received Dick Rowan's avowal in a most childish manner. But a few hours' consideration had set the whole in a different light. She went down to Hester's as soon as dinner was over, and asked for her aunt. Mrs. Yorke was in her own room, writing a letter, and she only glanced up with a smile as her niece entered.

"All well at Miss Clinton's?" she asked, folding the letter.

"Yes, very well."

"Anything new?

"Miss Clinton told me last night that her will is made, leaving everything to Carl, and that, if I marry to suit her, I am to have her jewels, shawls, and laces. I do not want them, though I would rather have fresh new things for myself, if they are not so rich."

"Whom does she wish you to marry?" Mrs. Yorke asked, directing her letter.

"She did not say," Edith replied in a constrained voice, looking down.

Mrs. Yorke glanced at her niece, then put her arm out and drew her close. "You have something to tell me, dear," she said.

Edith began to tremble. "Yes, Aunt Amy. Dick Rowan has been talking to me this morning, and, if you and Uncle Charles are willing, and if I should ever marry any one, I am going to marry him."

Mrs. Yorke's brows contracted slightly, rather with anxiety than displeasure. "Dear child, are you sure of yourself?" she asked. "One may have a very great affection for a person, and not be willing to marry him. Don't be hasty. Take time to think of it till he shall come back again. If you promise, you may regret it. I must say, dear, I think it selfish of him to speak so when you have seen nothing but birds and books, and do not know your own mind."

Edith raised her head from her aunt's shoulder. "Oh! Dick isn't selfish, and he only asked me to think of it, and to know that he wanted me."

It was useless to oppose. After a little more talk, Mrs. Yorke promised to consent if both were of the same mind after a year. "And now, Edith, I have concluded to start for home to-morrow, and I want to see Carl right away."

She did not say that she had only come to this conclusion since Edith had entered her room.

"And I also wish to see Mr. Rowan," she added. "Did he not mean to consult me."

"Oh! yes," Edith said eagerly. "He is coming up this evening; and, Aunt Amy"—very hesitatingly—"don't let me be married for a great while, till I am twenty-five, at least. Of course," looking up quickly, as if some doubt had been expressed—"of course, I think the world of him, and don't wish to marry any one else; but I cannot, *cannot* hurry."

Mrs. Yorke had a long conversation with her niece's lover, that evening, and laid down the law rather severely to him. No one but Edith, herself, and Mr. Yorke were to know of his proposal. "I do not wish her to be talked about, and assigned to any one, when nothing is decided," she said. "It is for that purpose that I am taking her away so soon, to prevent talk. If, when you come home next year, she wishes it, and nothing has happened to raise any new objection, I shall not oppose you."

He sat a moment silent. He asked nothing better than he had got; but his proud spirit rebelled at the manner in which the promise was given. He was tolerated be-

cause they could not help themselves.

"Do you agree to that?" she asked, after waiting a moment.

"Certainly!" he replied. "I forgot to say so, and to thank you, because, excuse me! I was thinking how much poorer an offering is a man's whole heart and faithful allegiance than a full purse."

"If you had millions, it would make no difference, Mr. Rowan," Mrs. Yorke said hastily, her color rising. "If I am not cordial in welcoming you into this relation, my reasons are not mercenary, nor—" her manner softened—"nor because I do not respect and like you."

She held her hand out to him. He bent gallantly over it, murmured a word of thanks, and took leave without saying any more.

He was willing, almost glad, that Edith should go home. He welcomed any stir and progress in events which would seem to pass the time more quickly along. Let him get over his year of probation, and, during it, be separated from her, if they chose. Her doubt and trouble in their new relations troubled him. When he should come again, all would be settled. He was full of hope and triumph, and far removed from jealousy. She had said that she should not think of marrying any one but him; and what Edith said was as sure as sunrise.

TO BE CONTINUED.

(IN MEMORIAM.)

A CONVERT.

1856.

(These lines express the feelings of one, now at rest, who was loved and honored by all who knew him—including, probably, those who cast him off.)

I.

Ah me! my alienated friends,
  Whose friendship, like a branch half-broke,
With all its mildewed blossoms bends,
  And piecemeal rots;—how kind the stroke
That bond—your bondage—sent to sever!
Yet, can I wish it? Never, never!

II.

I hear them tread your festal floors:
  When now the lights no longer burn,
Alone I haunt your darkened doors:
  The guests are gone; yet I return:
In dreamless sleep outstretched you lie:
I dream of all the days gone by.

III.

Against myself your part I take:
  "I was of those whose spring is fair;
Whom men but love in hope, and wake
  To find (youth flown) the worse for wear:
'Gainst the defaulter judgment goes:
I lived on trust, and they foreclose."

IV.

And many times I say: "They feel
  In me the faults they spare to name;
Nor flies unjust the barbèd steel,
  Though loosened with a random aim."
Officious zeal! for them I plead
Who neither seek such aid, nor need.

V.

Give up thy summer wealth at last,
  Sad tree; and praise the frost that bares
Thy boughs, ere comes that wintry blast
  Which fells the grove that autumn spares.
There where thou lov'st thou liv'st! Bequeath,
Except thy bones, no spoils to death!

VI.

To others sovereign Faith exalts
  Her voice from temple and from shrine:
For me she rears from funeral vaults
  A cross that bleeds with drops divine;
And Hope—above a tombstone—lifts
Her latest, yet her best of gifts.

AUBREY DE VERE.

THE LIQUEFACTION OF THE BLOOD OF ST. JANUARIUS.

NO. II.

WHEN was this liquefaction of the blood of St. Januarius first seen by men? It is not easy to answer the question. Some Neapolitan writers have maintained that it occurred probably on the very day when the remains of the sainted bishop were first solemnly transferred to Naples. For then, naturally and as a matter of course, the vials of the blood must have been brought into close proximity with the relics of the head. And this proximity, now intentionally brought about at each exposition, seems to be ordinarily the necessary and sufficient condition for the occurrence of the liquefaction. Others, however, prefer to be guided by positive historical evidence, and have come to a different conclusion. There is in existence a life of the saint written in or near Naples, about the year 920. It combines historical accounts and later legends, and evidently omits nothing which the writer thought would promote veneration toward the saint. It is diffuse on the subject of miracles. There is also in existence a panegyric of the saint, written perhaps half a century earlier still. No mention whatever is made in either of them of this Liquefaction. We may, therefore, conclude that in the year 920 it was not known. Four hundred and fifty years later, it was known, and had been known so long as to be reputed of ancient standing. About 1380, Lupus dello Specchio wrote the life of St. Peregrine of Scotland, who came to Naples about the year 1100, and died there probably about 1130. In that life it is stated that St. Peregrine came to witness this celebrated and continual miracle—*quotidianum et insigne miraculum*. Now, it may well be that the author, writing about two hundred and fifty years after the death of St. Peregrine, had access to documents and evidences clearly establishing this fact, although such documents do not now exist, five hundred years later, or, at least, have not as yet been exhumed from some dusty library, where they may be lying unnoticed. Or, on the contrary, it may possibly be that in 1380 Lupus believed that the miracle, so regular in its occurrence at his day, had regularly occurred since the year of the translation of the body, and took it as a matter of course that St. Peregrine had witnessed it; and so put that down among the facts of his life. But this, even though a harsh criticism, and one we think unwarranted, if not excluded, by the words of the life, would imply at least that, in 1380, the Liquefaction had occurred for so long a time that men had ordinarily lost the memory of its commencement.

Maraldus the Carthusian, who accompanied his abbot Rudolph to the coronation of Roger, King of Sicily, as historiographer, tells us in his *Chronicon*—or perhaps his continuator—how, in 1140, Roger visited Naples, and how there he venerated the relics of the head and of the blood of St. Januarius. The Liquefaction is not mentioned in so many words. But these relics would not have been singled out from all others in the city, and made so prominent, without

some special reason—a reason, perhaps, so well known and so obvious that it did not occur to the writer to state it explicitly, any more than to say that the king venerated the relics in the daytime and not at night.

The learned and critical Bollandists, who have carefully weighed all that can be said on this question, incline to hold that the Liquefaction commenced somewhere between the years 900 and 1000. Prior to the century between those years, St. Januarius had been ranked among the minor patrons of the church of Naples. After that century, he holds the most prominent place and rank in their calendar. This change is unusual and important, and must have been based on some sufficient reason. The most probable one under the circumstances—if not the only one that can be assigned—is that during that century the Liquefactions became known. The contemporary records of Naples for that time were very few; for it was a period of incessant warrings, devastations, and tumults. Those that did exist probably perished in the not unfrequent destruction of the monastic libraries. Still, some venerable manuscript may even yet come to light, telling us how on some festival day, or day of supplication, the relics were all on the altar, the vials of the blood near to the head; how some of the crowd that prayed before the altar saw that the blood in the vial had become liquid; how the wonderful thing was spoken of and seen by many; how, on other occasions, it occurred again and again; until at last it came to be regularly looked for, as a part, and the most wonderful part, of the celebration.

After 1400, the notices of the Liquefaction are more frequent. Æneas Sylvius Piccolomini (afterwards Pope Pius II.) gives an account of it. Robert Gaguin, the old French historian, narrating the journey of Charles VIII. into Italy, mentions his visiting Naples in 1495, and his witnessing and examining this miracle of the Liquefaction.

In 1470, Angelo Catone, a physician of Salerno, who devoted the later years of his life to literature and to travelling, has written a brief but clear account of it. Picus de la Mirandola, the wonder of his age, has also left his testimony as an eye-witness.

It is needless to say that, since the invention of printing and the multiplication of books, we have numberless accounts of it from travellers and authors, in Latin, Italian, German, Polish, English, French, Spanish, and every language of Europe.

Ever since September, 1659—ten years after the opening of the new *Tesoro* chapel—an official diary has been kept in it, recording day by day the expositions of the relics; in what state and condition the blood was found when extracted from the *armoire*, or closet; after the lapse of what length of time the change, if any, occurred; what was its course and character; in what condition the blood was, when safely replaced in its closet in the evening; and, generally, any other facts of the day which the officers charged with this duty deemed worthy of note.

There are also printed forms in blank to the same effect, which one of them fills out and signs in the sacristy attached to the *Tesoro*, and distributes each day of exposition to those who desire them. We have several in our possession.

Another diary is kept in the archiepiscopal archives. It was commenced long before that of the *Tesoro*. We had an opportunity of looking over it. Down to the year 1526, it seems to be made up from previ-

ous documents and extracts from various authors. In 1526, it assumes the character of an original diary. Here and there come intervals during which it appears not to have been regularly kept on. These omissions would be supplied from other sources, when, after a time, the diary would be resumed. From 1632 it is complete. We have before us a manuscript abstract of it, from which we will quote hereafter.

The church of Naples celebrates three festivals of St. Januarius each year; the feast proper of the saint, commemorating his martyrdom; the feast of the translation, commemorating the transfer of his body from Marcian to Naples; and the feast of the patronage, a votive one of thanksgiving. We take them up in the order of time as they occur each year.

I. The first Sunday of May is the feast of the translation. On the preceding Saturday—the vigil, as it is termed—a solemn procession, during the forenoon, bears the bust containing the relics of the head of the saint from the cathedral to the church of Santa Chiara, or St. Clare. In the afternoon, another more imposing procession conveys the reliquary of the blood to the same church, in which the liquefaction is then looked for. About sunset, both relics are borne back in procession to the cathedral and *Tesoro* chapel, and at the proper hour are duly locked up. On the next day, Sunday, they are brought out, first to the altar of the *Tesoro* chapel, and thence, after a couple of hours, to the high altar of the cathedral. In the afternoon, at the appointed hour, they are again brought back to the *Tesoro* chapel, and are duly replaced in their closet, or *armoire*. The same is repeated on Monday, and on each succeeding day of the octave up to the following Sunday, inclusive. Thus, for this festival in May there are *nine* succ sive days of exposition. And, in much as in the mind of the churc the vigil, the feast, and the octav are all united together, as the cele bration of one festival in a more s lemn form, so we naturally look o those nine expositions not as isolat ed and distinct, one from the other but as in some way connected t gether and united to compose a sin gle group.

The feast and its vigil are foun in ancient calendars of the churc of Naples. The octave was add about the year 1646, on the occasio of completing and consecrating th new *Tesoro* chapel, the work and th pride of the city. The processio on the vigil were at first directed t such churches as the ecclesiastica authorities might from time to tim select, to meet the convenience the wishes of the faithful. In 133 eight special churches were designa ed to which in an established ord of succession the processions woul thereafter go in turn each year. I 1526, it was stipulated between th city authorities and the archbisho that they should instead go in tu to six municipal halls, or *seggie*, the Neapolitans styled them, belong ing to as many civic bodies or corpo rations, which united, in some com plex and ancient way, in the munici pal government of the city: that is to the chapels or churches attache to these *seggie*. This regulatio was strictly followed until the yea 1800. The old mediæval usages an liberties had by that time becom weakened or had died out unde the influence of modern centraliza tion. The several old civic corpora tions of Naples, if they existed at all existed only in name. The halls o *seggie* had lost their original impor tance and standing. A new regula tion seemed necessary. From 180

town, the procession of the vigil has gone each year to the church of Santa Chiara.

II. On the 19th of September occurs the Feast of St. Januarius, the chief or proper festival of the saint, commemorating his life of virtue and his glorious death by martyrdom under Diocletian. It is traced back to the earliest martyrologies and calendars of the church; even those of the Greek schismatic church have preserved it. In Naples, St. Januarius being the patron saint of the city, the festival is, of course, one of high rank, and has an octave. Opening on the nineteenth, and closing on the twenty-sixth of September, it gives each year *eight* days more, on each one of which the relics are brought forth about 9 A.M., and are placed on the main altar of the *Tesoro* chapel, and, about 11 A.M., are carried thence out to the high altar of the cathedral, whence again in the evening they are regularly brought back to the *Tesoro* chapel, to be replaced for the night in their proper closets. On each day, the liquefaction is looked for. The reason already given in the case of the May octave applies here also. These eight days of exposition are not eight isolated or distinct days, without any connection. They should rather be looked on as forming a second group.

III. On the 16th of December is celebrated the feast of the Patronage of St. Januarius. This is a single day festival in annual thanksgiving for many favors received, and especially for the preservation of Naples, two centuries and a half ago, from the fate of Herculaneum and Pompeii.

Naples lies almost under the shadow of Mount Vesuvius, that terrible volcano which, after slumbering peacefully for an unknown number of ages, renewed its fearful and destructive eruptions in A.D. 79, 203, 462, 512, and more than fifty times since. The burning gas or the smoke from its crater has risen miles into the air, and has spread like a dark cloud scores of miles on one side or the other. It has thrown up stones, which fell in showers of lapilli ten miles away. Its ashes have been borne to Tunis and Algiers in Africa, and to Tuscany, to Illyria, and to Greece in other directions. Once they clouded the sky and filled the air even in Constantinople. Streams of molten lava have flowed down its sides, filling valleys that were broad and deep, and sending in advance a sulphurous atmosphere and a glowing heat which destroyed all animal and vegetable life, even before the fiery stream itself touched plant, tree, or animal. They roll on slowly, but so inflexible and irresistible that no work or art of man can stay the movement or control its course. Everything in its path is doomed to utter destruction. *Resina*, between Naples and the mountain, has been destroyed and rebuilt, it is said, seven times; *Torre del Greco*, near by, nine times. Other places have perished as did Herculaneum and Pompeii. On every side of the mountain, so fair to look on when peaceful, so terrible in its wrath, one may follow for miles on miles these ancient currents, radiating from the centre. Here the hard, dark rock rings, as iron would, under your horse's hoof. There, what was once a death-bearing stream of lava has been covered by time with a rich soil, on which vines and olives flourish. By the shore, you may see where they reached the water, and have added leagues of rough volcanic rock to the land.

Naples has often been violently shaken, and sometimes seriously injured; has often been in imminent

peril, but never was utterly destroyed. This brilliant capital, uniting in herself all that Italian taste admires of beauty and luxury—"*Vedi Napoli, e muori*"—lives with a sword of Damocles ever suspended over her. Each night as they retire the Neapolitans may shudder if they cast a thought on the possible horrors of the night they have entered on or what the morrow may bring them.

But men become callous even to such dangers as these, when often threatened and seldom felt. We can conceive how thoroughly all thought of them had died out in 1631, when Vesuvius, in a long unbroken sleep of one hundred and ninety-four years, had allowed six generations of Neapolitans to grow up and pass to their graves without any experience of its power. Earthquakes, explosions, flames, smoke, and streams of fire were all forgotten. Towns and villages, and gardens and vineyards, were dotting the base of the mountain or climbing its pleasant and fertile slopes. And among the many charming scenes in the neighborhood of Naples, there were then none more sweet and charming than those of the narrow tract between the city and Mount Vesuvius.

So it was on the morning of Tuesday, the 16th of December, 1631. Yet fair as was the scene on which the sun rose that day, it was to be greatly changed ere night. Early in the morning, the citizens were startled and somewhat alarmed by a very perceptible tremulousness of the earth under their feet. It increased in violence as the hours rolled on, and the atmosphere too, December though it was, became sultry and close. The innabitants of the beautiful villas and the farmers and country laborers, who had felt the trembling of the earth and the closeness of the atmosphere more sensibly than the citizens, and who saw at once that it was caused by the mountain, commenced to flee with their families for safety into the city. About 9 A.M. a cry of affright went up from the city and the country, as suddenly the mountain shook and roared as if in agony. All eyes turned to the summit of Vesuvius, only yesterday so fair and green. A huge turbid column of smoke was seen swiftly springing upward from its cone toward the sky. High up, it spread out like the top of a mighty pine or palm. The lightning flashed through this rolling, surging, ever-increasing mass as it rapidly expanded on every side. By 11 A.M., Naples lay under the dark and fearful cloud which shut out the heavens and darkened the day. The incessant trembling of the earth was perceptibly increasing in violence. Men felt that they were at the beginning of they knew not what terrible tragedy, before which they felt themselves utterly powerless.

The ever-open churches were soon crowded with fear-stricken suppliants. The cardinal archbishop at once directed religious services to be commenced in them all, and to be continued without intermission. In the hours of the afternoon there would be a procession through the streets near the cathedral, in which the relics of St. Januarius would be borne. Men prayed to be spared from the impending doom. The trembling earth might open to swallow them; the tottering houses might fall and crush them; or the mountain, whose sullen roar, like that of an angry monster, they heard amid and above all other sounds, might destroy them in some other more fearful way. They prayed and did penance, like the Ninivites of old. They sought to prepare their souls

for the death which might come to many of them.

To the gloom and horrors of the dark cloud of smoke, spread as a funeral pall over the city, was added, later in the day, a pouring rain. The water came down heated and charged with volcanic ashes. Night arrived, more terrible than the day. The continuous trembling of the earth had indeed ceased; but, instead, there came sharp, quick shocks of earthquake, four or five of them every hour, vastly increasing the danger of those who remained in their houses. Out-of-doors was the pouring rain and the intense darkness, rendered more fearful by the intermittent electric flashings of the cloud overhead. The few oil-lamps in the streets gave little light; some had not been lighted, others had been extinguished. The narrow streets sounded with shrieks of alarm and prayers for mercy. They were filled with those who chose rather the darkness, the rain, and the mud under foot, than the danger within their own chambers. And all through the city might be descried entire families grouped together, and, by the light of torches or lanterns, making their way to some church—for, all through the terrible hours of that long night, the churches still remained open and thronged, and the services still continued. Day came at length, if the dim, misty light could be called day. It brought no relief beyond its saddening twilight. All hearts were depressed and filled with gloomy forebodings. All felt that only by the mercy of God would they be rescued.

At 10 A.M. there came two shocks of earthquake severer than any that had preceded them. The waters of the bay twice receded, leaving a portion of the harbor bare, and twice rolled back furiously, rushing over the piers and quays, and passing into the lower streets of the city. A hoarse and violent roar was heard from the mountain. It was soon known that the sea of lava within its bowels had burst for itself a channel-way out through the northern side, and was pouring down in a rapid stream, widening its front as it spread into seven branches, and advancing directly towards the city. *Portici* and *Resina*, near the mountain, or, rather, on its lower slope, were seen quickly to perish. Portions of Torre del Greco and of Torre dell' Annunziata shared the same fate. It seemed to the affrighted Neapolitans, as they looked on the fiery streams pouring onward, resistless and inflexible, in their course of destruction, that death was coming to them by fire, more terrible far than death by water or by earthquake.

Meanwhile, the hour at last arrived fixed for this day's procession. The archbishop was to take part in it, and would himself bear the reliquary of the blood of St. Januarius. The clergy of the city would precede and accompany him, and the municipal authorities would walk in procession behind. Thousands were in the cathedral and would follow after, and tens of thousands crowded the streets through which its route lay. A common feeling filled all hearts alike; they prayed earnestly, if ever they did—for their lives, and their homes, their all was at stake.

The rain had ceased, but the dark cloud still hung overhead, and the ashes were still falling, and the air was close and sulphurous. As the procession issued from the cathedral, and while the archbishop stood yet in the square in front of it, a blaze of sunlight beamed around. The sun itself they did not see, but his beams found some rift in the mass of smoke surging overhead, and struggled through, throwing, for a few

moments, a glow of golden effulgence down on the cathedral and the square, and the groups that stood or knelt within it. The effect was electric. "It is a miracle! our prayers are heard!" was the cry that burst from the multitude. In a few moments the light was gone; but, with cheered and hopeful hearts, the procession moved on through the crowded streets to the gate of the city, looking directly towards Vesuvius and the advancing streams of lava. Here an altar had been prepared in the open air, psalms were chanted, prayers and litanies succeeded, and the archbishop, ascending the steps of the altar, stood on the platform, and, holding aloft the reliquary of the blood, made with it the sign of the cross towards the blazing mountain, and all prayed that God, through the intercession of their great patron saint, would avert the dreaded and dreadful calamity.

Ere the archbishop descended from the altar, all were aware that an east wind had sprung up, and that the smoke and cinders and ashes were being blown away over the sea. The mountain grew calmer, and at once ceased to pour forth such immense supplies of molten lava. The dreaded stream, no longer fed from the copious fount, soon slackened its movement—ceased to advance towards them—and, before their eyes, was seen to grow cold, and solid, and dark. When that procession, on its return, reached the cathedral, the sun was shining brightly and cheerfully. Well might they close with a solemn *Te Deum*, for Naples was saved. Outside of the city, five thousand men, women, and children had perished, and ruin was spread everywhere; within the city, not one building had fallen, not one life had been lost.

The eruption continued for some months after, but in a moderated form. The danger to the city was not renewed.

Therefore, in 1632, and in each year since, the sixteenth of December has been a memorable and a sacred day for Naples. It became the festival of the *Patrocinio*, or Patronage of St. Januarius. For a century and a half, it was kept as a religious holy-day of strictest obligation. But the sense of gratitude dies out equally with the sense of dangers from which we escaped in the distant past. Whether this was the cause, or whether it was deemed proper to yield to the so-called industrial notions that have prevailed in more modern times, we cannot say; but, for three-quarters of a century back, if we err not, this festival in Naples ranks only as one of devotion. For a number of years, its celebration was even transferred to the Sunday following. In 1858, it was transferred back to the day itself, and is now celebrated invariably on the sixteenth of December. On that day, the relics are taken from their closet and borne to the altar of the *Tesoro*, and thence to the high altar of the cathedral. After Mass, and the recitation of a portion of the divine office, they are borne in solemn procession through several streets in the vicinity of the cathedral, and, on the return, are brought again to the high altar, where there is the exposition of the relics with the usual prayers; and the liquefaction is looked for for the *eighteenth* regular time each year.

If the weather be rainy, the procession goes merely through the aisles and nave of the large cathedral and back to the high altar.

This feast has taken the place of another single-day festival, formerly celebrated on the fourteenth of Jan-

tury, and now merged in this votive feast a month earlier.

Beyond these ordinary and regularly established expositions, other special or extraordinary ones have been occasionally allowed, sometimes at the request of distinguished strangers, who visited Naples mostly in winter, and could not wait for the recurrence of the regular festival; sometimes to allow learned and scientific men, earnest in the cause of religion, to examine the liquefaction more closely and quietly than they could do amid the concourse of so many thousands on the regular days; and, sometimes, for special and urgent reasons of devotion or public need, as was that of December 16, 1631, of which we have just given the account. These extraordinary expositions were more frequent and more easily allowed two or three centuries ago than in later years. In fact, the latest one of which we can find any record occurred in 1702. Pope Pius IX. himself, during his exile in Gaeta, near Naples, waited for a regular day—September 20, 1849—to witness the liquefaction.

On a number of religious festivals during the year, it is customary to take out the bust of St. Januarius, containing the relics of his head, and to place it, with other relics of the saints kept in the cathedral, on the altar. To do this, it is, of course, necessary that the city delegate with his keys should be in attendance, and should co-operate with the canon or clergyman sent by the archbishop with his keys. Together they open the closet in which, under two locks, is kept the bust, and which, our readers will remember, is built in the massive masonry wall of the *Tesoro* chapel, immediately behind its main altar, and adjoining the similar closet in which is preserved the reliquary with the ampullæ, or vials, of the blood. As this reliquary of the blood is not to be taken out on these occasions, its closet is ordinarily left untouched. But, in some rare instances, it has been opened, and due record made of the state in which the blood was then seen to be. At some other times, also, the door has been opened by special favor, that strangers might at least take a similar view, if they could not be present at an exposition. We have the record of nineteen times altogether since 1648, when the door was opened for one or the other of these reasons, the last time being June 11, 1775, when the blood was seen *hard*. However, as to the number of such minor examinations, we apprehend that we should speak with some hesitation. There may have been many more of which we have not just now at hand sufficient information.

We have spoken of the official diary of the *Tesoro* chapel, commencing in 1659, and of the archiepiscopal diary, commencing as a diary in 1526, and both continuing, the latter with some *lacunæ* in its earlier portions, down to the present time. Of course, different hands have penned its pages as years rolled on; and it is curious and amusing to note their differences of character as shown in their styles. Even in so plain a matter as recording, day after day and year after year, the state and condition of the blood when extracted from its closet, the occurrence and character of the liquefaction, the prominent or important facts of each day, and in what condition the blood was when replaced at night in its closet—points which it was the duty of all to record—personal traits are unwittingly manifested. One writer evidently was fond of ecclesiastical ceremonies, and

he is exact in recording the character of the High Mass and of the processions: who and how many walked in them, how many altars were erected on the route through the streets, etc. Another was more of a courtier, and he carefully mentions the presence of cardinals, viceroys, ambassadors, princes, and eminent personages. A third was devoted to prayer, and his entries breathe his spirit of devotion in many a pious ejaculation. One tells you of a new musical *Te Deum* that was sung. Another had a painter's eye, and never fails to name, with minute precision, the varying shades of color seen in the blood. Another still, with more of a mathematical turn, is equally exact in setting forth to the very minute the times of the liquefactions which he records; while others, again, performed their duty in a more perfunctory style.

On the whole, these diaries are to us most interesting and unique, as well for the length of time they cover, and the evident sincerity and earnestness of the writers in stating faithfully what they saw—sometimes to their own astonishment or sorrow, sometimes with joy—as also for the wonderful character of the facts themselves which are recorded.

Of the archiepiscopal diary, we possess a manuscript abstract, kindly written out for us. From its pages we have made a summary of all the expositions of the blood of St. Januarius at Naples from the year 1648 to 1860, which we present to our readers in tabular form. We group them together in octaves, for the reasons already given, and because in that form several peculiarities are clearly seen which, perhaps, otherwise would disappear.

We give, first, three tables for the vigil, feast, and octave in May. The first one shows the state of the blood when taken out from its closet, giving to each day a column, and recording in each column the various conditions of the blood, distinguishing them as: 1. Very hard; 2. Hard; 3. Soft; 4. Liquid, with a hard lump in the liquid; 5. Hard and full; 6. Full, when, on account of that fulness, it could not be known whether the dark mass of blood within was solid or fluid; 7. Liquid. A second table will set forth, under a similar arrangement, the various lengths of time which elapsed from the taking out of the reliquary of the *ampulla* from its closet until the liquefaction was seen to commence. After enumerating the instances in which the time is clearly determinable, another line indicates the times when the liquefaction is set down as gradual, sometimes because the time was not clearly seen, sometimes, perhaps, because the recording was perfunctory. We add another line, embracing the various occasions when the diary either omits recording or indicating the time, or does so, vaguely or in such terms as "*regular, very regular, promptly, punctually, most punctually, without unusual delay, without anything new.*" We subjoin to this table other lines, showing on what days and how often the blood remained always fluid; or always fluid with a hard floating lump; or always hard; or always full, and so full that liquefaction was not detected. A third table, similarly arranged, will show in what condition the blood was when locked up at night in its closet. We also give three similar tables for the feast and octave of September, and similar accounts for the December festival and for the extraordinary expositions.

May, 1648, to May, 1860, inclusive—213 Years.

TABLE I.

State of Blood at the Opening of the Closet.

May.	Satur.	Sun.	Mon.	Tues.	Wed.	Thur.	Fri.	Satur.	Sun.
Very hard	2	....	1	1	2	....	2	2	2
Hard	156	119	207	203	168	139	123	113	113
Soft	4	8	1	3	2	5	3	7	6
Liquid, with hard lump	40	74	....	....	....	1	....	....	....
Hard and full	3	....	....	1	6	9	13	15	17
Full	....	....	....	4	33	56	63	75	73
Liquid	8	12	4	1	2	3	4	1	

TABLE II.

Times of the Liquefactions.

	Satur.	Sun.	Mon.	Tues.	Wed.	Thur.	Fri.	Satur.	Sun.
Under 10 minutes	88	67	85	44	27	23	18	16	16
Under 30 "	49	28	63	73	46	46	44	35	37
Under 60 "	18	9	8	36	42	25	19	17	13
Under 2 hours	5	4	2	1	5	6	5	11	7
Under 5 "	1	7	....	....	2	2	2	3	3
Over 5 "	1	....	1	....	....	....	2	2	4
Gradual	1	40	....	....	....	1	....	....	....
Vague or omitted	26	45	54	55	54	52	51	53	56
Always liquid, with hard lump	17	1	....	....	....	....	....	....	....
Always full	....	....	....	4	33	56	68	75	73
Always hard	1	....	....	....	....	....	....	....	....
Always liquid	6	12	....	....	4	3	3	1	2

TABLE III.

State of the Blood when Locked Up at Night

May.	Satur.	Sun.	Mon.	Tues.	Wed.	Thur.	Fri.	Satur.	Sun.
Liquid	131	203	204	174	145	130	122	121	130
Liquid, with hard lump	77	10	4	....	....	....	....	....	....
Liquid and full	....	....	5	35	33	25	21	14	8
Full	....	....	....	4	33	56	68	75	73
Soft	3	....	....	....	1	....	....	1	....
Hard	2	....	....	....	1	2	1	1	1
Hard and full	....	....	....	....	....	....	1	1	1

These tables present the course of the expositions for two hundred and thirteen times each of the nine days, in all, 1,917 expositions. They do not set forth the changes in color, in frothing and ebullition, in minor increases or diminutions of volume, and in occasional hardenings, of all which we shall treat further on.

From September, 1648, to September, 1860—212 Years.

TABLE I.

STATE OF THE BLOOD ON OPENING THE CLOSET.

SEPTEMBER.	19	20	21	22	23	24	25	
Hard	117	191	190	191	187	189	191	195
Hard and full, (*probable*)	24	....	....	....	....	....	....	....
Hard and full	58	....	....	....	....	2	1	1
Soft	1	....	1	....	....	1	1	....
Full	....	....	1	1	2	2	2	2
Liquid	12	21	20	20	23	18	17	14

SEPTEMBER.	19	20	21	22	23	24		
Under 10 minutes	35	32	62	59	59	51	51	55
Under 30 "	64	101	78	76	78	83	79	84
Under 60 "	19	24	17	21	10	18	21	15
Under 2 hours	19	4	5	4	8	4	8	7
Under 5 "	27	....	....	1	1	2	2	....
Over 5 "	13	...	....	....	....	....	....	....
Vague or omitted	23	30	28	30	32	35	33	35
Always liquid	12	21	21	20	22	18	17	14
Always full	....	....	1	1	2	1	1	2

TABLE III.

STATE OF THE BLOOD WHEN LOCKED UP AT NIGHT.

SEPTEMBER.	19	20	21	22	23	24	25	
Liquid	212	211	211	210	206	208	209	202
Liquid and full	....	1	....	1	3	3	2	8
Always full	....	....	1	1	2	1	1	2
Hard	....	....	....	....	1	....	....	....

These tables give two hundred and twelve expositions for each day, and thus for the whole group a second aggregate of 1,696 expositions. They do not, any more than the preceding ones, give an account of the changes to which the blood is subject, in color, frothing, or minor increase or decrease of volume. These points will be considered in their proper place.

The festival of the patronage on the 16th of December, established in 1632, has been celebrated 228 times down to 1860.

I. On opening the closet or safe the blood was found as follows:

Very hard,	2
Hard,	214
Soft,	1
Hard and full,	10
Liquid,	1—228

II. The variations as to times of liquefaction were as follows:

Immediately or under half-hour,	26
Under 1 hour,	29
" 2 "	41
" 5 "	42
Over 5 hours,	26
Always hard,	43
" full,	3
" liquid,	1
Vague or omitted,	17—228

III. The condition of the blood, when put up, was as follows:

Liquid,	131
" with lumps,	46
Soft,	5
Hard as found,	43
Full,	3—228

The extraordinary expositions were 43 in number. Of these 20 may be grouped with the December exposition, having occurred in the months of November, December, January, and February.

The blood was found: Very hard, 1; hard, 13; soft, 5; and liquid, 1. The times of liquefaction were: Under 10 minutes, 15 times; under 30 minutes, 1; under 5 hours, 1; remaining liquid, 1. Of course, on all the 20 days it was put up liquid.

Nineteen days may be in the same way connected with the May celebration, as they are distributed through the months of March, April, May, and June.

The blood was found: Very hard, 1; hard, 13; soft, 4; liquid, 1. The times of the liquefaction were: Under 10 minutes, 10 times; under 30 minutes, 3; under 60 minutes, 1; under 2 hours, 1; under 5 hours, 1; time not indicated in the diary, 2; and it remained liquid, 1. On every occasion it was put up in a liquid condition.

Four other times there were extraordinary expositions in July and September. Twice the blood was found hard and liquefied within half an hour each time, and twice it was found liquid.

Nineteen instances are recorded in which for various reasons the closet was opened and the reliquary seen in its place. Four times the blood was found very hard; six times it was hard; twice it was soft; four times it was liquid, and three times the condition is not recorded.

These tables present an aggregate of no less than 3,884 expositions within a little more than two centuries, of which number no less than 3,331 were marked by a complete or partial liquefaction. The exceptions are of various classes. The most numerous one comprises 320 cases, in which the ampulla, or vial, was found in the morning and continued during the entire exposition of that day so completely full, that it was impossible for an ordinary observer to say whether the blood liquefied or not.

The writer of the diary says on this point, A.D. 1773: "When the vial is full, some signs are at times observed indicative of a liquefaction, chiefly a wave-like motion when the vial is moved. But as this can only be seen from the rear (that is, as the light shines on it or through it from the opposite side), and only on close inspection and by practised eyes, and is not visible to ordinary observers standing in front, it is not here noted down as a liquefaction." In the diary of the *Tesoro* chapel, which we cannot now consult, they are probably recorded as liquefactions.

The next largest class of exceptions consists of the 171 cases in which the blood was found liquid in the morning, and was replaced in the closet in the evening still in a liquid condition. We should observe that not unfrequently in such cases the fluid mass became congealed or even hard during the day and liquefied again. Even when this does not happen, there are so many other and frequent changes as to color, to frothing, or to ebullition, and to change of volume by increase or decrease, that, even without the occurrence of liquefaction, the fluid blood presents many wonderful characteristics. Thus in our synopsis we have counted the octave of September, 1659, as presenting seven days during which the blood was found and remained liquid

The diary, taking up that octave day by day, states, that on the 19th of September the blood was found liquid, and, the reliquary being placed near the bust, there commenced an ebullition of the blood marked with froth. This continued, off and on, during the day. On the 20th the blood was again found liquid, and the ebullition and the frothing were repeatedly renewed as on the preceding day. On the 21st the blood was a third time found liquid, and on this day the ebullition was more continuous and violent. The 22d and the 23d and the 24th were marked by the same phases. The blood was always found liquid, and each day the ebullition was repeatedly resumed and sometimes was violent. On the 26th the blood was found in a soft or jelly-like state. It soon liquefied entirely, and during the day became covered with froth. The 26th—the eighth and last day—was like the first. The blood was again found liquid, and the ebullition was resumed, yet more moderately.

The two remaining classes, which our tables present as exceptions, will also suffer diminution if accurately examined. There are 44 instances in which the blood was found *hard*, and continued hard to the end of the exposition. Yet the diary records on several occasions the presence of one or more fluid drops, sometimes of yellowish serum, sometimes of reddish blood, which could be made to run to and fro on the surface of the hardened mass, and continued to be seen for hours, or sometimes even until the close of the day.

As for the 18 other instances in which the blood was found partly liquid and partly solid, the solid part floating as a globe in the fluid portion, and in which the same state of things was seen during the day and lasted until the closing, it must be observed that generally, if not always this floating solid mass graduall diminishes by a partial liquefactio or increases in bulk by a partial hard ening. Sometimes both these change succeed each other during the day In view of these facts, it would seen that these 18 cases, so far from bein looked on as exceptions, should o the contrary be rather set down special forms of the liquefaction.

No mere tabular summaries, lik those presented above, can give th salience which they demand to cer tain unusual facts and to many ordi nary but striking characteristics whic should not be overlooked. For thi it is necessary to go back to th diaries themselves, and to trustworth historical notices of the miracle.

On Saturday, May 5, 1526, th vigil of the feast of the translation the liquefaction is recorded to hav taken place as usual in the *Segg Capuana*, to which the procession were directed that day. On th next day, the feast, the blood wa found hard, and it continued har during the entire exposition. Th octave had not yet been established It continued hard all through th octave of the succeeding Septembe as also in January, May, and Sep tember of 1527, and again in Janua ry, May, and September of 1528 and in January, 1529. The lique factions were resumed on Saturday May 1, and continued on the nex day, the feast, and regularly durin the September celebration. Thus for nearly three years the blood re mained hard and solid, withou liquefying at any time.

The Neapolitans connect this un usual fact with the anger of God and his judgments, as manifested in the terrible pestilence which broke out in their city in 1526, and came to an end only in the early months of 1529, after causing 60,000 deaths in the

single year 1527, and, together with the war then raging, as many more in the ensuing year 1528.

Again, in 1551, in 1558, and in 1569, there was no liquefaction. On the contrary, for the two years 1556 and 1557, and again for the two years 1599 and 1600, and a third time for the single year 1631, the blood was always found liquid when brought forth for exposition, and never at any time was seen to become solid. Since the last-named year, it has occurred, in ten different years, that the blood was found and continued liquid during the whole of a single octave in a year; but never in both octaves. It never continued hard for an entire octave at any time, although at some few times the liquefaction occurred only on the second, the third, or the fourth day of the celebration; or, on the contrary, it was found and continued liquid for one, two, or three days at the commencement, and was found hard only on the second, third, or fourth morning. At the votive festival of December 16, it has repeatedly remained hard. The table numbers 44 such cases. Of these only 5 occurred in the first 90 years after the institution of the feast; the remaining 39 all occur in the last 78 years. This the Neapolitans explain by the special character of the festival. The other festivals have been instituted in honor of the saint; this one, to show their gratitude as a city for favors received repeatedly through his intercession. Hence, when vice is rife in the city, and especially when sins against religion abound, their professions of gratitude are wanting in the most necessary quality to make them acceptable; and the displeasure of heaven is marked by the withholding

Departures like these from the ordinary course, or any extraordinary delay in the liquefaction, or certain appearances of color in the blood, which they traditionally dread, fill the people with alarm and sorrow. From the many instances in the diary we give two, as showing this practical connection between the liquefaction and the religious feelings of the Neapolitans.

"1732, Dec. 16.—The blood was taken out, hard. Hard it continued until after compline (the afternoon service). The people were waiting for the miracle with great anxiety. Wherefore, instead of taking back the relics (to the *Tesoro* chapel) at the usual hour, they remained on the high altar (of the cathedral) until after 21 o'clock (2.30 P.M.); and the church being crowded with people, they recited the litanies several times. Rosaries were said, and sermons were preached. But the saint did not yield, which caused great terror; and everybody was weeping, So things were up to 24 o'clock (5.30 P.M.) At that hour, a Capuchin father in the church again stirred up the people to sincere contrition for their sins, and to acts of penance. While they were doing this, all saw that the blood was of a sudden entirely liquefied—a great consolation to all. The *Te Deum* was sung; and then, only at half-past one of the night (7 P.M.), the relics were taken to the *Tesoro* chapel."

"1748, May 7, Tuesday.—The blood was brought out hard. After 16 minutes, it liquefied. During the day it rose so high as to fill the vial completely. From the 8th to the 12th, the vial was always full, and the blood was seen to be one-half black, the other half ash-colored, for which reasons his majesty came a second time to see it, on Sunday afternoon (12th). When the king had left the *Tesoro*, his eminence returned to pray to the saint to vouchsafe some sign of the

miracle before the closing up (it was the last day of the octave). In the meantime the vast crowd strove to melt him by their cries and their tears. His eminence, having made his way out of the chapel with great difficulty, sent for a noble Capuchin, called Father Gregorio of Naples, who, in a most fervent sermon, exhorted the people to acts of faith and of sorrow for their sins. He then commenced reciting with them the Litany of the Blessed Virgin. During the recitation thereof, the blood was seen to sink half a finger, and to commence to move. Who can describe the weeping and the fervor? The *Te Deum* was sung; and the blood was put up, being at nearly its normal level, of its natural color, and with some froth."

No wonder the Neapolitans love St. Januarius as *their* patron saint when he thus yields to their fervent entreaties and prayers what was not granted to the pious curiosity of the king; nor, for this occasion at least, to the prayers of his eminence the cardinal archbishop.

The following briefer entries of our diary breathe the same spirit:

"1714, May 5, Saturday.—The miracle took place at once. On Sunday, after an hour and a half. During this octave, the blood showed a thousand changes, liquefying, hardening, and increasing in volume many times a day, in an unusual manner. God knows what will happen!"

"1718, Sept. 19.—The blood was taken out hard. After a quarter of an hour, it completely liquefied. During all this octave the miracle never delayed as much as an hour. This was truly a happy octave. There were no great changes; only a slight increase in volume."

It is tantalizing to pore over the diary. At times you almost fancy that you have seized the ver cess of liquefaction. Thus o day you read: "The bloo brought out, being hard and ordinary level. After fifteen m a drop of serous humor, of a yellow color, was seen to move on the hard mass. At the exp of an hour and fifty-six m the blood became liquid, w large spherical lump floating There was the usual pro through the streets, his em joining in. At 21½ o'clock 3 P.M.) the lump liquefied. blood was put up, entirely and at its ordinary level." 1771.) You think you see th of the process. First the dr yellowish serum; then a par quefaction, leaving a lump o matter; this gradually decr for three hours and a half, it entirely disappears, and the mass is fluid. If you read th lowing, you may feel surer th are on the right track: "The came out hard and at its or level. At the end of half an there was seen to run about c hard mass a particle of serou ter, inclining to a yellowish So it stood during the proc which was outside, through streets, his eminence the ca archbishop taking his place So it was when the reliquar brought back to the *Tesor* 23½ o'clock (about 5 P.M. serous matter changed into But the mass still remained Words cannot tell with what e ness and fervor the ecclesiasti the people continued at prayer nally, at 24¼ o'clock (5.45 the mass loosened in the vial half an hour later, that is, eight hours and fifty minutes o ing, the liquefaction took pl small lump remaining solid and

So it was put up." (Dec., 1768.)
ithstanding the change of the
cter of the yellowish serous
in the last cited instance into
lood, and the great difference
times, when the liquefaction
lace, there is a certain degree
respondence between the two
enough, perhaps to arrest the
on and excite expectations. But
no purpose. Such a drop was
on seven or eight other days,
a couple of hours or for the
day, without any liquefaction
ng. And in three thousand
hundred and odd cases of li-
tion, we have failed to find a
one in which such a drop is
to have preceded the liquefac-

act, the modes of liquefaction
various as we can imagine,
remarkable as the fact itself.
imes the liquefaction occurs or
ences at once, with little or no
At other times, it is delayed
quarter or for half an hour, for
wo, or three hours or more.
imes, though very rarely, it
en delayed nine or ten hours.
s is clearly seen in the tables.
unfrequently the change from
r to fluidity, whether occurring
r late, has been instantaneous,
r the whole mass at once—*in*
to d'occhio. Sometimes it is
l, lasting before its comple-
ver many hours; nay, some-
he ampulla is replaced in the
for the night before its entire
tion, a greater or a smaller
still remaining solid.
etimes the entire mass lique-
t other times, only a portion.
this is the case, the unliquefied
generally floats as a solid
or globe in the liquid part.
mes, however, one side of the
as liquefied; while the other
ed solid, and firmly attached
to the glass. Sometimes again, as in May, 1710, the portion next to the glass all around remained solid, thus forming, as it were, an inner cup, inside of which the other portion moved about in quite a fluid condition. Sometimes, during the process of gradual liquefaction, the upper part is quite liquid, while the lower part remains for a time hard and immovable in the bottom of the vial; or, again, the lower part liquefies first, and the upper portion, remaining hard, is seen either as a floating globe or as a lump attached for a time to the sides of the ampulla. And once, at least, the upper portion and the lower portion both remained solid and attached to the vial, while the middle portion was quite fluid.

We have already said something of the various degrees of liquefaction. Sometimes the blood is as fluid as water, flowing readily and leaving no coating after it on the glass. And, at other times, it may be somewhat viscous; and, if the reliquary be inclined from side to side, may leave behind a dark or a vermilion film on the inner sides of the ampulla.

There are likewise degrees of hardness. Sometimes the blood is only very viscous and grumous, or jelly-like. In the tables we call it *soft*. At other times, the diary notes it as hard, *duro ;* very hard, *durissimo ;* or even hard as iron, *duro come ferro*. When hard, it is attached firmly to the glass ampulla. Yet on two occasions, at least, the hard lump could move within, showing that it was then detached.

After having become liquid, or even when the blood was found liquid in the morning, it has often hardened during the ceremonial of the day, and then liquefied anew. One of the extracts we have quoted above refers to the frequent occur-

rence of this variation in 1714. But throughout the diary we find similar instances, where it hardened and remained hard for a few moments only or for one or two hours, during the public ceremony. This was sometimes repeated two or three times in a single day.

There is a special case, in which the mass hardens so frequently, and with such regularity, that it must not be omitted. We refer to the custom of suspending the ceremony for a few hours during the middle of the day. The Italians are very fond of a *siesta* in the early afternoon of a hot and oppressive summer day. Accordingly, unless there be something unusual to excite them, they are accustomed, on the later days of the octave in May, and sometimes of September, to yield to their beloved habit. The church grows very thin soon after mid-day. A few dozen pious souls may perhaps remain for their private devotions—about the number one would almost always find in the ever-open churches of an Italian city. Under these circumstances, the exposition is suspended. The reliquary, if on the high altar of the cathedral, is carried back to the *Tesoro* chapel, and is placed on an ornamental stand or tabernacle on the altar; and a silk veil is thrown over the whole. The door in the metal-work railing under the arch leading out into the cathedral is locked; and the clergy may retire, one or two remaining on watch. The reliquary continues on the stand, unapproached, but still visible, through the railing, to those in the cathedral. At 3½ or 4 P.M. the clergy return to resume the exposition; and the church is again full. The blood is very frequently found hard at that hour, and liquefies anew, as in the morning. This intermission and the attendant hardening and liquefaction seem to the Neapolitans so much a matt of course that we find no menti whatever of it in the diary, save th single notice that, on one day, al though the veil had been omitted the hardening nevertheless too place. The scientific men from Ital and from France and Belgium who have studied the liquefaction at various dates, all unite in commenting on this fact of the hardening of the blood during these mid-day intermissions, and in considering it, under a physical point of view, as a fact of the highest importance in deciding the character of the liquefaction.

There are other special circumstances under which the blood has not liquefied, or, having liquefied, has suddenly hardened again. The presence of open scoffers, or of declared enemies of the church, has sometimes seemed to have this effect. In 1719, Count Ulric Daun was viceroy in Naples. On Saturday, May 6, he came with many German officers lately arrived in Naples to witness the liquefaction, in one of the churches to which the procession went, as we have already explained, and in which the liquefaction was first expected. The viceroy with his personal staff was of course in his official *loggia* or gallery. The foreign officers were clustered together within the sanctuary. Some of them were Catholics, some Protestants. The blood was hard when brought to the altar, and remained hard and unliquefied for a long time. The viceroy at length sent an aid, with a command to all the officers to withdraw and stand outside the sanctuary. They obeyed, of course. "Scarcely was this done—the heretic officers thus withdrawing—when, in an instant, the entire mass became perfectly liquid, to the great joy of all. It was a miracle of miracles!" Some

tants became Catholics

nd *Celano* mention an-
Ve quote from the for-
a canon of the cathe-
sent at the time on
hile the relics were out
altar of the cathedral,
any nobles from beyond
wished to do homage
ad to witness the lique-
blood was extremely
, and the reliquary was
ed to those around, in
sed. In an instant the blood became hard and dry in the hands of the canon. Those near by, stupefied by this new prodigy, stood, as it were, nailed to the floor. Then the canon, moved by an interior impulse, raised his voice, and said aloud: 'Gentlemen, if there be any heretic among you, let him retire.' Immediately, one of the strangers quietly withdrew. Scarcely had he withdrawn, when the blood was liquid again, and was bubbling." Putignani adds: "The same thing is said to have happened on other occasions."

TO BE CONTINUED.

LUCAS GARCIA.

FROM THE SPANISH OF FERNAN CABALLERO.

II.

passed in this man-
was fifteen, and had
to one of those exqui-
gile creatures that, in
appear so rarely and
on. Lucas, who was
developed admirably.
outh of manly appear-
judicious and industri-
mers and managers of
ployed him in prefer-
s. Both inherited their
e—the oval face, fine
, large and expressive
small mouth, adorned
teeth, broad high fore-
e bearing of mingled
obility that distinguish

r had yielded complete-
ence of *La Leona*, who
living, and had made
rd in order to rule him
the more effectually. Too enervated and lazy to enter upon a new path, he went on selling his possessions to satisfy the woman's exactions, as an exhausted stream continues to flow in the channel it made when it was full and strong, without either the will or the force to open another. From the time that Lucas was able to work, he had maintained the house alone, with that mysterious day's wages of the laborer which God seems to bless, as he did the loaves and fishes destined to feed so many poor people. Else, how the *peseta*, sometimes two reals* a day can support husband, wife, generally half a dozen robust children; an old father or mother, or widowed mother-in-law, clothe them all and the head of the family in a very expensive

* From 10*d.* to 12½*d.* sterling.

manner,* pay house-rent and the costs of child-birth, sickness, and unemployed days; and still yield the copper they never refuse to *God's-namers*,† is a thing past comprehension, and belongs to the list of those in which, if we see not the finger of God or his immediate intervention, is because we are very thoughtless or voluntarily blind.

Lucas, who loved his sister above all things, seeing her entirely neglected by her father, had assumed over her the sort of tutelage, recognized and incontestable among the people, which belongs to the eldest brother—a tutelage which is annexed to the obligation of maintaining younger brothers and sisters if they are fatherless. This obligation and right instinctive do not constitute a law, nor are they laid down in any code, but are impressed by tradition on the heart, and have, no doubt, given rise to the institution of entails.‡ Lucas presented, also, the uncu
type of those chivalrous and
brothers that Calderon, Lo
other contemporary writers h
en us in their delightful pic
Spanish manners as models o
ty, delicacy, and punctilious h

As for Lucia, she was, as h
ther had been, loving, impr
and yielding. She regarded l
ther with the deepest affect
which respect mingled, witho
ening its tenderness.

One evening, when several
bors, who tenanted Juan C
house, were met together in th
one of them—it was the kins
of the departed Ana—said:

"Have you heard the new
is reported that *La Leona's* h
is dead. What do you say to

"That *La Leona* is just no
ing:

'My spouse is dead, and to heaven has
Wearing the thorns of a martyr's cro

replied one of the neighbors.

"There will be talk enoug
man, if it is true," replied th
speaker.

"Well, what do you want
say? I feel it for one."

"I feel it for *two*," added a
laughing.

"That is what I feel most,
tinued the kinswoman. "It is re
already that Juan Garcia is go
marry with the rag of a widow

"Woman! will you hold
tongue?"

"No; and I say more: I sa
I don't doubt it; for the wretc
him down, and holds him fro
neath, so that she can put h
the torture with "thou must
low this, or I will lay on the
that.'"

"True enough," observed th
er, "she has made a fool o
with drink; and, not satisfie
giving him wine, which is r

* We have thought it worth while to give the exact cost of the simplest dress—such a one as the poorest laborer is never without—of an Andalusian peasant:

Cloak,	260	reals.
Cloth jacket,	60	"
Cloth breeches,	60	"
Set of buttons (silver),	60	"
Idem for jacket,	36	"
Woollen sash,	50	"
Vest,	30	"
Linen shirt,	20	"
Linen drawers,	15	"
Calf-skin shoes,	22	"
Gaiters,	40	"
Stockings,	14	"
Handkerchief,	4	"
Hat,	30	"
Total,	606	"

—without the making, which is done by the women of the household.

What will be said to this by those who are all for utility, economy, and savings-banks, when the Andalusian rustic might, without inconvenience, go clad in a frieze sack, a pair of hempen sandals, and a rush hat?—*Authoress.*

† *Pordioseros*, those who ask in God's name—that is to say, beggars. For this and other delicate and tender epithets that the Spanish poor apply to the unfortunate, our stern language has no equivalents.

‡ The actual organization of the family throughout the kingdom of Aragon, the Basque provinces, and the mountains of Santander. It is this that makes the mania for codification that at present exists in Spain so much to be dreaded.—*Spanish Ed.*

and the legitimate child of the soil, she poisons him with bad brandy."

"The kite will get everything away from him by degrees, till she leaves him stuck, like a star lizard, to the bare wall," added another; "for she is more covetous than greediness, that 'walks one hand along the ground, and the other in the sky, and with its mouth wide open, that nothing may go by.'"

"She'll be Juan's third wife, and may die like the other two, and the four children he has under the sod. He must have some deadly exhalation about him, like a snake."

"Kill *La Leona!* As if that would be possible! It's my opinion that Death himself couldn't do it, with a century to help him. There was the cholera, that carried off so many good people; it never approached her door."

"The she-rake has no end of luck."

At this moment Lucas entered. It was Saturday evening, and he had come to spend the Sunday at home.

"Lucas," asked his kinswoman, "do you know that *La Leona* is a widow, and they say that your father is going to marry her?"

A thunder-bolt could not have hurt Lucas more suddenly than did these words; nevertheless, he maintained his composure while he answered:

"Either you are dreaming awake, Aunt Manuela, or age is getting the better of your understanding."

"Don't fling my age into my face, *Luquillo*," said the good woman, who was jocose. "I would rather you called me sly fox; it is permitted to say *old* only in the company of wines and parchments."

"Well, then, why were you born so long ago? But don't come to me with your troubles."

"Publish your decrees in time, my son, for this one is in everybody's mouth."

"They may say what they please behind my back. Regiments can't capture tongues and thoughts, but no one is going to speak against my father when I am present."

"I'll lay you something, Lucas, that he'll marry!"

"That will do, Aunt Manuela; you know the saying, 'Stop jesting while jesting is pleasant.'"

Like all men of stern nature, Lucas, when in earnest, had in him a something that imposed respect: the women were silent, and he went into his own dwelling.

He did not speak to his sister of the matter that occupied his thoughts so painfully, but, after giving her the money he had brought, remained a while talking cheerfully and affectionately with her, and then went in search of his neighbor, Uncle Bartolo.

He knew that the guerilla, on account of his age and good judgment, and because he had been his grandfather's friend, exercised great influence over his father, and could think of no one so suitable to confide in, and implore to interfere in the matter, and dissuade Juan Garcia, if, indeed, he entertained it, from such an outrageous project.

"Hola! What brings *Luquillo* with the step of a Catalan and face of a blacksmith?" exclaimed the old man, as Lucas entered.

The youth told his errand.

Uncle Bartolo, having heard him to the end, shook his head, as he remarked:

"Lucas, the proverb says, 'Between two millstones one had best not put his thumbs;' but—well, for your sake and Lucia's, the pretty dove! I will do what you ask, even if I lose—and I shall, for certain—

your father's friendship. I tell you though, beforehand, that interference will do no good."

"But, uncle, that which is never attempted is never done."

"Have I not told you I would try? You shall never say that you sought me and did not find me. I only want to remind you that counsels are thrown away upon the foolhardy, and perfumes upon swine. And to tell the truth, I would rather tackle one of those highwaymen of last year than your father; notwithstanding that the she-bandit has taken and done for him as easily as a spider would vanquish a fly."

Our old warrior went, the next day, to see Juan Garcia, whom he found indisposed.

"Hola! Juan," he cried, as he entered, "how are you?"

"Not so well as I might be, uncle," responded the invalid. "And you?"

"As well as can be, since I am a man of the old times, and not sorry for it: better suited beneath white hairs than white sheets. But," continued the guerilla, who in his long career had never studied diplomacy nor learned the art of preambling, "let us come to the point; for one needn't go by the bush where there's a high-road; they tell me, though I don't want to believe it, that you are going to marry."

Juan contracted his brows, and replied:

"And if I have never told any one so, how could they tell it to you?"

"Answer one question with another, to avoid committing thyself," is a rule of rustic grammar that the people have at their fingers' ends. Uncle Bartolo proceeded:

"It's easy to see how; you are thinking of it; and people nowadays are so sharp that they divine the thoughts. So that we may as well be plain—it is what you mean to do. Te truth, now."

"The truth!" responded availing himself of another s fuge. "Then, though—becai was not prepared to tell it—I not complied with the churc' year, I am to tell it to you! N 'He that reveals his secret, re without it.'"

"It is plain enough from crafty answer that your mi made up. So you needn't de nor put me off with palaver."

"The thing is yet in the and to be nibbled at," replied

"Do you know, Christian, you are about? For the begi of a cure is a knowledge of the ness."

"Yes, sir, I have my five counted."

"Yes, Juan, four of them u and one empty. But, my soi know me well, is it not so?"

"Yes, sir."

"You are sure that I am friend?"

"I don't say no to that, Uncl tolo."

"And you know the proverb 'An old ox draws a straigh row'?"

"Agreed, Uncle Bartolo; we that kind of wisdom years gi we are told that the devil is kn not because of his devilship, b cause he is the *old one*."

"Well, that being so, yo heed what I say."

"That remains to be seen."

"And you will consider n vice?"

"What is the meaning of : advanced guard, Uncle Ba Why do you sift and sift w falling through the sieve?"

"To fall with all my weight ing this, and no more: 'Don marry, Juan Garcia!'"

"Why not?—if you would please tell me."

"Don't marry, Juan Garcia!"

"Uncle Bártolo, don't leave your counsels like foundlings in the hospital, without father or mother. I must not marry—the reason?"

"Juan, 'where there has been familiarity, let there be no contract.'"

"If it were as you intimate, I ought to marry; for, if this woman has lost respect through me—"

"Stop, Juan; that'll do! Don't come to me with your '*mea culpas*.' There is always a pretext for wrong-doing. But you know very well that the woman has not lost respect through you. Nobody loses what he never had."

"Uncle Bartolo, by what I shave off, but that you comb gray hairs, and were my father's friend—*Vive Dios!*—"

"Tut, tut, man! Don't get excited, and talk nonsense! I did not come here to poke you up, nor to pick a quarrel, but with a very good intention; and, as the friend I am to you, to prevent your making an atrocious fool of yourself. Have you considered your children, and the kind of step-mother you are going to give them?"

"If she will be a wife good enough for their father, it appears to me that she will be a good enough step-mother for them; especially as, where they are concerned, what I do is right."

"Right! Now you are like the Englishman, Don Turo, that killed an urraca for a partridge, and then said 'all right.' Take notice, Juan, that they are not likely to be willing to live under that woman's flag. You are going to alienate them from you, and, 'withdraw thyself from thine own, God will leave thee alone.'"

"They will not be willing to live under her! What are you saying, sir? We shall see, however. 'Where the sea goes, the waves go.'"

"Well, Juan, we shall see that Lucas, who is high-minded, will not consent to let his sister live with a woman of evil note."

"The note I have put upon her, I will take from her. Do you comprehend? And Lucas will be very careful not to set himself up to crow while I live. There cannot be two heads, and, 'in sight of the public stocks, street-criers keep their mouths shut.'"

"Think, Juan, that your son should be the staff of your old age. You may provoke him so far that he will leave you some day without warning."

"Let him go; I have the means to maintain myself, and my wife and daughter."

"Ah! Juan, what have you left? Juice don't run out of a sucked orange. As if that woman had not swallowed your slice of field and olive-yard, leaving you nothing but the house; and that will go the same way the field and orchard went. As for making a living—you have thrown yourself away; your back is getting stiff already, and 'to old age comes no fairy godmother.' Where, then, are those 'means' to come from? What you are going to do is get entangled in debts; and, let a man be as honest as he will, 'if he owes and doesn't pay, all his credit flies away.'"

"*La Leona* has a gossip at the port that is a contrabandist; he is going to take me for a partner."

"*Only this was wanting!*" exclaimed the old man indignantly. "*You! you take to the path!** Does Barabbas tempt you, Juan Garcia? Have you lost your senses entirely, or are you fooling me? Sure enough,

* *Tomar la vereda*—Take another than the high or legalized way. Said of contrabandists.

'he that goes with wolves will learn to howl.' Don't you know that the devil takes honest gains and dishonest, and the gainer with them? But let us keep to the matter in hand. Juan, the woman has a bad name that neither you nor the king, if he tried, could take from her. She is bad of herself; and neither you nor the bishop, if he set his heart on doing it, could make her good. Moreover, 'a rotten apple spoils its company.'"

"Go on with the bad! 'Against evil-speaking there's nothing strong'; but, if she appears good to me, we are all paid."

"Juan, 'look before you leap.' You have not the excuse of youth for your indiscretion; you are more than forty years old."

"And have more than forty *arrobas** of patience, Uncle Bartolo. *Candela!* I have long sought and never found a friend that would offer me a sixpence, and have found, without seeking, one that gives me advice."

"Well, my son, your soul is in your palm," said Uncle Bartolo, rising. "Remember that there was not wanting a friend to give you good advice—a man of ripe brain, who warned you of the future—for this marriage is going to be the perdition of your house. And, remember what I tell you now, a day is coming when you will have eyes left you only that you may weep." With these words, Uncle Bartolo went his way.

"Son," said he to Lucas, who had waited for him in his house, "it was lost labor, as I foretold. But go, now, and mind what I say. Submit to what can't be helped, and don't be stiff-necked, for you'll surely come out loser. The rope breaks where it is slenderest. You are his son, and the authority belongs to him. You will only be kicking against the goad."

Lucas went back to the country and to work with a heavy heart. When he returned home on the following Saturday, he learned that the bans of his father's marriage were to be published the next morning for the first time. Grief made him desperate, and he resolved, as a last recourse, to speak himself.

We have already hinted at the cool and formal relation that existed between these two—thanks to the neglect the abandoned man had shown his children. For some time past, the excellent character of Lucas and the good name it had gained him had inspired Juan Garcia with that bitter sentiment which rises in the heart of a man who possesses the legal and material superiority, against the subordinate to whom he feels himself morally inferior—a sentiment of hostility that is apt to manifest itself in despotism.

"Sir," said the son, speaking with firm moderation, "they have been telling me that you are going to marry."

"They have been telling you what is quite true."

"I hoped that it was not true."

"And why? if I might ask."

"On account of the woman they say you are going to have."

"She is not, then, to your taste; and you think, perhaps, that I ought to have advised with you?"

"No, sir, not with me—I am of small account; but with some one that has more knowledge and judgment than I."

"So, then, it appears to you," said Juan, with repressed ire, "that your father needs counsel?"

"Yes, sir," answered Lucas calmly, "when he has a young daughter, and is going to give her a step-mother."

* An arroba is twenty-five pounds.

"For fear he might give her one that would eat her up, like the *Cancon!*"*

"No, sir, no; we understand now that people are not swallowed like sugared anises."

"Or make her work, being herself industrious, and not willing to sit hand upon hand like a notary's wife?"

"It is not that, sir; Lucia is not afraid of work. She knows that work is the honor of the poor."

"Or, perhaps, keep her at home like a chained dog?"

"No, sir; I am not thinking of that, for my sister, though brought up without a mother, is modest, and not a girl to be seen at the street door or with a hole in her stocking. She is used to the shade, but—"

"But what? Have done!"

"That which this woman will give her is evil, and may be her ruin."

Juan Garcia, who had with difficulty restrained himself, rushed upon his son, as the latter uttered these words, with his hand uplifted to strike. Lucas, perceiving the action, quickly inclined his head, and received upon it the blow that had been aimed at his face.

"God help me, father! what have I done to be chastised? Have I said anything wrong? Have I been wanting in respect to you? Father, just before my mother—heaven rest her!—died, she said to me, 'Lucas, watch over your sister.' I promised her that I would, and have kept my promise."

"She meant," replied Juan, somewhat softened by the memory of the mother evoked by her son, "she meant in case Lucia should be left without me. But, while I live, which is it that has the authority over my daughter?"

"Father, for the love of the Blessed Virgin, leave her to me! I will support her."

"Are you in your senses?"

"For God's sake, don't separate us! I will work with all my might to maintain us both."

"Separate you! Nobody has thought of doing it. You will come with her to my house."

"No, sir."

"How is that? What do you mean by 'no, sir'? Do you think you have a right to call your father to account? Is it not enough for you to know what his hands decide? Perhaps you would like to have another proof of what they are able to do?"

"My father may kill me, and I shall neither open my lips nor forget my duty; but—make me live with that woman—never!"

"We shall see about that, insolent upstart!"

"Yes, we shall see," said Lucas, as he went sorrowfully out.

Lucas was gifted with one of those noble and delicate natures that humble themselves in victory and grow firm in defeat; that is alike incapable of noisy elation in triumph, or pusillanimous abjection when prostrate. But the determination of his character was degenerating into stubbornness, as it always happens when will forsakes the guidance of reason to follow the promptings of pride. Therefore, though he had not, in the slightest degree, failed in the strict respect that morality enforces, neither the threats of his father nor love for his sister could shake the resolution he had taken in that decisive interview. On leaving his father's presence, he went in search of Lucia, whom he found weeping. For a long while neither spoke: brother and sister mutually comprehending the cause of the profound depression

* A monster they frighten children with.

of the one and the tears of the other.

"If mother could open her eyes!" at last exclaimed Lucia.

"They whose eyes God has closed have no wish to open them again in the world," replied Lucas; "but remember, that from heaven she always has hers fixed upon her daughter. I cannot help you; for, though I have tried my best to keep you under my flag, I have not succeeded: because, heart's dearest, there is no power in the world that can oppose a father's."

"But I am to do only what you tell me, Lucas, for my mother left me to you," sobbed the girl.

"Well, then, pay attention to what I am going to say.

"Bear your cross with patience; for that is the only way to make it lighter. Be a reed to all storms, but an oak to temptation. Never turn from the right path, though it be steep and sown with thorns. Always look straight before you, for he that does not do this never knows where he will stop. As for this woman who is going to be your father's wife, give her the wall; but remember that she is bad, and neither join yourself to her nor talk with her, except with reserve and when you must."

"Shall you do the same, Lucas?"

"I—I shall act as God gives me understanding."

Nothing was seen of Lucas on the day of Juan's marriage, and it was in vain that they looked for him: he had disappeared. Juan, who left no means untried to ascertain his son's whereabouts, learned some days later, from a muleteer who come from Tevilla, that he had enlisted. The father felt indignant at the contempt thus shown for his authority, and sorry to lose an assistant in his son: but found consolation in freedom from the immediate presence of an interested witness whose censur the fog, without form, voice, c tion, penetrated him with an ur fortableness from which there w escape.

Lucia went to live with her mother, and it is hardly necess relate what she had to endur particular from the daughters c latter, who, being both foolish ugly, naturally disliked one wh beautiful and wise; for she had menced by playing with swe the role of Cinderella that brother had recommended. little by little, the continual fr was wasting her patience, and i nation, repressed discontent, an cor were beginning to find pla her heart. She wished, somet to humiliate, by her advan those who were continually hun ing her, and grew presuming fond of admiration. So it i evil seeds spread and multiply prodigious rapidity: one suffic open the way and prepare the g for the rest.

While these things were pa a regiment of cavalry, comma by one Colonel Gallardo, came took up its quarters in Arcos.

Gallardo was rich, well-born, been good-looking, and a great comb. He was still the latter; the kind of conceit that is ofte result of living in the atmosphe adulation that surrounds the po ors of money and comman atmosphere that intoxicates r making them overbearing and lent, and apt to do, with great i tinence, things that would n tolerated in others. While aut is thus misunderstood, it is har be wondered at that it has lo ancient prestige, and is hated set at naught. Authority shou consecrated to its mission, and, its advantages, accept its respo

lies, the first of which is to give good example. Do those in place really think they owe the masses nothing?—that these are, at once, mothers to nourish, and incensories to deify them? Shall we ever go back, morally, to those remote times when men were both worthy and self-respecting, and neither admitted flattery nor refused to rule its reverence; for the latter was never so despised as it is at present; the former never so cringing.

But to return to Colonel Gallardo, who has given margin to those reflections.

This admirable person added to his other pretensions that of youth in its flower. His own having already gone to seed, the result was that, instead of appearing the young cock, he suggested the idea of a very old chicken. By grace of the peruke-maker, which, as everybody knows, consists in creating ringlets where there is no hair, he wore curled locks. He encased himself in a French corset, which gave him a slenderness a sylph might have envied. It was an article of his belief that amorous conquests were as creditable to a soldier as military ones; and he considered a little hare-brainedness in a man and a spice of coquetry in a woman the proper seasoning for each respectively. These things, united with vanity enough to fill the space left vacant in his heart and brain by the absence of other qualities, made of Colonel Gallardo one of those characters that are detestable, without being malevolent and ridiculous, though they do not

This cavalier, a bachelor, of course, like all of his stamp, had lodgings opposite the house of *La Leona*, whose daughters were not long in becoming acquainted with his attendants.

The preludes to acquaintanceship were couplets worded and sung with the evident intention of opening a flirtation. The soldiers took the initiative, singing to the music of their *guitarillos*: *

"If your person can be won
  By valor in the field,
Here's a man with sword in hand
  Will sooner die than yield."

Another followed:

"If for a a rustic's love
  You slight a soldier bold,
Base metal you will have
  Instead of shining gold."

To which the girls replied in a similar strain, declaring that they found it difficult to have patience with "these men of the fields," whom they describe as "persecutors of the ground" and "sepulchres of *gaspacho*."

Neither was the colonel behindhand in becoming enamored of the beauty of Lucia; nor was he the man to dissimulate his sentiments. And, alas! Lucia herself had ceased to be the discreet and modest maiden, who would once have shrunk offended from demonstrations that could not fail to give occasion for scandal.

The hopes of our decorated aspirant, who soon learned the interior circumstances of this family, rose high in view of the antecedents of the step-mother and the unhappy lot of the young girl. But he deceived himself. For, though vanity had led Lucia beyond the limits of prudence, she receded from corruption with all the energy of the honorable blood she had inherited from her mother. This resistance exasperated the step-sisters, who, wishing both to be rid of Lucia and to see her undone, hoped that the colonel would take her away with him, and laid a plan to accomplish the result they

* Small guitars.

desired. Having previously concerted with the lover, they carried out their project in the following manner: One night, when Lucia had gone to her room, and sat combing down her beautiful hair, the door opened suddenly, and admitted the colonel, hidden to the eyes in cloak and slouched hat, and accompanied by the daughters of *La Leona* in giggling triumph. They had hardly introduced him into the chamber, when, with jests and bursts of laughter, they turned and ran out, closing the door behind them and drawing the bolt.

Too much overwhelmed with indignation, terror, and shame to think of any means of escape, the unfortunate girl covered her face with her hands and remained silent. The colonel, also, who had been led by *La Leona* to think that it would not be difficult to propitiate Lucia by tender and gallant speeches, found himself without words in the presence of grief so real and so mute. For, unless a man is totally base, no amount of daring will enable him wholly to overcome the respect that innocence inspires.

"Am I, then, so disagreeable to you," said Gallardo at last, drawing nearer to Lucia—"I who have no wish but to please you?"

"Lucas! Lucas! O my brother!" cried the girl, bursting into sobs.

"I will go! I am going!" said the colonel, half-offended, half-compassionate; and he approached the door, but it was locked.

"You see that I cannot get out," said he, turning again toward Lucia.

"I know it," she exclaimed. "They wanted to ruin me, and they have done it! Have locked me in here alone with you! How can I ever bear to have any one look me in the face again! What will Lucas say? Ah, my heart's brother!"

"You are not ruined, child!" said the colonel, irritated. "I a friend to tragedies; heroic Lu frighten me. Believe me, I to go, and, to prove it, since not leave by the door, I will g by this window." With these the colonel wrapped himself in his cloak, and, mounting th dow-seat, sprang into the yard, was enclosed only by a low pa

Hardly had his feet touch ground when he felt himself a ed by an infuriated man, who trophized him with the most v insults. At the same momen *Leona* and her daughters ran s ing from the house, while the u py Lucia called from the winc a voice of anguish: "Don't him! It is my father!"

The man had drawn a but Gallardo, who was vi and wished to escape from th venture without hurting Lucia's er and without being recog pushed the assailant from him such force as to throw him up back; ran to the paling, leap and disappeared.

Juan Garcia rose from the g in that state of blind rage in men of his uncultivated natur at no obstacle and hesitate crime. Violently repulsing hi and step-daughters, who, alarm the result of their work, would detained him, he hastened t house, and was making direct Lucia's room.

"Lucia! Lucia! jump fro window!" screamed *La Leona* seeing a catastrophe. "Your fa going to kill you!"

Wild with terror, Lucia, who the enraged and drunken vo her father approaching her ch precipitated herself into the ya

"Run to the colonel's!" urg step-mother, with no intention but that of saving her life. "

the last one your father will suspect. It is the nearest house, and you can be hidden there better than anywhere else."

Lucia obeyed mechanically, guided by the instinct of self-preservation, the only motive that rules weak natures in moments of supreme peril.

Gallardo was excitedly pacing his room when she rushed in, pale as death, covered with her long black hair, cold and helpless with fear and desperation, and, sinking upon a chair, exclaimed:

"You have been my ruin! At least save my life!"

It is to be supposed that even the dry and sterile heart of this man would find, in such circumstances, sentiments and words to soothe the wretched creature thus forced to seek his protection. It is certain that, at the vision of her youthful and innocent beauty, seen through the prism of her tears, he became more enamored than ever, and took advantage of the distress, of which he was the cause, to advance his suit.

And the poor child, bereft of affection and support, having nowhere to lay her head, lacking firmness to resist and energy to act, unsustained by principle duly and constantly inculcated, which would have made her prefer misery to shame, allowed herself to be persuaded and retained, drawn by a love that began with the promise and conviction that it was to be unchanging and eternal.

The colonel soon left, taking with him, secretly, Lucia, who had already begun to feel contented in the atmosphere of tenderness and luxury that surrounded her.

The fit of passion that Juan Garcia had experienced, united with grief, shame, and remorse, so affected his constitution, already spent and worn by the life he had been leading, that he fell into an inflammatory fever, from which he never recovered. A little while before he died, he said to his old friend: "Uncle Bartolo, you hit the mark when you told me that the day would come when I should have eyes left only to weep. It has come, and—well, better to close them for ever."

Two years had passed since the events last narrated, and five since Lucas left home. His regiment was in Cordova, where a general recently arrived from Madrid was going to review the troops of the garrison.

The evening before the parade, Lucas was in the quarters with several other soldiers from Arcos, one of whom, with the careless and constant gayety which characterizes the Spanish soldier, and proves, to the extreme scandal and disgust of the votaries of utility, the non-material genius of the nation, was alternately touching his guitar, and singing:

"Oh! 'tis gay to be a soldier,
Standing guard with tired feet,
And head erect, in stiff cravat,
And nothing at all to eat.

"And, for the bread of munition,
He gets from the King of Spain,
To be 'Alert there, sentinel!'
All night, and never complain.

"This is the life of a soldier,
To march wherever he's led,
To sleep under alien shelter,
And die in a hospital bed."

At this moment the picket-guard, which had just been relieved from duty at the general's quarters, came up.

"Oh!" said one of the newly-arrived, "if the general's wife isn't a fine one! In all my travels I have never seen her equal."

"She is not his wife," replied another, "so drop the 'fine.'"

"And why should I drop it? Good words neither add to beauty nor take from it; but what do you know?"

"What they tell me; and, be-

sides, if she was his wife, he wouldn't keep her so grand; for that is the way with the *You-Sirs*, they spend more money upon their dears than they do upon their wives."

"Because they are afraid their mistresses will leave them for other lovers. What do you say, Lucas?"

"That it's like keeping a lead knife in a golden sheath," answered Lucas.

"The soul of this one may be of lead, or something cheaper, but her person—by the Moors of Barbary!"

"We hear enough," replied Lucas; "dress up a block, and it will look like a shopman. I tell you, these good-for-nothing she vagabonds appear to me more like bedraggled rags than women."

"Get away! If this Lucas hasn't always the rod of justice lifted! He has entered the uniform, but the uniform hasn't entered him. If you had been born king, they would have called you the *Justiciero*."*

The next morning the troops were drawn up in splendid array, the bands were playing, and the general, magnificently mounted, came galloping upon the field, followed, at a little distance, by an elegant open carriage, in which was seated a beautiful and richly dressed woman.

The carriage stopped near where Lucas and his townsmen were formed at the end of a line.

"That is the general's mistress," said the man at Lucas's right in a low tone. "Did I not tell you she was a sun?"

Lucas raised his eyes, and fixed them upon the woman, at the same instant starting so perceptibly as to attract the notice of his companions.

"What ails you, Lucas?"

"Nothing," he answered calmly.

But the glances of the occupant of the carriage had fallen u gallant-looking soldier who s near her, and a cry of deligh prise burst from her lips.

"Lucas," said his other n in line, "that lady is looki way, and making signs to yo

Lucas, pale but perfectly c ed, neither looked up nor rep

"Lucas, who can it be knows you; she is waving he kerchief, and seems as if she spring out of the carriage. I her! Say! who is she?"

"I do not know her," ar Lucas.

"By the very cats!" exclai first who had spoken, in an "may my end be a bad o isn't your sister Lucia! Look man! it is she!"

"I have looked at her, an you that I do not know h sponded Lucas.

"Look, now, look! the po thing is crying. She is not changed, only handsomer. Yo be blind not to see that it i sister!"

"I do not know her," repea young man, with the same com

There are men who feel pr ly, but exercise such self-contr they succeed in covering with tle of indifference the most and agonizing emotions — Scævolas, who astonish with tracting us. We like neith motive nor the effects of a s that parades itself so disda For, if in order to judge of al human, it is necessary to c them with the example of th of humanity — the God-Ma cannot fail to be repelled b arrogance when we reflect t most holy passion would have its tender and sublime sanctit it bravado had taken the p meekness.

* The doer of Justice.

The voice of the commanding officer was now heard prescribing the evolutions. When these were concluded, the troops marched to their quarters, where, gathered in groups, they made their comments upon the beautiful lady of the carriage, some of the soldiers from Arcos declaring that it was Lucia, others, who had not seen her so near, maintaining the contrary.

"Her brother will know," they exclaimed, running to find him.

"Lucas, is that grand, fine *You-Madam* your sister Lucia?"

"I don't know the woman. And now, comrades, no more questions; for I am not a repeating-clock, and am tired of answering."

Before half an hour had passed, an orderly arrived from the general in search of a soldier named Lucas Garcia.

Interiorly shaken by the indignation which he would not allow his face to betray, Lucas followed the messenger to a house of good appearance, and was shown into an elegant and luxuriously furnished cabinet. As he entered, a fair young girl robed in silk rose from a sofa, and ran towards him with open arms.

"I do not know you, my lady," said Lucas, quickly repulsing her with

"Lucas, my brother!" she exclaimed, bursting into tears.

"I have no sister," he replied, in the same tone as before.

"Lucas, my own brother, listen, and I will tell you what happened!"

At this moment, the colonel—that had been, and was now general—en-

"Ah! Lucia," said he, with ostentatious condescension, "so, then, you have already seen your brother."

"He will not know me," sobbed the girl.

"How is that?" asked the general, turning toward the soldier. "And why?"

"Because it would be a deceit, my general," answered Lucas, lifting his open hand to his temple. "I am the only one left of my house, and have no sister."

"I sent for you," proceeded the general, "to make you one of my orderlies, to keep you near me, have you taught to write, and fit you for a career. You will mount rapidly. I know already that you are intelligent and brave."

"I do not wish to learn to write, my general."

"And why?" asked the general, repressing his ill-humor, "since without knowing how to write, you cannot rise?"

"I do not want to rise, my general."

"The reason is evident," said the general, with a mocking laugh. "It is not strange that the heir of such a house should disdain the service of the king."

"He that sees not the king is king to himself," answered Lucas.

"What is there that you want, brother?" asked Lucia.

"I desire nothing but to serve my time out and return home."

"But who calls you there, if, as you say, you have no one?" questioned she.

"Love for my native place," he answered. "God give me rest in the soil that gave me birth!"

"Valiant goose!" exclaimed the general.

Lucas neither opened his lips nor moved an eyelid.

"Dearest brother! by our mother's memory, don't make as if you did not know me! You break my heart! Stay here."

"It would not suit me to be a stranger anywhere, madam."

"Enough!" said the general. "Let

the clown go, he will think better of it."

"I do not think twice of things," replied Lucas, saluting as he went out.

Lucia ran after him into the ante-room, caught his arm, and, pressing it against her bosom, cried in a voice of passionate and tender entreaty:

"Lucas! my brother! for God's sake stay! The general has promised me that he will do all he can for you; and he can do a great deal."

"The sack is not big enough to hold both honor and profit," responded Lucas, hurling his sister from him with all the loftiness of a proud nature and the brute force of an angry churl.

Lucia fell overwhelmed upon the nearest chair, and her brother went his way to the quarters with clinched fists and lips compressed—pale with lividness that ire stamps upon the faces of children of the south. Ire was suffocating him; for he could neither express it nor follow its vengeful impulses, which would not have been satisfied short of the commission of a crime; and of this he was incapable.

But, oh! for a war. The private soldier would have given in it a hundred lives if he had had ther pair of epaulets that would lift the rank required, in order to him to demand satisfaction villain who, after having sedu sister, had insulted him so im ly—epaulets that he would thrown away the next hour, l tened orange skins; for Luc not aspiring; neither fortune n attracted him. He clung to l dition, loved the labors of th was attached to his town and toms, and would not have ren the things that suited his tas in which he excelled, for the hoisting himself upon a p where he must always have l unwelcome stranger and i The very words were antipatl his innate devotion, to his c his province, the place where born, his lares, and his class the effort of the age is to dest beautiful instinct of the heart, tinually saying to the poor, rise! the summit is your go heights are common to all, infusing a vain arrogance i wholesome minds of those wh worthy and respectable in th they occupy.

CONCLUDED IN OUR NEXT.

EGYPTIAN CIVILIZATION ACCORDING TO THE MOST RECENT DISCOVERIES.

FROM THE CORRESPONDANT.

II.

THE SACERDOTAL CLASS.

EGYPTIAN civilization had its source in the priesthood. There is reason to believe that at first they exercised sovereign authority. "After the reign of the demigods and the Manes," says Manethon, "came the first dynasty, consisting of eight kings, who reigned for the space of two hundred and fifty-two years. Menes was the first of these kings. He carried war into foreign lands, and made himself renowned."

Menes, the chief of the military forces, effected a revolution which substituted a civil government for a theocracy. He was the first to assume the title of king, and he founded the hereditary monarchy of Egypt.

The separation of the sovereign power from the priesthood was maintained for a long time, for it is not till the twenty-second dynasty that we meet Pahôr-Amonsé, high-priest of Amon-Ra, whose name is still to be seen in the inscriptions at Thebes in a royal cartouche. Pihmé, another high-priest, also figures in the royal *legendes* among the historical representations with which the pronaos of the temple of Khons at Thebes is decorated. This sacerdotal revolution doubtless took place at the end of the seven generations of sluggish kings of whom Diodorus speaks. The twenty-second dynasty in fact left no traces in history. It is only known by its downfall. "And this leads us to remark," says Champollion-Figeac, "that there was perhaps some admirable conception, or profound combination, or happy inspiration in the monarchical establishment of a powerful nation in which the loss of the crown was the inevitable effect of the incapacity or the negligence of the family that had received it by the will of the nation. A Theban family preserved it for thirteen consecutive centuries, and furnished six dynasties of more than fifty kings. The first suffered from foreign invasion, and achieved the arduous labor of sustaining the government, finally restoring all the branches of public administration, and re-establishing the temples and the public works. They rebuilt Thebes, Memphis, and the principal cities, Lake Moeris, and the canals of Lower Egypt. They and their successors bore their victorious arms over distant lands and seas. The arts developed under the wing of victory. Public prosperity seemed to keep pace with these heroic achievements, and the reigning family to become more powerful and more firmly established by such great undertakings. Inaction succeeded to so much zeal. Ten inglorious kings ascended the throne, the last of whom were deposed by the priests.

The constitution of the country, favored by the state of affairs, provided for this disorder. A new family was called to reign."

Modern historians have represented the ancient monarchy of Egypt as subjected to the despotism of the sacerdotal caste. This assertion seems difficult to reconcile with the numerous inscriptions attesting that the principal functions of the priesthood were constantly assumed by the sons of the Pharaohs. An inscription in relief on the façade of the tomb of Koufou Schaf, whom M. Mariette believes to be the oldest son of Cheops, the builder of the great pyramid, depicts that prince wearing a panther's skin—a distinctive sign of high sacerdotal functions—and among his titles is found that of priest of Apis. According to a papyrus published by Baron Denon, the sons of the two Pharaohs must have filled the office of the high-priest of Ammon.

It is true these last-named princes belonged to the twenty-second dynasty, and at that epoch they had not had time to forget the usurpation by the high-priests Pahôr-Amonsé and Pihmé. It is probable that the king in causing this high function to be assumed by his nearest relatives wished to take precautions against the reaction of the sacerdotal class, always so powerful. But the monuments almost always show the priesthood living in strict and intimate alliance with the royal authority. Thus, while the younger sons of the Pharaohs performed the priestly functions, the children of the high-priests attended the royal children, and were employed in the highest offices in the king's palace. The office of high-priest of Ammon at Thebes, the sacerdotal city, was hereditary, as Herodotus attests in the following passage: "As Hecatæus, the h
gave his genealogy at Thel
made himself to be a descenc
god, through sixteen generati
priests of Jupiter (Ammon)
him as they did me, excep
did not give my genealogy
conducting me into a vast
apartment, they counted,
showed them to me, the larg
en statues of the high-pries
of whom, while alive, placed
age there. Commencing w
of the last deceased and goi
the priests made me rema
each of the high-priests was
of his predecessor. . . .
one of these statues represent
said, a piromis, the son of a
They showed me three hund
forty-five, and invariably a
was the son of a piromis."

It is not necessary to re
what degree the priests of
took advantage of the cred
Herodotus. Doubtless, the
high-priest in Egypt was he
as well as the throne, but it
less subject to the influence o
tic revolutions. We have ju
for example, the two sons of
filling the office of the high-p
Amon-Ra, king of the gods.

The sacerdotal class was t
soul of the Egyptian nation
completely embodied the
character, and traditions of t
ple that they may be said t
lived by their priests. They
the most powerful body of m
ever existed in the world be
Catholic clergy.

As we have seen in a pr
chapter, the independence
corporation was ensured by
territorial endowment. Ac
to Diodorus, "the largest pa
land belonged to the coll
priests. . . . They transr

descendants and
ion.".⁸

a possession of
hampollion-Fi-
cerdotal class
th a vast heri-
according to
new generation
s this right of
hat necessarily
hereditary, be-
their functions
of the land
member of the
damental prin-
titution of the
rpt depended."
ansmission of
:tion, and the
perty attached
l only take ef-
f the children,
lest, as in the
other children
ported by the
easily found a
in the perqui-
sacred or civil
number of the
dowments and
he Rosetta in-
)w so large a
ld live at their
must be added
royal treasury,
nerous salaried
ced every part
stration, apart
here. But in
families some-
: for want of

descendants, and thus a new path was opened for capacity without employment.

To form an exact idea of the influence exercised by the priesthood over Egyptian society, it is necessary to enter into some details upon their manners and kind of life, the duties which occupied them, and the extent of their knowledge of all kinds which they made use of to promote the civilization of their country.

Plutarch relates that the Egyptian priests abstained from mutton and pork, and on days of purification they ordered their meat to be served without salt, because, among other reasons, it whetted the appetite, inciting them to eat and drink more. He says: "They have a well apart, where they water their bull Apis, and carefully abstain from drinking the Nile water, not that they regard it as unclean, on account of the crocodiles, as some suppose—on the contrary, there is nothing the Egyptians reverence so much as the Nile—but they think its effect is to render them more corpulent. They are unwilling for Apis to become too fat, or to become so themselves, but wish their souls to be sustained by slight, active, nimble bodies, and that the divine part within may not be oppressed and weighed down by the burden of what is mortal.

"In the city of Heliopolis, or the City of the Sun, those who worship the divinity never carry any wine into the temple, because it is not suitable to drink in the presence of their lord and king. The priests take it in small quantities, but they have several days of purification and sanctification, during which they abstain entirely from wine, and do nothing but study and teach holy things."

Who would have expected to find among the priests of a pagan nation

the rules of abstinence now practised by the Catholic Church?—"that the soul may be sustained by slight, active, nimble bodies, that the divine part within may not be oppressed and weighed down by the burden of what is mortal." Was it not in these temperate habits, so in accordance with their spiritualistic doctrines, that lay, to a great degree, the secret of the moral influence of the priests, the real aristocracy of the country?

The prestige of the sacerdotal class was partly due to their costume and appearance. "In other places," says Herodotus, "the priests of the gods wear their hair long; in Egypt they shave. . . Every three days the priests shave the whole body, that no vermin may defile them while ministering to the gods. They wear only garments of linen and slippers of the papyrus. They are not allowed to wear other kinds. They wash themselves in fresh water twice a day and twice by night. Their rites are almost innumerable." On the Egyptian monuments of every age the priests of various ranks are easily recognized by their heads entirely shaven. They could only wear linen garments; woollen were forbidden. Besides the religious motives that induced them to adopt linen tissues, this preference was justified by its advantages. From linen could be made light robes of dazzling whiteness, which would reflect the sun's rays and engender nothing unclean.

All the ancient authors testify to the effect produced upon the popular mind by the imposing exterior of the Egyptian priests; their gleaming white robes, the habitual gravity of their deportment, their exquisite neatness, and the images of the gods worn on rich collars—all conspired to excite respect and veneration.

The most important duty of the priests, next to the functions office, was that of giving ad the king. "The priests," sa dorus, in a passage already "are the chief counsellors king. They aid him by their advice, and knowledge." In ing to the regulations for the tion of the king, and facilitati accomplishment of their dut have shown how their appli so important to the happiness people, was confided to the and patriotism of the chief But did they not render this ta possible by allowing the ki receive divine honors, exaltin pride by the ceremonies of actu ship, as attested by all the ments, and officially recogniz we shall presently see, by the dotal body itself, in the Rose scription?

In subjecting the Egyptians humiliation of this worship, superstitions still more shamef not the priests degrade ther facilitate the despotism of the The more enlightened and po the sacerdotal class, the more r sible before history for the of a nation which was the firs of civilization.

"In Greece," says Champ Figeac, "the service of the was the sole occupation o priests; in Egypt, they were men governing, so to speak, and people in the name of the and monopolizing the adminis of justice, the culture of the sc and their diffusion. We, the find members of this caste where, in all ranks of Egypti ciety, and we see by the gra the lowest grades that they attached by their titles or of religion and its ministrants. find in ancient writings the qualifications for the different

of the priesthood. "The monuments show that this class, with its infinite ramifications, was of every grade, the lowest of which was not despised. It was everywhere present by means of a vast hierarchy, which had every gradation from the all-powerful chief pontiff down to the humble porter of the temple and palace, and, perhaps, even their servant.*

In addition to their religious duties, the learned priests taught in the schools of the temples the arts and sciences, writing, drawing, music, literature, cosmogony, natural and moral philosophy, natural history, and the requirements of religion. The priest had charge of the finances, the assessment and collection of the taxes; priests administered justice, interpreted the laws, and in the king's name decided all civil and criminal cases. Another sacerdotal division practised medicine and surgery. It is known that the Egyptians were the first to make medicine an art founded on the data of experience and observation.†

One of the most numerous and most important of the sacerdotal divisions was the scribes, who transcribed the sacred books, the national annals, the documents of all kinds relating to the civil condition of families, property, justice, the administration, and, finally, the ritual of the dead, more or less extended, which piety deposited in the coffins of deceased relatives. Writing in Egypt dates from extreme antiquity. There are inscriptions still to be seen, perfectly legible, in the sepulchral chambers of the great pyramid, constructed by one of the first kings of the fourth dynasty.

Champollion-Figeac says the three kinds of writing, hieroglyphic, hieratic, and demotic, were in general use. He adds that "the hieroglyphic alone was used on the public monuments. The humblest workman could make use of it for the most common purposes, as may be seen by the utensils and instruments of the most common kinds, which, it may be observed, contradicts the incorrect assertions respecting the pretended mystery of this writing, which the Egyptian priests, according to them, made use of as a means of oppressing the common people and keeping them in ignorance."

No learned body ever understood the wants of its country as well as the Egyptian priesthood. And never was a public administration more solicitous of availing themselves of this knowledge for the general benefit. It is true, the annual uniformity of physical phenomena singularly facilitated the study and application of the laws necessary for the well-being of the people. The great and wonderful inundation of the Nile, occurring every year at the same time, covering the land with water for the same length of time, then subsiding to give a new face to the country and a fresh stimulus to the activity of the inhabitants, naturally imprinted on the nation habits of order and foresight which made it easy to govern.

The members of the sacerdotal class, then, were most intimately connected with the individual interests of the nation; they were the necessary intermediaries between the gods and man, and between the king and his subjects. Their concurrence in all public business was not less constant or less necessary. The religious nature of the inhabitants led them to offer invocations to the gods amid all their occupations, in peace and war, in public and private duties, at the ebb of inundating waters, the preparation of the land for the seed,

* *Égypte ancienne*, p. 117.

† Chemistry comes from Chemi—which means Egypt.—Ed.

and the harvesting of the fruits of the earth. The gods, manifesting themselves through the priests, directed the most important decisions, and sanctified by the expression of their satisfaction the possession of the harvest, the first-fruits of which were received as offerings.*

But that which gives a more just idea of the sublime *rôle* played by the Egyptian priests is the Rosetta inscription.† It is well known that this famous inscription is the reproduction of a decree made in 196 B.C. by the representatives of the sacerdotal body gathered at Memphis for the coronation and enthronement of Ptolemy Epiphanes. On account of its importance, we think ourselves justified in giving it almost entirely: "In the year IX.,‡ the tenth of the month of Mechir, the pontiffs and prophets, those who enter the sanctuary to clothe the gods, the pterophores, the hierogrammatists, and all the other priests, who from all the temples in the country have assembled before the king at Memphis for the solemnity of taking possession of that crown which Ptolemy, still living, the well-beloved of Pthah, the divine Epiphanes, a most gracious prince, has inherited from his father, being assembled in the temple of Memphis, have pronounced this same day the following decree:

"Considering that King
still living, the well-beloved
the divine Epiphanes, son
Ptolemy and Queen Arsin
philopatores, has conferred
of benefits on the temples
those who dwell in them,
general on all those who ar
his dominion: that being
the offspring of a god an
dess, like Horus the son
and Osiris, the avenger of O
father, and, eager to man
zeal for the things that per
the gods, he has consecrate
revenues to the service of the
in money as well as grain,
pended large sums in restori
quillity to Egypt, and cons
temples therein:

"That he has neglected n
in his power of performi
mane deeds; that in order
his kingdom the people an
citizens generally might po
abundance, he has repealed
the tributes and taxes estab
Egypt, and diminished the w
the remainder; that he has,
remitted all that was due h
the rents of the crown, eit
his subjects, the people of I
those of his other kingdom
these rents were of con
amount; that he has release
who were imprisoned and co
for a long time;

"That he has ordered
revenues of the temples, and
paid them annually in grai
as in money, together with
tions reserved for the gods
vineyards, the orchards, and
places to which they had a ri
the time of his father, sh
tinue to be collected in t
try;

"That he has dispensed t
belong to the sacerdotal tri
making an annual journey

* We have borrowed from Champollion most of this account of the services rendered by the priesthood to the Egyptian nation. It is true, it only gives the favorable side of that class, but, in speaking of the religion of the country, we shall endeavor to complete the picture and present it in its true light.

† The Rosetta Stone was among the valuable antiquities collected by the French expedition into Egypt, and given up to the English at the surrender at Alexandria. It was of black basalt, about three feet by two. The inscription on it was in three kinds of writing: the hieroglyphic, the demotic or enchorial, and the Greek. The upper and lower portions of the stone were broken and injured, but the demotic inscription was perfect. The Greek inscription was a key to the others, from which a complete hieroglyphic alphabet was composed.—Tr.

‡ Of the reign of Ptolemy.—Tr.

andria (the seat of royalty after the accession of the Lagides),

"That he has bestowed many gifts on Apis, Mnevis, and other sacred animals of Egypt; . . .

"It has, therefore, pleased the priests of all the temples of the land to decree that all the honors due King Ptolemy, still living, the well-beloved of Pthah, the divine Epiphanes, most gracious, as well as those which are due to his father and mother, gods, philopatores, and those which are due to his ancestors, should be considerably augmented; that the statue of King Ptolemy, still living, be erected in every temple and placed in the most conspicuous spot, which shall be called the statue of Ptolemy, the avenger of Egypt. This statue shall be placed near the principal god of the temple, who shall present him with the arms of victory, and all things shall be arranged in the most appropriate manner; that the priests shall perform three times a day religious service before these statues; that they adorn them with sacred ornaments; and that they have care to render them, in the great solemnities, all the honors which, according to usage, should be paid the other gods. . . .

"And in order that it may be known why in Egypt we glorify and honor, as is just, the god Epiphanes, most gracious monarch, the present decree shall be engraved on a stela of hard stone, in sacred characters and in Greek characters, and this stela shall be placed in every temple of the first, second, and third classes existing in all the kingdom."*

When we remember that the rule of the Greek conquerors had already been established in Egypt one hundred and thirty-six years, we judge, from the manner the Egyptian priests expressed themselves, of the persistent strength of this social organization imposed on the successors of Alexander in spite of all their power.

Therefore, says Champollion-Figeac, "the monuments of the times of the Ptolemies may be considered a key to the times of the Pharaohs, and the account of the ceremonies celebrated at the coronation of these Greek kings may very suitably be applied, by changing the names, to the kings of the ancient dynasties.

III.

THE MILITARY CLASS.

As we have already seen (Book I., chap. ii.), the profession of arms, as well as all other pursuits, was hereditary in Egypt, and those who followed it formed a distinct body still more numerous than that of the priests. They owned a part of the land, but were forbidden to cultivate it or to pursue any industrial labor. The fertile land assigned to every head of a family in the division which, according to Herodotus, was made under the first kings, was tilled by the laborers. It is easy to perceive the evils of this system, which for ever withheld from agriculture a multitude of young and vigorous arms. Herodotus estimates the number of the calasiries and hermotybies (the names of the warriors) at 410,000. We should doubtless modify the information given Herodotus by the priests, who had motives for exaggerating before a stranger the military forces of the country. But it is no less true that the number of able men withheld from agriculture by the Egyptian system must have been considerable. On the other hand, notwithstanding the numerous gymnastic exercises to which they were subjected, these exercises could not

* From Champollion-Figeac's translation.

have been as efficacious as agricultural pursuits in developing strength.

Wishing to elevate the noble profession of arms, they disparaged manual labor, and gradually left to slaves not only the trades, but even the agricultural pursuits so necessary to the existence and prosperity of a nation. Thanks to the salutary rule of hereditary professions, agriculture and other labor could not be entirely left to slaves, but labor alone attaches man to the soil; and there came a day when the military class was rooted out and transplanted beyond Egypt, which was left defenceless to its enemies. This is an important point in the history of the country which has not been sufficiently remarked.

Psammetichus, the head of the Saïte dynasty, was, it is said, the first king of Egypt who dared shake off the yoke of the laws imposed from time immemorial on royalty.* Relying on an army of foreign mercenaries, Arabians, Carians, and Ionian Greeks, he was not afraid of violating the privileges of the military class, and thus a revolution was effected in Egypt which became fatal to the country. "Two hundred and forty thousand Egyptian warriors revolted. . . . They therefore conferred together, and with one accord abandoned Psammetichus to go among the Ethiopians. Psammetichus, hearing of it, pursued them. When he overtook them, he implored them for a long time not to abandon their gods, their wives, and their children. Then one of them replied that everywhere . . . they could find wives and children." †

There are such bold colors in picture of Herodotus that moc requires us to efface them, bu may say that he depicts to the the brutal cynicism into which ness had caused the military cla fall. Whatever their wrongs or part of the king, it is difficult to a they were right in carrying thei sentment so far as to abandon religion, their families, and country. When, less than a cen after, the Persians, led by Camb invaded the land, the unarmed na could offer no resistance, and E was devastated. It had not recov from this disaster when it fell the power of Alexander.

The military system of an Egypt possessed, nevertheless, s ral advantages which should noticed.

First: Exemption from mil service ensured the tillers of the complete stability to their occupa so that war did not, as among mo nations, hinder the cultivation of land by enrolling the ablest pa the population and endangering subsistence of the country.

On the other hand, the posse of landed property guaranteed patriotism of the soldiers, wh Diodorus justly remarks, defe their country with all the ardor that they were at the time the safeguards of their property. Finally, the perpe of the military service in

* "The priests represented Psammetichus as the first Egyptian king to violate the sacerdotal rule limiting the king's ration of wine."—Strabo, *Geogr.* xvii.

† *Herodotus*, ii. Diodorus confirms this account, but its authenticity has been disputed by declaring that "the garrison of Elephantine, comprising only some hundreds or thousands of warriors, was the only one that could esc to Ethiopia." It was doubtless easier f garrison to cross the frontier which it v pointed to guard; but, supposing the Eg soldiers, dissatisfied with the violation c privileges, had concerted among themsel Herodotus declares, we do not see how Psammetichus could have hindered the de of so formidable an army. Besides, Her adds that he saw in Ethiopia a people kno der the name of *Automoles* (deserters), de ants of these Egyptian warriors. This tes is the more credible because Herodotus m journey not more than 150 or 160 years a death of Psammetichus.

wine. This is what the guards receive."

By this truly monarchical system, to which we venture to call the attention of the sovereigns who wish to retain their crowns, the whole army corps, and all the members of the military class, were successively admitted to the honor of guarding the sacred person of the king, which must have singularly augmented their devotedness and fidelity. This system had the great advantage of dissipating all feelings of envy with which privileged corps are regarded.

The Egyptian monarch doubtless found a solid support in this intimate union with the military class from which it sprang. King Psammetichus, the founder of the Saïte dynasty, was guilty of the capital fault of employing foreign troops, and violating the civil rights of the native soldiers. He thus caused the emigration of the entire national forces which we have already signalized as one of the principal causes of the downfall of Egypt.

From the time of the Persian conquest, the glorious *rôle* of the great Egyptian army was ended. History only mentions after this the exploits of the navy. Herodotus relates that Egypt furnished two hundred vessels for the fleet assembled by Xerxes for the subjugation of Greece. "The Egyptians," says he, "had barred helmets, convex bucklers with a wide bordure, spears for naval combats, and great battle-axes. Most of them wore cuirasses and long swords. Such was their equipment."

This fleet valiantly sustained the national honor, for the same historian adds a little further on: "In this combat (that of Artemisium, which preceded the great naval battle of Salamis) the Egyptians made themselves conspicuous among the troops of Xerxes; they did great things, and took five Greek vessels with equipages."

IV.

LEGISLATION—ADMINISTRATIVE JUDICIAL INSTITUTIONS.

The wisdom of the Egyptia was everywhere admired in a times. "I would remind the r accustomed, perhaps, to rega early history of Egypt as fabul somewhat uncertain, that obs rests on some points of its chron and the name and succession of of the kings, but not on its l tion, the wisdom of which wa mired by antiquity; and its eff the power and genius of the tian nation is attested by the ments still in existence.* Scripture itself seems to ratif eulogium in saying that "Mos instructed in all the wisdom Egyptians, and he was power his words and in his deeds."†

Unfortunately, all the Egy laws have not come down to u we have to resort to the incon testimony of Herodotus and I rus. But, as M. de Bonald sta is easy to recognize the g spirit of this legislation, which stantly contributed to stability l maintenance of ancient custom dently borrowed from patri traditions, and by the widest ap tion of the hereditary princip tending to every grade of so The details we have given conc the constitution of the famil about property, the distinctio tween the sacerdotal, military, a tural, and working classes, as w concerning royalty, appear suff to give the reader an approx

* De Bonald, *Théorie du Pouvoir*, I.
† Acts of the Apostles, VII. 22.

[illegible] political laws of the ancient Egyptian monarchy.

No [illegible] has yet been found of the municipal rights in ancient Egypt, but there is reason to believe that the [illegible] as Thebes, Memphis, Elephantine, Tanis, etc., had [illegible] suited to the genius of their inhabitants.

Each dynasty took for its capital the city from which it sprang. Thus the two first dynasties established the seat of government at Thinis and Memphis; the fifth at Elephantine; and the sixth at Memphis. Thebes only became the capital from the time of the eleventh dynasty.* Owing to this excellent custom, no city, under the ancient monarchy, could preserve its ascendency and attract all the sources of power in the country. Thinis, Memphis, Elephantine, Thebes, Tanis, Saïs, etc., were by turns the capitals of the kingdom, the centres of national activity, and the seats of sovereign power.

As to the financial laws, history has transmitted several the wisdom of which makes us regret the more those that have not come down to us. The object of the first was to proscribe idleness, which the Egyptians rightly regarded as a social evil. "Amasis," says Herodotus, "is the author of the law which obliges every Egyptian to show annually to the governor of his *nome* (province) his means of subsistence, and they who did not obey, or did not appear to live on legitimate resources, were punished with death. Solon, the Athenian, having borrowed this law from the Egyptians, imposed it on his fellow-citizens, who still observe and think it faultless."

The Egyptians, then, recognized this fundamental law—that man should live by the fruit of his labor, and we see with what rigor they enforced it.* In a well-regulated nation, where there is work for every one, no one, indeed, should be allowed to live at the expense of the community. The protection afforded human life in Egypt allows us to suppose that capital punishment was reserved for those who obstinately refused to gain their livelihood by labor or other honest means. We know from Herodotus that woman, as well as man, was subjected to the great law of labor. "The women go to market and traffic, the men remain at home and weave. Everywhere else the woof is brought up, the Egyptians carry it under. The men carry burdens on their heads, the women on their shoulders."†

The weaker sex was better protected from the violence of human passions than among other nations. "The laws concerning women were very severe. Those who violated a free woman were mutilated, for this crime was considered inclusive of three great evils, insult, corruption of morals, and confusion of children. For adultery without violence, the man was condemned to receive a thousand stripes, and the woman to have her nose cut off—the lawgiver wishing her to be deprived of the attractions she had availed herself of to allure."‡

We see the powerful protection assured to the family by the Egyptian laws in making woman respected and obliging her to respect herself.

Human life was equally protected. "He who saw on the way a man struggling with an assassin, or enduring violent treatment, and did not aid him when in his power, was con-

*Mariette: *Aperçu de l'Histoire d'Egypte*, p. 20 and 29.

*St. Paul says: "*Qui non laborat non manducet.*"

† *Herodotus*, lib. ii.

‡ *Diodorus*, lib. i.

demned to death." "He who had wilfully murdered a free man or a slave was punished with death, for the laws wished to punish not according to the degree of rank, but the intention of the evil-doer. At the same time, their care in the management of the slaves kept them from ever offending a free man.*

The law respecting loans was no less remarkable. It was forbidden those who lent by contract to allow the principal to more than double by the accumulation of the interest. Creditors who demanded pay could only seize the goods of the debtor. Bodily restraint was never allowed. For the legislator considered goods as belonging to those who acquired them by labor, by transmission, or by gift, but the individual belonged to the state, which, at any moment, might claim his services in war or in peace. It would, indeed, be absurd if a warrior, at the moment of battle, could be carried off by his creditor, and the safety of all endangered by the cupidity of one. It appears that Solon introduced this law at Athens, giving it the name of *seisactheia*,† and remitted all debts contracted under restraint. Most of the Greek legislators are blamed, and not without reason, for forbidding the seizure of arms, ploughs, and other necessary utensils, as pledges of debts, and for permitting, on the other hand, the privation of the liberty of those who made use of these instruments.

It is evident that civilized nations, from the earliest times, sought to oppose and repress the dangerous evil of usury, which inevitably leads to the oppression of the laborer and the degradation of labor. But the

Egyptians had an efficacious
of ensuring the payment of
in depriving those of sepulture
died without satisfying their
In such a case the body, af
embalmed, was simply depo
the house of the deceased
to the children. "It sometin
pens," says Diodorus, "that
to the prevailing respect
memory of parents, the gr
dren, becoming wealthier,
debts of their ancestor, had
cree of condemnation revok
gave him a magnificent
The same author adds, "It
mon to give the body of a d
parent as the guarantee of
The greatest infamy and p
of sepulture awaited those
not redeem such a pledge."

"Under the reign of A
says Herodotus, "the Eg
made a law allowing a pe
borrow by giving in pledge t
of his father. An additiona
allowed the lender to dispos
sepulchral chamber of the b
and, in case of refusal to
debt, he who had given such
incurred the following punis
in case of death, the impo
of obtaining burial either in
ternal sepulchre or in any ot
the interdiction of burying a
belonging to him."

This singular custom of ple
dead body could only exist in
where it was a religious oblig
preserve the body, and an
not to give funeral honors to d
parents.

The administration of jus
Egypt excited the admiration
philosophers and legislators
tiquity. Diodorus, who studi
system, found it superior to
other countries. To enab
reader to judge for himself,
give the essential details con

* *Diodorus*, lib. i.

† From σείω, *I shake off*, and ἄχθος, *burden*. See Plutarch, *Life of Solon*, xiv.

it. "The Egyptians," says he, "have carefully considered the judicial power, persuaded that the acts of a tribunal have a twofold influence upon social life. It is evident that the punishment of the guilty and the protection of the injured are the best means of repressing crime. They knew, if the fear of justice could be done away with by bribes and corruption, it would lead to the ruin of society. They therefore chose judges from the chief inhabitants of the most celebrated cities, Heliopolis, Thebes, and Memphis. Each of these cities furnished ten, who composed the tribunal, which might be compared to the Areopagus of Athens or the Senate of Lacedæmon. These thirty judges chose a president from their number, and the city to which he belonged sent another judge to replace him. These judges were supported at the expense of the king, and their salary was very considerable. . . .

The plaintiff in person stated his grievances, and the accused defended himself. There were no counsellors, the Egyptians being of the opinion that they only obscure a cause by their pleadings. . . . In fact, it is not rare," adds Diodorus, "to see the most experienced magistrates swayed by the power of a deceitful tongue, aiming at effect, and seeking only to excite compassion."

This organization seems adapted to secure the equity and impartiality desirable in the administration of justice. The selection of the judges from the principal citizens of the country, and their large salaries, guaranteed their ability and independence. At the same time, the restricted number of judges shows how rare lawsuits were in Egypt. It must have been so in a nation so wisely governed, in which order and peace reigned among all classes and in all families, and where the interests of every one were guaranteed and protected.

The study of the inscriptions shows that the civil offices were filled by citizens belonging to the sacerdotal and military classes.* Were these functions hereditary? The stability of the Egyptian institutions allows us to believe the transmission of the public duties must have been generally by inheritance.

A monument in the museum of Leyden shows us a family of the beginning of the twelfth dynasty, which for many successive generations was employed in the distribution of water in the district of Abydos.† But more important duties, requiring greater personal capacity or a special commission from public authority, must have been at the nomination of the kings or the governors of the nomes.

"A great number of administrative reports and fragments of registers of the public accounts are found in the papyri still preserved.

"The services employing the greatest number, and the most able men, were those of the public works, the army, and the administration of the revenues of the kingdom. Coined money was unknown,‡ all the taxes were collected in kind. There were three divisions on the land according to the nature of the rents: the canal (maou) paid its tribute in fish, the arable land (ouou) in cereals, and the marshes (pehou) in heads of cattle. A register was carefully kept, with an account of the changes, a statement of all the kinds of land in each district, and the names of the owners.

". . . . Many contracts of

* Ampère, *Des Castes, etc., dans l'ancienne Egypte.*

† Letter from M. de Rougé à M. Leemans, *Revue Archéol.*, vol. xii.

‡ We have seen by the law respecting loans, attributed to King Bocchoris, that coined money was known to the Egyptians at least eight centuries B.C.

sales and rents of land and houses, drawn up on papyrus, have been found among the family papers of the dead. They show with what guarantees and careful formalities property was protected in ancient Egypt."*

By this sketch, however incomplete, of the laws and institutions of ancient Egypt, we see they were, as Bossuet says,† "simple, full of justice, and of a kind to unite the nation. The best thing among all these excellent laws was—that every one was trained to observe them. A new custom was a wonder in Egypt. Everything was done in the same manner, and their exactness in little things made them exact in great ones. Therefore, there never was a people that preserved its laws and customs a longer time."

V.

A SUMMARY OF PRINCIPAL FEATURES OF THE SOCIAL ORGANIZATION.

We shall now give a brief review of the social and political institutions of ancient Egypt.

The priesthood, the guardian of religion and the laws, and the promoter of morality, was rendered perpetual by hereditary transmission in the sacerdotal families.

The army, the guardian of civil and political life, and the maintainer of order, was rendered perpetual by hereditary transmission in the military families.

Labor, the source of national and individual vigor, was rendered perpetual by the hereditary transmission of the agricultural or industrial pursuits in the families of the agriculturists and artisans.

Authority, the organ of the tional will, was maintained in i unity and perpetuity, by hereditary transmission in the royal family.

And all these classes, all these families, were guaranteed in their independence by the unchangeableness of their members, and the proprietorship of the soil and the trades.

Such were the foundations of the social constitution of Egypt.

With such fine order, to borrow the language of Bossuet, there was no place for anarchy or oppression. In fact, society was preserved from the abuse of power by the fundamental law of hereditary professions, which, ensuring to each family a fixed employment and an independent existence, prevented the arbitrary changes of men and property, so that opposition was not, as M. de Bonald happily says, in men, but in the institutions.*

It was by this combined action of the different social grades, that is, of royalty, the priesthood, the army, and the corporations devoted to manual labor, that Egypt attained such a degree of civilization, which left so great an impress on the ancient world, and the vestiges of which still appear so worthy of attention.

In consequence of this wise and powerful organization, peace and harmony seemed to have a long and unbroken reign in Egypt. The first symptoms of disorder and tyranny only appear under the kings of the fourth dynasty. When the knowledge of the true God was almost effaced from the memory of man, the kings, regarded with religious veneration, set themselves up for gods, and

* F. Lenormant, *Manuel d'Hist. ancienne.*

† *Discours sur l'Hist. univ.*: "The Egyptians observe the customs of their fathers, and adopt no new ones," says Herodotus.

* *Théorie du Pouvoir*, vol. i. book 1. From this work, now consulted so little, but nevertheless full of remarkable views respecting the different systems of social organization, we have taken the plan of this *étude* of the political institutions of ancient Egypt.

of despotism, en-
After overthrow-
nging, the nature
ligion, they favor-
ight the introduc-
which placed them
gave a divine au-
ver. "The priests
Herodotus, "that,
equity prevailed
prosperity of the
t. But after him
, the builder of
) reigned, and the
kinds of miseries.
e temples and for-
of sacrifices; then
ptians to labor for
ion of the impiety
r of the pyramids
racts from Mane-
important addi-
o built the largest
l by Herodotus to
t a despiser of the
ard repented and
k, greatly esteem-
e.

the national his-
by the discoveries
. A stone found
ramids contains a
n respecting the
Egypt. "It ap-
inscription," says
Cheops restored a
ding (dedicated
revenues to it in
d replaced the sta-
bronze, and wood,
sanctuary. . . .
" adds the learn-
that, even at that
period, Egyptian
rth with the great-

the royal despotism could not long prevail against the powerful social organization of which we have given a sketch, for, in re-establishing the worship of Isis, Cheops doubtless restored at the same time the national institutions, the violation of which has left so marked a trace in the historic traditions of Egypt.

To show our impartiality, we ought to state that many modern historians have judged Egyptian royalty much more severely than we. Among them, M. François Lenormant may be particularly mentioned.

"From the time of the oldest dynasties," says he, "we see existing this boundless respect for royalty, which became a genuine worship, and made Pharaoh the visible god of his subjects. The Egyptian monarchs were more than sovereign pontiffs, they were real divinities. . . . They identified themselves with the great divinity Horus because, as an inscription says: 'The king is the image of Ra (the sun-god) among the living.'

"It is easily understood what a prestige was given to the sovereign power in Egypt by such an explanation of royalty. This power, already so great among the Asiatic nations adjoining that country, assumed the character of genuine idolatry. The Egyptians were, with respect to their king, only trembling slaves, obliged by religion even to blindly execute his orders. The highest and most powerful functionaries were only the humble servants of Pharaoh. . . . For this *régime* to last so many ages with no notable modification, the Egyptians must have been profoundly convinced that the government they were under emanated from the divine will. *

* F. Lenormant, *Manuel d'Hist. anc.*, vol. I, p. 334.

Egyptian society stood on so firm a basis that it could be oppressed, but not overthrown, by the despotism of its kings. Property was so well secured by the general law of inheritance, the sacerdotal and military aristocracy was so firmly established in its independence, that the first excess of power only affected the laboring classes. Unable to dispose of t property of their subjects, the kings appropriated, as J. J. Rousseau justly remarks, "rather men's arms than their purse." It was thus they effected the gigantic work of erecting the pyramids by the enforced labors of a whole nation. Property was spared, but humanity was oppressed.

TO BE CONTINUED.

A WEEK AT LAKE GEORGE.

Most of our merchant readers will be able to recall a thousand pleasant reminiscences or anecdotes of the firm of Hawkins & Smith, wholesale cloth dealers, of our great metropolis. Mr. Hawkins is the dapper, fluent, old English gentleman, who meets all callers upon the house. He appears to be the very life of the firm, and sells the counters and shelves as clean as his own smoothly shaved, fair little face. He is fond of boasting that he never kept a piece of goods through two whole seasons. He is the only member of the firm with whom our agents and correspondents are acquainted. Rarely, indeed, does it enter anybody's head to inquire for Mr. Smith. But a silent, squarely-built, gray-eyed man, never to be seen in the salesroom, and only in the office at the earliest hours, looks as if he might be called Smith, or any other practically-sounding name; and on closer inspection this same individual appears to possess those qualities which would fit one to do and endure the grinding, screwing, and pounding, the stern refusing and energetic demanding, connected with the business of such a distinguished firm. Smith never boasts. He has a disagreeable way of chuckling, when he observes, before dismissing an idle employee, that *he* (Smith) came here (to New York) in his own schooner from home (Rhode Island) and, in six months, bought his share in the present business. Mr. Hawkins never alludes to him in conversation, but always greets him with marked respect, and, when late to business, with a nervous flush quite unpleasant to witness. It has been said by enemies of the firm that Hawkins is a first-class salesman because Smith does all the buying; and many quaint expressions have arisen regarding the fate of the American eagle whenever a certain coin passes between old Smith's thumb and forefinger.

Any one who has so far penetrated the nether gloom of our first story salesroom as to peep behind the little railing on the high desk, has seen a tall, pale, blue-eyed young man, with closely-trimmed whiskers, bending over the gas-lit figures and folios, the mysteries of Hawkins & Smith. Five years in this Hades, wearing and

over the perpetual riddle
ism, have worked a slight
ust between his brows, and
hin figure, and even blanch-
lelicate hands and hollow
but he is no more a demon
than you or I, or even Mr.
himself, but the jolliest
of jolly good fellows. If
long known Jack Peters,
iowledged this, be civil to
reader, henceforth, for his
I am this book-keeper's
n, George Peters.
e boys in the first floor whom
watches most. They will
with a laugh, the new clerk
t counter. Ask Mr. Haw-
he put at the first counter
e likes Jack Peters. He
er, George Peters, his cou-
Mr. Smith who the clerk
t counter is. He will an-
infernal fool that Hawkins
, because he always wants
oking figure-head."
st remark is historical, and
to illustrate many subjects
ity, modesty, and respect
nployers alike render deli-
e, George Peters.
ertain Monday evening in
Jack and I stood in the
esence of Hawkins and
the inner circle of the

'eters," said Hawkins, look-
h of us as blandly as man
k in such a place, "we have
luded that we can better
this week than next. No-
be going on, and so you
r be going off. Ah! ha!
my young friend, although
ustomary to grant vacation
cent employees, had better
), on account of your cou-
ely on his account!" add-
tle gentleman, dexterously, glancing the last part of his speech from me to his partner.

Jack nodded his thanks, and I endeavored to thaw the cold stare of the junior partner by a warm burst of gratitude, not altogether feigned. His glance, indeed, altered, but only to a sneer, and the labials of the word "puppy" were so distinctly formed that I could scarcely keep from disarranging them by a hearty slap.

Feeling checked and snubbed, I walked with Jack out of the store, but soon these feelings gave place to the excitement of our vacation.

"Jack, are the 'traps' all packed?"

"Everything is ready; all we have to do is to get aboard the boat. Hawkins told me on Saturday that I might get ready, but that it was necessary to stay over Monday in order to get you off with me. So I left word at home to have everything sent down by the boy."

We turned the corner, and, in a few minutes, were wandering through the cabins and gangways of the Albany boat. The "boy" on whom Jack had relied so confidently did not make his appearance until the last moment, and then professed utter ignorance of any lunch-basket. Jack was certain that he had put it with the trunk and satchels, and was but partially convinced when he found it, on our return, in the wardrobe of his bedroom. But we were on board of the *St. John*, and it only made a difference of two dollars in the cost of our supper.

Yes, dear reader, we were on board of the *St. John*, and moving up the Hudson; and, if you are pleased at finding us on our way at last, judge with what feelings we turned from the brick and stone of the great Babylon behind us to the towering palisades, the groves, and hills, and happy rural

sights about us. Jack and I were unable to get a state-room; all had been secured before the boat left the wharf. This, however, afforded little matter for regret, as we sailed through moonlight and a warm breeze beneath the gloomy Highlands, and watched the lights of the barges and tow-boats, like floating cities on the inky river. Scraps of history and romance were suggested at almost every turn of the winding channel, and as we passed old Cro' Nest, the opening lines of the *Culprit Fay* were forcibly recalled:

"'Tis the middle watch of a summer night,
Earth is dark, but the heavens are bright,
And naught is seen in the vault on high
But the moon and stars, and the cloudless sky,
And the flood which rolls its milky hue,
As a river of light, o'er the welkin blue.
The moon looks down on old Cro' Nest;
She mellows the shades on his shaggy breast;
And seems his huge gray form to throw
In a silver cone on the wave below."

The white schooners went through their ghostly parts in a way that would have shamed Wallack himself. We thought the performance of the sturgeons fully equal, from an artistic point of view, and, certainly, less objectionable from every point of view, when compared with anything we ever saw at the ballet; and, yet, we remembered that men and women were sitting wide awake through these late hours in the hot and crowded theatres of the city. Thus we were consoled for the loss of a state-room. But even in this peaceful enjoyment of nature we were not without drawbacks, and in the chapter of accidents must be recorded how and why we lost our places on the forward deck.

Scarcely had the steamer left her dock, when we were startled by a voice inquiring "if there would be any intrusion in case a party of ladies and gentlemen desired to while away time by singing a few hymns?" Jack and I turned in our seats. The inquiry had proceeded from an elderly individual, of general clerical appearance, and certain marks strongly indicating the specific character of the "Evangelical" school. A pair of "sisters" hung upon either arm, and all three settled into chairs in the middle of the deck. His question had been addressed to about two hundred ladies and gentlemen who crowded the forward deck. There were evident marks of dissatisfaction, but, as nobody spoke, our "Evangelical" friend thought proper to conclude that nobody was offended, and the hymn-singing commenced. Gradually congenial spirits, drawn by the sound, were to be seen approaching from various parts of the boat, and when Jack and I returned from supper, we found about twenty or thirty in various stages of excitement, and our clerical friend wrought up to a high pitch. Another minister, with a strong but wheezy bass voice, announced and intoned the hymns. At intervals in the singing, our friend arose and addressed the spectators. At one time he informed them that the feeling which animat the present assembly was love to th Saviour. At another, he thought tha perhaps there might be some presen who knew nothing about the Saviour to such he would apply the words o the apostle, "Be ye followers of me as I am of Christ." He said tha he had been a child of God fo thirty years, and knew by a certai assurance that he was a saved man Hallelujah!

"Evangelical" blood was up, an our friend turned from the contem plation of his own happy lot t worry something or somebody Jack's cigar caught his eye. It w the red rag to the bull.

"Young man! there ain't n

[illegible] There ain't no for'ard deck where you can puff that stinkin' weed of your'n!"

Jack [illegible] a forcible denial in [illegible], and, before I could [illegible], broke out with:

"I'd like to know what the Bible says against smoking?"

"You would, young man, would you? Well, I'm glad you would. I'm glad you have asked that question. Why, sir, the Bible says, 'Let no filthy communication proceed out of thy mouth'; and if that ar smoke ain't a filthy communication,' I'd like to know what is."

There was a general roar. "Come along, Jack," said I, "you are a Papist, and can't argue against a 'free Bible.'" So, retiring to the after-deck, which was covered, and concealed much of the landscape, we left our Methodist friends triumphantly shouting and keeping folks awake up to a late hour.

As the night passed, and our fellow-travellers dropped off one by [illegible] in their state-rooms or [illegible] of the cabins, we were [illegible] Gradually we retired within ourselves, and shut the doors of our senses.

"Wake up, old fellow, we are nearly in!"

I opened my eyes, and saw Jack's pale face smiling over my shoulders.

We landed at Albany, and after breakfast found ourselves settled in the Rensselaer and Saratoga cars, and, changing trains at Fort Edward, arrived at Glenn's Falls in about three [illegible]

Jack, who had often made the trip before, had set me reading *The Leather Stocking Series*, and I positively refused to budge from the town of Glenn's Falls until we had visited the rapids and descended into the cave which Cooper has immortalized in the first chapters of his most interesting romance, *The Last of the Mohicans*. The falling in of the rock at different periods, and the low stage of the water in the summer season, prevented us from recognizing the old shelter of Hawkeye and his party.

But there is the cave, and there are the rapids—both are shrines of American legend; and we felt better pleased with ourselves for our pilgrimage. Of course we had missed the stage which takes passengers from the station to Caldwell at the head of Lake George. We wandered a short time about town, found out that there were a number of Catholics in it, and that its president, Mr. Keenan, was a well-known Irish Catholic. We also visited a beautiful church, the finest in the town, recently completed by Father McDermott, the pastor of the English-speaking Catholic congregation, there being also a French-Canadian parish in the place.

As may be easily imagined, we had no mind to walk over to the lake, or to pay ten dollars for a vehicle to carry us as many miles, and Jack was beginning to grumble at my curiosity when we met a farmer's wagon—with a farmer in it, of course. The latter offered to take us over for fifty cents a head, as he was going in the same direction. Never was there a better piece of good luck. There are several Scotch families settled on French Mountain, at the head of the lake; our driver was one of their patriarchs. He literally poured out funny stories of the "kirk" and "dominie"; and although some of the jokes were very nearly as broad as they were long, Jack and I were forced to hold our sides while the "gudeman" sparkled and foamed, like a certain brown export from his native country.

During a momentary lull in the conversation, I took occasion to inquire with respect to a black woolly-coated

dog, who followed the wagon, if he were a good hunter. "Yes," said Jack, with a contemptuous smile at the subject of my inquiry. "He is what is called a beef-hound."

"Hoot, mon," said his owner, "that dog would tree a grasshopper up a mullen-stalk."

It was in no sad or poetical mood that we passed by "Williams's Monument" and the scene of Hendrick's death and Dieskau's defeat, or saw at "Bloody Pond" the lilies bending over the sedge and ooze which served of old as the last resting-place of many a brave young son of France. We did not think of the fierce struggle which had here confirmed our Anglo-Saxon forefathers in possession of this soil. All this comes up now as I write; for, certainly no sober thought entered our brains until, as we turned round a mountain-side, I saw Jack take off his hat. I looked in the direction of his respectful nod, and—oh! what a vision!—the deep blue lake sank from view in the embrace of the distant mountains. Its winding shores and secret bays, curtained with veils of mist hanging in festoons from boughs of cedar, birch, maple, and chestnut, were like enchantment in their endless variety of form and shade. No less the work of magic were the islands. These, owing to the reflection of the water, appeared to hang over its surface as the clouds seemed to hang over the peaks above. To stand suddenly in view of such a sight might have startled and awed even lighter souls than ours. Here, indeed, our hearts were lifted up and thrilled as we thought of the gray-haired apostle and martyr, the first European who sailed upon the water before us—the Jesuit Father Jogues, who also gave it on the eve of Corpus Christi its original name—Lac du Saint-Sacrament. Our Protestant tradition, following the courtier taste of liam Johnson, has handed d name of Lake George, but that the hope of every l American antiquity who ha its shores may not prove v that time, in doing justice to restore to the lake its first lovely title.

A few small sails on the w the smoke from the village at broke the spell and reminde we were still among the h man.

Caldwell is made up of house, several churches, store and shops, a saw-mill, an streets of separated dwelling The grand hotel is near the s occupied by Fort William and is called by that name, a towards Ticonderoga, altho view is cut off midway by th ings of the lake. Old Fort is overgrown with cedars and and only a few feet of ruined remain. The scene of the of Fort William Henry is nearly as we could reckon f Cooper's description, a swamp however, is said to have gr tered the topography of the this point, and certainly it is locate Montcalm's old c ground during the siege des *The Last of the Mohicans.*

Leaving such questions to tiquarian, perhaps, dear rea will ask one with a practica for the present and future, How do they provide for the at the Fort William Henry ? that were indeed an ill-time tion for us. Perhaps, if I ha the proprietor to allow me t upon his fare in the pages CATHOLIC WORLD, he wou done so in a manner satisfa all parties; but, as no such idea occurred at that time, I

ed to confess that I was afraid that it was too good. Be it said to our shame, we did not promenade upon the magnificent piazza, nor did we stop to taste the alluring fare of the Fort William Henry. What else did we come for? Why, to see Lake George, of course, and to have a good time; and we did both, although we went without lunch for some hours that day.

Scarcely had I claimed our baggage at the stage-office, when Jack came up from the beach with a radiant countenance. "It's all right!" adding, "I've got just the boat we want. Five dollars for the rest of the week. Take hold of that trunk, and we'll get under way as soon as

Perhaps, dear reader, in your wanderings through life it has never been your happy lot to be absolute master of the craft on which you are sailing. Do you think that you have fathomed the mystery of such lives as those of Captain Kidd and Admiral Semmes?

Do you imagine that life on the ocean wave means sleeping in a berth and pacing a quarter-deck? Ah! that was truly independence day to us. The wind blew fresh and strong. We hoisted our india-rubber blanket on an oar. Coats and collars were packed away in the satchel, our "worst" straw hats were pulled down over our eyes, and, as we sat with loosened flannel in the bottom of our heavy skiff, and listened to the rippling water, we quite forgot that it was past lunch-time. The warm south breeze, and that peculiar fragrance which popular fancy has associated with the name of cavendish, brought us in full sympathy with the naval adventurers of other days, and we blessed the memory of Sir Walter Raleigh, "as we sailed."

The upper portion of the lake, through which we are now passing, though surrounded by hills, has enough farming land and farm-houses on their slopes to give it that placid, tranquil beauty which is always associated with views on the English waters. As it widened from three-quarters to as many full miles, we passed several beautiful residences, two of them belonging to Messrs. Price and Hayden of New York City. Opposite these, on the eastern shore, is a handsome property belonging to Charles O'Conor, Esq., one of the most distinguished members of the New York bar, and well known throughout the United States. Just abreast Diamond Island is the residence of Mr. Cramer, president of the Rensselaer and Saratoga Railroad, and while sailing past the lovely group of islands known as the "Three Sisters," the property of Judge Edmonds, we saw beyond them the white walls of his cottage peeping out from the green foliage of the western shore, about three miles and a half from Caldwell.

As the sun sank below Mount Cathead, back of the pretty little village of Bolton, we landed on a little islet in the Narrows near Fourteen Mile Island.

I was quite curious to find out what preparations Jack had made, and lent a willing hand at the long narrow trunk. In the tray was a small cotton tent, made according to Jack's own order, and slightly larger than the soldier's "dog-house." A keen little axe in Jack's quick hand soon provided a pair of forked uprights and four little pins, an oar served for a ridge-pole, and our shelter was up before the sun was fairly below the real horizon. Out of the same tray came a quilt and two pairs of blankets, which I was ordered to spread on the india-rubber. My task accomplished, the smell of

something very much like ham and eggs recalled me to the beach. We supped, that night, by the light of our camp-fire, and it was only after a night's heavy sleep that I was able to examine the rest of Jack's outfit. A small mess-chest, which bore marks of his own clever fingers, occupied one division of the bottom of the trunk. The rest of it was shared by apartments for clothing, provisions, and a humble assortment of fishing-tackle and shooting material. The gun lay strapped to one side of the trunk, and a couple of rods on the other.

"Very neat, Jack," said I.

"You are right; I built it myself, all except the walls and roof, seven years ago."

I am sorry to confess that I did not get up that morning until breakfast was ready. Jack did not complain, but I saw by his quiet smile that some kind of an apology was necessary.

"Jack, I'm as stiff as a clothes-horse, and sore from head to foot."

"Why," he asked, "didn't you dig holes for your hips and shoulders, as the Indians do?"

"The holes were all made, only they were in the wrong places."

After breakfast, we broke up our camp and rowed over to Fourteen Mile Island. On the way we had another view of Bolton, behind us, and the countless islands in the Narrows, through which we were shortly to sail. The little village of Bolton lies on the western shore opposite Fourteen Mile Island. It contains a hotel, several boarding-houses, a pretty little P. E. church, and a forest of flags, every house seeming to have its own staff. One of the islands, near Bolton, was shown us as the point of view from which Kensett's picture of the Narrows was painted. At Fourteen Mile Island we found a quiet little hotel, which serves as a dining-place for excursionists from Caldwell. A few regular boarders seemed to be enjoying themselves, and I noticed an artist's easel and umbrella on the porch.

We soon left with a good supply of butter, eggs, milk, and fresh bread. After rowing a few miles through the maze of islands in the Narrows, one of which is occupied by a hermit artist named Hill, a "transcendentalist," the wind arose, and we sailed under the shadow of Black Mountain through the wildest portion of the lake. On the western shore, savage cliffs were piled in utter confusion, now rising, like the Hudson River Palisades, in solid walls above a mass of *débris*, now hanging in gigantic masses over the crystal abyss below. On the eastern shore, Black Mountain rises above any other height on the lake, and the view which we beheld as we passed from Fourteen Mile Island down the Narrows is one of the finest in the world. Now we were drifting under the cliffs at the base of the mountain, and, looking up its abrupt sides—a series of rocky spurs covered principally with hemlocks and cedar—we saw two eagles soaring above the thin clouds which floated half-way up. Throughout this portion the lake varies from one to two miles in width.

Oh! what a cozy little nest in the hills at the northern end of Black Mountain! A few farms, and a sleepy old mill that looks as if it never was made to run, lie on the sunny slope retiring into the hills which forms a pass over to Whitehall. No wonder they call it the "Bosom!"

Here, in a little graveyard, we saw the tombstone of a Revolutionary soldier, and the old farm-house, at which we stopped for dinner, with its loom and spindle and bustling old housewife, formed a good specimen of that

tance while Jack's trout were frying over the little camp-fire now gleaming in the twilight.

Supper having been despatched, I heard Jack approaching, while engaged in washing the dishes on the beach—an occupation which time and place can often rob of all its offensiveness, wherefore, most delicate of readers, I am bold enough to mention it.

I looked at Jack from my towel and tin plates, and great was my astonishment to behold him in complete hunting-dress, gun in hand, and all accoutred for the chase.

"Why, Jack! what's afoot?"

"No game yet," he answered, smiling; "but I'm to leave you to-night."

"What! to sleep here all by myself?"

"Why, yes—you are not afraid, are you?"

"No, not afraid exactly."

"The fact is," said Jack, "a fellow over at Hague promised me a deer-hunt last year, and if I can find him to-night I shall go out with him to-morrow. You can't shoot, have no gun, and are not much of a walker, so I am sure you would be bored to death." (I nodded.) Jack continued, "I will walk over to-night, and if I do not meet the hunter will be back bright and early to-morrow morning. If I do not come then, please row over for me to-morrow evening."

"All right, *mon capitaine.*" And, with a wave of the hand, Jack departed, and I was alone.

The embers of the camp-fire began to brighten as the darkness fell. The birds and squirrels disappeared. The trunk was stowed safely together with its mess-chest and provisions, and the blankets were spread in the little tent; the milk-jug and butter-bowl were secured by stones in the water, in order to keep them cool. I began my rosary for night prayers, and roamed through the grove over to the northern side of the point, in full view of the steep promontory on the opposite shore. Beyond our own smooth camping-ground the western shore surged up again in all its former wildness. The beads passed slowly through my fingers, and it seemed as if the beauty and loneliness of the scene were absorbing all my faculties, and withdrawing me from instead of raising my thoughts to God and heaven.

Finally the moon arose. A thousand scattered beams shot through the dark foliage, and lit up patches of the lawn over which I had just passed. The wind had died away, and the light fell in unbroken splendor upon the broad mirror before me. The few thin clouds, veiling small groups of stars, the frowning cliffs and sombre woods—all were reduplicated in the unruffled water. Far to the south, Black Mountain closed up the view, which sank in the east behind the low ranges of hills, all dark below the rising moon. The last bead fell from my fingers, and praying God to forgive anything inordinate in my enjoyment of his creatures, I gave up to the intoxication of the scene. The hours passed rapidly while I dreamed of the days of Montcalm and Abercrombie, and saw in fancy the fleets of canoes and batteaux passing and repassing in victory and defeat the rocks upon which I was sitting. Had my mind ever reverted to the possibility of being obliged to give a public account of itself, I might have composed some lines, had some "thoughts," or done something worth recording. Alas, dear reader, do not consider me rude if I confess that I did not think of you at that time. For, indeed, I did not think of anything, but left my fancy to be sported with by im

three little steamers continually plying about this portion of the lake, complete the impression that it is a place of pleasure, ease, and holiday. The Narrows, completely filled with islands, where every stroke of the oar reveals new vistas and endless changes of scene, I can compare with nothing, and, indeed, it would seem as if they were a unique creation. These extend for two or three miles to where Black Mountain begins. And as for the rest, my ignorance is also at a loss for a comparison, and I can only think of what Lake Como might have been if adorned with islands, if its peaks were lower and covered with foliage, and if the hand of man had never wrought upon its native beauty.

That evening I rowed over for Jack. He had not yet arrived, although the sun had set when I arrived, as agreed, at the little hotel at Hague. Something unusual was going on, and I made various guesses as to the reason why so many well-dressed maids and shaven yeomen were gathered on the porch. Seven o'clock came, and yet no Jack. I eagerly inquired after supper, resolved not to risk the chance of being obliged to depend upon myself for a cook. The dining-room had been cleared of every table save the one which I occupied, and shortly after I had come out from supper I saw the young people crowding into it. I had now begun to suspect what was the matter, when an honest-looking young gentleman, fresh and fragrant from a process to which he shortly afterwards urged and invited me, approached and said: "Stranger, you're camping on the p'int?" To this piece of information I nodded a genial assent.

"Lookin' for your pardner?" asked the pleasant young man. I nodded again. "Well, he'll be in soon.

Whitehall, and the cars thence to Albany and New York. Our tent did not blow away that night; and, although the storm beat fiercely, not a drop of water touched us, thanks to the little furrow which Jack had traced with a sharp stick, to carry off the drippings from the tent-cloth.

Starting bright and early next morning, we rowed past a steep smooth cliff running almost perpendicularly for about four hundred feet and then down into the lake.

"That's 'Rogers's Slide,'" said Jack.

"The deuce it is! He must have worn a stout pair of pantaloons!"

"Oh! but he didn't actually slide, you know!" replied Jack, and then proceeded to recount the famous escape of Major Rogers in 1758, who here eluded the pursuit of the Indians, and, having thrown his knapsack over the precipice, turned his snow-shoes and made off by another route.

In a few hours, we had left our little boat attached to the steamer to be taken back to Caldwell. A stage ride of several miles brought us to Ticonderoga and Lake Champlain. That same evening, at ten o'clock, we snuffed the hot and fetid of the great metropolis, and M morning saw us re-enterin shades of Hawkins & Smi word to Jack and a stare at n the only greetings of the junic ner, as he passed through the room.

"Ah, boys!" said the cheer kins, "glad to see you; l if you've been having a goo Plenty of bone, muscle, and skin, eh? I guess Mr. Smi think that it pays to give you *rest.* You haven't been wastin money at Long Branch or Sa I'll bet."

Thus ended our summer va and if we did not have enou venture to pass for heroes, enough game for sportsmen, enough sights for artists, or enough of the past for antiqu or measure miles and heights for the scientific—in short, if pear as two vulgar and thor commonplace clerks, smokin boating through our holiday note, dear reader, that even s we can take delight in Lake G then, go and make the trip aft own fashion, and see if you ca it more or better.

ritory, for the reason that there was no idea of nationality, and consequently no unity of action, among the aborigines in their resistance to the new-comers. Supported by their home governments respectively, they grew from mere settlements to be important colonies, at peace with each other as far as their own individual relation was concerned, but always liable to be embroiled in the incessant quarrels of their countrymen at home. The sturdy Hollanders were the first to succumb to what might be called foreign influence; then the French settlers, deserted by France, laid down their arms before their English conquerors, who, in their turn, by the Revolution of '76, yielded their dominion to the Thirteen Colonies, which embraced within their limits much of the territory and most of the descendants of the original colonists of at least three of the nationalities which first effected settlements on the Atlantic coast. From this period we may date the origin of American nationality. In its infancy, it included nearly four millions of men of various races, creeds, opinions, and sentiments. For the first time in history was proclaimed the perfect equality before the law of all persons of European origin, as has since been extended that grand principle of human equality to men from every part of the earth. In forming a code for itself, it rejected what was contrary to this dogma, and adopted everything that was beneficial in all other forms of government. From Holland, it took the Declaration of Independence, that great manifesto of popular rights; from England, the writ of habeas corpus and trial by jury; from France and Spain, many of those equitable constructions of the civil law which regulate the rights of property and the domestic status of individuals. To all these were added the beneficent constitution under which we have the good fortune to live, and the many excellent laws, local and national, which, in conformity with that instrument, have been enacted from time to time.

But custom is said to be stronger even than law, and hence we can understand that the vivifying principle of the government itself was generated from the peculiar circumstances amid which the first settlers of America and their children found themselves, without local monarchical traditions, an hereditary aristocracy, or laws of primogeniture. With, as a general rule, little private fortune or means of subsistence other than that derived from manual labor and individual enterprise, the American colonist, no matter of what nation, was naturally disposed towards popular government, and to proclaim and admit general equality. It is undoubtedly to the existence of these robust social and economical habits in the early settlers—which, finding expression in their new-found political power, were embodied in the fundamental laws of the new nation by the fathers of the republic—that we are primarily indebted for the wise and moderate scheme of government we enjoy, and which it is our duty to preserve and perpetuate unimpaired to posterity.

It was thus by a combination of circumstances hitherto unknown that our country became clothed with all the attributes of nationality pecul' to itself—its subsequent progress, as we may presume its future greatness, having no parallel in the annals of other lands. That we are a nation possessing an appropriate autonomy capable of sustaining all the relation of war and peace with other countri and exercising supreme authori over all our integral parts and indivi dual members, no sane man uninfluen

[illegible] lawyers or [illegible] political passions of [illegible]. Who would so [illegible] that this republic [illegible] petty sovereignties in [illegible] is coequal [illegible] the others combined, [illegible] the axiom of Euclid, [illegible] is greater than its [illegible]-American, then, is [illegible] principle of unity [illegible] It gives dignity and strength [illegible] country abroad, and assures peace, concord, and security at home. While allowing all possible latitude to subordinate members in the management of their domestic affairs, it reconciles and harmonizes the conflicting and sometimes antagonistic interests of different sections, concentrates on works of vast commercial and national importance the collective powers of all, directs the foreign policy of the government for the general good, and arrays the power of the people for the common protection and defence. True, some years ago, many persons held contrary opinions, and in the attempt to carry them out unhappily caused one of the most calamitous civil wars of modern times; but, like the tempest which sweeps over the gigantic oak, swaying its trunk and loosening the ground around it only that its roots may strike deeper and firmer into the earth, our country has passed through the storm unscathed and now rests on a basis firmer than ever. The past and its errors, however, we can easily forget; the future is ours; and who shall hold us harmless if we profit not by our dearly-bought experience and the lessons which every day teaches us?

One, and not the least potent, of the causes which led to that fratricidal struggle was the advocacy of what was called "manifest destiny," and, in its application, very often a dishonest doctrine. It is not unnatural that in a young and sanguine republic, whose short history is so full of successes, many ardent propagandists of freedom should be found, who without calculating consequences would like to extend the benefits of our political system not only to the utmost confines of this continent, but over all Christendom; but this feeling, though creditable, is hardly one to be encouraged. It leads, as we have often seen, to a national lust for the acquisition of our neighbor's territory, to the undue extension of our boundaries, disproportionate to even our ever-increasing population, and to the weakening of the bonds that hold together the comparatively settled states of the Union, by the bodily introduction of foreign elements into our polity at variance with our real interests. The annexation of Texas and the acquisition of our Pacific territory, though productive of many tangible advantages, were undoubtedly some of the remote, but, nevertheless, very important, influences which, operating on the public mind, tended to unfix our loyalty to the whole country, and to induce us to view the recent forcible attempt on its integrity with feelings somewhat akin to indifference. That enlargement of the national domain was so sudden and immense that men's minds, accustomed to defined limits, failed to realize it. Patriotism is not a mere sentiment, but a love of something of which we have some accurate knowledge, whether associated with a particular race, locality, or historical record, or all together; and hence, when we could not understand how in one moment what we had thought was our country, the object of our affection and source of our pride, was extended thousands of miles and millions of acres, our imaginations

could not keep pace with the monstrous growth of the country, and we fell back on our native or adopted states, and felt prouder of being known as Virginians or Vermonters than of being United States citizens.

It is not at all improbable that posterity will see the whole of North America united under one government, but this consummation, so devoutly to be wished, to be permanent and salutary, must be the result of time and the observance of the laws of right and justice, for nations as well as individuals flourish or fade in proportion as they follow or despise virtue. It must also be when our population is not forty millions, as it now is, but quadruple that number, and when our sparsely settled territories are well filled with citizens, their resources in full process of development, and their varied interests assimilated with those of other portions of the country. Steam and electricity may do much to bring about such results, foreign immigration more, but a proper administration of our own laws, and a judicious, liberal, and conciliatory policy towards our American neighbors, most of all.

Happily for us, we are at present on terms of friendship with all nations, and, remote from Europe and Asia, we are not likely to become involved in the complications and disputes of the Old World. Still, no human penetration can foresee how long such a desirable state of accord will exist. The monarchical states of Europe are not very sincere friends of republicanism, and, should war occur between us and them, our greatest difficulty would be to defend our already too extensive frontiers from their attacks. Why, then, should we increase our danger by enlarging them? A good general never lengthens his lines unless he has proportionate reinforcements to them.

As to becoming propaga republicanism in Europe, the attempt, in this centur would be both injudicious less. The impious atroc dark designs of the secret there, who profane the wo and blaspheme against all have put so far back the true freedom in the old cou they who sincerely desire liberal system of laws are seek under the shadow of protection and security eve sacrifice of their political If we truly wish for the spre institutions, let us use exam than precept, and prove, by t administration of our own respect for the doctrines of Ch and, by proper regard for laid down by the church, th licanism has ceased to be a ment, and has become a pra glorious reality. Such a res be an argument so cogent sophistry could refute it and could combat its logic. We member, also, that the grea mies of free government after all, kings and nobles, b deluded men who have band selves in every part of Eu tensibly as republicans, but as the destroyers of all law a These men, it is well know the inspired word of God his very existence, conten ignore the first principles o and scoff at the beautiful virtues which bind the wife tionate duty to the husband child in love and gratitud parent. Empires are governe by force, republics through ol and yet those pretended ap freedom acknowledge no la their own and that of their

Human laws, no matter by whom made, or how just they may be in letter and spirit, are mere pieces of paper or parchment if the people are not disposed to obey them, and this disposition can only come through religion. For, as man is constituted, he becomes amenable to the opera-ion of the divine law of obedience efore he comes under the edicts of uman legislation; in other words, he a Christian or the reverse before he a lawyer or responsible to the emporal law. "The characteristics f a democracy," says Blackstone, are public virtue and goodness as to s intentions;" and Napoleon I., hough by no means as good a hristian as he was a far-seeing states-an, when about to reduce chaotic rance to order and decency, found necessary first to restore religion nd recall her exiled priesthood.

Unfortunately for us, this spirit of religion is not confined to the other de of the Atlantic. We find it ady making its way into American ciety, though as yet it assumes more e character of indifferentism. We l ourselves a Christian people, yet s than one-half of the entire com-unity ever enter a church for devo-nal purposes from one year's end another. Recently, too, we notice, our larger cities particularly, exhi-tions of the same wicked spirit hich animated the Carbonari and cialists of Europe, and which veals itself in many expressions of mpathy for the infamous Commun-s of Paris in the columns of me of our newspapers and the eeches of more than one promi-nt politician. This insidious dan-r to our venerated institutions ght to be closely watched and mly repressed. It is opposed ke to private virtue and public rals, and, if ever allowed a ntrolling influence in the state, would sweep away every safeguard that stands between the citizen and the passions of the mob. No person who values the blessings of domestic peace or venerates the memories of our ancestors, no true American, can tolerate for a moment these communistic and socialistic designs which are creeping in amongst us, utterly foreign as they are to our soil and the genius of our people and government.

While thus excluding vicious principles from our shores, we ought to, as we have ever done, continue to welcome the oppressed and impoverished people of the Old World, and, as far as is consistent with the public safety, to extend to them every facility to a participation in the political as well as the material prosperity of the country. They are our relations. Very few of us, going back two or three generations, but will find that his ancestors were also immigrants, like those who to-day seek our protection and hospitality. Since the formation of our government, eight millions of them have made their homes in the young republic, helping to develop our resources, commerce, and manufactures, and always proving faithful to their obligations of allegiance in peace as well as in war. An enlightened and tolerant treatment of our immigrants is both charitable and wise; and the best evidence that we have profited by our superior political and educational advantages, is our readiness to make allowance for the intellectual defects and antiquated habits of those who have left home and country to join their lot with ours. The exclusion of any class of citizens from a participation in the benefits of our government, on account of religion or previous nationality, never has had, and is never likely to have, the countenance of the people of this country. The spasmodic efforts of those

fanatics, vulgarly but not inappropriately called Know-nothings, which have been made occasionally, were directed against Catholics, but they never reached the dignity of national movements, and, being the offspring of disappointed ambition and blind prejudice, withered before the scorn and contempt of all good men. Politically, there can be little possible danger arising from the exercise of the elective franchise by all citizens of foreign birth, even conceding their inferiority in some respects to the native-born, as the former number less than one-eighth of our entire population, and these, in the natural course of events, will disappear from among us, their children born here growing up thoroughly imbued with the spirit and liberality of our institutions. Even to-day the immediate descendants of adopted citizens hold, under both the great parties that divide the country, many high places of honor and trust, and perform their duties with an ability and patriotism that reflect credit on the American name. The nationality that would deal harshly or jealously with friends or neighbors because they were born in a foreign land, or are poor in the world's goods, is not American, and is more fitted for the latitude of London or Peking than of New York or Washington.

We are well aware that there are many things in the conduct of some of our adopted citizens that we find difficulty in understanding, and which require all our good-nature to overlook or palliate. A great famine, we might say a succession of famines, the misgovernment of England, and the oppression of the worst class of alien landlords with which a people ever were afflicted, have driven among us, within a quarter of a century, over two millions of the inhabitants of Ireland. Having been denied practically all participation in th ernment of their own countr never have had an opportur acquiring that steady habit of tl and reflection necessary to them to judge of the relative or demerits of the manifold p measures which the exigencie free nation are, from time to tir senting for popular endorse and having unlimited confide those who profess to be their in their new homes, they fall a prey to the demagogue ar political charlatan. The vict long, cruel, and unrelenting ty and ardent lovers of their fathe their hatred of England is, if ble, stronger than their love fc land. In fact, those two engr passions sometimes so absorl minds that prudence, toleratio even self-interest are forgotten. circumstance, while it may be table to themselves, cannot t regretted by us for many re but more particularly because ders their assimilation with th majority of our people more and difficult, and operates a their material advancement, an sequently against the welfare o children. In the abstract, we c blame our Irish immigrants f fond devotion to their natal co nor for their hatred of her oppr on the contrary, we admire it a as it works no injustice to th to the country they have selec their future home; but we do emphatically deprecate the cc of those among them who, tı on such natural and generou ings for selfish purposes, turn aside from their duty as parent citizens, and, assuming to be leaders, have swayed them i interest of this or that faction, v neglecting at the same time th formance of duties to the exe

of which any one might be proud to devote his life.

Let us illustrate what we mean. There are, at least, two and a half millions of Irish in the United States, the great majority of whom, for very sufficient, if not obvious, reasons occupy socially and pecuniarily a very inferior position to that which their natural abilities would entitle them, yet we see how little effort is being made by their countrymen, of more education or larger wealth, to assist them. The Catholic Church has done much, but the church, necessarily, can only attend to their spiritual wants and to the education of their children; the temperance and benevolent societies are good in their way, but their power is limited, and their sphere of action very restricted; but we look in vain for an organization that will take by the hand the bewildered and uncertain stranger as he lands at Castle Garden or in the harbor of Boston, shield him from the temptations and villany which mark him out as a victim from the moment his foot touches the firm earth and his battle of life commences, find him employment in the great centres of trade and commerce, or conduct him safely to the broad extending fields of the free and fruitful West. If he be a farmer or agricultural laborer, as the majority of Irish immigrants are, what society of his countrymen is prepared to defray his expenses to the rural districts, where labor is always in demand, and wages high, or help him to locate on the Western lands, which can be had almost for the asking, and where he can bring up his family in comfort and happiness? If half the money and one-quarter the time and labor which were recently so foolishly expended in futile efforts to free Ireland and invade the British dependencies had been used for the benefit of the poorer class of our Irish immigrants, how many thousands of them might now be enjoying happy homes in our fertile Western states and territories, instead of infesting the purlieus of New York, underbidding each other for precarious and unhealthy employment. How many victims of disappointed hope or mistaken confidence might have been rescued from the slough of despondency and degradation into which they have fallen, and placed in a position of at least comparative independence. The liberation of Ireland through the instrumentality of her exiled children is an old and a splendid dream, but it is only a dream so long as the present relations exist between this country and England. We yield to no one in appreciation of all that is noble in that pious and gallant nation, and would, perhaps, sacrifice as much as the most enthusiastic of her sons to see her not only independent, but in the enjoyment of the fullest liberty; but no person who has ever casually studied the relative strength and resources of England and Ireland, and who has had any practical experience of the enormous expenditure of life and money so unsuccessfully incurred by the people of the South, even when military training and available population were so evenly balanced, can for a moment believe in the success of any attempt of the people themselves to separate forcibly one from the other.

But whatever the people in Ireland may see fit to do or dare, the organization of armed men in this country to assist in that purpose is most reprehensible and fraught with the greatest mischiefs. For any person within our limits to attempt to levy war on a country at peace with the United States is clearly illegal. If he be a stranger, it is a criminal

abuse of our hospitality; if a citizen, he disregards his oath of allegiance. Such a movement gives color to the assertions of the worst enemies of all foreigners, the Know-nothings, who accuse Irishmen of not becoming citizens in the true spirit of their oath, but merely pretended ones, whose object is to use this country as their *point d'appui* for ulterior objects. Besides, such societies have a tendency to unsettle the minds of the people, and divert them from the main objects of their self-expatriation—free homes and altars. But even if Ireland were to-day independent, not one-tenth of the Irish in America could or would return. The mass of them are permanently attached to America by affection, association, or interest; their children are growing up around them, naturally imbued with a love for this, the country of their birth; their property and business are here; some are too old to be retransplanted, and others young enough to prefer seeking fortunes in our stupendous and but yet only partially developed commonwealth, to spending a lifetime in the necessarily limited sphere of enterprise presented by so small a country as Ireland under the most favorable auspices. True patriotism should, therefore, dictate to the Irish-American the wisdom of promoting the welfare of this large majority of his countrymen who, for good or evil, must pass their lives with us. And what a vast and enticing field is thus presented to the successful merchant and ardent Irish nationalist! If they cannot free Ireland, they can by their money and their intelligence free tens of thousands of their countrymen from the slavery of poverty and dependence, from the vices of the cities and the degradation of the factories and the coal-mines. Such an effort, judiciously made, apart from the b
would confer on so many
deserving citizens, and the
able argument it would p
practical, disinterested s
would, if the occasion sh
present itself, enable the pers
nefited to assist in their turn
of true Irish nationality. Tl
thing so successful, it is sai
cess, and while the sympathi
nations, particularly of our
easily enlisted in favor of ar
ed nation like Ireland, ther
rally observable an implied c
she is misgoverned because
ple have not the capacity to
govern themselves. At hc
certainly have not been al
try the experiment, but here,
institutions already firmly es
vast mineral, agricultural, a
mercial industries to invite
bor and excite their ambi
with an area of unoccupied
most beyond conception,
incapable of profiting by the
tages, either as individuals c
tual co-operation, expose th
to the suspicion of being de
that organizing faculty an
grasp which create and su
dependent governments.

Without intending to dra
vidious distinction between
of citizens and another, we n
to the German immigratio
country as an admirable ex
the benefits arising from org
and mutual support. It is
mony of purpose that has
the Teutonic element, thou
means the strongest in our pc
a preponderating influence i
of the Western states, and
prietorship of innumerable
both sides of the Mississip
Coming from a self-governin
and leaving behind an exten
ing and manufacturing co

the German immigrant has of course many advantages over his Irish fellow voyager, but those who have closely watched the progress of both races in America assert that it is to the admirable system of mutual help and protection enjoyed by the former that his great industrial progress is mainly due.

We are satisfied that there are many wealthy citizens of Irish birth in this city and elsewhere who would gladly contribute of their superabundant means to assist their less fortunate fellow-countrymen, were any feasible project inaugurated by which they could do so practically and efficiently, and we trust that there are among us adopted citizens themselves—persons who, abandoning chimerical schemes of conquest and invasion, would devote their time and ability to assist those of their helpless countrymen who have come and are coming among us. Every intelligent agriculturist that can be planted on the virgin soil of our now waste public lands, every ingenious mechanic that is furnished with employment in our workshops, and, we may say, every stalwart laborer that is removed from the overstocked labor market of the East and assisted to the towns and smaller cities of the South and West, adds to the general wealth of the community, increases the strength and glory of our republic, and conduces to its growing intelligence and morality.

The pursuit of wealth, however important, is not of course the primary duty of man, considered either as an individual responsible being or as a citizen. Religion, in its proper practical sense, is not only the source of happiness for mankind in this world and the next, but is absolutely necessary for the preservation of all well-regulated society, and it is on this account among others that so many admirers of American institutions have seen with regret that a large portion of our immigrants from the continental countries of Europe evince a complete disregard for the plainest forms of Christianity. Now, the founders of this government were essentially a religious people. The Catholics of Maryland and the Puritans of New England; the Virginia Episcopalians and the Pennsylvania Quakers, feared God and revered his laws, as far at least as they understood them; and the excellent institutions which those men of diverse opinions, but honest intentions, originated and transmitted to us, are but the reflex of that reverential and devotional spirit. We admire the thrift and enterprise of our German fellow-citizens, we admit their general good order, taste, and proficiency in art, particularly the beautiful one of music, and we know how many fine churches and hospitals they have built and are sustaining, but it cannot be denied that there is a great deal of indifferentism, and even worse, among the anti-Catholic portion of them, the outward evidence of which may be found in the complete disregard that is so generally manifested for the holiness of the Sunday. We are not of those who would deny to the hard-working and hard-faring classes their proper share of innocent and healthful amusement on the only day in the week that they can escape from labor, but this recreation should be preceded by some act of devotion, some solemn and open recognition of our dependence on the great Giver of life and happiness. Still, whoever visits our saloons and pleasure gardens on a Sunday will find them thronged with persons of all ages and both sexes from early morning till midnight, while churches that would gladly receive them are comparatively deserted. Luther's revolt

against the church has much of this to answer for, but Kant, Fichte, and other so-called philosophers of more modern times have much more; for while the " Reformers " only unsettled the religious mind of Germany, and partially succeeded in alienating it from the Catholic Church, the schoolmen succeeded in making atheism fashionable among the intelligent classes by covering it with a thin veil of learned mysticism. This want of proper deference for the day set apart by the church, and by all Christian sects, for special reverence, and the observance of which is even enjoined by our common and statute law, is, we maintain, not only unAmerican, but is likely to produce a general contempt for all law, and lead to a weakening of the sense of that obedience which every individual citizen owes to the public authority.

In thus alluding to the characteristics of some of our adopted citizens, we have touched only on those of the two most numerous re-

presentatives of European n: ties, not because there are no whose deficiencies, from an A: point of view, are not as ap but from the fact that we c from their numerical strength trinsic qualities, they are dest exercise a marked and extens fluence on the future characte country. In feeling or tempei they are not opposed to us each other. The vivacity ar excitability of one race fine complement in the solidity an ter-of-fact disposition of the o union of qualities which, goverr properly managed by the p genius of Americans, will in all probability lead to results in t tant future of the magnitude of we scarcely dare to dream. No ever possessed the advantage we, native and adopted, enjoy. avail ourselves of them in sucl ner that posterity may look b us, as we to the Revolutionary f with unmingled feelings of gr: and admiration.

OUR LADY OF LOURDES.

FROM THE FRENCH OF HENRI LASSERRE.

(*Concluded.*)

PART X.

II.

ANOTHER episode.
There are, in civil life, men whose appearance is precisely that of a soldier. Though they have never seen service, every one who meets them and does not know them takes them

without hesitation for veterans. have the rather stiff carriag step, disciplined appearance, ar cealed good-fellowship belong the profession. They are sp common in the mixed service as the customs, the waters and i which, though purely civil ir nature, borrow their degrees o and their methods from the :

army. On the one
have, the private
and a domestic life;
ey are bound in a
y the manifold re-
n entirely military
due the peculiar
hich I speak, and
one is familiar.
have ever seen a
cer in citizen's dress,
air and his bristly
ing to turn gray; if
d in his energetic
traight and verti-
are hardly as yet
ch seem peculiar to
ces; if you have
forehead, rebellious
which seems made
kepi or tricorne,
eyes which by day
o brave danger, but
gentle at the fireside
he children's heads;
this characteristic
need to introduce
Lacassagne, officer
use at Bordeaux—
well as I.
vo years ago, I had
ng him at his house,
s Farines, No. 6, at
struck at first by his
e and his air of

with the somewhat
s habitual to men
t was the object of

id I, "I have heard
ourney to the Grotto
or the profit of some
ust now making, I
e it from your own

the Grotto of Lour-
ountenance became
dear remembrance
lines.

"Be seated," said he, "and excuse the disorder of our establishment. My family leaves to-day for Arcachon, and everything is topsy-turvy."

"Do not mention it. Tell me all about these interesting events of which I have already heard, but only confusedly."

"For my part," said he in a voice choked by emotion, "I shall never in my life forget their smallest details.

"Monsieur," he continued after a moment of silence, "I have only two sons. The youngest, about whom I am going to tell you, is called Jules. He will come in before long. You will see how sweet, pure, and good he is."

M. Lacassagne did not tell me all his affection for this youngest son. But the accent of his voice, which became gentle and as it were caressing in speaking of this child, showed me all the depth of his paternal love. I understood that in that strong and tender feeling was concentrated all the force of this manly soul.

"His health," continued he, "was excellent until the age of ten.

"At that period there came on unexpectedly, and without apparent physical cause, a disease the importance of which I did not at first appreciate. On the 25th of January, 1865, when we were sitting down to supper, Jules complained of a trouble in his throat which prevented him from swallowing any solid food. He had to limit himself to a little soup.

"This state of things continuing next day, I called in Dr. Noguès, one of the most distinguished physicians of Toulouse.

"'The difficulty comes from the nerves,' said he—which gave me hopes of a speedy cure.

"In fact, a few days afterwards, the boy was able to eat, and I thought all was over, when the trouble return-

ed, and continued with occasional intermissions till the end of April. It then became fixed. The poor child had to live entirely on liquids; on milk, the juice of meat, and broth. Even the broth had to be very clear, for such was the narrowness of the orifice that it was absolutely impossible for him to swallow anything solid, even tapioca.

"The poor boy, reduced to such miserable diet, was becoming visibly emaciated, and was dying slowly.

"The physicians, for there were two—as I had from the outset requested a celebrated practitioner, Dr. Roques, to consult with Dr. Noguès—the physicians, I say, astonished by the peculiarity and the persistence of this difficulty, tried vainly to discover its precise nature, that they might apply a remedy. One day, it was the tenth of May—for I suffered so much, sir, and thought so much about this illness that I remembered every date—one day, I saw Jules in the garden running with unusual haste, and as it were precipitately. Now I dreaded the least agitation for him.

"'Stop, Jules!' cried I, going to him and taking his hand.

"He broke away immediately.

"'Father, I cannot,' said he. 'I must run. It is stronger than I.'

"I took him in my lap, but his legs moved convulsively. Soon after the movement passed to his head and face.

"The true character of his disease had at last declared itself. My poor child was attacked by chorea. You are no doubt aware, sir, by what horrible contortions this disease is usually marked."

"No," said I, interrupting him, "I do not even know what it is."

"It is what is often called *St. Vitus's dance.*"

"Yes, I have heard of that. Go on."

"The principal seat of th
was in the œsophagus. Th
sions which I had just witne
which were continued at
from that time, put an en
perplexities of the physician

"But though they now ur
the difficulty, they could 1
come it. After fifteen m
treatment, the most they coul
control these violent extern
toms; or really, in my own
these disappeared of thems
the efforts of nature alone.
to the contraction of the
had become chronic and
all appliances. Remedies
kind, the country, the bath
chon, were successively and
employed for about two ye
the treatment seemed only to
the disease.

"Our last trial had been
son at the sea-side. My
taken our poor child to St.
Luz. I need hardly say
the state in which he was,
of his body was everythir
only object was to keep h
We had from the first su
his studies and stopped
on his part, whether of
mind; we treated him like
Now, his mind was natural
and inquiring, and this pri
intellectual occupation g
much *ennui.* The poor bo
so ashamed of his trouble;
other children in good healt
felt himself as it were disgr
under a ban; so he kept ap

The father, deeply moved
memories, stopped a mo
check a rising sob, and cont

"He kept apart. He
When he found some interest
he would read it to distract
At St. Jean-de-Luz, he saw o
the table of a lady who live
neighborhood a little notic

[illegible] Lourdes. He read it, and seemed to have been very much impressed by it. He said that evening to his mother that the Blessed Virgin could very easily cure him; but she paid no attention to his proposal, considering it as only a childish idea.

"On our return to Bordeaux—for a little while before this my station had been changed, and we had come to live here—on our return to Bordeaux the child was absolutely in the same condition.

"That was last August.

"So many vain efforts, so much science employed without success by the best physicians, so much lost trouble, had by this time, as you will easily imagine, discouraged us most completely. Disheartened by the failure of all our endeavors, we gave up all kinds of remedies, letting nature act alone, and resigning ourselves to the inevitable evil which God was pleased to send us. It seemed to us that so much suffering had in a certain way redoubled our love for this child. Our poor Jules was tended by his mother and myself with equal tenderness and solicitude continually. Grief added many years to our lives. You would hardly believe it, sir, but I am only forty-six years old."

I looked at the poor father; and at the sight of his manly face, upon which grief had left such visible traces, my heart was moved. I took his hand and pressed it with cordial sympathy and real compassion.

"Meanwhile," said he, "the strength of the child decreased perceptibly. For two years he had taken no solid food. It was only at great expense, by means of a liquid nourishment in preparing which all our ingenuity had been taxed that it might be substantial, and by most extraordinary care, that we had been able to prolong his life. He had become frightfully thin. His pallor was extreme; he had no blood showing under his skin; you would have said he was a statue of wax. It was evident that death was coming on apace. It was not only certain, but imminent. And, though the uselessness of medical science in the case had certainly been clearly shown, I could not help knocking once again at its door. I knew of no other in this world.

"I applied to the most eminent physician in Bordeaux, Dr. Gintrac. Dr. Gintrac examined his throat, sounded it, and found, besides the mere contraction which had almost entirely closed the alimentary canal, some most threatening roughnesses or small swellings.

"He shook his head, and gave me little hope. He saw my terrible anxiety.

"'I do not say that his cure is impossible,' said he; '*but he is very ill.*'

"These were his exact words.

"He considered it absolutely necessary to employ local remedies; first injections, then the application of a cloth soaked in ether. But this treatment prostrated the child; in view of the result, the surgeon himself, M. Sentex, employed in the hospital, advised us to discontinue it.

"In one of my visits to Dr. Gintrac, I communicated to him an idea which had occurred to me.

"'It seems to me,' said I, 'that if Jules *had the will*, he could swallow. Does not this difficulty perhaps come from fear? Is it not perhaps that he does not swallow to-day merely because he did not yesterday? If so, it is a mental malady, which can only be cured by moral means.'

"But the doctor dispelled this my last illusion.

"'You are mistaken,' said he. 'The disease is in the organs themselves, which are only too really and se-

riously affected. I have not contented myself with looking at them, for the eye may easily be deceived; but I have sounded them with an instrument, and felt of them carefully with my fingers. The œsophagus is covered with little swellings, and the passage has become so small that it is ***materially impossible*** for the boy to take any food whatever, except liquids, which can accommodate themselves to the size of the opening, and pass through the pin-hole, as I may call it, which still remains. If the enlargement of the tissues proceeds a few millimetres further, the patient cannot live. The beginning of the trouble, the alternations which characterized it, and its occasional interruptions also bear out the result of my examination. Your child, having once recovered, would have continued well if the difficulty had been in his imagination. Unfortunately, it is organic.'

"These remarks, which had been already made to me at Toulouse, but which I had gladly forgotten, were too conclusive not to convince me. I returned home, with death in my soul.

"What could now be done? We had applied to the most distinguished physicians both of Toulouse and Bordeaux, and all had been unavailing. The fatal evidence was before my eyes; our poor child was condemned, and that without appeal.

"But, monsieur, such cruel conclusions cannot easily remain in a father's heart. I still tried to deceive myself; my wife and I continued to consult; I was thinking of hydropathy.

"It was in this desperate state of things that Jules said to his mother, with an air of confidence and absolute certitude which strongly impressed her:

"'Mamma, neither Dr. Gintr any other doctor can do anythi my trouble. It is the Holy who will cure me. Send me Grotto of Lourdes, and you w that I shall be cured. I am s it.'

"My wife reported this propo me.

"'We must not hesitate!' cr 'He must go to Lourdes. An as soon as possible.'

"It was not, sir, that I was f faith. I did not believe in mi and I hardly considered such ordinary interventions of divine er as possible. But I was a f and any chance, no matter ho significant, seemed to me not slighted. Besides, I hoped without any supernatural occur the possibility of which I di wish to admit, this journey have a salutary moral effect o child. As for a complete cure, not entertain the slightest idea of a thing.

"It was in winter, at the begi of February; the weather was and I wished to wait for a fine on Jules's account.

"Since he had read the little n eight months before, at St. Jea Luz, the idea which he had ju pressed to us had never left Having expressed it once wi any attention being paid to it, h not introduced the subject a but the thought had remained in and worked there while he wa dergoing all the medical trea with a patience that had to be to be appreciated.

"This faith, so full and com was the more extraordinary be we had not brought up the ch any unusual practices of piety. wife attended to her religious d but that was all; and, as for m I had, as you have just heard,

sophic ideas, tending quite the other way.

"On the 12th of February, the weather promised to be magnificent. We took the train for Tarbes.

"During the whole journey, Jules was gay, and full of the most positive faith that he would be cured; his faith was overpowering.

"As for myself, I encouraged, but did not share, this confidence; it was so great that I should call it exaggerated, did I not fear to be wanting in respect for the God who inspired it.'

"At Tarbes, at the Hôtel Dupont, where we put up, every one noticed the poor child, so pale and wasted, and yet with such a sweet and attractive expression. I mentioned at the hotel the object of our journey, and in the good wishes and prayers which these good people made for us there seemed to be a presentiment of success. And when we set out, I saw plainly that they would await our return with impatience.

"Notwithstanding my doubts, I took with me a small box of biscuits.

"When we arrived at the crypt above the Grotto, Mass was being said. Jules prayed with a faith which shone out in all his features, with a truly celestial ardor.

"The priest noticed his fervor, and when he had left the altar, he came out of the sacristy almost immediately and approached us. A good idea had occurred to him on seeing the poor little one. He proposed it to me, and, turning to Jules, who was still on his knees, said:

"'My child, would you like to have me consecrate you to the Blessed Virgin?'

"'Indeed I would,' answered he.

"The priest immediately proceeded with the very simple ceremony, and recited over my child the sacred

"'Now,' said Jules, in a tone which impressed me by its perfect confidence, 'I am going to be cured.'

"We went to the Grotto. Jules knelt before the statue and prayed. I looked at him, and can still see the expression of his face, his attitude, and his joined hands.

"He rose, and we went to the fountain.

"It was a terrible moment.

"He bathed his neck and chest. Then he took the glass and drank several mouthfuls of the miraculous water.

"He was calm and happy, gay in fact, and radiant with confidence.

"For my part, I trembled and almost fainted at this last trial. But I restrained my emotion, though with difficulty. I did not want to let him see my doubt.

"'Try now to eat,' said I, handing him a biscuit.

"He took it, and I turned away my head, not feeling able to look at him. It was, in fact, the question of the life or death of my child which was to be decided. In putting this question, such a fearful one for a father's heart, I was playing, as it were, my last card. If I failed, my dear boy would have to die. This test was a decisive one, and I could not see it tried.

"But I was soon relieved of my agony.

"Jules's voice, joyous and sweet, called me:

"'Papa! I have swallowed it. I can eat, I knew I could—I had faith!'

"What a surprise it was! My child, who had been at death's door, was saved, and that instantly. And I, his father, was a witness to this astonishing resurrection.

"But, that I might not disturb the faith of my son, I checked any appearance of astonishment.

"'Yes, Jules, it was certain, and could not have been otherwise,' said I, in a voice which I made calm by great effort.

"There was in my breast, however, a whirlwind of excitement. If it could have been opened, it would have been found burning as if full of fire.

"We repeated our experiment. He ate some more biscuits, not only without difficulty, but with an increasing appetite. I was obliged to restrain him.

"But I could not refrain from proclaiming my happiness, and thanking God.

"'Wait for me,' said I to Jules, 'and pray to the Blessed Virgin. I am going to the chapel.'

"And leaving him for a moment kneeling at the Grotto, I ran to tell the priest the wonderful news. I was quite bewildered. Besides my happiness, so unexpected and sudden that it was terrible, besides the confusion of my heart, I felt in my soul and mind an inexpressible disturbance. A revolution was going on in my agitated and tumultuous thoughts. All my 'philosophical' ideas were tottering and crumbling away.

"The priest came down immediately and saw Jules finishing his last biscuit. The Bishop of Tarbes happened to be that day at the chapel, and he wished to see my son. I told him of the cruel illness which had just had such a happy end. Every one caressed the child, and rejoiced with him.

"But I meanwhile was thinking of his mother, and of the joy in store for her. Before going to the hotel, I ran to the telegraph office. My despatch contained only one word: 'Cured!'

Hardly had it gone before I wanted to recall it.

"'Perhaps,' said I, 'I have been too hasty. Who knows if he w have a relapse?'

"I did not dare to believe blessing I had received; and did believe in it, it seemed was going to escape from me.

"As for the child, he was without the least mixture of d tude. He was exuberant in and perfect security.

"'You see now, papa,' said me every moment, 'it was on Blessed Virgin who could cu When I told you so before, sure of it.'

"At the hotel, he ate with cellent appetite; and how I e watching him!

"He wanted to return on the Grotto to give thanks for liverance, and actually did so.

"'You will be very grateful Holy Virgin, will you not?' priest to him.

"'Ah! I shall never forget he.

"At Tarbes, we stopped at t tel where we had put up the d fore. They were on the look us. They seem to have had think I told you) a feeling th would be successful. There great rejoicing. People ga around us to see him eat with ish everything that was served the table; to see him eat h who the day before could only low a few spoonfuls of liquid. time seemed to me long by.

"This illness, against whic science of the most able phy had failed, and which had jus so miraculously cured, had two years and nineteen days.

"We were in haste to return mother, and took the express for Bordeaux. The child was come with fatigue by the jo and I should also say by his

tions, were it not for his peaceable and constant calmness in spite of his sudden cure, which overwhelmed him with joy, but did not astonish him. He wanted to go to bed on reaching home. He was extremely sleepy, and took no supper. His mother, who had nearly died of joy before our return, when she saw him so exhausted and refusing to eat, was seized by a horrible doubt. She told me that I had deceived her, and I had the greatest difficulty in making myself believed. But how she rejoiced when, the next morning, Jules sat down at our table, and breakfasted with a better appetite than ourselves. It was not till then that she became reassured."

"And since then," I asked him, "has there been no relapse?"

"No, sir, absolutely none. I may say that the cure progressed, or rather consolidated itself, considering that it had been as complete as it was instantaneous. The transition from a disease so fixed and obstinate to a perfect cure was made without the least gradation, though it was without apparent disturbance. But his general health improved visibly, under the influence of a restorative regimen, the salutary effects of which it was full time for him to experience."

"And the physicians? Have they testified to Jules's previous condition? Certainly they should have done so."

"I thought so too, sir, and mentioned the subject to the Bordeaux doctor who had been the last to attend my child; but he maintained a reserve which prevented me from insisting. As for Dr. Roques of Toulouse, to whom I wrote immediately, he hastened to recognize in the clearest terms the miraculous nature of the fact which had occurred, and which was entirely beyond the powers of medicine. 'In view of this cure, so long desired and so promptly effected,' he said to me, 'why not quit the narrow sphere of scientific explanations, and open one's mind to gratitude for so strange an event, in which Providence seems to obey the voice of a child?' He rejected most decidedly, as a physician, the theories which are always produced on such occasions of 'moral excitement,' 'the effect of the imagination,' etc., and confessed frankly in this event the clear and positive action of a superior Being revealing himself and imposing himself on the conscience. Such, sir, was the opinion of M. Roques, physician of Toulouse, who knew as well as myself the previous condition and the illness of my son. There is his own letter, dated February 24.

"But the facts which I have just related are also so well known that no one would care to contest them. It is superabundantly proved that science was absolutely powerless against the strange disease by which Jules had been attacked. As for the cause of his cure, every one can place it differently, according to the point of view which he chooses to assume. I, who had previously believed only in purely natural phenomena, saw clearly that its explanation must be sought in a higher order of things; and every day I gave thanks to God, who, putting an end to my long and cruel trial in such an unexpected way, had approached me in the way most adapted to make me bow before him."

"I understand you, and it seems also to me that such was the divine plan."

After these words, I remained some time silent and absorbed in my reflections.

The conversation returned to the boy so wonderfully cured. The fa-

ther's heart came back to him, as the needle does to the pole.

"Since that time," said he, "his piety is angelic. You will see him soon. The nobleness of his feelings is visible in his face. He is well-born, his character is honest and dignified. He is incapable of lies or meanness. And his piety has not been at the expense of his natural qualities. He is studying in a school close by, kept by M. Conangle, in the Rue du Mirail. The poor child has quickly made up for his lost time. He loves his studies. He is the first in his class. At the last examination, he took the highest prize. But, above all, he is the best and most amiable. He is the favorite of his teachers and schoolmates. He is our joy, our consolation, and—"

At this moment the door opened, and Jules came with his mother into the room where we were sitting. I embraced him affectionately. The glow of health was on his face. His forehead is large, high, and magnificent; his attitude has a modesty and gentle firmness which inspires a secret respect. His eyes, large and bright, show a rare intelligence, and absolute purity and a beautiful soul.

"You are happy to have such a son," said I to M. Lacassagne.

"Yes, sir, I am happy. But my poor wife and I have suffered a great deal."

"Do not be sorry for that," said I, going a little away from Jules. "This path of grief was the way which led you from darkness to light, from death to life, from yourself to God. The Blessed Virgin has shown herself twice in this event as the mother of life. She has given your son his temporal life in order to give you the true life which knows no end."

I left this family, so greatly blessed by our Lord, and, still under the impression of what I had heard and seen, I wrote, with my heart [illegible] the feelings produced, what yo[illegible] just read.

PART XI.

Let us return to Lourdes. [illegible] had passed, and human ir[illegible] had been at work. The sur[illegible] ings of the Grotto, where the I[illegible] Virgin had appeared, had ch[illegible] their former aspect. Without [illegible] anything of its grandeur, this [illegible] spot had put on a pleasing [illegible] Yet unfinished, but fairly aliv[illegible] workmen, a superb church, p[illegible] crowning the Massabielle [illegible] was rising joyously to heaven. [illegible] lofty heights, so abrupt and u[illegible] vated, where formerly the feet [illegible] mountaineers could scarcely de[illegible] were covered with a green[illegible] and planted with shrubs and fl[illegible] Among dahlias and roses, daisi[illegible] violets, beneath the shade of a[illegible] and cytisuses, a path, broad [illegible] highway, wound in sinuous [illegible] from the church to the Grotto.

The Grotto was enclosed [illegible] chancel by an iron railing. [illegible] the roof a golden lamp had [illegible] suspended. On the rocks, [illegible] had been pressed by Mary's [illegible] feet, clusters of tapers burne[illegible] and night. Outside the enc[illegible] the miraculous spring fed [illegible] bronze lavers. A canal, sc[illegible] from sight by a little building, [illegible] ed a chance for those invalid[illegible] wished to be bathed in this l[illegible] water. The mill-race of Sav[illegible] changed its bed, having bee[illegible] into the Gave, further up. [illegible] Gave itself had withdrawn [illegible] what, to give room for a fin[illegible] which leads to the Massabielle [illegible] Below, on the banks of the riv[illegible] ground had been levelled, and

own and walk,
...
had been accom-
going on amid
se of the faith-
...thrown by
the grotto—the
invalids who had
any hearts who
f so many souls
and life, alone
these gigantic
ches the sum of
When God, in
es to call men
of his works, he
...ers, or tax-
es to collect the
... his creatures
istance. The
erse repudiates
he God of free
consent to re-
is not sponta-
with a cheerful

was gradually
and the mill-
sides were level-
ted, and path-
he now famous
other of Christ
lory to the eyes

laborers, su-
ing, suggesting
tting his own
set a misplaced
badly-planted
ardor and holy
nd figures of
h, occupied, by
rebuilding of
m, a tall man,
emed to make
present. His
black cassock

rendered him conspicuous to all eyes. His name will be speedily guessed. It was the chief pastor of the town of Lourdes, the Abbé Peyramale.

Every hour of the day he thought of the message which the Blessed Virgin had addressed to him; every hour he thought of the miraculous cures which had followed the apparition; he was a daily witness of countless miracles. He had devoted his life to execute the orders of his powerful Queen, and raise to her glory a splendid monument. All idleness, all delay, every moment wasted, seemed to his eyes a token of ingratitude, and his heart, devoured by zeal for the house of God, often broke forth in warnings and admonitions. His faith was perfect, and full of confidence. He had a horror of the wretched narrowness of human prudence, and scouted it with the disdain of one who looks upon all things from that holy mount whereon the Son of God preached the nothingness of earth and the reality of heaven, when he said: "Be not solicitous . . . seek first the kingdom of heaven, and all these things shall be added unto you."

One day, while standing before the miraculous fountain amid a group of ecclesiastics and laymen, the architect offered him a plan for a pretty chapel which he proposed to build above the Grotto. The curé looked at it, and a flush rose to his cheek. With a gesture of impatience he tore the drawing into bits, and tossed it into the Gave.

"What are you doing?" cried the astonished architect.

"Look you," answered the priest, "I am ashamed of what human meanness would offer to the Mother of my God, and I have treated the wretched plan as it deserved. We

do not want a country chapel to commemorate the great events which have taken place here. Go, give us a temple of marble as large and as high as these rocks can sustain—as magnificent as your soul can conceive! Go, and do not check your genius till you have given us a *chef-d'œuvre;* and understand that, if you were Michael Angelo himself, it would all be unworthy of her who has appeared in this spot."

"But, *monsieur le curé*," observed everybody, "it will cost millions to carry out your ideas!"

"She who has made this barren rock send forth its living stream—she will know how to make faithful hearts generous," answered the priest. "Go, do what I tell you. Why are you afraid, O ye of little faith?"

The temple rose in the proportions designed by the man of God.

The good pastor, as he watched the progress of the various works, often used to say:

"When will it be granted me to assist, with my priests and people, at the first procession which goes to inaugurate in these hallowed precincts the public worship of the Catholic Church? It seems to me that then I could sing my *Nunc dimittis*, and die of joy." His eyes filled with tears at the thought. Never was there a deeper or warmer desire than this innocent wish of a heart given wholly to God.

Sometimes, at hours when the crowd was thin at the Massabielle Rocks, a little girl used to come and kneel before the place of the apparition, and drink of the miraculous spring. She was a poor child, and meanly clad—nothing marked out from the common people about. And if the pilgrims were all strangers to the place, no one suspected that it was Bernadette. This privileged soul had withdrawn into silence and concealment. She went daily sisters' school, where she simplest, and strove to be t unnoticed. The numerous whom she was called upon to never disturbed her peace o which ever retained the me its glimpse at heaven and the parable Virgin. Bernadette these things in her heart. came from all quarters, mirac being worked, the temple wa Bernadette and the holy pa Lourdes awaited, as their c joy, the day which was t to their eyes the sight of pr the true God leading their with cross advanced and flyi ners, to the spot of the appa

III.

In spite of the bishop's the church in fact had not y possession, by any public ce of this spot, consecrated f It was not till the 4th of Apr that this was done, by the in tion and blessing of the sup tue of the Blessed Virgin, wh placed with all the pomp cu on such occasions in the rusti bordered with wild flowers the Mother of God had appe the child of man.*

The weather was magnifice young spring sun had risen, vanced in a blue and cloudle

The streets of Lourdes wer ed with flowers, banners, g and triumphal arches. The the parish church, the chap

* This statue, made of fine Carrara life-size, was presented to the Grotto c by two noble and pious sisters of the Lyons, Mesdames de Lacour. It was according to Bernadette's particular in by M. Fabish, the eminent Lyonnese The Blessed Virgin is represented as I described her, with scrupulous rega smallest details, and rare talent in exe

the churches of the neighborhood, rang out joyous peals. Immense numbers of people flocked together to this great festival of earth and heaven. A procession, such as had never been seen by the oldest inhabitant, moved from the church of Lourdes to the Grotto. Troops, in all the splendor of military attire, led the way. Following them were the confraternities of Lourdes, the societies for mutual aid, and other associations, with their banners and crosses; the Congregation of the Children of Mary, whose long robes were white as snow; the Sisters of Nevers, with their long black veil; the Daughters of Charity, with their great white hoods; the Sisters of St. Joseph, in dark mantles; the religious orders of men, the Carmelites, the Brothers of Instruction and of the Christian schools, and prodigious numbers of pilgrims, men and women, young and old—fifty or sixty thousand persons in all—wound along the flowery road leading to the Massabielle rocks. Here and there, choirs and instrumental bands gave a voice to the popular enthusiasm. Last, surrounded by four hundred priests in choir dress, his vicars-general, and the dignitaries of his cathedral chapter, came his lordship, Mgr. Bertrand-Sévère Laurence, Bishop of Tarbes, in his mitre and pontifical robes, with one hand blessing the people, and bearing his crosier in the other.

An indescribable emotion, an exaltation of feeling, such as only Christian people assembled before God can know, filled every heart. The day of solemn triumph had at last come, after so many difficulties, struggles, and disasters. Tears of joy, enthusiasm, and love ran down the cheeks of the people, moved by an impulse from God.

What indescribable joy must have filled the heart of Bernadette on this day, as she led the Congregation of the Children of Mary! What overwhelming happiness must have inundated the soul of the venerable curé of Lourdes, who was no doubt at the side of the bishop, singing the hosanna of the victory of God! Having both had to labor, the time was certainly come for them to enter into their reward.

Alas! one would have sought in vain among the Children of Mary for Bernadette: among the clergy surrounding the bishop, the Abbé Peyramale would not have been found. There are joys too sweet for earth, which are reserved for heaven. Here below, God refuses them to his dearest children.

At this time of rejoicing, when the bright sun was shining on the triumph of the faithful, the curé of Lourdes, laboring under a disease which was expected to result fatally, was a victim to intense physical sufferings. He was stretched on his bed of pain, at the head of which two religious watched and prayed night and day. He wished to rise to see the grand cortége pass, but his strength failed him, and he had not even a momentary glimpse of its splendor. Through the closed shutters of his room, the joyous sound of the silvery bells came to him only as a funeral knell.

As for Bernadette, God showed her his predilection, as usual with his elect, by giving her the bitter trial of pain. While Mgr. Laurence was going, accompanied by countless numbers of his flock, to take possession of the Massabielle rocks in the name of the church, and to inaugurate solemnly the devotion to the Virgin who had appeared there, Bernadette, like the eminent priest of whom we have just spoken, was prostrated by illness; Providence, perhaps, fearing for this well-beloved child a temptation to vainglory, de-

prived her of the sight of this unprecedented festivity, where she would have heard her name on the lips of thousands, and extolled from the pulpit by the voice of enthusiastic preachers. Too poor to be taken care of in her own home, where neither she nor her family would ever receive any gift, Bernadette had been carried to the hospital, where she lay upon the humble bed provided by public charity, in the midst of those poor whom the world calls unfortunate, but whom Jesus Christ has blessed in declaring them the possessors of his eternal kingdom.

IV.

Eleven years have now elapsed since the apparitions of the most Holy Virgin. The great church is almost finished; it has only to be roofed, and the holy sacrifice has long since been celebrated at all the altars of the crypt below. Diocesan missionaries of the house of Garaison have been stationed by the bishop near the grotto and the church, to distribute to the pilgrims the apostolic word, the sacraments, and the body of our Lord.

The pilgrimage has taken dimensions perhaps quite without precedent, for before our day these vast movements of popular faith did not have the assistance of the means of transportation invented by modern science. The course of the Pyrenees Railroad, for which a straighter and cheaper route had been previously marked out between Tarbes and Pau, was changed so as to pass through Lourdes, and innumerable travellers continually come from every quarter to invoke the Virgin who has appeared at the Grotto, and to seek at the miraculous fountain the healing of all their ills. They come not only from the different provinces of France, but also from England, Belgium, Spai
sia, and Germany. Even fr
midst of far America, pious
tians have set out, and cros
ocean to come to the Grotto o
des, to kneel before these
rocks, which the Mother of C
sanctified by her touch. An
those who cannot come writ
missionaries, and beg that a l
the miraculous water may be
their homes. It is thus dist
throughout the world.

Although Lourdes is a smal
there is a continual passing
fro upon the road to the gr
stream of men, women, pries
carriages, as in the streets of
city.

When the pleasant weather
and the sun, overcoming the
winter, opens in the midst of
the gates of spring, the faithful
neighborhood begin to bestir
selves for the pilgrimage to
bielle, no longer one by one,
large parties. From ten, twe
fifteen leagues' distance, these
mountaineers come on foot in
of one or two thousand. Th
out in the evening and wa
night by starlight, like the she
of Judea, when they went to t
of Bethlehem to adore the ne
infant God. They descend
high peaks, they traverse dee
leys, they cross foaming torre
follow their course, singing the
es of God. And on their w
sleeping herds of cattle or of
awake, and diffuse through
desert wilds the melancholy
of their sonorous bells. At
break, they arrive at Lourdes
spread their banners, and form
cession to go to the Grotto.
men, with their blue caps and
shoes covered with dust from
long night march, rest upon a
stick, and usually carry upon

gently crosses their fields. But the stream laughs at their dikes of wood, earth, and pebbles.

"We will stop these drops of water," the fools repeat in their delirium.

And they heap up enormous rocks; they join them together with impenetrable cement. And notwithstanding, the water does leak through in a thousand places. But the men are numerous—they have a force greater than the armies of Darius. They stop up the thousand fissures, they fill up the cracks, they replace the fallen stones; and at last a time comes when the stream cannot pass by. It has before it a barrier higher than the pyramids, and thicker than the famous, walls of Babylon. Beyond this gigantic obstacle, the pebbles of its dry bed are shining in the sun.

Human pride shouts its pæan of triumph.

Meanwhile the water continues to descend from those eternal heights where it has heard the voice of God; and millions of drops, coming one by one, stop before the barrier and rise silently against this granite wall which millions of men have built.

"Look," say the men, "at the immense power of our race. See this enormous wall. Raise your eyes to its summit; admire its astonishing height. We have for ever conquered this stream which comes from the mountains."

At this moment, a thin sheet of water passes over the cyclopean barrier. They run up; but the sheet has thickened—it is a river which is now falling, scattering on all sides the upper rocks of the wall.

"What is the matter?" they cry on all sides in the doomed city.

It is the drop of water to which God has spoken, and which proceeds invincibly on its way.

What has your Babel-like wall accomplished? What have y
with your herculean effort
have changed a quiet strea
formidable cataract. You
stop the drop of water; bu
resumes its course with the
of Niagara.

How humble was this
water, this word of a child
God had said, "Pursue thy c
How insignificant was this
water—this shepherdess b
candle at the Grotto,—th
woman praying and offering
quet to the Blessed Virgin—
peasant on his knees! A
strong, how apparent, impass
invincible was this enormo
upon which all the force of
nation, from the policeman
gendarme to the prefect a
minister, had labored fo
months!

But the child, the poor
the old peasant, have resume
course. Only now it is not
candle or a poor bouquet th
fies to the popular faith; it is
nificent monument which the
are erecting; they are spend
lions upon this temple,
celebrated throughout Chris
Their opposers thought to p
some scattered believers; b
they come in crowds, in imme
cessions, displaying their ban
singing their hymns. The
pilgrimage without precedent
peoples now come, borne up
iron roads by chariots of f
steam. It is not now a littl
borhood which believes—it is
it is the Christian world
coming from all directions,
drop of water which men tried
has become a Niagara.

God has finished his wor
now, as on the seventh day,
entered into his rest, he
signed to men the duty of

, and the formidable re-
of developing or com-
He has given them a
dant grace, as of other
urden remains on them
and ... it. They
it a hundredfold by
bly and holily in the
providence; they can
itful by refusing to enter
ler. Every good thing
is entrusted to human
terrestrial paradise was
on the condition of la-
keeping it—"*ut opera-
ret illum.*" Let us be-
at men may not reject
done for them, and that
by earthly ideas or ir-
break in their guilty or
ds the sacred vessel of
which they have re-
t.

VI.

e persons mentioned in
f this long history are
e prefect, Baron Massy,
t, Mayor Lacadé, and
ld are dead.
em have made several
nce on the road to for-
ouland has left the Min-
c Worship (for which he
em to have been well
e care of the Bank of
Dutour, the procureur-
become counsellor of
I. Jacomet is the chief
of police in one of the
of the empire.
Croisine Bouhohorts
, Mme. Rizan, Henri
c. Moreau de Sazenay,
ozat, Jules Lacassagne,
whose cures we have
still full of life, and tes-
r recovered health and strength to the powerful mercy of the apparition at the Grotto.

Dr. Dozous continues to be the most eminent physician of Lourdes. Dr. Vergez is at the spring of Barèges and attests to the visitors at this celebrated resort the miracles which he formerly witnessed. M. Estrade, whose impartial observations we have several times given, is receiver of indirect contributions at Bordeaux. He lives at No. 14 Rue Ducau.

Now, as formerly, Mgr. Laurence is Bishop of Tarbes. Age has not diminished his faculties. He is to-day what we have represented him in this work. He has near the Grotto a house to which he sometimes retires, to meditate in this spot, beloved by the Virgin, on the great duties and the grave responsibilities of a Christian bishop who has received so wonderful a grace in his diocese.*

The Abbé Peyramale recovered from the severe illness of which we spoke above. He is still the venerated pastor of this Christian town of Lourdes, where his record is left in ineffaceable characters. Long after he is gone, when he rests under the sod in the midst of the generation which he has formed to the Lord; when the successors of his successors live in his house and occupy the great wooden chair in his church, his memory will be living in the minds of all; and when the "Curé of Lourdes" is mentioned, every one will think of him.

Louise Soubirous, the mother of Bernadette, died on the 8th of December, 1866, the very day of the feast of the Immaculate Conception. In choosing this festival to take the mother from the miseries of the world, she who had said to the child, "I am the Immaculate Conception," seems

* Mgr. Laurence died at the Vatican Council in the winter of 1869–70.

to have intended to temper the bitterness of the loss to the heart of her survivors, and to show them as a certain pledge of hope and of a happy resurrection the sign of her radiant appearance.

While thousands go to the Grotto to contribute to the splendid church, Bernadette's father has remained a poor miller, subsisting with difficulty by manual labor. Mary, the daughter, who was with Bernadette at the time of the first apparition, has married a good peasant, who has become a miller and works with his father-in-law. The other companion, Jane Abbadie, is a servant at Bordeaux.

VII.

Bernadette is no longer at Lourdes. We have seen how she had, on many occasions, refused gifts freely offered, and repelled the good fortune which was knocking at the door of her humble cottage. She was dreaming of other riches. "We shall know some fine day," the unbelievers had said at the outset, "what her pay is going to be." Bernadette had in fact chosen her pay, and put her hand on her reward. She has become a Sister of Charity. She has devoted herself to tend in the hospitals the poor and the sick collected by public benevolence.

After having seen with her own eyes the resplendent face of the thrice holy Mother of God, what could she do but become the compassionate servant of those of whom the Virgin's Son has said: "As long as you did it to one of these my least brethren, you did it to me."

It is among the Sisters of Charity and Christian Instruction at Nevers that Bernadette has taken the veil. She is called Sister Marie-Bernard. We have lately seen her in her religious habit at the mother-house of this congregation. Though she twenty-five, her face has ke character and the charm of hood. In her presence, the feels moved in its better part indescribable religious sentime one leaves it embalmed in t fume of this peaceful inn One understands that the Ho gin has specially loved her. wise, there is nothing extraor nothing which would make h spicuous, or would make one the important part she has this communication from hea earth. Her simplicity has no touched by the unexampled which has been taken in her concourse and enthusiasm multitude have no more troub soul than the turbid water o rent would tarnish the impe purity of a diamond.

God visits her still, not bright visions, but by the sacr of suffering. She is often suffers cruelly; but she be pains with a sweet and almos ful patience. Sometimes the thought her dead. "I shall just yet," she would say, smili

She never speaks, unless que of the favors which she has r

She was the Blessed Virgin senger. Now that she has gi message, she has retired in shade of religious life, wisl be unnoticed among a nun companions.

It is a trouble to her wl world comes to seek her in th of her retreat, and when so cumstance obliges her to ap fore it again. She fears the this life. She lives in the l of the Lord, and is dead to t ities of the earth. And th which we have written, and speaks so much of Bernadett Marie-Bernard will never rea

THE RIOT OF THE TWELFTH.

...te in our comments on
...he 12th of July last in
...asioned by the Orange
commemoration of the
...e Boyne; but as what
...say relates to general
...ther than to particular
...marks will have suffer-
...m the delay, and will
...nce of being more care-
...nd duly weighed than
...an earlier day. The tra-
...not likely to be soon

...ar press of the city have,
...re have observed, with
...exception, taken the
...t, however ill-advised
...ie Orange procession, it
...of the Orangemen, and
...of the citizen was in-
...he police order prohibit-
...order was also an act
...e, as dictated by fear of
...mob; and hence its revo-
...ie governor, and his ex-
...solution to sustain the
...the law, and to protect
...procession by all the
...essary, at his command,
...nd manly interference in
...berty and law. The sec-
...of city and country see
...se order prohibiting the
...dictated, it is assumed, by
...clergy—only a proof of
...of the Catholic Church
...and republican institu-
...the action of the govern-
...bravery of the military
...the crowd, and killing
...ng a large number of citi-
...most part innocent, except
of idle curiosity, an assurance much
needed, that Protestants have as yet
even in this country some rights
which Catholics are bound and can
be compelled to respect.

The view taken by the sectarian
press is ridiculous, as well as malicious. The Catholic Church was
the victim of the riot, but her only
responsibility for it was in warning
her children against it, and bidding
them to let the procession alone, and
not to go near it. If she had been
heeded, there would have been no
riot, no disturbance. The question
was not a Catholic question, and the
church had nothing to gain by pre-
venting the procession, still less by a
riot to break it up. The pretence
that the rights of Protestants are in
danger from Catholics in this country, where the Protestants outnumber
the Catholics as eight or ten to one,
is too absurd to be even a passable
joke. Do the sectarian journals
count one Catholic more than a
match for eight or ten Protestants?
That were a greater compliment to
us than we deserve. We are afraid
the sectarian leaders have bad consciences, which make them cowards.
Catholics cannot show the least sign
of vitality, or make the slightest
move for the practical possession of
the equal rights guaranteed them by
the constitution and laws, but they
take fright, tremble in their shoes,
and cry out: "Liberty is in danger!"
the Pope is going to suppress American republicanism, strip Protestants
of their rights, cut their throats, or
reduce them to be " hewers of wood
and drawers of water " to—the Je-

suits. They are dreadfully alarmed, or affect to be, and create a panic throughout the whole country. But, dear frightened souls, there is no occasion for your alarm, unless you suppose you cannot be free if everybody else is not enslaved. Even if we were the majority of the American people, as we are not, nor likely to be to-day, to-morrow, or the day after, you would be in no danger, for we understand liberty as well as you do, appreciate it more highly, love it better, and have made greater sacrifices for it than you can imagine. Not a few of us have fled hither from the tyranny and oppression of Protestant governments, expatriated ourselves for the sake of liberty, and do you believe us such fools as to destroy it the moment we have found it?

This talk about the hostility of the church to liberty and American republicanism, when not malicious, is sheer nonsense. The acts Protestants allege to prove that the church is hostile to liberty, prove the contrary; for they were acts done against tyrants and despots in defence of liberty, both civil and religious. What were her long struggles against the Franconian and Suabian emperors, but struggles on her part for the freedom of religion, the basis and principle of all true liberty? Why did the popes deny to kings and emperors in the middle ages the right of investiture by the cross and ring, but because to have conceded it would have enslaved the church to Cæsar, and destroyed the independence of religion and the freedom of conscience? Know you not that it was under the fostering care and protection of the church that grew up the freedom and independence of all modern nations? What nation, state, or people has she ever deprived of independence or liberty? If

she has asserted the rights of eigns, and condemned seditio bulence, conspiracies, insurr rebellions, on the part of the she has been equally prom determined in asserting the and franchises of subjects, censuring, excommunicating even deposing, when professin Catholic, the tyrant who de and oppressed them. The principles of justice and equa which American republican founded were taught by hood ars in their monasteries, an claimed from the Papal thro before the landing at Plymo the Pilgrims from the *Mayflo* the settlement of English colo the banks of the James. D friends, read and try to unde little of history, and dismiss y fears, or, if fear you must, fear salvation of your own souls ter.

The fact is, we are a little tient when we hear Protesta pressing in grave tones and serious face their apprehensio the spread of Catholicity will the destruction of American Considering what Protestant and by what means it was intr and has been sustained, it much as if Satan should exp rious apprehensions that the of the Gospel may tend to struction of Christian piety an lity. We find among Protestan and not a few, who, when the of liberty, mean liberty for a for Catholics as well as for n tholics; but your true-blue ant, who is imbued with the and genuine spirit of Protest would seem unable to unders liberty anything but his right ern, or by religious liberty a but his right to reject the abuse the Pope, calumniate

poil the church, and exterminate or [illegible] Who has not heard of Tyburn, and who went there—of the infamous penal laws against Catholics of England and Ireland, to say nothing of other [illegible]—and were not these [illegible] enacted and enforc- [illegible] colony of Virginia, and [illegible] a capital offence in Mas- [illegible] for a priest to set his foot [illegible] colony, or for an inhabi- [illegible] or give him even a [illegible]? Did not Massa- [illegible] and send from Boston [illegible] body of men, who shot [illegible] Rasle, a missionary to [illegible] Indians, at the head f his congregation as they came rth from Mass and massacred them? id not an American Provincial ongress enumerate among their rave charges against George III. he fact that he had granted freedom f worship to Catholics in the neigh- oring province of Canada? Was ot Guy Fawkes' Day celebrated in oston with the usual anti-popery emonstrations down to the epoch the Revolution, until protested gainst by some French officers, who me with the army from France to d us in gaining our national inde- ndence? Yet Protestants do not ush to call Protestantism the friend, d Catholicity the enemy, of lib- ty!

Protestants have very short memo- s if they have forgotten these ings, or else they suppose that tholics have no memories at all if ey suppose that we can permit em to claim, unchallenged, to be d always to have been the party liberty. It is not, however, the angest delusion of Protestants, d is only of a piece with their de- ion that Protestantism is Christi- ity and sustained by the Holy riptures. But let this pass. We yield to no one in our devotion to liberty or in our readiness to defend the rights of the citizen. We have no sympathy with the rioters of the Twelfth of July and not one word to offer in their defence. They broke both the law of the church and the law of the land, sinned against God, and committed a crime against the state. But we venture to deny that the police order forbidding the Orange procession infringed the liberty of any citizen or deprived the Orangemen of any right they had or could have on American soil. No men or class of men have the right, in the performance of no civil or religious duty, but for their own pleasure or gratification of their own passions, to do any act or make any display in the judgment of the police certain or very likely to provoke a riot or breach of the peace. This is common sense, and, we presume, common law.

The Orangemen were required by no duty, civil or religious, to celebrate the battle of the Boyne by a public procession in the streets of our city, nor were they called to do it by any sentiment of patriotism—not of Irish patriotism, for the battle of the Boyne resulted in the subjugation, not the liberation, of Ireland—not American patriotism, for the event was foreign to American nationality. No foreign patriotism has any right on American soil. The event commemorated is wholly foreign to our patriotism. It occurred in a foreign country before our nationality was born, and has no relation whatever to any American sentiment. No procession not in honor of religion or some religious event, and wholly disconnected with American interests or sentiments, has any right on American soil, and can only take place by courtesy or sufferance, indifference or connivance. The prohibition of the Orange procession by

the police would have deprived the Orangemen of no right which they had or could pretend to have in this country; and if the procession was designed or even likely to irritate a portion of our citizens, and to provoke a riot, it was not only the right but the duty of the police, as conservators of the peace, to prohibit it, and as far as possible to prevent it.

But the right and the duty of the police do not stop here. There is another side to the question. Every peaceable citizen has the right to walk the streets without being insulted or having his feelings outraged. Processions, banners, songs, tunes offensive, and really intended to be offensive, to any portion of the community, and in commemoration of no American event, in satisfaction of no American sentiment, or in the performance of no civil, military, or religious duty incumbent on American citizens, are never allowable, for the insult and outrage offered to the feelings and sentiments, no matter of what class of the population, is purely wanton, malicious, and wholly unjustifiable. Of this sort is manifestly the insult and outrage offered by Orange processions, banners, songs, and tunes to all of our Irish fellow-citizens not of the Orange party; and these fellow-citizens of Irish birth or extraction, though they have no right to take the law into their own hands, have undoubtedly the right, on American soil, to be protected by the American authorities from insult and outrage to their feelings and sentiments, just as much as persons have the right to be protected from indecent sights in the public streets, or the display of obscene pictures and images in the shop-windows.

But these Orangemen—very few, if any, of whom, we are told, are American citizens—outrage American as well as Irish manhood. Their

celebrations here are an
every true American, for th
honor of principles and de
rent to every American. he
them to bring their old
hither from a foreign land
reprehensible, even if thei
were not utterly disgraceful
but they become a gross out
the real character of their qu
their loyal countrymen is co
The deeds of the party in Ire
represent are such as are co
by every distinctive Americ
ple, and a more infamous
would be difficult to find
country on earth. They
the party that in Ireland fo
foreign invader and a chief
against their own country,
at once traitors to their
nation. They represent t
that enacted the infamous an
izing penal laws which dep
loyal Irish—who in the batt
Boyne fought for and at
mand of their rightful kin
rebels, traitors, foreign inva
enemies—of every vestige of
religious liberty, even mal
crime for a father to teach
child letters, and doomed
scendants, till within our own
to the most cruel, heartless, a
less oppression ever endure
people in the world; they
the party that, after the Pre
and Jacobin movement of
which some Catholics had
veigled by the promise of
for their religion, and left
fighting and to bear almost
penalty of defeat, were the
of the savage butcheries inf
the Orange yeomanry on t
olic peasantry, even on th
had taken no part in the m
and were innocent of all of
cept that of sighing to be
from bondage, and treated

ust as wild
t to hunt out
they can be
rate in their
their songs
of treachery,
tion, oppres-
d wholesale
the history
nd heathen-

re cruel and
edeemed by
ied by more
re deserving
d, than that
n represent
s it no insult
s for them
in our faces
h the blood
good, brand-
te, and wet
symbols of
n, and reli-
ersecution?
a, they dare
lic of their
eir infamy?
ofess to ab-
and oppres-
a sovereign
world that
lum to the
, the down-
nd of every
s our man-
tyrant, the
or, to come
age his vic-
r we profess
m? What
is noble and
Americans
to protect
er even the
e.

when only
ng the pro-
procession a

violation of freedom and a cowardly yielding to Irish or Catholic dictation. It was no such thing. The Orangemen had no right on their side, and were entitled to no protection. Liberty was on the other side, and its vindication and the right of asylum required us as Americans to protect the victims of the Orange party who had sought refuge with us from Orange insult and outrage on our own soil. His excellency the governor of the state also took only a hasty and a very incorrect view of the case in revoking the very proper order of the police. We are as far as he can be from yielding to the dictation of the mob. When a mob has collected, it must be admitted to no parley, and the only answer to be given to its demands is the reading of the riot act, and a whiff of grape-shot or a shower of musket-balls. But no threats of violence should ever deter authority from doing what is right, and, in this case, right was not on the side of the Orangemen. Authority must be just as well as firm. The threats of violence were wrong, but they did not put the Orangemen in the right. Authority was bound to protect the Orangemen from actual violence, but it was not bound to protect them in the performance of acts which they had no moral or legal right to perform, and which it was foreseen, if permitted, would lead to violence. One wrong is not redressed by permitting another that must provoke it.

His excellency's revocation of the order of the police prohibiting the Orange procession, and promise to protect the procession by all the force at his command, cannot be defended on the ground that the party opposed threatened violence in case the procession took place, unless it be assumed that the Orangemen had a perfect moral or legal right to

march in procession through our streets in their regalia, and with their insulting banners flying and bands playing offensive marches. But they had no such right, as we have seen, and the party making the threats, however wrong the threats were, had the right to be protected from the insult and outrage offered to their feelings by such a display. The vindication of liberty did not require the procession to take place, for liberty is not infringed where no right is violated or abridged; and the assertion of the majesty of the law never requires protection of a wrong because they who would be aggrieved by it have threatened, if permitted, they will attempt by violence to right themselves. Neither American liberty nor law required the Orange procession to be permitted, and if both liberty and law required a mob, when collected, to be dispersed and the violence suppressed, they both also required the protection of American citizens from public insult and outrage. His excellency forgot the duty of protecting American citizens from wrong, and thought only of protecting a foreign and wholly un-American party in committing it.

Yet we have no doubt that the mistaken conduct of the governor—an able man, a good lawyer, and for the most part a worthy chief magistrate of the state — was chiefly prompted by the clamor against Catholics, and the charge brought against his party by its opponents of acting under the dictation of Catholics, who, of course, it is assumed, act always under the dictation of their clergy, and was intended to refute the charge by showing his readiness to protect even Protestant Orangemen, and shoot down their hereditary enemies, though Catholics. The charge, we know, was made against the party now in power in

this state; but his excellen
not have allowed, it woul
It is no doubt true that, h
votes of citizens who hap
Catholics, he would never
governor of the state, and
would be, at least for the
a hopeless minority; but w
allow that Catholics have
upon the fact, or asked any
their right as simple Ame
zens, and we know that
obtained less than their eq
even in this city, where
probably count not much
one-half of the population.
charge is a mere party tric
ed, through the sectarian
against Catholicity, to thro
ty now in out of power.
vernor seems to us to ha
into the trap his political
set for him, and has no
damaged the political prosp
of himself and of his party

The clamor against the
account of its Catholic le
supporters means only tha
are anxious to become the
party out of power in
would as willingly receive
of Catholic citizens as doe
ty in power, and when in
did, we believe, more for
than the party now in p
ever yet done, though it,
promised less. Catholics h
had any reason for giving t
to the Democratic party b
doing so, they followed, w
terestedly, their honest poli
victions.

The pretence of Protest
Catholics in or out of office
cally under the dictation
clergy, and in reference to
interests as such, is too n
false to mislead anybody.
prominent politicians, in o
office, who happen to be

are the last men in the world to listen to the dictation of the clergy or to act in obedience to the orders of their church, and they take infinite pains to prove that their religion has nothing to do with their politics, in order, we suppose, to escape the suspicion of being influenced in their political conduct by regard for Catholic interests. Their party standing is more to them than their Catholic standing, and they consult rarely the wishes or interests of their church, and usually only the wishes and interests of their party and its leaders. All the offices in the state or nation might be filled by Catholics, the constituencies remaining unchanged, without any more advantage accruing to the church than if they were all filled by Protestants. Catholics and Protestants alike, when in office, consult their constituencies, and act in the way and manner they judge most likely to secure votes to themselves or their party.

The fact is, Catholicity has never placed any man in city, state, or nation in office, and never yet has any man in our country been elected to office because he is Catholic. The Catholics who are in office under the municipal, state, or federal government, in congress, in the state senate, or the assembly, are there not because they are Catholics, but because they are Democrats or Republicans, or because they are of Irish, German, or some other foreign origin, and have or are supposed to have influence in securing the so-called "Irish vote," the "German vote," or the "foreign vote"—distinctions which should have no place in American politics—not because they are Catholics, and supposed to be devoted to Catholic interests. There is an "Irish vote," a "German vote," a "foreign vote," but no "Catholic vote," and, the constituencies remaining the same, Catholic interests would be just as safe in the hands of American Protestants as in the hands of Catholics elected to office, not for their Catholicity, but for their real or supposed influence with our naturalized fellow-citizens; and perhaps safer, because Protestants would be less likely to be suspected of acting under Catholic influence, and therefore could act more independently.

It is, we think, a mistake on the part of our politicians who are Catholics, whether in or out of office, to be so anxious not to be suspected of acting under Catholic influence and in view of Catholic interests. The church asks only what is just, only to be protected in the possession of the equal rights before the state, guaranteed to her by the constitution of the state, and which are not always respected by the popular sentiment of the country. The care which politicians take to show themselves independent in their political action, if Catholics, gains them no credit, and a frank, open, straightforward, and manly course would gain much more respect for themselves and for their religion. Indeed, their sensitiveness and overcaution on this point tend to excite the very suspicion they would guard against, or the suspicion that their conduct is diplomatic, and that they have some ulterior purpose in reserve which they artfully and adroitly conceal. The church is supposed by Protestants to be the very embodiment of craftiness and dissimulation, always and everywhere intriguing to get the control of the secular power, and to wield it in her own interest regardless of all rights and interests of the citizen who happens not to be Catholic. Hence, every Catholic politician is suspected beforehand of craft, intrigue, of crooked and underhand ways, lacking frankness, openness, and straightfor-

ward honesty. The only way to repel this false and unjust suspicion is for such Catholics as are politicians to show in an open and manly manner that neither they nor their church have any sinister purpose, and that in being devoted to her interests and acting under influence as good Catholics, they have nothing to conceal, and no ends to gain for her incompatible with their plain duty as American citizens, or which they fear or hesitate to avow in the face of all men. The best way to quell a wild beast is to look him steadily in the eye, and show that you do not fear him.

But to return to the question more immediately before us. If the press and the executive had looked at the subject from the point of view of common sense, as a simple question of right and wrong, without prejudice against Catholics or in favor of Protestants, and without any wish to charge or acquit any party of being under Catholic influence, they could not, it seems to us, have failed to see that liberty was violated in permitting, not in prohibiting, the Orange procession. Party or sectarian prejudices obscured the judgment, and many lives of innocent persons were lost in consequence.

It is contended by some that if a procession of Catholic Irish in honor of St. Patrick is allowed, the Orange procession of the Protestant Irish should also be allowed; either permit both, or prohibit both. The celebration of St. Patrick's Day as a festival of the Catholic Church, which it is, even by a public procession through our streets, if peaceable and orderly, is a right guaranteed in the freedom of the Catholic religion under our constitution and laws, and so far differs totally from the Orange procession. As a purely Irish national festival, it can be celebrated here only by courtesy, as is St. George's Day by the Englis Nicholas's Day by the Dutch, Andrew's Day by the Scotch; foreign nationality has any rig American soil; otherwise, Am nationality would not be indepe and supreme on American ter No foreign national festival commemoration or honor of and interests or sentiments fore American nationality and in and sentiments, can be publicl brated here except by indiffe courtesy, sufferance, connivanc tional comity, or international

This rule, however, does not to religious festivals and celebr whether Catholic or Protestan cause in the eye of the state a gion is catholic, and not na and, therefore, never a foreig any nation. Protestants c claim Orange celebrations as a though the Orangemen are all Protestants, because the event brated is a foreign political, not gious event; yet they have the to institute and celebrate festi honor of Martin Luther, John vin, John Knox, and other Prot reformers; for these being the f ers of their religion are as suc foreigners. Catholics may als brate here any of the festivals church in the way and mann prescribes, because they are rel festivals, and the right to cel them is included in the freed conscience; so may they celebrat licly the birthday of the Holy F his return to Rome from his e Gaëta and Portici, the complet the twenty-fifth year of his p cate, or his liberation, when eff from his present imprisonment the recovery for the Holy See possessions of which she has bee rilegiously despoiled—because, chief of their religion, he is n eigner in America.

dies, roughs, and disorderly persons in our large towns, nobody denies; but we must remember that there are plenty of the same class not of Irish origin, and there have been riots, and riots of a very grave character, in which the Irish had no hand, though of some of them they were the victims. We have seen more than one American mob in which the chief actors were respectable, well-dressed Protestant American citizens.

There are Irishmen who are wealthy and wear fine clothes that are no credit to their race or their religion, but the Catholic Irish as a body constitute a sober, quiet, peaceable, intelligent, religious, industrious, and thriving portion of our population, and no American-born citizen has any right to say a word in disparagement of them. Indeed, we may say of the Catholic population of the city generally, that it is that portion of the population that it can least afford to spare. Were the city to lose them, it would lose the very population that has contributed, and contributes, the most to its high moral and religious character, to its industry and wealth, and on which its prosperity chiefly depends. With all their faults, and they are many, and many more in the eyes of the Catholic than of the Protestant, they are, as they should be, decidedly the best people going. Their vices are on the surface; their virtues lie deeper, and are many, solid, and d
We bless God that we are
ted to call them brethren, a
we are with them in the unity
and communion, though we
to be an American of the
generation, and it was our mis
to be reared a Protestant.

We think the conduct of the
cratic party towards their C
supporters is discreditable. An
may feel itself honored that
the votes of the great body
Catholic citizens, whether nat
or native-born citizens, and n
will suffer in the end by insis
justice to Catholics and to C
interests. Any party, by fran
fearlessly sustaining the equal
of Catholics with Protestant
maintaining the freedom and in
dence of religion, will not onl
truly their country, and resp
the demands of American patr
but they will best ensure its o
manent prosperity, power, a
fluence. They who scorn and t
on the church may flourish
time like the green bay tree,
the end they will wither and d
their places be sought, an
found. It is well for every p
party to remember that God
and that they who scorn his
whom he hath purchased w
own blood, will in turn be scor
the "King of kings, and L
lords."

deplored and denounced that unjustifiable attempt at the national sovereignty which suddenly drew on us the danger of Prussian occupation of the city and the horrors of civil war—perhaps both of these scourges. Our indignation was profound. One blamed the government for having too readily abandoned Paris to the danger of insurrection; another maintained that by establishing itself at Versailles with the national assembly, and defending the environs of Paris, it saved France. Another declaimed with bitterness, sometimes against the culpable indifference of the national guards, which left everything to be done, and sometimes against the audacity and wickedness of the leaders of the mob that, without any pretext, was dragging France, all bleeding from the wounds incurred in war, into a bottomless abyss. We all felt there was something beneath all this: it was the shameful defection of a part of the troops of the line which had rendered such cruel misfortunes possible. If the army were to countenance the insurrection, that would decide the fate of France —*Galliæ finis!*

It was easier to deplore the gravity of the evil than to point out a practical means of remedying it. There was great diversity of opinion respecting the latter. Should recourse be had to material force or to a spirit of persuasion and conciliation? The use of material force might inflame the rebellious party still more, and cover Paris with blood and ruins. The success of moral influence was hardly possible with insurgents who began by assassinating Generals Lecomte and Clément Thomas, and deliberately advocated a social revolution.

At three o'clock, a well-known inhabitant of the Place Vendôme, who had already distinguished himself by his courage in the insurrectic June, 1848, in which he was o the first wounded, came to ann to me the formal intention c national guards of his battali retake the place from the insuı come from the faubourgs. He th that by a bold stroke they effect their object without a sh(is sure that the friends of order ed by all means to avoid the ding of blood. Some momen ter, one of my friends, who bea of the great political names of Fı and is destined to render his cc eminent service, after the examı his family, because he is at o man of superior intelligence an interestedness, very liberal and religious, announced to me th: national guards of his arrondiss(were animated with the best tions, and comprehended the u necessity of maintaining order i midst of the inextricable chaos which we had fallen. He was self a powerful example of the lution and self-sacrifice inspire an enlightened and generous p: ism. A retired officer from the of his marriage, he had organiz the beginning of the war, th tional guards of that section c country in which his estate Later, when the army of G(Chanzy made his evolution fror Loire toward the Sarthe, he res his military life, and took an : part as captain of the staff in the (tions and struggles of the army west. The very day he returned t life, he took the cars to spend days at Paris, where several me of his family awaited him. I rived there on the eve of the teenth of March. Instead of r ing to the country, like so other Parisians, he enrolled his the following day as a simple ber of the national guards, re

the employees of the minister of justice came to beg me to carry to her brother the final consolations of religion. I had seen him some days previous, and his end seemed near. It was with the greatest difficulty she had left the Ministère and the Place Vendôme, and she feared it would be impossible for me to return with her. But, unwilling her brother should die without the sacraments of the church, she succeeded by her prayers and tears in reaching me, and was willing to brave everything again in order to enable me to go to him.

I assured her I would unite my efforts to hers, and, though conscious that the ecclesiastical costume had, since the downfall of the empire, been disagreeable to the Parisian revolutionists, I added that we should succeed. I set out that very instant with one of the employees of the church.

The Place and the Boulevard de la Madeleine were quiet and nearly deserted. The Rue Neuve-des-Capucines was livelier. At the entrance of the Place Vendôme, I found myself in presence of the national guards, who did not much resemble those belonging to that quarter. They were very numerous. Their language was in the main rather noisy than threatening. The words "citizen" and "republic" were constantly on their lips. They allowed no one to stop, and showed themselves severely rigid towards the passers-by that wished to contemplate a spectacle so new in this pacific and wealthy quarter.

I had not yet arrived at the angle of the Rue Neuve-des-Capucines and the Place Vendôme, when an outpost of the national guards, arms in hand, cried to me in somewhat rough tone: "Citizen, no one is allowed to stop!" It was the very place and the time to stop to accomplish my holy mission. I explained briefly, but politely, the motive that to the Place Vendôme: it was tion of giving a dying person succor of religion; and, to le doubt of the truth of my sta I pointed out the lady, ba tears, at my side, and the er of the Madeleine. "It is im citizen," was uttered on al "the *consigne* has forbidden asked to see one of the office saw plainly I should be ob parley, but, in view of a duty s and urgent, I resolved to us means. A sergeant present self with that important an what ridiculous air which the conviction among the low that public affairs could not tained without him. I ex my wish. "You cannot pa mildly insisted. "The *consigne* bidden it, and to-day he is ver ous." I asked the reason of ceptional severity. "It is, y citizen, because the bourgeoisi quarter have been making a to-day, and this must not be ed."

This observation, one of tl characteristic I ever heard life, was made with a seri which would have dispelle at another time less distres my heart as a priest and a man.

Convinced that nothing w effected with this sergeant, w more self-sufficient than wi asked to see the captain. H to me with a dry and lofty air mildness of my language an less the sad motive also tha to the Place Vendôme spee dified. After refusing me, an ing to renewed entreaties, he permission to enter the Pla dôme, on condition that I remain all night. That was tent of the right allowed hin

uently hear-
, according to
the sergeant,
y his dissatis-
hat the bour-
ad been mak-
nat I could not
hat I was very
understand a
a dying person
on, and that I
: to judge this
other autho-

with an emo-
ned, changed
n, who vainly
xts to oppose
besides, to be
ith the com-
hers were con-
for orders, and
s embarrassed
been more ac-
han to give or-
of the nation-
ny me to the
of justice, not
an instant, and
ie entrance of
ucines. Not-
c character of
eated like one
geoisie of the
t be pardoned
ket during the
had strength-
he Place Ven-
enceforth the
onest people.
ed to allow it
h extreme cir-
ersons who re-

panied by my
ho was armed.
y lighted. We
d us the group
hat barricaded
addressed me

these words in a confused but very respectful tone: "How sad all this is, monsieur l'abbé, and how wrong not to arrange everything so every one can remain at home and quietly attend to his business!" I evidently had with me one of the too numerous workmen of Paris who love order and peace, but who dare not, or who do not know how to, resist the bold ringleaders who take them from their work and lead them astray. The fear of not speaking with sufficient calmness and caution, while I was at once afflicted and exasperated, induced me to be reserved. I merely replied that I shared his sentiments, and that very probably reason would prevail in the end.

Every moment we met armed groups. As far as I could judge, from rapid glances over the Place, some were discussing with vivacity the events of the day: others, like mercenaries, without dignity and without conscience, appeared to have no other care than to smoke and drink. The insurgents I met did not conceal the suprise that the presence of a priest in their midst during the night caused them. Those who thought I had been arrested, and was on my way to the post of the *état-major*, where I had seen more than one spy or Prussian led during the siege, did not deprive themselves of the pleasure of aiming a joke or an insult at me. Those who thought I was going to fulfil the duties of the holy ministry saluted me with respect. They were far from resembling in their equipments and deportment the national guards of the quarter of St. Roch or the Madeleine, but when I compared them with those I found the next day in the same place, after the criminal and bloody fusillade upon citizens only guilty of calmly expressing their love of order and their devotedness to the national assembly,

they were comparatively disciplined and civilized.

The ante-room of the minister of justice's residence was guarded by insurgents, who allowed no one to enter or go out without particular scrutiny. I quickly made known to the leader the object of my mission. He listened to me with evident curiosity and self-sufficiency, and, after affecting to consider, he motioned me to proceed. The court was occupied by another post that watched the entrance to the offices and hôtel of the minister, and the avenue that led through the gardens to the Rue de Luxembourg. No light was to be seen in the apartments. A profound silence reigned everywhere. No other employee remained at the minister's than the brother-in-law of the young man to whom I was carrying the last consolations of religion. He received them with more calmness and serenity than might have been expected, humanly speaking, of a young man of twenty-two years of age, when one looks forward to a long life; but what a double grief for a family to find themselves at once in the presence of death and a band of insurgents!

A quarter of an hour after, I left the *ministère* with my national guard, who treated me with a respect more and more deferential. The lady who had gone to the Rue de la Ville-l'Evêque to find me was also struck with his excellent appearance, and commissioned me to give him a small sum of money. I begged him, as delicately as possible, to accept it in aid of his family, who might be in need for want of employment. He seemed very much touched by this generous attention, and, as much to satisfy my curiosity as to prevent the difficulty of expressing his gratitude at a time when he was officially charged with guarding me, I concluded to address him : questions.

"From what quarter of Pari you?"

"I am from Bercy, monsieur l'a They sounded the rappel this eve I set out with my company. ' told us we were appointed to a important patriotic mission. A ed at the Place Vendôme, we ordered to guard it rigorously."

"But why so rigorous a g in a quarter where there are very excellent people, who love and peace above all things?"

"Ma foi, monsieur l'abbé know nothing at all about it. cy is perfectly quiet. This qu is no less so. I do not unders it. They ordered us to come, we had to obey."

"But did you not at Bercy confidence in M. Thiers as we we? Do you prefer Assi, Flou Blanqui, and Felix Pyat to him?"

"Our employers have al spoken very highly of him. good workmen call him a grea triot, and not a mere pretende so many others. He promise liberty and work, and would ce ly have kept his word. So we committed a great piece of fo ness in allowing him to go to sailles. God grant it may no for a long time!"

"But what becomes of your all this time? Do you think state of thing favorable to the rests of the workman?"

"Ah, monsieur l'abbé, work thing but little thought of now, yet the longer we delay resumi the more unfortunate we are. T are among us so many sluggard madcaps! . . ."

My excellent guard was expla to me in his own way how the workmen, who wished in 1848 t tain the right to labor, had, sinc

years previously. Paris is rather the theatre than the author of the revolutions that take place there.

Revolutionists and rioters belong to all parts of France and Europe, and in disastrous times they hasten to Paris, hoping to catch fish in the troubled waters.

I have studied all the large cities of Europe from a political and social point of view. For reasons too extended to be enumerated here, not one is like Paris, the rendezvous of all suspicious and corrupt characters—of the unfortunate who are at variance with the laws of their own country, and of men of no class who are ready to become revolutionary agents—and these are the worst of all. After the siege it had endured, the state of agitation and prostration resulting from so great a struggle, so much suffering, and so many deceptions, could not fail to attract the leading charlatans and rogues of all parts of Europe. It is not to the honor of the popular class at Paris, the most frivolous and the most credulous in the world, that these new-comers met with a success beyond their expectations, for they became in a moment our masters. Thanks to this cosmopolitan invasion, and also to the departure of too large a number of genuine Parisians who feared the Prussian bombardment less than the mob of international agents, Paris, the brilliant centre of elegance, art, and of intellect, as well as a financial and political centre, became, according to the expressive comparison of the *Times*, an infernal caldron, which terrified all Europe, and in which mingled and seethed all human passions.

The party that was playing its part at Paris was not Parisian or French, but exclusively social. It was a flock of birds of prey, a herd of roaming wild beasts, who had hastened from the four cardinal points to fall o capital of France, which a five m siege had weakened. The In tional agents wished to foun Commune, and, to realize the of the Commune, which espe clings to locality, home, the fi the steeple, the associations an ditions of domestic interest, they moned to Paris all their boon panions of the Old and the New and forced the real inhabitar Paris to take refuge in the pro or abroad. It was a revolting cism, pregnant with disaster.

At half-past two, some pe filled with terror and indignatio tered the Madeleine to inform a sinister catastrophe. The of the pacific manifestation, wh proposed on the eve to traver principal streets of the city, c *Vive la République! Vive l'O Vive l'Assemblée Nationale!* ha come the victims of a horrible a cade. After passing through th de la Paix, a large number of re ed citizens of Paris, unarmed influenced only by the patriotic of securing, by the most inoff means and for the benefit of all citizens, the triumph of equity and a spirit of conciliation, had met at the entrance of the Vendôme by a murderous fu from the insurgent national g The reports of the number o killed and wounded varied, must have been considerable.

At the same time, I saw fro outer colonnade of the Mad the shops hastily shut up and fleeing in disorder from the dir of the Place Vendôme. Ever expressed wrath and constern Some national guards of the arrondissement hastened to around the church to watch ov public security.

I made inquiries about the

The second patrol, stationed in the middle of the street, allowed me to pass without objection. It was composed, like the first, of national guards of all ages, but not of all conditions: they were from the most uncivilized class of the faubourgs. Their accoutrements were not uniform or neat. Some appeared quite satisfied; they were the youngest; others had a less blustering manner; but all felt an instinctive joy to rule over the most brilliant part of Paris, and inspire the citizens with a lively terror.

Before I came to the third patrol, placed at the opposite end of the street, I noticed on the pavement many stains of blood. It was in fact only a few steps distant that, only a short time before, the victims of the fusillade fell. I will not attempt to describe the anguish that filled my soul at the sight of this blood of my countrymen, shed by insurgents without country and without God. In the midst of my great distress I recalled the sublime cry of Monseigneur Affre: "Let my blood be the last shed!" I ardently prayed in my turn that the blood of these innocent and peaceful victims might be the last poured out, but it was to be feared that the revolutionary and social crisis, that weighed on Paris like a horrible nightmare, would only end, as it had commenced, by a terrible effusion of blood.

There was no difference between this patrol and the preceding, except that it was more actively vigilant. The chief of the national guards that formed it, and who seemed surprised to behold me, having asked where I was going, and what I was going to do, sent two men to conduct me to the post that guarded the entrance to the Place Vendôme. During the siege of Paris, I one day passed along the formidable defences of the Point-du-Jour at Auteuil. The consigne there was of a different degr mildness and condescension fror at the entrance of the Place Ven which the insurgents evidently to make their headquarters, and they were entrenching thems The national guards that def the entrance were less blusterin more numerous and more de than those of the evening b They allowed me to pass w hindrance; many of them must felt that where the dead and dyi to be found is the proper place minister of Jesus Christ. A se was ordered to accompany me Ministère de la Justice, where tended to go first. He poss neither the intelligence nor the ness of the national guard that e ed me the night before. He rather an animated machine t man. Not a word, not a ge not a change in his features wondering what he was thinki I ended by doubting if he thou all. I should render him this j —that, from a material point of he discharged his commission irreproachable exactitude.

I experienced an undefinabl pression in the Place Vendôme, duced by a twofold contrast, tl membrance of which will n effaced to the latest moment c life.

This Place, with which Louis adorned Paris, was first callec Place des Conquêtes, to recal brilliant victories which had se to France the fine provinces we have just lost a large part ter most lamentable reverses. sumptuous edifices, built accordi Mansard's plans, which form contour, render it in an archite point of view the finest Pla Europe. Destined by Louis to bring together the royal li and imprimerie, the academie

notwithstanding my natural love of observation. Some—a small number, however—received me with coarse insults and horrid laughter. A few steps from the Ministère de la Justice, a national guardsman, who was talking and gesticulating with uncommon vivacity, stopped to address me, while shaking his fist at me, this singular apostrophe: "When shall we be delivered from those wretches?" I will not relate other pleasantries of this nature of which I was the butt: this one is only too much. Their authors had doubtless learned to know and judge the clergy by the violent diatribes of citizens Blanqui and Félix Pyat.

Others, on the contrary, saluted me with a respect and cordiality which I was careful to return politely. They were honest workmen who had doubtless had intercourse with their parish priests, or whose children attended the catechism classes or the schools of the religious congregations, and received a benefit which they understood how to appreciate. There were strange contrasts in this mixture. Not to forget a single characteristic detail, I caught some observations that denoted on the part of their authors serious regrets for the dreadful catastrophe which terrified the whole city.

If, among the insurgent battalions chosen to fire on the inoffensive inhabitants of Paris, there were some to deplore the horrors of civil war, how many might not have been found in the other battalions! If the ringleaders could be separated from those whom they lead, and the deceivers from the deceived, the number of the latter would be considerable, and the former somewhat modified. One of the most serious faults of the workman of Paris is the incredible facility with which he enters into all the hollow schemes of the rogue and the charlata tempt him, and sacrifices t mad ambition and culpable j his peace, his property, his and his life.

My guide, or rather my gu peared insensible to the ins well as to the salutations I r on the way. Arms in hand, impassible and solemn, it w now and then he cast toward inquisitorial glance, as if to his authority and my c ence.

I made known the object mission to the leader of the the Ministère de la Justice. a young and well-bred office listened to me with attention, plied, after saluting me twice politeness full of respect, tha at liberty to do all I wished.

I found the sick person I h the evening before in the hôte minister of justice, exhausted citement that was hastening l He could see from his sick- that occurred on the Place. corner of the apartment his endowed with the higher C virtues, and an aged lady w did not know, but who was p their mother, were weeping o public as well as their own woes. I had promised the si son the night before to vi again in three or four days, l could not enter the Place V without indicating the precis I wished to go to, and co have a better means of asce where the victims of the fusill been transported, I briefly ex the reason of my unexpected gave him some religious enc ment, which was to be the learned that the dead and w removed from the Place ha carried to one of the neig houses occupied by the adn

of remorse. He was not wounded, but only had a sudden nervous attack, that affected him in a manner painful to behold. He did not appear to understand anything, and was suffering from contractions and contorsions of a truly frightful character. I approached him—tried to calm him with some kind words, and then recommended him aloud to the care of the two infirmarians of the International society. The national guards who surrounded him appeared touched to see manifested for one of their number an interest equal to that I had just shown for the victims of devotedness to the cause of law and order.

Before leaving the Place Vendôme I wished to ascertain if any of the victims had been taken to the ambulance of M. Constant Say. This was one of the six ambulances I was appointed to visit during the siege, to administer religious aid and awaken the moral sense of the soldiers who were sick or wounded. This ambulance was kept in perfect order. More than once, in observing the meals of the wounded, I envied them the healthful and abundant nourishment served up to them during the interminable months of December and January. They were treated as real members of the family, and were truly the spoiled children of the house. They were daily visited by one of the most celebrated physicians of Paris, who lavished on them the most intelligent care, and by the minister of Jesus Christ, who no less kindly spoke to them of God, their souls, their absent mothers, and of their temporal and eternal welfare. It could not be otherwise in a family whose extensive industrial establishment and inexhaustible charity are such a benefit to the laboring classes of Paris. I had the consolation of seeing all the soldiers who were taken to this ambulance leave i Christians and better French

As to the rest, during th siege, the solicitude of the I for the sick and wounded was truly admirable, and th I am bound in justice to ac the ambulance of M. Consta may be equally given to the re appointed to visit: the aml of M. Frottin, formerly mayc first arrondissement, in the Honoré; that of M. Jour member of the Institute, in t du Luxembourg; of Dr. Mois physician of the Hôtel Dieu Rue Richepanse; of Madam nin, of the Point du-Jour at and, finally, the ambulance founded and directed at Gre some laboring women of arde and a devotedness that wor ders, and transferred after th bardment of Grenelle to the ficent hôtel of M. le Comte d'Argenteau on the Rue de S

I was also aware that there v some wounded soldiers in M ambulance. The brutal inva the Place Vendôme had pr me from visiting them the t previous. To go there, I was to cross the entire Place. It more like a field of battle Place. Here were stacks o there were caissons full of s further on were delegates of t tral committee of the Hôtel c who where transmitting orde feverish haste, and everywhe the insurgents who had jus and who were ready to tak aim.

I had no longer an armed to accompany me. During n which I frankly acknowledge have seemed much shorter o nary occasions, I was again ject of insult and sarcasms no seasoned with wit from some

of saying: "If the rest of the bourgeoisie resemble this one, Paris is certainly ours."

I was as much saddened at the dejected and disconcerted appearance of most of the inhabitants of this quarter, as I had been alarmed by the boldness and audacity displayed on the Place Vendôme by the workmen of the faubourgs, old criminals and revolutionists from all countries, who held possession of it. There was more stupor than indignation among the former. They hardly ventured to the doors of their houses, they spoke in low tones for fear of being compromised. This unfortunate attitude of the lovers of order only encouraged the energy and boldness of the enemies of society. I comprehended for the first time how a handful of factionists had been able in 1793 to terrify and decimate the better part of the community, who were ten times as numerous. The very day when the lovers of order will say to those of disorder, with the same energy and firmness as God to the waves of the sea, "Thou shalt go no further!" Paris will have no more to fear from anarchy and revolution, and France will no longer oscillate between the equally deplorable extremes of despotism and license.

If this simple and impartial account, intended to cast a little light upon one of the saddest and most execrable episodes of the revolution of the eighteenth of March, could also have the effect of calling the more particular attention of the lovers of order and stability, of whatever nation and party, to the dark aims of the International league of demagogues who, under the mask of workingmen's associations, prudential interests, and mutual protection, aim at the denial of God, the destruction of family and country, of public capital and private savings, of the domestic and political hierarchy—in a word, the destruction of all those principles which are the foundation of society; and also of thoroughly convincing the better classes of Paris and all the larger cities of France, that the promoters of disorder and anarchy, though now recruiting from the lowest social grades of Europe, are only strong in consequence of their own inaction and regard for self; that such power is only derived from their own want of discipline and energy; that they would only have to enroll, organize, and assert themselves to utterly destroy it—I shall have realized one of my most ardent wishes, and labored in my sphere of action for the consolidation of the social edifice and of public order, so profoundly shaken.

It was nearly six o'clock when I reached home. I had passed a little more than three-quarters of an hour among the insurgents and the wounded of the Place Vendôme. God alone knows with what emotion and earnestness I implored him that I might never be subjected again to such a trial to my heart as a priest and a Frenchman.

Here ends my first account, drawn up at the end of March. I need not add that my prayer was not granted. The Commune was founded in blood and terror, and was to end in a fiendish debauchery of madness and crime.

TO BE CONTINUED.

must rise Fervorously to our Morning Prayer." It is practical enough for any one, perfectly clear, intelligible, and interesting; and, at the same time, no one can find in it any want of devotion or spirituality.

It is divided into four books, as stated in the title; the first, second, and fourth treating of the purgative, illuminative, and unitive ways respectively; the third being concerned with "What Belongs to a most Perfect Practical Performance of Our Actions," which illustrates in detail the general principles laid down in what precedes.

We are under great obligations to the editors for having brought into notice, and into general use, as we trust, this treasure of Catholic piety. It will be of inestimable value to all who desire to lead a really spiritual life and to practice the "adoration" of which it treats, which is nothing else than complete self-renunciation and devotion, in the true sense of the word, to God and to his service.

IGNATIUS LOYOLA, AND THE EARLY JESUITS. By Stewart Rose. London: Longmans, Green & Co.

We have several excellent biographies of St. Ignatius in the English language, but the present one is likely, we think, to become the most popular. It is carefully compiled, written in that literary style and with those graphic sketches of surrounding circumstances which modern taste demands, and published in an elegant manner. Its principal distinctive excellence consists in the portraiture of the early life of Ignatius as the accomplished, valiant, and Christian knight, whose noble and chivalrous character formed the basis of his future heroic sanctity. We welcome any work which may make the illustrious founder of the Society of Jesus and his Institute better known both to Catholics and Protestants, and we hope for a wide circulation for this ably and charmingly written biography.

MOUNT BENEDICT; OR, THE V
TOMB. By Peter McCorry.
Patrick Donahoe.

The burning of the con
Charlestown, and the accom
horrors of that fearful nig
subjects worthy of a graphic
tion, well calculated to poi
ral and adorn a tale. We
our disappointment in this
written, no doubt, with a g
sign. The conversations a
and pointless, and too mucl
book is occupied with the ir
talk of the "conspirators."
test against the introduction
into story-books. The int
the story is marred by these

MR. P. DONAHOE, Boston, :
ces as in press an account
"Passion Play" at Oberam
Bavaria, from the pen of t
George W. Doane, Chancell
Diocese of Newark. It will
cated to the Rt. Rev. J. R.
D.D., Bishop of Newark

THE Catholic Publication
will publish, early in No
Mary, Queen of Scots, and h
Historian, by James F. Meli
book will contain the articl
appeared in THE CATHOLIC
on Mr. Froude, as well as
deal of new matter. In fact
ticles as they appeared in
THOLIC WORLD are almost
rewritten, and many new f
duced. It will be a complet
tion of Mr. Froude's romanc
tory.

ERRATUM.—In the article
Reformation not Conserva
733, 1st column, 16th line
bottom, for *French* soverei
Frank sovereigns. Christer
founded some centuries bef
was a French sovereign or
kingdom, in the modern sen
word *French*, or France. Th
were a Germanic race, and
man was their mother-tong

tion it takes is not controverted. But the lawyer says it does not meet the question, that is, we presume, the question as it is in his mind, though he had not previously expressed it. He says:

"The note given me does not meet the question. It is claimed that the church is infallible because a divine institution—that is, because established by God.

"Now, admit it to be a divine institution, if it is to be presented for our acceptance, it must be for the acceptance of our fallible reason.

"For example, when the missionary carries the church to the heathen, does he not present it for their rational acceptance? And if so, does he not ask their finite judgment to pass upon and accept the infinite and the absolute?

"Now, the point is this: if the thing or truth presented be infinite and absolute, and the person to whom it is presented be imperfect, fallible, and conditioned, how can the truth—or the church, if you please—appear otherwise to him than according to his finite and partial interpretation of it?

"The question in respect to the absolute is, not whether it be *really* true and absolute or not, but to what extent does the normal affirmation go respecting it. In short, must not the same argument obtain against the church as against the Bible?

"It comes to the question of *authority*; and, if all intelligent authority resides in *the person* (and certainly each one must, from the nature of his constitution, be his own authority), then it follows that no authority whatever can reside in the state, the church, or in any mere institution or being *outside* of the person, whether that church or institution assume divinity or not.

"The authority is not in *the so-called fact*, but in *the person* to whom the so-called fact is presented, and who is called upon to pass upon it.

"The Baconian system is false, because it makes the so-called fact the authority for itself; when plainly the very existence or comprehension of the so-called fact depends wholly on the *person* to whom it is presented."

The objection is, apparently, the objection we ourselves bring to the Protestant rule of faith, r Bible interpreted by pri ment. The Bible may b of God and infallible, bu pretation of it, or my pri ment in interpreting it, is f therefore I have in it a only a fallible rule of fait church may be a divine and by the assistance of Ghost infallible; but her addressed to my intellig must be passed upon by judgment, which is finite a therefore incompetent to the infinite and absolute. the Catholic rule no more fallible faith than does the rule. The principle of the the lawyer urges is that a intrinsic, not extrinsic; c from without, but from wi the mind, and can never than the mind itself; and fallible, there is and can be lible authority for faith or b objection is simply that a authority for the mind in faith is impossible, because is not itself infallible, and incapable of an infallible sent. This, we believe, is tion in all its force.

The objection rests on t ples, neither of which is first, that the mind or intel versally fallible; and, secon authority in matters of fait mind itself, not out of it, a fore, belief in anything o authority is impossible.

1. The intellect is not univ finite, and does not and ca all things; but it is neve what it knows, and in its o is infallible; that is, the i not false or fallible in what for every one who knows k he knows. The judgment fallible only when and whe

what is implicit, for nothing can be asserted in the conclusion not already implicitly asserted in the premises; yet the assent is by virtue of the evidence or authority intrinsic in the object, as in intuition. All this means that we know objects because they are and are placed in relation with our cognitive faculty, not that they are because we know them, or because the mind places them, or makes them its object. If the lawyer's rule, that authority is not in the object but in the mind or person, were true, there could be no fact of knowledge, either intuitive or discursive, because the mind cannot know where there is nothing to be known.

Faith or belief agrees with knowledge in the respect that it is intellectual assent, but differs from it in that it is mediate assent, by an authority extrinsic, as authority or evidence, both to the object and to the person. The authority or evidence mediates between the mind and the fact or object, and brings them together in a manner somewhat analogous to that in which the middle term in the syllogism brings together the two extremes and unites them in the conclusion. If the evidence or the authority is adequate, the belief is reasonable and as certain as any conclusion of logic, or as the immediate assent of the mind in the fact of science or knowledge. I am as certain that there is such a city as Rome, though I have never seen it, that there was such a man as Julius Cæsar, George Washington, or Napoleon Bonaparte, as I am that the three angles of the triangle are equal to two right angles. It is on this principle the lawyer acts and must act in every case he has in court. He summons and examines witnesses, and relies on their testimony or evidence to obtain a conviction or an acquittal, except in a question of law; and then he relies on th or the court. If there is no ty *outside* the person, that is thority not in his own mir does he summon and exam cross-examine witnesses or the judge? Why does he n the facts and the law out of " inner consciousness," as c modern historians the facts th us for history? As a lawy friend would soon find his p if he carried it into court, o as an effectual estoppel to th tice of his profession.

The lawyer asks, " When t sionary carries the church heathen, does he not preser their rational acceptance? so, does he not ask their fini ment to pass upon and acc infinite and absolute?" We our friend would argue bett this if he had a case in c which anything of importa pended. When presented brother lawyer opposite with t sion of the court of appeals his case, would he attempt t or pass upon the judgment court before accepting it, o he not be content with simp fying the fact that the decis been rendered by the court of or court of last resort? \ quite sure that, if he were on fensive, and adduced the (of the court of last resort bar action, he would be very f allowing his brother oppo question the judgment. No he as a lawyer dream of r the decision because his ow had not passed upon its meri when once assured that th had rendered it, he would a and submit to it as law, not own judgment, but on the a of the court itself. All he wou himself to do would be to ve

my reason by its own light. But what is evident to me by the light of my own reason, I know, and not simply believe. As belief is always on extrinsic authority simply accredited to reason, this goes so far as to deny that any belief is or can be rational, and that any authority or any amount of testimony is sufficient to warrant it, which, as we have seen, is much farther than the lawyer can go in the practice of his profession, or any man in the ordinary business of life.

We do not think our legal friend has duly considered the reach of the principle he lays down. Even in the so-called positive sciences, the greater part of the matters accepted by the scientist are accepted on extrinsic authority, not on personal knowledge. No geologist has personally observed all or even the greater part of the facts he uses in the construction of his science; no geographer, however great a traveller he may have been, has visited and personally examined all parts of the globe which he describes; the botanist describes and classifies more plants, the zoölogist more forms of life, than he has personally seen, and the historian deals almost entirely with facts of which he has no personal knowledge. Eliminate from the sciences what the scientist has not observed for himself, but taken on the reported observation of others, and from the garniture of every mind what it believes or takes on extrinsic authority, not on his personal knowledge, and there would be very little left to distinguish the most learned and highly educated man from the untutored savage. In all the affairs of life, we are obliged to rely on extrinsic authority, on evidence neither in the subject nor in the object, on the observations and testimony of others, and sometimes on the obser-vations and accumulated testi of ages, especially in wise and dent statesmanship; and if we suddenly deprived of this auth evidence, or testimony, and re to our own personal knowledg tuitive or discursive; society v come to a standstill, and would fall below the level of the New lander, for even he inherits som sons from the past, and associate his observations some observ of others.

We presume our friend the l means nothing of all this, an mistake arises from not sharpl tinguishing between the motiv credibility and the authority, o one hand, and the authority and it authorizes, on the other. Th istence of God is a fact of sci though discursive, not intuitiv ence. That God is, as the theolo say, *prima veritas in essendo, in scendo, et in dicendo*, is also a tru science—is a truth we not s believe, but know or may kno it can be proved with certain natural reason prior to faith. G truth; it is impossible for him since he is *prima veritas in dicend* primal truth in speaking, and neither deceive nor be deceive he is *prima veritas in cognoscen* the principle of all truth in kno

This granted, the word of must be true, infallibly true. we can go by science or c knowledge. Now, suppose the yer to have full proof that it re God's word that is announc him, would he not be bound t lieve it true, nay, could he in th ercise of his reason help believ true, prior to and independe any consideration of its conten what it is that God says? Go neither deceive nor be dece therefore his word must be true

We need not now go into the historical proofs of the identity of the Catholic Church with the apostolic body, for that is easily done, and has been done over and over again; besides, it lies on the very face of history, and Pius IX., the Pontiff now gloriously reigning, is as easily and as certainly proved to be the successor of Peter as Ulysses S. Grant is proved to be the successor in the presidency of the United States of George Washington, the schism of Jefferson Davis to the contrary notwithstanding. Moreover, if the lawyer doubts, as we presume he does not, the identity, we hold ourselves ready to adduce the proofs whenever he calls for them. Assuming, then, the case to be as stated, we demand what in the whole process of acceptance of the faith the missionary proposes to the heathen is irrational, or not satisfactory, to the fullest demands of reason? In fact, the points to be proved are exceedingly few, and those not above the reach of private judgment, or difficult. The authority of our Lord as a teacher come from God was proved by miracles. These miracles the church witnessed and testifies to as facts, and so far her testimony is unimpeachable, Their supernatural and miraculous character we can ourselves judge of. Whether they prove the divine authority of Jesus or not, is also a matter of which we are competent to judge. His divine authority proved, his divinity, and all the mysteries of his person can be rationally accepted on his word, and what his word was, the church who received it is competent to declare. There really, then, is nothing to be proved which the church herself does not either prove or supply the means of proving in order to render belief in what she claims to be, and in what she teaches, as rational or reasonable as belief in any well-ascertained fact in natural science. motives of credibility whicl brings with her and presents understanding of all men whc her accredit her as the divine pointed depositary and teacl the revelation God has made tc and all the rest follows of itself the syllogism the conclusion f from the premises.

The lawyer does not admit i rejects the whole, because he all belief on extrinsic authority. is not this because he mistak meaning of the word *author* used by theologians and philoso| We have generally found tha men who object to belief on aut understand by authority an or command addressed to the will out including anything to co the reason or to motive the ass the understanding. This is nc cisely the theological sense c term. The theologians unde by authority in matters of fai thority *for* believing as w an order *to* believe. It i reason which authorizes the and is therefore primarily a ity for the intellect, and fu it an ample reason to believe.

Authority addressed simply will ordering it to believe, and the intellect no reason for bel can produce no rational belief, a duce no belief at all, and this v sume is what, and all, our legal means. Taking authority in his we entirely agree with him, ex command from God is always son for the intellect as well as der to the will, since God is *veritas*, and can command only v true, reasonable, just, and right. command is his word, and an from him to the will is *ipso j* reason for the understanding, si higher evidence of truth th word is possible. With tl

the intellect as well as to the will, and a sufficient reason for believing as well as obeying, the lawyer's principal objection is disposed of, and the acceptance of the faith is shown to be a rational acceptance.

But, conceding the infallibility of the church, since her teaching must be received by a fallible understanding, why is belief on the authority of the church less fallible than belief on the authority of an infallible book, interpreted by the same fallible understanding? You say to Protestants: The Bible may be infallible, but your understanding of it is fallible, and therefore even with it you have no infallible rule of faith. Why may not the Protestant retort: Be it that the church is infallible, you have only your fallible private judgment by which to interpret her teachings, and, therefore, with your infallible church have only a fallible faith?

More words are usually required to answer an objection than are required to state it. We do not assert or concede the fallibility of reason, intellect, or private judgment in matters which come within its own province or competence. Revelation presupposes reason, and therefore that man is capable of receiving it; consequently of certainly knowing and correctly understanding it, within the limits of his finite reason. We do not build faith on scepticism, or the incapacity of reason to know anything with certainty. Reason is the preamble to faith, and is competent to receive and understand truly, infallibly, if you will, clear and distinct propositions in their plain and obvious sense when presented to it in words spoken or in words written. If it were not so, all writing and all teaching, all books and all sermons, would be useless. So far the Protestant rule and the Catholic are the same, with this difference only, that, if we happen to mistake the sense of the chur is ever present to correct th and to set us right, while the F ant rule can give no further ex tion, or add a word to corr misapprehension. The teachi the church need to be unde but not ordinarily to be interp and, even when they do ha be interpreted, she is pres interpret them, and declare libly the sense in which th to be understood. But the from beginning to end, must b preted before it can be unde and, while private judgment or may be competent to underst when it is interpreted or exp it is yet only a fallible interpret incompetent to explain to the standing its real sense.

The church interprets and e herself; there are books, als carry their own explanation them, and so need no interpr or further explanation; but ma the Bible is not such a book. inspired; it is true; it is inf and is, as St. Paul says of all ture, divinely inspired, "profit teach, to reprove, to correct, struct in justice, that the m God may be perfect, furnis every good word and wor Tim. iii. 16, 17); but it bears face the evidence that it was ad to men who were already be and already instructed, parti least, in the truths it teaches forces, and that it was not wri teach the faith to such as l knowledge of it, but to correct to present more fully the faith tain points, to point out the d enjoins, to exhort to repentan reform, and to hold up a tives, on the one hand, the judgment of God upon tho disregard his goodness, or his mercy, or abuse his long

whole revelation, whether written or unwritten, and in this tradition she has the key to the real sense of the sacred Scriptures, and is able to interpret them infallibly. Tradition, authenticated by the church as the witness and depositary of it, supplies the knowledge necessary to the understanding of the sacred text. Read in the light of tradition, what is implicit in the text becomes explicit, what is merely referred to as wholly known becomes expressly and clearly stated, and we are able to understand the written word, because tradition interprets it for us, without any demand for a knowledge or judgment on our part that exceeds our natural powers. Our judgment is no longer private judgment, because we have in tradition a catholic rule by which to judge, and our judgment has not to pass on anything above the province of reason.

The objection we make to the Protestant rule, it must be obvious now to our friend, cannot be retorted. The Protestant must interpret the sacred Scriptures by his private judgment, which he cannot do without passing upon questions which transcend its reach. The Catholic exercises, of course, his judgment in accepting the infallible teachings of the church, but he is not required to pass upon any question above the reach of his understanding, or upon which, by his natural reason, he cannot judge infallibly, or with the certainty of actual and complete knowledge. He is not required to pass upon the truth of what the church teaches, for that follows from her divine institution and commission to teach the revelation God has made previously established. He has simply to pass upon the question, What is it she teaches, or presents clearly and distinctly to my understanding to be believed? and, in passing upon that quest judgment has not to judge thing beyond or above reas therefore, is not fallible any m in any other act of knowledg

There is another advant Catholic rule has over the P rule. In this world of p change, and with the restl ever-busy activity of the hum new questions are constantly up and in need of being a and so answered as to save t and integrity of the faith. T having once spoken is he silent; it can say nothing m make no further explanation faith to meet these new q and tell us explicitly what t requires or forbids us to beli regard to them. Hence, Pr never know how to meet them new or further explanations cisions are constantly needed, be needed to the end of time the explanations and decision church, amply sufficient whe not seldom, through the subt activity of error, and its u efforts to evade or obscure th become insufficient, and nee selves to be further explain applied so as to strike head the new forms of old er deprive them of their last sub These explanations and deci necessary, and which can be i made only by a living and e sent infallible authority, can fallibly made, if at all, on the ant rule. Even the creed church, though unalterable, from time to time not devel but new and further expla to meet and condemn the ne of error that spring up, and serve the faith unimpaired an late. How is this to be done bly by a book written two t years ago and private judgn

THE HOUSE OF YORKE.

CHAPTER XV.

VOILA CE QUI FAIT QUE VOTRE FILLE EST MUETTE.

MADAME SWETCHINE says: "The wrongs which the heart resents most keenly are impalpable and invisible." We may parody this, and say, with equal truth, that the troubles most difficult to bear are frequently those which, to indifferent observers, seem scarcely worth mention. There is dignity, and a certain stimulating excitement, in great affliction and great wrong; but a petty persecution, which we would fain treat with contempt, but which, in spite of us, pierces with small, envenomed points to our very hearts, is capable of testing our utmost endurance. Who does not know how one malicious, intriguing woman can poison a whole community, break friendship that would have stood the test of death, and destroy a confidence that seemed as firm as the hills? The smiling malice, the affected candor, the smooth insinuation, the more than infantine innocence—happy he who has not learned by bitter experience these tactics of the devil's sharp-shooters!

Of such a nature was the earlier stage of the persecution suffered by the Catholics of Seaton. Servants were daily insulted by mistresses less well-bred than themselves. They had to swallow a gibe with their Friday's eggs or fish; they were entertained with slanderous stories regarding the priest they loved and reverenced. This was, of course, without provocation. Who ever knew an Irish servant-girl who attacked the religion or irreligion of her employers? Workingmen could not go through the streets to and from work without being forced to to revilings of their church. was carried to such an exten they soon found themselves ol to relinquish their open-air lour places, where they had smoke talked after the day's work was and shut themselves into their h Nor were they allowed to rem peace there. Nearly all the lived on one street, running fro bridge up the west side of the and called Irish Lane. When found that they would not con to be insulted, the mob that gat in the streets every evening ma up this lane, calling out to the challenging, taunting them. not one word or act of retal could they provoke to give the excuse for the violence which were thirsting to commit. I Rasle had given his people stri orders to remain in their house make no reply, no matter wha said to them, and to defend selves only if their houses were en into. They obeyed him wi tonishing docility.

When, later, the people of S found themselves covered witl grace before the country for outrages on Catholics, they str throw the odium on "a few row or on workingmen from other employed in the Seaton ship-y and in a sketch of the town i *History of Maine*, written sinc time, the Catholics are accus being themselves the cause of own troubles. Both these state

delightful to go out ..t recess and play without being assailed by blows or nicknames! How proud they were when Father Rasle came in to give them his weekly instruction in religion! It was quite different from their accustomed ideas of school-life.

Mrs. Yorke was much disturbed by this arrangement. "Edith will have to give up her new friend," she said decidedly. "I honor Miss Churchill for acting up to her principles, even when it is sure to bring her into a disagreeably conspicuous position; but there is nothing that obliges us to share her danger. When a person comes out of the ranks for conscience' sake, let her stand alone, and have the glory of it."

Edith objected at first, but her aunt insisted, and the girl soon saw that, though it went against her feelings, it was right to obey.

"We are not Catholics, my dear," Mrs. Yorke said; "but it is our duty and wish to protect you from insult. We have suffered in doing so. You know we have given up going to meeting, the sermons were so pointed, and given up the sewing-circle, because we could not go without hearing something offensive, and your cousins find it unpleasant to go into the street even. As to your uncle, his defence of the religious rights of your church exposes him to actual danger. Our life here is nearly intolerable, and this will make it worse if you and Miss Churchill continue to visit each other."

Fortunately, Miss Churchill anticipated this, and herself put a temporary end to their acquaintance—"till better times," she wrote.

"She has behaved well," Mrs. Yorke said, after reading the note. "And now, Charles, I wish that you would show a little prudence, and let events take their course v interfering. Why should yc anything? It does no good.'

"From which motive wou wish me to be silent," her hı asked quietly—"from cowar selfishness?"

She made no reply, save tc her hands, and wish that sh never come to Seaton.

"Now, Amy dear, listen to re her husband said.

"You know, Charles, it i disagreeable to have to listen ı son," she objected pathetically

He laughed, but persisted have heard you say many a that disinterested and intellige were to blame in withdrawing public affairs, and leaving th the hands of dishonest polit You said, very sensibly, that, i men were not strong enough t vent abuses, they should at lea test against them, and let the see that patriotism was not dead. Perhaps, you added, s protest might shame others int ing you. Oh! you were el on that subject, little womar quoted from *Tara's Halls*. Tl was that even the indignant br of a heart in the cause of showed that truth still lived, was some good. What do yo milady? Was it all talk? A going to fail me? 'I appeal Philip drunk to Philip sober.'"

Mrs. Yorke was smiling, ar face had caught a slight color. repetition of her own sentimen encouraged her, as the recoll of our own heroic aspirations does help us in weaker momen

His wife pacified, Mr. Yorke out to work off his own irri He would not have had her kr but he had been attacked i street that very day when stc to speak to Father Rasle.

tion, and another reference to Johnny O'Brian. A Portuguese barber had made an idiotic speech, and various town-officers, and prominent Know-Nothings, all more or less illiterate, had spoken, and all had seasoned their discourse with Johnny O'Brian. Finally, the Rev. Saul Griffeth had held his hearers spell-bound while he described, in glowing phrases, the inevitable and complicated ruin of the country in case Catholics should be admitted to equal rights, or any rights at all, and had painted a dazzling picture of the country's future glories should Catholics be excluded. And here again the perennial Johnny O'Brian figured.

In the midst of a cold and threatening silence, Mr. Yorke got up. Never was his voice more rasping, his mouth more scornful, his glance more full of fire. "It was happy," he said, "for one man that the Reverend Mr. John Conway was not Calvin; for, instead of being content to burn Servetus, he would first have tortured him, till even the flames would have been a relief. As for the Reverend Mr. Griffeth's companion pictures of the country's future, they were daubs such as no sensible man would receive as true representations, and the young man who painted them probably believed in them no more than he had believed in the precisely contrary views which he had expressed within a few years in the speaker's own hearing. With regard to the other orators, he did not know what that illiterate and idiotic Portuguese barber had to do with the town affairs of Seaton, and he congratulated the rest on the possession of O'Brian, who had certainly godsend to them. So lon shred of that devoted child they would have something But the reasoning in the mos speeches to which he had had reminded him of the L Sgarnarelle, *le médecin mal* They had put their premises middle ages of Europe, an conclusion in a little New E town of the nineteenth 'Voilà ce qui fait que votre muette.' What, in fact, are to talk about?" He then to state his own views.

It is said of the French mists under the first empire, their scorn of the emperor, a determination to regard hi foreigner, they used to pronou name so that it seemed to be a twenty syllables. Mr. Yorke h faculty. His enunciation wa and the letter *r* very promine the mere pronouncing of a n could make an insult. At manner had commanded silen one liked to be the first to hi it became too scathing presen when one gave the first fain of disapproval, the storm bro He tried again and again to but they would not hear him. and jeers arose, and cries o him out! Down with him!"

"Touch me if you dare!" facing them, and lifting his They stood aside, and he out, and went home, not ve pleased.

CHAPTER XVI.

BY THEIR FRUITS YE SHALL KNOW THEM.

MR. YORKE went home from that first town-meeting, and opened his Bolingbroke to look for a s He found this: "The incivi

were trivial, but they called out the spirit of the martyrs.

Cold weather seemed to cool the zeal of the Know-Nothings; but with another spring it kindled again, making the Catholic school its principal point of attack. Anonymous letters were written to the teacher, threatening her if she did not give it up. The *Herald* contained, week after week, insulting and scarcely veiled references to her; and the children could not go through the streets unmolested. But no notice was taken of these annoyances, and the school prospered in spite of them. The children came unfailingly, not, perhaps, without fear, but certainly without yielding to fear. They were deeply impressed by the position in which they found themselves. All their childish gayety deserted them. They gathered and talked quietly, instead of playing; they drew shyly away without answering when the Protestant children attacked them. "Keep out of their way, and never answer back," was the charge constantly repeated in the ears of these little confessors of the faith, and they obeyed it perfectly. Dear children! may they never lose in later years that faith by which they suffered so early in life. Herewith, one who watched and admired their constancy sends them loving greeting.

When the first examination for prizes took place in this school, Mr. Yorke was present, and made an address; and when it was over, he and Father Rasle walked away together.

"I am obliged to go away. to be gone a month," the priest said. "I must go to-night. But I do not like to leave my flock to the wolves. There is no help for it, though. The bishop wishes to see me at Brayon, and I must visit the Indians on Oldtown Island."

"I advise you, sir, to go as ly as you can, and let no o you go or know that you are g Mr. Yorke said.

Father Rasle looked sur "Why, you do not imagine th person would molest me?"

"I do not imagine, but I a that the Know-Nothings wo anything," was the reply. "I safe to give them an opportur mischief."

Still the priest looked incre

"I cannot see why they touch me," he said. "I hav nothing to provoke them. Tl sult us, they tell lies, and I resent it. Do you know the that have been brought to n week? I find them am He laughed pleasantly. "S they represent the church! tholic man, they say, wanted t a hundred dollars. Now, to t much at once would be a mort but to steal ten cents would b a venial sin. So my brave C steals ten cents, and, after a ten cents more, and so on, has the hundred dollars. B means, he secures his money, guilty only of a thousand veni which he gets forgiveness for l ing the priest fifty dollars. T one of Mr. John Conway's Here is another that was pul in the *Herald*, with my nam the others in full. You kno Mrs. Mary O'Conner's husban ly died in California. Well, tl *rald* says that the poor widow to me, weeping and lamentin she had not even the consolat seeing her husband's grave; told her that, for thirty dol would have him buried here had saved thirty dollars, earr washing, and she brought it Three days after, I told her tl husband's body had been mira

is that? I have been in the Catholic Church forty years, and I never heard of a Holy Ghost.' Now, sir, this, of course, seems to you idiotic; but a Protestant doctor of divinity keeps such books, and gives them to people to read, and repeats such falsehoods in his sermons. You see what you have to expect."

"Shall I, then, publish a card denying the truth of these stories?" Father Rasle asked, with an expression of face which showed his distaste for the task.

"No one will read it if you do," was the reply. "You must leave all to time. At present, for you to be accused is to be condemned. Who was it—Montesquieu?—who says, 'If you are accused of having stolen the towers of Notre Dame, bolt at once'? That is your case. Whatever they may charge you with, consider yourself convicted."

They had by this time reached the priest's house, a little cottage close to the corner of the two streets. Mr. Yorke declining an invitation to enter, they leaned on the gate a few minutes to finish their talk.

"You must not judge our country by what you see here," Mr. Yorke said. "What you complain of is merely the abuse of a good gift. A priest of your church has expressed himself very well concerning these difficulties. 'It always pains me, in such periods,' he says, 'to hear men express doubt concerning our institutions. As for me, I would rather suffer from the license of freedom than the oppression of authority. War is better than a false peace; riot better than servitude; heresy better than indifference. But none of these things,' he adds, 'is to my liking. And may the good God preserve us from them all!' That was Father John, an American priest."

"Ah! I know him," Father Rasle said brightly. "I happenec once in his company. We steamboat, and some minis ed into controversy with h tholic Christianity degrades the minister said. The cannot hold any communica God. If he should be cast a desert island, he would b God. All must come to hin the church. He has in hi power to reflect the divine 'You mistake,' says Fath 'and I can show by a famili Suppose that every man in t should insist that his timep correct, and should refuse late it by any other. Of cc chronometers would all wag veral ways, no two alike, a would be a ceaseless wrangl what was the time of day, a man would think that he ca sun in his pocket. To the (the meridian and the alma watch is right! That is Pı ism. Now, the Catholic ha: itual dial also; but since h that it is a fallible instru keeps it regulated by the gr of the church. The conse truth and harmony. Every conscience ticks alike; and, meridian-gun of the great is fired, every man says, 'I o'clock. Amen!'"

Mr. Yorke's warning was ed, for the event proved th: Rasle would scarcely have lowed to leave the town wit lestation had it been known was going. No one knew ever, but the priest's hou Mr. Yorke, and the man wl him over to Brayon that nig

"I do not think that any tion was needed," Father R to his companion, as the through the dewy woods by "But since it was as easy

see every Catholic driven out of the town."

If there was ever a moment in Mr. Yorke's life when he regretted being a gentleman, it would be safe to say that this was that moment. To talk with such a man was folly. But if some muscular Christian had entered the scene opportunely, and applied to the town-officer's back a score or so of such logical conclusions as he was fitted to understand, or had enlightened his cranium by propounding to it an argument from an unanswerable fist, Mr. Yorke would, doubtless, have left the office with a smile of serene satisfaction, and a conviction that the dramatic proprieties had been sustained. No such person appearing, he went away with anything but an amiable expression.

His next visit was to the Rev. John Conway. The minister had just finished his breakfast, and came into the room with a comfortable, deliberate air, rather exasperating to a man who was not only indignant, but fasting. His guarded look showed that he expected an attack.

By an effort, Mr. Yorke greeted him courteously, then began: "I come, sir," he said, "to ask you to raise your voice and use your influence to put a stop to such outrages as were committed last night, and bring the perpetrators of that to punishment."

Mr. Conway seated himself with dignity, cast down his eyes, puckered his mouth accurately, put the tips of his right-hand fingers to the tips of his left-hand fingers in an argumentative manner, and spoke slowly and solemnly:

"I am sorry that any violence has been done. But when a community becomes incensed by encroachments which threaten their most sacred interests, and when they find that the laws are not stringent enough to afford them security from an i
foe, we cannot expect that t
act with that calmness and d
tion which is to be desired. I
cate—"

"You are not in your pulpit
ing to blockheads!" Mr. York
forth. "I came here to talk c
sense."

A cold glimmer showed un
minister's lower eyelids, and
went over his face; but he ha
self-control than his visitor, or
not that sense of outraged just
decency which, to that visitor'
made forbearance a vice, cons
ly he said nothing for a n
There was, indeed, no more
said. Mr. Yorke rose and v
the door, but stopped there.
appeal was vain, warning mi
be.

"I warn you, sir," he said
Protestant—that your course
only dishonest, but impolitic
are working so as to secure t
triumph of those you hate,
bring about your own ruin.
anti-Catholic mobs are not
tant, except as they protest
all religious restraint. The
Catholicism most, simply beca
the strongest religion. You m
think, perhaps, that you use th
you mistake. They use yo
they despise you. They spe
fair now, because you stand b
them and the law and give
certain respectability. Indee
only power is derived from yo
when they shall have crushed
licism, if they ever do, they wi
the same weapons you have
in their hands against you.
hope that by the course you are
you are going to make Bap
Congregational, or Methodist
members; you are going to m
fidels."

A sense of the utter useless

that respect, she thought as little about it as possible. Perhaps her only definite thought was that Dick might have waited awhile before speaking, and let her study more; for study had now become impossible. She wanted to be in continual motion, to have work and change. A deep and steady excitement burned in her cheeks, her eyes, her lips. Her piety, instead of being tender and tranquil, had grown impassioned. To die for the faith, to suffer torments for it, to be in danger, that seemed to her desirable. She almost regretted that she had home and friends to bind her. If she were still with Mrs. Rowan, in the little house that was under that clay-bank, then she would be free, and perhaps they would kill her. She had scarcely been to Mass that year without thinking how glorious it would be if a mob would break in and kill them all. Her imagination hovered ceaselessly over this subject.

Seeing her uncle coming, she waited for him. "We must make up our minds that we have not seen the worst that they will do, little girl," he said. "There is no law."

She smiled involuntarily.

"Why, are you pleased at that?" he exclaimed.

"There might be a worse fate than dying for one's faith, Uncle Charles," she said, clasping her hands over his arms.

He laughed, and patted her cheek. "Is that your notion?" he asked. "If it is, remember that I have a word to say about it. I shall fight hard before you are made a martyr of. I see what you have been reading—Crashaw's *St. Theresa*:

> 'Farewell, house, and farewell, home:
> She's for the Moors and martyrdom.'

Do I guess and quote rightly, mademoiselle?"

She only smiled in reply. But well she knew that she had been reading from a deeper book than Crashaw.

A few nights after, the C[...] school-house was blown up [...] gunpowder, and left a perfect [...] "Of course!" said Mr. Yorke.

"The teacher has taken th[...] dren into the galleries of the ch[...] Patrick said.

"The church will be dest[...] then," replied his master.

It was not destroyed altoge[...] once, however, but every windo[...] was broken. This was done in [...] daylight, just after a summer s[...]

Mr. Yorke put himself befo[...] mob, entreating them to forbea[...] trying to push back the fo[...] ones, but without avail. "[...] listen to him! His niece is a [...] lic," they cried. "To the ch[...]

Two or three gentlemen dr[...] in their buggies, and sat at [...] distance while the work of d[...] tion went on, and several [...] lingered on the outskirts [...] crowd. In a neighboring stre[...] of sight, Edith Yorke stoo[...] Clara, and listened to the so[...] breaking glass. For a mome[...] tural indignation overcame p[...] her heart. "Oh! if I were a [...] sand men on horseback," s[...] claimed. "I'd like to ride [...] down, and trample them under [...] Then the next moment, "Oh [...] wicked I am!"

"You are not wicked!" Cla[...] angrily. "I won't have yo[...] such nonsense."

Clara was in that state o[...] when she must scold somebod[...]

Of course the authorities took [...] tice of this affair. The teacher [...] glass reset, and continued her [...] Mr. Yorke wrote to Father Ra[...] vising him not to return to Sea[...] a while, and a lull succeeded.

And now the Yorkes took [...] and felt not quite alone, for C[...] coming home, and Dick [...] would soon be there, and [...] Cary was coming down.

TO BE CONTINUED.

need only consult the lives of such saints as have been thus favored.*

The psychological condition or state which is somewhat vaguely termed ecstasy has always possessed peculiar interest both for the theologian and the physician; and, although numerous definitions of it have been attempted, it is extremely difficult to convey to the general reader a clear idea of its distinctive nature. The word itself usually signifies a condition in which the mind and soul is transferred, or placed out of its usual state.

St. Augustine called it "a transport, by which the soul is separated and, as it were, removed to a distance from the bodily senses," and, following this definition, Ambrose Paré, the father of French surgery, terms it "a reverie with rapture of the mind, as if the soul were parted from the body." St. Bonaventure, the contemporary and biographer of St. Francis of Assisium, says that ecstasy "is an elevation of the soul to that source of divine love which surpasses human understanding, an elevation by which it is separated from the exterior man." St. Thomas Aquinas, Cardinal Bona, and other theological writers give similar definitions; while among medical authorities, Briquet, J. Franck, Bérard, Thomas King Chambers, Guislain of Brussels, Clymer, Gratiolet, and many others describe its symptoms and discuss its pathological relations.

Well-marked ecstasy and the stigmata have but seldom been united in the same individual, and still more rarely have these extraordinary manifestations been subjected to the searching tests of science.

It will not, then, be amiss to present the readers of this ma with a brief description of th notable illustration in recent of these marvellous phenom the case has acquired a Eu celebrity, attracting the scrut many savants, and forming th ject of an interesting memoir professor in the Belgian Unive Louvain. From his descript the facts, which he was offici pointed to investigate in thei tific bearings, we shall conde following account.

In the rich and industrial p of Hainault, in Belgium, is ed the village of Bois d'Haine midway between the towns of roi and Mons. It is mainly c ed of cottages occupied by w in the neighboring manufa and in one of the poorest o Louise Lateau, the subject notice, was born January 30, 1

She is the youngest of thr dren, all daughters; and th rents were poor working strong and ordinarily healt never subject to any nervous rhagic disease. The mother living and in good health; th died during an epidemic of pox at the age of twenty-eight ise, then two and a half mon contracted this disease from ther, but made a rapid recover family continued to struggle poverty, the children's food poor and scant—"plusque says Dr. Lefebvre—but they theless grew up robust and When only eight, Louise was in the temporary care of a p woman in the neighborhood the latter's son was engaged door work. A little later s

* See among others, Salvatori's *Life of Veronica Giuliani*, pp. 100–108, and the exhaustive *Christliche Mystik* of Görres, in which is given a full account of Maria Möri, the "Ecstatic of the Tyrol.'

* *Louise Lateau de Bois d'Haine: s Extases; ses Stigmates. Etude Médi* le Dr. F. Lefebvre, Professeur de P Générale et de Thérapeutique. Louv 12mo, pp. 360.

during the illness of her relatives, and falsely accused by her mother (who seems to have been a person of difficult temper) of being the cause of all the family's misfortunes, she remained invariably calm and cheerful. Another of her most striking traits was her charity for the poor; "poor herself, she loved to relieve the poor," and many instances are narrated of her devotion to the sick and helpless during the cholera that raged at Bois d'Haine in 1866. From her infancy almost she was exceptionally devout, and her piety was always practical, and devoid of affectation and display. In her interior and religious life, as in her domestic duties, she was simple, earnest, and discreet.

A recollection of these details of her character and antecedents is necessary for the proper appreciation of the phenomena now to be described. These are of two distinct kinds, having no connection but their accidental association in the same individual; and that they may be more clearly understood, they will be considered separately, first the stigmata, then the ecstatic trances, and, thirdly, the nature of the evidence upon which the extraordinary facts rest.

I.—THE STIGMATA.

The first occurrence of the bleeding was noticed by Louise on Friday, the 24th of April, 1868, when she saw blood issuing from a spot on the left side of the chest. With her habitual reserve, she mentioned it to no one. The next day it recurred at the same spot; and she then also observed blood on the top of each foot. She now confided it to her director, who, although thinking the circumstance extraordinary, reassured her and bade her keep the facts to herself. During the night preceding the second Frid lowing, May 8, blood oozed the left side and from both fe toward nine o'clock in the m it flowed freely from the bac palm of each hand. At this ture it seemed impossible lon keep the matter secret, an confessor directed Louise to c a physician.

Recognizing the medical c ter of the case, the periodical ing, and the ecstatic trances subsequently occurred, the ec authorities felt constrained to its investigation in the hand medical expert, and for this pose called in the aid of Dr. vre. A more judicious choice not have been made, as this g man had long devoted himself study of nervous affections, an passed fifteen years in medical c of two hospitals for the insan in lecturing upon mental dise the University of Louvain.

Of the minuteness of his exa tion, and of his credibility as ness, each reader can judg himself.

If, during the course of the from Saturday to Thursday ne the hands and feet be examine following facts are revealed: C back of each hand there is a patch about half an inch (two half centimetres) long, of a mo hue than the rest of the ski and glistening on the surface the palm of each hand a simila patch was seen, equally red, an responding exactly with the s that on the back. On the sol back of each foot are found s marks, having the form of a pa ogram with rounded angles, three-quarters of an inch (thre timetres) in length.

On examining these spots magnifying-glass of twenty diam

upon pressure. On examining these points with a magnifying lens, most of them looked like minute cuts in the skin, of triangular shape, as if made by the bite of microscopic leeches: others were semilunar in shape, and some quite irregular.

The quantity of blood that flows through the stigmata each Friday is variable. During the first months of the flow and before the commencement of the ecstatic attack, it was abundant, and often lasted twenty-four hours—from midnight to midnight—and it was estimated that as much as one litre, or seven-eighths of a quart, was discharged from the nine wounds. An exact estimate of the amount was difficult, from the fact that most of the blood was absorbed by the cloths about the chest and limbs. But, as the result of his personal observations, Dr. Lefebvre states that at his first visit, August 30, 1868, both the duration and the quantity of the flow had already begun to diminish: beginning at midnight, it stopped about four or five o'clock the next afternoon; yet he counted on that day fourteen large linen cloths (the largest being twenty inches by eight, and the smallest twenty inches by six) completely saturated. Besides this, the left foot was still enveloped during the ecstasy, and there was a pool of blood on the floor as large as two hands. He thinks he rather understates the amount of blood then lost if he estimates it at two hundred and fifty grammes (a half-pint). This, however, he gives as the mean quantity lost, it being sometimes more and sometimes less.

Sometimes the bleeding ceased about midday, and two Fridays passed without any hæmorrhage, the ecstasy occurring as usual. On one of these occasions the stigmata remained unchanged, but on the other the usual vesicle formed, yielding rous discharge of a delicate ro: but no blood. After this the bleeding resumed its regular every Friday, and the bloody let on the forehead, which appeared exceptionally, was n played each week.

The blood, which was ca examined, had neither the tint of arterial nor the dark hue of venous blood, but wa violet red color, like that of pillaries or minute vessels whic the veins and arteries. It natural consistence, and clott dily upon the cloths and up edges of the wound. With his colleagues who were ex microscopy, Dr. Hairion, pr of hygiene and dermatology (t ory of skin diseases), and D Kempen, professor of anatom Lefebvre made several careful scopic examinations of the which showed a perfectly trans plasma or blood fluid, with t and white corpuscles of o blood in proper proportion.

The stigmata are manifestl ful; for, although the girl was ex ly reluctant to speak of it, Dr. vre was satisfied, by careful vation of her attitudes and exp before the ecstasies began, th suffered acutely.

The bleeding stopped at d hours, as has been stated. following day—Saturday—th mata were quite dry, with littl of dried blood here and there c surface. Not a trace of supp ever occurred from the wounc the girl, who a few hours a much difficulty in using her or in standing on her feet, is engaged with her morning hold duties, or walking a mile half to her devotions at the church.

less as a statue, with the body bent slightly forward; the bleeding hands enveloped in cloths and resting upon her knees, the eyes wide open and rigidly fixed as described. The expression of the face is that of rapt attention, and she seems lost in the contemplation of some distant object. Her expression and attitude frequently change, the features sometimes relaxing, the eyes becoming moist, and a smile of happiness lighting up the mouth. Sometimes the lids droop and nearly veil the eyes, the brow contracts, and tears roll slowly down the cheeks: at times again she grows pale, her face wears an expression of the greatest terror, while she starts up with a suppressed cry. The body sometimes slowly rotates, and the eyes move, as if following some invisible procession. At other times she rises and moves forward, standing on tiptoe with her hands stretched out, and either clasped or hanging open like the figures of the *Orantes* of the catacombs; while her lips move, her breathing is rapid and panting, her features light up, and her face, which before the ecstasy is quite plain, is transfigured with an ideal beauty. If to this be added the sight of her stigmata: her head encircled with its bloody chaplet, whence the red current drops along her temples and cheeks, her small white hands stamped with a mysterious wound from which bloody lines emerge like rays —and this strange spectacle surrounded by people of all conditions, who are absorbed in respectful attention and interest—some idea may be gained of what Dr. Lefebvre often witnessed at Bois d'Haine.

About half-past one o'clock, she usually falls on her knees, with her hands joined and her body bent forward, while her face wears an expression of the profoundest contemplation. She remains in this attitude about half an hour, then ris resumes her seat. About two the scene changes. She first little forward, then rises—slc first, then more quickly—anc by some sudden movement jection, falls with her face ground. In this position she on her chest, the head restin the left arm, her eyes clos mouth half-open, her lower stretched out and covered heels by her dress. At three she makes a sudden moveme arms are extended at right with the body in cross-like while the feet are crossed, th instep resting on the sole of t She maintains this positior about five o'clock, when she s ly starts up on her knees in t tude of prayer. After a few r of profound absorption, she r her chair.

The ecstasy lasts until ab or seven o'clock, the attitu expression of face varying acc to the mental impressions, terminates in an appalling The arms fall helpless along the body, the head drops forw the chest, the eyes close, th becomes pinched, while the f sumes the pallor of death: same time the hands beco cold, the pulse is quite imperc a cold sweat covers the bod the death-rattle seems to be h the throat. This condition last fifteen minutes, when she r The bodily heat rises, the p turns, the cheeks regain thei but for some minutes more hangs an indefinable express ecstasy about the face. Su the eyelids open, the feature the eyes look familiarly at su ing objects, and the ecstasy is

If the different phases of t oxysm be carefully watched, i

the conjunctiva * is touched, which produces a slight winking or contraction of the lids. A bright light or other object may be suddenly passed without effect before the eyes, which gaze vacantly into space.

The sense of hearing is equally blunted, and insensible to ordinary sounds. On several occasions, a person standing behind her has shouted loudly into her ears without exciting the least evidence of being heard. Except upon the conjunctiva, as mentioned, general sensibility seems to be completely in abeyance. Numerous experiments were made to test this fact.

For instance, the mucous membranes of the nose and ears were repeatedly tickled with a feather without exciting any reflex contraction; a strong solution of ammonia held under the nose produced no effect. The skin, being less sensitive than the mucous membranes, was pricked with a needle, and a pin thrust through a fold of skin on the hands and forearm; the point of a penknife was also driven into the skin until it bled freely, without producing the faintest muscular contraction or indication of sensibility.

A still more decisive test was made with an electro-magnetic battery, † the electrodes of which were placed on the front of the forearm where the skin is very thin and sensitive, and the strongest possible current passed through the muscles for more than a minute by the watch without eliciting the least evidence of pain, and the electric brush was equally powerless. The poles were likewise applied to different parts of the fa violent and prolonged cont of the facial muscles induc without the slightest winking o sign of sensibility or suffering

Such is the condition of the functions during the first par ecstasy, but some modificati observed during the second. while lying prostrate on the fl pulse becomes almost imperc and an ordinary observer woul detect it at all, although Dr. L was sure it never ceased to be Its frequency was at the san greatly increased; so that, w could be counted, it often rose or 130 in the minute. The ments of respiration now b more and more feeble, and th est attention is needed to ma that they exist, the rhythmic tion of the little shawl that her shoulders being often th appreciable evidence that th not totally suspended.

Another remarkable fact, w contrary to the general physic is that the rate of the pulse a of respiration are directly in an proportion; both Dr. Lefebv Dr. Imbert-Goubeyre having that, while the pulse rose fro 130 per minute, the respiratio mally averaging 20 to 25) sin or even 10 in the same peric proportion as the pulse and br become feeble, the skin loses tural temperature, and is bath cold sweat. As was stated, r occurs in ten or fifteen m the pulse regains its force and frequency, respiration increas the natural standard of bodi is restored. The ecstatic thus at once from her trance into dinary life without any interr stage of transition. No he stiffness of the joints, or otl comfort is complained of; th

* The thin, transparent membrane that covers the eyeball, and is reflected upon the inner surface of the lids. It is one of the most delicate and sensitive portions of the body.

† This test is often applied for the detection of feigned convulsions, etc., by criminals and other malingerers; its efficacy will be appreciated by any one who has tried to hold the poles of a powerful battery.

cians. As an example of the uncertainty of her privacy, Dr. Lefebvre states (in a note) that, on the 11th February, 1870, he was unexpectedly passing through the neighborhood, and, as it chanced to be on Friday, he thought he would stop and see Louise. He knocked at the door—was at once admitted, and went straight to her little room without stopping to speak to the family. It was a quarter to four in the afternoon, and she was completely alone, lying prostrate on the floor, with her arms extended as described, and insensible to all that was passing around her. The bleeding limbs were wrapped in the usual cloths, of which he counted nine. The blood which trickled from her forehead was dried; and, lifting up her little white cap, he noticed the circle of bleeding points on her forehead, which presented the usual appearance. The feet had not been bleeding; on the right hand the flow was just stopping, while on the left the blood was still distinctly flowing from both stigmata. Having ascertained these points, he quietly left the cottage without her having been aware of his visit.

As a general answer to the objection of insincerity, Dr. Lefebvre appeals to both moral and physical proofs. As the most convincing of the former class, he cites the general good repute of Louise, which was never doubted, even by those who most resolutely questioned the nature of the phenomena she presented: her brave and humble life, her contempt for presents or money, her simplicity and avoidance of all parade; her extreme anxiety to conceal the first evidence of the stigmata even from her own family. If, as occasionally happened, money or presents of any kind were offered to her mother or sisters, their wounded pride was unmistakable; and when the

Archbishop of Malines, after
examination of Louise, once
the family if they had no req
make of him, they only entreat
they might be relieved of visit
left undisturbed.

To meet the physical obj
raised to the theory of the sti
he tried the effects produced b
ping, caustics, and various bli
agents. The first of these ha
or no force; for, besides the di
of exhausting the air under
upon the hard and uneven sur
the back of the hand, it is ne
to cut the skin to make the
flow, and, when the amount dr
the surface flows out, the bl
ceases at once.

Caustics produce a destruc
the skin at the point to whic
are applied, and after five
days an eschar is detached, l
a sore but not a bleeding surfa
if bleeding exceptionally occ
ceases very soon, and the l
process is slow and always follo
an indelible scar. This in no
accorded with the facts observ

The blistering hypothesis
less improbable, as this class
tants produce a special form of
mation of the skin, during whi
epidermis is raised from the d
an exudation of serous fluid.
process much more resembl
vesicles that preceded the sti
bleedings, it was examined with
er care. The characteristic c
cantharides or ammonia was
perceived, nor could the p
spangles of the Spanish-fly ever
tected with a magnifying lens.
mus paper, moistened and app
the wounds, gave no evidence
application of acids. In addi
this, there was no inflamed
around the stigmata, as is co
around the edge of blistered su
and their development was n

right was bleeding freely, while the left was dry.

Lest some subtle doubter might object to this experiment that, by some indiscretion on the part of the examiners, the girl might perhaps have discovered their intention, and applied her secret irritant to the hands before their arrival, Dr. Lefebvre resolved to repeat the test with still more conclusive precautions.

The gloves were therefore again applied on a Tuesday with the same care as before, and the next day were removed for a few moments, and the hands found in a perfectly healthy and natural state; they were then re-applied as before. On Friday morning, they were taken off before a new set of witnesses, when the stigmata of both hands were found bleeding freely as usual.

In his appendix, Dr. Lefebvre states that this glove test was suggested by Mgr. Pouceur, who superintended the theological part of the inquiry at the request of the Bishop of Tournay, and to whose tact and intelligent liberality he pays the highest compliment.

These experiments, and the inferences that they logically involve, convinced Dr. Lefebvre that the hypothesis of fraud in the production of the stigmata was untenable.

It would be easy to show by similar proofs that the ecstatic trances could not have been feigned. But for this purpose it will suffice to recall the reader's attention to the numerous trials that were made to test the subject's sensibility to external impressions. Those made with the electric current alone are decisive upon this point, for it may fairly be said that the strongest and most resolute man could not possibly resist some exhibition of feeling powerful magnetic battery w torting his muscles.

In a subsequent part of his Dr. Lefebvre enters into an tive medical study of the fa served, the discussion of whic be out of place in this magazir shows conclusively that, a they have some points in cc the ecstatic trances essentiall from hysteria, catalepsy, an allied disorders of the nervc tem; while animal magnetisı various subdivisions of "Bra hypnotism, and electro-bio equally powerless with som lism or the theory of spiritu unravel the phenomena prese this simple peasant girl c d'Haine.

The reader who desires to this inquiry is referred to Dr. vre's work (pp. 162 *et seq.*) Fournier's article entitled rares" in the fourth volume *Dictionnaire des Sciences M* which is replete with curio mation upon the subject of mata.

So convincing are the sta of Dr. Lefebvre, who never into the advocate or mistakes theories for facts, that the narrates has been accepted faith, and republished within sent year by two of the leadi nals* of this country and En

In one of these, Dr. Day, don, discusses the probable the phenomena with con liberality, while the learned contents himself with repor extraordinary facts.

* *The Journal of Psychological Med* York, Oct., 1870. *Macmillan's Maga* don, April, 1871.

"Woe, woe, for the priestly tribe this hour
On the Feine Hill have sway!
Glad am I that scarce their shapes I see;
Half-blind am I this day.

"Woe, woe, thou Palace of Cruachan!
Thy sceptre is down and thy sword;
The chase goes over thy grassy roof,
And the monk in thy courts is lord!

"Thou man with the mitre and vestments broad,
And the bearing of grave command,
Rejoice that Diarmid this day is dust!
Right heavy was his clenched hand!

"Thou man with the bell! I rede thee well,
Were Diorraing living this day,
Thy book he would take, and thy bell would break
On the base of yon pillar gray!

"Thou man with miraculous crosier-staff,
Though puissant thou art, and tall,
Were Goll but here, he would dash thy gear
In twain on thy convent wall!

"Were Conan living, the bald-head shrill,
With the flail of his scoff and gibe,
He would break thy neck, and thy convent wreck,
And lash from the land thy tribe!

"But one of our chiefs thy head had spared—
My Oscar—my son—my child:
He was storm in the foray, and fire in the fight,
But in peace he was maiden-mild."

Then Patrick answered: "Old man, old man,
That pagan realm lies low.
This day Christ ruleth. Forget thy chiefs,
And thy deeds gone by forego!

"High feast thou hast on the festal days,
And cakes on the days of fast—"
"Thou liest, thou priest, for in wrath and scorn
Thy cakes to the dogs I cast!"

"Old man, thou hearest our Christian hymns:
Such strains thou hadst never heard—"
"Thou liest, thou priest! for in Letter Lee wood
I have listened its famed blackbird!

"I have heard the music of meeting swords,
And the grating of barks on the strand,
And the shout from the breasts of the men of help
That leaped from the decks to land.

"Twelve hounds had my sire, with throats like bells,
Loud echoed on lake and bay:
By this hand, they lacked but the baptism rite
To chant with thy monks this day!"

Oisin's white head on his breast dropt down,
Till his hair and his beard, made one,
Shone out like the spine of a frosty hill
Far seen in the wintry sun.

"One question, O Patrick! I ask of thee,
Thou king of the saved and the shriven:
My sire, and his chiefs, have they their place
In thy city, star-built, of heaven?"

"Oisin, old chief of the shining sword,
That questionest of the soul,
That city they tread not who lived for war:
Their realm is a realm of dole."

"By this head, thou liest, thou son of Calphurn!
In heaven I would scorn to bide,
If my father and Oscar were exiled men,
And no friend at my side."

"That city, old man, is the city of peace:
Loud anthems, not widows' wail—"
"It is not in bellowings chiefs take joy,
But in songs of the wars of Fail!

"Are the men in the streets like Baoigne's chiefs?
Great-hearted like us are they?
Do they stretch to the poor the ungrudging hand,
Or turn they their heads away?

"Thou man with the chant, and thou man with the creed,
This thing I demand of thee:
My dog, may he pass through the gates of heaven?
May my wolf-hound enter free?"

"Old man, not the buzzing gnat may pass,
Nor sunbeam look in unbidden:
The King there sceptred knows all, sees all:
From him there is nothing hidden."

"It never was thus with Fionn, our king!
In largess our Fionn delighted:
The hosts of the earth came in, and went forth
Unquestioned, and uninvited!"

"Thy words are the words of madness, old man,
Thy chieftains had might one day;
Yet a moment of heaven is three times worth
The warriors of Eire for aye!"

Then Oisin uplifted his old white head:
Like lightning from hoary skies
A flash went forth 'neath the shaggy roofs
Low-bent o'er his sightless eyes:

"Though my life sinks down, and I sit in the dust,
Blind warrior and gray-haired man,
Mine were they of old, thou priest overbold,
Those chiefs of Baoigne's clan!"

And he cried, while a spasm his huge frame shook,
"Dim shadows like men before me,
My father was Fionn, and Oscar my son,
Though to-day ye stand vaunting it o'er me!"

Thus raged Oisin—'mid the fold of Christ,
Still roaming old deserts wide
In the storm of thought, like a lion old,
Though lamblike at last he died.

nated in various combinations of second-class political intrigues, and allowed himself to be made the conceited tool of one of them, under the full persuasion that he had become the imposing leader of a party.

The general now began to think, with excellent reason, very sound judgment, and profound calculation, that it was time for him to be more considerate. The reader will pardon us the expression, which, in his case, meant to enter upon a life of usefulness and devotion to the interests of the country—without sacrificing his own, it will be understood. Influenced by these grave considerations, our young leader subscribed to newspapers, bought books and read some of them, though he soon forgot precisely which he had read and which not; wrote a memorial on river navigation, and another upon the *Renta del Excusado;** made short speeches as a preparation for longer ones, which succeeded very well and met with the entire approbation of his hearers; and, in the time it takes to say a devout *amen*, exchanged the rakish air of the young blood for the pompous tone of the prominent and influential citizen.

Our friend, as may be seen, had reached his apogee: in confirmation of which—among other sacrifices made to seriousness—he had procured a good cook, and loosened the lacings of his stays.

Nevertheless—since there is a difference between a serious man and a moral one—our hero maintained a sort of toned-down dissoluteness behind the scenes, where he and his intimates entertained themselves in conversations tissued with a variety of subjects, such as the discourse *A* and the scandal *B;* the concordat

* Name given to the subsidy formerly levied by the King of Spain for carrying on wars against the infidels.

and the theatre royal; the ı and the *danseuse;* the bish the prima donna; the cro cards; erected a throne to Ta quia; proposed an apotheosi dustry; and passed a vote of upon the luxury of novenas.

"Look here, *little one!*" him just such another "*little* a breakfast party—where cha was made to represent the ı good society that the grea of the guests lacked—"what come of *La Lucia?*"

"She was not very well, aı her in Sevilla," responded the

"Doesn't it strike you th losing her varnish?"

"At twenty-one, man?"

"It is not singular," remar elegant son of a capitalist (th had been educated in France that age, one who lives fast *retour.*"*

"The existence of *camellia* that of roses," quickly added whose Christian name of B they were in the habit of con into *Boni.*

Having constituted himsel separable copy of the engraı risian, and not wishing to fall his model in anything, *Bon* allowed the capitalist to ex idea without instantly reprod in different words, always ende to surpass the original in eleg licisms; in scepticism of th material, and cynicism of tl approved kind, and in extrem tation of the fashionable forei nerism.

"You ought to place thi *dis*-lucent among the numbe thousand-and-one Didos," s would-be Gaul.

"Lay her aside with last yea *fanées,*"† the copy hastened t

* On the wane. † Faded

within myself, although my face denoted the gravest sympathy for his situation, I led him to a closet, took out a case of pistols, which I opened, and, handing him a weapon, said, as I bowed his dismissal, 'Here is a remedy for all your troubles.' My mendicant turned upon his heel and left; and you may be sure that I have rid myself of him, *une bonne fois pour toutes*."*

Boni's mirth was overpowering.

Gallardo and the rest of the Spaniards were silent.

"You must positively put this joke into some paper," said the capitalist's admirer, between his paroxysms of laughter.

"*Mon cher, à quoi bon?*"† responded the hero of the anecdote, with an air of modesty.

"To show people how to get rid of impostors," answered Boni; "to furnish a specimen of your humor—to let it be seen that you are as richly endowed by nature as by fortune—to give circulation to an entertaining item—and to—"

"And could a paper be found that would print such an iniquity as an entertaining item!" shouted the old general, no longer able to contain his wrath. "Is it the mission of the press to propagate such ideas and sentiments? God help us, sirs, if there is no one left in Spain capable of a blush! Can the press parade infamy shamelessly, and no one be found to repudiate the impudence that relates such a scandal in terms of laudation; or appeal from it to the noble and generous instincts, and sense of public decorum, of good and true Spaniards? Have we become as positive as the written law? In former times, gentlemen, not all gave, but the few that denied did not boast of their refusal. Charity made men

* Once for all. † What for, my dear?

sorry to say no, even to im
and, having said it, they woul
been silent about it for shame.
rice was looked upon as
the disgraceful vices which
for public opinion required
kept out of sight."

"Uncle, for God's sake!" er
Gallardo.

"For God's sake what, ne
"Speak with more modera
"When I do, look towar
quera for sunrise."

"Don't feel apprehensive, g
said the capitalist, *Je sais vi*
respect your family, and know
make allowance for gray ha
the ill-humor of advanced ag

"Yes," instantly added the s
shadow, "*carte blanche* belon
dies, children, and—"

He was going to add *old n*
a look from the general silenc

"No, nephew, don't be ap
sive," said the latter. "The w
of a gentleman are for nobl
than the punishment of insult

"Come, let us talk of so
else," said Gallardo's intima
ious to change the subject, b
in his heart, as were all th
guests, of the lesson the b
had received from so wort
authorized an antagonist.

"It is not possible, Gallar
you will allow Lucia to be
deemable lien upon you.
tell you, my boy, that it wou
pretty piece of folly on your
create an obstacle to your fu
tablishment.'

"I don't see that—in ord
a deputy, senator, or—"

"Oh! you're on the wron
Your political ideas absorb a
thoughts; but I have been t
one of her friends—that the
ter of Don Juan de Mone

* I know how to behave.
† Don John made of Money.

"*Taisez vous, mon cher*," entreated the model, in a low tone.

"I am not in the humor," replied the copy, in excellent Spanish.

"Of course he ought to marry," said all the rest.

"Let us understand each other, gentlemen," said the old general. "I think, Gallardo, that you ought to marry, not the mushroom of the millions, but Lucia."

These words were received with clamorous disapprobation.

"You take advantage of your *rôle* of Nestor, general," exclaimed the capitalist.

"The hero of former times dotes—I would say *radote*. I propose a vote of censure!" hiccoughed the copy.

"S-s-s, Boni. *Le vous en prie!** Do you want to get another broadside from the disabled old pontoon? Don't provoke him, for the next time neither prudence nor contempt will enable me to keep my temper," murmured his patron.

"The general is jesting. A gentleman of his fine delicacy cannot mean to counsel one, in Gallardo's position, to marry a woman of light reputation," said Gallardo's friend.

"I do it because I have delicacy—a plant that strikes so deep when once it has taken root, that neither the silver plough nor the golden spade which cultivates the field of ideas of the present day can turn it out. I counsel a man who has done a wrong to repair it. I advise one who has been the ruin of an honest girl to become her defender. And the more public he has made her position, the more he is bound to set her right in the eyes of others. If the future looks smiling, I counsel it all the more earnestly, that the past may not reproach him. In my days, gentlemen, marriages were not dis-

* "Hush, I beg of you."

cussed in semi-public m
The only counsellors were, ac
to the circumstances, the he
honor, and the conscience.
added the old man, rising, "r
timents are as much out of h
with yours, as my person is
place in a reunion of gay
men. Gentlemen, I salute yo
phew, good-by. Do not ask
your brilliant wedding if you
with the million-heiress of the
ces. If with Lucia, I will b
groomsman."

With these words the nobl
ran took his leave.

"Style of an epic poem," s
pseudo-Parisian.

"Tone of an *elegiac lyric*,"
mered the copy. "One woul
the governor had been drinkin
kind of palate-skinning Catala
instead of the excellent, exquis
lectable, delicious— "

"Enough, *Boni*," interrup
friend, indicating to him w
foot the urgent necessity of
discretion.

"The general has, so to
one foot in the grave, and, na
all looks to him *de profundis*
observed Gallardo's intimate.
we live in a positive age, an
conform to the step of its mar
do otherwise would be to ma
selves antiquated and ridiculo

Days followed days, eacl
bringing to our hero its busin
velty, interest, and forgetful
those that had preceded it.
in the meantime, saw her me
subsistence failing without inf
him; for, with the reawakene
ments of duty and shame, ca
comprehension of her guilty
dence, and sense of the doul
miliation of soliciting and rec
She had lived for some time
sale of her valuables, but t
source was almost exhausted.

La Giralda for insignia, and the verdure of its orange groves for adornment; the city that is at once gay as a village maiden and imposing as a queen; beautiful as a young girl, and full of wisdom and memories as a matron; graceful as the Andalusian of to-day, and chaste and noble as the Castilian dame of olden time.

Lucia found herself in Jerez alone and without resource, but, by favor of her good angel, met Uncle Bartolo at the inn where she alighted. The visible presence of the former would not have rejoiced her more than did the sight of this old friend of her family, to whom she told the whole of her sad story, adding that now she knew not what to do, since she dared not seek even a servant's place.

"My daughter," said the old guerilla, "you grew vain in the fiend's own house of *Leona*, and forgot that wings were given to the ant for its destruction. If you had shown that wretch a repulsive face, he would not have ventured to do what he did. What motive, will you tell me, could a *You Sir* have for playing clucking fox to a little country girl, but to make of her a mark for shame?

"However," he continued, seeing that Lucia's tears began to flow, "far be it from me to hack at the fallen tree, or double the burden of the ass that is down. The baptism of repentance opens the fold, and your repentance is sincere, because you return to poverty, when, if you had chosen otherwise, profligates would not have been wanting, in the great city, to complete your ruin. Come with me, and I will talk to Lucas. It is his duty to take care of you."

"He will never forgive me, Uncle Bartolo!" exclaimed Lucia sadly. "He has said that he had no sister, and no one can make him say the contrary."

"True," replied the gueri
Garcia heads are harder tha
I learned that by experien
your father—Heaven rest hin
ried *La Leona*. But this i
thing, for, notwithstanding
father did so badly, Lucas
ed out well. And it is a g
easier to yoke two that are
blood than to unyoke two
devil has united. We will
helping us, and, in the n
you shall come to my hou
is no great abundance, but
is not wanting."

The next day saw Uncl
and Lucia travelling along
which we described at t
mencement of our story
mounted upon a little ass,
agile good old man follo
foot. At nightfall they rea
cos.

Alas! for the one who,
to his native place, instead
riencing pure happiness,
heart torn by grief and shan
his parents dead, the house
was born the property of
and sees, in the looks of n
cold disdain instead of tl
smile of recognition and we

Uncle Bartolo took Lucia
house, and, while they were
supper, went himself to that
who, on receiving his disch
returned to Arcos and to
among the day-laborers, an
his aptness and diligence,
much credit that several
jobs and positions had alr
offered him. As will be sup
had found his father's hc
But as his kinswoman still l
he hired his former habita
she assisted him.

Uncle Bartolo entered,
Lucas had finished his sup

"Sit by, Uncle Bartolo,"
young man.

behind you the trust you received from your mother, and, without commending yourself either to God or the devil, shouldered your gun and made off; knowing that for six years, walled up in a uniform, you must lose sight of your charge; knowing, besides, that you were leaving her in a house where wickedness was well established. And so what happened, happened. The past is past, and can't be mended now; but after this, do you think it is right, Christian, that your sister should have no one to turn to when she leaves her sinful life?"

"She ought to have remembered in time that every uphill has its down."

"But, my son, is not this to

> 'See the ulcer, see the woe:
> Shut the purse, and naught bestow'?

This is to have bowels of a pagan toward a poor creature that they pushed and pushed—a child that did not know what they were doing."

"Uncle Bartolo, ignorance does not take away sin."

"Do you think, if you had had your evil hour—suppose it for instance, only—and had robbed or done something that had dishonored you, and had gone to your sister, that she would refuse to own you? I'll be bound she wouldn't!"

"Well, I should have acted badly. But the case is impossible, for it would have been my care not to put myself in her way. 'He that touches his own with his leprosy, gives it to them, and does not cure himself.'"

"Lucas, my son, the sentence says, 'Act with good intention, and not with passion!'"

"And the proverb says that 'blood boils without fire,' Uncle Bartolo."

"Lucas, for the love of the Blessed Virgin! How can he who shows no mercy hope for the mercy of

God? Do a good deed, and
you lie down, though it be
mattress of rushes, you wil
without bad dreams, and as
as if it were a bed of feathers!

"You are wasting words,
Bartolo. Even if I am conc
for it, I will not hear that vil
spoken of, and so—stop!"

"Go to, then, *Cain!*" exc
the good old man as he rose tc
"and God set a mark on you
did on the cruel brother t
cursed! I'd rather have he
her sin and her repentance, th
with your virtue and your pric

To paint the grief of the wr
Lucia when Uncle Bartolo in
her of the no-result of his n
would be impossible.

"Holy God!" she exclaim
tween her sobs, "only witl
shall I find mercy! Ah! how
ed this brother in the days
happy childhood, when I was
cent, and he was all my conso
Then he could not do enou
please me, and used to swear
to abandon me!"

"Come, come, dry your tea
daughter, said Uncle Bartolo.
frightened partridge is the
get skewered.' What do you
of an unnatural, without bow
compassion? You have m
the roof of my house is not so
that it cannot shelter you.
have you shall share, and yc
help my poor Josefa. She h
come a potsherd, and dor
much rest, for 'woman's work
and to be done again.'"

When the other inmates
house slept, Lucia kept lonel
and wept the things that had
ly made her happiness—her p
her innocence, and her broth
fection. Wandering in the va
of her recollections, she foun
affliction and consolation in re

THE LIQUEFACTION OF THE BLOOD OF ST. JANUARIUS.

NO. III.

But this is far from being the general rule. In 1543, the diary mentions the presence of Muleasses, Bey of Tunis, a Mohammedan, and records his expression of astonishment at what he beheld. On several other occasions, Mohammedans were witnesses of it; some became Christians. Protestant travellers from England, Denmark, Sweden, and Germany have written accounts of what they themselves saw. On four of the six occasions when the writer of these lines was present, he can bear personal testimony to the presence of Protestants.

It is narrated that the liquid blood has been known to solidify instantly, whenever the reliquary passed into the hands of a particular canon, in his turn of office, to be presented by him to the people, or when certain persons approached to venerate and kiss it, and would as quickly liquefy again when they withdrew. A notorious case is mentioned by the Bollandists, and by other authorities, of a prince, whose name, for family reasons, was not given—for the matter was published in his lifetime. At his approach the liquid blood used to become solid. His personal character left no doubt on the minds of the Neapolitans why this happened.

We have already spoken of the notable differences of color, on various days, or parts of the same day. The diary registers them as *bright*, *beautiful*, *vermilion*, *rubicund*, or as *dense* or *dark*, or *blackish*, or *ash-colored*, or, again, *pale* or *yellowish*. Sometimes the whole mass was of one uniform tint. Sometimes there were several tints in different parts, as in 1748, when, as we saw, one portion was blackish and the other ash-colored, the vial being then full, and the blood liquid, as afterwards appeared.

Again, the liquid blood is sometimes quite quiescent, yielding, indeed, to every movement of the ampulla, as water would, but when the ampulla is at rest on its stand, remaining in it as tranquil as water, with a level and smooth surface, and without the least indication of internal movement. Yet often it gives forth a froth or foam, which covers a part or all of the surface, which stains the glass dark or vermilion, and the remains or traces of which may be noticed on the mass when indurated afterwards; that is, if this foaming has continued until a solidification on the altar, or until the reliquary is locked up in the evening. Very often this foaming will cease after lasting half-an-hour or an hour. Its ending and disappearance is as fitful as its beginning.

Sometimes the motion is greater, and of a different character—an ebullition or boiling, as the Italians call it. Portions of the liquid blood are thrown up a quarter of an inch, or more. Sometimes this bubbling has been very violent, some of the liquid being thrown up into the neck of the ampulla to the very top.

On December 16, 1717, it is recorded that, before the liquefaction took place, and while the blood was still hard and solid, "an exhalation was seen to rise from the hard mass,

corded in the diary, to which we should add, perhaps, an equal number for the first category. A complete period, so to call it, of the fulness may vary, therefore, from a few moments to five consecutive days.

The second class comprises ninety-four instances of fulness opened and not completed during the octave. The varieties in these are even greater than in the former class. In *nineteen* cases the fulness, or, at least, its last phase, commenced on the closing day; in *five* cases, on the day before; in *nine*, on the third last day; in *eleven*, on the fourth; and in *twenty-two* on the fifth day, counting from the closing of the octave; in *twenty-six* cases, the fulness began on the sixth day; and in *two* cases, as far back as the seventh day, counting from the close of the octave. We have here twenty-eight of these incomplete periods, longer than the longest of the closed or complete periods, just mentioned, still further complicating any question as to the lengths of these periods of fulness.

Whenever, during an octave, the ampulla is locked up at night *full*, it will be found *full* the next morning. When it is locked up at the close of an octave in that state, it will be found in the same at the first opening of the next celebration, months afterwards. We said that the mass changed its volume only when in a fluid condition. We may now venture to add that such changes take place only in public, and never while the blood is closed up in the closet, or *armoire*. In examining the diary very carefully, we find that, in the vast majority of cases, the level of the mass as stated when taken out—whether it be at the ordinary level, or somewhat elevated, or very high, or full—perfectly agrees with the level at which it was stated to stand when last p whether the day before or close of the preceding octave. number of cases, indeed, the silent or obscure on the poir its language often seems to this fact, or to take it for g Nowhere does it state the rev general terms; and we cannot single instance recorded which lishes the contrary. The bl always found at the level at w stood when last put up.

These ninety-four unclosed p were, therefore, prolonged next festival, when the ampul taken out still *full.* Some o periods had just commenced last day; others had lasted days after the day of their mencement. Is there any r difference in their closing? the day; for they all, with th ceptions, closed on the first the incoming octave, if they h over to May or September, December 16, if that was th exposition. In regard to time is no rule. The most nu class, containing twenty-six ins varied from *immediately* to *nin and a half;* nine times the liq tion occurred in less than one and nine times it delayed mor three hours—the other eight t lay between the two. The t two cases of the next highes present the same diversities of from *immediately* to *nine hours half.* Nine instances were un hour, eight were over three the remaining five lay betwe two divisions.

The more those periods of are examined, the more clearl it appear that they follow no s and can be classified or acc for by no law. We see the swelling and increasing its v and filling the ampulla, and cc

kissed the relics in the hands of his eminence in the *Tesoro*."

However, the diary mentions that he did witness the liquefaction itself at the next regular day in May, with all the people.

Other instances are given in which viceroys and nobles and princes waited until they were tired out. Soon after their departure, when the faithful and fervent people might freely crowd the chapel and pray, the liquefaction would occur.

It is impossible to exaggerate the firmness of their faith or the depth and tenacity of the affection of the Neapolitans for this *their* miracle. Whatever else happens to their fair city, nothing must interfere with their devotion to St. Januarius and the proper celebration of these festivals—neither wars nor pestilence, nor eruptions nor earthquakes, nor change of rulers. Once a battle raging in the streets prevented an outdoor procession. But, within the cathedral, there was a procession through the aisles and nave, and all things else went on as usual.

Oddly enough, the greatest disturber, to judge by the simple-minded writers of the diary, has been—rain. Not that the weather has any direct influence on the liquefaction or its circumstances. Quite the contrary. The blood liquefies all the same, and with as many attendant variations, whether the day be fair or rainy, whether the season be so dry that the farmers are complaining of drought, and prayers have been ordered for rain, or whether it has been raining incessantly for weeks and months, to the injury of the crops, and in the churches they are praying for fair weather; in summer, when the sun is pouring down his almost tropical beams; and in winter, when the procession is confined to the cathedral because it is too cold to go out into the streets, or becau
ground is covered with snow.
meteorological changes have
parent influence on the lique
or its characteristic circumstan

But at Naples they sometim
terrible deluges of rain—steady
pourings such as one may
only within or close to the
Sometimes these have come
at the hour to interfere wi
grand afternoon procession
vigil in May, forbidding it, c
crously disarranging it, and
monks, friars, priests, semir
canons, and people alike to
the ranks and seek immediat
ter in the neighboring sho
houses. However, come what
at the worst, his eminence,
highest ecclesiastical dignita
sent, with a few attendants of
proof hearts, would carry th
in a sedan chair or a carr
might be, to the appointed pla
it not all punctually set dowr
diary; at what corner, or i
street, the procession was brol
and who then carried the re
and whether still on foot o
carriage, and how many cour
ly accompanied him? We r
sure that on arriving at their c
tion they never failed to fi
church, despite the rain, and
the absence of fashionable or
ed by devout souls, who love
saint more than they feare
such weather.

Passages in the extracts w
made from the diary, and ma
er passages we might quote, i
the feelings of alarm which
hearts of the Neapolitans wh
liquefaction fails to occur, o
tended by circumstances whi
traditionally dread. St. Janu
their patron saint. This eve
ring liquefaction is, in their eye
petual and miraculous sign

To complete our statement, we must, perhaps, go still further back, and inquire how it has come about that a portion of the blood of a Christian bishop, beheaded in the year 305, under Diocletian, and in virtue of edicts by that emperor for the suppression of Christianity, should, after the lapse of so many centuries, be now found in a glass ampulla, or vial, at Naples. To some, this primary fact may, at first sight, appear as strange and as extraordinary, if not as unaccountable, as the subsequent liquefaction itself.

To an Italian Catholic, indeed, a doubt on this head would scarcely present itself. The usages and the thoughts of his ancestors in the faith have come down to him so naturally that they form, as it were, part of his being. He thinks, and feels, and knows as his fathers did before him. In such cradle-lands of Christianity, and among a people that has never swerved from the faith since the early ages of the church, there is what we might term an inherited Catholic instinct, a readiness and a correctness of Catholic thought in religious matters, which those of other lands that received the light of Christianity only at a later period, and consequently have not such a bond of ancestral connection with the Christians of the days of persecution, can only reach by study and cultivated piety. However, even a moderate acquaintance with the usages and customs of those early ages will show in many instances that what some have considered peculiar national traits of perhaps later growth are in reality deeply rooted in the customs of those ancient times; and that many a point, often set down as a fond fancy or a singular product of superstition, is firmly established as a truth, by historical research into their records.

This is the case with the ç
before us.

As we study the daily life ‹
early Christians, passed un‹
cumstances so very differen
those of our modern life, an‹
to realize to ourselves their tl
and aspirations, their motiv
modes of action, nothing
out in bolder relief than their
conception of the honor an
of martyrdom. In the e
pages of *Fabiola* and of *Cali*
learned Cardinal Wiseman a
Newman have made thes‹
Christians live again before
we catch some insight int‹
enthusiasm on this subjec
them, a martyr, dying for tl
of Christ, was—and truthf
hero of the highest grade.
love than this no man hath
man lay down his life for his
John xv. 13.

They could never sufficientl
him. For, honor him as the)
all they could do would fall
ly short of the honor whi‹
had already bestowed on his
heaven, and that which he w‹
stow on his body in the resur
A martyr's blood, in their vie‹
next in rank to the blood of
viour.

Their daily life made ma‹
the prominent subject o
thoughts. Day after day, tl
their brethren seized, imprisor
tured, and put to death for tl
Each day, any one of the
might be seized and led to
dom. The greatest of all tri
and the surest passport to e
lasting bliss, was to persever
the end in that conflict; the ;
of all misfortunes was to fail
nounce or deny the faith f‹
of death. Each one strove ‹
himself ever ready for the trial
pastoral injunctions; their mu

of sponge or of cloth so saturated would be kept as a precious jewel in a locket of silver or gold, and be preserved in the oratory or chapel of a Christian household, or even be reverently borne on the person. Ordinarily, however, the vials or vases into which the martyrs' blood had been gathered, or the open vases containing the saturated sponge or the bundle of blood-stained cloths, would be placed with the body in the tomb; or the vials might be built into the masonry of the tomb, near the head, in such a way as to be partially visible from without.

The *Acta Martyrum*—the official records of the sufferings, death, and deposition or burial of the martyrs, written out at the time by appointed officers of the church—bear frequent testimony to the widespread existence of this custom. Other Christian writings, in prose and in poetry, refer to it frequently. We find it prevailing at Rome and in all Italy, in Carthage, in Sebaste, in Nicomedia, in Gaul, and throughout the church. It was the universal custom.

About the time when the body of St. Januarius was transported from the original tomb where it had been laid during the persecution, to the church of St. Januarius, *extra muros*, at Naples, similar translations of the bodies of martyrs took place elsewhere. St. Ambrose, the great Bishop of Milan, gives an account of such a ceremony for the martyrs St. Gervase and St. Protasius, and again for the martyrs St. Vitalis and St. Agricola. He mentions finding in the tombs, in both cases, the blood of the martyrs which had been gathered and placed there. St. Gaudentius, Bishop of Brixia, about the same time, mentions a similar fact. Some centuries later, the northern barbarians were making raids into Italy, and had repeatedly bro to and desecrated the sepul the catacombs, either in me tonness or in search for the t which they thought might be there. In order to save the ed relics of the martyrs fro outrages, the popes open tombs of the martyrs in the of the catacombs then acce a great portion being already up, either by the falling in roof or by the act of the Ch centuries before—and transfe remains to the churches wit city for greater safety. In the tombs, these vases wer found, and hundreds of th now in the churches or in the museums of Rome. Three c ago, Bosio, and after him Boldetti, Mamachi, and other trated into the catacombs, s them anew, and came upon s those portions which had no disturbed at the time of the removal. In such portions few unopened and undisturbed of martyrs were found. Wit the remains of the body—bon dust—with sometimes the ruste ments of the instrument of and frequently the vial, or a of the martyr's blood. Dur last forty years, the work of i gating the catacombs, whic been intermitted, has been ta afresh and prosecuted with e ness and skill by F. Marchi, C Rossi, and other eminent arc gists. They still come occas across the tombs of martyrs, e ly untouched since the day of sition, and within them, or mortar by the head, the va blood are still found. When vials are so placed in the mo to be visible and accessible without, the thin glass has ge been broken. But the botto

church of Naples, together with the other relics of St. Januarius, is under the circumstances *prima facie* evidence of its own authenticity—evidence which cannot be impugned, except by attempting to overturn a well-known and universally admitted usage of the early Christian church, or else by a supposition, equally gratuitous and absurd, that the ampulla which originally was in existence, and was prized beyond measure and carefully preserved, was somehow lost, and another fraudulently substituted in its stead. We need not recur to the olden traditions of the church of Naples or its legends concerning this relic—traditions and legends found, too, we believe, among the Greeks, whose intercourse with Magna Grecia, as Southern Italy was called, was more intimate and continued longer than with any other portion of Italy. We scarcely need the testimony of *Fabius Jordanus*, quoted by Caraccioli, going to show that, so far back as A.D. 685, it was the custom of the clergy of Naples to bear the relics of the head.

The historical evidence in favor of the genuineness of the relic is ample and satisfactory. There would not be a moment's hesitation on the point but for the very vain hope which some minds may entertain that, by declining to admit the genuineness of the blood, they will somehow escape the difficulties of the liquefaction. As if the liquefaction of any other substance, with all the circumstances which characterize the liquefaction at Naples, as we have set them forth in our previous articles, would not be for them as hard if not a harder nut to crack than the liquefaction of the blood of St. Januarius!

Having, therefore, established the genuineness of the relic, the next question which presents itself is this: Are we to attribute the amou the blood still to be seen with ampulla when at its ordinary and its condition when hard, continuous action of natural c or are we to recognize in points the effects of that sup ral force to which the lique itself is to be attributed? W would not the agency of n causes have resulted in a gre duction of the original volume blood, and in a far different co of the residuum, at the present

We know pretty accurate composition of human blood. proportions of the several ingr going to constitute it may somewhat according to the hea the food of individuals. W entering into the refined, and not fully accepted results of th qualitative analysis, it will be cient to give the following ta the constituents of the healthy of man:

Water, . . .		790·37
Albumen, . . .		67·80
Oxygen, . . .		
Nitrogen, . . .		
Carbonic acid, . .		
Extractive matters, .		10·98
Salts, ...		
Coloring matter, .		
Fibrine, . . .		2·95
Hæmatine, . .	2·27	
Globuline, . .	125·63	
Blood globules,		127·90
		1,000·00

Water constitutes nearly fou of the entire quantity. If it be off by evaporation, only a dr would remain behind.

When blood issues from the v first passes through the process gulation, the successive steps of have been carefully examined. fectly liquid as it comes ou blood soon thickens, throug action of the fibrine it contains, firm, elastic, uniform, jelly-like Soon drops of clear, amber ed fluid begin to exude fro

decomposition would have gradually passed through into the outer atmosphere, and only the dry solid residuum would be left, as we ordinarily find it in the ampullæ from the catacombs. The case of the ampulla containing the blood of St. Januarius is not open to these doubts. We are not able to say, indeed, whether it was actually closed in either of the modes we have indicated. As it stands in the present reliquary, of which we have given an account, the mouth enters so deeply into the upper mass of soldering within the case that the eye cannot discover the manner of closure. Before it was placed in this reliquary, five hundred and seventy or seven hundred and thirty years ago, this could probably have been seen; but we have found no record throwing light on the subject. We presume it was done in one or the other of the modes we have described. It is certainly so tightly closed that not a drop of the liquid blood within has ever been known to ooze out.

But this ampulla has not been lying in the low and equable temperature of an underground vault of the catacombs. It has been preserved in the upper and variable atmosphere of a city, subject for many centuries to the excessive heats of almost tropical summers, and to the cold winds that blow down at times from mountains covered with snow. By no law of physics could a mass of blood so situated escape the natu quence—a vast diminutio by the loss of water and of gases. The film that interior of the smaller am in the same case or reliqu the film seen in the whole broken ampullæ of the and churches generally, think, what would have natural course.

That the larger ampul on the contrary, have lost the volume of its conten should still be four-fifths though for centuries expo have said, to heat and cold- general permanence of bu character should be main though eighteen or twen year the mass alternates f id to a fluid condition, a through many subordinat of color and volume—tl seem to us not only utter cable, but directly contrar know of physical laws. them along side the grand liquefaction itself, as bein measure its characteristic tants. Still, should any these questions too obsc peremptorily decided, we now discuss them. We willing to let them stand c the more prominent and and more tangible questi liquefaction itself. Of tha now proceed to treat.

TO BE CONTINUED.

THE WAYSIDE SPRING.

FROM THE FRENCH OF ALPHONSE DE LAMARTINE.

As here is quaffed a sweet forgetfulness
Of the long journey yet to go,
So unto all who through life's pathways press,
Lord, from thy rock let waters flow!
Let thy sweet grace refreshment be!
On earth we wander wearily,
And in a thirst that will not cease.
Oh! let each dry and dusty lip
From thy deep hidden fountain sip
Sweet draughts of love and peace.

Ah! every soul drinks its own cup of bliss.
Some the delights of glory bless;
One finds it in a little daughter's kiss,
Another in a wife's caress.
The secret friendships of the heart,
The rapture of creative art,
Each hive its own sweet honey stores;
To every lip let torrents burst
From life's great fount; but I—*I* thirst
For the eternal shores.

Earth's dreams are but a bitterness to those
Whose yearnings are for love divine.
No rivulet sparkles here, no runlet flows,
To satisfy this thirst of mine.
What shall assuage it? The desire
That heavenward ever doth aspire,
And sigheth ceaselessly;
The sweetness that in suffering lies,
And tear-drops showering from my eyes,
Are hope's one draught for me.

VALENTINE.

FROM THE REVUE DU MONDE CATHOLIQUE.

"FRANKLY, my dear friend, tell me, is she not charming? Does she not lend a certain grace to her white dress, and a brilliancy to her blue ribbons? Is she not the prettiest flower in my garden?"

"And my Alfred, dear Madame de Guers, does he not look well by her side? Are there many young men in our village who appear to such advantage near this fair and graceful darling, now in the flower of her youth?"

"What you say is true, my friend. We have both of us, thank God, fine children—noble, virtuous, and good; and I hope they will be happy."

"They will make a very handsome couple, at all events," concluded M. Maubars, rubbing his hands and smiling contentedly.

Thus spoke two old friends, as they sat quietly, one summer evening, in the shadow of the hop-vines of a pretty green arbor, and talked away in this simple, lively, and joyous manner, while they observed their children as they appeared here and there in the garden-walks.

When people have passed fifty, and known each other since they went to the same school in childhood, and during the long succeeding years have resided pretty much in the same place, they are very apt, when talking together, to speak openly from their hearts, especially if those hearts are filled to the brim and running over with justifiable paternal pride and motherly tenderness.

And it was true that the dear . the only and cherished son Maubars, was handsome, hon tive, and gifted, and, thanks fortune which he would inherit, one day take his place amo most respectable citizens of th vince. As to Madame de this fair and worthy old lad white hair, in whom all the souls of the little town salute recognized a sister, all the p benefactress, and all the affli friend, she had never been a m She had married late, less fr clination than duty, to obey of her parents and fulfil a project; she had cared for, w admirable devotion, and sup with a no less admirable equal temper, the precocious infi and frequent brusqueries of Guers, who, as former captai vessel, had lived a silent, s deserted life in an old cold-l little house on the coast. B happy day the sun seemed to brighter for her, and the radia timent of an unknown hap mingled with her tears and h grets, as one of the friends childhood, a poor widow, in confided to her the educatio guardianship of her deserted What a complete happiness, v recompense for all the sunless the gloomy and heavy hours, s fully supported! M. de Guers, t very ill at the time, consented ceive the child, on condition, added peremptorily, "that she be kept very neat and mak

about in the garden-walk, as running from side to side to form their bouquet they chanced so often to meet. But, under the arbor, they were more grave, calmer, and certainly more mature, and they spoke of business.

"If you will permit it, my dear friend, I should like the young couple to live in my house," said M. Maubars. "It is, I may say, without vanity, one of the most comfortable and best furnished in the town. As to me, you know, I am becoming a monk, or a bear, or a house-rat. The rolling of the half-dozen coaches and the three or four cabs our town possesses is sufficient to trouble my digestion, and almost deafens me; so I think, in order to plant my cabbages in peace, I had better lodge in the pavilion of my large garden at Vaux, which is not more than a league from the town. My good old Baptistine will accompany me, and keep the pot boiling. Every evening the children can come and see me, that is, every fine evening; and you can have them right by you—nothing to do but cross the street, and walk a few steps on the quay, ring the little bell, the latch will fly up, and there will be Valentine in a clean dress and red ribbon coming to meet you, for her delicate hearing would distinguish your step among a thousand others on the same pavement."

"Poor dear child! I don't want to be selfish, and yet it is hard to part with her," murmured Madame de Guers, while stifling a sigh.

"Do you call that parting with her, when I tell you she will be right under your eye? And then, my dear friend, I must tell you you have become very worldly of late. You are obliged to accompany Valentine to this and that soirée, and it fatigues you, absorbs and puts you out altogether. When it comes my Alfred's turn to do all this fo you will see how you will im and old ladies always recov naturally. Confess it, my dea dame de Guers, have you n some time been very neglige yourself and your old people?"

"Alas, yes! poor good old pe replied the respectable lady, sweet smile. "Yet every mo after Mass, I stop to see them. my child monopolizes much time I should give to them, b loves them too: she has so lent a heart! How often I seen her, when quite a child, from her weekly allowance t jujube for old Manou, who h tarrh so badly, and tobacco f rine, whose happiness is in sm And how she takes care of when necessary, my friend! merry she makes them, and co them, and reads them good and the Scripture she expla prettily! In truth, this humble will not perish with me: I have one to whom I can confide it."

This demands an explan Madame de Guers was not o excellent, tender, and devote ther, a constant and generous but she was, at the same time foundly pious and sincerely c ble. The death of M. de had left in her soul a bitter a cret sorrow, which she had been able to console. The lieutenant of the service, in sp the solicitations and tears Christian and devoted wife, ha farewell to this world in a m far from exemplary, dying, w doubt, peaceably and bravely e but without repentance, without without penitence, neither fixi eyes on the cross nor listening absolution of the curé. So, f poor, tender soul of the wife remained a gnawing regret, a

replied the adopted mother with a sigh of relief. "Assuredly," she continued with a sweet and mischievous smile, "I am very sure that it is not with dowry or business that they are entertaining themselves just now."

This you may be assured of, my readers, for, just then, Valentine, spreading into a sweet smile her fine and delicate lips, while her brilliant eyes sparkled above the cheeks as rounded and satiny as the petals of her roses, said to her partner, who was coming toward her:

"You had better believe me, Mr. Alfred. We will not go to Paris. Paris is very far off, and it costs a great deal to go there. But we will go every evening and see dear papa in his little pavilion at Vaux. Won't it be charming to do just as we did when we were little, ten years ago, just us two alone, you and I, running through the ruts and the fields, gathering the new hay and the herbs covered with dew?"

And the simple child, clapping her white hands, gently smiled still more joyously at the innocent, truant projects with which she proposed to inaugurate their future housekeeping. Then, Alfred having offered his arm, she accepted it a moment in order to adjust with her young intended some other detail of great importance, which she must tell her mamma immediately — mamma holding her breath meanwhile, hearing vaguely the murmur of the wind in the arbor and smiling with tenderness as her child approached.

"Mamma," cried Valentine, throwing her arms around her mother's neck, and with a caressing and infantine movement mingling the waves of her lustrous hair with the fine, heavy gray curls, "did you not say that the anniversary of your birth would come in two weeks, the second of next month, and that you woul
see Alfred and me choose
to celebrate our betrothal?"

"Yes, my darling," repl
dame de Guers gently.

"Very well, dear mam
all arranged; we will exch
rings on the same day that
so dear a mamma. But I
decided anything about th
tions?"

"I have at least thought
my child. We will have,
the greater part of those of
society, and especially, yo
stand, all your young friends

"Yes, just as you wish.
to be only for the even
mamma?"

"Ah! my little ambiti
wishes to give a whole da
fête."

"Indeed I do, mamma
dreamed of it even, so I ma
confess. I want particularl
morning to have those I i
to myself; I will receive the
them, and serve them with
hands. O mamma! it wi
nice, in the shady part of the
among the flowers, to set t
tables, and have an excellen
fast, good wine, cakes, a ro
Pierrot the violinist with hi
and the baskets all filled w
ers! And my guests will be
prised, and so pleased, my d
mamma!"

"But who are they, then?

"Your old women, dear n

Madame de Guers's respon
take the pretty brown hea
charming child in her t
hands, and to press it tend
long upon her lips, while
shivering of admiration a
made her heart beat.

"It is said," she replied at la
table shall be set for fifteen, a
shall be cakes and violi

friend and protectress, pressed it between her own, and repeated in mourning accents:

"Miss Valentine, you deserve to be truly happy; you know how to give blessings like the good God, whose care and pleasure it is to think of the poor."

Thanks to the pleasure of such a repast and so much time so happily spent, the old guests lingered around the table in the garden, and exceeded the limits of the morning hours. When at last they wended their way homeward, accompanied by the good sister who took care of them, they met on the road several of those invited for the afternoon, friends of Valentine mostly, accompanied by their mothers, in elegant toilets, and coming in great pomp to offer their compliments.

"Why, how is this, my dear? Have the old pensioners of Madame de Guers come to congratulate you?" asked Rosine Martin, one of the young ladies, as she entered and embraced her friend.

"Yes, Rosette, on this occasion I gave them a little *fête*. They breakfasted here and drank my health; and, do you know, Pierrot played the violin, and old Manou was so excited she actually danced a minuet."

"Do you hear what Valentine is saying?" whispered Madame Martin to her friend and confidante, Madame Fremieux. "I always thought Madame de Guers put on the airs of a great lady, and, of course, will leave the same to Valentine, as foundress of charitable institutions. Insupportable, is it not? And charity costs something too. It is well to make a parade of it, whether one has it or not; and the question is, whether it is prudent to put such ideas into the child's head, when she will give her at the very most two poor thousand francs?"

"Provided that charity is a
like any other, and often m
prudent than any other," add
tentiously, Madame Fremieu
she pulled out with her righ
the crushed ruche of her gre
dress.

"What an odd fancy you h
these old gossips, Valentine
Adeline de Malers, anothe
friend, a pretty young woman w
handsome children, whom
gaily into the garden. "Th
go, charmed with your recepti
repeating your name to all the
of the town. Well, it is a go
while you are waiting and l
little to do, and nothing much
See what will become of the
you will be mamma in your t
dear!"

"Do you think so, Adeli
cannot agree with you," repli
entine, blushing a little. "M
good mamma Marie always
time to give me all her care, h
and her watchfulness, and ye
sure she never neglected the
old friends. It seems to m
when one becomes a moth
desires to heap up a treasure o
actions, and multiply one's
and virtues, in order that G
requite the little good one
graces and benedictions o
dear little heads."

"You always have a sent
way of seeing things," replied A
stooping and arranging with h
fingers the white plume that
the hat of baby; "but I doub
Alfred Maubars will give th
light to the chapter; for, m
one, husbands are not nonen
the future organization of a
hold; their decrees are ine
and must be listened to."

"O Adeline! do you reall
that Alfred would wish to
my doing a little good in a

must confess you do things royally. It certainly cannot be these ladies, with their small, very small fortune, who have by themselves given us such a *fête* as this. And then, it is not according to their tastes. If by accident they should have a little too much money, they would have less pleasure in offering a ball to their friends than a breakfast to their old poor."

"My dear Madame Martin, when one does as one can, one does as one should," replied, with a deep bow, M. Maubars, responding to her compliment to himself. "As to these ideas of our excellent friend Madame de Guers, you see, we must not be surprised at them. She has always lived a little above our so-called middle society; she is a woman—how shall I say it?—well, of the old *régime*. In her devotions, in good works, and perseverance, she has grand ideas; the commandments of Christ, the love of her neighbor, the good of the poor. It is all beautiful, Madame Martin, and sits superbly on a woman like her, grave and dignified, with such handsome white hair."

"But for the little one—for Valentine—do you think, M. Maubars, that it will suit her as well?" replied, quickly, the lady, with a mocking smile.

"Oh! why not? Everything becomes a child. All these fine devotions are an occupation for the widow and an amusement for the little one. It is much better to direct her by caring for the poor than by ruining the reputations of others and seeking false excitements. Wait till Valentine becomes the wife of Alfred; that will change everything, you know, neighbor. The dear child will only have one end, one duty, one love—her husband."

"Do you really think so, neighbor?" interrupted Madame Martin, in a jeering tone.

"It is, at least, what all women promise at the altar, madame. And Valentine will do as she promises, I am certain. A child so docile, a nature so pliable, and a heart of gold. Yes, madame; I do not doubt, if my Alfred wishes it, she will prefer the road to the market or the grocery in preference to that of the church. And as to the refuge of which you speak, Madame de Guers will take care of that, as it will be her only occupation. My daughter-in-law will visit it occasionally in her leisure moments."

"It will become her well to adapt her household to his wishes; for every one knows, neighbor, your son brings her a fortune far superior to her own."

"Alas! yes, you say truly; her dowry is the only weak point."

"The little one will have scarcely anything, will she, M. Maubars?" asked the lady precipitately, in her ardent, almost joyous curiosity.

"Oh! a modest cipher, but enough. There is nothing to complain of. If it had been less, I confess I do not know what Alfred would have done. The needs of luxury are so numerous nowadays, and it costs so much to live, my dear lady!"

"Yes, we all know that," replied the prudent mother. "This is the reason I calculate, and economize, and stint myself every day for the love I bear Rosette. According to my ideas, it is a culpable charity that does not consider one's own first."

At the enunciation of this wise maxim, M. Maubars sighed profoundly. At the bottom of his heart he could not help wishing, in the interest of Valentine and Alfred also, that Madame de Guers, his dear old friend, had less tenderness and greatness of soul, less gen-

having sought her white marriage robes. Alas! it was a robe of mourning that covered her now, poor little one! She had again become an orphan; her sweet and careless happiness of the young daughter, the cherished child so tenderly protected, was all gone, destroyed for ever, for ever lost with the last swallows that fled from the woods with the first falling leaves. The most devoted care, the greatest affection and constancy, could not preserve to her this nervous and tender mother, whose life here below was sad enough, and whose death would have been sweet, had she not so felt for and trembled for her child. Her illness, however, had been long and courageously combated, and for some time there was hope of triumph over the disease, until one day, when Valentine was absent on a pilgrimage to a neighboring chapel, a sudden hæmorrhage set in, and Madame de Guers, feeling it necessary to use what strength she had left, sent for several papers, and with pain wrote for her adopted daughter directions which were not to be opened until a month after her death, when the first transports of grief were over.

The fatal moment then came, and by one of the last auroras of September, soft, fresh, and almost veiled, Valentine found herself on her knees by the bedside of the dying, exchanging the last adieux with her tender benefactress, the devoted mother who, from her infancy, had so unceasingly studied her happiness. The poor child remembered no more: grief had completely prostrated her, and she forgot her own existence until one evening, returning to consciousness, she found herself clothed in deep black, and alone with Marianne, the old and faithful servant, who wept low by her side and tried to console her. Then, M. Maubars and Alfred had come, and felt a secret consolation ii of her sadness. It was s toning and strengthening one's self still loved whi stances had separated he upon whom she had lavis wealth of affection. It i consolations offered by father-in-law and betrothe of the highest order of mo not very profound, perhap were truly affectionate and at least, Valentine thoug they had power to alleviat and restore her heart's ser

"What would you, my c are all mortal," said the fu "But we can still console and live almost happy in t the friends that remain to

Alfred did not even say But he looked at her ten a gentle expression of in pity; he quietly took the l and thin hand that lay la her black drapery, and pr tween his own, while he n

"Poor dear Valentin friend, so dearly loved." simple words, this look, tionate gesture from the fri childhood, seemed to op heart-broken young girl a sure of hope and consolati

The days, however, r grief was not less profound stant, or less bitter, but necessarily more contained, signed, was borne more v secret, giving place to aust the serious preoccupation The time came, naturally, v ness had to be spoken of tine. Until then, with r her grief and her weakness, spared her every propositi discussion on the subject.

"I will do all that is n murmured the poor child.

know with what end, a work of mercy that I wished to succeed and prosper a long time, even when my presence and aid would have, by the will of God, been withdrawn from my poor old *protégées*. This charitable foundation has been for me the object of grave and disquieting cares, that till now I have never found necessary to confide to you. I have just learned that the proprietor of the building that shelters my poor old pensioners, having some speculation in view, has decided to take possession of it and its dependencies himself, or will only permit me to retain it under conditions too exacting to be in harmony with my slender resources. Many people of judgment whom I have consulted have all counselled me to choose another abode and there install my pensioners. If I had found myself, as formerly, alone in the world, I should not have hesitated to do so; but to find a suitable house and pay several debts of my poor little hospital—for times have not been good for a few years past—I should have had to have laid out at least twenty thousand francs, almost the half of my present fortune; and could I deprive you of so important a sum—you, my best loved and only heiress, who cannot have the same reasons for being interested in the existence of the work, and therefore its continuation?

"This idea has not seemed possible to me, my dear child; therefore I have made no reserves, no stipulations in the interests of my poor old dependants, leaving it to your reason, not less than to your generous heart, to decide what you find best to do. Perhaps the advice, the support of the new family into which you are going to enter, of my good friend M. Maubars, whom I have always known so loyal and just, will be at your service, and, without impoverishing yourself, you ‹
those whom I have always
so much to see prosper. 1
vice, then, of these friends, my
ter, consult your own faculti
strength, and, above all, do n
pitate anything. It would ha
too painful for me to have
the thought of relinquishing tl
which has been so dear and
ing, therefore I speak to y
to-day, confident you will unc
me in this as in everything els
in any event, I hope that Pro
will continue to watch over t
dest foundation for his glo
whatever you decide to do, n
and tender child, be assur
will have my approval and m
ing.

" Farewell, joy and consola
my old years, sweetness of
my dear daughter. I will no
you in the presence of my
he will deign to hear my pray

Thus the letter finished, a
sad and continued voice of l
rin, which seemed to die out
murs, was only replied to by t
and bitter sobs of Valentine.

At the end, the young gi
bling and half-tranquillized, ap
ed the notary, turned towa
her mild countenance, where
smile of gratitude and tender
ready commenced to shine as
tive and light ray in the mids
tears.

" Monsieur Morin, in four
I will be twenty-one," said she.
haps the proprietor of the
will wait till then. I shall
then, will I not, to give the
thousand francs necessary for t
chase of the house?"

A profound silence, soon in
ed by a feeble murmur, gre
first these words of the orpha
Maubars rose from his chair,
ged his shoulders slightly, ap

But from time to time a deeper and more sombre shade spread over her eyes, an expression more desolate fixed itself on her lips. When the caressing and persuasive voice of her future father-in-law ceased to be heard, she sadly bent her head, and replied:

"Alas! Monsieur Maubars, I see we can never again understand each other. I am not free, as you appear to think. What my dear and worthy protectress would have done, I must do for her."

"But, my child, reflect: you cannot sacrifice your little fortune."

"And this fortune, to whom do I owe it, then—I, a poor, abandoned orphan, who, without the generous protection of this inestimable friend, would have been sent in years gone by where you would place these poor infirm people—in a hospital. Oh! my good Monsieur Maubars, if my benefactress had in dying left some debt of honor that I should pay, would you advise me to cancel the obligation—you who are so just and honorable?"

"But, dear young lady, the case is different; your excessive delicacy leads you astray."

"It is only different in one respect: it is more grave and solemn. This is a sacred debt that Madame de Guers has contracted toward God and toward the poor, to satisfy the yearning of her soul. To-day this debt is transmitted to me. I recognize it; I receive it with the rest of her heritage; I promise to use, if necessary, all my resources, all my time, all my strength to pay it as I should."

The young girl, pale though resolute, rose in pronouncing these words, and extended her little hand, that had ceased to tremble, as if she called upon all the strangers assembled to witness her irrevocable decision, her generous determination. The old frequenters of the mansion scarcely recognize her: she s to have grown taller, ripene moment, and was transfigured. former sweetness, so timid and ing, did not abandon her, but mingled in it an expression of cible courage and inflexible i ty; the weak and feeble chil disappeared, and in her pla peared a woman—loyal, intrep signed, ready for every devoti every sacrifice, even of the and most cherished affections heart.

M. Maubars was undeceiv was with an expression eviden extreme surprise and marked tent that he fell back a few and bent his whitened head: " sist in hoping, mademoiselle, th will still reflect," said he, in impressed with remarkable co "Otherwise, you understand, w doubt, our projects must u some modification. Conside such obstinacy on your par most unhappy precedent for th being and peace of your future hold."

At this brutal menace, at th saddest moment, perhaps, of h Valentine became still paler a look more sombre, but she trembled nor flinched, acceptin out a murmur and in silence bitterness of the duty she ha embraced. Only, by an ol tender habit of childhood, wi remains of a hope perhaps, he more eloquent and earnest tha was fixed upon Alfred—the the betrothed, whom, for so a time, she had been accustor consult in any sadness or disqu But Alfred, before the mute a of this regard, was not moved bore with his father an air of and dissatisfaction.

"I am sure you will reflect

tion strengthened by the secret prayers and solitude of her affliction.

"My dear," said Adeline to her at the end of her arguments, "if you grow poor by this foolish liberality, and if, half-ruined, you are obliged to give up M. Alfred Maubars, you will be an old maid, I warn you."

"I have always been a happy young girl, I can be a tranquil and contented old maid. Happiness has no age," replied Valentine, with her calm and tender smile.

"My dear, the obliged are generally ungrateful; gratitude from the poor is a rare and uncertain commodity."

"I know it; but the satisfaction of an accomplished duty is immense, and the grace of God infinite. Besides, I shall be so happy to realize the intentions and to continue the work of my mother, who is in heaven."

Adeline shrugged her shoulders with a gesture of impatience. "But your poor old folks won't live for ever, and when the last one has disappeared, your work will be finished, and you will be alone. Besides, in devoting yourself in the flower of your years to their catarrhs and their rheumatisms, do you know, my poor child, what you renounce and what you lose? Come here, Bertha, my treasure, kiss me, Max, you dear little angel. . . . Look at them now, you wicked little obstinate one, and tell me, as you examine them well, if all the happiness, all the glory of a woman, does not consist in raising, caring for, and cherishing such charming little loves."

At these words, Valentine drew the little ones to her; kissed each of their pretty white foreheads, and laid her hand gently on their blonde heads; for she had at heart that tender and deep love of children that God has given innocent young girls, in order that one day their m[illegible] duty may become their tru[illegible] sweetest happiness. And for [illegible]stant perhaps the caressing lo[illegible] she fixed upon them becam[illegible] tender, deeper, and more tear[illegible] stooped then a moment tow[illegible] earth; then resumed her s[illegible] and replied peaceably and [illegible] signation:

"God has given me my [illegible] —children, Adeline, who ha[illegible] need of me, for they are s[illegible] poor, and feeble. Besides, m[illegible] friend, when the last of the[illegible] old people shall have gon[illegible] will remain to me the foundat[illegible] hospital. I will open it then [illegible] children, to young and poor c[illegible] In this way, I too will have [illegible]mily—my family blessed by [illegible]

"It is fanaticism, truly, an[illegible] gin to despair of your fut[illegible] dear friend," cried Adeline, s[illegible] and discontented to find he[illegible] tures so energetically repulsed [illegible] then, why do you persist in [illegible] ing in the world, that will onl[illegible] believe me, disdain for your h[illegible] coldness and raillery for yo[illegible] rous devotion? Why do yo[illegible] once adopt the cornette and s[illegible] the Sister of Charity?"

"Because, thus far, God ha[illegible] commanded me," replied the [illegible] geous child, modest and r[illegible] "My duty lies near these old [illegible] here my place is marked [illegible] have nothing else to do but [illegible] stand, adore, and obey. A[illegible] I have friends among my [illegible] I esteem and love the[illegible] Why should these friends a[illegible] me because a sacred duty c[illegible] portion of my time and my s[illegible] and I must consecrate mysel[illegible] My destiny is no doubt chan[illegible] my heart will never chan[illegible] from those I should have lo[illegible] memory will never be detac[illegible]

ing finished the reading of the Scriptures to the old Genevieve, she heard in the street, quite close to her, a great noise of carriages, rolling joyously towards the church, from which resounded the sounds of a *fête*, and, looking out the window to explain the cause of the tumult, she saw in the first of the carriages, ornamented with wedding favors, bouquets, and ribbons, two friends of her childhood: the betrothed of that day, Alfred Maubars and Rosine Martin. There passed over her face a calm smile, vague and almost dreaming; then a fixed and disturbed look, for at the bottom of the page, as she read, were these words: "*It is not good for man to be alone.*"

But almost immediately resounded in her ears the caressing and infantine voices of childhood, those of two little orphans, her cherished dependants, who had taken the places of Babet and Manou, dead full of years, and now quietly reposing in their graves. At the joyou Valentine was once more l and, with a calm smile, bendi head as if she recognized her she said:

"Yes, indeed, it would t to be alone, but those are n who know how to love. Dea ma told me so, and well sh what she said. Come, Marie Louisette, let me say the with you." The little ones ap ed, knelt down, and she la hands on their heads, and their browned foreheads. A fore she made the sign of th she regarded them earnestl with a joyful, softened, pea and triumphant gaze, even pression of indifference and fulness to the carriage that w ing towards the church, and s at last full of gratitude and l benediction and prayer, and her eyes to the clear and blue that caressed her with its gold-

---

TRUE FAITH.

Faith is no weakly flower,
By sudden blight, or heat, or stormy shower
To perish in an hour.

But rich in hidden worth,
A plant of grace, though striking root in earth,
It boasts a hardy birth.

Still from its native skies
Draws energy which common shocks defies,
And lives where nature dies!

E. Casv

tence of their country. The Commune did not conceal its affection for such auxiliaries, but its caresses were to some of a more serious and compromising nature.

Formerly, the most ultra never dreamed of giving up their patriotism. It was reserved for the members of the Commune to divest themselves of this old prejudice of all nations. They vehemently demanded, during the siege of Paris by the Prussians, the most extreme measures—a general sortie, "*des battailles torrentielles*," and fighting to the last. When conspiracy made them masters of Paris, their violence and ferocity against the Prussians changed to obsequious devotedness and civilities of the most amicable nature. Their dishonest protestations were displayed in the columns of the official journal of the Commune with a coolness that makes one blush. The delegate of foreign affairs treated the Prussians, who had just lacerated and humiliated France, and bombarded its capital, as if they were our most faithful allies, and were sacrificing themselves heroically for our safety.

The generals of the Commune, who had been imprisoned some weeks before by the government of the national assembly as Prussian spies and agents, made no change in their patriotic course. The delegate of war, General Trochu, recalled at the tribune, "is making a series of rigorous arrests, the object of which is to assure to the enemy the freedom the pending negotiations confer on them."

The politicians and chemists of the Commune proved they had been in a good school by borrowing two ideas of M. de Bismarck and M. de Moltke, the very names of which now inspire horror—the system of hostages and the use of petroleum. To ensure the entire payment of the exorbitant requisitions on the invad-

ed provinces, and somewh
the limited enthusiasm mai
the humiliated and sufferi
tants, the Prussians retaine
notable individuals as hos
sent them to the prisons of
Citizens Ferré and Raou
found this system too ing
convenient not to be adopt
took as hostages, and i
them at Mazas and La Ro
priests and laymen who,
to the opinion of these ser
tors, had been more devot
cial and national interest
those of anarchy and dema

Fourteen months ago, a
dictionary was discovered in
quarters of the Internat
which was a list of such w
tro-glycerine and picrate c
um, and a recipe for sulp
carbon, and the chlorate a
ate of potassium. At the
recipes were these words, s
of the uses to which they w
applied: "To throw from
dows: to be thrown into th
If the most formidable of
not to be found there, it i
the citizens of the Commun
yet learned in the school of
engineers the art of destroyi
and monuments by means
leum.

In continuing the accou
horrible deeds of the Con
find consolation as a Fren
the thought that the murd
incendiaries of Paris denied
their God, but their country
they were members not o
criminal, but a foreign leag

THE CLOSING OF THE MAI

In following with serious
the various evolutions of t

into the hands of the committee of public safety and the central committee. On Wednesday, the seventeenth of May, in going to administer the last sacraments to the daughter of a concierge in the Rue de la Victoire, I found the ninth arrondissement hemmed in by the insurgents, who were making frequent arrests. Thanks to one of the most ultra journals of the Commune that I pretended to be reading very attentively, I passed through their inquisitorial ranks unimpeded.

On the eighteenth, which was Ascension day, the church of St. Augustine was closed, and one of the vicars and the organist were imprisoned. All the offices of the day were celebrated at the Madeleine, attended by a numerous and very devout congregation; but, so far from yielding to any illusion about the fate that awaited me, I begged Dr. B. de L——, a parishioner of the Madeleine, to enable me after vespers to see M. Jacquemin, one of the physicians of the prison of Mazas. There was every reason to believe I should soon require his kind services. I was already acquainted with M. de Beauvais, the second physician at Mazas, whose courageous devotedness I was subsequently to experience, and who had already been so thoughtful as to give me news of the curé of the Madeleine and of the Archbishop of Paris. After my interview with Dr. Jacquemin, I felt some embarrassment about returning to my residence. The Rue de la Ville-l'Evêque was filled with an armed band of the national guards. The house of the Sisters of Charity, opposite the Presbytère, was guarded by two sentinels. The sisters had been expelled, and the girls' school confided to some *citoyennes*, who, according to the unruly tongues of the quarter, had been replaced at the prison of St. Lazare by th ters of Picpus, who were accu a series of crimes, each one m traordinary than the rest. I bou on the previous day, one of th journals of the Commune, and, with this new kind of a safe-co I took a roundabout way to th la Ville-l'Evêque, in order to the national guards as much a sible. Once their protection have been eagerly sought ag robber or assassin, but since th of the Commune respectable feared and fled from them a worst of evil-doers. And the ne litary organization will doubtles to undergo a radical transforn for it will be difficult for it t above the moral discredit into it has fallen.

Some moments after, a priest, who had gi en himself u indefatigable zeal to the servi the ambulances, notified me th order had been signed to clo churches and arrest the priest in Paris. I went to see one devoted *confrères*, M. de Bre and consult with him abou means of preserving the hol charist from profanation. Th surgents had already thrown or carried off in their cartridge- the sacred elements in some churches. At this very tim church of St. Philippe-du-Roul entered by the insurgents, an want of priests they arreste employees who were guardin church. The Madeleine of the arrondissement was the only c that was still open.

Although, after the arrest Deguerry, a part of the valuab the church had been carried safe place, I employed the fir ments of Friday, the nineteer confiding the remainder to son men of the working-classes. I

er. "If you continue to treat me in this way, I shall seat myself without another word, and force alone shall tear me from this sanctuary."

He made a sign to his followers to moderate their civic indignation, but without being heeded. I now sought to lead them into a discussion, hoping to appease them and preserve the church from devastation by making them incapable of justifying their acts and outrages. For two hours—hours that seemed ages—I was obliged, under the greatest peril, to defend myself as a man and a priest against these emissaries, who were as ridiculous as they were odious. I will relate the principal points in this interchange of observations.

I first asked why I was arrested. At this question the delegate of the committee of public safety replied by a torrent of accusations and maledictions against the "miserable quarter of the Madeleine, the most hostile in Paris to the *régime* of the Commune." He was not wholly wrong in this, for at the last elections the parish of the Madeleine, which comprises about forty thousand inhabitants, did not give more than a hundred votes to the candidates of the Commune. In the eighth arrondissement, where the church is, of about nineteen thousand votes, only five hundred voted for the Communist members. He added: "You must therefore expiate your conspirations in favor of the Versailles assassins." Here the delegate was no longer right. But it was evident that I was arrested because I was the "citizen director of the Madeleine," and they would make me expiate the sympathy and concurrence that the parishioners of the Madeleine had the unpardonable offence to refuse the Commune. To gain more time and thus calm their fury, I spoke of political affairs. My observations visibly disconcerted my interlo The epithets, *canaille*, *crapul* assassin, became more and rare, and their revolvers, at fi actively and impertinently exe were returned by degrees to cases.

Another incident that migh been fatal to me served still m disconcert them. During th half of the reign of the Com the affair of the bodies found Laurent, Notre Dame des Vic and Notre Dame de Lorette h unfortunate effect. Disregardi reports of the physicians and was clearly evident, the revolu papers, the *Journal Officiel*, a clubs exclaimed at the scandal. most abominable crimes were i ed to the clergy, against wh diabolical persecution was exci extravagant accounts and vil tures. In vain were these ex gances met by decisive reason reasons themselves became ne jects of crimination and inve which gave me great concern.

The vaults of the Madelein at this epoch filled with bodies. ing the siege of Paris by the sians, the bodies of several ge and foreigners of distinction been deposited there till they be carried to their distant tombs. I had for several days on the explanation I could gi specting these bodies so as to these furious madmen, but had none. The time had come w needed it.

"It is in this miserable pari the Madeleine," exclaimed the gate of the Commune with a of contempt and hatred, "th shall discover the infamy o priests. I will bet," continue turning toward his agent, "th shall find here more horrible than at St. Laurent and Notre

II.

THE PREFECTURE DE POLICE AND MAZAS.

It is no easy matter to describe the singular scene at the préfecture de police, usually so quiet, so disciplined and solemn. This establishment had become noisier and more picturesque than a fair-ground. By way of contrast with the usual proceedings, robbers and other criminals now issued decrees of arrest and imprisonment, and they who were arrested and imprisoned were lovers of order and their duty.

The entrance was guarded by a crowd of national guardsmen, who had stopped drinking and smoking to laugh at the unfortunate victims of the hatred of the committee of public safety, who were arriving in large numbers. I had seen at the Madeleine the delegate who ordered my arrest give the staff-officer appointed to conduct me a five-franc piece to pay for the carriage. This honest man found it more suitable to leave this expense to his prisoner, and keep the five francs himself. It was a little contribution to the expenses of the war that I cheerfully paid. Like the misanthrope of Molière, I was almost glad to see the masters of Paris throw off the mask and add niggardliness to all kinds of violence. It was pleasant to be able to testify that a staff-officer of the Commune, the friend of Ferré and Raoul Rigault, the confidential agent of the committee of public safety, and one of the great dignitaries of the préfecture de police, committed a theft at my expense, and with an unceremoniousness that could not be found among the robbers and pickpockets of the worst quarters of the barriers.

After waiting three hours, I was summoned before citizen Fe
member of the Commune de
to the ex-préfecture de police
signifies in common langua
préfet de police. He appea
be from twenty-six to thirty y
age. He was no longer the te
student and the burlesque wr
the small journals of the Lati
ter, who gave himself up to p
on those rare festivals when t
ceeds of his pen allowed hi
vel at the public balls at the
way of the Observatory. I
exchanged his worn clothes
more elegant suit, his old poin
for a cap with gold spangles.
lessly seated in a superb arm-c
the luxurious office where De
Maupas, and Pietri had labo
gave orders to his subordinat
the solemnity and self-sufficie
a pasha. I am mistaken; th
pashas I saw while travelling
East were only inferior rulers
him; he realized with admirab
cision the fantastic idea I had
of a Chinese mandarin of th
class.

After making a salutation wh
doubtless did not find propor
to his dignity, I requested pen
in respectful and sufficiently h
tones to appear as promp
possible before the *juge d'insti*
He interrupted me in a dr
haughty tone: "Be silent, c
You are here to listen to me, a
to talk!"

I had never met with so hu
ing a reception. It is true
never been in the presence o
lence personified. I imme
drew from my pocket a num
the *Journal Officiel de la Co*
which I had been carefully k
for three days, and which con
a recent decree by virtue of wh
individuals arrested should
before the *juge d'instruction*

noise. Some cried as loud as they could bawl: "Vive la République! Vive la Commune!" Others thought they were at a club, and, all speaking at once, advocated in discordant tones the abolition of capital, the death of the priests, the freedom of woman, and other benefits of social revolution.

Just after midnight, a confederate officer was brought into one of the neighboring cells who was indebted to too copious libations for the eloquence of a Demosthenes and the strength of a Hercules. This patriot thought himself confronting the Prussians, among whom he made frightful carnage. "Now it is your turn, you bully of a Bismarck! Now you, William, you rascal! You shall see what a patriot and a republican can do!" Then he would throw himself on to the door of his cell, and pound and kick it. This continued till daybreak. The heroic avenger of the national honor made me forget for a time the singular insolence of Ferré, and more than once I laughed at his manly eloquence and glorious feats in battle. I took pleasure in retaining, in the midst of the extravagances and crimes of the Commune, a bitter remembrance of the crushing and humiliating proceedings of Prussia.

On Saturday morning I wrote to M. Moiré, the *juge d'instruction*, asking to be heard in the course of the day. At half-past three I received a reply. It was an order to Mazas. No illusion was longer possible. The advocates of legal forms must expect to be shot without form—a respect for which would doubtless have been a poor consolation in falling under the bullets of assassins, but it is well to observe that such judicial modes are unknown among the cannibals themselves. Among the prisoners who accompanied me were, with other ecclesiastics, the Laurent Amodru, the vicar of Dame des Victoires, and th de Marsy, the vicar of St. Vin Paul. Both came to me and fested a sympathy that began t the gloomy perspective of M. de Marsy was full of ani and his cordial devotedness more benefit to us in a moral material sense. And I beca separably attached to M. Amodru. He was my neighb at La Roquette, and his enco example, even more than his p religious ministrations, aided enduring the greatest trials fearful abode. I wish to giv public testimony of my profou titude. We were transported of those cellular vehicles, th sight of which inspires horr disgust, and arrived at Mazas past five. They kept us s nearly two hours in a kind of cage, which made me wish f of those which contain th beasts in the Jardin des Plant

Though separated from o ther, we were able neverth exchange some words. "I indignity," exclaimed a young al guardsman, who had ref serve the Commune, "to shu in this way as if we were robl

"Cheer up," replied an o with a cultivated and symp voice. "In these days, hon are placed here, and robbers without."

Exhausted with fatigue, I neither sit down, lie down, o read. I can understand thes rous precautions for the disci Cartouche, Troppman, and lard. Would there have be great social danger in shutting in an apartment where there bench? I learned afterwa the Archbishop of Paris had th

than examining my pockets, my books, and even my portemonnaie.

The next morning I asked to see one of the physicians of the prison. It was Dr. de Beauvais's day, whom I had already seen at the Madeleine. As he was under the surveillance of the agents of the Commune, I made no sign of recognition. I made known to him the intolerable treatment I had received, the bad state of my health, and the physical impossibility of remaining in my cell. I added that I simply wished to inform him of my situation, but by no means to claim a favor.

He replied that, in consequence of my state of health, I had a right to change my cell. He ordered one to be given me in the first story.

The energy of my language had such an effect on the infirmarian and pharmaceutist of the prison that they hastened to manifest their sympathy. My new warden was perfect. In spite of the severity of the discipline, I could, thanks to them, obtain news of M. Deguerry, Mgr. Darboy, Mgr. Surat, and of M. Bayle, the vicar-general of Paris, who was in my neighborhood. Hitherto I could only give an idea of their trials and those of the other hostages of the Commune by relating my own, only most of them had been incarcerated seven weeks, and I only four days.

Sunday was, relatively speaking, a comfortable day. I guessed, on Monday morning, from the general sound of the tocsin, that the Versailles troops must have entered Paris. The pharmacist and wardens confirmed the supposition. "Courage," they said to me, "perhaps in a few hours, or to-morrow at the latest, you will be free."

I offered up my thanksgivings to God, and hailed the first dawn of light on Tuesday as the happy day of my deliverance, and the ance of all my companions i vity.

III.

LA ROQUETTE—MASSACRE (HOSTAGES—FOUR DAYS OF /

A brilliant sun lighted th of Mazas. We were, then, a return to Paris, from which w ed a thousand leagues distant, within its limits; we were to once more those who were us, and endeavor, according measure of our strength, to h moral and material wounds n the most shameful and odi *régimes* that ever burdened a (people. I forgot all my fatig my sadness, all my anguish, reawakening of hope and prayed with the enthusiasm exile who had despaired of e ing his country again, and tc he was, by an unexpected about to be restored.

At a quarter before ten, tl of my cell was opened. A w did not know ordered me to my effects and go down. M verance, then, was nearer a than I had hoped. All my were packed in a few minu took all the money out of m except enough to pay for a c and give the driver a generou *boire*. I was too happy not to make those around me hap descending I distributed all tl ney I possessed. They shut in one of the compartments prison parlor. After some n they took me to the directc asked me if I had any obser to make. "None," said I, " that I am ignorant why I am l here."

His face, and the faces

our being sent to La Roquette. It was not best to enlighten them yet, but I resolved to do so at a later moment. With almost certain death staring us in the face, I thought it proper, and especially more Christian, to modify my attitude. Until now I had taken an energetic stand against the agents of the Commune, and sometimes expressed my indignation. I now resolved to speak but little, to pray a great deal, to encourage those of my companions who should need it, and to arm myself with patience and meekness toward our persecutors.

The charitable young pharmacist of the prison, who, the night before, so gladly announced our approaching liberation, was stationed in a corner of the vestibule to give us a last proof of his sorrowful sympathy. This was not only a kind but a courageous act at a moment when a single smile of compassion might be regarded as treason. A week after, a young man, kneeling by the body of M. Deguerry in the lower chapel of the Madeleine, stopped me to express his joy and his grief. It was the pharmacist of Mazas.

An enormous cart, surrounded by armed national guards, awaited us in the first court. I at once bethought myself of the carts that during the Reign of Terror conveyed the victims of the committee of public safety to execution. And we too were to go in the same direction, toward the Barrière du Trône. Such coincidences could not fail to strike any one familiar with our revolutionary history. Fifteen prisoners mounted the cart, among whom I noticed M. Chevriaux, the principal of the Lycée at Vanves, who bravely wore his ribbon of the Legion of Honor; Père Bazin; M. Bacues, the director of St. Sulpice; an honest workman, and some members of the national guards, guilty of not having sacrific[e]
idol of the day. They wer[e]
ecclesiastics.

We were told that the re[st]
had not been sent to La Roq[uette]
night before with the first hos[tages]
patched was that a third vehi[cle could]
not be procured. Mgr. Darb[oy]
Deguerry, Mgr. Surat, and]
jean had suffered very much a[t]
the prolonged severity of th[e]
discipline had, in particular
the archbishop's health. T
been obliged, only a few h
fore his departure for La R
to apply blisters to him.]
all showed themselves, by th
ness and patience, superior
sad condition.

At the sight of M. Perny
Houillon, apostolic mission
China, whom the Commune
pidly arrested on their way
Paris, M. Deguerry said
Darboy: "Only think of th
Orientals coming to seek ma
in Paris! Is it not curious
the way, they had to encou
threats and outrages of a rat
Men *en blouse*, ragged child
women, or rather furies, wi
stop and enter the vehicles:
les chouans et les calotins!"–
we wish to cut them in piece[s]

It was revolting, monstro
yet something still more hide
reserved for us. We were
in our turn, not by the m
but by the national guards w
charge of us. I could unc
the threatening attitude of a
excited mob, led away by its
stincts and the speeches of
gogues, but I had never
thought it possible, that an
force could basely insult and
en those whom they were c
deputed to escort to a place
ishment. I had not suspect
a degree of vileness in human

THE DÖLLINGER SCANDAL.

FROM THE HISTORISCH-POLITISCHE BLAETTER.

DURING the course of the year 1857 we published in these pages an exhaustive article on the philosophy of Baader. Before the article was sent to press, the editor of Baader's complete works gave to the public the author's correspondence in another volume, the appearance of which occasioned the most painful surprise among the admirers of the great thinker. The book showed that, in his later years, Baader's mind was out of harmony with the church; and that his tone towards it had grown to be one of bitterness even. As was wont to be the case in those happier days, the editors of these pages turned to Dr. Döllinger for an explanation of the glaring contradictions between the earlier and later views of Dr. Baader. The result was a postscript to the article above referred to, written by Dr. Döllinger, and which may be seen in the fortieth volume of the *Historisch-Politische Blätter*, p. 178.

In this postscript, Dr. Döllinger pointed out from the correspondence itself what were the reasons of the change, and showed that Baader's animosity against the church rested only on extraneous and accidental causes, and had nothing to do with his philosophy. "No further key"—these are Döllinger's concluding words—"will be needed to understand how the broad chasm that separates the calm convictions of the ripe man in his prime from the passionate, almost childlike, outbursts of mental impotence of the old man in his decline, was overleaped."

These lines were written by Dr. Döllinger thirteen years ago, a[n] have often read them since. St[ep by] step, he has himself proceeded [in a] course towards the church whi[ch he] so severely censured in the ph[iloso]pher of Munich.

The fall of the two men is [to a] certain extent the same. The [grey-]haired church historian, too, is [sepa]rated by a great chasm from wh[at he] was in his prime—at a great di[stance] from the convictions that guide[d him] when he was in the zenith of [his in]tellectual power.

His deportment and langua[ge be]tray signs of ungovernable pa[ssion,] incompatible with the self-poss[ession] of a man who understands hi[s own] mind.

We have a right to seek i[n his] case, also, for a psychological [explana]tion of the change that has le[d him to] the very reverse of what he wa[s. In] his case, as in that of Baader, [it will] be seen that the reasons have n[othing] to do with his erudition as a c[hurch] historian; that they are of a [purely] "extraneous and accidental c[harac]ter." But, indeed—and this [is the] great difference between the tw[o—in] Baader's case, the motives wer[e of a] private, domestic nature; in th[e case] of Dollinger, they are of a publi[c and] political nature. To express i[t in a] word, it is the spirit of the tim[e and] of the world that has carried D[öllin]ger into the fatal gulf. Dölli[nger's] fall, his breaking off from all h[is] in the past, is only a piece [of the] political history of Bavaria duri[ng the] last twenty years. The Counc[il and] the definition of the 18th of [July] have only hastened the matter;

importance. We have already referred to the revelations in question as throwing light on the internal history of Bavaria, and on Döllinger's dangerous complication with certain tendencies of the late government; but we must return to the subject, and treat it more particularly. We refer especially to the academical oration held by Dr. Döllinger on the 13th of March, 1864, on King Maximilian II.

In his oration, he happens to speak of the remarkable interest felt by the deceased monarch in historical research, and reveals to the world a very strange, "a more secret" motive for the royal interest. The reader, to understand the full bearing of the history which we give below entire on Dollinger himself, must bear in mind the peculiar characteristics of a man who has lived more among his books than among men. It would be hard for any one to be more subject to external influences than Döllinger is, and, at the same time, to be less conscious of their presence or effect. He unconsciously puts forth to-day, as the result of his own experience, what he happened to hear expressed yesterday by another. Döllinger is always the product of his surroundings, and hence his change, as he lost his old friends, one after another, by death or by alienation, and fell in almost exclusively with the society of the so-called "Bernfenen." This explains also how it came to pass that many younger men, and the members of the scientific guild—for example, his little Mephistopheles, Huber—exercised so unwarranted and increasing an influence over him. Bearing all this in mind, it is impossible to overestimate the effects and influence of the overtures which King Maximilian made to Dr. Döllinger. He was completely intoxicated by them, and his new

friends found means to pre
return to his sober senses.
pression made on Döllinger
conference in question mu
been the more lasting, as D
the acknowledged head of th
montane party, could not ha
ed to stand any higher in hi
ty's favor than any other
abused class. To express th
matter in a few words, we
vinced that the careful obse
discover the later as oppose
earlier Döllinger in the follo
count, or in his cradle.

The following extract is f
oration above referred to:

"As I have permitted m
refer to the deeper though
guided the king in his gov
and especially in his attitude
science, I may also recall
other communications whic
ceived from his own mou
upright, faithful Christian, he
in the lasting future of Chr
and, therefore, could not
that its divisions and the str
the different confessions sho
tinue for ever; that Christian
waste their powers in mutua
The division, he was of opin
had its time, and God had p
it for some high purpose;
time, even where not entir
was near its end; and he
firmly that in spite of all p
bitterness, in spite of the sor
of self which had intruded it
the controversy, the day of u
Christian nations would co
the promise of one fold and o
herd be fulfilled. And the gre
siastical bodies of the We
once reconciled and work
more than redoubled intellect
or upon the Græco-Russian
the latter would not long r
powerful magnetic influence
Or, on the other hand, wh

would kiss; for only through history, as established by the most thorough research, could men know their own past and others' past, their own and others' failings; through it only was there any hope of begetting a conciliatory and pacificatory frame of mind.

"Thus the field of historical science seemed to the king like the Truce of God in the middle ages, or like a sacred city in which those elsewhere at variance found themselves at peace together; and, urged on by the same desires, endeavored to slake their thirst at the same fountain of truth, and grew into one communion.

"Out of the scientific fraternity of historians would one day proceed, so he hoped, after the trammels of confessions had been done away with, a higher union, embracing all historical, all religious truth, a brotherly reconciliation, such as patriots and Christians alike hoped and prayed for."

All this Dr. Döllinger spoke with all the warmth of personal conviction. Although the whole is evidently a thrust at the idea of a confession and against the church as an organization, Döllinger does not append one word of correction in the name of the church. We cannot, however, help wondering that a critic so acute, a thinker so profound, as Döllinger should have surrendered himself to such a politico-religious system. It is easily seen that there are three separate, and in part contradictory, ideas in the royal programme, and all three have this in common, that they are totally irreconcilable with the idea of a divinely instituted and saving church.

In the first place, there is mentioned St. John's church of love, Schelling's church of the future, on which subject Döllinger was otherwise perfectly innocent. An ideal which contemplative enthusiastic charac .King William the Fourth migl ish, and which might also c place in the thoughts of the rian king, could scarcely hav attraction for Döllinger. Bu otherwise with the second ide King Maximilian had elaborat is, with the idea of a German r church; and, finally, with th idea, that of the absorption of confessions into a universal r of *savants*, and the church world-academy of science. H thread of the supernatural i pletely lost, though, perchan king himself was not aware of is this not the most utter ration

If, now, we look at Dölling claration of the 28th of Ma will find these two ideas stand in bold relief. The odious an of Germanism and Romanis indeed be in harmony with th ing political spirit; it certainl compatible with the idea of t tholic Church. Whoever pr in the name of nationality to of any member of the church a "Roman party," either knows n he is doing or must wish the "(national church" in schism. this there is but one step, a not a hard one for the pride of i or the haughtiness of science, position occupied by Döllinge declaration to the archbish which he places the scientific nity of historians as the high thority over the church, and m the court of final appeal in mat faith. And yet the learned gent although he signs himself o Christian," will have us consid a Catholic.

It is impossible to look in abyss into which this once clear has fallen without a feeling of Is it not sufficient to open th of every one that the apost

he did not leave a disciple after him. Whilst he expatiated in the endless world of book in a manner hitherto unparalleled, perhaps it became impossible for him to prepare the living materials which young men needed, and lost the gift of sociability.

Böhmer became more and more aggravated as he proceeded, till, finally, his anger culminated in the following anecdote: He said that, when Döllinger visited Frankfort last, he had had a walk with him through the city, and Döllinger had spoken to him about his literary plans. He, Böhmer, remonstrated with him, and inquired why he did not fulfil his older promises; why he did not continue his unfinished church history. Whereupon Döllinger, stopping and swinging his cane, said with a smile: "You see, I can't do that; for now my researches have brought me to such a pass that I cannot make the end of my history tally with the beginning; the continuation of my church history would be entirely Protestant." I see Böhmer this moment before me with the same grim visage which he wore as he closed this story with the words: "*He—he* said that!"

Still, in 1860, Döllinger's great work, *Christianity and the Church in the time of their Foundation*, appeared. Embracing the results of the latest research, and written in the most charming manner, this book touched and strengthened many a Catholic heart, as it did my own. But Döllinger has made that same beautiful book a sad memorial of his fall. He had written the book when he was sixty years of age, but when, in 1868, the second edition of it appeared, it was discovered that he had omitted some of the principal passages of the first edition, bearing upon the promises to and the establishment of the primacy; and what he h
omitted, he had changed in t
terests of liberalism, and all w
giving any ground for the alter
without a single note even.

Döllinger has a wonderful m
for everything in the world of
but very little for what concer
own person or his own acts.
he wrote his declaration to the
bishop of Munich, he seems to
quite forgotten the intentional
rections" of his celebrated
Otherwise, he would not have r
to the approval which it me
from the whole of Catholic Ge
and raised the question, Whic
he meant—the true one of 1
the altered, not to say the fa
one of 1868? Moreover, he,
inspirer of *Janus*, recalled, i
last-named book, the little l
left in the edition of 1868 fav
to the primacy, for the reason
"contradicted all opinions
fathers, and the principles of
tical theology." In other
Janus has completely and fla
nied the primacy.

It is hard to calculate w
blessing Dollinger might hav
the means of to his contemp
and to posterity, had he con
to make the rich treasures
knowledge accessible to Christ
as he had done in his work of
The Almighty, who had pre
him upright during the war
passions of these later years,
have decreed him doubtless
old age had he remained true
resolution not to divide his p
to live an unprejudiced vot
science. It was to be oth
That book was the last fruit
professional activity of the his
The historian was now to b
the bitter party-man, not to s
future Bavarian senator, and
writer, a mere political pampl

ble for were he the chief pastor of a diocese.

The opinion expressed in an appeal to the Catholic ladies of Germany on the subject of the higher schools, made him lose his patience altogether. The outbreak of the Seminary question in Spiers was in his view another attempt of those infected with the "Roman" spirit against free German science, and it found him, even if not publicly, on the side of the decided opponents of the bishop's rightful claim in the matter.

Very nearly at the same time, the then Bavarian minister of worship made a report to the king on the occasion of a vacancy in the theological faculty of Würzburg, in which he painted the clergy educated in the German College at Rome in no flattering terms. An accidental circumstance threw suspicion on Döllinger as the instigator of it. The pamphlet "for the information of kings," which appeared in the beginning of 1866, represented Döllinger, although only under the general name "of the Munich school," as the real actor in the minister of worship's puppet-play. There was a report that in the Spiers matter, speaking of the attitude of the bishops, he had said: "They are attempting to misuse the king's youth!" How much of this had its foundation in truth, to what extent the statements of the pamphlet were based on a change or mistake between the ministry and cabinet, must remain undecided.

The pamphlet referred to created no small excitement, however; and, precisely two years before the appearance of the notorious articles on the Council, was exhaustively replied to in the *Allgemeine Zeitung*. The style and other accidents would lead to suppose that the "amanuensis," since known more of, had here made his *début*. The reply was no[t]
futation. It was made up of [a]
of counter-complaints, and, wi[th]
exception of the attacks on t[he]
suits, the Roman party, and th[e]
seminaries, these articles conta[in]
kernel of the articles again[st]
Council published two years
In spite of all this, however, [D]
ger is represented in these arti[cles]
of the same unaltered mind wi[th]
er members of the faculty, Ha[neberg]
and Reithmayer.

"If there was no ground of [suspi-]
cion during all these long ye[ars]
reason to believe that thes[e]
were hankering after dangero[us no-]
velties, how comes it recentl[y]
such suspicions are aroused,
that they have always been
same mind?" It is now certa[in]
this unanimity has since cease[d]
it is clear that Döllinger's mo[]
accusation—"not a soul belie[ves]
—must have been unjustly b[]
by him against his colleagues.
articles also quote the words
Tübingen theologian: "The su[]
has spread further—Döllinge[r]
Michelis are no longer inn[ocent]
What says the Tübinger of th[e]
ing of these two men to-day?

On the first of January, 18[]
Hohenlohe ministry took cha[rge of]
the ship of state.

It will not be claimed that [Döllin-]
ger's influence increased with [the ac-]
cession of his old friend Prin[ce Ho-]
henlohe to the ministry; it [is]
more probable that the prince
have found the learned prof[essor a]
powerful obstacle in his way.
prince had formerly been con[sidered]
unexceptionable in his religiou[s views]
and relations; but in order t[o dissi-]
pate the bad odor in which [he stood]
in the highest circles, suspe[cted as]
he was of favoring Prussia, he
no better method than to enc[ourage]
the superstitious fear of the Ult[ramontanes]

the sense approved by Holy Mother Church."

The foreign office and its zealous co-operator, the learned professor, now began their campaign against the Council. The reporter of the Leipzig *Grenzboten* of the 24th of June, 1870, thus expresses himself on the subject: "The alarming circulatory dispatches of Prince Hohenlohe have turned to political account the results obtained by *Janus*, and introduced them into governmental and diplomatic circles." The Bavarian ambassador, a man of no distinction and one who favored the "Curia," was recalled and replaced by Count Tauffkirchen, the most talented diplomatist at that time at the disposal of the government.

His operations in Rome were very influential; and if the matter furnished by the events in the Council became immediately the subject of discussion in the press and in the literature of the day, the Bavarian Embassy is not entitled in the least to the merit of it. The rest was accomplished by Döllinger, as is now well known, and by his intimate young friend Lord Acton.

About the end of the year appeared the pamphlet, *Considerations for the Bishops of the Council on the Question of Papal Infallibility*. This time he appeared again anonymously, but without making any extra effort to conceal himself as the author. A little later, he appeared under his own name in the official organ of the new Catholic theology, the *Allgemeine Zeitung*, in the "Declaration in the matter of the address touching Papal Infallibility," on the 19th January, 1870. From this declaration, says the Lepzig correspondent more than once referred to above, proceeded his agreement with the views of *Janus*.

The publication of his name was no sooner made than the party of progress took it as a signal to him their own entirely.

This had already been done press; now it was accomplisl the House.

On the 7th of February, Dr. a deputy, seized the opportunit sented by the debates on the dress" to drag Dollinger int field against the "patriotic" n ty. He read the most objectic and most venomous parts of the ' siderations" and "Declaration, imputed these views to the ma of the House as their own opi endeavoring to drive them to d themselves for Döllinger and a the Pope and the Council. "patriotic" majority had taker not to embitter the debates by ducing questions ecclesiastical them; but now a defence was for. The stenographic repor scribes the scenes, which were with the following words from D Törg:

"I have been on the most int terms with the gentleman Deputy Völk so formally parad fore the House, for years. I b acquainted with him shortly the time of the 'genuflexion tion' in Bavaria; and, surely, n then imagined that a time come when Dr. Döllinger wou thus quoted before the whole I by Dr. Völk. I consider it a te misfortune, and accept it as yes, gentlemen, as a personal m tune. Dr. Döllinger was an autl for me; he is such no longer; l has fallen the victim of blind p and lost the calmness necessa the forming of an opinion; ar is no longer in a condition to fo late a dogmatic question as a th gian ought to be able to form one."

But that is not what Döll wants. He now stands in dre

importance. And the great storm of an ovation given to Döllinger is meant not so much for Döllinger himself as for its influence on the king and his government.

The king must a second time be made to serve the cause of German liberalism. We said it in the beginning: as soon as the little German Empire is established, the party will want a "German National Church" for their little empire. We did not think, indeed, that any attempt at this would be made so soon; for, a year ago, men who knew what they were talking about assured us that so long as the old king lived he would not permit the peace of religion to be disturbed; but that it would be otherwise with those who came after him. But now that the king has become German Emperor, unanimous reports of the contrary come to us. "The idea of the establishment of a German National Church is taking deeper root, to all appearances, in the government circles." So a relatively unprejudiced Berlin correspondent lately reported. The rest of the tale is told by the debates in the chamber of deputies.

The party are anxious to strike the iron while it is hot; not without reason was the party battle-cry spoken during the war—all our noble blood were shed in vain did not the stroke which freed us from France sever the Catholics of Germany from Rome—"War against France and against—Rome!" Even Dr. Michelis joined in the cry.

If it was very desirable that the Bavarian king should take the initiative in the matter of the imperial title, it was also very desirable that the first step for the establishment of the "German National Church" should proceed from the Munich.

The King of Bavaria to the "new Luther" wl Frederick of Saxony had b ther of old; and on that a is promised the surname o This is the meaning of th telegram of the tenth of M Dresden—"him, the e thinker who publicly pro dissatisfaction with the dog pal infallibility!" When th tatives of high offices in M to set themselves up public manders in the military ec society, one need not be s the progressionist intrusive rashly sporting with the m principle itself. Thus on understand how any one c bold as to encourage the fall by insinuating a pro no one might fear a ma Could the necessary numb church servants have be the programme was that th Bavaria should give the National Church" its first the Munich places of wor wish to be excused from further the plan which fin make true the saying: " to misuse the king's youth

We are not deceived. S plan fail, another will be accomplish what is intend linger has been in relation sian diplomats since 18 ever, neither he nor the ne Empire has the divine pro the church has; and wher and the bishops are, th church.

Let all Catholics gat closely yet about the cent We can do no better serv world. God will take care

overgrown, weakly-looking wooden house tells its story, not of greatness gone by, but of greatness planned and never accomplished—a pitiful comment on the uncertainty of human affairs! It happens thus: Some settler, sadly miscalculating his resources, projects a palace in the wilderness on a scale of city splendor; that is, with parlor, dining-room, kitchen, bedrooms, and the little elegances of pantries and closets. The sides are enclosed, the roof is on, and the revenues he counted on as certain are not forthcoming. Then do papered walls and panelled doors with brass knobs, and visions of portico and piazza, all float away to the blue clouds; the hapless dreamer fits up one corner room for the reception of his whole household until he can find another *location*, and take a new start in the search after fortune, and so abandons his rickety palace to the lord of the soil. As the boards blacken in wind and storm, and one end blows down perhaps in some rough northwester, it gains the name of being haunted; and to ride past such a skeleton thing by moonlight or in the dim twilight, with the utter desolation of all around, and the yawning blackness of cavities which should have been doors and windows, it requires no great stretch of imagination to picture an unearthly head peeping out here and there. Very bold yeomen are known to always whip their horses to a full gallop as they approach and pass the fearful spot; and as for women and children, under that strange fascination by which the supernatural repels and yet attracts, they always gaze intently, and as surely "see something"!

Although goblin visits in our land are just now rather on the decline (except in a regular business way), there was a time when strange sights were seen and strange things happened; and, although it may seem almost ble, it is a fact well establi history that it was generally Dutch settled here, to that headed, reasoning nation, s likely to be deceived on any that most of these revelatior made.

This certainly ensures for tl the firm belief of all mankind. an imaginative Hibernian or a light-hearted Gaul announce sion, it must be taken with son allowance for flights of fancy, et but when a phlegmatic, coo ed Hollander declares he has *spook*, you may believe as if your own eyes.

For the precise period mos fic in signs, sights, and drea must go back to the early d our state, yet not to the *first* *Their* troubles, so numerous tl scarcely possible to number had their origin in things ta and so closely did these troubl daily on all sides, that the tl of the first colonists were engrossed by the things of To such a point did this dov tendency reach, that they at times in danger of relapsi heathendom, as may be see the reports sent back to Amst and yet extant among colon pers, that they possessed school-houses nor churches. did possess, however, three u sources of annoyances and —an Indian warfare, neigh their eastern boundary cf un ed audacity, and domestic bic in the perpetual strife kept tween Manhattan and Ren wyck.

What might have happene Indians had been treated wit mon justice and honesty can only conjecture; but their began at the beginning. It is

more spiritual life, and to gather around them by degrees all that troop of unearthly beings well-known in the mother country. Little children were encouraged to be good and expect Santa Klaus, and bad ones were no longer frightened into propriety with the threat of being devoured by some hideous Waranancongyn with tomahawk and scalping-knife.

One of the spots first renowned for ghostly adventures was a pleasant little valleylike place, on the northern limits of the town, called Medge Padje (now Maiden Lane), where a clear stream ran between grassy banks, so gentle and noiseless that it carried the gazer's heart back —far back over the ocean to the canals of Faderlandt, and was a perfect relief from the lashing waves of the great North River. Hither, on pleasant summer afternoons, many a gude vrow would turn her steps with her troop of sturdy urchins, and, work in hand, knitting, knitting, all the way. But they were always careful to return before dark; for such fearful tales had been told, principally of a tall woman in white who always vanished in the direction of Golden Hill (now John Street), that no one cared to make her acquaintance.

Long years after this, when the palisades marking the extent of the city had been removed as far north as what is now Warren Street, and a field of barley flourished on the Heerewegh (now Broadway), somewhat about the present City Hall, we again hear of the same apparition. The Rev. John Kimball, passing along the little stream rather late at night, heard steps, and, looking behind him, saw the spectre; of course he fled. Doubtless she was the bearer of some important message from the spiritland which she was anxious to communicate, but, as no one ever stopped to listen, what it was can now never be known.

Mr. Watson, in his *Annals of New York*, relates a story given by a military gentleman of his own encounter with an apparition in that same place. The captain declares, and doubtless believed, that he bravely attacked it, and discovered only a mischievous mortal in disguise; but it is hardly probable that any mortal in his senses would be personating a ghost at midnight on haunted ground, so that the tale, being rather one-sided evidence, is doubtful.

Another solitary place was Windmill Lane,* which led from Broadway between Cortlandt and Liberty Streets down quite a steep hill, in a northwest direction, to the river edge, where stood a windmill. There was a time when this lane was the most northern street in the settlement; then house after house began to be built around the old mill, and the city crept up gradually in that direction. Among those who made their homes there was a French lady, Madame Blompeaux, who had crossed the ocean to teach the rising generation all she knew—French and embroidery. Two paths led to her establishment, one through the Lane, the other through a wheatfield, where now is St. Paul's church, and both were beset with spectres. Alas for the scholar kept in after the others were dismissed! Lightly did the offended majesty of madame weigh in the balance compared to what might possibly beleague the path homeward. There was a legend of a tall Indian who was always digging about for his bow and arrows, and a little short Dutchman about a foot high in breeches and cocked hat, who, the moment he found them, sprang into

* Watson's *Annals of New York*.

was in debt to the company," and whose opinions on the subject were of course of no consequence. As for pulling down the house recently erected, Herr Van Slechtenhorst pointed to the fact that Fort Orange stood on the very soil of his employer, and that it was his intention at some leisure day to annihilate it. So went matters, until at last, when Stuyvesant ordered a solemn fast, and Van Slechtenhorst absolved all in his latitude from obedience, human patience could stand it no longer, and the insulted autocrat rushed to Albany in the swiftest sailing sloop that could be found; there, as has been said, to meet his match.

But our business is not with these belligerents, but with those peacefully disposed burghers, who had grown tired more and more, year after year, with this turmoil, which seemed now to have reached its height. Armed soldiers were in their midst (for seven had been sent up from Manhattan), and when the talk was of razing houses, why, even the neighboring Indians came crowding in to ask what the *Swannckins* were about.

Happily another home opened to them, and very many packed up all their worldly goods and migrated. This home was the region about the Kaatskill. One part of the mission of Herr Van Slechtenhorst when sent over the ocean was "to acquire by purchase the lands around Kaatskill for the greater security of the colonie, as they were forming companies to remove thither." *

On the land thus obtained, they had nothing to fear from Indian opposition, and the kind of domestic life they coveted is pictured in a lease yet extant in the Van Rensselaer family, dated 1651, wherein the tenant binds himself to "read

* O'Callaghan, *Hist.*, vol. ii. ch. iv.

a sermon or portion of Sci every Sunday and festival t neighboring Christians, and tc hymns before and after p after the custom of the C of Holland." Years in that nook of creation brought few changes; their habitations had to be grouped together som town fashion, and were dignifi a name much too long, and u nounceable except by a Dutch to but well loved because traceal Holland; and there life afte passed away like great waves stream—one disappears and an takes its place.

Such were the mortal inhab of the place; but the invisible tion of the community—their was Legion! It seemed the place of refuge for all sorts of less personages who had been i ed and expelled from other pl indeed, if a census had been take cording to the old wives' stories, aggregate numbers would have up near half the population (village.

In one portion of the spot might truly have been calle supernatural reservation was a ravine, which bore traces of h once been the bed of a mo stream. At this period time before the old French wa sole inhabitants were a moro looking woodman and his age ther, and their dwelling-place miserable hut perched on rock so hidden by gnarled and twiste and a dense undergrowth of as to be almost invisible to a its occupants. Why they estal themselves in that uninviting or what were the events of thei previous to their appearance their unintelligible English fa communicate, nor was there a the sullen taciturnity of both o

mortal is admitted to the society of spirits, an oath of secrecy is imposed under a penalty few would care to brave. She cited the cases of several imprudent individuals who, having violated this compact, suffered fearful consequences. One was Alice Pearson, of Byrehill, somewhere about 1588. Having been introduced to the invisible world by a friend, and joined them in "piping, mirth, and good cheer" (to use her own words), she was warned that, if she ever related what she had seen, "she should be martyred." One day, when she began to speak of these things, an unseen blow took away her breath and left an ugly mark on her side; heedless of the warning, Alice continued her revelations until she was burned as a witch, thus fulfilling her doom.* Every one in the Highlands knew, too, the terrible visitation that had lighted on one kirk for having pried into secrets merely to publish them. Every one knew that he was a mere wandering gypsy in the universe, and would be to the end of time.

Effie generally concluded her oracles with the remnant of an old song, written about fairies particularly, but equally applicable to any unearthlies. It was called

"*God a Mercy Will.*

"To be sung or whistled to the tune of *Meadow Brow* by the learned; by the unlearned, to the tune of *Fortune.*

"A tell-tale in their companie
They never could endure,
But whoso kept not secrecy
Their deed was punished sure.
It was a just and Christian deed
To pinch such black and blue."
Etc., etc., etc.

Poetica Stromata.

As this bore the antique date of 1648, and was written by Corbet, Bishop of Norwich, it was co[…] ed good authority for anything[…]

This, then, explained the u[…] silence of Jans Van Dorp, […] also half-reconciled his gude w[…] endure her unsatisfied curiosity[…] wonder and to be afflicted nigh[…] night by his truant absence wa[…] enough, but to have seen him […] in blue smoke would have […] worse.

Things were passing thus i[…] sequestered little spot, while th[…] world without was agitated […] mightier events—the opening […] of the Revolutionary war. It is […] ful whether the faint rumors […] which penetrated the seclusion […] would have excited the least […] tion, except for the fact that […] the only earthly topic on whic[…] Van Dorp nowadays man[…] the least interest. Every Dut[…] lager, whose business led him […] great cities, was questioned and […] questioned on his return as […] precise state of things, with […] nuteness which would have do[…] nor to that renowned lawyer […] Adrian Van der Donck, the fir[…] landed in the New Netherland[…] one little gray newspaper that […] ed weekly, and had hitherto ci[…] ed among his neighbors until […] quite illegible, was now pack[…] mediately in his great-coat […] and taken to his ghostly partn[…] this was a perfect labyrinth of […] ry, and furnished texts for n[…] sage conjecture and dubious […] of the head. Some hinted th[…] Van Dorp might mean to […] execution the threat he had b[…] often heard to hurl at his in[…] helpmate when her vexatiou[…] bility exceeded all bounds of […] ance—that he'd be off to son[…] But time puts an end to all […] although it does not always […] things to universal satisfaction.

* *Trials from the Criminal Records of Scotland.* By R. Pitcairn, Esq.

The *Fraction au Centre* in the German Parliament limits its activity by the following principles:

"I. The fundamental characteristics of the empire as a confederation (*Bundesstaat*) shall be maintained. Conformably to this principle, all efforts shall be opposed that tend to modify the federal character of the constitution of the empire, and the spontaneity and independence of the several states in their interior affairs shall only be sacrificed when the general interests evidently require it.

"II. The material and moral welfare of the popular classes shall be urgently insisted upon. The civil and religious liberty of all the subjects of the empire shall be secured by means of constitutional guarantees, and religious associations, in particular, shall be protected against legislative encroachments.

"III. The *Fraction* weighs and forms resolutions in accordance with these principles, upon all questions submitted to the deliberation of the parliament, but without forbidding isolated members to vote in the assembly contrary to the decisions of the *Fraction*."

The *Fraction* remained faithful to these principles during the session of the parliament that has just closed. It avoided all extreme views, and manifested no systematic hostility to the government. Nevertheless, the very fact that it is composed of Catholics firmly resolved to defend the rights and liberties of the church against all attacks, and that these Catholics were elected from the most prosperous and intelligent sections of Germany, where pseudo-liberalism thought its rule immovably established, sufficed to excite against the *Fraction* a coalition of all who were opposed to the church. Their invectives began with the debates on the address. The form of address proposed by the national liber ty contained, besides some e sions in praise of the historic of the adversaries of the Papa following sentence: "The da interference with the national of other kingdoms will, we never return under any pret under any form." This senten structive of all national right evidently aimed against Ro was partly acknowledged: th lian revolution was not to be ed by diplomatic representati the accomplishment of its d against the visible head of the c Naturally, it would not have red to any one to impose al passiveness on the powerful G Empire in its relations with boring states. The party of th *tre* drew up a counter-schedule, did not contain the propositi absolute non-intervention we just referred to, but which was theless in conformity with the a of the liberals. This counte dule did not demand, either c or indirectly, any intervention vor of the Pope: it containe ing that clashed either with th ernment or the other partie consequently was not the obj criticism in any quarter. So this, that the *Allgemeine Zeit* Augsburg, the chief organ o religious liberalism, could n guise its preference for the sc of the *Centre* as to its subst well as form. Nevertheless, the *Centre* remained wholly defensive, and its orators ex the greatest moderation, a rea of invectives was raised agains and the church by the journa all the other parties and by t liament. Even the so-called vatives took sides against the whose motion, thanks to the cries, only obtained sixty vo

accused the *Fraction du Centre* to Cardinal Antonelli of having assumed an attitude hostile to the government of the empire, and that the cardinal had expressed his disapproval of this attitude not only before the Count de Tauffkirchen, but in a letter addressed to the leaders of the *Fraction.* This assertion being repeated in several quarters, the said leaders denied it in the journals. Driven to the wall, the *Deutsche Reichscorrespondens* then brought up the case of the Count de Frankenberg already mentioned, and at last Prince Bismarck himself declared the blame really proceeded from Cardinal Antonelli. This induced the Bishop of Mayence to ascertain the correct account of the matter from the cardinal. His eminence replied that it had been incorrectly reported to him that the *Fraction du Centre* had insisted upon the Emperor of Germany's intervention in favor of the Pope, and that, under the existing circumstances, he had declared such a step inopportune. At the same time, the cardinal assured the Bishop of Mayence and his friends that he had a particular esteem for the members of the *Fraction du Centre* and its proclivities. Thus failed the effort made at the court of Rome to bring discredit on the *Fraction* among Catholics, for at once a great number of Catholics gave in their full adhesion to the *Fraction*, and besought it to persevere courageously. This effort had, moreover, a comic side, for until now the *Fraction* had been represented as the servile tool of the Roman curia, whence it received its orders on all important questions.

No general interest would be felt in all these facts, if they were not the clear prelude of an act the consequences of which cannot be foreseen. It is not the acts of the *Fraction du Centre* that provoke tl lent attacks against it: it is it existence that is considered a Those hostile to the church h: culated, without distinction of that the very first diet of the G Empire would aim a blow at manism" in Germany, on th of which would afterwards national German church, that finally end in a cosmopolitan manitarianism," without d without sacraments, and with tars—the very *beau idéal* o masonry. Everything, in fact ed propitious for the realizat this hope. The two principal lic nations successively con the Roman race suffering fr cessant convulsions, the head Catholic Church a prisoner Vatican, and, finally, a schis seemed likely to arise on acco the dogma of infallibility—all s to form a breach by which hoped their opponents wou overcome. Only, as an ancient says: "Man proposes, but G poses!"

The election of the Prussi puties and the members of th man Parliament has already lyzed the action of these regen of humanity, by rousing the lics to an energy not easily surmounted. The complete of the representatives electe their bold stand, showed it wo quite useless for the legislati semblies at Berlin to make rious charge against Catholicis the contrary, it was hoped at that the initiative would be ta Munich, where "the Luther nineteenth century" had rai standard of revolt against th man Pontificate. But Munic likewise under the influence sions. It was supposed tha Hefele, the Bishop of Roth

uch a report will never be published r drawn up by the authorities, conequently the formation of a private gency to effect such an object is an rgent necessity. Perhaps this report ight at last put an end to the onstantly repeated accusations of e base ingratitude of Catholics gainst the Prussian government. l'he clear judgment of Frederick Villiam IV., and the constitutions hat sprang from the events of 1848, uaranteed a liberty of action to the 'atholic Church and its organs vhich had not existed in any German tate since the peace of Westphalia. l'he Prussian Catholics displayed a ively gratitude for this, and flattered hemselves with the hope that several rying injustices which weighed on hem would be removed, especially n the conferring of public offices nd the nomination of professors at he universities. This hope was then he more reasonable, because, in the 'ar against France, Catholics, as vell as Protestants, shed their blood n the battle-fields, and submitted to he heaviest requisitions. The relirious orders particularly signalized hemselves by their services, as the ecently published report of the 'nights of Malta (Catholics) prove. 'nfortunately, this hope has already riven place to serious preoccupation.

Prince Bismarck appears no longer ble to endure repose. Having vanuished our foreign enemies, he seems o aim, unless all appearances deeive us, at making adversaries of the 'atholics of Germany and causing hem to feel the weight of his hand. 'erhaps he is influenced by the conideration that military unity, to be on a solid basis, should be founded on, or crowned by, political and relíious unity. At all events, this is the pinion of the liberal party, whose ourse involuntarily recalls the exression of Tacitus, "*Ruere in servitium;*" whereas, while M. de Bismarck was rising to power, they abused him beyond all bounds. These worshippers of success have for allies the Catholics who are not willing to submit to the decrees of the Council of the Vatican. In the jargon of the liberals, these Neo-Protestants are designated as old Catholics, while the immense majority of Catholics who now, as formerly, consider the authority of the Pope and bishops in religious things as higher than that of certain professors, are styled Neo-Catholics, absolutely as if they had abandoned the faith of the church. A foreigner would find it difficult to understand how it is possible to give a completely opposite meaning to the real signification of a word, and this in a country like Germany, which prides itself on its intelligence.

But it is not the anti-religious journals alone that take this liberty. M. de Mühler himself, the Prussian minister of the public worship, treats the Catholics who remain faithful to the decrees of the Pope and bishops as rebels to the government. Immediately after the suspension of the council, he took under his protection the professors, even those who were priests, who refused to submit to the decisions of the council and the bishops, and encouraged them in their revolt against ecclesiastical authority. Recently, *à propos* of the affair of the Bishop of Ermland, he went so far as to submit to the ministry of Prussia, composed exclusively of Protestants, a resolution to ascertain what Catholics should be considered as orthodox, and he ordered a priest named Wollmann, who had been excluded from the fold of the church by major excommunication, to retain his professorship as religious instructor in the Catholic college of Braunsberg. The students, unwilling to receive religious instruction from a fallen priest, left the col-

arbitrary ministry. At all events, I imagine these deputies will smile with pity when they hear themselves styled unpatriotic by some parties in imitation of a part of the journals hostile to the church, or even accused of conspiring with foreigners or the *Internationale*. Some papers, in fact, have not shrunk from the ridicule attached to such foolish accusations. Does not this having to resort to such imputations prove the want of any serious charge against the members of the *Centre?* They are evidently not credited by those who make use of them, nor is any attempt made to convince others of their truth.

The members of the *Fraction du Centre* figure, for the most part, among the notabilities of their districts. Many of them have occupied or occupy some public office with honor: and several have, for many years, showed their constant zeal in the old Prussian house of legislation, where they had a seat, and gave their devoted support to the government in the crisis of the year 1848 and the following year, often at the expense of their popularity. They were often known to defend the authorities against the attacks of those who are now endeavoring to excite the government against them.

In support of what I have just stated, it is sufficient to recall the names of those whom the confidence of their colleagues chose as a committee of the *Fraction du Centre* in the German parliament and the Prussian house of representatives. I will mention M. de Savigny, the son of the illustrious jurisconsult so well-known throughout the whole world, who was formerly Prussian minister at Brussels, and latterly the representative of the King of Prussia at the Diet of Frankfort; M. Windthorst, who was president of the house of representatives in] and twice minister of justic kingdom; the Baron d'Ar vice-president of the upper the kingdom of Bavaria; M. linkrodt, the counsellor of tl sian regency; the Prince c wenstein; the Count de La Velen, a hereditary member Prussian house of lords, etc haps I may be permitted to also my brother, a counsello Prussian Court of Cassation, one of the most active leade conservative party when the ment was the object of the m lent attacks.*

He who consecrates his ti strength to the cause of just religious liberty, or uses the arena of political combat, sh expect to reap any gratitude, leaders of the *Centre* and thei could not foresee that they be exposed to the calumnies alluded to. The only app grievance uttered against the verian and Bavarian meml their *Fraction* is, that the for approved of the annexation country to Prussia, and th used its influence to prevent from joining the new Germa pire. But these deputies ha ed publicly that, these m having been decided by vot were ready not only to fall the new order of things, but deavor to strengthen it, whi not be the case if the r liberal party is not opposed, dent tendency of which is n

* The modesty of the eminent auth article did not permit him to mention name among the most illustrious memb *Fraction du Centre*. It would be ungr to supply this omission by adding to th champions enumerated above the m multiplied labors, marked by his superi gence and ardor of feeling, are at once to Germany and the church.—(*Note of tor.*)

enormous material resources of the state at his disposal, to enter into a combat against people who can and will only oppose him passively, as is suitable in the defence of a cause which represents the most powerful interests of humanity.

But perhaps all these hopes are illusory; perhaps we are about to see in our Fatherland the beginning of a sad and fruitless struggle, such as has so exhausted the strength of other countries by giving a free course to the most dangerous passions. In this case the Catholics of Germany should prepare themselves to endure a long succession of contradictions, for their moral courage will be severely tried. They will have to make sacrifices of a for their faith, recalling the of the Gospel that comm not only to render to Cæ things that are Cæsar's, but God the things that are God's ever may happen, whatever the consequence of such a s the church of God, which ways been victorious throu tience, will never yield either assaults of unbelief or the att a false science, that in its seems to declare anew: *Erit Deus.* Truth is great, and it w vail: *Magna est veritas et lebit.*

A. Reichensper

Cologne, Aug., 1871.

THE MOUNTAIN.

The mountain's sides are green anear,
  In clouds is lost its snow;
And he who climbs that Alpine height
  Shall earth and heaven know.
Lo! like a temple to the skies,
For toil, for prayer, for sacrifice,
Its green and snowy heights arise.

A thousand pilgrims wander up
  To yonder blue abode,
And some are lost, and some are slain,
  Or robbed upon the road.
Far up the holy hermits dwell,
And sounds the monastery bell
The safe and ancient way to tell.

And they who mount that highest steep
  Are tired and sad and poor,
But lo! a starry house is there,
  And angels at the door.
Rich joy for poverty and pain
They give, that summit to attain:
All earth they leave all heaven to gain.

Faith, which looks up out of the blackness and shadow of death into the full-orbed splendor of the sun of righteousness, may not inappropriately take for its symbol the "stimulating negation" of the poet.

Thus do the three primary colors, blue, green, and red, represent the triad of Christian graces, the primary virtues of the Christian life—faith, hope, and charity, or love.

But leaving the poetry of color, we come to the subject of its place and function as it imprints itself on the myriad forms of the organic world. The question has been asked, Are all these tints of nature in the flower and shrub, the gorgeous plumage of the bird, only meant to please the eye of man and to gratify the artistic sense? Is there a deeper, subtler purpose running through all this apparently wanton pageantry, aside from the delight which it affords the mind of man, and looking only to the perfecting and preservation of the organism itself?

A utilitarian age has answered in the affirmative, and the researches of Darwin, Wallace, and others are daily opening new vistas into this interesting field of inquiry.

Darwin was the first to establish the fact that the bright coloring of flowers is for the purpose of attracting insects in order to accomplish their fertilization, and deduces the general rule that all flowers fertilized by the wind are of dull and inconspicuous colors. In the animal kingdom the principle of assimilation guides and modifies coloring in conformity with surrounding nature, and it is, therefore, to a great extent, protective.

The lion inhabiting the desert is of the color of the sands, so as hardly to be distinguished at a short distance. The leopard lives in jungles, and the vertical stripes on its body harmonize admirably with the vertical reeds of its tangled la
completely conceal it from vie

In arctic regions, white is t
vailing color, as here reign pe
snows; therefore, it is that tl
is only found *white* in this p
the globe.

The curious fact that amon
the female is usually of a du
tral tint, while the male mon
the bright colors, is accounted
the principle of protective c
the female needing the obscu
forded her by her sober pl
When there is an exception
rule, the protection is affor
some other way. And this l
to the subject of *birds' nests.*

Wallace, in a chapter on th
ry of birds' nests, divides the
two classes, those in which tl
are protected by the shape c
tion of the nest, and those in
they are left exposed to view
then gives the following law:
when both sexes are of strikin
and conspicuous colors, the
of the first class, or so as to c
the sitting bird; while, whenev
is a striking contrast of col
male being gay and conspicu
female dull and obscure, the
open and the sitting bird exp
view."

In connection with the sub
protective coloring, the phen
of *mimicry* is not the least c
Wallace gives several instan
butterflies, moths, snakes, etc.
the coloring of protected fan
imitated by weak and unpr
ones not in any way allied to
A large and bright-colored bu
the heliconidæ of South A
which is protected by a disag
quality affecting its taste, thus
ing it secure from insect-eatin
is imitated by a smaller and
family, resembling it so com
as to be quite indistinguishabl

laborateurs, to enrich our English libraries with these splendid patristic translations.

A Life of St. Augustine is also promised to accompany the selections from his writings. From this we can scarcely expect as much satisfaction as from the other parts of the undertaking. The theology and opinions of the writer must unavoidably prevent him from understanding and correctly representing a Catholic bishop and doctor, and giving a perfectly complete and correct account of the state of the church during the period in which he lived. No one but a Catholic can achieve this task with success, although a Protestant who is sufficiently learned, accurate, and skilled in the art of composition, may make a perfectly satisfactory translation of Catholic works. It were much to be desired that some competent Catholic scholar would give us a biography of St. Augustine so complete and perfect that it would supplant all others, and take rank as the standard history of his life and times.

LIGHT IN DARKNESS. A Treatise on the Obscure Night of the Soul. By the Rev. A. F. Hewit, of the Congregation of St. Paul. New York: Catholic Publication Society. 1871. Pp. 160.

This is a very small volume in bulk, and of very modest pretensions, but of great merit, and treats with much truth and justice a very important subject. It belongs to what is called *Mystic Theology*, and gives us in a small compass the simpler elements of the science of the saints, and cannot fail to interest all those who are entering upon a life of Christian perfection, whether in religion or in the world. The "obscure night of the soul," as St. John of the Cross calls it, is experienced in some degree by all whom the Holy Spirit is conducting through purification, not to be effected without pain and sorrow, to the highest and closest union with God possible while we are still in the flesh. It is a deprivation of all sensible sweet
devotion, a desolation, a d
of all but the very highest f
of the soul, in which all is
hard, and the soul discerns
ray of light to relieve the d
that seems to pervade and
her every act, and everythin
listless, prayer demands an
and brings no consolation, a
ditation is painful and fruitle
obscure night of the soul,
times called passive purga
supernatural, the gift of th
Ghost, and is intended to
soul, to test its faith and con
to purify it, and enhance it
by bringing it in the end int
union with God.

If carefully distinguishe
sadness and melancholy, wh
spring from the physical c
tion and a variety of natural
this inward desolation, in wh
soul longs for light, for spirit
and to behold the counten
the Lord, is a great good,
proof that the Holy Spirit
left us, but is present within
preparing us for the joyful d
will dawn in the soul, and p
to ascend to the Mount of Visi
the saints. Sensible sweetne
visions, which are not seldor
rienced by one just entering
gious life, are baits to lure u
to save us from discouragem
they cannot create in us a
and solid piety. Whom the L
eth he chasteneth, and sc
every son that he receivetl
more profitable to the soul
obscure night in which th
hides his face from us, and le
desolate, and yet does not l
nor cease to love and care f

Father Hewit explains th
ces and solidity, the certai
infallibility, of the science
saints; shows the princip
which it rests; describes th
lation of the soul due to th
pline to which the Holy Spi
jects the aspirant to Christ
fection; gives plain and si
rections to distinguish it fro

for the use of our church choirs. The selections, from a purely musical point of view, are as good as publications of this nature generally contain.

THE PICTORIAL BIBLE AND CHURCH HISTORY STORIES. Abridged. A Compendious Narrative of Sacred History, brought down to the present Time of the Church, and complete in one Volume. By the Rev. Henry Formby. New York: The Catholic Publication Society, 9 Warren St. 1871.

This is a book which deserves to find a place as a text-book in all Catholic schools, and to be put by all Catholic parents into the hands of their children. Even the very little ones will be found capable of comprehending the easy and familiar English of the narrative; nor can too much stress be laid on the importance of thus familiarizing them from the start with the history of God's dealings with men. For this purpose, the plan of acquainting them with the Bible history simply is far from sufficient. It leaves too great a gap between the past and the present—as if sacred history had virtually come to an end eighteen centuries ago, and since then everything had been merely secular and profane. A well-instructed child needs to have the whole of sacred history, from the creation of the world to the usurpation of Rome by Victor Emanuel, laid before his eyes in a series the connections of which are plain and unbroken. Such a simple historical knowledge will be apt to prove the best safeguard of his faith in a time when there is no longer any great temptation for him to abandon it in favor of misbelief, but when open unbelief in the providence of God is fast becoming his only real enemy. The task which Father Formby has undertaken, of presenting this history in an easy and compendious form, is one which he has very satisfactorily accomplished, and for which there seemed to be a crying need.

We can only hope that An
Catholics will make haste t
themselves of the results of
bors. The book is an att
one, very fully illustrated l
tures which, if they are not
called artistic, have at all
the merit of being often sugg
and the letterpress will be
good reading by older reac
well as by the young ones.

THE ILLUSTRATED CATHOLIC FAM
MANAC FOR THE UNITED STA
THE YEAR OF OUR LORD 1872.
lated for different Parallels of L
and adapted for use through
Country. Illuminated cover
pp. 144. New York: The (
Publication Society. 1872.

There are many good work
done for our Catholic comi
and here is one of them. A
annual at a trifling price, yet
per, typographical executio
illustrations, wonderfully att
now finds its way to over s
thousand Catholic homes, an
to perhaps a quarter of a mil
Catholic readers informatio
struction, and entertainment
The material is new and heal
is a commentary on the comi
of saints. Catholics are not
state or country, of one age
tury. We are a brotherho
bracing all. The young grow
wish to know of the past glo
the church as the old love to
of them; and all desire infor
of the actual life of the chur
God's hand is not shortened
nineteenth century. He ov
the great and wise, and revea
self to little ones, now as
Bernadette Soubirous, whos
ness is given, kneels there,
cluster round her to hear th
derful history of Lourdes. Th
martyred Archbishop of Pa
be viewed with interest, a
sketch of him will be impri
all minds. The beautiful p
of Adelaide Procter and Eug
Guérin bring to mind the repr

made by an American lady fully qualified for the task.

An excellent portrait of Mother Julia embellishes the book.

The Four Great Evils of the Day. By Henry Edward, Archbishop of Westminster. London: Burns, Oates & Co. 1871. Pp. 142. For sale by The Catholic Publication Society, New York.

The Four Great Evils exposed in these four lectures are the Revolt of the Intellect against God, the Revolt of the Will against God, the Revolt of Society against God, the Spirit of Antichrist. The author shows how the revolt against the Roman Church and the Vicar of Christ results in atheism, immorality, social anarchy, and the disruption of the whole fabric of Christianity, involving the destruction of the human race, and of the world, the Catholic Church excepted, which is preserved by miracle to the end of time. These lectures are very timely, and ought to be read by every reflecting person. The Archbishop of Westminster is equal to the greatest of our modern prelates in his clear insight into Catholic principles, and thorough knowledge of the atheistic and communistic tendencies of Protestantism. Hence the respect, fear, and hatred with which he is regarded by the enemies of the church. One thing especially noticeable in these lectures, and which we have observed with peculiar pleasure, is the exhibition of the intellectual as well as moral degradation of modern infidelity. The superstition and absurdity into which the proud rebellion of the mind against the authority of the church has plunged it is shown by Archbishop Manning, in a different way from that employed by Dr. Newman, but with a force equally irresistible. We recommend all our intelligent readers, and we presume that all our readers are intelligent, who desire to master the true and pure principles of the Catholic religion in their relation to the errors and disorders of the day, to obtain and study carefully all the works of the Archbishop of Westminster.

A Critical Greek and English Concordance of the New Testament. Prepared by Charles F. Hudson, under the direction of Horace L. Hastings editor of *The Christian*; revised and completed by Ezra Abbot, LL.D., Assistant Librarian of Harvard University. Second edition, revised. Philadelphia: J. B. Lippincott & Co. 1871.

This handy little volume is evidently the result of a good deal of painstaking and conscientious labor. As the production of several hands, it is a monument of somewhat heterogeneous scholarship. It professes to be "critical"; and critical and scholarly we are sure it is, so far as it is indebted to the contributions of Dr. Ezra Abbot, a gentleman whose minute bibliographical knowledge is only equalled by his rare modesty, and by his readiness to place his learning at the disposal of others. To his careful hand, we take it, is due the collection of various readings as given by Griesbach, Lachmann, and the latest editions of Tischendorf and Tregelles. The student will find in this compilation a mass of information which we do not remember to have seen in so compact a form elsewhere. For the rest, the work will doubtless fulfil the purpose announced by the editor-in-chief, as a "book available to the mere English reader," and will be welcomed by evangelical ministers of all denominations who may have felt more or less keenly the need of supplementing the defects in their early classical education by some easy artificial helps. How convenient, for example, when we run against the word γυνή, to find, on the authority of Messrs. Hastings and Hudson, that, in a given number of passages, the majority in fact, it signifies *woman*, undoubtedly *woman*, whereas in several other given pas-

ject of this handsome brochure—the theme of so many thousand eloquent pens and voices. The celebration in the Province of Baltimore, however, was an exceptional one, as became the oldest See in the United States. Besides the addresses, letters, and resolutions, etc., which we naturally look for in such a publication, it includes encyclical and other letters from His Holiness, and some historical and chronological matter which the reader will find highly useful.

THE MARTYRS OF THE COLISEUM; or, Historical Records of the Great Amphitheatre of Ancient Rome. By the Rev. A. J. O'Reilly, Missionary Apostolic at St. Mary's, Capetown. London: Burns, Oates, & Co. 1871. For sale by the Catholic Publication Society, New York.

The basis of the narratives of this volume is furnished by the ancient *Acts of the Martyrs.* The story of several of the most illustrious martyrs of the early ages is told by the author, according to history and legend, with some embellishments of imagination, poetry, and fancy. There is also an account of the history of the Coliseum itself, as far as knowledge or probable conjecture can furnish it. The author's style is warm, exuberant, and brilliant. The volume is instructive and entertaining, and ought to be a favorite, with young people especially.

MANUAL OF PIETY, for the use of Seminarians. Second American Edition. Baltimore: Published by John Murphy & Co., 182 Baltimore Street. 1872.

This is a new edition of an excellent and well-known manual for seminarians. It can hardly be too highly commended either as regards matter or form. It contains an immense amount of matter in a very small space, and the type is clear and beautiful.

MR. ROBERT CODDINGTON has in press, and will publish about Christmas, *The Vicar of Christ; or* [...] *tures upon the Office and Prerog*[...] *of our Holy Father the Pope,* b[...] Thomas S. Preston, pastor [...] Ann's Church, New York, and [...]cellor of the Diocese. It w[...] published uniform in style wit[...] other volumes of Father Pre[...] lectures.

THE Catholic Publication S[...] will publish, November 1, [...] *Queen of Scots, and Her Latest E*[...] *Historian,* a narrative of the pri[...] events in the life of Mary S[...] with some remarks on Mr. Fro[...] *History of England,* by James F[...]line. This work will contain [...] only the thorough criticism o[...] Froude's *History of England* [...] as made in the five articles o[...] subject in THE CATHOLIC WO[...] articles which have attracted [...]ral attention, and put Mr. F[...] upon his defence—but also a [...]plete narrative of the life of [...] Stuart, with a review of those [...]umes of Mr. Froude's history [...] noticed in the articles.

MR. P. DONAHOE, Boston, will publish *To and from the Passion at Oberammergau, Bavaria,* fro[...] pen of the Rev. George H. D[...] Chancellor of the Diocese of [...]ark. It will be dedicated to th[...] Rev. J. R. Bayley, D.D., Bisho[...] Newark.

KELLY, PIET & Co. announc[...] in press *The Martyrs of the Colis*[...] by Rev. A. J. O'Reilly.

BOOKS RECEIVED.

From CHARLES SCRIBNER & Co., New [...] The Holy Bible according to the Auth[...] Version (A.D. 1611), with an Explanat[...] Critical Commentary, and a Revision [...] Translation, by Bishops and other Cle[...] the Anglican Church. Edited by [...] Cook, M A., Canon of Exeter. Vol. I. [...] 1. Genesis—Exodus.

From KAY & BROTHER, Philadelphia: [...]lection of Leading Cases in the Law o[...]tions in the United States, with Notes a[...]ferences to the latest Authorities. By [...]erick C. Brightly.

THE

ATHOLIC WORLD.

VOL. XIV., No. 81.—DECEMBER, 1871.

THE RECENT EVENTS IN FRANCE.

have no occasion to dwell on sastrous events of the war of econd French Empire with a, nor on the still more disas- esults of the feeble efforts of the vised republic to drive back erman armies from French soil. are too painful to be dwelt on, re, probably, as well known to eaders as to ourselves. We however, remark that we regard a mistake to represent the war nprovoked by Prussia. The that declares the war is not al- responsible for it. Prussia, by uplicity, her aggressive spirit, er menacing attitude to France, to the French government am- ason, according to what has een the usage with European s, for declaring the war.

have never been the partisans uis Napoleon; but it is only justice to say that by his con- ns of January, 1870, he had l to be the absolute sovereign ance, and had become a con- onal monarch, like the Queen of Great Britain and Ireland, and the declaration of war against Prussia in July of the same year was not his personal act, but the act of the Liberal ministry and the French people, influenced, not unlikely, by the secret societies that had sworn the Emperor's destruction. Perhaps, when the facts are better known, it will be clearly seen that the Emperor had really no alternative but war with Prussia, or the loss of the French throne for himself and dynasty. Though unprepared, he chose the war, as offering at least a chance of success, and it is not improbable that the result would have been less disastrous both for him and the nation if he had been loyally sustained by the French people, and had not had a more formidable enemy in his rear than in his front. The influences that compelled him to consent to the declaration of war were unfriendly to him, and both before and after the declaration were, not unlikely, indirectly controlled by that astute but unprincipled diplomatist, Bismarck,

at present Chancellor of the new German Empire, and through whose adroitness Germany has been Prussianized.

It now also appears that the disaster of Sedan was far less the fault of the Emperor than of his marshals, who acted without his orders, and without concert with one another. If Marshal MacMahon had fallen back on the capital, as Trochu says he advised, instead of attempting to relieve Metz, and given the nation time to rally and concentrate its forces, it is probable the empire would have been saved, and the Prussians been ultimately defeated and driven beyond the Rhine. Even after the disaster of Sedan, the integrity of French territory might have been saved, and peace obtained on far less onerous terms than those which were finally imposed by the conqueror after the surrender of Paris, but for the Parisian mob of the 4th of September, which compelled the Corps Législatif to pronounce, illegally of course, the escheat of the Emperor and the empire, to proclaim the republic, and to suffer a so-called government of defence to be improvised. The disaster of Sedan was great, but it was a mere bagatelle in comparison with that of the revolution effected by the Parisian mob acting under the direction of the secret societies, whose destructive power and influence were so well and so truthfully set forth by Disraeli in his *Lothair*, one of the most remarkable books recently published, and which shows that its author fully understands the great questions, movements, and tendencies of modern society. That revolution was the real disaster, and Paris, not Prussia or Germany, has subjugated France. The French, excepting a few lawyers, journalists, literary dreamers, and the workingmen of the cities and towns, who demanded "*la république democratique* [...] *ciale*," had no wish for a re[...] and were, and are, decidedly a[...] publican at heart. The men [...] posing the so-called governm[...] defence were, for the most par[...] who had not, and could not i[...] it, the confidence of the nation[...] men without faith or solid pri[...] theorists and declaimers, utterl[...] titute both of civil and milita[...] pacity, distrusted, if not detest[...] all Frenchmen who retained [...] sense of religion or any love of [...] try surpassing their love for the[...] theories. France, perhaps, [...] have been saved by a loyal su[...] of the empire, and a hearty co-[...] tion with the Imperial gover[...] under the Empress-Regent, eve[...] the disaster of Sedan, but n[...] overthrowing it, and plungin[...] nation into the revolutionary [...] The government of defence [...] hastened the catastrophe by d[...] ing the Imperial government, c[...] niating it, and publishing ever[...] of falsehood against it that r[...] could invent or render plausil[...] the event has proved, and a[...] world is beginning to see and [...]

But for the socialistic revolut[...] is now known that, even afte[...] surrender of the Emperor, the [...] rial government could have obt[...] peace without any mutilatio[...] French territory, and on ter[...] hard, at least such as coul[...] borne. France would have su[...] the mortification of defeat, and [...] have been compelled to inde[...] as a matter of course, Prussia f[...] expenses of the war; but she [...] have suffered no loss of territor[...] would have remained, defeate[...] deed, but not conquered. E[...] would have mediated effectua[...] her favor, for the balance of [...] requires her preservation; bu[...] European nations could not

of loyalty towards him, and abandons him as it did his greater uncle the moment he becomes unsuccessful. It never felt that it owed him allegiance, and how could it since he professed to hold from it? His government was based on a plebiscitum, and could it bind the nation? It was created by the people, was their creature, and can the creator be loyal to or bound by his own creation? The nation can be bound only by a power above itself and be loyal only to an authority that comes from a source independent of the people.

Louis Napoleon held from 1789, and had the weakness to believe in plebiscitums. He seems never to have understood that universal suffrage can only create an agency, not a government. He was a disciple of the political philosophers of the eighteenth century, who erected revolution into a principle. These philosophers of the eighteenth century made no account of the continuity of the national life, of national habits, customs, and usages, and assumed that the convention might draw up an entirely new constitution according to an abstract and preconceived theory, without regard to the antecedents or past life of the nation, and without any support in the spiritual or supernatural order above the nation, get it adopted by a plurality of votes, and safely rely on *l'intérêt bien entendu*, or enlightened self-interest, to preserve it and secure its successful practical workings as the fundamental law of the nation. The whole history of France for nearly a century, without any reference to our own experience, refutes the absurd theory of the philosophers, or sophists, rather. A French gentleman, still living, told us, before the recent collapse of the second French Empire, that he had witnessed seventeen revolutions or changes of government in his native country, and he is in a fai living to see the number inc least to a score. No go created by and held from th can govern the people; an son alone or the calculation rest were sufficient to susta ernment, no government cal constitution would be n Paper constitutions are worth so far as they express the li stitution of the nation. " tions," Count de Maistre has "are generated, not made"; merit of the American co is in the fact that it was b the American people, not them.

France was originally co by the king, the nobility, the with some feeble remains of Roman municipalities, subs revived and expanded into *état*. The balance of her constitution had been distur true; the church and the nob been greatly enfeebled by the ate growth of monarchy on hand, and the expansion of munal power on the other; four fundamental elements national constitution still sub more or less force down to volution of 1789. That re swept away king, church, bility, and proclaimed th *état* the nation, without an cal organization or power t stitute legal or legitimate gov No nation is competent to c itself, for till constituted it i mass of individuals, incapabl legal national act. Since the has been trying in vain t something out of nothing, a continually alternating betw mob and despotism—despoti pressing the mob, and th deposing despotism. She moment has no legal gov

their own heads. They throw her now as a sop to Cerberus.

The power of religion to sustain authority against the insurrection and rebellion of subjects, and liberty against the tyranny of the prince, is in her being an organic power in the nation, but independent of the national will, holding from God, not from the nation or its sovereign, and free to declare and apply the divine law alike to prince and people. Nationalized, she has no support outside of the nation, no power not derived from it, and can give the nation only what it already has in itself. It must follow, not lead the nation, and share its fate, which it has no power to avert. What can the Russian Church do to restrain the tyranny of the Czar? Or the Church of England to check the progress of the revolution now going on and threatening to sweep away king, nobility, and the church first of all? What can it do before the democracy become omnipotent? Why is it that no Gentile nation has ever shown any recuperative energy, but because Gentilism, as the name implies, is nationalism, and the nation has in it only a national religion, and nothing outside, above, or independent of the national authority? The Gentile religion, deprived of catholicity, had to follow the nation, and to share its corruption and its fate. When the nation fell, it fell with it; and the nation, when it fell, fell for ever, and disappeared from the list of nations. Protestantism in its essential principle is a revolt against catholicity, and the subjection of religion to the national will. It is essentially a revival of nationalism, or Gentilism, and hence a Protestant nation has no recuperative energy, and, were it to fall, its fall would be like that of a Gentile nation, a fall without the power to rise again. So it must be with every nation that has only a national or a nationaliz gion.

Napoleon, who wished the only as an adjunct of his own never understood anything of He saw that the church w conservative than Protestanti in fact so by virtue of her Cat that she had a stronger hol French people, and could se better than any Protestant se he did not see that the church for a political end, is ne powerless even to that end, a she serves a political end onl she is sought for her own s cognized and supported for gious end, or as the free an pendent kingdom of God o Not understanding this, he her unrestrained liberty, and by his own legislation to subj in his own dominions to l will, and to compel her ei support his policy or to feel weight of his vengeance. Sl support him, wear his livery, bidding, hold his enemies to enemies, or he would not tole at all. She, as the church could not accept this positi sink into a mere national however powerful the natio asserted her independence, independence alike of him an he professed to govern. H manded her to obey him: sh ed. He quarrelled with her, her supreme pontiff from his despoiled him of his estates, soned him, was excommunica came powerless before his was defeated, lost his thro was sent by his conquerors his life away as a prisoner land on the barren isle of St. leaving French society har disorganized than he found it

The Restoration which was a return toward legitim

under it France actually recuperated with a rapidity which seems marvellous to unbelievers. But it humiliated the nation, because it was imposed on it by foreign bayonets, and its work of reparation and expiation necessarily made it unpopular with all who had profited by the plunder and confiscations of the Revolution, or by the wars of the Empire. The spirit of 1789 still possessed a large portion the population. The Bourbons turned, also, with the old Gallican traditions of the relation of church and state, which had lost the monarchy, and prepared the people for the old revolution. They would have the church, indeed, but they would never recognize her rightful supremacy; and, though giving France really the best government she had had for a long time, they at length fell before the intrigues of a younger branch of the family, supported by the combined factions of the Bonapartists, republicans, and so-

The monarchy of July or the Barricades was, notwithstanding the pretences of the *juste milieu*, or doctrinaires, a purely revolutionary government, improvised in the interests of disorder, without a shadow of legality, and without anything, in the nation as in religion, on which it could rest; and from the first it was spurned by the legitimists, the old national nobility, by the peasantry, the larger part of the republicans, and supported only by the *bourgeoisie*, or business classes, and the Bonapartists, the latter of whom hoped to make it a stepping-stone to the restoration of the Napoleonic empire. It had no hold on the nation, no power to reconstitute it on a solid and permanent basis; and so, as a new generation appeared on the stage, it fell without a struggle before the Parisian mob. It was indifferent rather than avowedly hostile to the church, but it gave free scope to the infidel press, warred against the Jesuits, and maintained the infidel university in the monopoly of education. It, however, indirectly served the cause of religion by the little court favor the bishops could obtain, and who, in consequence, retired, and looked after the interests of religion in their respective dioceses, so that when a Parisian mob overthrew the citizen-king in February, 1848, and proclaimed the republic, the church was really more influential in France than she had been since 1682. She had influence enough to displace the party that made the revolution from the control of public affairs, to defeat and crush the reds and communists in the terrible days of June, 1848, to save French society from utter dissolution, and maintain order under a republic proclaimed by the friends of disorder. We are far from being convinced that, if the bishops and clergy had continued to show the energy in supporting the republic that they did in wresting it from the control of the infidels and destructives, they would not have been able to reconstitute French society on a Catholic and a republican basis, to the advantage alike of religion and society.

Certain it is, the church, though not officially supported by the republic, and had many and bitter enemies in France, was freer under it than she had been since the great Western Schism, and had a fair opportunity to prove to the world that she is wedded to no particular form of government or political organization, and can subsist as well, to say the least, in a republic as in a monarchy. We thought at the time, and we still think, though no enemy to monarchy and no blind defender of republicanism, that the French bishops and clergy committed a grave

blunder in abandoning the republic and surrendering French society to the nephew of his uncle—a member of the Carbonari, a known conspirator against the Pope in 1832, and a favorite with the red republicans and socialists. It would be difficult to estimate the damage they did to France and to the cause of religion throughout the world. It will cost, perhaps, centuries of bitter struggle and suffering on the part of Catholics, to repair the sad effects of that blunder. But French Catholics had for ages been accustomed to rely on royal support, and they lacked the robust and vigorous habits under God of self-reliance. The bishops and clergy could easily have marched to a martyrs' death, but they had with all their experience never learned the folly of putting their trust for the church in princes. They remembered the Reign of Terror; they remembered, also, the flesh-pots of Egypt, and shrank from the hunger, thirst, and fatigue of the desert.

The new emperor found the French people divided into three principal parties—the church or Catholic party, which included the Bourbonists and the better part of the Orleanists; the republican party, properly so-called; and the socialistic or extreme radical party, represented in the recent civil war by the communists of Paris and of all Europe. His policy on commencing his reign was avowedly to keep the control of all these parties in his own hands, by leaving each party something to hope from his government, and allowing no one to gain the ascendency, and, as far as possible, engrossing the whole nation in the pursuit of material goods. He acknowledged the sovereignty of the nation, professed to hold from 1789, and favored universal suffrage, which was in accordance with the views of the republican party; he adopted measures to secure em ment to the working-men o cities and towns, among whon the great body of the socialis communists, by his encourag of expensive national and mun works; and, to retain his ho them and to protect himself fro assassins of the secret societi made his Italian campaign, the Austrians out of Italy, and pared the way for Italian unific and for despoiling the Holy F of his temporal possessions an ereignty; raised the salaries p clergy as servants of the state repaired churches and abbeys tional monuments at the nation pense, to please and secure the c party. But he suppressed the dom the church had enjoyed the republic, maintained the "or articles" of his uncle, and all th Gallican edicts and legislation a the freedom and independen the church in full force, tr that she would see a compen for her loss of liberty in the incr pomp and splendor of her w or the gilded slavery to whic reduced her.

The recrudescence of infi atheism, or materialism was a m feature under the Second Em and the influence of religion and hourly declined; and all th dom and energy of the govern seemed exerted to *despiritualiz* we may be allowed the word French nation, to extinguish ever remained of its old chi sentiments and its old love of once so powerful in every F heart, and to render the nation i only on things of the earth, ea His policy, being always that of measures, disguised as moder was not suited to make him friends. His Italian campaign a Austria was pushed far enoug

ing and governing France was not in laboring to maintain an equilibrium of parties, but in throwing himself resolutely on the side of the party, in studying and sustaining, without any compromise with the enemies of God and society, real Catholic interests, and in surrounding himself by thorough-going Catholic statesmen. Catholicity alone offered any solid basis for the state or for authority, order, or liberty. The other parties in the nation were all, in varying degrees, the enemies alike of authority and liberty, and none of them offered any solid basis of government. He should, therefore, have placed his whole confidence in Catholic France, and set them aside, and, if they rebelled, have suppressed them, if necessary, by armed force. Had he done so, and acted in concert with the Holy Father and the religious portion of the nation, he would have reorganized France, given solidity to his power, and permanence to his throne. But from policy or from conviction he chose to hold from 1789, and was incapable of understanding that no government that tolerates the revolutionary principle, or is based on infidelity or the rejection of all spiritual or supernatural authority above the nation, can stand. So-called self-government, without the church of God, teaching and governing all men and nations in all things spiritual, is only a delusion, for the nation needs governing no less than the individual.

But as we have already hinted, there are remoter causes of the present condition of France, and, we may add, of all old Catholic nations; and Catholics must not throw all the blame of that condition on the governments or the revolutionary spirit of 1789, still so rife. They have been and still are the great majority in all these nations, and why should they not be held responsib prevalence of the revolutio it, and for the bad secula ments they have suffered t the church? Why have th ed an anti-Catholic public c grow up and become pred Why have they suffered t and interests of religion to ficed to the falsely suppos and interests of the secula Can they pretend that no l taches to them for all this?

France has, at least s death of Philip the Second been the foremost Catholic r the world, and for a muc time the leader of modern civ and in her we may see th that have produced her ow that of the other old Catl tions. France, in this her moment, has not, we b single Catholic in the ad tion. The president is a b no religion; the minister o affairs is no Christian, and l a man of very small abili minister of worship and i says he is moral, but he is no Catholic. The transitio ment, opposed as it is by all er parties in the nation, must at present seek to gain port of the bishops and c what we call the church p Spain, though the majority tholics and have votes, the ment is in the hands of the of the church. In Italy, a h infidels and miscreants though the great body of th are Catholics and have vote trol the nation, to violate w nity every principle of priv and of international law, t cate the property of the ch of religious orders, and t the Holy Father, take poss his capital, and hold him

between politics and religion, and that he who would serve God must leave the affairs of state to men of the world; which is, in effect, to deliver them over to the control of men who are servants of Satan rather than servants of God. The state has, therefore, been given over to the Enemy of souls, because Catholics were led, through a one-sided asceticism, to neglect to keep it in their own hands, and the church has been suffered to be despoiled, her pontiffs, priests, and religious have been suffered to be massacred, for the lack of a little resolution and energy on the part of Catholics to defend their religion and the sacred rights of their church and of society entrusted to their courage and fidelity. Thus a handful of Jansenists, Protestants, Jews, and infidels in France were permitted to establish a reign of terror over twenty-five millions of Catholics, exile their bishops, massacre or banish their priests and religious, suppress religious houses, close the churches, prohibit Catholic worship, abolish religion itself, decree that death is an eternal sleep, and substitute for the worship of the living God the idolatry of an infamous woman, placed upon the altar and adored as the goddess of Reason. All this time, while all these horrors were enacted in the name of the nation, the twenty-five millions of Catholics, except in Brittany and La Vendée, made hardly a show of resistance, and suffered themselves to be led as sheep to the slaughter, forgetful that they owed it to France and to Christendom to sustain and govern their country as a Christian or Catholic nation. It is a duty to pray, and to pray always, but sometimes it is a duty for Christians to fight, and to have not only the courage to die in the battle for a holy cause, but to generous souls the far more difficult courage, the courage to kill. We have observ French Catholics no lack against a foreign foe, even of more than doubtful ne justice, but a fearful lack against the domestic foe, late communist insurrectio They seem restrained by conscience.

Another reason may pr found in the fact already h the mass of Catholics h trained and accustomed t external authority; to look tion and support not to God selves, but to the secular gc They have not been accu rely on spiritual authority al the secular sovereign as a so *pus externus.* This had nc sequences so long as th sovereign was faithful, and under the direction and au and in concert with, the Pontiff; but it had a most effect when the sovereign ecclesiastical matters in name, and when he turne the Pope, and sought to s church in his dominions t control or supervision, w not seldom the case. But and people, accustomed to l secular authority to guar against the entrance of th became slack in their vigil remiss in acquiring habits liance, and, with the inspirati Holy Ghost, of self-defence quently, when kings an ceased to keep guard, or w turned wolves themselves, Protestant revolt, the f powerless, knew not to who for support, and had no res to yield themselves to be by schism, heresy, or aposta is now the case with the g of the Catholic people in a tholic countries. With the

volution and
s, the sover-
it a single ex-
ed or turned
d there is not
y Father can
ith the kings
either hostile
while the old
the secular
for the mo-
es nearly the
ics in all old

wing out of
in the habit
ce the rise of
g on the ex-
clusion of the
Holy Ghost.
in the church,
s through her
; he dwells
faithful, and
m, and gives
elf-reliance to
tism assailed
f the church,
for Catholics
o its defence,
pirit that dis-
not assert it
be the spirit
it of error, in
, the blessed
already in his
may be that
call the ex-
Holy Ghost,
ch as a teach-
, has caused
t body of the
inspirations
oly Ghost in
Catholic will
appreciate as
the external
her suprema-
accept *ex*
and infalli-

bility of the successor of St. Peter in the See of Rome, as defined in the recent Council of the Vatican, and should be no better than a Protestant if we did not; but that external authority is not alone, or alone sufficient, as every Catholic knows, for the soul, and its acceptance is not sufficient for salvation. The Holy Ghost must dwell in the individual soul, forming "Christ within, the hope of glory." We do not mean to imply that any of our ascetic writers or spiritual directors overlook the need of the interior inspirations and guidance of the Holy Spirit, or fail to give it due prominence, but that its authority has not had due prominence given it in our controversial literature and in our expositions of Catholic faith intended for the public at large.

All these reasons have combined to reduce France, so long the foremost Catholic nation in the world, to her present pitiable condition, hardly more pitiable than that of Italy, Spain, Austria, and the Spanish and Portuguese states of this continent. What is the remedy, or is there none? We do not believe there is no remedy. We do not believe it, because the church proved her power in France under the Republic of 1848; which originated in hostility to her still more than to monarchy; we do not believe it, for we see Catholicity still able to convert the heathen; we do not believe it, because we see Catholicity vigorous and flourishing, and every day gaining ground in Protestant nations, where the church has no external support, and receives no aid from the state, and is thrown back on her own resources as the kingdom of God on earth, as she was under the pagan emperors. These facts prove that she is by no means effete, or incapable of making further conquests. Her decline in old Catholic nations

is no sign of weakness or decay in her, but is due to the imperfect training, to the timidity and helplessness of her children, deprived as they are of their accustomed external supports.

The remedy is not, as De Lamennais contended, in breaking with the sovereigns and forming an alliance with the revolution; but in training her children to those interior habits and robust virtues that will enable them to dispense with the external props and supports of civil society, and in asserting for herself in old Catholic nations the freedom and independence she has here, or had in pagan Rome, though it be done at the expense of her temporal goods and of martyrdom. The people of God, under the Old Law, sought support in an arm of flesh; the arm of flesh failed, and they were carried away into captivity. The arm of flesh fails the people of God again. There are Christians, but there is no longer a Christendom. Modern society is hardly less pagan than the ancient society the church found when she went forth from Jerusalem to convert the world. There is no reliance to be placed in the horsemen and chariots of Egypt. The whole world is to-day, as in the time of the apostles, a *missionary* world; and, perhaps, the greatest embarrassment of the Holy Father is encountered in the fact that Catholics in old Catholic nations cannot see it, but persist in being trained and governed as they were when there was a Christendom. Everywhere the church is by the defections of the governments become again in all nations a missionary church, and her bishops and priests need everywhere to be trained and formed to be wise, persevering, and effective missionaries. Catholics must everywhere be made to understand that it is not the church that needs the state, but the state that needs the church.

France without the church has no power to reorganize the state. She has not yet subdued the revolutionary elements which have so confused her, nor loosed the hold of the conqueror upon her throat, and her present improvised government deserves the confidence of no party in the nation. In itself, the Thiers government is utterly powerless. It needs the church, and cannot stand without her. French Catholics should understand this, and boldly assume the lead of public affairs, if they are men and love their country, and make, as they now can, the republic, under an emperor, king, or president, it matters not much which, a truly Catholic republic, and France, now so low and weak, may become again the nucleus, as under Clovis and St. Clotilde, of a reconstructed Christendom, constituted differently as to politics, it may be, but unchanged as to religion from that which has now passed away. The church never dies, never changes, and cannot be other than she is; but the political organization of Christendom may change with time and events. It changed when the barbarian nations displaced the Roman Empire; it changed when Charlemagne closed the barbarous ages, and opened the way for the feudalism of the middle ages; it changed again when, through the revolution inaugurated by Luther, absolute monarchy succeeded to feudalism in Catholic hardly less than in Protestant Europe; and it may change again when order succeeds to the present revolutionary chaos. It is not likely that Christendom will be reconstructed on its old political basis, whether it is desirable that it should be or not, and, for ourselves, we think that all who hope to see it so reconstructed are sure to be dis-

We think it not impro-
vhen Christendom is re-
it will be politically, on a
nd anti-monarchical ba-
bsolutism, whether that
r that of the people, is
e with the recognition of
sovereignty, and conse-
religion. Neither form
n can form the political
onstructed Christendom;
babilities are that, when
into their places, and
der begins to emerge, it
ed on some form of re-
, in which the organic
take the place of the

nt condition of things is
d; but we see nothing
hould lead us to despair
e. Catholics in old Ca-
s have needed, and per-
eed, to learn that this
subsist and conquer the
ut any external support
lar government, but that
ernment cannot subsist
ge properly its duties to
ut the church. We who
estant countries, and see
y dissolving before our
o need to be taught that
have already learned it
But the mass of Catholics
olic nations, even of the
well as the uneducated,
imperfectly understand
sequently render it diffi-
mpossible, for the church
ly and promptly the mea-
ght judge the most pro-
t the wants of the times.
see that the old Christen-
me, beyond the hope of
Providence, it seems to us,
ed the present state of

f their inopportune con-
nd to force them to learn and profit by the lesson which every day becomes more and more necessary for them to heed, if the prosperity of religion is to be promoted, the salvation of souls to be cared for, and the preservation of society assured. The measures taken are severe — very severe, but there are scholars that can be made to learn only by the free use of the ferula. Especially do the Catholics of France need to learn this lesson, for in no other country have Catholics made their religion so dependent on the secular order.

The fall of France, notwithstanding the faith, piety, and charity of so large a portion of her people, will probably prove only a temporary injury to Catholic interests. France has fallen because she has been false to her mission as the leader of modern civilization, because she has led it in an anti-Catholic direction, and made it weak and frivolous, corrupt and corrupting. Providence is severely punishing her; but he has not, we trust, cast her off for ever. She has in her bosom still millions of Catholics, and these have only to come forward in the strength of their religion, displace the enemies of God, take themselves the management of the affairs of the nation, and show the wisdom and energy they did in 1848, when they put down the red republicans and socialists. They will then enable France, in spite of the grasp of the conqueror and the fierce opposition of the destructives, to recover, slowly and painfully, it may be, but nevertheless to recover, and to prove herself greater and more powerful than ever. When France becomes once more a really Catholic nation, the revolution will be extinguished, infidelity will lose its popularity, atheism will no longer dare show its head, and a reaction in favor of the church will take place, so

strong and so irresistible that the whole world will be affected by it, and the nations that have so long been alienated from unity will be brought back within the fold.

The only obstacle to this grand result which we see is in the timidity, in the lack of energy on the part of Catholics in the assertion and defence of their religion, or in their want of courage to confide alone in God for success. Adversity, we think, can hardly fail to reform and reinvigorate them, and to direct their attention to their true source of strength as Catholics or the children of God. They will learn from it to adhere more closely to the Chair of Peter, a rely more on the internal di of the Holy Ghost, and less o aid of the secular order. No the present state of things impo ditional labors as well as suf on the bishops and clergy in o tholic nations, and requires som difications of the education o priesthood now given in our naries. Our Levites must be t for a missionary world, not f old Catholic world; but this alarm no one; for the great labors and sacrifices in the ser God, the greater the merit a reward.

A MEMORY.*

'Twas only a prayer I heard
In that vast cathedral grim,
Where incense filled the air
And vesper lights burnt dim.

'Twas only a woman's form,
Kneeling with upturned face,
That looked through the pictured altar
Up to the throne of grace.

Clasped in her small white hands
An amber rosary telling;
While from her glorious eyes
Teardrops fast were welling.

No thought for the world without,
No thought for the stranger near,
As pausing and sobbing she murmured,
"O Mother of sorrows, hear!"

And I, in a land of strangers,
Joined in the pleader's prayer:
Praying for her that I knew not,
To Her who I felt was there.

* By one who is not a Catholic.

may more easily tear himself out from the central whirl than draw back from that smooth outer circle.

Besides, there was doubt. He who can do many things must needs choose, and, where circumstances are passive, choice may be difficult. Carl inherited his father's talent, and had more than his father's force. He sketched and painted exquisitely, and, when he drew the portrait of one he loved, the picture breathed. Many a lady, disappointed with the stiff presentment of her beauty achieved by other artists, had entreated him in vain to become her limner.

"Ransome paints my nose, and hair, and shoulders all right," one said. "I cannot find fault with a line. But for all the soul he puts into them, my head might as well be a milliner's block. I suppose it is because he thinks that a fine body does not need any soul. Such a contrast as I saw in his studio, the other day! He had two or three portraits of Mrs. Clare, painted in different positions, and he displayed them to me, going into ecstasies over her beauty. 'Yes, yes,' I answered; but I was not enchanted. 'She is one of the few dangerous women,' he said, meaning that the power of her loveliness was irresistible; but I could not understand his enthusiasm. Presently, I espied, in a corner of the room, on the floor, half-hidden by other pictures, a face that made me start. I did not think whether or not the features were perfect, the hair profuse, the tint exquisite. I saw only a luring, fascinating creature, who, with head half-drooping and lips half-smiling, gazed at me over her shoulder. There were no red and white. The face looked out from shadows so profound, they might be of a midnight garden at midsummer, when the moon and stars are hid in sultry cloud, or from the shrouding arras of a lonely chamber wicked old palace, or from hanging portal of the bottor I would walk through fire t back one I love from follow a face. 'It is wonderful!' I ed. 'Why do you hide it by far superior too anything have here.' I thought that l some did not seem to be much ed by my praise. 'I did not he said. 'Carl Owen You Of course, I could not say a The situation was emba 'Would you think that t same as these?' pointing to traits of Mrs. Clare. I coul resemblance. 'They are th he said, looking mortified. I knew what he meant in say she was a dangerous woman did you paint that, Mr. Yorl lady asked abruptly, turnir Carl.

"In order not to be attr. it," he replied gravely. "D leave on you the impression thing snakelike? In painti I broke the spell. Alice M me to paint it. She said, ' fascinated only by that which not analyze. Catch the tr the power is gone.' She w She is always right. Nothi shallow as an evil fascination

Yet, in spite of every pro success, Carl turned aside f He had found out that th above all, needs happiness. study, think, and work, w heartstrings are strained to b but he who, with his hand t pen, the brush, the chordec or the chisel, waits till those influences which he is gifted ceive shall move him, mu every pulse stilled by a perf tent. Pain distorts his work. tunes his music, blurs his col ens his thought, and makes h

. Nor is this in purely natural
ne; for the artist whose strug-
ul ignores all else to grasp
ernatural gives only a blunt-
through a turbid medium.
pencil failing, there was dip-
r, and literature, particularly
ism.. Something must be
His idle and aimless life had
e a torture. Therefore he
l, and read, giving much time
guages. "Languages," he was
to say, "are as necessary to a
who would always and every-
have his forces in hand, as a
of keys is to a burglar."
conversation which Carl held
dith, just before she left Bos-
ay have been instrumental in
ng him. The two stood to-
, in one of the lance-windows
ghted Hester's library. Hes-
l her mother were up-stairs, and
was no one else in the room
gene Cleaveland and his little
r, Hester's child. The little
as gravely and patiently striv-
pick up, with dimpled fingers,
: of pink light that fell on the
rough a pane of colored glass
window-arch, and Eugene was
rely explaining to him why he

nd so," said Carl, after a si-
"Mr. Rowan is your ideal

was his way of intimating his
edge of existing circumstances,
e spoke carelessly, watching the
en.
have no ideal of man," Edith
l briefly; and, after a moment,
e: "A person may be excellent,
ut being ideal." She thought a
nt longer, then said: "Men
ars have to be set at a certain
ce before they shine to us. I
ot sure but Tennyson could
a fine hero of a poem of Dick.
as heroic qualities. I do not analyze nor criticise my friends, but I perceive this in him: he is capable of proposing to himself an object, and following it steadily. Every one is not."

Carl Yorke's countenance changed. And yet he knew well that she had not dreamed of reproaching him.

"What are you studying Spanish for?" Miss Clinton inquired fretfully, one day. "You might as well learn to dance the minuet."

"When one has so many castles in a country, one would like to know the language," he said.

"Pshaw!" exclaimed the old lady. "Don't waste your time. No language with a guttural in it is fit for a well-bred person to speak. Besides, to speak Spanish properly, you must wear a slouched hat and a stiletto, or a ruff and feather. I have no patience with this mania for tongues. English and French are enough for any sensible person. Italian is boned turkey. What book is that you have brought in?"

"De Maistre, *Les Soirées de Saint-Pétersbourg*."

Miss Clinton laughed disagreeably. "'The prophet of the past,' is it? Who is it says that he has '*une grande vigueur, non pas de raison, mais de raisonnement*'? Are you studying sophistry or Ultramontanism? *A propos*, there are pretty doings in that absurd little town where your people live. That ungrateful paper which you used to edit has been abusing your father like a pickpocket, on Edith's account, I suppose. You wouldn't tell me, but Bird found out; and she says that he doesn't dare stir out-doors."

"It is not true that he is afraid," Carl said; "but he is insulted. In Seaton, 'the pen is mightier than the sword,' without doubt. I would like to see it tried if the horse-whip might

not in this case be mightier than the pen."

"You see, now," the old lady said, "what mischief all these religions make. The basis of every so-called religion is hatred of every other so-called religion. And here you are poring over De Maistre! Pshaw! Read *The Age of Reason.* Here it is."

Carl was silent a moment, struggling with himself. Then he said, "I have gone round the circle, and come back to a faith in faith, and the sneers or arguments of the atheist have no more effect on me. I have found that mocking is neither noble nor manly, still less womanly; and I look back on my days of scepticism as on the freaks of a presumptuous child, who fancies itself wiser than its parents, when it is only more foolish. I have done with Tom Paine and his brotherhood."

It is always hard to even seem to exhort our elders, and especially so when they are our intimates; and Carl spoke with such an effort that his words seemed to be a passionate outburst.

Miss Clinton looked at him a moment in silent astonishment, then laughed shrilly. "'*What is this that hath happened to the son of Kish?*'" Then changing suddenly, she rang her bell. "Bird," she said, when that person appeared, "I want you to read the paper to me. There is a beautiful case of poisoning, this evening. Young Mr. Yorke is too pious for secular reading. He has turned preacher, Bird. You and he can sing psalms together."

"Alice, I accept one dogma of your church," Carl said afterward to his friend. "I must believe in purgatory, for I am in it."

"I am rejoiced to hear it," she replied, yet looked at him sadly. She would so gladly have spared him any pain. "Purgatory is the high-road to heaven. Of course you are getting your moral p tive arranged, you must feel fortable; but once started in will arrange itself."

"Suppose that I should fa asked.

"I dare say that you will one sense," she replied. "M propose to themselves great e ways do meet with a sort of as the flower fails in order t place to the fruit. Each gre cess, *being unique* of its kind in its own way. You canno surely, but success must come, or later."

"You speak as if I had all ty," he said, not without imp

She looked up vividly. "Yo all eternity, Carl!"

He made no reply.

"Let me quote a favorite of she said:

> "'That low man goes on adding one t
> His hundred's soon hit.
> This high man, aiming at a million,
> Misses a unit.
> That, has the world here—should
> the next,
> Let the world mind him!
> This, throws himself on God, an
> plexed,
> Seeking, shall find him.'"

"I understand you," he sai a slight shrug. "But, do I l apostle?"

"You might be," she ans "You could influence a class the preachers cannot reach. gion has been too much confi ascetics, or to those who und mate the power of the be What we want most now are tians who can outshine sinn grace, fascination, and learnin these reckless days, people w receive a check from those they know would gladly imp utter prohibition; but one o own might put a limit. We scholars who will acknowledg

drawal at the time when they must have been startled into thinking of her in some other way than as pensioners, never entered her mind. Besides that momentary and almost unconscious complaint, she had but one thought: God alone had loved her, and she must be alone with him. She could no longer do anything for any person; and since no one belonged to her more than to any other, nor so much as to others, no one had any claim to intrude now.

The sisters were faithful to their charge. Of the many who came with tardy devotion, she heard nothing; of Miss Clinton, sitting in her carriage at the door, with two men waiting to carry her up-stairs in a chair as soon as she should have permission, the attendants did not speak to her; of Carl Yorke, haunting the place, and sitting hour after hour in the parlor, waiting for news, she never knew.

One day, when Carl had sat there long, with only one prospect of news before him, the priest came down, and entered the room. Carl lifted his face from his hands, and looked at him, but could not speak.

"Let us think of heaven!" said the priest.

Of some actively religious persons, we might think that they parody the paradox, and say, Give us the luxuries of piety, and we will dispense with the necessities; but this woman had been other. No great work could be pointed to that she had done or attempted: her life had flowed like an unseen brook, that, hidden itself, is only guessed at by the winding line of verdure which betrays its presence. She was one of those piteously tender and generous souls whom everybody makes use of, and nobody truly thanks. Seldom, indeed, do we find one so just and truly kind as to think for those who do not deman thoughtfulness. It is the cl and the pushing who poss land.

A part of Miss Mills's fort given to the church, the r left conditionally. She kne Clinton's caprice well enough it possible that Carl might unprovided for at the last n In such a case, he was to heir, after a few legacies ha paid. But if Miss Clintor should be favorable to him, was to go to Edith.

On Miss Clinton, the effect death was terrible. She alte refused to believe that it ha place, and reproached them ing her of it. When Bird t discreetly to draw a pious from it, the old lady flew into paroxysm of rage that she frig them. She seemed to be point of having convulsions. went to the funeral without where he was going, and the was never again mentioned hearing.

But that silence was not fo ness, they saw plainly; for, fro time, Miss Clinton never herself to be left alone a m Bird read to her till far in night, watched her fitful slu and was ready with cheerful in whenever the old lady open frightened eyes. The light went out in her room, but wa brightly burning—a small screening the face only of the By day, Carl had to read to her ing stories or tell the gossip town.

When spring came again, s unable to leave her room, an short time, was confined to h and from querulous became headed.

Carl made a desperate eff

The Catholics did not raise their voices. Those who mourned their deserted altar, mourned in silence ; the rest went back to their whiskey-drinking, their quarrelling and stealing. That was what the atheists meant by peace. " The lion and the lamb had lain down together," but the lamb was inside the lion.

On the surface of these halcyon circumstances, Carl Yorke found his lotos-flower growing. Everybody was smiling and conciliatory. Congratulations, not always overdelicate, on his accession to fortune met him at every hand, and callers became more frequent, in spite of a reception as cool as politeness would allow. In fine, the Yorkes, having suffered a temporary eclipse, shone out again with dazzling lustre, regilt by their new prosperity. If they bore themselves rather haughtily in the face of this subservience, we can scarcely blame them. We can forgive, we may not care for, the frowns that darken with our adversity ; but the smiles that brighten when fortune brightens, must, in a noble nature, awaken a feeling of involuntary disgust.

Dr. Martin and his wife called a few days after Carl came home. It was rather an embarrassing call, for there was scarcely a non-explosive subject on which they could speak, but by dint of careful management on the part of the ladies, and a determination on the part of each gentleman that he would not be the aggressor, no accident happened. Mr. Yorke and the minister exchanged a few remarks on agriculture, Clara hovering between them, and volubly smoothing the asperities of their uphill talk. Mrs. Martin and Melicent were kindred souls on the subject of worsted work, and grew quite intimate over a new pattern and a rainbow package of wools. Mrs. Yorke

acted as presiding deity, and ɩ ped a smile or a word at the time, and Carl was somewhat cally amused by the situation therefore amusing. The visitor asked for Edith, but she declir come down. When they had however, she spoke kindly ɔ Martin.

" He asked me once," she " if, when I came to die, I ɛ need any one but Christ. I not answer him, for I did not ' stand then that he was attacki doctrine of extreme unction, a timating his belief that Ca think only of the priest, and all of God. But I noticed tl showed a great deal of feelin when he said, ' If you have you need no one else,' there tears in his eyes. Since then, liked him. I think he is mi: rather than malicious."

Mr. Yorke looked gravely niece. " I sometimes thinl said, " with Pope, ' that th nothing needed to make all ɪ and disinterested people in the of one religion, but that they talk together every day.' If would ask what you believe, ɛ ten to you, instead of tellir what you believe, and abusin much strife might be avoided.

" I think that Dr. Martin's in coming here was good, Yorke said. " He knows t are going away, and wishes ɪ in peace."

" Carl, have you settled wl are going to be ?" Edith vent ask when he joined her after the garden.

" No," he answered, with tion. " Something depends. at the north pole, and al lead south. Meantime, I idle."

She waited for him to ɔ

made a crayon group of his father, mother, and sisters. Mrs. Yorke insisted that he should paint his own portrait separately for her. Being in a bitter mood one day, he sketched himself as Sisyphus standing on the hill-top, and watching the great stone, which he had just rolled painfully up hill, roll down again of itself. Edith sat by him, saying a word now and then, and watching his work.

When his hand paused to let his imagination picture first the dull misery in the face of the dazed and baffled giant, she said quietly, "What great bovine creatures the Titans were, after all! I did not admire them much, even when you read me the translation of the *Prometheus*. All that splendor of soul was Æschylus, not the fire-stealer. But wasn't it a beautiful verse: 'Stately and antique were thy fallen race'?

"Still, the mastodon is stately and antique, too. The Titans were too easily conquered. They cut like great melons. If their spirit had been equal to their size, they would have snapped the Olympians like dry twigs beneath their feet."

Carl knew full well that she was talking *at* him, but he was in no mood to be either shamed or inspired. He wanted to be coaxed. The manliest man has his time of not only wishing, but needing, to be coaxed, if only he would own it.

She stretched her hand, and softly, inch by inch, drew the porte-crayon from his yielding fingers. "Please, Carl! The picture would haunt me, though it were out of sight."

It was better than a wiser word. Carl's face cleared.

"I am going to paint your portrait in oil," he said, "and keep it myself. Shall I?"

"I will be your rich patroness, and you a poor artist," she said. "I order my portrait of you, and will pay—let me think what!
be a red gold medal of tl
maculate Conception, or a lit
ny crucifix, with the figure i
whichever you choose. The
be a poor lady, and you a ric
and you shall buy the pictu
and—what will you give me
I know what I like that you

"What do you like?" asl
placing a large sheet of c
board on his easel.

"A tiny brooch, that yo
wear, with a carbuncle in it.
fess to you that I have longe
It is like a coal of fire. It
beautiful. You know I have
sion for gems. Flowers m
sad, but gems are like heave
and hopes that never fade.
no object in nature that deli
like a beautiful gem. They
good acts of the earth. A
an act of love, a sapphire a
faith, an emerald an act of
diamond an act of joyful ad
Pearls are tears of sorrow
dead, opals are tears of sor
sin. The opal, you know, is t
gem that cannot be imitated.'

"So you wanted the carl
Carl said, much pleased.
didn't you say so before?"

"I waited till I knew tl
cared nothing about it," Ec
swered.

"But I do value it ver
now, young woman; and if yo
where it is, you will bring it t
once. I am impatient to see

She went out and got the
It was a smooth, oval sto
deep-red color, with a tin
flickering in it. The lapid
been too true an artist to s
stone with facets, and the re
a little crystallized poem. Ec
it on black velvet, and held it
Carl to see. "There!" sh
It had never occurred to him

pressed it; their best clothes, given by Mrs. Yorke, were donned; and their hair combed down so smoothly that it seemed to be plastered to their heads. Woe to that child who should rumple a hair or disturb a fold when all was done! Since her accession to fortune, Edith had given the family, among other things, a clock—they had formerly reckoned time by the sun—and, at precisely half-past nine, Joe sat himself in the south window to watch for the teacher. According to Mrs. Patten's notions of propriety, it would be indecorous for any of them to be seen outside the door on Sunday till after the instruction. The house was as clean and orderly as such a place could be made; the sacks of straw and dry leaves that answered for beds were made into two piles, in opposite corners, and used as sofas; the calico curtains that divided the bedrooms were artistically looped; a vast armful of green boughs concealed the rocks of the rough chimney, the sticks laid there to be lighted to get dinner by, and the pots and pans in which that dinner was cooked. Green vines and flowers and moss were placed here and there, and the door by which Edith entered was always made into a sort of triumphal arch, where she stood a moment to exchange her first salutation with the family. They were drawn up in two lines, to right and left, the girls headed by their mother, the boys by their father, and as that pretty creature appeared in the door, with her air of half-conscious shyness, and wholly unconscious stateliness, like a young queen appearing to her subjects, the feminine line dropped a short courtesy, and the masculine line achieved a simultaneous bow, both so crisp that they gave a sensation of snapping. What a beautiful salutation was that low, deliberate "Good-morning!" of hers; and could equal in grace that slight ing, half bow, half courtesy, which she greeted them! Op the door was a little stand, chair behind it, and the whole pany stood till Edith had tak seat there. She never did so out a blush of humility.

To one less earnest, and le occupied by the real work sh to do, this ceremony would seemed sufficiently ludicrous. perhaps, we should say, rath one less tender of heart. But Yorke saw only the eager gra and desire to do her honor, th ple earnestness and good fait that mingling of poverty and which silently showed all the of poor Mrs. Patten's life. F that was done was hers. W her, the children and their would have been almost as clo

There is a certain arrogan affability with which the rich times approach the poor, as t wealth and education constitut essential difference which the elaborately anxious should no much humiliate their *protégés.* the intelligent poor are very to perceive, and inwardly, i outwardly, to resent. Others a the rude manners of those they would benefit, in order t them at ease—a good-natured take, but one which inspires cont and weakens their influence. Yorke's quick sympathies and cate intuitions rendered it impo for her even to make either of missteps. She carried herself perfect dignity and simplicity kind, and even affectionate, w lowering herself into a caressi miliarity, and thus gave th sample of exquisite demeanor, at the same time, set them as at their ease as it was well

danger of death, any person who knows how can baptize it."

She said no more, but, after distributing some little presents to the children, as her custom was, and sitting by the baby a few minutes, went home. The mother was very pale. She sat looking at her child, and seemed indisposed to speak. There was even a sort of coldness in her manner when she took leave of her visitor.

The children went out, and looked after the lady as long as they could see her, then gathered in a whispering group about the door. They felt, rather than knew, the impending sorrow. Joe went, stool in hand, and sat down by his wife. Her lips began to tremble. She was only a woman, poor soul! and wanted comfort, not only for the grief before her, but for the new and terrible fear that had risen up in her heart while Edith Yorke spoke.

"Joe," she said unsteadily, "that girl is very learned. Dr. Martin can't equal her. She makes everything awfully clear. She leaves no hole for you to crawl out. If baptism isn't what she says, then there isn't any sense in baptism."

"Yes," sighed Joe, "she's a mighty smart gal."

"Then," the mother whispered sharply, "if what she says is true, what's become of our other children, Joe?"

He looked up with startled eyes. He had been thinking of their present sorrow, not of the past. It is only the mother who for ever carries her children in her heart.

"There are three children gone, Joe," she said imploringly.

He dropped his eyes, and considered anxiously, not so much the fate of his lost children as the fact that Sally looked to him for help. A shallow head goes with a shallow heart, and his first thou
merely how he should e
weight of his wife's depende

"Oh! you broken reed!
claimed, with suppressed pa

Thus apostrophized, Jo
desperate, and that desper
parted to him an air of
decision and authority.

"I tell you what it is,
said, "these rules and re
are very well for learned
they're to blame if they d
'em. But I don't believe
Lord is going to punish us
young ones for what we do
nothing about. He kno
enough that we'd a had 'e
soul of 'em, baptized, if
thought he wanted us to.
I don't begrudge the young
ing baptized. So don't you
Sally, but he'll sly 'em in s
poor little creters! Why,
s'pose that, while we wer
here and crying over our
bies, and saying, 'The Lo
and the Lord hath take
blessed be the name of th
that just at that time he'c
out of sight somewhere,
pinching on 'em and hurtin
for his own amusement, w
scared little faces looking up
It don't stand to reason, Sa

The first tears she had sh
from the mother's eyes
down her cheeks. "Joe,"
gratefully, "you've got son
tion in you, after all."

Edith went home that d
troubled heart. Two or th
on the way she stopped, ha
a mind to turn back, but
She was too agitated to k
or to eat. One thought
mind: a soul just slipping a
earth waited on the thresho
should open for it the gate o
The thought was overpowe

came swiftly in, and knelt by the cradle, leaving Carl standing in the doorway.

"Thank God! I am in time," she exclaimed. "I have come, you dear parents, to baptize this child, if you will permit me. You were not to blame for the others, because you did not know. But now you know. Consent quickly; for it is almost gone!"

"Yes, yes!" said the mother. "Make haste!"

Edith called the children, and made them kneel about the cradle, with their hands folded, palm to palm, and she scarcely noticed that Carl came in and knelt behind them.

"I am so anxious to do it rightly," she said, with one swift glance round the circle. "I never did it before, but it is very simple. I am very unworthy, and am afraid. All of you must say an Our Father for me."

Edith put a crucifix in the father's hands, and, as he held it up, bowed herself, and kissed the floor before it. Then she lighted a wax candle she had brought, and gave it to the mother to hold. Lastly, she knelt by the head of the cradle, and poured out a little vase of holy water.

"What is the child's name?" she asked, quite calm by this time.

Mr. and Mrs. Patten looked at each other. There had been many discussions between them on the subject, and at this moment neither of them could call to mind a single desirable name which had not been appropriated by their children, living or dead.

"I would like to name him for my father," Edith said. And they consented.

The words were spoken, then Edith leaned quickly, with a triumphant smile, and kissed the new-made saint, and whispered something to it.

The child had been lying
stupor for several hours, bu
whisper he opened his eyes,
ed them in a solemn and ste
on her face. There was so
in the look significant and
like; and, so looking at her,
ly died. Only a sigh, and
half-drooped, that was all o
But who shall say what it
heaven?

It was quite dark when
went home again. The s
was still, and perfumed wi
fern and wild violets, and th
ran along with them now
sound like a child talking
They walked hand in hand
by that sound.

"I am very, very happy
Edith.

Carl said nothing, but
short.

"Have you lost the trac
asked.

There was still a momen
ence, then he said in a stifle
"I have found it again."

Poor Carl! his finding
path was heroic. For an in
flower-wreathed wicket had se
swing across his way, and a
delight to lead from it. H
it, and walked on.

After a minute, Edith rec
that she had brought a seco
dle. They stopped and lig
then resumed their walk. S
the candle in her right ha
left she placed in Carl's agai
air was so still that the yello
waved only with their moti
the light of it made a hal
them, and brought out lea
flowers, and drooping branch
shone a moment, then disap

That ancient forest had
over many a human group
the unknown centuries of
dusky hunters in the chase o

AN ENGLISHMAN IN CHINA.*

In November, 1867, Mr. T. T. Cooper, an English gentleman who describes himself as a "pioneer of commerce," undertook an overland journey from Shanghai to Calcutta with the hope of discovering some shorter and more direct line of communication between India and China than that lying through the province of Su-tchuen and Eastern Thibet, the only route at present open. The undertaking was not a successful one, Mr. Cooper having been stopped and imprisoned at Weisee-foo, in the province of Yunnan, in July of the following year. This detention was the work of the Thibetan lamas, who have no desire for a free trade which will interfere with their monopolies, and who are, as a matter of course, violently opposed to the introduction of a religion which will weaken their own hold upon the people. Mr. Cooper, although an English Protestant who was contented to describe himself on his travels as a disciple of Confucius, and who took pains to inform the lamas that he could readily sympathize with their dislike of foreign innovations in religious matters, did not fail to share the effects of that distrust of foreigners which is so carefully kept alive in China by the governing classes, the literati, and the priests. While imprisoned at Weisee-foo, his interpreter, a Chinese Catholic, overheard the following conversation between two Mandarins, one of whom was Mr. Cooper's jailer, wh
to say the least of it, not rea

"Just as Philip took his p
der the window, Tien asl
Atenze Mandarin if he had :
foreigner who had passed
Atenze on his way to Tali-f
ing, 'We have him here in
mun.' His guest replied, '
cursed barbarian! what is
heard he was writing all the
was in my town, and drav
country. The son of a d
writes with a pen that req
ink. I suppose he has com
the country; and his peo
come to take it by-and-b
have got him here; why d
kill him?' To this my frie
replied, 'Why, it's no use to k
he has no money. We have
ed him; he has nothing; a
we are considering what to
him.' When Philip had got
he was so completely overv
that it was several minutes b
could proceed: when he ha
ered a little, he went on
late what the Atenze Manda
in reply. The ruffian evide
ed foreigners, for he said, '
him. You dispose of hin
when I return from the figh
kill those sons of dogs, the m
ries on the Lan-tsan-kiang: 1
fast converting the Lu-tsu, a
will very soon be masters
country, and we shall be kil
kill them all, I say.'"

A day or two later, our t
who seems to be very plucky
of courage, managed to effec
cape, but only to retrace his

* *Travels of a Pioneer of Commerce in Pigtail and Petticoats; or, An Overland Journey from China toward India.* By T. T Cooper, late Agent for the Chamber of Commerce at Calcutta. With Map and Illustrations. London: John Murray. 1871.

Cooper contracted into Philip, for convenience's sake, was the eldest son of a family which had been Christians for several generations. "His superior education rendered him, save in dress and manner, quite different to ordinary Chinamen, whose natural superstition and prejudice were replaced by intelligence, strengthened by the study of European philosophy and theology, while a knowledge of the Latin, English, and Chinese languages made the term of interpreter in his case no empty title. Such was my interpreter, who proved, as I expected, a useful servant and intelligent companion."

Having procured the services of these men, however, Mr. Cooper found it impossible to induce them to start from home until after the Christmas holidays were over; so that it was not until the 4th of January, 1868, that he finally left Hankou for the interior. He had previously taken the advice of the English secretary of legation at Pekin to conform himself in all respects to the line of conduct pursued by the missionaries, and had, during his month of enforced inaction, been trying to accustom himself to the pigtail and petticoats in which he was to introduce himself to the Chinese public. He had also been obliged to relinquish the idea of making scientific observations while on his journey, in order to avoid shocking the inveterate prejudices of the people against the use of instruments for that purpose. Even in keeping a daily record of his travels, he found it necessary to be constantly on his guard against their suspicious curiosity. One amusing instance of his caution in this respect, characteristic alike of our traveller and of his friendly enemy, is worth quoting:

"Round the fire of the little courier hut where we put up for the night, we were joined by a lama, w
he said, *en route* for Bathang.
the unwelcome addition of
dier spies to our party, it had
necessary for me to wait till
asleep, to write up my jou
was hard at work about m
when the lama returned to th
pretending to have left his
book behind; and seeing me
in writing, he became very
to know what I was doing.
owned to recording a simpl
tive of the day's journey, he
have reported that I was takin
of the country for some sinis
pose, so I replied that I was
my prayers, a ceremony whic
formed every night. This is
common occupation of the
themselves, but he was surpris
a merchant should write pray
I told him that I always
them after they were writte
would commence as soon as
finished. He waited, and
commenced to read my journ
in a monotone like that in wh
lamas recite their litanies.
reading thus for nearly half a
I stopped and asked my fri
recite his prayers for my bene
mising to pay him for the se
and off he started and kept
without ceasing until dayligl
morning, when he awoke m
received his fee of one rupe
declared that I must belong
Yellow religion, but I assur
to the contrary, merely sayi
my religion much resembled h
He was evidently puzzled, bu
ed at my having made use
services as a priest, and beg
to allow him to keep under m
to Bathang."

His inability to serve the i
of science was perhaps not a
of a nature to be very serio
by our traveller, whose chief

in bearing he really was—that I accepted his invitation, and sat down again; and in a few minutes all the other merchants, except two young men, who were permanent guests, left, and a serving-man then laid out the table, placing a pair of ivory chop-sticks, tipped with silver, for each of us, and brought in the dinner, consisting of fish-soup, boiled and fried fish, stewed ducks, mutton, and fowl. We took our seats—the host last—and were then handed cups (about the size of a large breakfast-cup) of rice, and in the interval before the soup and fish were brought in, baked melon-seeds were placed before us on small plates; these we nibbled at for a few minutes, until our host, taking his chop-sticks up, put their points into a plate of fish, and, looking round the table, bowed to us, whereupon we simultaneously helped ourselves, and commenced our meal. I kept up a lively conversation on the subject of foreigners and their wonderful inventions during the dinner, which I thoroughly enjoyed. When we had finished, we all stood up, holding our chop-sticks by the tips with both hands horizontally in front of our foreheads as a sign of thankfulness, and also respect to our host. We then sat down again, and little kettles of hot Samshu were brought in, and we commenced to drink wine with each other. The two young merchants soon became very loud in my praise, saying that I was quite different to the foreigners in Hankou, I was more like a Chinaman; but were very anxious to know if I was of the same religion as themselves; and when I told that I was a Christian, repeatedly embraced me, calling me a brother. We sat over our Samshu and smoked for a long time, the absence of anything like constraint among us, and the genuine hospitality of our host, mak-

ing the hours pass qui
that I was seeing Chinese
standpoint hitherto unknow
Europeans, especially Eng
and I felt much gratified wit
first admission into the priva
the people whose manners an
I had adopted. During the f
in the house I saw no fem
the exception of a servant,
ever in the house of any re
Chinaman meet the womank
ing the greater part of a ye
among this people. . .
was going toward the hotel
not help reflecting on the
had just left, so different i
spects from any previous id
formed of the Chinese cha
which, though I had dwelt
in their country, I confess wi
I had until now known no
could not help contrasting t
tion my host had given m
stranger and a foreigner,
which he would probably
ceived at my hands had h
me in Shanghai, when, as
with us Englishmen, he wo
likely have had to come
office without the least polit
agement from me, and ha
acted his business standi
which I should probably l
missed him with a gesture
tience. It seems a great pit
Englishmen, being such a gr
mercial people, do not assoc
selves more with the people
whom we trade. In China,
do wisely to remember the o
which tells us to 'do in Ro
Romans do,' and to meet
nese more on a footing of
in fact, adopt as much as
their ways of business, and
means do away with that s
go-betweens which is so de
to us in all our dealings
people, of whom we real

purer faith." Yet when he meets "apostles" of what he supposes to be a "simpler and purer faith," he can hardly preserve a decent gravity in contemplating either their methods or their results. "By their fruits ye shall know them" is naturally the last reflection suggested to the mind of a Protestant when he considers missionary work. The application of the text would be so speedily fatal to his Protestantism that the instinct of self-preservation keeps him from making it:

"The *Société des Missions Etrangères*, which from its headquarters in Paris directs the affairs of this mission, is most careful in the selection and training of the candidates for missionary life. As their work lies much among the wealthy and educated, though the poor and ignorant are by no means neglected, every missionary sent to Sz-chuan is specially educated for the purpose of meeting the Chinese literati on equal terms. They land in China generally as young and newly-ordained priests, under vows by which the rest of their lives is dedicated to the Sz-chuan Mission. Once having entered upon their work, they never abandon it, nor return to their native country; indeed, it is impossible for them to do so, for I have good reasons for stating that any recreant who may seek, in violation of his engagements, to quit the country, is certain to be apprehended by the Mandarins and sent back to the jurisdiction of the mission. This has an apparent connection with the edict of Khang-hi, which accorded toleration to those missionaries only who would swear never to return to Europe. The young missionary on entering China strips himself of his nationality; he shaves his head, and adopts the Chinese costume, and conforms in all respects to the Chinese mode of life. His first two years are spent either at one of the principal mission stations or at some out-station, in close attendance on an old and experienced father, under whose care he systematically studies the language and the manners of the people to whose service he has devoted his life. He is also trained in the working of the mission, and, as soon as he is a proficient in the language, is appointed to a permanent post under general orders from the bishop of the district to which he has been sent from Paris. It can easily be imagined that a mission numbering its converts by tens of thousands, and carrying its labors over such a vast extent of country as Western China and Eastern Thibet, must be a well-organized institution systematically administered. Taking advantage of the division of all the provinces into districts, each district is worked by the mission with more or less activity, as the disposition of the people will allow. The apostolic bishop resident at Chung Ching exercises a metropolitan authority over four other bishops, who reside at Cheu-tu and Swi-foo, in Sz-chuan, Yun-nan-foo in Yunnan, and in Kwei-cheu, and Bishop Chauveau at Ta-tsian-loo. The latter has charge of the mission stations of Eastern Thibet established at Bathang, Yengin, and Tz-coo, on the western banks of the Lan-tsan-kiang. I was informed that there were, in 1868, three hundred French missionaries, besides native priests and catechists, engaged in the missions working in the above provinces. The pay of a missionary varies from one hundred taels * per mensem—the salary of a bishop—to twenty taels, the scanty stipend of the simple fathers. Out of this they provide themselves with everything. At small out-stations, of course, the

* Not quite $170.

Chauveau, to whom Mr. Cooper gratefully records his many obligations, and whom he calls the ablest man and kindest friend he found in Western China, he made acquaintance with some of the Thibetan lamas, and visited their lamasery, of which he gives an interesting account. The chief lama paid him a visit at his hotel, and, as he showed a good deal of curiosity concerning his intentions, Mr. Cooper proceeded to define his position by remarking that he had heard that the lamas were averse to French missionaries entering their central kingdom, and added that he was not surprised that a great religious country like Thibet should object to the introduction of a new religion. The lama, unused to the easy way in which a travelled Englishman can carry his religion, was amazed, but on learning that Mr. Cooper was not a Frenchman, but professed a different faith from theirs, being in fact a simple disciple of Confucius, quite indifferent to new creeds, and disposed to look with friendly eyes upon all religions whatsoever, he became at once more cordial, invited him to the lamasery, warned him of a conspiracy against his liberty, and cautioned him to avoid identifying himself in any way with the Catholic missionaries. Mr. Cooper's return call upon his new friend was not in all respects pleasant:

"Crossing the courtyard, the lama led me up a flight of stairs into his room, which differed from those occupied by the other lamas only in its furniture and superior cleanliness. The other rooms were dirty, and contained nothing save a small stove in the centre of the floor, and a large wooden bucket, somewhat like an attenuated churn, and containing the everlasting butter-tea of the Thibetans. My host's room, however, had
in it several chairs of
and round the stove
thick woollen carpe
was invited to squat.
fortably seated mysel
ed in lama robes br
cups, one of which
with butter-tea, and,
mark of hospitality, b
huge pat of rancid bu
large as his fist, and
cup, which he polit
me; then, filling his c
way, he invited me
him. Good manners
drink, and I succeede
a mouthful of the gr
well-feigned pleasure,
observing, nodded h
bending gracefully fo
flourish, stirred round
butter in my cup with
and again pressed m
would have given w
been spared this sec
calling up all my reso
another gulp, and h
my pipe, while my
sipped his melted
much gusto as an a
his full-bodied port.

"Expressing a wis
lamasery, I was sho
the lama, and visited
temple, where he da
prayers to the Gran
said; meaning, I pre
It was a superb little
end a railing, richly o
gilded, fenced off int
gilded image of Bud
feet high, sitting in a
posture, enveloped in
pery of silk gauze. I
walls were rows of n
geon-holes, about a
each of which was a
of solid gold, about tw
There could not have
a hundred of these in

formed him that I was desirous of seeing the building, and, giving him my card, desired him to present it to the chief lama, with a request for permission to view the lamasery. He requested me to remain at the gate until his return, and took my message to the chief lama. . . . From where I stood I could see but little of the interior building. As much, however, as was visible proved that the fame of the Bathang Lamasery was justly deserved. In the centre of the block of buildings, the roof of the sacred temple was plainly visible, its massive gold covering flashing and gleaming in the sunlight with dazzling brilliancy. On the roofs, and, indeed, everywhere, the place was literally alive with roosters, which kept up an incessant crowing, blending in a chorus with the chants of the lamas. These birds are sacred to Buddha, and number, I was told, more than a thousand. None are ever killed, and their ranks are constantly swelled by the donations of the country people, who bring the chickens to the lamasery as religious offerings. The birds are all capons, and, like the lamas, live a life of celibacy. Not a single hen is allowed to come within the building. Everything in the sacred edifice is dedicated to the worship of Buddha, and supposed to be free from the contamination of the outer world.

"I noticed several nuns about, with shaven heads, but dressed in the ordinary garb of Thibetan women, with this difference, that the color and material of their dress were the same as those of the priestly robes of green stuff. These nuns are the abject slaves of the lamas, performing all the drudgery of the house in common with youthful novices or deacons. They, however, in the outer world enjoy, like the lamas, a superior social position, and command considerable respect from of the lay people. The shut themselves up entirel series, like cloistered nuns mish religion, but often their families, and work at hold duties and in the fielc nuns, like the priests, p strictest chastity, dedicati selves entirely to the wc service of Buddha. But, own observations, and from ly expressed opinion of the bitants of Thibet, which I quent opportunities of hear is a thing unknown among hood, and the lamaseries ar ter than dens of debauchery had begun to be impatie long absence, the lama retu a message that my presenc desired within the build would unsettle the priests devotions, but if I wished an offering in the shape or anything else, it would l ed. As this concession o of the chief lama was me expression of good-will, I messenger a tael of silver, a feeling of disappointment home. I afterward found t reason to congratulate mys exclusion from the lamaser of its inmates were suffe small-pox. This fearful dis mits great ravages among t tan population; of whom alr fourth person is disfigure effects. . . . When ca in a town, the lamas co families attacked to remo mountains, and seal up thei Should the sick persons b to bear removal, they are s the house, all communica them being prohibited, an to die or recover, as the be."

It was in a great measu

nearly reduced the party to starvation that Lo-tzung was only too glad to leave him and take shelter with an uncle. Later on, at Weisee-foo, as we have already related, he was imprisoned, and narrowly escaped with his life, only to begin at once to retrace his steps homeward. On reaching Kiating, on his return journey, he met for the first time traces of Protestant missionary work, and tells an amusing story about it:

"On the second day, a Chinese Christian called upon me, from whom I learned that a Protestant missionary had visited the city in the early part of the year, and had distributed a good many religious books; one of which, in the possession of the landlord of the hotel, proved to be a copy of the New Testament in Chinese. The owner produced the volume, and, adjusting his spectacles with a solemn air of wisdom, turned up the passage which runs as follows: 'It is easier for a mule [the camel in the English version] to pass through the eye of a needle than for a rich man to enter the kingdom of heaven.' Having read these words, he looked over his spectacles at me, and asked in a very contemptuous voice if it was possible for any man to believe such a statement, and if foreigners really did believe the statements made in this book? It had been my invariable custom since commencing to travel in China to avoid religious discussions, and always to proclaim myself a disciple of Confucius, so I now replied that I was not a teacher of religion, but only a humble disciple of Con-fu-dzu, but as to the statement about the mule passing through the eye of a needle, I thought I could explain that; and then proceeded to interpret the word 'needle' as used in the passage referred to. This somewhat mollified mine host, who remarked that he had no doubt that teachers found great diffic writing the flowery langua it would perhaps be as well did not write religious books Chinese under such circum When I was alone, I could regret that the praiseworth of the missionary in Kiating been more successful. How soon as it becomes safe for E to travel in China, there doubt but that the self-deny hard-working Protestant mis will enter upon a new and e field of labor, in which their devotedness, and well-know influence will doubtless win f if not success, at least ad from their supporters at hom

After leaving Hankou for hai, he again came upon the —apparently without great g tion:

"As we steamed past the Yang-chow, in the province o hoei, we saw the British flee had been sent up to demand tion for an outrage commi some Protestant missionari had been beaten and otherw treated. The sight of a Brit on the Yang-tsu for such a was curious indeed, and have no doubt, have don toward convincing the pe Yang-chow of the force of tantism, if not of its pacific For myself, I remember the French missionaries, whose source had been flight into m fastnesses, and then recall th given by the Master to the for drawing his sword aga high-priest's servant; and it hard to reconcile the prese fleet at Yang-chow for such pose with the doctrines prof his servants. Probably, times have changed sinc

rucified, and suffer-
nd it may now be
dient to proclaim
ie cannon's mouth,
oats to exact repa-
lern martyrs."
ave of our travel-
unate experiences
im from undertak-
rney, though by a
the following year,
nsuccessful result.
vell worth reading,

simply as an entertaining record of travel in a little known country; although to a Catholic it has the further interest of furnishing another of those involuntary testimonies from Protestant pens, which record the unvarying failure of their own missionary enterprises in producing any beneficial effect upon the heathen, and the exceeding heroism and devotion and the uniform and great success which as invariably characterize our own.

THE ISLAND OF SAINTS.

n lavish in her gifts
d, once so famous
hool of the godly
ugh fallen from her
gh no longer the
science, she is still

d romantic shapes,
and of stormy capes;
nd the tangled brake,
and the sunlit lake!"

ous cliffs protect
her shores are in-
t magnificent bays
r bosom is stored
tals, and the most
world crowns her
very geographical
antageous one, for
were, an advanced
kirts of Europe—
ute to the great
l she offers the first
American mariner.
nd green, her land-
d;" pellucid lakes
or the hills, rocks,
heir margins; here
ins of unequalled

verdure; there, garden-like tracts where the myrtle, the rose, and the laurel need no culture; where the evergreen arbutus, in wonderful luxuriance of growth, appears to be indigenous; where every spot is enamelled with flowers and fragrant herbs.

Beautiful Ireland! most picturesque land on the face of the globe! Alas! why not also the richest and happiest?

Religion and learning early found a welcome home in this "emerald gem of the ocean." Even in the dark days of paganism, the priest-and-poet Druid of Erin appears to have been superior in intelligence and culture to his brethren of England and of the Continent; and when Christianity was first preached in the land, no other people ever welcomed it with such ardent enthusiasm as did the Irish; no other people ever clung to their faith with such inviolable fidelity as Irish Catholics have since done.

During the five centuries that followed the apostolic labors of Saint Patrick, so great was the multitude of holy personages who trod in the

way which he traced out; so eminent the sanctity of their lives; so illustrious their learning, that Ireland received the proud title of "Island of Saints and Doctors." The number of her churches was infinite, and her monasteries and convents were at once the abodes of piety and the sheltering homes of the poor and the stranger. Her theological schools and colleges were the most renowned of Europe. Their halls were open to the students of every clime, "who," says Moreri, "were there received with greater hospitality than in any other country in the Christian world." Hither, as to the "emporium of literature," the youth of France, Germany, and Switzerland repaired in search of knowledge. But to the English nobility and gentry especially, the Venerable Bede tells us Ireland showed the most cordial hospitality and generosity, for, great though their numbers, they were *all* most willingly received, maintained, supplied with books, and instructed without fee or reward."

And the tide of sanctity and learning overflowed the shores of the holy isle; many were the pious missionaries who, in those days of religious fervor, went forth to labor for the salvation of souls among the nations of Europe. The memory of their works is still preserved in the countries which reaped the fruits of their zeal. The Italian town, San Columbano, still bears the name of the great Columbanus, a native of Leinster; and St. Gall, in Switzerland, still reminds us of his friend and disciple Gallus. The hermitage of Saint Fiacre, another Irish saint, is still one of France's consecrated spots; and the memory of the Connaught man, Saint Fridolin, "the Traveller," is still blessed on the banks of the Rhine. The famous universities of Paris and of Pavia owe their origin to the learning and industr ment and John, both] From Ireland the Anglo-Sa rived their first enlightenm till the thirteenth century t ture of Scotland was the sp vince of the Irish clergy.

"When we look into th astical life of this people," learned Görres, "we ar tempted to believe that son spirit had transported ove the cells of the Valley of the all their hermits, its monast all their inmates, and ha them down in the Western isle which, in the lapse of t turies, gave eight hundred saints to the church; won Christianity the north of Bri soon after, a large portion c pagan Germany; and, whi voted the utmost attentio sciences, cultivated with esp the mystical contemplatio religious communities, as w the saints whom they produ

Numerous vestiges are s found in Ireland of those da thusiastic faith. Ivy-grown and churches, and the habit saints; and the emblem of creed, now rudely cut on pill now exquisitely carved in fin tions, are to be met with scatt the whole length and bread land—"memorials," we are celebrated archæologist, "n the piety and magnificence o whom ignorance and prejuc too often sneered at as b but also as the finest works tured art, of their period, n ing."

In the wild and lonely v Glendalough, County Wick yet to be seen the remain noble monastery, "once the] of the Western world," found beginning of the sixth ce

ind which a city
d, decayed. Gloo-
ompass the silent
ninhabited glen, in
he ruins of shrines
teen centuries ago
onor of their God
d thankful in the
immortality—men
their youth rever-
as a more than

> e these silent shades
> of days departed,
> votive maids
> and heavenly-hearted !"

mbled dismantled
ig oratories, broken
nonumental stones,
ager to be distin-
s, abbots, and re-
the wasted remains
one of those mys-
tall and slender
ads, still strong and
tinel guarding the
t. It is impossible
ie of sterner, more
. On the shore of
lakes that lie em-
len, rises a beetling
of which Saint Ke-
lived while pursu-
study and contem-
his name is even
this same cavern,
by the name of
led," the illustrious
Laurence O'Toole
ve ofttimes mused
he was abbot of

of Meath we find
int Columb's house
, the elegant poet,
of so many monas-
ne-roofed construc-
itecture, seeming
of an oratory
ion.

On the celebrated Rock of Cashel stands a group of ruins unparalleled for picturesque beauty and antiquarian interest. The most ancient structure, with the exception of the Round Tower, is Cormac's chapel, built by Cormac MacCarthy, the pious king of "deep-valleyed Desmond," in the beginning of the twelfth century. It also is a stone-roofed edifice, with Norman arches and an almost endless variety of Norman decorations. Near it rise the magnificent cathedral founded by Donogh O'Brien, King of Thomond, about 1152; and on the plain beside the rock, Hoar Abbey, the ancient castle of the archbishops, a perfect Round Tower, and numerous crosses.

And one of the grandest of these ancient holy piles, Newtown Abbey, now lies a crumbling heap on the banks of the Boyne. What it once was may, however, still be conceived of from the exquisite beauty of some of the remaining capitals, vaulting, and shafts, and from the many fragments of its noble windows which are strewn about the neighboring cemetery. This, alas! like many another of the magnificent ruins of Ireland, has been used as a quarry; not by the unlettered peasant, who is rarely found wanting in a devotional feeling that leads him to regard antiquities, and especially those of an ecclesiastical origin, with a sentiment of profound veneration; but by contractors for the erection of new buildings, and sometimes even by men of station and education, who seem to have forgotten that age and neglect cannot deprive structures once consecrated to God, and applied to the service of religion, of any portion of their sacred character.

Bective Abbey, not far from Newtown, is another wonderful wreck, which seems to combine ecclesiasti-

cal with military and domestic architecture in the most singular manner. It presents indeed a striking evidence of the half-monk, half-soldier character of its founders. Battlemented towers, cloister-arches, and rooms with great fire-places; the flues carried up through the thickness of the walls, and continued through tapering chimney-shafts, seem to have made the Abbey of Bective a kind of monastic castle, and previous to the use of artillery it must have been a place of great strength.

Perhaps one of the most beautiful edifices ever erected in Ireland was the church of Killeshin, near Carlow, once decorated with richly sculptured capitals representing human heads, the hair intertwined with serpents. This magnificent building was more hardly treated by the destructiveness of an individual who, about forty years since, resided in the neighborhood, than by the storms and frosts and thunderbolts of ages. The detestable vandal wantonly defaced the exquisite capitals, and almost entirely obliterated an Irish inscription which extended round the abacus!

On the romantic shores of the beautiful Lake of Killarney stands the venerable ruins of Muckross Abbey. No vestige of its former grandeur remains; "its antic pillars massy proof" are all ground into dust, and a magnificent yew-tree that has grown in the very centre of the wreck spreads its mighty, sombre branches like a funereal pall over the fallen temple. And in the lake on the "holy island" of Innisfallen, on a gentle verdant slope, surrounded by thick groves, are still to be seen the few crumbling stones that mark where stood the abbey once so renowned throughout Christendom for its learning and piety.

But it would be a vain task to attempt to enumerate all the beautiful memorials of Ireland's spl whose ivy-grown ruins still ado land they once made so famou

"Her temples grew as grows the gra

and popular tradition tells u numbers have been hidden mortal eye, ever since the monks who prayed within the barbarously driven forth or slai

"In yonder dim and pathless wood
Strange sounds are heard at twilig
And peals of solemn music swell
As from some minster's lofty towe
From age to age those sounds are he
Borne on the breeze at twilight ho
From age to age no foot hath found
A pathway to the minster's tower!

Mingled among the mossy m of fallen altars; among the mo ing stones and the rusted of crumbled cloisters; beneat "churchyard's bowers"; by the hillsides; on the margins of th lit lakes, or under the shadow mysterious Round Towers, lie, a countless, the defaced, mutilate blems of Ireland's heart-deep f broken crosses—innumerable b crosses—eloquent of the pie those by-gone days, eloquent ruthlessness of the devastator. are found scattered over the island, and are as various in styles as in the perfection o workmanship — some, differi nothing from the pillar-stones pagans, save that they are sculptured with a cross, to ma graves of the early Irish sa others have the upper part shaft hewn into the form of a from which the arms and the t tend. Crosses, highly sculp appear to date from the nint twelfth centuries. In these the instead of being simply cut in face of the stone, is represente ring, binding, as it were, the arms, and upper portion of the together. There are scores of beautiful remains in Ireland, b

Stones very similar, but perforated, are also found in Ireland, in Scotland, and even, it is said, in India. What may have been their origin is completely unknown.

The most remarkable of the pillar-stones is found at the celebrated hill of Tara, in the county of Meath. Dr. Petrie thinks that this monument is the famous Lia Fail, or Stone of Destiny, upon which, for many ages, the kings of Ireland were crowned, and which is generally supposed to have been removed from Ireland to Scotland for the coronation of Fergus Mac Eark, an Irish prince—a prophecy having declared that in whatever country this stone was preserved, a king of the Scotic (ancient Irish) race should reign. The learned Doctor refers to some MSS., not earlier certainly than the tenth century, in which the stone is mentioned as still existing at Tara. "If this authority may be relied on," says Mr. Wakeman, "the stone carried away from Scotland by Edward the First, and now preserved in Westminster Abbey, under the coronation chair, has long attracted a degree of celebrity to which it was not entitled, while the veritable Lia Fail, the stone which, according to the early bardic accounts, *roared* beneath the ancient Irish monarchs at their inauguration, remained forgotten and diregarded among the green raths of deserted Tara." Deserted Tara! thirteen centuries have passed away since the kings and chiefs of Ireland were wont to assemble in the royal city—

"Tara, where the voice of music sung,
And many a harp and cruit responsive rung,
And many a bard, in high heroic verse,
The deeds of heroes gloried to rehearse.
And many a shell went round, and loud and long
Rose the full chorus of the festive song.
Ah! who can tell how beautiful were they—
The Fenian chiefs—how joyous, young, and gay!
Each stood a champion on the battle-field,
And but with life the victory would yield."

Thirteen centuries have p
away since the work of decay b
and nothing now remains of i
cient grandeur. All has been
away, save some faint indicatio
the site of the noble banqu
hall, whose magnificence wa
vaunted in bardic song and
and the raths upon which the p
pal habitations stood.

These raths or duns, whic
found in every part of Ireland,
consist of only a circular intr
ment, but most frequently fo
steep mound, flat at the top
strongly intrenched. The work
ally enclosed a piece of ground
which, it is presumed, the hous
lesser importance stood, the n
being occupied by the dwelling
chief. The circular enclosures
rally contain excavations of a
hive form, lined with uncem
stones, and connected by pa
sufficiently large to admit a
These chambers or artificial ca
are supposed to have been
houses for food and treasure
places of refuge for the womer
children in time of war.

In the centre of the pri
mound of Tara, the Forradh,
stands the Lia Fail—the great p
stone—the stone of destiny—n
from its primitive site to its p
in order to mark the grave—
croppies' grave," it is called—of
men killed in an encounter
British troops during the risi
1798.

By the side of the hoary rui
the earlier monastic houses
most invariably seen one of
singular and, for many cent
mysterious edifices, the R
Towers. The question of the o
and uses of these remarkable ve
long occupied the attention of
quaries. They were supposed to
been built by the Danes, or to

...n of Indo-Scythic origin, ...contained the sacred fire ...ce all the fires in the king... ...annually rekindled. There ...st as many theories con... ...em as there were towers, ...cceeding theory appeared ...the subject in deeper mys... ...ever—a mystery that was ...until dispelled for ever by ...Dr. Petrie. This gentle... ...ecided that the towers are ...n and of ecclesiastical ori... ...were erected at various ...tween the fifth and thir... ...turies—that they were ...answer, at least, a twofold ...y, to serve as belfries, and ...or places of strength, in ...sacred utensils, books, ...other valuables were de... ...d into which the ecclesi... ...hom they belonged could ...ecurity in cases of sudden ...d that they were probably ...when occasion required, as ...nd watch-towers. These ...were arrived at after a ...atient investigation of the ...l peculiarities of the ...ms, and also of the reli... ...nes generally found in ...with them, and the vexed ...at rest.

...of a hundred and eigh... ...se buildings have been ...the greater number in ...of some only the foun... ...; others are almost ...artificial shape. They vary ...y to a hundred and ten ...ght, tapering gradually to ...t, and terminated by a ...l stone roof. The Tower ...in, near Dublin, is nearly ...t perhaps the most noble ...found at Monasterboice, ...mbines, with the magnifi... ...we have described, and ...own ruined churches, to form a group of sacred antiquities unsurpassed in interest and picturesque beauty.

Frightful as were the devastations of the Danes in Ireland—the unhappy land bore the brunt of their fury—and frequent as was the pillage of religious property, there have been found many beautiful relics of sacred objects belonging to the sacked and ravaged abbeys and churches. In newly-ploughed lands, in the beds of rivers, in the heaps of crumbled stones around the ruins, in the bogs have been discovered, among many other interesting evidences of early Irish civilization, pastoral crooks and crosiers, chalices of stone and of silver, and ancient quadrangular bells of bronze and of iron. These last appear to have been in use in Ireland as early as the time of St. Patrick. Some of them, we are told by Cambrensis, were so highly reverenced that both clergy and laity were more afraid of swearing falsely by them than by the Gospels—"because of some hidden and miraculous power with which they were gifted, and by the vengeance of the saint to whom they were particularly pleasing, their despisers and transgressors were severely punished."

The crooks and crosiers are in general of exquisite workmanship, exhibiting a profusion of ornament of extreme beauty. Among these relics has been found one which affords the most striking evidence of the proficiency that Irish artificers had arrived at in many of the arts previous to the arrival of the English. It is known as the Cross of Cong, and was made at Roscommon, by native Irishmen, about the year 1123, in the reign of Turlogh O'Connor, father of Roderich, the last king of Ireland. The form is most elegant, and it is completely covered with minute and elaborate ornaments, a portion

worked in pure gold. The ornaments are, for the most part, tracery and grotesque animals fancifully combined, and similar in character to the decorations found upon crosses of stone of the same period. In the centre, at the intersection, is set a large crystal, through which is visible a piece of the true cross, as inscriptions in Irish and Latin distinctly record.

The copies of the Gospels and of the sacred writings which had been used by the saints of Erin were often preserved by their successors enclosed in cases of yew, or some wood equally durable. Some of these deeply-interesting evidences of Irish piety and learning have come down to us, and are to be seen in the collection of the Royal Irish Accademy at Dublin. One of them, the Caah, is a box about nine inches long and eight broad, formed of brass plates riveted together, and ornamented with gems and chasings of gold and silver. It contains a rude wooden box enclosing a copy of the ancient Vulgate translation of the Psalms in Latin, written on vellum, and, it is believed, by the hand of Saint Columbkille, "the Apostle of the Picts." It seems to have been handed down in the O'Donnell family, to which the great saint belonged.

Another most interesting relic, also in the collection of the Academy, is the Domnach Airgid, which contains, beyond a doubt, a considerable portion of the copy of the holy Gospels used by Saint Patrick, and presented to him by Saint Macarthen. This MS. has three covers; the first and most ancient, of yew; the second, of copper plated with silver; and the third, of silver plated with gold.

Beautiful—sadly, solemnly beautiful—are the remains of Ireland's ancient grandeur; but though he
dor may have passed away;
she be no longer "the school o
tendom"; though her abbe
monasteries, her churches and
and sculptured crosses, lie
heaps of wayside ruins, still he
her wondrous faith, is fres
strong as in those bygone ag
it was in those days of old wl
fervent piety of her sons led t
distant lands, apostles of religi
science, so is Ireland's faitl
warm and active as ever. In
struggles, in all her sorrows, h
has stood by her side to
consolation and to ward off d
O lovely, unhappy isle!
chief of reliquaries," thou
shamrock be watered with te
thou hast the better part!

> "And if of every land the guest,
> Thine exile back returning
> Finds still one land unlike the re
> Discrowned, disgraced, and m
> Give thanks! Thy flowers, to yo
> Transferred, pure airs are tasti
> And, stone by stone, thy temple
> In regions everlasting!"

Will "the bound and suffer
tim" ever again breathe freely
religious freedom and politic
dom ever again stand hand
on the dewy turf of Erin?—
Lia Fail ever again roar bene
seat of an independent Irish r
these are questions which Tim
can answer. But whatever fa
be reserved for long-tried Ire
the future, however disconsol
present, every Irishman's heart
glow with pride and love w
remembers the glory of he
days—glory such as no other
ever possessed—glory of wh
centuries of relentless tyran
deprive her—the glory of
been, when all was dark arou
home of learning and the fat
of saints!

THE LEGENDS OF OISIN, BARD OF ERIN.

BY AUBREY DE VERE.

II.

THE DEATH OF OSCAR.*

" SING us once more of Gahbra's fight,
  Old bard, that fight where fell thy son:"
Thus Patrick spake to vexed Oisin,
  And the old man's wrath was gone.

" Thou of the crosier white! whoe'er
  Had seen that plain with carnage spread,
Or friend or foe, had wept for Eire,
  And for her princes dead!

" There lay the arms of mighty chiefs:
  There kings in death with helms unbound.
A field of doom it was; a place
  By deadly spells girt round!

" Upon his left hand leaned my son:
  His shield lay broken by his side:
His right hand clutched his sword: the blood
  Rushed from him like a tide.

" I stayed my spear-shaft on the ground:
  O'er him I stooped on bended knee:
On me my Oscar turned his eyes:
  He stretched his hands to me.

* The substance of this poem will be found among the translations of the Irish Ossianic Society.

"To me my Oscar spake—my son—
The dying man, and all but dead:
'Thou liv'st! For this I thank the gods!
O father!' thus he said.

"'Rememberest thou that day we fought
Far westward at the Sith of Mor?'
Caoilte spake: 'I healed thee then,
Though deep thy wounds and sore:—

"'No cure there lives for wounds like these.'"
Here ceased the lamentable sound.
Five steps the old man moved apart;
Then dashed him on the ground.

"My Oscar stared upon his wounds;
To fields long past his thoughts took flight:
'My son, I cried, thou hadst not died
If Fionn had ruled the fight!'

"O Patrick! I have sung thee lays,
Emprize of others, or my own;
Where he was bravest all were brave;
But his, and his alone,

"The gracious ways, the voice that smiled,
The heart so loving and so strong:
The women laughed my harp to hear;
They wept at Oscar's song!

"All night we watched the dying man:
To staunch his blood we strove in vain:
We heard the demon-loaded wind
Along the mountain strain.

"All night we propped him with our spears:
To staunch his blood we strove in vain:
Till, drenched in falling floods, the moon
Went down beyond the plain.

"Alas! the dawning of that morn,
My Oscar's last! With barren glare
It flashed along the broken arms,
And the red pools here and there.

"Then saw we pacing from afar,
A kingly form, a shape of woe:
King Fionn it was that toward us moved
With measured footsteps slow:

"King Fionn himself; and far behind
Came many warriors more of Fail,*
Down-gazing on Baoigne's clan,
Death-cold, and still, and pale.

"There lay all dumb the men of might;
There, foot to foot, the foemen, strewn
Like seaweed lines on stormy shores,
Or forests overblown!

"Oh! then to hear that cry far borne
On gales new-touched with morning frost
As though he heard it not, the king
Came, striding o'er that host,

"Seeking the bodies of his sons.
So on he strode through fog and mist;
And we to meet him moved; for now
That Fionn it was we wist.

"'All hail to thee, King Fionn! all hail!'
He answered naught, but onward passed
Until he reached that spot where lay
My Oscar sinking fast.

"'Late, late thou com'st: yet thou art here.
Then answered Fionn, 'Alas the day!
My reign is done since thou art gone,
And all this host is clay.'

"My Oscar gazed upon his face:
He heard the words his grandsire said:
He heard, nor spake: his hand down fell;
And his great spirit fled.

* "Inisfail"—Ireland.

"Then all the warriors, far and near,
Save one that wept, and Fionn, my sire,
Three times upraised a cry that rang
O'er all the land of Eire.

"Fionn turned from us his face that hour:
We knew that tears adown it crept:
Never, except for Bran his hound,
The king till then had wept.

"He shed no tear above his son;
Tearless he saw his brother die:
He wept to see my Oscar dead,
And the warriors weeping nigh.

"This is the tale of Gahbra's fight,
Where all the monarchs warred on one;
Where they that wrecked him shared his fate,
And Erin's day was done.

"On Gahbra's field the curse came down:
Our voice is changed from that of men:
We sigh by night; we sigh by day:
We learned that lesson then.

'Oh! many a prince was laid that day
In narrow cairn and lonely cave:
But all the fair-famed Rath thenceforth
Became my Oscar's grave.

Patrick, I pray the Lord of Life—
Patrick, do thou his grace implore—
That death may still my heart ere long:
This night my pain is sore."

closed and stript of all the exterior emblems they could destroy.

Some of us were confined in the first story of the western building where the hostages were who came the night before. The second and third stories were occupied by those sentenced by the court of assize of the Seine.

The remainder, and I was of the number, were sent to the third story of the eastern building. The first story was occupied by about forty Parisian guardsmen, prisoners of the Commune; the second story by a somewhat larger number of *sergents de ville*, who were found at Montmartre in the affair of the eighteenth of March. In consequence of the defection of a part of the line, they fell into the power of the insurgents. There were also on the same story a dozen artillerymen, likewise prisoners. The third story, where I was conducted with seven ecclesiastics and three laymen, was already occupied by a hundred soldiers, some of whom, on their way through Paris at the time of the proclamation of the Commune, refused to serve it, and others had been taken prisoners in the engagements between the insurgents and the regular army. The following night, three vicars from Belleville and St. Ambroise were imprisoned with us.

The cells of La Roquette are extremely plain. They are about one mètre and a few centimètres wide and two and a half mètres long. No chair, no table: the only article of furniture is an iron bedstead. Neatness is the least thing to be remarked concerning them. It was very evident that several generations of criminals had occupied them without rendering them any more agreeable. This was not all. The first night I found myself among two kinds of insects whose names are unmention-

able. When in the warm cli
the East, and in the villages
thern Spain, I found myself *a*
ses with these nocturnal ene
had at least the consolation o
ing my taper, of complaini
next day to the hostess, a
changing my room or the inn
at La Roquette none of these
was possible. Having no c
sit on, I remained seated on n

I must, however, mention c
vantage at La Roquette of wh
were deprived at Mazas: the
discipline was not as rigorous
prisoners could at certain m
of the day see each other in th
or in the passage of the sto
occupied. Each window ligl
cells separated by a strong pa
but between the partition a
grating of the window, comn
both cells, is a space through
the occupants can talk, and ev
a book. I could thus exchang
pious thoughts and fortifying
tions with my neighbor, the
Amodru. During the day we
of God, of death, eternity, of
sistance we could render our c
ions: during the night, we re
with horror the lugubrious fir
seemed to be devouring the
city.

The very night of our ar
battery of seven large marine
set up at Père-la-Chaise be
discharge shells and petroleum
on different parts of Paris. A
only a few mètres from our
it shook our cells and stun
with the frightful detonatio
the whir of the projectiles
above our heads. This batt
not cease its incendiary w
the following Saturday, the
seventh of May, at half-past
the moment when the regula
gained possession of the ce
Some days before my arrest,

illusions and material and moral ruin."

We quote these words to show that M. Deguerry had no grave fears respecting his situation. The archbishop and he both knew that the death of the hostages had been discussed by the Commune, but they were convinced that these threats would never be executed. What reasons had they for such an assurance? Had they received an absolute promise? Were they ignorant of the revolutionary orgies of Paris, and the brutal hatred of its tyrants? Did they think, having nothing to reproach themselves for, that no one could conceive the idea of putting them to death? I was vainly endeavoring to find an explanation of this assurance when Mgr. Darboy joined us.

If his health was affected and his body enfeebled, his mind was undoubtedly clear and sagacious. He not only took broad and correct views of the events and men of the times, but he displayed an acuteness almost caustic. The consciousness of his ecclesiastical dignity and his intellectual strength suggested to him many observations, full of animation and reality, respecting the incredible humiliations that he had received from Raoul Rigault and other heroes of the club, or *estaminet*, who thought they were aggrandizing themselves and acquiring claims on the admiration of posterity by their absurdity and impertinence. He bitterly deplored the weakening of the public sense of respect for authority, and thought, without a reformation in this respect, Paris and the whole of France would never recover from their misfortunes. To support these observations, Mgr. Darboy recalled the conclusion of one of his last pastoral letters, in which he predicted that, if society persisted in disregarding the precepts of the Gospel and abandoning the principles of r
and morality, it would be liab
terrible overthrow.

I, in my turn, recalled to
collection that a democratic
had not hesitated to condem
language as bearing the imp
exaggeration, so desirous was
Paris should be divested of
ligious belief or practice. I
membered the article spoken
seemed pleased to hear it quo

The archbishop knew I ha
been arrested the week befo
was aware that, in consequenc
former functions, I had frequ
tercourse with the political
After questioning me respect
religious condition of Paris a
parish affairs, and inquiring
Mgr. Buquet, who, notwiths
his great age and notoriet
bravely remained at Paris, re
quite providential service in t
cesan administration, of which
the only member free after th
and incarceration of M. Jou
the Conciergerie, and M. I
the Prison de la Santé, Mgr.
added, in a tone that exclu
personal preoccupation:

"What is thought of the si
and fate of the hostages in th
cal world of Paris?"

"Thanks to the confidenc
ed by the Commune, hone
monseigneur, are daily takin
When the committee of publi
came to prove my mistake in
lowing in their traces, I onl
four persons in Paris with w
could converse, and that ra
the events of the day:—M. L—
chief secretary of the Crédit I
M. G——, a former depu
Seine-et-Marne; the Count de
an old officer; and M. G—
president of the Conseil de F
at St. Eustache, imprisone
short time, though eighty-fo

ply of bread and
t his house which
ess to distribute to
arties des Halles.
wish to know the
political and di-
ew at Paris, you
nced to mine, and
my modest *régal*
igneur's appetite."
aid Mgr. Darboy,
Commune has not
epress your spirits.
an answer to my

honesty and intel-
your arrest, mon-
of the other hos-
Prussians and the
pahle of reviving
tom. I have been
representatives of
owers have taken
from danger, and
vernment at Ver-
sibility of directly
nsider it a duty to
forts."
f this," replied the
arked satisfaction.
under this diplo-
at Protot declared
ommune had taken
obedience to the
s of the lowest de-
they should possi-
ecution necessary,
one or two officers
gents de ville, and
mber of the clergy.
have entire confi-
dness of God and
y conscience."
ended these words,
two, the warden,
the signal for
[illegible]. His confi-
[illegible] would have
[illegible] if, after
[illegible], I had

not firmly resolved not to yield to my illusions. And afterwards, in writing an account of this final interview to an eminent friend of the archbishop and my curé, I said: "While they seemed to have no fears, I had no hope."

This was on Wednesday, the twenty-fourth of May. Some time after, about seven o'clock, I observed, through the bars of my cell, a strange movement in the large interior court. There was a great difference between Mazas and La Roquette. At Mazas, the prison discipline was in sufficient vigor, but at La Roquette there was no order and no discipline. This prison, placed between the Faubourgs St. Antoine, Ménilmontant, and Charonne, was at the mercy of all the wild beasts of these quarters, who knocked around and roared without any restraint. Some men of sinister appearance went from the office to the western building where the first hostages were kept, some armed with revolvers and others carrying mysterious documents. The director of the prison, with his red girdle and pantaloons, gave, or rather received, orders with an air that might be regarded as embarrassed or satisfied, according to one's idea of his principles. The bad wardens did not conceal their joy, the good ones disappeared in consternation. A citoyen of imperious manners and wild aspect, before whom some bowed and others trembled, proceeded like a man in a fit of madness or intoxication towards the western building. I had not then sufficient presence of mind to recognize him, but I was convinced afterwards that it was Ferré; others, with less probability, declare it was Raoul Rigault. These two rivals of Robespierre would figure equally well at the post of infamy.

Most of the windows were closed in the first story of the western part

facing us, where the principal hostages were incarcerated; a few were open, revealing empty cells. At the same time, the windows of the second and third stories, occupied by those condemned by the court of assize, were filled with prisoners who were wondering, with a lively curiosity, at the meaning of the unusual spectacle which had struck us.

My anxiety became more and more intense, when I saw an officer of the insurgents half open the door that led from the court to the office, and say, with a solemn voice: "Are the *hommes de guerre* ready?" Without being thoroughly initiated into the military language, I understood they were about to shoot the whole or a part of us. I threw myself on my knees to implore God to grant us all strength and courage. A few minutes past eight, I was stunned by a horrible firing. Six almost simultaneous discharges of chassepots, succeeded by some single reports, resounded in the prison court. A deadly silence succeeded this noise, and revealed to me that only a few steps distant had been committed one of those monstrous crimes that constitute an epoch in the history of the human race.

From the prayers for the dying I passed to the prayers for the dead. Never had I so thoroughly sounded the depths of God's mercy. I no longer conjured him, but claimed an indemnification, worthy of him, for the victims of so base and execrable an outrage. I never could have survived this excess of man's iniquity, if I had not felt myself sustained by an assurance of the eternal goodness and justice of God.

When I rose, the mournful noise of the clarions and drums, and the dismal rumbling of a cart towards Charonne, seemed to put an end to this tragedy.

Wednesday night was truly a night
of torture for me. Every ins
outer and inner doors of the
were opened to bring in, o
away, victims. A court ma
rather banditti under the g
judges, held a session in th
The unfortunate men, who w
pected of "complicity with th
ans at Versailles," or who re
die for the Commune under
ders of old criminals, were m
ly sacrificed. With the so
drums and trumpets mingl
noise of the carriages that
the suspected to La Roque
carried to Père-la-Chaise the
had been shot, and the bomb
trole. At the same time th
tery battery did not cease its t
and the flames that were con
the monuments of Paris ca
lurid gleams into our cells.
reader for a moment take m
and he will feel that no des
could equal so overwhelming
tacle.

Being on the eastern side
prison, which has no direc
munication with the western
still ignorant on Thursday n
of the names of the victims
night before. Two faithful
came at an early hour to an
the fatal news, and give me
the same details of this sad
According to them, the emiss
the Commune were the only
es of the execution: it was th
difficult to obtain a precise,
pecially, a complete account
of these wardens, who went
as he could to the place of
tion, received orders to aid th
cutioners in placing the bodi
a cart which was to take the
corner of Charonne, at the ex
of Père-la-Chaise. It is to
tails, and those of other w
and the prisoners of the weste
that I owe the following parti

tained that the money of the six victims was afterward stolen from their cells, and their books and papers cast into the fire. Some weeks after a half-burned breviary was seen in one of the closets of the ante-room of La Roquette. It is thus the Commune respected the last wishes and testamentary dispositions of its victims.

Those who were shot on Wednesday and the following days, and all the prisoners whom the committee of public safety reserved for the same fate, were victims of their devotedness to two noble and grand causes. They were persecuted through hatred of religion, the abolition of which the Commune had inscribed in its sacrilegious programme, and through hatred of the country represented by the French army and the national assembly at Versailles, who were defending order, liberty, honor, civilization, and the faith against barbarians.

After the massacre on Wednesday, the hostages could entertain no further illusion as to their fate. This was only the commencement of a bloody drama. Everything convinced me it would only end with the last of the hostages. Then we entered upon a long agony of four days, the sad changes in which no human tongue could describe. I will confine myself to enumerating without comment the most remarkable incidents.

On Thursday noon, we were allowed recreation together in the same court as the day before. Our faces were sadder, but our hearts were as courageous. The laymen manifested a cordial sympathy for the clergy and a like serenity. It was evident that all put their confidence in God—a confidence that is not vain. I conversed twenty minutes with Père Olivaint. Smitten in his dearest affections, he still had a gracious smile on his lips. I attempt to depict the expre his face or repeat his conv His face had something abo ly supernatural, and his wor those of an angel. At the tion of Mgr. Surat, M. Ba Père Olivaint, the priests vow, if God would deign t them from the jaws of death, brate a Mass of thanksgiving or of the Blessed Virgin on Saturday of every month space of three years. I among the laymen a face fa me. I inquired his name. that of one of the most in and most courageous comn de police. It was he whom ernment appointed in Januar to make me a domiciliary seize my papers, by way of e my support of M. Thiers as date, and my opposition to sures that had brought de on the empire and threatene very moment to cover Pa blood and ruins. By a stran of fortune, our struggles in directions had brought us to t fate, which neither of us had anticipated. If I had n afraid of recalling a delicate brance, I would have assu of my absolute forgiveness my devoted regards. Towards of our recreation, one of th from the battery of Père-la broke, with a loud explosion, in the wall under which w walking. In ordinary ti should have shuddered an flight, but now it scarcely ex tention. In separating, we b another farewell till we met below, or in heaven: we know which.

In the evening we notice fires in Paris, and learned t insurgents were setting fire tc

were amusing themselves in discharging their guns against the prison walls: I assure you, no one was shot."

Then, knowing we were to undergo the same fate in a few hours, he eagerly proposed to the clergy of our story a lottery which, according to his delicate calculations, would procure him some profits without depriving him of the objects of art he was proud of fabricating. For eight days I was obliged to swallow such humiliations, which revealed poor human nature in quite a new aspect. The selfish proposition of this deceitful employee was rejected promptly, but we concluded to continue our daily gratuity, in gratitude for services he was always promising, and which were never performed.

When he left our story, he always went directly to the office to give an account of what he had seen or heard. We had not only to resist ferocity, but also craftiness and duplicity.

It was in the plans of the Commune that none of the hostages should escape death. The next Sunday, the first object that struck my eyes at the office of La Roquette was the list of their names. There was a horizontal mark against the names of those who were to be shot: when the execution was accomplished, they added a vertical mark, thus forming a cross. Every name had a horizontal line before it. If my memory does not deceive me, they followed the order of the list in the executions.

About two o'clock, three shells from the battery of Père-la-Chaise hit the prison roof only a few mètres above our heads, and covered the court with tiles and fragments of the chimneys. Some of the prisoners protested against the danger of these projectiles exploding in their closed cells and had the doors opened; others did not seem to h
stunning incident: absorbed i
er, they were more preoccupi
eternal than temporal things.

The shells that hit our pris
an indication of the rapid p
of the French troops, but th
gress threw us into the most p
ing and intolerable of situatio
could only expect our safet
the Versailles army; we ough
in consideration of the genera
ests of civilization, and our
terests, to desire ardently its t
But it was no less evident t
nearer the army approach
more imminent became our enc
the perspective which was o
hope of safety, inevitably ann
at the same time our destructi
the illimitable consolations of
had not raised us above our
tunes, we should have been
to the anticipated horrors o
lasting woe. In such cruel h
comprehend the words of th
Man, who, in the garden of
mani and on Golgotha, drank
dregs the chalice of all humil
all sorrows, and every kind of a
in order to sanctify them.
God, my God, why hast thou
doned me?" should not be se
from these other words, which
all despondency and presage
derful recompense: "Fathe
thy hands I commend my spi

IV.

LA ROQUETTE—INSURRECTIO LIVERANCE—CONCLUSIO

The close of the day on
was exceedingly gloomy. Th
events took place in the
court of the prison as on Th
evening. At the sight of the
rious agent who held a list
hand, each one said to himsel

The constantly increasing noise of the firing announced the approach of the contending parties. 'he barricades of the Château d'Eau had been valiantly taken by the Versailles troops: the Commune, in session at the Mairie du Prince Eugène, was obliged to beat a retreat. By a great effort, the scattered members succeeded in gaining the office of La Roquette, to conduct the labors of the cosmopolitan banditti. Between the army of deliverance and us were still those men of blood, whose last ravings were so many decrees of death and incendiarism. It is said that Ferré sprang like a tiger about to lose his prey, crying in a hoarse voice: "Make haste! shoot them, the *chouans!* Cut their throats, the robbers! do not leave one standing! Citoyens and citoyennes of the faubourgs, come and avenge your sons and your fathers, basely assassinated!" The unhappy men had no time to lose; the Versailles troops, on the one hand, were entering the Boulevard du Prince Eugène; on the other, they surrounded Père-la-Chaise; but, by an intolerable fatality, the source of our safety was at the same time that of our destruction.

A few minutes past three, the heavy bolts of our cells flew back with unaccustomed quickness. I was on my knees, saying, with a voice almost extinct, the office of the Eve of Whit-Sunday. My neighbor quickly opened the door of my cell. "Courage," he said, "it is now our turn; they are going to take us all down to shoot us!"

"Courage," I replied, "and may the will of God be done!" I had on my clerical costume, and advanced into the corridor where priests, soldiers, and national guards were all mingled together. The priests and national guards appeared calm and resigned, but the soldiers cc
believe in the fate that awaite
"What have we done tc
wretches? we fought agai
Prussians! we fulfilled ou
What are they going to shoot
No, it is not possible!" Son
ed cries of anger, others re
silent and motionless as if th
in a dream. The priests kne
tify themselves by a last abs
one of them urged the sol
imitate us, and addressed the
words of encouragement.

A voice with a metallic ri
denly rose above this confuse
"My friends, those ignoble
have already killed too ma
not allow yourselves to be mu
join me; let us resist; let u
Rather than give you up, I
with you!" It was the voic
warden Pinet. This generou
Lorraine, aghast at so many
could no longer stifle his indi
Charged to open our cells slo
deliver us two by two to th
gents, who were waiting for u
he had fastened the door of t
story behind him, rapidly ope
cells to advise us and aid in
ing a resistance, ready to sac
life in aiding us to save ou
first, I could not believe in s
heroism. The Abbé Amod
in his turn, and joined his p
tions to those of Pinet: "Le
submit to be shot, my frienc
defend ourselves. Have co
in God; he is for us and
he will save us!"

There was a difference of
some hesitated. To defend o
objected one, would be mad
should only incur a more crue
Instead of being simply s
shall be slaughtered by a
consumed in the flames. "
call up the national guards,"
ed a simple fellow (I had

the office, and boldly attack the Commune!" the Communists, frightened at our resistance and the rapid progress of the French army along the Boulevard du Prince Eugène, hastily fled from La Roquette in the direction of Belleville. The rabble, astonished at this sudden removal, were convinced of the great danger, and fled after them. The prisoners were restored to liberty, and naturally cried: *Vive la République! vive la Commune!*

Availing themselves of this confusion, the lay hostages who were to have been shot with us escaped from La Roquette: almost all succeeded in crossing the barricades or hiding till the next day in the late haunts of insurrection. Some of the clergy imitated them; others, particularly Mgr. Surat, who was dressed as a layman, hesitated. The wardens, from motives more praiseworthy than prudent, urged them to fly. This course seemed to me disastrous. The neighborhood of the prison was in the hands of the insurgents, whose irritation knew no bounds. I thought it my duty to warn the first vicar-general of Paris, and said to him through the bars: "Take care; to leave is certain death; to remain, uncertain!" I ascertained afterwards that I had not been heard. In going out of the prison, he was murdered in a frightful manner, with M. Bécourt, the curé of Bonne Nouvelle; M. Houillon, a missionary of the Missions Etrangères, and a lay prisoner. Some priests succeeded in concealing themselves in the Faubourg St. Antoine, and some returned to the prison.

Notwithstanding the departure of the insurgents who were to put us to death, we were still exposed to sudden attack and every danger while the prison gates were unfastened. I therefore protested in violent terms to the two wardens, who, frightened at the terrible consequenc would result from a return of surgents, urged us strongly to c and go out. "We will not g I replied; "the Versailles troc be here in a few hours: if a fortune happens to us by you on you will fall the respon Fasten all the prison doors, an open them to the Versaillais."

They warmly reproached an obstinacy they thought mus fatal to us, but they faithfully my orders.

At eleven o'clock at nigh firing, which was not far off, The frenzied demagogues w uttered powerless threats agai We kept a strict guard, and se began to hope. At a quarter three, the firing recommenced Père-la-Chaise. Every hou seemed an age. There was a dable barricade in the Rue Roquette in front of the prison tacked on the side of the B it would have opposed a form resistance on account of its stee but, owing to the winding and c tric course of the French army, surgents, stormed from the heig cupied by our troops, left the ba in disorder, and a battalion of m took possession of La Roquette resistance, that at first was onl ness, ended miraculously. I the great festival of Whit-S After four days of the greatest that can be imagined, we were trary to all expectation, resto life and liberty.

While some of the prisoners "Vive l'armée! Vive la Fr the most of them, affected by of sleep and the mental tortur no human tongue could expres sisted in regarding our liberat insurgents disguised as marines. began a singular negotiation be the prisoners and the marin

no one would believe in, the horrible deaths of Mgr. Darboy and M. Deguerry. My two *confrères* at the Madeleine expressed the same doubt, the same incredulity. When at vespers I was about to ascend the pulpit to recommend the victims to the prayers of the faithful, they advised me to defer it, hoping the fatal news would not be confirmed.

I had told it to more than one hundred persons, begging them to inform, in their turn, the other parishioners of the Madeleine, but when, in an affecting but cautious and brief manner, I requested the faithful gathered at the foot of the altar to pray for the pastor of the diocese and the curé of the parish, basely shot on the twenty-fourth of May, in the prison of La Roquette, a cry of grief and horror escaped from every soul; the men and the women rose up in confusion, as if to protest against it; the gravest and most reverential for a moment seemed to lose their balance. Among the confused voices around the pulpit, these words were the most distinct: "No, no, such a crime is not possible!"

My moral conclusions will be simple and brief. It would be an insult to the reader to dwell on the great lessons to be drawn from such sorrowful and overwhelming catastrophes.

First Lesson. Divine Providence never chastised and enlightened a nation by severer blows. It behooves us therefore to consider the grave and exceptional malady that is afflicting society, and seek an efficacious and permanent remedy for it. We are all suffering from the evil, and we all should be preoccupied about the means of recovery.

Some days after leaving La Roquette, I wished to revisit the places where I had been imprisoned, in order to retrace, with precision, the events that took place in days of the Commune. I one of the most intelligent a religious *juges d'instruction* bench of the Seine. I vis him the places of the grea rest, Mgr. Darboy's cell, and on the circular road where der of the six principal hosta place. The warden tool Troppmann's cell. "I supp within a few days," said magistrate of the Seine, "th nals like Troppmann were species that required fifty years to develop in the grades of society. After the I witnessed at La Roquett convinced they are to be f thousands in Paris." T *d'instruction* replied that all t istrates who studied the of those grades had the sa viction. It would therefore ply folly not to consider the most suitable to counteract disorder.

Second Lesson. In the hor tastrophe that has just rev many material or moral sor one is more or less responsi culpable. Every one should *meâ culpâ*, and seek to becom The most guilty are certa turbulent working classes, th gogues, the International, th societies, outlaws, and gove without morality, but they a not guilty. Literary men fuse in their pernicious publ the poison of scepticism and rality; artists who are wantir spect and decency; the jour the rich and influential *bo* which defend the principles of conservation, while by their on the Holy See, the clergy, church generally, they sap t foundations of morality; po who brutally proclaim, with

GOD IS OUR AID.

A CHRISTMAS STORY OF '67.

In the dim twilight of an October evening, a rich man prepared to leave the vast treasures accumulated by a fruitless life. Fruitless, I say, for though his increasing millions ranked him a merchant prince of the great metropolis, yet the gold had hardened and crusted and metallized his heart—fusing a subtle poison that destroyed the softer instincts of his nature. Therefore, instead of bearing upward a Godward soul on prayerful incense, those last pulses concentrated in one bitter feeling against the daughter whose faith had won from him the intense hate of his life. The owner of millions each year increased his avarice, bowing him low before the god of the nineteenth century, and inciting the struggle, the sacrifice, the sin, for place and station and gold, literally proving the poet-king's cry,* " *Quoniam omnes dii Gentium dæmonia!* " So, while the stormy gusts swept up the avenue, and the lowering sky increased the night, the old man gathered his failing strength for the last great effort. "Hold me, William, support me ere it is too late. Quick! give me the pen, I must sign while yet my hand has power." Then they put the pen in his trembling hand, his stalwart son supporting him, and all the fiercer passions played upon that cold face, and in those cruel eyes, as he wrote the signature disinheriting the child of the wife whose fair face looked in silent reproach from the portrait opposite. And William Stanfield folded the paper and locked it

* "For all the gods of the Gentiles are devils."

in the escritoire, and old Th
the iron heart "slept the la
But this Stanfield, he of the s
tan stock, had not always b
First, he married his wife a
boy of twenty—a gentle New
girl—who had left William
William, so staunch in his l
the heritage left by the A
stock. But Thomas laid h
love to rest within the quiet
acre" of the village church,
wandered to New York to
fortune. Fate did not with
favors from this sturdy son,
and conquered her; for he
termined to succeed, and di

And strange to say tha
time human softness yet liv
the dross and corruption of t
for Thomas Stanfield was
means indifferent to certa
ences. So, one bright C
morning, he found himself
Orleans, and, stranger still
his partner, Mons. Crécy, p
him to listen to the magnifi
vice at —— Church. The m
exquisitely appealing, thril
nobler attributes of man's b
ture; and so this worldly m
forgot to speculate or dream
for two long hours, and
while his soul absorbed it
inspiration. If there is a
when the hardness of huma
solves and merges into its
essence, it is when music ge
it to its higher affinities, and
en rapport with God. And
man of gold listened to the
prano, and far beyond the
grating caught a glimpse

long after the
rhen Etienne
dine at the
on near the
cely realizing
ound himself
lid bays, with
distance.
cied South al-
nt Christmas,
n on the trees
eading to the
breath of the
air. This to
omed to ice
, was a most
his stroll over
afforded real
ested on the
as it is called
d of business
Mons. Crécy
t was strange-
soft voice was
panying harp,
ognized the
had absorbed
ning service.
di, suscipe de-
ll earnest and
s, it must be,
d to M. Cré-
r Madelaine,"
at dinner he
es that had
d the grating
d those shy,
e in the heart
nder, and in
a bride to his
York.
and only the
household.
the marriage,
ather Jean, at
with such an
the maiden
Puritans, so
ence or his
ce overcame

the scruples of the good priest, and Thomas Stanfield finally triumphed, giving some vague promise in reference to the children. He fully intended evading the fulfilment of the promise, for soon after his marriage he acknowledged thus much to his wife, who, with tears in her dark eyes, said she would only pray for God's grace to change him. So, almost as a curse it seemed, for three years no child came to bless the marriage. True, the young wife was very dear to this stern husband, but the element which had strengthened his forefathers still waxed strong within him, and the self-asserting dogmatism heired from John Carver's band sounded in the stern words that answered his wife when, with quivering lips, she told him of his little daughter's advent. He kissed the pale young mother tenderly and lovingly, but even in that hour he did not restrain himself from replying, "She belongs to me!" and Madelaine understood too well what those words implied. So she only whispered, as her white face grew whiter, "*I will leave her to God.* May our Holy Mother care for her!"

Then the gentle soul departed with the cross upon her bosom, and those last words on her lips, and many, many years after Thomas Stanfield heard repeated in his dreams, "God shall help her."

And a judgment rested on the rich man's harvest, for this warm-hearted, earnest Southern wife was very dear to him. But the child grew in loveliness, and her impulsive nature felt the need of more than her cold father accorded. Firm as he had been in reference to the child, it seemed strange that he evinced so much indifference to her education, for though she had been baptized in his own church, and sent to Protestant schools, yet very little care was be-

stowed upon her religious instruction. When she grew old enough, she accompanied her father to church, and through the long sermons her weary little eyes would often close. She went merely from habit, because her father wished her with him, for there was nothing in the cold, formal ritual, if that bare service can be called a ritual, to attract or warm her heart; but it was part of her duty to go; and so she went. Thus her childhood passed, and so her girlhood opened. Children rarely exert the reasoning faculties, accepting with boundless trust what is proposed by their elders. Faith and confidence are largely developed, therefore a grave record is written of those intrusted with these young immortals. But when reason waked and the heart expanded, this warm loving nature asked for more than what was offered, and her soul felt starved, hungry for the food it found not. Thomas Stanfield was now devoted to his business, from nine in the morning, when his *coupé* drove him to his office, to six in the evening, when his key opened the massive door of his palace—his whole soul entered into the fascination, the strife for increasing millions. And at night, as he sat silent in his high carved chair, the closed eyes and set features told that the scheming still continued. Was it strange, then, that the young girl yearned for something more than her home offered? Well, one September evening, soon after their return from the country, the servant handed in a card, bearing the simple inscription, "Kenneth C. Arnaud." Then Mr. Stanfield, disturbed in the midst of some speculation, testified by a grunt his welcome to a distant relative of his wife. "This is Miss Stanfield, my daughter," he said, as he seemed to remember that another person occupied the room. The stranger was a courtly, h gentleman, and started as rested on the young girl. like my cousin Madelaine," "as I remember her in n hood." For the first time man seemed to realize th blance, and turned to exar fair girl who was his c "Yes," he faintly assent the conversation dragged th half-hour's duration, when naud rose to go. But this his last visit, for he passed th in the city; and many evenin him at Mr. Stanfield's hous Madelaine sang to him the loved best. Then a new life to the young girl, and her h a strange happiness it ha known before.

The Advent season came of joy and gladness in the that celebrate this season, bu ly remembered or noticed in ing congregations; and on Sunday that Mr. Arnaud for of the family party, he propo Madelaine should accompan St. ——'s church, as the m always attractive there. Stanfield was half asleep, w name of this Roman Catholic startled him. "Only to liste music, papa!" she laughingly to his frown, and she wer ritual was new to her, the s strange mystery, but she watched it all, listening to th site bursts from the choi sounded the "Alma" with i cadence. and the heart of th girl thrilled within her. Sh not explain, but she felt a st traction that drew her aga will to this beautiful ritual came the lovely benediction, devotion of the kneeling h the solemn censer's cloudli ing, the elevation, and the

because the ties binding her to her father appealed to her heart, and she dreaded an anger which she knew would never forgive what he considered so fearful an error.

But one cold morning in the winter of '61, the telegraph bore to New York tidings of the secession of Louisiana, then the sons of the sunny South rallied to her standard, and for four long years a bloody war desolated that section. She, the young wife, had never given her thoughts to politics, nor did she understand why hate and bitterness waged with such deadly strife between the two portions of a country which she so dearly loved; but her husband decided for her, and, feeling that her life was only a part of his, she followed. And those were years fraught with agony—years that recorded suffering that aged more than time had power to accomplish; for over each battlefield brooded a great host of prayer—prayer born of love intensified, and of partings which would know only the meeting above; and the race schooled by those years grew, developed, lived, more than generations ordinarily experience in a whole lifetime.

Col. Arnaud won a soldier's reputation, and the autumn of '64 found him, with his fine regiment, encamped a few miles below the Confederate capital. Madelaine soon followed him to Richmond, bringing her little family, her boy Kenneth and a baby daughter. The winter was very trying to this delicate woman, for the city was crowded with refugees from all parts of the Confederacy; every square inch was occupied, and therefore comfortable accommodations were impossible to find. Then the depreciated currency rendered the price of necessities almost fabulous, so that barely to live required great sacrifice and control. But the cour-ageous wife and devoted : gathered her little ones, and c edly dwelt in one small room, to welcome her husband wl his brief furloughs allowed l spend a day with her. But th culmination approached, ar troops that wore the tattere were soon to furl the cross that had proudly waved ove a gallant fight; and on or wintry morning she heard th boys shout " Extra! extra!" a Franklin Street was echoin news of the fierce battle belo mond. Madelaine had not s husband for almost four wee her heart sank as she listene will get a paper," she said, an ing her nurse with the childr descended to the street to p one.

Poor young thing—she little ed how literally she had follow Scriptures, for she had forsa things, and he, her brave hu was all she had to cling to; a —but she was too truly a wo control, and she fainted wh read the cruel words that told husband's fate. A night of followed, and the roll of the lance in the early gray of th morning startled her from h bled sleep. They, those of l gade, in their faded gray bo to the small chamber whe young wife waited, and pal ghastly she saw him laid up bed, where he was soon to sl long pulseless sleep. All tha could render to sweeten the p dying was offered, for the j rang with the grand charge l led, and his deeds of daring v household words in the crowde federate capital. But the gre had gone forth, and the priest church came to offer the last lations.

twenty-five, and two children depended on her for support. What could she do, and how must she act? In her agony, she cried, "Save me, O Father, for without thine aid I am lost!" Then the crucifix fell from her letter, and, clasping it, she drew her boy to her, and, kneeling, prayed: "Lord, thy enemies and mine have risen up against me: I therefore cast myself at thy feet to implore thy succor."

The soft eyes of the little one gazed into her own, and, nestling closer, he asked:

"What makes mamma so sad?"

There are seasons in life when suffering is too great for expression, when tears refuse relief, and the overcharged heart, paralyzed by pain, seems incapable of pulsation. Then even speech fails; and the poor, desolate woman only pressed her child closer, and appealed to her God for protection.

Thus days passed, and she seemed unable to act, for at the South all was poverty and desolation, while she dared not anticipate what awaited her in New York. But the few dollars were growing less, and her children required food, so she decided to try the great city, and thither with her faithful nurse she journeyed. Her mother's note gave her strength, and she often re-read the faint tracery on the faded paper.

"For, my darling child" (the note read), "should you ever wander into the dear fold of your mother's church, feel always that my blessing will rest upon you, and though I may not live to guard you, yet my prayer will be then as it is now for God to be with you.

"MADELAINE CRECY STANFIELD."

And though she did feel crushed and desolate on that stormy September evening which found her in the great city, still a strength came which she had never known, felt that God would prot
Through the crowd at the d
wended her way, and thenc
midst of a pouring rain to
boarding-house, where she pa
night. The next morning s
an old servant who had kn
as a child, and, with tears st
from the old eyes, she took
small but respectable house
town-part of the city, where s
ed two rooms, and commen
new life. A touching sight i
see her in her sad mournin
she so fair and fragile, yet
that three depended upon h
tions, she rose to the emerge
determined to succeed, or di
service. She had brought a
a priest of her church, and
she applied. He was very k
promised to do all that he co
at the same time told her tha
were not easily obtained, and
mended her to watch the new
And she did search the jour
voting herself to answering a
ments, but, save a few ques
replies, nothing came of this a
Meantime she began to
pinchings of want, and vent
try sewing, but how was she
tain work? "Go yourself, r
young mistress," said the go
negress—"go yourself; and
kind Lord bless you!" And, sh
and nervous, she applied to
chant down-town. She could
ly find words for her request,
pale face appealed, and sh
away her parcel. Tireless w
continued efforts, and all t
snow and ice she persevered
work. "God will help her
dying mother had said, and t
the darkness of her life's sto
tried to comfort herself with
surance.

"Bring a light," sounded a gruff voice.

"Don't you see dat de poor chile has no light for herself? Stonishing de fools dat libs in dese parts!"

A kind voice asked, "Is there no money? Take this and buy a candle." The speaker was a shabbily-dressed man, but the whole aspect showed that he had known better days. He remained with the injured man, and while they go to find a light I leave them. . . .

The snow was falling in great white feathery flakes, covering the dark alleys and darker tenements with its soft downy covering, and the little ragged, barefooted gamins of the great city were shrieking and screaming with delight; but not to build mimic forts or to join the army of snow-ballers did our little wanderer pause. "Mamma shall have some money," he said, "and I will begin to work for it, so I will go to the streets where the fine houses are, and there the men will give me work." Only eight years old was this little soldier in the grand army, but his noble face was radiant with the workings of his soul, which no poverty could injure. His little clothes were patched and scanty, and his poor little frozen toes came through the holes in his worn shoes; but the eyes shone with a light that could not be dimmed, and the firmly-set lips told that he was quite determined to do his best on that afternoon. At first he shrank from the cutting wind that swept from the East River, but, with hands in his pockets and cap pulled down, he ran on till he came to Broadway. Crowded with the happy crowd of the vast metropolis, the great highway was gay with bright faces on this eve of the feast of joy. Windows bright with presents for the favored children of fortune, shops thronged by smiling mothers eager to gratify their pampered d
and child-infant as he was, tl
one paused to look at the prett
but tears filled the large blu
and he said, "Oh! I can't
these things, for poor mamma
and wants food." At that m
a gentleman passed, and th
went up and pulled his warn
coat, "Will you give me som
sir?" But the creature, a f
able young fop in tights, sho
off, and passed on. Then
another, this time a respectabl
haired worthy, and, running i
the same appealing voice asl
same question. But the su
merchant, hurrying home, wa
upon some new speculatio
suddenly disturbed, was nc
amiable, as he replied, "Be
little vagabond!"

This time the policeman ca
and taking him by the arm
ordered him to move on. An
on the eve of this blessed f
when the great city joyed i
household, there was no grain
wee waif, no crumb for th
estray, who was struggling agai
power of the ebb which fa
sent to test his strength for th
after. On, on past the Fifth
Hotel, through Madison Square
ing at the glittering icicles or
ing snow-drifts, shivering o
frozen pavements, on he tra
faintly trying for that which s
for ever denied to him.

"*I will* find it for her," h
"for the beautiful angel, our
Mother, told me that she sh
taken care of. I see her now
in the clouds." And up in the
sky, far beyond the pure, be
flakes, he gazed, half-hoping th
Mother of Christ would smile
again. And did she not eve
hover over the young boy-w
Did she not pray that he, too,

but ere he returned to his own home, and the young wife waiting him, he went back to the station-house to look after "the pretty young-one" who had died with the cross in his hand; for he fully expected to find him dead on his return.

"We have had hard work to bring him back, Murphy," said the doctor, as the man walked up to the child. "Only five minutes more, and the cold would have reached the little heart, which was losing all sensation. We have had a time of it, and he has just fallen asleep. These are what we found on him. The card was fastened to his worn jacket, and the crucifix has also a name engraved." And picking up the card from the table the policeman read, "Kenneth Arnaud, 312 East —— Street." On the back of the silver cross was the name, "Madelaine Crécy, August 15, 18—."

"Poor little child! said the policeman. "I'll take him home, for his house is near my own."

So he wrapped the sleeping child in an old blanket, and carried him through the storm. A light glimmered on the first-floor front room as he approached the house, and the man stepped in to inquire about his young charge. As he opened the rickety door, the wailing voice of a woman smote him with the agonizing pain it expressed. "The gentleman may remain," she said, "but for God's sake find my child. O sir! bring me back my child!" and her sobs and moans were heart-rending. The negress rocked to and fro with the little girl, trying to keep her warm and still her feeble cries for bread, chanting the while in dull monotone, a habit peculiar to her race, and which at this time increased the oppressive gloom of the place, not at all relieved by the flickering tallow-candle, nearly burned out—on the small bed in the corner the wo
gentleman lay groaning in
and impatiently awaiting a mes
he had summoned—a sad ev
that announced the blessed fes

At this time the policeman
with his club, but receiving
swer, and not caring to wait
cold, he once more opened the
Standing mute on the thresho
the scene at first deprived h
speech, then walking to the
of the room, he asked, "Is th
ther of Kenneth Arnaud here
I have found a child of that
who wore a crucifix on whic
engraved 'Madelaine Crécy.'"

With one wild scream the
answered, "He is mine!" and,
clasped him to her heart, th
eyes unclosed, and the feeble
voice whispered, "Darling ma
I asked them all for work
might buy you bread, but—oh
head hurts, for a wicked man
me away from a gentleman wh
in his carriage. But, mamma,
cry, for she—the one with the
—will care for us. Oh! I hav
seen her, and I waked to fin
own eyes where hers had
Dear mamma, keep me with
away from the cruel man, and t
oh! the cold snow!" And hi
frame shivered with the recoll

"Madelaine Crécy!" the sic
muttered on his couch in the c
And the policeman approached.
sir, that was the name on the
fix, and I thought the little
was dead when I picked him
front of the millionaire's hou
Fifth Avenue."

"My God! and it was my s
who cast him from me! Wi
take a message to that hous
good man? Do not refuse n
gold shall pay you well. I—
that millionaire, and an avengin
has crushed me." With his

CATHOLICITY AND PANTHEISM.

NO. XII.

THE COSMOS IN TIME AND SPACE.

THE supernatural moment unites created personalities to the infinite. By the moment of substantial creation the first duality is established between the infinite and the finite. This duality is brought into harmony and unity in the Theanthropos, who knits together the finite and the infinite in the oneness of his single personality. But as the hypostatic moment united only created natures to the infinite, another moment was necessary, namely, a medium between the Theanthropos and substantial creation. This is the *supernatural,* which, by raising created persons above their natural sphere, enables them to arise, as it were, to the level of the infinite, and establishes a communication and intercourse between them. This we have shown in the preceding article. The question which now remains to be treated of at present is the following: *Who or what is to be the medium of communicating the term of the supernatural moment to created personality?*

Although God, in acting outside himself, might have effected everything immediately by himself, without allowing any play to second causes, yet, following the law of his wisdom, he exerted immediately by himself as much power as was required to set second causes in action, and then allowed them to develop themselves under his guidance. The law of wisdom is the law of sufficient reason, which implies that no intelligent agent can, in acting, more power than is absolute sary to attain its object; fc otherwise would be to let the of action not necessary to a object go to waste, and be e without any possible reason. the necessity on the part of nite to admit secondary ag the effectuation of this momer ever that was possible, in observe the law of wisdom. ing this theory to the externa we see that the substantial hypostatic moments were immediately by God himself, no secondary agency could ployed therein; but the supe moment was effected by God the agency of the Theanthro merited it by his own acts of value.* Hence, as the Thea is the meritorious cause of th natural moment, he is pre-e its mediator, and therefore th um of communicating it to personality. This consequ Christ being the medium of t munication of grace, in forc being its meritorious cause, i dent that we know of none ever disputed it. The only which remains to be solved— tion of the greatest import: this: When the Theanthro living on earth, he would co cate the term of the supe moment in the personal int and intimacy in which he li

* Council of Trent.

nity; the other, by which we tend to the act of creation.

But there is this difference among others between us and the infinite, that *he* possesses in himself and by himself the force of concentration and expansion, whereas our force is borrowed and communicated to us by means of *instruments*, which his infinite wisdom has prepared. Life is kept in us by something *forcing* to us the *instruments* to which God has communicated the power of sustaining and repairing it.

We subsist by the invisible force contained in an organism. The same must be said of the force of expansion. We cannot act outside ourselves, on any being at all capable of resistance, by the simple direct act of our will, but must make use of instruments, among which our body is the first.

Now, the reasons of this are, that, if we possessed the force of concentration and expansion in ourselves and by ourselves, it would follow that, as these two forces constitute the essence of life, we should have life in ourselves and by ourselves, we should be to ourselves the reason of our being and subsistence, and consequently we should be infinite and not finite. Hence, pantheism, which admits the unity of substance independent and self-sufficient, and all else as phenomena of this substance, rejects all idea of instrument in metaphysics, and all idea of sacrament in theology.

Nor would it do to say that God might communicate that double force to us immediately by himself without the aid of any instruments. For two reasons we must reject such a supposition: First, the law of secondary agency, which requires that created substance should act, and it would not for any purpose do so were God to do everything immediately by himself Second, the law of communion, so necessary to tl
ty of the cosmos, which is fo
exclusively upon the action
element upon the other, e
communion would be merely
ary and fictitious.

We conclude: An instrume
metaphysical idea is an o
containing a force of conce
and expansion. A sacramen
an instrument, must therefore
organism containing a force
centration and expansion; an
organism is something outw
sensible, it follows that a sac
must be also outward and s
And as the force which the
ment is designed to convey
gether supernatural, it follows
sacrament must be an instrun
conveying supernatural forc
may, therefore, define a sac
to be a sensible instrument or
ism containing a supernatura
of concentration and of expan

But it is evident that no instr
no organism in nature, is capa
conveying a supernatural fo
concentration and of expansi
that would imply an act supe
its nature, which is a contra
It follows, therefore, that this
natural force must be commu
to the organism by the The
pos, otherwise it could neve
its destination and office. Th
anthropos, in order to be the
of communicating to all hum
sons in time and space the su
tural term, which is nothing e
a supernatural force of concen
and expansion, must comm
and unite his infinite energy a
tion to an external organis
thus himself convey through t
ganism the supernatural life.
this union of the infinite energy
Theanthropos with an outward
nism must not be successive o
porary, but permanent and

Hence, the different moments of the sacramental extension of the Theanthropos:

1. A moment of supernatural generation by which the Theanthropos attaches his infinite energy to a visible instrument, permanent in time and space, and through which he confers a similitude of himself and the other divine persons; a similitude in essence, in intellect, in will, in feeling, in aspirations, in an initial and germinal state, and which establishes the incipient and germinal union of human persons with the Trinity.

2. A moment by which the Theanthropos attaches his infinite energy to a visible instrument, and through which he carries that initial and inchoative similitude and union to a definite and determinate growth.

3. A moment by which the Theanthropos attaches his infinite energy to a sensible instrument, in order to communicate to human persons the power to perpetuate his sacramental extension in time and space.

4. A moment by which the Theanthropos communicates his infinite energy to human persons, to exalt their natural force of expansion, and enable them to propagate the human and supernatural species.

5. A moment by which the Theanthropos attaches and unites the *real substantial presence of his person*, that is, of humanity and divinity, both subsisting in his single divine person, to a sensible instrument, in order to communicate to human persons his real, substantial, theanthropic life, in order to put all human persons of all time and space in real living communion with each other, by meeting in him and through him as a common centre, and in order to reside continually in the visible cosmos.

The third and fourth moments follow necessarily from the others, both having the like office.

The first of the
perpetuate the
of Christ. An org
motion requires the
persons; consequen
ral organism on the
tension of Christ, i
plied to human per
agency of human
ed and fitted for su
other visible instru
particular theanthr
tached.

This third mom
also for another ob
transmitting whole
without any error, l
tercourse, of the wh
trines which are t
supernatural intellig
the first moment.
way can be though
whole and entire th
doctrines, the object
tural intelligence, th
tercourse, the only s
losophical manner
doctrine. Hence,
also, a moment was r
the Theanthropos, a
ite energy to a parti
would fit human per
fallibly the whole bo
came to reveal, and
sacramental extensio

The fourth mom
natural union of sexe
generation.

Human persons
the first moment to
order, their personal
sarily become sup
more the highest p
act of expansion, w
fusion of their united
Consequently, it was
Theanthropos should
lar supernatural ene
of the sexes with a v
generation, in orde

These are the three leading principles, according to which infinite wisdom resolved the problem of the end of the external action: highest possible variety, highest possible unity, highest possible communication.

Now, let us see if and how the effectuation of real cosmos was governed by these principles.

In view of these principles, God effected substantial creation and the hypostatic moment, by which the whole substantial moment was united to the person of the Word in the bond of his divine personality.

Was the problem of the highest possible variety and the highest possible unity and communication in the person of the Theanthropos resolved? It was, so far only as nature and substance were concerned; because the hypostatic union only wedded *human nature*, and through it all inferior natures, to the person of the Word. But this unity and communication excluded, and had to exclude, all human personalities. It excluded them in the fact; it had to exclude them, otherwise human personality would have ceased to exist. Here the problem must be resolved anew—how to raise human personality to the highest possible union and communication with the Theanthropos. Another moment was effected to initiate the solution of the problem; and this was the supernatural moment. By it human personality, by being endowed with a higher similitude of the Trinity and the Theanthropos, and by receiving higher faculties, is brought into a real and particular union with the Word, and through him the other persons of the Trinity. But the supernatural moment does not resolve the problem yet; because the union which results thereby is union between human persons and the Word as God, not a union between human

persons and the
Word made man.—
A real and efficie
two terms requires a
tween them. Now,
term establishes a
human persons and
not a relation betwe
Theanthropos, beca
spiritual and incor
relation between pe
of body and soul m
not spiritual only, b
Hence, if we excl
stantial presence of t
as such, we have a
persons united to th
real efficacious unio
sons united to th
On this suppositio
would lack the high
and communication,
to realize the end of
tion. But, admit t
sence of the Thea
and space, admit th
corporating and indi
in human persons,
wisdom and beauty
flashes at once up
the whole cosmos, a
human nature of Ch
by the hypostatic
Word; all human
rated body and sou
and soul of the Th
up into his body and
ed, as it were, in th
them, and in them
closest possible com
the divinity which
tain. In this plan
holds together and
harmony, and beaut
But, if the real sub
of the *Theanthropos*
in order to bring hu
to the highest poss
communication with
thus realize the end

vaded by him, when so closely and so intimately united to him as to feel his flesh come in contact with their flesh, his blood glowing in their blood, his heart beating against their hearts, his mind illumining and guiding their minds, his will captivating and mastering their will, his divinity ennobling and exalting their whole being and faculties—I say, when the cosmos of personality is thus united to the Theanthropos, does it not represent most vividly the infinite being of God? Does the infinite in looking at such a cosmos see anything but as it were one Theanthropos filling and pervading all?

As to expressing the action of the life of the infinite, and thus raising the acts of a human person to the digty and value of theanthropic iife, it will appear evident if we recollect that the life of the infinite establishes the eternal religion in the bosom of God which expresses itself in the mystery of the ever blessed Trinity. For the Father, in recognizing himself intellectually, and as it were theoretically, produces an intellectual image of himself, absolutely perfect in every sense. Both in recognizing themselves aspire a practical acknowledgment of themselves, the Holy Ghost, who completes the cycle of infinite life, and perfects the eternal religion.

Now, this eternal religion are human persons destined to express, to realize in themselves, that they may be a most perfect image in their action and life of the life of the infinite. This they could never do either naturally or supernaturally. Naturally, because such acknowledgment requires an infinite intellect to apprehend the infinite excellence and perfection of God, and an infinite power of appreciation to value, esteem, and love it practically. Now, naturally these faculties of human persons are simply finite. Even the light of grace, which strengthens the r
intelligence, and the supern
force, which corroborates th
cannot do it, because in their
also finite. It is, therefore, t
nite intellect and will of the
thropos which alone can app
him intellectually and love
he deserves. Now, the myst
the Eucharist enables huma
sons to partake of this intellect
volitive recognition of the infi
their union with the Theant
When, after the solemn and
moment of feeding upon the fl
blood of the Theanthropos,
myself to adore God, to renc
the homage of adoration w
owe him as creature, then I a
alone with my limited underst
and will. It is with the inte
the Theanthropos, which p
and illumines my intellect,
recognize theoretically his infir
fections. When at the same n
I turn to him to offer him the
of my love, I cling to him th
with the finite, limited, circu
ed power of my natural or su
tural will, but of a will unc
guidance, the mastery, the
sion, the infinite power of exp
of the will of the Theanthrop
der the immense weight of hi
and when I yield my heart t
berant joy and complacency
infinite loveliness and bliss, it
the little vessel of a heart,
can contain but a finite joy,
heart under the pressure of
jubilee, which gushes up fr
heart of the Theanthropos an
flows into my heart, and m
swim in a joy and a delight
to those alone who have ta
Thus, with the Theanthropos
bosom, pervading my mind, m
my heart, my flesh, and c
me toward him even as the
groom draws his bride to hir

will. Thus, in union with the Theanthropos by the eucharistic presence, they come in communion with all the objects which are to bring them to perfection by a gradual development and transformation.

Take the corporal presence of the Theanthropos away, and the supernatural faculties would only be in communication with the infinite, but not with the finite; with God, but not with his cosmos; because these faculties could never come in contact with the whole cosmos, except inasmuch as it exists and lives in the Theanthropos.

This argument introduces us to another. Every elevated person, to live fully and perfectly, must be in communication not only with the infinite and the finite as to nature, but also as to personality. Every elevated person must commune in a real, living, actual, quickening manner with elevated persons in time and space. The perfection of unity of the cosmos claims this communing, as it is evident; and the fulness of life of each particular person demands it, because life in its plenitude* results from communing with all its proper objects.

Now, how to bring together all elevated persons living at a distance of time and space—some in the initial and germinal state, others in the state of completion and palingenesia? We come into communion with things and persons distinct and separate from us by time, space, or individuality, by a *medium* common to us and those things or persons we wish to enter into communion with. Thus, I come into communication with persons at a certain distance from me by the mediums of light and air, which are between me and them, and common to both. Suppose I was

* We speak of initial plenitude.

speaking, the air which exi
tween me and my hearers w
the common medium of com
tion. In articulating, I woul
the air which surrounds me,
strokes would be transmitt
particle to particle in every
until they would reach the
my audience, and thus a com
tion by speech would be est
between us. If, therefore,
vated persons must come in
with each other, there must l
thing which will bring the
ther—a medium common
all—to make them commu
each other. Now, this me
the real substantial presenc
Theanthropos incorporating
in all elevated persons. I c
with the Theanthropos, with
nity and his humanity, with
telligence, his will, his he
body: I appropriate him to
another communes likewi
the Theanthropos; and thus
brought together, we come in
we are united in the same lif
gence, will, heart, body; thus
and live in one common thea
life. This is the foundatio
of that sublime, magnificen
bling doctrine of Catholic
communion of saints—commu
all persons elevated to the su
ral moment. Communion!
the medium which brings the
ther? It is the real, living,
tial presence of the Theanth
corporated in them, and o
they have fed and shall feed
nity.*

How beautifully, how divi
this communication of the Th

* We hold that an elevated person
to the substance of the Theanthrop
not always actually united to his bod
this sacramental union only lasts as
species would naturally last, yet is
so united in a spiritual though not les
ner.

We feel that withal the arguments we have brought forward in vindicating the beautiful and sublime dogma of the real presence of the Theanthropos in his cosmos will have no effect on some minds, unless we remove the metaphysical difficulties which are raised against it, and show consequently its possibility. Therefore, we willingly hasten to the task. And as these objections are very popular, we shall put them in the popular form of a dialogue. The dialogue is between W. and D., the first a Protestant, and the other a Catholic.

W. I shall begin by a very strong objection. I cannot conceive the possibility of the body of a full-grown man being within the small portion of space filled by a wafer. Christ was a full-grown man. He is so now. How, then, can he reside or be contained in such a small particle of space as the host?

D. You will be kind enough to observe what the Catholic Church teaches, that it is the *substance* of the body and blood of Christ, which is under the modifications of bread and wine.

W. Suppose it is; what difference does that make?

D. All the difference in the world. Pray, what is a substance?

W. It is that part of a being which remains immutable amid all the vicissitudes and changes of the being. These changes or vicissitudes are called accidents or modifications; that which remains always the same and immutable is called substance.

D. Right; and, pray, has substance any dimensions, has it length, br height, or depth, or is it what sophers call a simple being?

W. It must have no dime because dimensions may chan vary, and the substance must ways the same.

D. Then substance is a sim ing, that is, it has neither depth, length, or breadth.

W. So it would seem, an I recollect aright, all the met cians worth the name hold it

D. Right again; and, if y member, Leibnitz calls it a *m* a unit, and distinguishes tw of substances, the simple a composite. The simple is o stance; the composite is an gate of simple substances o Thus, bodies are an aggregate stances or units.

W. Well, suppose that bo to substance are an aggregate ple units, what of that?

D. Why, then your objec answered.

W. How?

D. Did we not say that t tholic Church teaches that it *substance* of the body and bl Christ, which is under the m tions of bread and wine? not agree upon the theory th stance has no dimensions? not admit that a body is an gate of simple units, as to sub and that consequently in that it has no dimensions? Then ters not how large or how sm may imagine the wafer to be, not make the least difference; that our Lord's body in th Eucharist is there in its subst as an aggregate of simple un consequently has no dimensio occupies no space whatever remark, that what happens particular case happens in ev

in the Old Testament, who were united to Christ by faith and charity. As to children and grown-up persons who never communicated, we answer that we are giving the general law, and not accidental cases. The foundation, therefore, of the communion of saints is the union with Christ, real and actual, of the supernatural faculties. The perfection of the communion of saints is the real presence and incorporation.

D. But it *does* remove it. And let me tell you that you Protestants, in fighting against the dogmas of the Catholic Church, commit two very serious faults: First, you do not provide yourselves with philosophy enough to cope with her. Secondly, you do not sound the depth of her statement. Then it generally happens that, when you think you are proposing your strongest objections, and you are very sure you have her in a corner, you are merely combating a phantom of your own imagination.

Now, let us see if the substance of the body of Christ can be in different places at the same time. To do this, we must examine the other question, How can a simple being reside in space? Metaphysicians teach that a body may reside in space in two ways, according as it is considered either in its phenomenal representation or in its real objective nature and substance. In its phenomenal representation, a body resides in space by contact of extension; in its real objective nature and substance, by acting upon it. I lay my hand flat upon the surface of a table, and suppose I consider both my hand and the table in their phenomenal extension. Under this respect, all the points and parts which form the phenomenal extension of my hand come in contact with all the respective parts of the table which my hand is able to cover.* Under this respect, a body naturally *cannot* be in different places at the same time without a contradiction, because the supposition would imply that the parts of my hand which are in contact with the respective parts of the table are also in contact with parts of other bodies at any given distance.

But if we consider a bod[y] its phenomenal extension, b[ut] real objective nature and su[bstance] the case is different; becaus[e] have seen, the body as to stance is simple and une[xtended] and therefore, as such, it ca[nnot re]side in space by contact of e[xtension] inasmuch as its parts touch nomenal parts of space; fo[r it has] no parts which may touch. it follows that it resides in every other simple being, th[at is, by] acting upon it.* In this cas[e] in its substance and objectiv[e] does not reside in space ex[cept by] its action upon it.

Now, naturally, a body ir jective nature and substance ed in its action to a certain space, and cannot extend it beyond it. But there is no contradiction in supposing body may be endowed by th[e] with the power and energ[y] upon any indeterminate am[ount of] space at the same time.

Now, with regard to the our Lord, we have seen tha[t] the holy Eucharist in its state, and consequently is the real action. The miracle in is, that the infinite power of t[he] to which it is hypostaticall[y] intensifies its natural sphere upon space, and makes it ex[tend to] thousands of places at the sa[me time.] To conclude: The question, body of Christ be in differen[t places] at the same time? resolves it this other: Can the substanc[e] body of Christ act really a[nd] in different places at the sam[e time?] Who could give a reason wo[rth any]thing to show that it cannot could prove any contradictio[n]

* "Corporalia sunt in loco per contactum quantitis."—*St. Thomas.*

* "Incorporalia non sunt in loco p[er contac]tum quantitis sed per contactum *virt[utis]*

of that law which causes blood to flow from the wounds of a corpse if the real murderer lay his hand on the dead body.

These replies, or attempts at a natural solution, are antiquated. We need not seriously consider them.

In the last century, the objectors took a very different ground. The whole thing, they said, was a device of the priests. Some called it a "trick of long standing and great ingenuity"; others stigmatized it as "one of the most bungling tricks ever seen."

This style of objection still holds its own.

During the present century, another style of objection has come into vogue, based on the ever-increasing spirit of rationalism. The laws of nature, we are told, are invariable and supreme. No violations of them are possible. All miracles—in the sense of occurrences above and beyond those laws of nature, occasional interruptions in the grand scheme of universal order, law, and causation—are to be at once rejected. "The idea of *their* possibility can only occur to those who have failed to grasp the great inductive principle of invariable uniformity and law in nature." "It is hardly a question of evidence. The generality of mankind habitually assume antecedently that miracles are now inadmissible; and hence, that, in any reported case, they must in some manner be explained away. . . . . Of old, the sceptic professed he would be convinced by seeing a miracle. At the present day, a visible miracle would be the very subject of his scepticism. It is not the attestation, but the nature of the alleged miracle, which is now the point in question. It is not the fallibility of human testimony, but the infallibility of natural order, which is now the ground of argument." (Rev. Baden Powell, *Order of Nature.*)

We have not the space to
this theory at length, and
that it is at bottom anti-chris
pantheistic, contrary to the
principles of true philosoph
is it necessary for our purpo
so. All the philosophical
tions in the world will not pr
man having eyes that, becau
laws of nature are immutal
miracles are therefore imp
the blood which stands in
pulla was liquid when taker
is solid at the conclusion.
that it was hard, and sees t
now fluid. He will laugh
philosopher and believe h
eyes.

Neither is it necessary to
at length the opinion acc
blindly by Protestants, that
of miracles has long since p
that miracles have entirely
since the days of the apost
God can work miracles, wh
can limit him in the exercise
power, either in time or place
did not the Saviour promise
tinuance of signs among th
believe—a continuance to w
put no limitation?

The assertion that the
Church is erroneous, and tha
quently there can be no mi
her fold, is more than akin
words of the Pharisees to t
man, whom our Lord had
to sight: "*Give glory to G
know that this man is a sinner.*
appropriate answer was: "*If
sinner, I know not: one thing
that whereas I was blind, no*
(John ix. 24, 25).

We therefore leave the gen
ject of miracles to be tre
others; and we confine ours
the fact of the liquefaction.
as in every other case of
miracles, the decision depend
ly on the character of the te

each series are so alike that they might be interchanged. The general hygrometric condition of the atmosphere evidently has no perceptible influence for or against or on the liquefactions.

Nay, more, it frequently happens that the blood, after liquefying, grows solid again on the same day, and then liquifies, perhaps solidifies anew. and liquefies a third time. All these changes have sometimes taken place within one hour. Now, did the atmosphere, during that hour or during that day, pass through corresponding extreme changes of its hygrometric condition? Ordinary men did not feel them. Meteorological observers have not noticed them. Registering instruments do not record them. And yet, the habit of watching their neighboring and often threatening volcano has made the people of Naples as observant of such changes as sailors at sea, and has given to that city one of the ablest schools of meteorology on the Continent.

We may well conclude, therefore, that the liquefaction of the blood of St. Januarius is not the deliquescence of a solid body, arising from humidity of the air to which it is exposed.

Is it the melting of a solid substance through the action of heat?

This is a more important question. Many of those who charge bad faith and trickery on the "priests and monks" officiating at the expositions, maintain that it is by an adroit application of heat that the liquefaction is brought about. Others, who admit the sincerity and good faith of the Neapolitan clergy—which, knowing the men, they feel cannot be impugned—still attribute the liquefaction to the heat of the altar, all ablaze with lighted tapers, and of the crowd thronging the chapel, and packed most closely just in the sanctuary itself and around the altar.

We undertake to show th: liquefaction is in no way prc by or dependent on heat.

I. Often, when the crowd is est, and the heat most intens in September—the liquefactior layed for hours; perhaps do occur at all, or only a portion fies, while another portion r solid.

II. On the contrary, it has red quickly and for the entire even though the crowd was c ratively small. This is esp seen in the extraordinary expo even in winter, when not a sc persons were present.

III. It has taken place in th air, while the reliquary, place right in an open framework, ar aloft above the heads of the p was borne in procession throu streets; and this in the winter r of December and January, a as on the vigils at the beginn May.

IV. It has occurred on days snow covered the streets, or th was so excessive as to cause th al procession through the str be dispensed with. As the ch in Naples are not heated, th perature within the cathedra have been very low, probab above 45° Fahrenheit.

V. This very question has submitted to scientific investi The professors of the Royal U sity of Naples, headed by Dr. *las Fergola*, the most eminent cist of the faculty, instituted a ber of interesting observations, Dr. Fergola published. We from his work a table giving t tual temperature in a number stances, as shown by a standar mometer which they stationed altar in close proximity to th quary at the time of the li tion:

they did, and as Dr. Fergola maintains in his essay, that the liquefaction of the blood of St. Januarius evidently does not depend on the degree of heat to which it is subjected during the expositions.

VI. The same conclusion may also be reached by a single consideration. When a solid substance is liquefied or melted by heat, it will continue liquid if the heat is kept at the same temperature or rises. It will resume its solid condition only when the temperature falls below that degree which is the melting point of the substance.

Now, in those summer days which we have spoken of—such as the six days of May, 1795, marked in the table of Fergola—days on which the Neapolitans seek the repose of a *siesta* — the hottest hours are from 12 M. to 3 P.M.. During these hours, the temperature is naturally higher than it was at 9.30 or 10 A.M., or is afterward at 4 P.M., or later. Yet the blood, which liquefied at 9.30 or 10 A.M., almost invariably becomes solid again during these hottest hours, if the reliquary be placed on the altar and a silk veil thrown over it, and it liquefies again during the afternoon exposition, although the heat of the day is then sensibly diminishing.

The more accurately and carefully the facts of the liquefaction are studied, the more clearly do we see that it does not depend on temperature, general or local. It is not produced by the action of heat.

This exclusion of the agency of heat has "considerably exercised" some of the opponents of the liquefaction of the blood of St. Januarius. Confident that all miracles are, now at least, inadmissible, and that this and every other alleged miracle is susceptible of a natural explanation, if we only knew it, they eagerly catch at any, even the most ed and improbable theories, them forward with equal in ateness and confidence.

We have heard it said: (ples is an exceptional, volc trict. There may exist th occult or obscure volcanic which suffices to produce t faction; who can tell what results may come from a con of all the volcanic agencie work in that vicinity?

Is Naples the only volc trict in the world? Does a volcanic district present anyt this liquefaction, or calcu throw light on it? Even in is there another similar e And has not this liquefact tinued regularly, even when was quiescent for a long years. Previous to Decemb the volcano had slumbered i tranquillity for nearly two (A French traveller tells of tl of cattle he saw browsing w very crater itself, then a va valley sunk in the plateau the top of the mountain. this while the liquefactions c as they had done before, anc have done ever since, in o sons of quiet, and in seasons volcanic eruption.

And then, we ask, what o or indication is there giving (of this natural influence or la what sort of a natural law which acts only on one si of blood, and has not actec thousands of others in the sa ditions.

Again, it has been urged, the same strain, that our kn of the laws of nature is still perfect. Many laws are as y covered. Every year is ma some advance in our knowl them. It by no means foll

fore your eyes, it will increase, sometimes with froth, sometimes even bubbling more or less violently, sometimes retaining a perfectly tranquil and level surface; sometimes rising very slowly, sometimes rapidly; and it may continue to rise until it fills the vial. Or again, if the vial be full, or nearly full, the liquid within it will sink, either suddenly or gradually, hour by hour, with or without froth or bubbling, until it occupies perhaps three-fourths of the space. These changes take place in summer and in winter indifferently. They are entirely independent of the temperature. They evidently set aside the second law we have recited regarding volume.

III. A third law of nature is, that her steps are forward and not backward. A movement once made is never revoked. Chemical changes are progressive, and, so long as the ingredients and agents remain the same, they never go back to repeat a combination which has once been made and then changed for another.

Yet continual repetitions of the same forms, combinations, or conditions of the substance within the ampulla are a special characteristic of the liquefactions.

We will produce, hereafter, in a fitting place, evidence that for centuries the ampulla has not been opened, and consequently that its contents have not been changed. Nevertheless, the alternate hardenings and liquefactions, the variations of color, the frothing, and the ebullitions, and the increases and decreases of volume, have continued to succeed each other, and to be repeated hundreds, some of them thousands, of times.

Nay, leaving aside for the moment these longer periods, and confining our examination to the ten or twelve hours of a single day, during which the ampulla is all the while the public gaze, and any interf of chemical art with the cont absolutely impossible, we sti these repetitions of the same f combination. The blood wa when first taken out, it lic stood liquid for an hour o solidified again, and again lic Perhaps it solidified a third tir a third time liquefied. It con ed to froth, and it ceased, the menced again, and again cea changed color, and again re to the prestine tint. It chan bulk, either increasing or dec and again returned to its level.

This reiteration of some o of these changes, in a sing while the ingredients in the a are evidently neither added diminished, is contrary to the of nature. The opposition i the same in character, but fested in vaster proportions evidence compels us to that the substance in the a has not been changed or m with for years, and even for turies; while yet these reite ever continue. The argun the same in both instances.

There is no uncertainty as facts of the liquefaction or th known laws of nature which v referred to. Nor is there an that the facts are violations o laws. Other laws of nature, be discovered, may fill gaps knowledge, and may complen laws already known. None discovered to contradict or them. It is as vain to wait discovery of some unknow which may account for the t the liquefaction, as it would look for some other unknown nature in virtue of which lived again, and came forth f

liquid was obtained, it would observe the law of constant volume at the same temperature, and would not so frequently either decrease or increase its bulk. In one word, man has no power to set aside the laws of nature as we plainly see them set aside in this liquefaction. We are forced to conclude that it is not his work. The liquefaction which is seen at Naples is not, and cannot possibly be, the natural result of any art or skill, or of any blundering of the Neapolitan clergy.

This will be made still clearer if circumstances allow us to examine somewhat in detail, as we hope to do in a closing article, the various solu-tions which have been proposec the attempted imitations of this faction. Their signal failure in instance serves as practical con tions of the conclusion to whi have been already led. If wi aids of science and skill at their mand, men have failed to repr the liquefaction of the blood Januarius, is it not clear tha priests and monks of Naples a competent of themselves to pr the original?

The liquefaction must be, : Neapolitans hold it to be, a *i* —a fact contrary to the laws ture, wrought by the power o for a purpose worthy of himsel

---

THE PRINCETON REVIEW ON DR. FABER.*

TWENTY years ago, Dr. Newman delivered a series of lectures on "The Present Position of Catholics in England." The scope of these lectures was the exposition of the English Protestant view of the Catholic Church. Dr. Newman showed, with an ability, skill, and cogency of argument, a mastery of language, a wealth of illustration, and a keenness of satire which even he has rarely equalled in his voluminous writings, what is the nature, origin, basis, and life of this view. Its sustaining power, he proves, is *tradition*, its basis *fable*, its life *prejudice*, its protection *ignorance*. We take the liberty of recommending this volume to the writer whom we are now intending to criticise, to the conductors of the distinguished review for whi writes, and to the clergy and re laity in general of his eminent spectable denomination. The nation to which the British Lio roused, and the fierce assault he made upon the illustrious a who entered his cage and too by the beard of prejudice, so of such ancient growth, and so erable in his own eyes, is an evi of the power of Dr. Newman's and the efficacy of his weapon. exposure which he made of o the apostate traducers of the C lic religion, after whom the E public for a while ran open-mou gave occasion to a prosecutio libel, as the result of which Dr. man was condemned to a fine imprisonment. It was a striking tration and confirmation of wha Newman had so boldly dec

* *The Princeton Review*, October, 1871. Art. II.: *The Life and Letters of Frederick William Faber*. By Rev. William Scribner.

learned to exercise their minds, to compare thought with thought, to analyze an argument or to balance probabilities. The Catholic Church appeals to the imagination, as a great fact, wherever she comes; she strikes it. Protestants must find some idea equally captivating as she is, something fascinating, something capable of possessing, engrossing, and overwhelming, if they are to battle with her hopefully: their cause is lost unless they can do this. It was, then, a thought of genius, and, as I think, superhuman genius, to pitch upon the expedient which has been used against the church from Christ's age to our own; to call her, as in the first century Beelzebub, so in the sixteenth Antichrist; it was a bold, politic, and successful move. It startled men who heard; and whereas Antichrist, by the very notion of his character, will counterfeit Christ, he will therefore be, so far, necessarily like him; and, if Antichrist is like Christ, then Christ, I suppose, must be like Antichrist; thus, there was, even at first starting, a felicitous plausibility about the very charge which went far towards securing belief, while it commanded attention.

"This, however, though much, was not enough; the charge that Christ is Antichrist must not only be made, but must be sustained, and sustained it could not possibly be, in the vastness and enormity of its idea, as I have described it, by means of truth. Falsehood, then, has ever been the indispensable condition of the impeachment which Protestants have made; and the impeachment they make is the indispensable weapon wherewith to encounter the antagonist whom they combat. Thus you see that calumny and obloquy of every kind is, from the nature of the case, the portion of the church while she has enemies—that is, in other words, while she is militant—her position, that is, if she is to be argued with at all; and argued with she must be, because man, from the very force of his moral constitution, cannot content himself in his warfare, of whatever kind, with the mere use of brute force. The lion rends his prey, and gives no reason for doing so, but man cannot persecute without assigning to himself a reason for his act, he must settle it with his conscience, he must have sufficient reasons, and, if good reasons are not forthcoming, there is no help for it, he must put up with bad. How to conflict with the moral influence of the church being t[he] problem to be solved, nothi[ng] but to misstate and defame; the alternative. Tame facts, elabora[te] tions, subtle presumptions, will with the many; something which a dash, something gaudy and something inflammatory, is the in request. He must make up [h] then, to resign the populace to t[he] of the Catholic Church, or he m[ust] der her to her greater confusion.' maintain, *is* the case; this, I [say,] *must* be the case; bad logic, fal[se] and I really do think that candi[d] whatever persuasion, though t[hey] not express themselves exactl[y] words I have used, will agree w[ith] substance; will allow that, putti[ng] the question whether Protestant[ism] be supported by any other met[hod] controversy—for instance, by sin[...] blishment, or by depriving Cat[h...] education, or by any other viol[ent] dient—still, if popular controvers[y] used, then fable, not truth; calu[mny] justice, will be its staple. Strip [its] fallacies and its fiction, and w[...] you?"*

Where would the Rev. M[...] ner be if his article were [...] of its fallacies and its [...] What would become of the [...] *ton Review* if it should publis[h] and favorable account of the writings of Dr. Faber, with potent antidote administere[d] with that sweet draught o[f] waters which might otherwis[e] too alluring to some of th[e] and candid members of the [Presby-] terian flock? The writer of [...] cle, who has evidently been e[...] in the old-fashioned Protesta[nt] tion about the Catholic Chu[rch] fallen in love with Dr. Faber [...] works, and with the greates[t] ness and candor has opened [...] to the public. We can see reflected in his pages the a[...] ment which came over hi[m] began and went on from vo[...]

* *Lecture IV.*, p. 206. Dublin. Thir[...]

writings of the elo-
in, and from page to
[illegible] biography.
with equal distinct-
fell back on the old
r, the old prejudice,
iolent effort, in order
self against the new
l beamed on his mind
sentiments which had
en into his heart.
e he could not deny
asure of communicat-
easure he had found
resbyterians, he could
g that they also need-
, and could find none
swer except the old
ose shelter he had hid-
Suppose that a num-
and inquisitive Pres-
l be induced, by read-
of Dr. Faber's life and
ed by one of their own
chase or borrow the
so much delights in?
should come to the
the beautiful charac-
is a fair specimen of
the Catholic religion
hat his doctrine is
the Catholic doctrine
m the lips of all our
from the pens of. all
iters? Suppose these
hould meet with some
g somewhat of the
F. Faber, should lis-
ersation and hear his
uld perhaps attend a
reat? We ask the
is a Catholic, but as
ask it, and simply
is a question of the
antage-ground by the
ies. Does not any
hereas we have need
g than a fair chance
guidence, the excel-
[illegible] of the two

religions, in order to hold our old ground and gain new, the Presbyterian has lost the greatest advantage he has hitherto possessed, as soon as the frightful cloud of odium which the old Protestant view has thrown around us has been dissipated? Therefore, that odium must be kept up; that antecedent impossibility that there can be any truth in the claims of the Catholic Church because it is so very wicked, must be placed as a bar to the ingress of every argument. So has the Rev. Mr. Scribner reasoned and acted. We will not impute to him a deliberate and conscious purpose to falsify or calumniate, and are willing to admit that he is probably in a great measure the victim of the gigantic fraud which he indorses and recommends. His language about the Catholic Church and her hierarchy is of that kind which might justly cause the cheek of any one not steeled to the endurance of the grossest insults to mantle with indignation. But, when we reflect on the fact that many honest, candid, and well-disposed minds are duped to such an extent by this fraudulent Protestant tradition that they are almost incapable of seeing anything except through its medium, we are more inclined to pity than anger. It is a great misfortune, even when it is not a wilful fault, to be under the control of this horrid delusion, this gloomy nightmare, which besets the very cradle, haunts the nursery, and sits brooding and glowering on the breast of so great a multitude of our fellow-Christians. We will, therefore, try to do something to relieve them of this incubus, and to lead them to think and feel more rationally and justly about Catholics and their religion. We will take the expression of the common Protestant view by the author before us in its objective

sense, without reference to his personal and subjective motives in repeating such ignominious charges, and simply examine them in themselves and with reference to the grounds on which they rest.

The first passage we quote is the last sentence of the article. It is expressed conditionally as to the form, because the direct statement of the author was quite different, and apparently contrary to it. Yet it does not appear that the author entertains any doubt, or at least intends to suggest any doubt, of its truth :

"We may admit that the Papacy is the Mystical Babylon, the Scarlet Woman, the Antichrist drunk with the blood of the saints, 'the great Whore which did corrupt the earth with her fornication,' and yet believe that God has a people in the Church of Rome who live and die within her pale."

Here we have what Dr. Newman calls the "expedient of superhuman genius," the startling, fascinating, terrifying idea, the Protestant view, which forestalls all argument by prepossessing the imagination with a nightmare of preternatural horror. The writer has had this image before him from a child. He alludes to it as something well known to his readers. It is like the "Old Smoker" in the chimney, or the goblin in the garret, or the mad bull around the corner, waiting to execute vengeance on naughty little girls and boys who ask questions. We find it very difficult to argue seriously against this chimera. It is like arguing against the odd fancy of the eccentric Jesuit Hardouin, that the North American Indians are the descendants of devils. It is revolting or ludicrous as it is looked at in different lights. It appears to our mind to be vulgar, silly, superstitious, and fanatical. Not, of course, because it is the use of

language and imagery tak
the Scripture, but because
wholly arbitrary, fanciful, a
warrantable use and applic
such language and imagery
like the grotesque use of S
names and images by the far
the Cromwellian revolution.
assumed as something cert
well known that the Papacy
told and described in these p
visions and predictions, as
and well known as the interp
of Joseph's dream, the dre
the chief butler and chief
Pharao, the vision of Nab
nosor, or the Messianic predi
Daniel. Nothing short of th
justify the manner in which
tant writers apply these term
Roman Church, and shut
calm and sober consideratio
claims and doctrines by an
to the prophecies respectin
christ and Babylon. You ca
gue from a mere hypothesis
were a fact or a certain tr
this case, the entire probabili
hypothesis depends on first
that the Roman Church re
sesses and exhibits the qualiti
must belong to the objects
prediction. A sober and rati
quiry into the real meaning
sublime, terrible, and obsc
phecies exacts, first of all,
of the interpretation of the
It requires, moreover, an exam
and due appreciation of the
tions of Catholic commentat
must be dispassionate and s
in its character. Now, the
Protestant application of the
phecies to the Roman Chu
none of these characteristi
finds no countenance from a
ers before the time of the s
Reformation. It was invent
used as a convenient and
weapon of assault. It is reje

"With the exception of a few such men as Faber, it is not to be believed for a moment that the educated prelates and priesthood of the Romish Church have themselves a particle of faith in what they teach the people concerning their Popish legends. We do not know what to think of the man who does not feel intense indignation at the bare thought of Pope, cardinals, and priests all encouraging the people to reverence the disgusting pretended relics with which their churches are filled. Let it be remembered that the highest Romish authorities in all countries continue to this day to give their sanction to *what they know to be imposition* on the credulity of the people; and can it be doubted that even the most bigoted person, if he knew the real facts, would question the truth of a system which rests so extensively on known and deliberate deception?" (p. 528).

There is something which seems so honest and unpremeditated about this outburst of indignation that we are disposed to give the author the benefit of that excuse of childlike simplicity which he so kindly makes good in behalf of Dr. Faber. He has no thought of proving his assertions, does not seem to think they require any proof, or that they can be questioned by any one who is not ignorant and bigoted. *Let it be remembered*, he says, as of something learned in childhood, like the rules of grammar or the date of the discovery of America. Evidently, here is the old Protestant view, the old tradition, which has all the force of an infallible authority. Now, it is not the fault of Presbyterians and other Protestants that they have had this prejudice instilled into their minds in youth. While their ignorance is invincible, it is also inculpable. But if they adhere to it without reason, through supine indifference to truth or affection for their old prejudices, when their attention has been called to the reasons and motives for doubt and examination, they become morally blameworthy.

A simple denial of the truth accusations made in the for paragraph, on our part, is eno destroy all their prestige in the of any candid and intelligent I terian who is not ignorant or b Our word carries as much weight as that of the conduc the *Princeton Review*. And w emphatically, invoking God as ness to our sincerity and truth item of the foregoing accusatic is an atrocious calumny, anc who have uttered it are bo prove it or retract it, even have been themselves deceive have had no intention to calu This is all the reply we have t to the attack on the personal and integrity of the Catholic hood. But in regard to the top of relics and miracles, we wil word out of charity to our bew and indignant friend, and to him who are willing to hear th side.

Disgusting pretended relics. is the sense of that word *disg* Does it mean that real relics gusting, or that pretended rel disgusting because of the impo If it mean the former, we understand the feeling any than we understand the feeli one who is disgusted with t niture which has been in the for a long time. You cannot the question in that way. Th way of arguing the matter at a discuss the matter itself. If th of the saints are entitled to rev and have a secret, miraculous the feeling of disgust is simply normal and senseless feeling, ought to be suppressed by an the will. If it is a question the genuineness of the relics, who is not grossly ignorant of can be unaware of the fact tha the second century down, re

a similar sentence on the whole body of their modern descendants, it would be well to examine somewhat carefully the evidence in the case. For instance, to confine ourselves to modern times, there are: the liquefaction of the blood of St. Januarius; the ecstatic virgins of the Tyrol, and the recent similar case in Belgium; the miraculous conversion of the Jew Ratisbon; the case of Mrs. Mattingly of Washington; the miracles of Lourdes; the miraculous cure of a young lady at St. Louis, attested by three physicians; the miracles wrought by the relics of F. Olivaint, the martyr of Paris; the miraculous conversion of sixteen Mohammedans at Damascus, one of whom has suffered martyrdom; and many other events, believed by a vast number of intelligent persons, upon grounds of evidence, to be supernatural and miraculous. We do not ask our Protestant friends to believe these things on our word or without evidence. We simply say that it is the part of good sense and necessary for you, if you expect to sustain your own cause against us, that you should examine these things, and, if you deny altogether this whole class of professed facts, should give good reasons for it. Will you rule the whole case out of court by a sweeping principle that these things are in themselves impossible and incredible, and therefore false? We defy you to do it without subverting the whole basis on which rests the belief in the miracles of the Old and New Testaments. Moreover, we defy any one to evade or rebut the evidence of some of the miracles we have mentioned, especially the cure of Bourriette at Lourdes and of Mrs. Mattingly at Washington. We mention these, because we have given the evidence of the former in our own pages, and of the latter in the edition of the works of Bishop Engla[nd] pared for the press by the au[thor of] this article more than twent[y years] ago. The authority of the Church, nevertheless, and t[he] of the Catholic faith, do not manner rest on any one or all t[hese] of the visions, revelations, or [miracles] in question as their basis, an[d] ground of a divine faith. highest value, even when fully is to confirm and enliven our truths of which we are pr[...] certain.

The Rev. Mr. Scribner s[...] great truth that "one grea[...] taught by this biography Faber] is the lesson of c[...] (p. 531). He is also so o[...] correct in his remark that "[...] does not require us to admi[t] be true which is false," that [...] der he took the trouble to [...] Moreover, we cannot and [...] wish to dispute his right "[...] nounce a flaming Roman C[...] professor a child of the de[...] shows himself to be one." [...] wish to add to his statem[ent] more, which is that justice [...] as well as charity, that one not make atrocious charges [...] opprobrious epithets witho[ut] quate proofs and motives. reverend gentleman conside[...] coolly and deliberately, and [...] Protestant reader of this arti[cle] sider and judge of the f[...] sentence:

> "It would not be enlightene[...] which would make us think t[...] haps, after all, *the licentious Rom[...] lic priests of Spain and Italy, and priests of Ireland*, are Christia[ns]" (p. 531).

Charity! We do not a[...] charity. We spurn with ind[...] any such despicable count[...] charity as that which is here

The insult offered to the clergy of Ireland is equally offensive and touches us still more closely. It is not so bad an epithet which is applied to them, but, while it is vague enough to make it difficult to seize and expose the precise calumny which the writer intends to fasten, it is forcible enough to make it as insulting and opprobrious as any epithet which a gentleman could well use, or a refined and scholarly periodical suffer to appear on its pages. It is like the gross caricatures of *Harper's Magazine*. We blush at the thought of noticing such an aspersion on the Irish clergy. The priests of Ireland *brutal!* The Irish people are not a brutal people, and it is impossible that a brutal clergy should spring from them. The clergy are loved by their people, they cannot therefore be brutally cruel; they are respected by them, and therefore they cannot be brutally vicious. They are educated men; they meet noblemen and gentlemen on equal terms. Irish society is cultivated, refined, and polished, and the Catholic priests of Ireland are respected by the respectable Protestants of Ireland. Such an accusation as this could not be made in Dublin, or on the floor of the British House of Commons, without calling derision on the head of the unlucky person who ventured to use a sort of language about Catholics, which polite society is beginning to regard as unfit for its ears.

It is no wonder that a gentleman so prejudiced against the Catholics and their religion as Mr. Scribner has shown himself to be, should be astonished or puzzled at the conversions which have taken place in the past twenty-five years:

"How one educated in the Protestant faith can become a sincere Papist it is difficult for us to understand, and to many minds the thing seems impossible" (p. 510).

He tries to diminish, and … possible to shirk the diffic… laying the blame on Anglican… Puseyism:

"It must be remembered th… Anglican or Puseyite to become… lic is a very different thing from… version to Romanism of any oth… gent Protestant."

The perusal of Dr. N… *Lectures* will show that the… tant view and the Protestan… dice have had as deep and … hold in the English Establish… in the Kirk, and, therefore, t… culty remains where it wa… although we may allow that… churchman is logically near… Catholic than is a Presbyteria… are plenty of cases of the co… of those who were brought u… other Protestant churches. Phillipps, Stolberg, and De Ha… Lutherans. Mr. Lucas was a… and F. Baker was brought u… thodist; Dr. Brownson was … rian, and Judge Burnett was … bellite. There are numbers… verts in the United States f… Lutherans, Presbyterians, Me… Baptists, Unitarians, and o… nominations. It does not a… case that some of the best kn… the converts who were broug… various sects became Episc… first, and afterwards Catholic… as our author asserts, they… by that step "almost Ca… And how did they first beco… vinced of those "almost C… doctrines, and altogether … principles which they only … followed out when they beca… tholics? Then, again, we h… two Drachs, the two Ra… Hermann and Veith, who wer… ites. Infidels, too, have be… verted, as well as Protesta… Jews; men of every countr…

He was no adherent of any softening, modifying, minimizing school. He was not like any of those whom Protestants are wont to regard with favor as belonging more to themselves than to us, as a sort of secret, unconscious Protestants, who are only externally united to the Roman Church, while their spirit is alien from her spirit. There was nothing of Pascal, Martin Boos, or Hyacinthe about him. He was not even one of those who stopped short at the line of strictly defined and obligatory doctrine, as if afraid of being extreme Catholics. He was no Gallican, no rigorist, no advocate of anything that might be called Neo-Catholic or Anglo-Catholic. Even in regard to minor and accessory matters, to modes and ways in which there is great room for variation in opinion and practice, he preferred those which characterize the genius of the Italian and Spanish nations, and which seem to the colder and more reserved temperament of the English to be the most remote and foreign to their tastes and intellectual habits. He endeavored to divest himself of everything which bore the semblance of conformity even in accidentals to Anglicanism, and to throw his whole soul into what he considered to be the most perfectly Catholic mould. He outran in this many both of the old English Catholics and of his fellow-converts. Especially in regard to the devotion to the Blessed Virgin Mary, he made himself the champion of the most exalted views concerning the power and glory of the Mother of God, and the importance of her cultus in the practical teaching and piety which is directed to the end of the conversion and perfection of souls. He followed St. Bernardine of Sienna, St. Alphonsus, and the V. Louis Grignon de Montfort, and his entire spiritual doctrine is derived

from similar sources, as
flowing from the very topmos
of mystic contemplation, ab
clouds, and far remote from t
and ken of ordinary mortals.
theology, which is remarkab
for accuracy and depth, he
follows those authors whose
accords with the strictest crit
Roman orthodoxy. It is n
anything in Father Faber w
peculiar and self-originated, c
he brought over from his Pr
education, and has mixed witl
lic doctrine as a clarifying ing
that makes his books popul
Protestants, and has excited
miration of the writer in the *A*
Review. F. Faber's doctri
sanctity are purely Catholic p
The homage which he has
is homage paid to the school i
he learned, and the mast
models he followed. The
shows the quality of his pa
the fineness and whiteness of h
"Men do not gather gra
thorns or figs of thistles."
reverend friend were more
iar with the lives of the Sa
the works of Catholic spiritual
he would cease to wonder
Faber and his works. We ca
him to whole libraries of w
which the characters and act
a multitude of similar m
women are depicted, and
countless forms of the same
truths and holy sentiments
sented. Those who "practi
terities" to the greatest poss
tent, the solitaries of the des
holy monks and nuns, the sa
the most heroic type, are p
those who were marked at th
time by their entire conformit
doctrine and spirit of the
Church, their profound humil
their ardent love of the gre
and Saviour of mankind. Con

those like him, with
-fervent Catho-
l a "different spirit,"
being "full of self-
nd these select few
idence in their own
sheer nonsense, and
ittle of words. We
nd to possess the
liness of character,
r graces, or the exalt-
F. Faber. But all
he genuine Catholic
our holy mother the
and possess in any
uine Catholic piety
ates, are, so far, like
same spirit is in all,
the frail and sinful
sins with contrition,
h imperfect who are
God's command-
e or less diligence,
vanced in Christian
ess of life. Those
se and counterfeit
ge in the spiritual
self-confidence, and
re willing victims to
e devil, and seek to
saints in order to
-love and win ap-
ther sinners, except
ore of the hypocrite
y generally become
into open sin, and
ir wearisome part,
truly humbled and
se are the persons
fferent spirit" from
es the true children

That F. Faber
mon chords which
the great Catholic
the fact that he is
spiritual writer of
hundred thou-
works, in some six
ges, had been sold
and they still continue to circulate everywhere. It is not a little remarkable that the same chord is obedient to his touch in the hearts of so many Protestants. What genius, learning, reasoning, philosophy, cannot do, the faith and love which spring from prayer and penance accomplish with ease. It is a remarkable fact, and we call the attention of Catholic preachers and writers to it, as well as that of Protestants. One who disdained the thought of diluting Catholic doctrine to suit the delicate palate of the age, who was regardless of the opinion of men, who plumed his pinions for a kind of audacious flight into the lofty ether in which saints alone are wont to soar and poise in contemplation, who threw off all drapery from the glorious form of Catholic truth, and loudly called on all men to gaze and worship, is the one who wins the confidence and captivates the hearts of the greatest number of the church's lost and estranged children. We trust that his works will win their way, and exercise their gentle, attractive force still more extensively among evangelical Protestants. The recommendation of a Presbyterian pastor, which goes forth under the sanction of Princeton, will, we trust, produce its full effect, and excite the pious curiosity of a great number of readers to become acquainted with the biography and writings of the gifted, lovely, holy poet, priest, and teacher, who has been called the Bernardine of Sienna of the nineteenth century.

We have endeavored to bring out into strong relief what is really of the greatest moment in the article of the *Princeton Review*, and what the weak though violent counter-protests only make more prominent and definite, that the concessions to the personal and doctrinal purity of Father Faber are a yielding of the most grievous

of the charges against Catholics and their religion. It argues, we hope, a change in the spirit and manner of maintaining the controversy with us which is coming on. The teaching of Father Faber is admitted to contain the "essential truths of the Gospel," and his most distinctively Catholic and Roman doctrines are admitted to be "not incompatible with piety." The conclusion is rigidly logical and irresistible, that Calvinists must consider the controversy between us as one not respecting *directly*, but only *indirectly*, the essential, fundamental dogmas and precepts of the Gospel and Christianity. Let them, then, realize this view to themselves, think in accordance with it, and regulate their conduct and language in harmony with it. Let them no longer ignore and practically abjure the Christian church from the fourth century to the present moment, and confine their sympathies to an imaginary primitive period and the sphere of modern Protestantism. Let them study ancient, mediæval, and modern Catholic authors, read history and theology, and learn to discuss the real issue with us. The Chinese metl warfare, charging upon us with aloft, bearing the hideous fig the beast with seven heads a horns, with outcries and sho derision and vituperation, wı answer any longer. Those choose to follow such tacti soon be forced to throw theii into the air and take to flight. too late to frighten even Presb children with such nonsense. weakness and helplessness of tl Irish Catholics, and of the h of Catholics in England, mad for a long time the easy vict oppression and calumny. B day for treating the Catholics English-speaking world with l tiness and contumely has pas We desire, however, no reve retaliation. We ask nothing c testants except that they wil the truth. In the words of l lembert: "The truth, and r but the truth—justice, and n but justice—let that be our s venge!" *

* *Monks of the West*, Introduction, l graph.

LIMITATION.

Through limit and hindrance man works: no limit hath God,
need;
But his wind is musical only when prisoned in the cane of th

AUBREY DE VE

gallery represents the preparatory school; the boxes, the pupils in philosophy.

However, it is difficult to believe that artistic taste and love of music are the sole motives which cause the public to fill the halls of the opera-house. Forty years ago, the works of Mozart, of Weber, and other masters were well appreciated by connoisseurs, but they did not meet with as much success from the public as modern operas enjoy to-day. Or is it rather that Donizetti and Verdi, Meyerbeer and Offenbach, understand the art better than Mozart and Weber, Spohr and Spontini? We cannot admit it. The reason must be elsewhere, and surely, gentlemen, you wish to know it.

In a pamphlet published ten years ago, Richard Wagner says: "The essential foundation of art, as practised generally in our day, is industry: its moral end is gain, its æsthetic intention to kill *ennui*."

This richly endowed artist has in view his colleagues in dramatic music, the composers of opera. He knew these men well, and understood himself how they set to work. But in the words quoted he has perfectly explained the end and tendency of modern opera.

The end is no other than gain; and, as means conducive to this end, effect is necessary, which must be attained at any price. Industrialism, that tyrant of our age, has also submitted the opera to its power, and under its domination the art exhausts itself forcibly, because tied to the fly-wheel of the artistic fabric. To produce effect, to surprise and bring out something which has not yet been seen—these are the objects of actual dramatic music. To this end is sacrificed not only art, but also all that exists—religion, politics, morality, and truth. This unfortunate

course has been inaugurate Italians. In their dramati Donizetti and Verdi have so for effect, theatrical success, this end have completely s dramatic truth. For love they have trodden upon law, and even reason. The do of sense over mind is the teristic feature of their musi

But it is among the Fre this style has attained its perfection, and even among man composers, who, for effect, have Frenchified the The most skilful author of s operas, Scribe, has offered h these greedy musicians for and shows his readiness to all to it. Scribe understood risian public for which he He knew its weakness, and succeeded in imposing the taste of that public on th civilized world.

In the texts furnished by S is intended for scenic ef means are employed to re end. The requirements of truth and of morality, even sense, are sacrificed to the effect. Frivolous and i allusions, which offer gross the impure fancy, and neces the imagination of innocence ful scenes, as, for example *Diavolo*, where a young girl and goes to bed before the a scenes of the bath, as in th *nots;* scenes of seduction, a *bert le Diable;* political a exaltation of and homage revolutionary passions, as *Muette de Portici;* base fla the irreligious opinions and p of the day; even, in fine, s culiarly religious, that are the piece to produce strik trasts, and bring out vc scenes better—these are th

sought but for effect, and had no regard to dramatic truth. In this manner, Meyerbeer has become not only the most famous, but also—and this is the principal thing--the richest musician of the entire world. He knows his business, as no one before has known it.

Meyerbeer is distinguished particularly for his predilection for religious scenes. With consummate skill, he uses them to produce striking contrasts. None of his last operas fail in this spicy seasoning. As a Jew, he is impartial among the different Christian sects. He maligns and mocks them all. In *Robert le Diable*, it is Catholicism which is put under contribution to furnish material for his religious scenes; in the *Huguenots*, he abuses Protestantism in the same manner and to the same end.

Marcel, a personage insignificant and dull, a fanatical Huguenot, interrupts everywhere the action of the piece with a Protestant canticle, always inopportunely and without reason, but producing always a grand effect by contrast. It is the air of the canticle of Luther: "Our God is a tower of strength." The success of the *Huguenots*, this opera being so much a favorite, rests almost entirely on the contrasts produced by this canticle.

In the first act, a merry company of cavaliers is found at table drinking and singing a riotous song. Marcel, the incomprehensible solitary, proceeds to thunder out, with a loud voice accompanied with brazen instruments: "Hear me, strong God! My voice is raised to thee." This canticle, in the midst of jovial drinkers, intermingled with the song they are singing—how can it fail of effect? In the second act, there is a very violent scene. At the instigation of Queen Margaret, the Count St. Bris has proposed his daughter to the Chevalier Raoul, who refu
Valentina, the daughter, desp
scorned, complains; Queen l
preaches peace; all shout a
and Marcel adds his chor
thundering voice, "God, o
and protection, listen to ou
Is not this a shameful prostit
sacred things? But it prod
fect; and our opera-going
which boasts of its delicate
enchanted with it, and imagi
the violent impression prod
these contrasts is a religio
edifying sentiment.

In *L'Africaine*, the last pro
of Meyerbeer, he introduces u
diately, in the first act, to a si
the secret council of the K
Portugal. It is understood t
grand inquisitor and a certai
ber of cardinals play the p
rôle. Finally, Vasco de Gam
demned, loaded with chai
thrown into the deepest d
Why? Because he has a
the existence of distant and u
lands of which the Scriptu
not speak. You know well t
clesiastical dignitaries have
had the habit of refuting with
and a prison novel ideas and
tific discoveries. At least, l
scene the public is convince
with the aid of stunning
This same opera, so much ap
contains also a very piquant a
intrigue. There are several
es of prayer, then a large ve
the stage, and finally a man
tree, which spreads death. W
agree that it is the possible a
impossible.

However, it is not the Jew
beer who has pushed to the e
his musical industry. Th
Offenbach has gone much
The former speculated princip
the curiosity of the unreflectin
es; but while his art is und

in general: "Finally, all our dramatic representations should be such that Plato could tolerate them in his republic, that Cato could listen to them with pleasure, that vestals could witness them without wounding their chastity, and, what is more important, that Christians could listen to them."

You will say this is too antiquated a principle. Among the greater part of our amateurs at the theatre it will only provoke expressions of doubt; they will say that this poor Wehrenfels is far behind modern civilization. Notwithstanding, no one undertakes to refute this principle, to demonstrate that these requirements are groundless. But as long as they are not refuted, we must consider them justified, and we ask if they should not be applied to the opera. Is not the drama when sung to be submitted to the same true moral and æsthetic laws as the drama recited?

To the phenomena of life as produced before our eyes, we apply the scale of conscience and of reason. Why should it not be our right and our duty to apply them also to the opera, and to regulate our conduct from the result of such an examination? No one will deny that this question is well founded. Nevertheless, it would meet with much resistance. Our enthusiasts of the opera have tacitly agreed that, where it is a question of opera, good sense and conscience should be silent. But ourselves, gentlemen, ought never to abandon these principles. We should no longer be Christians, if we did not apply to the opera the principles we practise in our lives.

Let us, then, apply these principles to the music of our day. What must we do if it be condemned for frivolity, for immodesty and abuse of religious things? If we find that the scenes are arranged solely with a view to effect, and in disregard of good sense and logic? and conscience, by comm condemn this degradation the deception with which t dation is presented as ver What must we do, in pr these great accusations ag dern opera?

Would you condemn your reason and your cons cause you are promised am Would you wish, as a retur money, to have sung on words you despise, words y repulse if they were spoken you put a temptation be children, in leading them t ra—these same children w tried to bring up in honest gion, in piety, and the o of all Christian duties? D lieve that at the opera, whe is made a plaything, where posed to contempt, attacke lumniated, they will learn and to obey it? Will t good morals, decency, and from the dancers of the ba is sufficient to place before questions; you will ansv yourselves. But why this s ticism? What will result f

Will my words succeed i dramatic music from its ba and making it enter on Will the thousands and of individuals who find thei pleasure in modern opera tice of them at all? I do upon that. But I hope w dence, gentlemen, that n will engage you to exam closely the subject of whic been treating. You will your judgment from char criticism and enthusiastic of sensuality; but you will yourselves, by vigorously your Christian principles. are thus affected, my words borne fruit.

obey the mandates of their supposed superiors, knelt at the feet of the holy prelate and begged his forgiveness for the crime they were about to commit. It is not claimed by the apologists of the Communists that their illustrious victims were guilty of any offence against the state, or that even the form of a trial was accorded them; and yet there are to be found many persons, considering themselves honorable and intelligent, who openly or secretly applaud that glaring and cruel act of injustice, and who thoroughly sympathize with the European revolutionists—those enemies of all law, who, if they had the power, would repeat in every city in Christendom the late disgraceful scenes of Paris. It is a melancholy fact that outside the Catholic Church the horrible murder of the venerable Archbishop Darboy and so many of his clergy has been the cause of ill-disguised congratulation, not only among those who are in direct affiliation with the revolutionists, but amid the sects who profess to regard the Decalogue as part of their fundamental doctrine. Have we yet heard from the thousands of pulpits and hundreds of newspapers, occupied and controlled by the various Protestant sects, one open and manly protest against the atrocious criminals who have so recently sullied the fair fame of France by deeds that would have disgraced the most degraded forms of savage life? Not one.

A fact like this, so patent and portentous, while it shows how large a portion of civilized society has fallen away from the plainest teachings of Christian charity and justice, must necessarily lead to the inquiry as to the best means of arresting, and, if possible, correcting so monstrous an evil. Recognizing it as such, it is our duty fearlessly and persistently to endeavor to correct it, for "*Felix qui potuis rerum cognoscere causa*" ways be a true maxim, even w are engaged in the study of th of human miseries and disaste a view to their alleviation.

In contemplating the man which now afflict Christian soci creation and formerly the o creature of the Catholic Chu must recollect that God has nc to his church the gift of being th ble preserver of the faith in every and at all times, no more than guarantee to all people civi and wise government. Ther doubt that the church is the tre in this world, the leaves of wh the health of mankind, "*et quis putavit si perierint nationes qua cisti*" (Wisd. xii. 12); but wh accuse her of countenanci disorders which have arisen t the rejection of her authority, which she has ever been stre opposed? Our Lord himself c plates the rebellion of natio people against his doctrine. angel of the Church of Ephe Spirit said, "Be mindful from thou hast fallen: and do penan resume thy first works. Or if hold I come to thee and will m candlestick out of its place, thou dost penance" (Apoc. Even the presence of the pri among us in adequate numbe assurance against schism and lity. Though we may have confidence in their sanctity a soundness of their teachings, not always be certain that the of their holy calling will be per with uniform discretion, intell and zeal, or that the hearts c congregations will respond on a sions and amid all circumsta the teachings of their pastors true that at all times and in all the soldiers of the Cross have themselves the faithful guardi

another. It does not appear to be a part of the providence of God that man should simply grow into a knowledge of the doctrines of the church, in the same manner as he advances to bodily maturity, but by intelligent and persevering teaching and diligent practice. In our world, every year brings new-comers on the stage, and the message to the Church of Ephesus was, "*Age pœnitentiam et prima opera fac.*" The Catholic clergy inherit a tradition, long anterior to that of the past century, of being the patrons and the cultivators of the human mind, and they still should remember these true and ancient glories of their sacred calling. The language of the sacred liturgy on the day of Pentecost is beautifully expressive on this subject:

"*Da tuis fidelibus*
In te confitentibus
Sacrum septenarium."

Sacrum Septenarium — the sacred seven gifts of the Holy Ghost, amongst which we find the "spirit of understanding and of knowledge." All the gifts of the Holy Ghost doubtless require to receive their due share of honor and cultivation. But in a generation which has gone so widely and so terribly wrong by the way of a perverted and deceived intellect, the cause of faith in the world demands that the battle be fought with a special determination on the ground of the intelligence. If Satan relies on the perversion of the mind for leading them away from belief in the truth and divinity of the revelation brought by Moses, and perfected by the coming and ministry of one greater than Moses, St. Michael must contend with Satan for the possession of the body of Moses. The more the spirit of deception that has gone abroad seeks to discredit the Mosaic revelation, which is the forerunner in the world of the

revelation of Jesus Christ, th we must diligently persevere a sist that all who are willing t should stir up within the the gifts of the spirit of underst and knowledge, and qualify selves to resist and confront th of error wherever they meet and on all fitting occasions. Catholic family ought to be a or focus of Christian informati every household there ought books containing the narrative works of God through the line great saints, beginning from cred narrative of Moses dow to the present time. Sacred is the true tower of strength cause of faith.

This study should not, as heretofore generally been, conf ancient history; for, though w find in the Old Testament th derful working of God in hi course with his creatures, and veloped and completed his wo promises to his chosen peop have, under the new dispe and in the history of the C Church, as indubitable proofs promises and fulfilment of them fulness of time by our divine The history of the Popes, for ex from St. Peter to Pius IX., is with providential incidents, as ing the worldly and baffling called wisdom of the sceptical perpetual rejuvenation of the herself when apparently crush disintegrated beneath the lo kingly oppression and the lawl of the mob, is in itself not perpetual miracle, but the e fulfilment of the promises of the der to be with her all days e the consummation of the world. lives of the grand throng of martyrs, confessors, and missi —the glory and pride of the —their sufferings, triumphs, an

the creation of the world, he remarks:

"Jesus Christ rested in the tomb from the work of redemption on the Sabbath or seventh day, and arose again from the dead on the first day of the week. For this reason, the Christians no longer keep holy the original Sabbath, but the Lord's day, or first day of the week, in memory of the resurrection of Jesus Christ."

And again, after relating the dispersion of the builders of the Tower of Babel, he draws this beautiful comparison:

"The nations of the world suffered a great punishment upon their pride in the confusion of their speech, and in their separation one from another. Jesus Christ has in part removed this punishment; for he has again made all the nations of the earth one religious family in his church, under the supreme government of the successor of St. Peter, and as partakers of one and the same sacrifice at the altar."

In allusion to the well-known story of the sale of Joseph to the Egyptians by his brethren, he says:

"Joseph, hated by his brethren on account of his love of virtue and innocence, and sold by them for a slave into the land of Egypt, is a striking figure of Jesus Christ hated by his own people on account of his love of justice and sanctity, and delivered up by them bound into the hands of the Roman governor, Pontius Pilate."

Father Formby's diction and treatment of his subject are varied and suited to the epoch which he describes. In the early pages of his book, he adopts the figurative orientalisms of the Hebrew writers, but further on he sobers down to the less florid and more matter-of-fact style of modern times. His descriptions of the crusades and the origin and growth of the religious orders are exceedingly graphic and correct,t of course merely outlines o would fill books enough to m an ordinary library if written tail, and his summing up of called reformation is deserving ticular notice.

"There is something worthy carefully observed as regards testantism which began in the century to cause whole nations ples to renounce the faith and d of the Catholic Church. But great heresies, such as that of Ar had a similar ruinous effect in c great falling off from faith withou of the world following in their w testantism cannot simply for thi by itself be understood to be th which St. Paul refers. What is able, however, in Protestantism though Dr. Martin Luther and t who were leaders at the time forn the disciples of which called th by the names of their masters—a rans from Luther, Calvinists fro —Protestantism has long ago c be the name of any particular Lutherans, Calvinists, Anabaptis ans, and all the different sects wh at this time, as regards what is Protestantism, are just as goo tants the one as the other. T and do, dispute with each oth what is to be held to be true as doctrine, but as regards Prot they are all quite agreed. H then, those who are complete with each other about Christian to agree completely about 'Protes The reason is, that Protestantis has but one solitary doctrine and tary precept, viz., '*Depart from t Church*.' All who satisfy this on entitle themselves to the name testant.' It is true that, up to th time, those who have protested the Roman Church have gene the credit of deserving to be, in or other, known as Christians; b rapidly ceasing to be the case. tantism' has now come to be the the confederacy of almost all wi ception whose cry is, 'Depart Roman Church,' so that there wo to be no rashness in recognizing departure (*discessio*) which St. Pa

pen of the Archbishop of Westminster has often astonished our mind. From hints given in the preface to this last publication, we get, in part, an explanation. It appears that his Grace employs a skilful stenographer to take down and then copy for the press his extemporaneous lectures. In this way, one who has a mind stored with the acquisitions of a lifetime, and is gifted so unusually with the *copia fundi*, can accomplish what could otherwise be done only by a man of more leisure than is enjoyed by the active prelate of the London diocese.

These four lectures make a pendant to the last four published, and complete the general view of the subject. They are like all the works of Archbishop Manning, of which our opinion has been so lately expressed. We need, therefore, only to announce the publication of these new lectures, and our readers will understand for themselves the value and interest they possess.

THE TRADITION OF THE SYRIAC CHURCH OF ANTIOCH, concerning the Primacy and the Prerogatives of St. Peter, and of his successors, the Roman Pontiffs. By the Most Rev. Cyril Behnam Benni, Syriac Archbishop of Mossul (Nineveh). London: Burns, Oates & Co. 1871. For sale by The Catholic Publication Society, 9 Warren Street.

This unique production symbolizes the contrariety and unity of the East and West in a singular manner. It begins at both ends, and finishes in the middle, where the appendices usually put at the end are snugly sandwiched between the Syriac original and the English translation. This translation has been made by the Rev. Joseph Gagliardi, and is, of course, at that end of the volume which, to our Occidental habits of thought, appears to be the natural beginning. The Syriac begins at the opposite end, and thus both languages have their own way, and the book will answer equally well for the reader in Nineveh and the one in London. The tradition of the Church of Antioch, w Peter established his first scarcely inferior in interest portance to that of the Church. The learned prel gathered together the best a authentic testimonies to th macy of the Roman See fro ments both ancient and liturgies, official acts, and of prelates and learned me Catholic and schismatical. ferences are most carefull and the whole work is crit scholarly. It is published i handsome and ornamental st cannot fail to interest the the learned, and all who are ed in theological pursuits. timonies to the authority Holy See which it contains valuable, and as they are gi clear English translation, ically arranged, and accomp full explanations, they are i ble to any person of ordin cation. We cannot flatter o that we have very many am subscribers who will be appreciate the beauties of riac original.

THE LIFE OF JESUS THE CHRI Henry Ward Beecher. Ill New York: J. B. Ford & C Vol. I.

The publishers of this wo given it a very handsome e and adorned it with a num excellent illustrations of sce places in Palestine. The a at reproducing some of th celebrated representations Lord are, however, not suc As for the work itself, it is a to imitate the fascinating an lar style of Rénan in such a to satisfy those Protestant call themselves Evangelical the author has the art of p the multitude cannot be ques That he is an artist in the and truest sense we cannot And, so far as more solid q are concerned, he is not to l pared for a moment, in res

change of scene the infant church appears clothed in new beauty, in new holiness, in new strength. It is much to be desired that Catholics of the present day should become acquainted with the religious life of their brethren of the early church. No other study is so well calculated to enliven our faith, animate our hope, inflame our charity, and incite us to that heroic virtue so necessary to perseverance in the present age. *Cineas* tends to promote this study, and as such we welcome it, commend it to the perusal of every Catholic, and thank the translator and publisher for the care with which they have performed their respective tasks.

THE LETTERS OF MADAME DE SEVIGNE TO HER DAUGHTER AND FRIENDS. Edited by Mrs. Hale. Boston: Roberts Brothers. 1871.

THE LETTERS OF LADY MARY WORTLEY MONTAGU. Edited by Mrs. Hale. Boston: Roberts Brothers. 1871.

These two books, simultaneously issued from the same press and edited by the same author, bear strong marks of similarity and contrast. Each, in its way, has long been looked upon as a model of epistolary correspondence in its appropriate language, and each is defaced by that superficial, not to to say anti-Christian, philosophy which prevailed among the "higher classes" in France and England during the last and the preceding century. The French authoress, however, has somewhat the advantage of her English sister, not only in the possession of a language especially adapted, by its grace and flexibility, to this species of composition, but from the fact that she lived surrounded by a strong Catholic public opinion, which, with all her cynicism and fashionable scepticism, she could not wholly disregard. We find, therefore, in many of her letters, particularly those to her daughter, flashes of true, genuine moral sentiment, which are the more striking from contr the worldly tone which g characterized her life anc spondence. Lady Montagu contrary, was brought up hard, unsympathetic schoo was inaugurated in Englar the frenzy of the Reformat subsided, and with all her womanly elegance we cann upon her otherwise than a tellectual pagan. We may from cover to cover of Mrs edition of her correspond vain to find one religious se that would not have been as priate in the days of Ho Zeno as in the eighteenth of the Christian era. This more singular when we r that these gifted women, ma husbands far their inferior tally, and, as it appears, me the sake of conventionalism, unnatural effort transferr love women usually bear partners of their joys and to their offspring, and cent their affections and hopes i children. With our children apt "to assume a virtue if w it not," yet still we find the intellectual mothers writing daughters in strains which, positively immoral in the sense of that term, certainl not actively conduce to stre them against the temptati which they were constant rounded, or to elevate their above the glitter and hollow the society in which they wer ed to move. Both these disting writers were well-bred, thor educated according to the i their times, and were the ass of generals, statesmen, poe artists, and their frequent an liar reference to the then men of their respective co are not only interesting, structive, as giving us a view interior life of many emine sonages hitherto known to by their public acts; but w consider how many unexcept

every thirty-three and a third years [the time has been estimated as much shorter in regard to what we are going to state], the entire property of the country, its countless millions, are administered or acted upon by a single officer, the Judge of the Probate Court, or other officer of the law, elected by the people, and thus incidentally by the masses themselves. Thus the various elections, which we so heedlessly disregard or pass by, are, in fact, the casts of the die that determine the fate of the nation, its prosperity, happiness, and honor. The importance, therefore, of the law regulating these elections in their varied relations may be estimated from this fact.

That numerous questions and contests should have arisen in a country where so many offices are to be filled, and where elections are so frequent, is not strange, and that the decisions of our own courts upon these litigated cases should have become numerous and controlling is a natural result. The law of elections has been greatly developed and expounded in this country in recent years. The leading cases bearing upon these subjects have been skilfully and carefully collated by Mr. Brightly, illustrated by his own notes and references, and presented to the legal profession and the public in the volume before us. He could not have selected a theme of greater interest or importance to our country, especially at this time, than the law of elections. He has handled it with the same accuracy, learning, and industry which have always characterized his works, and elevated his reputation as a jurist and author. The present work carries with it an interest far more general than professional works usually possess, and may l with improvement and plea all who are fond of a g readable book, who seek fc knowledge on a matter of v lic import, or who take an in the purity of elections, a general morals and welfar commonwealth. We comn their perusal.

THE title of Father Doa book is to be *To and fron sion Play in the Summer of* will soon be published by nahoe, Boston.

MR. P. O'SHEA announ press, and to be publishe scription, *The Lives of Bishops of the Catholic Chu United States*, by Mr. Ri Clark, A.M. The work wil lished in two large octavo and will be ready about th December. These volu contain the biographies c deceased members of the A Catholic Hierarchy, from liest dawn of Christianity continent to the present will trace the history of th through the important ep of Archbishop Carroll, an icle with graphic effect th sacrifices, and achievement fifty bishops who have bee to their reward.

THE Catholic Publication will soon publish a new e Father Young's *Office of* greatly enlarged and impro

THE volume of *Sermons of ist Fathers for* 1870 will be delivery on the 25th of No

should be definitively answered. Pulpits, forums, and the press, in their respective spheres, have discussed the matter from almost every stand-point, and some of the ablest thinkers, particularly in the Eastern States, have devoted their time and erudition to the elimination of order out of the chaos of crude and transcendental opinions which of late have filled the pamphlets and books of so many writers in Europe and America on the subject of education. Theories innumerable have been advanced, and historical precedents quoted in favor of particular systems, without much approach to unanimity, and still the problem remains as ever unsolved.

Amongst other expressions of opinion on this all-important subject, we have before us a long and very elaborate essay in the *Congregational Quarterly* of Boston, strongly in favor of the continuance of the public-school system as received in that classical city, and as earnestly endeavoring to demonstrate that, unless the Bible, "without note or comment," prayers, hymns, and piety, be taught in the state schools in conformity to the statute of 1826, these institutions will become worse than useless, and should be discountenanced. In the language of the writer: "The school system which requires the ethics can receive them only as indissolubly one with the religion, and the state that cannot sustain a statute like the Massachusetts law of 1826, which requires the principles of piety as well as those of morality to be taught, cannot sustain a common-school system."

As a counterpoise to our New England contemporary, we find in the last number of the *American Educational Monthly*, a magazine published in this city, as stout a defence of secular education, while exhibiting a decided preference for the removal from our public schools of the Bible and the discontinuance of all teachi religious character. Its ar on these points, if less sub more practical than those *Congregational*, and some of t it adduces in support of its vi thus plainly stated:

"It is well to repeat here what in the beginning: that knowled virtue itself, but only the hand virtue. This is the lesson of Con statistics—a state having a first-cl versity as well as the usual net common schools: in every ni seven-tenths marriages there is su one divorce. Ohio, which has versity comparable to Yale, and common schools are presumably ter than Connecticut's, has but one in twenty-four marriages in a muc population. There are graduates mon schools who make it their b to procure divorces by observi scribed forms, yet without the kn of one or other of the parties—con the spirit of the law."

From the contemplation of and other results of our co schools, in which piety and m are supposed to be taught, the in the *Monthly* concludes th better for us to "leave devotio struction to those whose busi is—to parents and clergymen.'

Another writer, the editor of the most widely circulated sectarian weekly newspapers, decided advocate of the public system as at present existin forward among others the fol novel argument for its perpetui

"We hold, therefore, that it is u sary and unwise to disperse or r bute our common-school pupils in dance with the dogmatic or eccles leanings of their parents respect that the inconvenience and cos doing would immensely overbala benefits. We should need fa schools; yet our children would t travel much further to reach one preferred theological stripe than

we assert the day-schools should also take their part in supplying food to the ever-expanding and question-asking minds of the American youth.

The formation of character, one of the great objects of education, should be conducted on principles somewhat similar to those of domestic economy. We do not eat all the sweets at one time and the sours at another, the solids at one meal and the dessert at the next, but by a judicious admixture of both produce a savory and salutary combination which gives health and strength to the body. It may be said that mere secular education—such as geology, geometry, history, natural philosophy, botany, astronomy, etc., as taught in our common schools—presents no opportunity for moral instruction. Nothing can be more fallacious. That great master of dramatic literature, Shakespeare, whose knowledge of the springs of human action has seldom been equalled, has told us that we can find books in running brooks, sermons in stones, and good in everything. Properly directed, the anatomy of the smallest insect, equally with the contemplation of the vast firmament with its countless planets and stars, may become a silent and involuntary prayer to the Creator of all things. There is not a force, physical or deduced, that is revealed to the mind of youth that ought not to be made to bear with it some conception of the unseen Power that presides over and governs the universe, and the teacher who neglects to place before the minds of his pupils the moral to be drawn from those symbols of the Creator's almightiness does but half his work, and that the less nobler part. Leaving dogma and doctrine aside, are the generality of our public-school teachers capable or disposed to thus draw from nature the beautiful lessons of God's

wisdom and powe
book contempl
should be b
fancy to the gra

Some persons
connection with
youth as if it we
sentiment or a ho
occasionally ind
more serious dut
and political adv
complied with.
is a matter of ev
ling and guiding
mankind individ
lectively, and as
for our actions e
ment of our life,
form or another
our every pursuit
true among full-
men, is it not ap
tem of youthful
dissociate religio
dies in early li
the world viciou
who would eithe
the practice of h
and morality, or
rance would mal
butes of Christi
worldly interests
cation, therefore,
religious instructi
during their hou
half of their you
cation at all, at l
sense of the wo
them expert fina
cians, but it can
right, truthful, a
zens. In this re
the writer in the
he says, "We c
outset to the im
it be not the ab
of separating
from any practic
education."

But we do no

of freedom to me if, as the *Congregational* suggests, I must see my child forced into a common school, to listen to the reading of a Bible which I believe, at best, to be a mutilated and perverted copy of the Holy Scriptures, and be obliged to repeat prayers and hymns that too often, alas! are but blasphemies against the holy name of him who died on the cross for man's redemption?' In one case the body alone suffered, in the other the eternal salvation of immortal souls is imperilled. Even the framers of the constitution, that noble document about which so much is said and so little understood, having surveyed their work, and finding it defective in respect to providing guarantees for the perfect freedom of religion, hastened by an amendment to supply the deficiency. "Congress," they ordained, "shall make no law respecting the establishment of religion, or prohibiting the free exercise thereof,"* and our own state, on November 3, 1846, by its constitution, emphatically declares that "the free exercise and enjoyment of religious profession and worship, without *discrimination or preference*, shall for ever be allowed in this state to all mankind." (Art. I. sec. 3.)

Does the state derive its authority to teach religion to our children from God? If so, where is its authority? The writer in the *Congregational* evidently considers the Bible an authority on matters of faith and discipline. Yet we fail to find in the inspired writings any authority for the state of Massachusetts, or any other purely political corporation, to teach the doctrines of Christ. But, if the state have a right so to teach, it has a right also to decide what shall be taught, and this, of course, must depend on the cha-

* Amendment proposed March, 1789.

[illegible]
the state for [illegible]
as yet, [illegible]
ed Protestant [illegible]
fixed state religion, [illegible]
on the popular ele[...]
faith and ideas o[...]
would like the adv[...]
teaching in scho[...]
prayers, hymns, a[...]
more explicit on th[...]
children to be ta[...]
cording to the parli[...]
of the Church of [...]
total depravity noti[...]
ers of Calvin; are [...]
to deny the divini[...]
the Unitarians, an[...]
ments with the Un[...]
we, in fact, bringi[...]
the world to be lial[...]
indoctrinated into [...]
Methodism, Congr[...]
byterianism, Mugg[...]
monism, or any o[...]
sand "isms" born [...]
mother of dissent, [...]
Reformation? Or [...]
them treated to a [...]
every one in turn [...]
wheel brings their [...]
surface? The ide[...]
absurd, and yet it [...]
sequence of the C[...]
sition that the sta[...]
gion in its schools [...]
ing liable to be c[...]
time by any of th[...]
"isms," must of n[...]
own ism, and, havi[...]
authority, who can [...]
But, says the write[...]
tional, and those wh[...]
we do not violate [...]
science, we only "a[...]
ing of the Bible, "[...]
ist does not believe,'[...]

* See page 387, Octob[...]
gregational Quarterly, [...]
State—Religion in its Sch[...]

and accomplished gentleman, would not be a very safe teacher in a school composed in whole or in part of Catholic children. Any person who could endorse as he does Draper's absurd assertion that the *Imitation of Christ* was the forerunner of the Reformation, call the illustrious Fénelon a Jansenist, style millions of his fellow-citizens by the cant epithets of "Romanists" and "Papists," and coolly declare that Catholics do not believe in the Bible, is evidently unfitted to form a correct opinion on any religious subject, much less to be entrusted with the instruction of youth.

"But," says the writer above quoted, "the safety of democracy requires compulsory education. The work cannot be entrusted to churches, or to corporations, or to individuals." Now, this may mean very little or a very great deal. If it mean, as he hints in another part of his article, that the state has an absolute right to teach a particular religion or any religion at all in its public schools, and enforce attendance therein, for the preservation of our democratic form of government, we entirely dissent from his proposition. The very essence of a free government lies in its recognition of religious liberty and the natural rights of individuals, and our best guarantees of freedom rest on the fact that majorities, which for the time being represent the power of the state, all potent as they may be, cannot set aside the fundamental law, and dare not infringe on the civil or religious liberty of the citizen. No state could or ought to attempt an exercise of power so utterly despotic and foreign to the genius of our institutions.

We are aware that of late it has been customary to denominate our form of education as the American system, for the purpose, doubtless, of exciting public prejudice in i
The system is not by an
American in the national se
is purely local, and of Pr
origin and growth. When
England colonies by persecu
violence secured for themse
formity of worship, such as
they established schools, i
prayers, hymns, and piety we
ad libitum, with all the raw-h
bloody-bones anti-Catholic
which the descendants of
grims mistook for veritable
Being all of one mind, such
of training could have no
ble evil effect on the pupi
they did not hear intolera
falsehood in the school, th
pretty certain to hear ther
meeting-house. But time
strangely altered since ther
writer in the *Congregational*
to admit. "The reason ou
system had to be modified,"
"was not that it was *per se* ri
the day it was enacted, but be
foreign immigration and the
of time had produced an
revolution in the religious
the people, and required t
justment of the civil cree
school system." In no sen
can this system of public e
which is sought to be thrust
be called American, except,
as contradistinguished from
England, France, Germany,
and other so-called despot
tries, in all of which the
national plan, more or le
rally, prevails. In the la
countries particularly, one
and the other Protestant, the
of secular education has b
and abandoned, and the wi
the new system has been pr
yond peradventure. If it b
can to tax citizens for the
of schools and compel t

the public schools, and must either send their children there or pay for their education elsewhere. This double payment, in most instances, they cannot afford. How many tens of thousands of parents are there not among us whose scanty means will not permit them to indulge in the luxury of seeing their children instructed in the ways of true religion, and who are consequently compelled, if they desire even a primary education for their offspring, to send them to schools which they neither admire nor would select if they had a free choice!

We are accused of being hostile to the Bible. Such is not the fact, and those who make the assertion are well aware of its falsity. The Bible has always been an object of especial care and veneration in the Catholic Church. It is one of the sources of her authority and the muniments of her holy mission. What we object to is the profanation of its sacred character by unworthy and profane hands. It has repeatedly pained us to see even "King James's Version," imperfect as it is, scattered broadcast by the agents of the Bible societies in hotel and steamboat saloons, barbers' shops, and bar-rooms, not to be read, but to be devoted to the meanest purposes of waste paper. The treatment of the holy book in some of our public schools is little better. If any person doubts that Catholics venerate and read the Bible, let him go to our large Catholic publishing-houses and see the numerous and splendid editions of the Old and New Testaments which are constantly being issued from their presses.

Though on principle we decidedly object to the reading of the Bible in our public schools, our greatest objection is to the schools themselves. We hold that the education that does not primarily include the religious element is worse than no educati all, and, we hold, also, that the has no right to prescribe what of faith, doctrine, or religious pr should be taught to the chi of its citizens. We claim that C lic parents have a right to de that their children shall be edu by Catholic teachers, be instr from Catholic books, and at all t particularly during hours of stud surrounded as much as possible all the influence that the church, whose bosom they have been a ted by baptism, can surround t This can never be done in our lic schools. However high the sonal character of the teache those institutions, and wha may be the peculiar merits of discipline and success in tu out smart accountants and supe thinkers, we maintain that, in th mation of character and the cu tion of the spiritual and better pa our nature, they have been and necessarily be failures. What p can read without a shudder the fo ing extract from a Boston pap garding the recent investigation *savant* who, it is well known, friend to Catholicity or the teac of the church:

> "Professor Agassiz has of late gi portion of his valuable time to an in gation of the social evil, its cause growth, and the result has filled him dismay, and almost destroyed his fa the boasted civilization of the ninet century. He has visited and noted the houses of ill fame throughout th of Boston, and has drawn from the tunate inmates many sad life stories his utter surprise, *a large number unfortunate women and girls trace fall to influences which surrounded th the public schools.*" *

It has been already stated, o authority of the *Educational Mo*

* *The Pilot*, Nov. 4, 1871.

Connecticut, the ...ed and nursery ...any there is one ...inety-nine mor- ...have the un- ...Agassiz, after ...of the malign in- ...ols in the sister ...reason to doubt morals exists in be traced to the so, is it not time ...n of instruction, ...ould be discon-

...terial point of ...hools have been In the efforts, ...ust believe, to ...om from the ...rd of Education ...cities have al- ...r usefulness for ...imary rules of arithmetic, and ...mathematics, can ...nity, but, when ... of study are ... question again ...logy, for exam- ...esting science, ...has led to more ...e sophistries of As at present ...without expla- ...a, it cannot help ...o the faith, and ...morals, of the ...ned minds of the ...ry, it is impossi- ...ut careful revi- ...it without con- ...disputed events ...garding which ...holics can never ...gine a history of ... the great facts ...e Old World by ...lishment of the the Popes, the

"Truce of God" and the Crusades in the middle ages, the great rebellion against spiritual authority—miscalled the Reformation—the penal persecution of the Irish Catholics, and the French Revolution left out? At best, such a book would be a sorry compilation of dates and miscalled facts, and yet to describe those great epochs in European history with any degree of accuracy would necessarily offend the opinions or prejudices of either Protestants or Catholics. If history be "philosophy teaching by example," we must look for it somewhere else than in our public schools.

But, because we are opposed to the existence of common schools, are we therefore against popular education? On the contrary, the efforts of the humbler class of Catholics throughout the country to secure education for their children independent of state interference are almost incredible.

In this city alone twenty thousand children are annually taught in the free schools attached to the various churches, at an expense of a little over one hundred thousand dollars, independent of the thousands who attend the pay-schools of the Christian Brothers of a high grade.*

Let us now sum up in brief our objections to the further continuance of the present public-school system:

I. All education should be based and conducted on true religious principles.

II. The state has no right to teach religion in its schools.

III. State or public schools without religion are godless.

IV. As such, they are incapable of forming the character of our children, or teaching them morality according to the Christian principle.

* For the benefit and edification of our readers, we subjoin an official tabular statement of the attendance on, and expenses of, the Catholic free

V. In endeavoring to avoid what is called sectarianism, they defeat the ends of even mere secular education.

Now, it may be asked, What remedy do we propose for the evils which our public-school system has already produced? What substitute are we prepared to offer that will both satisfy the demands of religion and the requirements of the state? We answer, by the establishment of denominational schools for Catholics, wherever practicable, under the supervision of the proper ecclesiastical authorities, and likewise for such of the sects as do not approve of mixed schools. How are these schools to be sustained? In either of two ways. If the state will insist on levying a general school tax, let it be divided *pro rata* according to the number of

pupils taught
denomination
proper propos
non-religious
amount thus a
tholic school
with a board a
to be compose
of clerics and
sary, let the st
cials to see tl
attendance a
way, which to
ferable, would
ther the scho
the parents of
of no denomi
ty of educati
Compulsory e
well in countri
but an automa
be moved by
based on pri
ple are made
not the gover
and where th
of the masses
used for the b
tary rulers; b
republic, the
in individual e
fame, and hon
of every on
who has ene
to win them,
that parents, a
lic parents, w
duty in respec
education of
struggles they
making to s
schools, despi
which they are
would be ren
ergy if that d
were removed

The advant
the adoption
manifold and

It would s

day schools of the city of New York for the present year:

Location of Schools.	Daily attendance.	Annual Expenses for the support of schools
Nos. 272 & 274 Mulberry St.,	1,100	$6,000
Barclay and Church Sts., .	573	3,118
New Bowery and James Sts.,	1,400	9,000
No. 29 Mott St., . . .	1,225	5,745
Nos. 54 & 56 Pitt St., and 264 Madison St., . . .	1,680	9,500
Nos. 8 & 10 Rutgers St., .	1,050	5,000
Leroy St., ...	1,000	5,500
Nos. 300 & 302 East Eighth St.	1,600	7,000
Nos. 121 & 123, and 135 & 137 Second St., ...	1,420	5,970
Nos. 8 & 10 Thompson St., .	240	2,000
No. 208 East Fourth St., .	1,700	6,217
No. 48 Fourth Ave., . .	200	2,000
Nos. 511 & 513 East 14th St.,	1,250	10,000
No. 32 West 18th St., and 111 West 19th St., . . .	720	5,000
No. 118 West 24th St., and 236 West 26th St., . .	140	1,120
Nos. 333 & 335 West 25th St.,	650	3,000
No. 209 West 30th St., and 211 West 31st St., . . .	400	1,600
No. 143 West 31st St., . .	400	1,200
East 36th St., near Second Ave., ...	1,250	6,000
No. 309 East 47th St., . .	130	2,660
East 50th St. and Madison Ave., ...	350	1,000
East 84th St., near Fourth Ave., ...	560	4,000
West 131st St., and West 133d St., near 10th Ave., .	320	1,200
West 125th St. and Ninth Ave., ...	130	1,000
	19,428	$104,430

der the head of tea-room, supper, dinner, or board bill, but is covered up under the head of postage-stamps or other 'incidental' expenses. How much of the $60,000 goes in this way, it is, of course, impossible for us to know."

Is it any wonder, then, that, in view of such extravagant use of the public money, of which the above is only a specimen, the education of about one hundred thousand children, the average attendance at our public schools, should cost over three millions of dollars, or at the rate of thirty dollars *per capita*, while in the Catholic free schools one-fifth of that number are taught at an expense of one hundred thousand dollars, or at the rate of only five dollars a head, per annum?

Are the Catholics competent and prepared to assume the duties and responsibilities of the education of the vast number of children of their communion who now attend the public schools? Most decidedly. As to our ability to teach, we point with something like pride, certainly with satisfaction, to the success of our numerous colleges, seminaries, and convent schools, to the latter in particular, where are always to be found among the pupils a respectable minority composed of daughters of many of our most intelligent Protestant families. We call attention, also, to our twenty-four city free schools, now in full operation, many of which, though of recent origin, will compare favorably with the oldest of our common schools. Besides the professors of our colleges, who are constantly preparing young men for the ministry and for the scarcely less responsible duties of teachers, and such orders as the Christian Brothers, we have many trained lay instructors ready and anxious to devote themselves to the good work of Christian education. Then, again, there are numbers of Catholic teachers now in the [pub]lic schools, male and female, of whom we know personally would prefer to give their se[rvices] exclusively to the training of ch[ildren] of their own faith if such an op[portu]nity presented itself. Said o[ne of] this class, a teacher of over t[...] years' experience, on a late oc[casion] to the writer, "If I dared, I [would] like to expose the dangers a[nd ab]surdities of our school system; [but I] cannot, for I would surely be [turned] out and dismissed, and then [what] would become of my wife and [fami]ly? I wish we had separate s[chools] for ourselves, and then I wou[ld] like teaching even at a less [salary] than I now receive."

We submit the considerati[on of] this very grave and, in our min[d, most] important question to the serio[us con]sideration of our patriotic and [na]tive countrymen, no matter o[f what] creed or opinion, having an [...] confidence in their sense of [justice] and equity. To the fanatical [portion] of the community who will [not lis]ten to reason, we have only [to] say: Though you may prete[nd not] to know it, and may even be [uncon]scious of the fact, your instin[ct tells] you that the present system [of edu]cation saps the foundation of t[he Ca]tholic religion, and it is for this [reason] you hold so tenaciously to it; [let] us add, the system itself, being [...] undermines all religion and [...] likewise. But such is your [...]tion and hostility to our religi[on that] to so undermine it you are wi[lling to] see your own faith, whatev[er it] may be, ruined and wrecked [so long] as you can accomplish your [object], and the next generation becon[e...]ists and sceptics, totally de[void of] all faith. Holding the politi[cal pow]er, and in spite of your boa[sted fair] play and in defiance of the [...] our free institutions, you ar[e]

phold your system and tax support against our con- religion, freedom, s, and the spirit of Ame- utions. Your efforts to powers of our government, nent of our natural, divine, l rights, will ultimately end rn confusion. They are y of some half-crazed theo- l follower of Fourrier and unists than of a citizen of public. The government that robs a parent of his rights and his children is neither free nor democratic, but is the aider and abettor of that system of free-lovism which is said to have originated in pagan Sparta, and has culminated in our own country at Oneida. But let it be understood that, as Catholics and free citizens, we proclaim our rights, shall resolutely defend them, asking for nothing which we are not willing to grant to others, and being content with no less for ourselves.

ONE CHRISTMAS EVE IN LA VENDEE.

in '93—that horrible '93, name makes our blood our hearts beat with a ror and security, as when the painted panorama of l or some scene of crime and despair long since it brought vividly before aphic power of eloquence e words have a spell in ascinates us, and defies us without pausing to look mories they evoke. Well, s tragic '93 that I am eak. But not to describe It only makes the frame , a most veracious story, the spirit of that wonder- here we see all that was oveliest in humanity shine side of its most criminal ig aberrations.

istmas eve fourscore years ertile soil of La Vendée, streams of patriot blood, under a deep quilt of the landscape slept as in a death-sleep under a pure white pall. Hills and plains were garmented in white. The snow had fallen heavily during the night, and its untrodden purity was as smooth and uniform as the blue of the winter sky, that looked down upon it and grew pale. The cottages that dotted the fair expanse hardly broke its uniformity, for they too were liveried in white, the roof thick thatched with snow, and the whitewashed walls only a degree less dazzling than the brightness of the ground. The hedges that divide the fields in La Vendée as in England were filled and covered with snow, and the hoar-frost like a fairy lace-work glittered and shone on the soft, unblemished surface, and the trees with rolls of snow resting on their bare gaunt arms held up clusters of icicles that sparkled like crystals in the tepid December sun.

The village of Chamtocé lay in this white landscape; and in the middle of the village stood the church, and close by the church the presbytery.

On the road that led from St. Florent to Chamtocé a young, lithe figure was crushing the crisp white carpet with a long, elastic step. His face was concealed, the upper part of it by a cap drawn low over his forehead, and the lower part by a woollen scarf wound round his throat, swallowing up the chin and nose in its capacious folds. The weather was not cold enough to need this ostentatious display of *cache-nez;* true, *la nappe blanche de la Noël* (white cloth of Christmas), as the peasants call it, was spread, but there was not a breath of wind, and it was not freezing. It had frozen during the night just enough to sprinkle the hoar-frost abroad and hang a thin fringe of glass from the roofs of the houses and deck the trees with icicles, but this was not what the Vendéans called freezing. The Loire pursued its journey majestically to the sea unchecked by the icy hand of the black frost, the cruel black frost, that had but to blow with its bleak breath for one night on the strong deep stream to paralyze its waters and chill their moaning into icy dumbness. So, the cold was not bitter. The traveller knew it, too, for on coming to a point of the road where it turned abruptly, and disclosed the church with its slim, gray belfry, and, on the rising ground beyond it, a windmill, still as spectre suspended midway between the white earth and the pale sky, he looked cautiously up and down the road, assured himself there was no one in sight, and then, raising his beaver cap, stood bare-headed in the attitude of a man saluting some object of love and veneration.

"Nearly four years since I knelt under the shadow of thy walls, and now I have come home, and thou dost greet me with the same unchanged, unchanging welcome!"

He replaced his cap, drew it low over his face, and contin
way.

"Home, did I say?" he n
presently. "Have I still a l
come to? Gaston most l
gone, fallen like the best bl
La Vendée in God's and th
cause. And Marie!"

A sudden flush suffused th
ed cheek. The pilgrim wa
with a quicker step, and was
the gate of the presbytery.

"Ah! here it is, just as I
the little wicket that opened
with a ready welcome. A go
to begin with!"

He pushed it and walked o
door of the dwelling-hous
ajar; winter and summer it w
shut; he pushed it open, and
ed gently at a door on the le

"Come in!" said M. le C

And François Léonval
and stood face to face with t
father he had known on
Nearly four years had pass
they had parted, and the ol
who had baptized him, and
him, and wept with him
his mother's grave, was j
same as when he had left h
nign, cheerful, a trifle more
perhaps and a good deal wh
the same in everything else—
was changed within. He lo
promptly, closed his book, an
with a giance where "chari
thinketh no evil" deprecated
tain vague mistrust, he said:

"What can I do for y
boy?"

"Monsieur le Curé! mo
Is this the welcome you give

"François! my son! my b
ed!" And the old man held
arms, and the two clasped eac

"Ah! my son!" exclaim
curé, when his emotion left hi
er to speak, "this is an hou
suffering for; it pays me fo

he little did I dream
joy before we met in
and my boy! Bless
Our Lady of Mercy,
atched over you and
ack to me! I never
your face before I

not, mon père!" said
ing, and embracing
ou know the prodigals
rn sooner or later; be-
nised to pray me safe
to go to heaven till I
o get your blessing.
your promise?"

Does a father forget
you have travelled a
will tell me all pre-
t you must have need
rmth. Victoire!"

l gouvernante appear-
cognising François her
tled into a smile of
y and she embraced
r with motherly affec-
owered him with ques-
never waited to hear
e she bustled about
ning backward and
e kitchen, and mak-
all speed the very
could supply. The
s soon spread, and the
after the first outburst
ubsided, her presence
sed relief, said with a
in his voice and look
on François's heart:
ois, François, it was
ve me all these years
or a word. Gaston
long time that either
ed from the country,
ere still fighting, and
either case only the
r into trouble that
rising, or the want
ges, and I believ-
ing; but when two

whole years went by, and still we had no news, what could I think but that you had fallen? Victoire, put on your hood, and go—but stay—no, I had better go myself. We must run no risks: there is a price on your head, you say? I will go myself. These are times when we need the cunning of the serpent more than the innocence of the dove. Alas! what does innocence avail my little ones? But shame upon me for an ungrateful wretch! Does it not avail them the palm-branch and the crown, and are not the purest of the flock chosen for a sacrifice to plead for the guilty?"

Thus discoursing, he wrapped himself in his heavy serge cloak, and clutched his stick, and went in search of Gaston, but not without first speaking a word in Victoire's ear.

And who was Gaston? Gaston was cousin-german and adopted brother of François. They had been brought up from infancy together by Gaston's mother. When they were both sixteen, she died, leaving the lads to the care of the good God and Monsieur le Curé, and bidding them love each other like true brothers, and live together in the comfortable cottage, which, being her own, she bequeathed them as a joint legacy till either should marry, and then, if they chose to separate, the one who left was to have compensation in a sum of money to be kept by M. le Curé till the event entitled either of the youths to claim it. Besides the cottage, their mother, for both the lads looked on her as such, left two thousand francs, to be equally divided between them when they came to be twenty-one. This was the wedding portion she had brought to Gaston's father, and as she had adopted François, and given him a true mother's love, she wished to divide her all, share and share, between him and her own son.

Gaston had a goodly inheritance of land from his father, so she was not impoverishing him by sharing her own with his brother, and he could never feel in after-life that she had wronged him. So Jeanne Léonval thought, at least. And perhaps she was right at the time. But as years went on, Gaston saw things differently; his ideas about the value of money changed, and with them his notions regarding right and justice, and he began to feel an undefined vexation and sense of injury on the subject of his mother's will. For Gaston had a worm at his heart—the worm that entered the heart of Judas, and sucked it dry of love, and truth, and mercy, and led him at last to deicide and despair. He loved money, and he was growing to love it more every day; it was filling up his heart, and making him hard and selfish, and brushing off the bloom of his boyish freshness. He was growing into a miser. Nobody noticed the growth. Gaston did not suspect it. He lived like other people, frugally but abundantly, in the homely manner of his mother and the people of his class. He wore good clothes, and the same as those around him. But though he did not take to the ways and crotchets of the miser of the story-book, his heart was none the less developing the miser's spirit, and growing rapidly absorbed, to the exclusion of all other aims, in the love of money. He grudged more and more parting with it, and he longed and pined more greedily after its possession. François, who lived with him, saw nothing of this. He saw him indeed eager and active in turning his land and stock to account, vigilant to seize every opportunity for gain, sharp at striking a bargain, chary of spending his money on many innocent pleasures that tempted the self-denial

of older and
was right
were plenty
spend their
made it, and
ton prudent
by for the
ones who wo
by. So arg
handed Fran
wisdom of h
practise it, a
franc in his p
one in want of
as Gaston, he
a different mo
He gave to
be driven fro
not come in t
gave to the c
hearth wante
ed for bread,
supply both.
lage but love
smiled a bless
as he passed.
forgave him.
enough to
share in his
coming to Fra
But when the
the money th
his handed
disowned the
ment for the
Gaston felt th
he felt he was
and robbed o
wrathful agai
çois. In the
ment, he spok
çois, and repr
come betwee
But François,
lessness of a
about the mo
motive of hi
thought it wa
jealousy agai
who had com

mother's love, and, with of a generous nature, gave him his unjust re- offered to give up all nditionally to his cou- leave the cottage, and ensation, provided only give him back his love iaston was not utterly d the generosity and is cousin disarmed him, im out of his unworthy e embraced him, and forgive him, and they others from that out. avarice twined round t, and choked his best his finest impulses, but crush out his love for hat grew and flourished ongst weeds. So they er till they grew up to and then an event oc- distant town of Cha- which was to make a e lives of both.

the curé's died, leaving hild, whom she implor- to receive and take care as alone in the world; s no one to whom the bequeath her except Chamtocé. Great was y of the worthy priest ived the intelligence of ath, accompanied by the gacy of a grand-niece, t that he would enter on at once. Victoire to council, but, instead m out of the difficulties n, she staggered him by meant to buy a cage *petite* in the window ? That was the only f taking her in. Why, fight for room that ; were not the wo- , it would be simply an to fit herself and her *effects* into the space allotted to her at the presbytery; and where, in the name of common sense, did M. le Curé think she could make room for another inmate? The curé admitted the inexorable logic of this fact, and immediately proposed adding another room to the house; this was the Vendéan's ready way of simplifying difficulties when his family outgrew his dwelling. Victoire said of course that this remedy was open to them, but what were they to do with *la petite* till the room was built? Hang her up in the window? M. le Curé rejected the cage alternative, and suggested his niece be sent to one of the farmers' wives' for the time being. "Which of them?" Victoire begged leave to inquire. Mère Madeleine would take her and welcome, but she had four sons at home, so that would not do. Then there were La Mère Tustine and La Tante Ursule, and a great many other estimable matrons who would gladly give her a shelter, but between their hospitality and Marie's acceptance of it there stood some impediment in the shape of sons or brothers that shut the door on the young stranger. The curé and his gouvernante were puzzling over the case, and seeing no way out of it, when François Léonval came in. The curé loved all his children, but, if there was one that he loved better than all, it was the child-like, open-hearted François. He told him at once of his trouble, and asked him what he was to do. François solved the difficulty instanter by offering him the spare room at home—his mother's formerly, and never occupied since her death—assuring the curé that he and Gaston and Gervoise, their old *bonne*, would take every care of his grand-niece, and that, far from being in the way, she would be quite a godsend to them all in the dull cottage. The curé smiled

with a deeper thankfulness than the young man understood at the biblical simplicity betrayed in this proposal, and it took a good deal of argument to make François see that the scheme was not practicable; but when ultimately he did see it, he was ready with an amendment which the curé saw no fair reason for rejecting. This was that Mlle. Marie was to be installed in her uncle's room, and he was to come and stay with the brothers while another was being added to the presbytery. This point settled, the first thing to be done was to get possession of Marie. The curé would have gladly gone to fetch the poor little orphan himself, but this was Saturday, a very busy day for the country priest, and to-morrow would be Sunday, a busier day still, and when it was quite impossible for him to be absent. But François here again came to the rescue. He would drive over to Chapelle-aux-lys, put up for a few hours—it was a good three hours' drive—and be back by nightfall with the legacy. François Léonval was perhaps the only youth in the village to whom such a mission could have been entrusted without its provoking a stream of chattering comments on all sides, but the curé knew that not even that queen of gossips, Tante Ursule, would find a word to say against it in his case. So he gave his blessing to François, who ran home as fast as he could, put the strong bay mare to the cariole, and was soon trotting over the snow on the road to Chapelle-aux-lys. This was how Marie came to Chamtocé.

In due time the room was built, the curé took leave of the brothers, and returned to the presbytery, where Marie reigned henceforth with soft, despotic sway over himself, the stiff old Victoire, and all who came within her kingdom. She was soon the

acknowledged belle of Ch
and the number of her admi
the zeal with which they c
for her hand in the village d
the honor of carrying her red
co *Heures* to and from ch
Sundays and fête-days, be
serious complication in the e
of the venerable curé. For
loved him with the love tha
out fear, and had no secre
him; old and young went
with their *confidences* as a m
course, and the rival candid
Marie's favors carried thei
and fears and complaints of
of each other to his symp
ears with merciless garrul
was no small thing to bear
den of this confidence, to
to these knotty cases, and
advice and sympathy befitti
particular one. The curé,
sure, had more experience th
men in this kind of diploma
ing been the bosom confida
the swains who had sighed
belles of Chamtocé these for
past; but he declared that
lovers gave him more to do t
whole generation together.
were nine eligible *partis* goi
all nine were competing for h
good man was driven to h
end. Marie remained sere
different to them all, and nev
a glance of encouragement
above another, nor could he
detect the faintest sign of pre
toward any of them. He t
fuge, therefore, in perfect ne
and refused to interfere in be
any of the suitors. She was
enough to bide her time a
their fidelity before she ado
choice so important to them
herself. Marie was fifteen wh
came to Chamtocé. The
tion had broken out in Paris a
spreading rapidly through th

Gaston quarrelled. Both wanted to go, both were equally good for the service; the recruiting officer, unable to choose between them, declared they must decide for themselves. The only way to do this was to defer it to the curé. They walked off to the church, where the old man was speaking plain, soul-stirring words of encouragement and exhortation to a throng of men and women, the men exulting, the women weeping, but all of one mind and heart in the cause, and ready to give their best and dearest to serve under the banner of the fleur-de-lis.

Marie was kneeling close by the altar, amidst a group of weeping mothers and sisters. Her eyes were dry, but dim and restless; she spoke to no one, but turned constantly toward the door, as if she were watching for some new arrival. When the brothers came in, there was a movement, the crowd made way for them as they walked up to the altar, and hushed their sobs to hear what they were going to say.

"Monsieur le Curé," said Gaston, "only one of us may enlist, and you are to choose between us; which of us may go and fight for the king?"

"Ah! my children, what is it you ask of me! How can I choose!" exclaimed the old man, clasping his hands. "You are both dear to me; I would have you both fight for the king and win a crown of glory. If you fall fighting in defence of God and his altars, yours will be the crown of the martyrs. Which is most pure at heart, strongest in faith, most worthy to serve in the cause of God? He alone can tell!"

"François! François!" cried many voices in chorus, and the people gathered round the poor man's friend, and blessed him, and bid him joy of being chosen for the good fight.

"So be it!" said the curé; and

François knelt d
laid both hands
blessed him.

Marie was a
spectator of the
still on her knees
rails with both ha
the strain left the
less. François w
had followed M
the church, and i
of the two, and
up to Marie and
her. He did not
not look at him,
it was François.

"Marie!" he
hand on her arm.

Then she turn
his eyes, and th
they loved each o

"If I fall, you
Marie, and pray
çois, taking her h

"Yes."

"And, Marie, i

"We will com
and bless God to

"You will wait
a day?

"I will wait fo
my life."

They sent up
silence, then kiss
parted.

As François lef
Gaston, who wa
great concern eve
thers walked ho
coursing with full
den and solemn p
entered the cott
straight to his r
with a small deal

"*Frère*," he
much to trouble
property, but wh
keep for me. M
ing to speak of, s
in all; here is the

:ven that sum but for the cattle at Easter. Do the :an for me with it; lay it or grain—whatever brings mes go. The sheep were investment the last two 'ish I had done more in but I was never overwise oney, and this will thrive our hands than in mine, I would rather you didn't ut long at a time, as you ur own; gather it in soon od stroke, and let it grow good sum; it's not safe in to leave one's money any business."

astonishment had grown tion by the time his bro- ht this speech to an end. t mean, this sudden desire ney and let it accumulate? ad all his life been as care- ais-d'or as of carrots or l gave them away as read- asking; and now that he to face the cannon, and ong chance of never need- gain, he was smitten with desire to have them in- multiply. Though Gas- othing, François read this his eyes.

think I've put my heart in ," he said, laying a hand 's shoulder, and looking to his face; "I'd hand it your own, to do as you it, if I were alone in the t I'm not, *frère*. I've an- ink of now."

away his hand, and avert- quickly, but Gaston saw ver, and the drops gather e, truthful eyes. He saw glance, and followed the gure, as it disappeared his room, with an expres- face that it was better for çois did not see; if he had looked at his brother then he would have read a secret that would have pierced his heart like a sword. Gaston stood staring after him as if he had been turned to stone, his features fierce and hard-set, the veins in his forehead swelling and throbbing, all his frame shaken by a vehement struggle. Gaston mastered it, his face relaxed, and he went in after François.

"*Frère*," he said, "you may trust me," and held out his hand to him.

François clasped it, but looking at his brother with a puzzled smile:

"Trust thee!" he repeated, "as if I needed thy pledge for that! Brother, I trust thee as I trust my soul."

"And, *frère*, as Monsieur le Curé said just now, the best and purest are chosen for the sacrifice; if—"

"*Vive Dieu et le Roi!*" cried François, raising his cap. Then he was silent a moment before he said:

"If I fall, you will be a good brother to Marie, and do what you can to comfort her."

"And the money, what shall I do with it?"

"Give it to her."

The brothers embraced, and set out in search of M. le Curé. He blessed them all once more, and the brave young fellows fell into ranks with the soldiers, and marched off singing their battle-psalm, their hearts beating with high hope and faith and courage; while brave Vendéan mothers followed them out of the village, speeding them with blessings and cries of *Vive Dieu et le Roi!* It echoed through the gathering twilight with a strange, inspiring pathos. Quiet and darkness fell upon Chamtocé, the shadows died out of the silent church, the red flame of the sanctuary lamp rose and fell, flickering like a crimson pulse in the gloom,

smoke of the battle, in the dreary watches of the bivouac, in the many miseries of his soldier life, was a mirage that had tempted him along the desert path, only to mock him when he neared it, and fade out of the sky like a false and fickle star. No; he had not the courage to tell him that Marie was his brother's wife.

When the curé entered the cottage, he found Gaston sitting down to his dinner alone. Marie had gone to nurse a sick neighbor's child. The curé was glad of her absence. It made his mission easier. "*Mon garçon*," he said at once, "I bring news that will startle you, and I am thankful to be able to break it to you before Marie hears it. Your brother is come back." The curé expected his announcement to startle Gaston, as he had said, but he was not prepared for the effect it produced. The young man stood bolt upright, looked at the curé with wild, scared eyes, and dropped again into his chair without uttering a word.

"Have you told him?" he gasped, after an interval of silence that the old priest felt himself incapable of breaking.

"No; her name was not mentioned by either of us."

"Ha!" Gaston drew a breath of relief; "then perhaps—who knows? He may take it less to heart than we fear?"

"I don't know. At his age, four years is a long absence; still we cannot tell. But at any rate, my son, you must come and give him a brother's welcome, and do what a brother's love can do to lighten the disappointment to him."

He took Gaston's arm, and they went out to the presbytery together.

The curé's heart belied his words when he held out the hope that François' love might not have borne unchanged the test of absence. He

knew the youth ...
it. And he was righ
The meeting betw
was quiet, but none t
The curé told Franço
happened; how faith
kept her troth; hopin
and Gaston had give
how at length he ha
listen to Gaston; an
and with a sad heart,
to both their entre
heard him to the end
voice of heart-rendin
said:

"It was my fault,
blame thee. God's w

He held out his
clasped it, and the bro
a moment face to f
Both were very pale,
François who was th
two.

Gaston went home
watched his figure a
garden and down the
appeared like a blue
white background, an
upon the curé's nec
like a woman.

Before many hours
on tiptoe with alarm
A shepherd had arrive
the news that one
captains had passed th
in disguise, and been
pelle-aux-lys, whence
started in pursuit of h
a large price on his
bleus were so enrage
for his desperate ex
having baffled them
they were resolved to
ter to the people that
and would set fire to
than let him escape.
herd who had been in
the service of the Mar
cognized François E
road, and, guessing

ad sent a trusty messenger ord afterwards to Chamtocé. n was the only person, be- e and Victoire, who his brother's arrival so far, n Gervoise came in with this hich she caught from the vil- sips on her way from even- ers, his first impulse was to the presbytery, and warn his to start at once, and seek fer hiding-place. He went kly, but, as he had his hand ricket, he saw Marie coming the cottage. She was the son he wished to meet just t he could not avoid her with- ting surprise in her mind, and suspicion. So he tarried till e, wondering why she walked ly, as if she did not make was waiting for her, or as if— n's heart whispered to him— uld rather he went without to her. Why? Was it pos- truth had come to her ears ? He could not believe it, as with a painful quickening ulse that he saw her at that pace.

e you waiting for me, Gas- e said simply.

I am going in to Monsieur for a minute; I will be back y. Are you not well, Ma-

, *mon ami*, quite well, only d cold."

lrew her shawl closer round a little shudder, and passed entered the cottage. Gas- art leaped up as if an adder ng it, and then sank as y with a horrible faintness. ned against the snow-stuffed nd felt as if the very life ozen within him. The blood o his throat; he put his hand rehead as if a spasm of pain ned him; but soon rousing himself from his absent attitude, he walked on to the presbytery. But he did not enter it. He did not see it, in fact. He walked on and on like a man in a dream, looking neither to the right nor the left, and when suddenly he remembered where he was, and whither he was bound, he had left the village more than a league behind him, and was standing on the sloping beach of St. Florent, under the shadow of its semicircular hills that look down upon the Loire, where the little islet of —— sits like a brooding swan midway in its waters. The night had fallen, but the moon was not yet up, and the darkness was only lightened by the snowy reflex of the landscape. A bank of cloud hung like a heavy curtain over the hill, and hid away the moon. Somehow Gaston was glad of the darkness. But it was in vain that he strove to make it dark within. No outer darkness could conceal from him the workings of his heart. He saw into its troubled depths as clearly as if a thousand moons had been shining in the purple vault above him. He saw the tempter busy with his fiercest instincts, and he saw what a base and miserable tool he was. Ay, but desperate as well as base. Much must be forgiven to a desperate man. Here was his whole life wrecked. His wife's affection and trust—he felt it had not yet grown to love—was lost to him; his gold was lost to him—his precious, darling gold, that he had hugged to his heart till it grew to be a part of it, a second wife; and he must give it up just at a moment when he wanted it as he had never done before, and had laid out all his money, and had not a louis to ring on his hearthstone except this gold of François'. A curse upon the hour he took it! François would never ask it back—never accept it, most

chair in the chimney-corner, and nodding significantly at the knitting that lay on her knees. The noise he made drawing a stool to the fire awoke her. He asked where her mistress was, and Gervoise told him that Marie had come in for a few minutes and then gone out again, and that they were not to expect her home that night, as the child was worse. He was glad of her absence; yet it frightened him. Was it a pretext—was she shrinking from him, afraid or loath to meet him! At any rate, it changed his intention of starting at once; he decided that he would wait till all the village was up and astir for midnight Mass, and then he would slip off and ride hard, so as to reach Chapelle-aux-lys and be back again before daylight and Marie's return. He said he did not care to eat anything, and went up to his room. He locked himself in, lighted his lantern, and pulled out the fatal money-bag; he felt he must strengthen himself by the sight of the gold, and count over his treasure once more, to make sure it was worth the price he was going to pay for it. This done, he flung himself undressed on the bed, and, worn out by the conflict of the last few hours, was soon sound asleep. But he had not been asleep long before he was aroused by a long knocking at his door, and a rough voice demanded admittance. Gaston sprang to his feet.

"Who's there?" he said.

"*Les bleus.* Open in the name of the republic!" and the speaker dealt a blow on the door that nearly broke it in.

Gaston opened without further parley, and six men entered the room.

"What do you want?" he asked.

"We want one François Léonval who is concealed in this house. Tell us where to find him and we will go, and do you no harm; but if yo to shirk it—" The man sw brutal oath, and pointed his pis Gaston's head.

But Gaston Léonval had a déan's spirit withal. It was r dastardly personal cowardice tl would betray his brother; he fe cold touch of the muzzle on hi head, and, quietly pushing it he told the man he might sear house, and he wished him joy found what he was lookin "We had better begin by th houses and the garden," said th who seemed to take the lead; "t you stay inside to prevent any while we are outside." And l the room, followed by all bu soldier, who remained to r guard over Gaston.

But a safer and stronger se was keeping watch by the wre brother, urging him with terrible er and show of reason to sa word that would free him for Only an hour ago, he was res to run great risks to say it, and he had only to make a sign, an no risk whatever, and he coul bring himself to do it. Con that moonshine! It had made man of him. He went to the dow and looked down into the den to watch the proceedings c soldiers. Then he heard them s ing the rooms below, banging and overturning everything, and sently the officer came up again.

"Hearken, *mon garçon*, it's n trying to play hide-and-seek wi *bleus*," he said, "you won't find swer. Now, once for all, whe this François Léonval?"

"I tell you he's not here," re Gaston doggedly; "if he was, would find him."

"Most likely, if we had tim lose hammering at the walls

up the chimneys; but *les*
rather more expeditious way of
work. When we can't bag
le, we fire it. So walk out,
will set a light to the house
ke a little Christmas bonfire
If he's a coward, he'll soon
it! If he's a brave man, why
out in a blaze, and that's as
death as another. So here
e me the light!"
ized the lantern, took out
et, and deliberately advanced
the bed.
d!" cried Gaston, clutching
retched arm; "the man you
arch of is not here; he is at
bytery."
les laid down the light.
here," he said to the soldier
remained in the room; "we
istle for you when it's time
is."
escended the stairs quickly,
ston heard the door close,
r the five figures disappear
e road. After that he seem-
ll into a sort of stupor, and
thout moving hand or foot,
stolidly out of the window,
e soldier waited in silence for
nised signal. It came at last,
g the silence like the hiss of
and Gaston knew that his
was in the hands of the tor-

oner was he alone than a
f demons seemed to people
m, filling it with hideous
d voices, mocking and scoff-
asking him what he had
th his brother. He stamped
and dashed his hands through
and began to walk rapidly
down. But the spectres kept
h him, grinning and hooting
eating with maddening itera-
What have you done with
other?"
at had he done with him?" cried Gaston aloud—"why, only what François would have done with himself sooner or later. And was he to let his house be burnt down and his gold melted to postpone the day perhaps for twenty-four hours? Pshaw! what an idiot he was to take on so about it. It was all that whistle that set his nerves on an edge. Why did it keep on hissing and hissing? The *bleus* and their capture were half a mile out of ear-shot by this. Fate had been good to Gaston, and served him much better than he could have served himself. It had taken the matter out of his hands, and he had been no more than a passive agent in its grasp, in the grasp of law and might—ay, and right too. When François came back like a simpleton and thrust his head into the lion's mouth, what could he expect but that it would close on him and crunch him? It was over now. Marie would never hear of his return and need never curse the day she gave her hand to Gaston, and Gaston might sleep in peace, and without being haunted by terrors of his brother's return." Thus did he argue with the fiend and strive to beat him off, and stifle remorse that had entered his soul, and was gnawing at him with fierce, relentless tooth. But it would not do. Across the legion of fiends there flitted visions of the past, that he could not shut his eyes to, struggle as he would. First, there rose before him a curly-headed little brother whose small arms were round Gaston's neck, clasping him as they lay in a little cot beside their mother, breathing softly in sweet child slumber; then he beheld a frank, bright boy kneeling with him beside that mother's death-bed, while she blessed them and promised to meet them in heaven. Then the boy was a youth who stood with his hand on Gaston's shoulder, and looked

into his eyes, and said: "Brother, I trust thee as I trust my soul!" This faded away, and he saw the same youth bronzed and war-worn, and betrayed in his manly trust, but still holding out his hand to Gaston, and saying with the well-remembered voice, now husky with the strong man's agony: "I do not blame thee, brother; God's will be done!" Slowly but vividly the visions rose before Gaston's soul, and he could not but look on them, and, as he looked, sweet memories of his childhood rushed upon him like a torrent and bore him down; his boasted courage was gone, his pride, his love, his gold melted away like false phantoms, and he was alone with his sin and his despair. He remembered François' noble unselfishness, his truth, his grateful love of their common mother, his reverence for her lightest wish; he remembered his many acts of kindness to the poor and the suffering, and how he had seen him followed by blessings from the old and young whom his generosity had helped and comforted; and oh! bitterest of all was the memory of their parting, when François gave him his little hoard in trust, and bid him take care of Marie. And this was the brother he had sold! O God! It was all too horrible to be true. Gaston seized the bag of gold, rushed from the house and into the stable, and, without waiting to saddle her, leaped on his mare's back, and dashed off in pursuit of *les bleus*. They were only six, and he had gold enough to buy them if he only came in time. The mare flew as if she knew what hung on her speed, dashing up the snow that spattered her flanks and enveloped her rider in a moving cloud as they galloped along. The moon was still magnificent, and the stars shone down with the same calm splendor—the patient, far-away stars that 1793 years ago rang ou glad tidings to the watchers o hills of Judea: Glory to God! to men! Gaston, as he flew pa scene of his recent struggle, chill of supernatural terror freez to the marrow of his bones. stars stooped down till they se to touch him, and pierce hin needles of fire; the hills, the uncompromising hills, shook pale brows at him, and turne ran with him through the wa snow; and above them, fro battlements of heaven, rang myriad voices in ecstatic song: to God! Peace to men! Bu and anon, breaking the high h ny of that song, came a shriek a mocking fiend: "What hast done with thy brother?"

The mare took a longer strid put out her strength with a su increase of vehemence as they to a turn in the road where it c the river and rounded the ba the hills. Gaston's heart leaped his throat, as he caught the ha ing of hoofs ahead. Thank he he was in time. The hor came in sight. They slackene speed, nay, they were dismo now. Out in the open road w shelter of any sort in sight? did it mean? The mare stro A few more pulls, and she wo up with them. Gaston could guish the trim figures of the so and François's loose peasant But now he lost sight of them; had moved behind a hedge. for a moment. The six slim f emerged from the snowy foregr and six muskets gleamed hori in the moonlight.

"Hold! in the name of he hold!" shrieked Gaston.

He flung down the bag, that and sent the gold rippling o ground—but it was too late;

him that one François Léonval, who had born arms for nearly four years against the republic, and taken refuge the day before at Chamtocé, whither the soldiers of the republic were bound in pursuit of him, had, in order to prevent the shedding of innocent blood, left his native village in the night, and of his own free will given himself up to justice. He had died like a soldier, worthy of a better cause, and had begged the writer to bear his last words to the curé of Chamtocé, which were that he was happy to give his life for God and the king; and he prayed a blessing on his brother, and Marie his sister-in-law, and begged them and the curé to be mindful of him in their prayers. He fell crying *Vive Dieu et le Roi!* which treasonable words had been enough to shoot him again if he were alive; but being dead, the writer, who respected a brave man, though he was a traitor, conveyed them in fulfilment of his promise to François Léonval.

Soon after this event the Reign of Terror came to an end. The fertile fields of La Vendée smoked once more under the furrowing ploughshare, and peace and plenty smiled upon the land. Absent ones returned to gladden many hearts, and to tell the story of their short and wonderful campaign, and brought back glory-laden banners, tattered and blood-stained, to hang in the village church, as trophies of Vendéan valor, to show future sons of La Vendée how their fathers had fought the good fight. Once more there was marrying and giving in marriage, and toil and prosperity reigned in Chamtocé.

When the winter snows had twice melted off the hills, and the snowdrops peeped up under the grimy hedges, like white-robed little choristers singing their glad good-by to the winter, and the lusty young spring had laid his emerald finger on the earth, the bells rang out their full, exhilarating peal, and a gay procession wound its way to the church, where Monsieur le Curé in his surplice and stole awaited the bridal train. His voice shook, and big drops rolled down his aged cheeks, as he laid his hand on the two bowed heads and called down the blessing of the God of Abraham on Marie and François Léonval. This was his last ministration. He tarried long enough to bless the marriage of his two best-loved children, and then he went home. They laid him to rest beside a humble grave that was always freshly decked with flowers. It bore a white stone cross and a marble slab, on which it was recorded that François Léonval in life was a brother with a noble heart, and in death a martyr who had died for a noble cause, and that, like his Master, "having loved his own, he loved them to the end."

which is in fault; that its irrepressible tendencies are to raise one class by depressing another, and to create a countless multitude of tastes and wants which can be gratified by none but the favored class who are the possessors of great wealth.

They fret vainly—beating against the little that remains of ancient bulwarks erected to shield them, as if by destroying these their condition would be improved—and indulge an idle dream that women's suffrage will remedy the evils, real or imaginary, of which they complain. "Let us vote," they say; "let us have some voice in regulating our own affairs, and, if we do not succeed in shaping them entirely to our wishes, we shall at least reduce the number and weight of our grievances, be enabled to open new channels through which we can attain the independence we desire, and, by making our presence felt as an element of the body politic, be acknowledged as an existing fact that is of some importance to the nation."

It is indeed an idle dream! The mind of every intelligent person must, upon a very little reflection, discover innumerable reasons why woman must cease to be woman, wife, and mother, before she can exercise the elective franchise to any purpose.

As a true American woman, we cannot regard the clamor which has been raised upon the subject of woman's rights with the entire contempt it has met in many quarters. There is an invisible current of sad and mournful facts underlying this agitation.

If "material prosperity" is the key-note of Protestantism—as the testimony of its own writers would seem to prove—the development of material comfort and luxury is its highest expression. In all the appliances, arrangements, and habits of our domestic and social life, there has been a constant and alarming increase of expense during the past fifty years. New fashions have been invented, new wants created and multiplied, so rapidly that the supply, never exceeding the demand, has altogether exceeded the means of a great majority of our people. The few who were able to indulge in each novelty as it appeared have gone to surprising lengths; while the many, whose revenues were wholly inadequate, have strained every possible resource to keep pace with their wealthy leaders in expensive follies. Crime, bankruptcy, widespread ruin, and desolation have followed, of course. Multitudes have been left in poverty, with all the habits, tastes, and aspirations which wealth alone can gratify, and of these multitudes a large proportion are women. Accustomed to affluence, they are determined not to accept poverty—the synonym for *disgrace* in their circle—and eagerly cast about them for some avenue of escape. Hence the frantic efforts to obtain entrance into new paths, hitherto untrodden by woman, for securing the object of their ambition.

Woman has a right to be all that her Maker designed when he created her as a "help" to man. He is not of more importance to society in his own place than she in hers. He would not render himself more ridiculous by forsaking his own duties and avocations for the care of the household, the kitchen, and the nursery, than she would by abandoning these for the public employments of men. The present state of affairs is sufficiently deplorable, but I do not see how such an exchange would mend the matter. Nor can we see any remedy, but by returning to old-fashioned ways. Very comfortable ways they were, too, however dis-

lation, or state in life is so simply and clearly defined for her, that to mistake or err is impossible, except through wilful dereliction: For the child, reverence and submission to parental authority; for the maiden, humble devotion to the plain every-day duties of home, and a modest reserve that seeks the seclusion from which she must be

"Wooed,
And not unsought be won";

for the married woman, respect for him who is "her head, even as Christ is head of the church"; entire devotion to his spiritual and temporal interests; and a loyal fealty to the sacred gift of maternity, by which the First Great Cause brings her into most intimate communion with himself; permitting her through its penalties, as one of Eve's daughters, to offer her portion of expiation for the sin of that first parent, before his holy altar. For the mother, this tender Mother of souls provides abundant consolations and counsels in every hour of need, with measureless grace and strength to enable her to discharge perfectly every duty towards the young immortals committed to her keeping.

In no feature of the maternal care and solicitude with which the church surrounds her daughters is the contrast with the cold neglect and indifference of Protestantism more striking, than in the treatment extended by each system to those women who remain in a state of celibacy.

The condition of such under the Protestant *régime* is truly pitiable, and the very title of "old maid," with rare exceptions, entails odium and contempt more surely than moral depravity.

Hence the dread entertained by the girl in Protestant society for a single life, and the universal impression that to be married is t great object of her existence. that escape from the sacred some duties involved in th should too frequently be the :

Even mothers encourag daughters in this view of the and enter into their conspira securing husbands with mi zeal. Very little reflection is to the question whether the are suited for each other, or tual attachment sufficiently st enable them to bear jointly th rous and inevitable trials wh tain to every state and cond life. The attention is chiefly ed to considerations of a wic ferent character, relating wh pecuniary affairs. It is a mos lar fact, in connection with th of our subject, that—the great *ratum* once secured—the you too generally begins at once gard and treat the husband she has been so anxious to the adversary to her intere happiness, instead of adopti old-fashioned idea that he is h friend. Strange as it may see is a very common mistake i days, and the source of much tic discord and misery.

A lovely young mother— the fairest and most intelligen mens of the modern Americ man whom we are so happy know—said to us, the othe "My boys are well provided any event, and, if they were no could fight their way in the like others; but, I assure you, bestir myself to make such pr for my girls as will secure the being ground to powder by husbands!"

This from a most devoted a emplary wife, happy in a hu who dotes upon her, was suffi surprising.

rights upon the ruins of her ancient safeguards.

Woman's suffrage — should they obtain it—will only betray their feet into a political slough, and bespatter them with political defilements from which none but an omnipotent power can rescue and cleanse them. Woman has everything to lose and nothing to gain in this movement, for, after all, men will manage affairs to suit themselves. The Almighty pronounced no idle decree when he said to the woman: "Thou shalt be under thy husband's power, and he shall have dominion over thee."

EVER.

THE steadfast gaze brings out the star,
That, like an eye
Set in the sky,
Its sweet light shedding from afar,
At morning dawn, and still at even,
The night alway,
And livelong day,
There twinkles ever, deep in heaven:

Thy constant prayer so reacheth Love,
That, like the star,
Seeming so far,
Its glad strength sending from above,
To youth's fair dream, and memory's smart,
To grief's sad moan,
And joy's sweet tone,
Aye burns for us, deep in God's heart.

Then, led on by her sympathy for him, she told her own past, there on the spot where it had occurred.

These confidences drew the two together, and formed a bond which was never broken.

A man's manliness can scarcely bear a severer test than when he becomes the pet of woman. One is sometimes astonished to see how characters, apparently fine, deteriorate under that insidious influence. But Dick Rowan was too grateful and modest, and too little selfish or vain, to be injured.

"He is not quite like us," Mrs. Yorke said, "but he is more natural and original, and is, altogether, a remarkable young man. Edith has reason to be proud of his homage. He certainly behaves exquisitely toward her."

Mr. Yorke, refusing to be influenced by feminine raptures, was fain to take the young man out of the house, in order to talk with him uninterruptedly. He displayed the improvements he had made in the place, his avenues, now as hard as cement, his terraces, smooth and green with turf of velvet fineness. There were vines here and there, disposed for effect, like drapery in an artist's studio, and many a flower which bloomed now for the first time under Seaton skies. They stopped at last beside a clover-plot, thick with crowded trefoils and blossoms. Its surface was unsteady with bees, musical with a low hum, and all the air was sweet with the breath of it.

"If I were not disgusted with Seaton," Mr. Yorke said, "I should like to spend my summers here, and carry out my plans for the place; but when we go away, probably in October, I shall never wish to see the town again. There is no security here."

Dick leaned thoughtfully on the fence, and watched the bees come and go over the clover, and took off

his hat to shake his hair loo
fragrant air. "I think, sir,
ton may be in future all the
this trouble," he said slowl
tone of the place is low, I l
well, but it is in a fair way o
ing ashamed of itself, and so,
ing. When people have wr
and stand by them stubbor
to have them go on, and fir
themselves what their princ
to. Conviction reaches th
through their own experienc
you hear no more about th
It is, of course, a slow way,
sure."

Mr. Yorke made a grim
quoted President Mann: "
mighty is not in a hurry, an

Carl had gone to Brag
went quite unexpectedly,
Dick Rowan came, and
see Edith's lover till he ha
week in Seaton. He came l
evening after tea, when th
people were in the cupola
down the bay, for the
They waved their handker
him, and his mother ran out
him.

"My dear son!" she e
embracing him as joyfully
had been gone a year. "I w
watch for you, lest I should l
pointed. I pretended I di
pect you. But you may kr
a hypocritical pretence it w
I say that your supper is a
though, to be sure, breakfas
and supper have been kept
every day."

While speaking, she led hi
little northern parlor, which
summer dining-room.

Carl looked at his mothe
smile, but tears rose to his ey
was not one to take even a
devotion as a matter of cou
just now he found it peculiar
ing.

the house that night highly pleased with his visit.

"They seem to me perfectly kind and natural people," he said to Dick, as they walked through the woods together. "Your Edith, it is true, is rather grand, but in a sweet, child-like way, and Miss Melicent seems disposed to be a little on the high horse once in a while, but not much. I always thought that accomplished ladies were more airy, but I don't see that these do any great things."

"True," Dick answered; "but mark the things which they do not do."

They were much together after that, and Mrs. Yorke and her daughters went on board the *Halcyon*, and were entertained there. Carl had been afraid to have his mother venture on board the ship, and had charged himself especially with the care of her, but his solicitude was not needed. He was both pleased and amused by the simplicity and tenderness with which their gigantic host smoothed every smallest obstruction from her path and spared her every exertion. There had been a momentary flash of angry surprise when he saw his mother lifted over an obstructing timber in Captain Cary's arms; but the sailor's face was so absolutely anxious and kind, and Mrs. Yorke laughed so merrily over the *naïf* gallantry, that he instantly perceived the folly of resenting it.

"My dear," Mrs. Yorke whispered to Clara, "he is like one's grandfather, grandmother, and all one's aunts and uncles, in one. It's a pity he hasn't a wife, he would be so good to her."

Clara blushed slightly. She had been thinking some such thought herself.

The intercourse gave the Yorkes a fresh and novel sensation. It was so different from anything they had

ever had before, a
time, so pleasant
breath of pure sea
and scented draw
were not so mu
tion that they cou
this simple, unco
in which they found

Captain Cary li
nation to the story
experiences. As a
ship, and completel
everywhere, he co
hend how one part
could exercise such
ercion over the oth
me that the Cath
done something out
said. "There's usu
sides, you know,
would justify such a

"There is just t
Yorke replied, ra
"It is so easy for
to be fair, and, at th
put themselves to t
of investigating, to
probably fault on
then fancy that the
tice. On the con
have done great inj
certainly, rendered
slipshod judgment.
cases where the fai
side, and other cas
in the end there
both sides, the res
rests on the one wh
sor, and provoked t
endurance. I am
sir; but I am alway
off-hand way of sayi
bably fault on both
don't know, let the
know, and not give
all. I do know, a
provocation was gi
tholics have been e

"There have bee
Cary," Edith said,

tive, you therefore are useless. I visited once, in Europe, a spot where a temple had stood. Nothing was left of it but a few broken fragments lying about, and a single beautiful pillar that stood alone. Was that pillar useless? No; in its way, it was very eloquent. No one could look upon it without trying to fancy what the whole edifice might have been; and you may be sure that the traveller's imagination did its best in rebuilding that temple. So, now, you shall be the little caryatid of the church in Seaton. You have the gift of silence: use it. Be as obedient and quiet as that solitary column, and let the world guess from you how fair must be that structure of which you are a part."

Edith turned from the window, where she had stood to read her letter, folded her arms up over her head, and said to Dick Rowan, sitting there, "Can you fancy me supporting an entablature?"

"No," he answered; "for then there would have to be others like you."

Edith blushed, and dropped her arms; for they were all looking at her, and their faces, as well as Dick Rowan's answer, reminded her that she was beautiful. She gave him her letter to read, and went to sit on the window-sill beside Clara, and listen to the talk of the three gentlemen on the piazza. The two families were dining together that day, and Mr. Yorke, with his son-in-law, and Captain Cary, were smoking their cigars outside. Inside the window nearest her husband, Mrs. Cleaveland sat in a low, broad arm-chair. A nurse in a white cap had just placed on her knees Hester's second son, an infant of six months old. As it lay slowly and deliciously waking up, both nurse and mother gazed down upon it with adoring eyes. Master Philip, this baby's predecessor, was his face in one arm of his n arm-chair, being in tempora grace. Original sin was very and active in this child. I full of vitality and determinati just at that age when will is well developed, and memory derstanding still dormant—t for childish atrocities. The moments when the child's lif burden to him, by reason great number of things wh wished to do, and meant to could not remember that h not do. He had a chronic d pull out the baby's eyelashe winkeys," he called them, make it smile in season and violently drawing the corne mouth round toward its ears. ever an infantine shriek was h was always understood that Philip was in some way acco Another fancy of his was t holes in paper, or any delic easily perforated fabric, w plump forefinger. He could greater pleasure than to seat with some precious volume him, and go gravely and indus through it in this way, leaf from cover to cover. There deed, a long list of indi against this unhappy child. little forefingers tied together his back, and a dilapidated bo on the carpet, showed plainly what his offence was at this ti

In the background, Carl w ing marvellous stories to the half-brother, Eugene; an Yorke and Milicent, in the ce the room, were coaxing some of his adventures from Dick He had to be persuaded be would speak much of himself.

"Isn't he magnificent?" whispered to Edith, meaning Cary.

had been describing an
craft, the *Humming-bird*,
had once darted in and
hinese coast, smuggling
very teeth of an English
Seeing the addition to
he threw the end of his
and moved his chair

ould like to be a sailor!"
ara with enthusiasm.
iry leaned forward, with
his knees, in order to
more on a level with the
"And how would you
ailor's wife?" he asked.
e had the greatest possi-
n for Miss Clara Yorke,
d her by far the cleverest
a he had ever known, it
to say that the thought
further than that had
l his mind, till he saw
eyes and color with
ised his question. The
ical. He straightened
gain, and, in the first
possibility, did not hear
it rather tardy reply:
ds on who the sailor is."
as confounded between
re, and astonishment.
iad seemed to show that
mation was not impos-
st, think of—that it had,
rred to her own mind.
most likely to scorn the
for all that, a momen-
nced before his eyes of
would be if he had a
own to love and serve.
e of his choice should
ever occurred to this
He could at any time
l a common person,
people would have
l enough for him; but
is nature a capacity for
ip which made him
ch an alliance.

Presently, Edith's cool voice stole through the chaos of his mind. "You can go to sea with Dick and me, Clara."

The sailor started, and fell from the clouds. His face became overcast, and, with a deep sigh, he seemed to renounce a long-cherished hope.

With a laugh and a toss of the head, Clara rose from her lowly seat, and, stepping out through the window, began to promenade up and down the garden-walk. She saw through this great, transparent creature perfectly, and was amused, and she knew not what else. One could not be angry with the fellow, she said laughingly to herself. She had been looking up to him with enthusiasm, as to some antique bronze or marble Argonaut, or other hero of simpler times. Now that was changed, and she was on the pedestal, to be worshipped by him. It was preposterous, but not altogether disagreeable.

Meantime, Captain Cary was confiding his distress to Edith. "I hope that your cousin didn't think I was fool enough to dream of her being my wife," he said, looking down. "What I said was a slip of the tongue, and I didn't know the drift of it myself till I saw how she took it."

"Oh! never mind," Edith answered. "Clara is always jesting, and twisting people's meaning. She knew you meant no such thing."

He sighed, and said no more.

If Clara had expected the sailor to watch her, she was disappointed. He went into the parlor, and when, later, she entered, brilliant with exercise and mischief, he was sitting by Carl, and listening with as sober a face to the stories that young man was telling Eugene Cleaveland as if he were listening to a sermon. Clara passed near them, to hear what it might be which produced such so-

lemnity in the man and such a trance of interest in the child.

"Then," Carl was saying, "Taurus sent to the Great Bear to say that he should like to have something out of the golden dipper about the middle of the next month, for all the little stars would grow dim about that time, and need something to polish up with. And the Bear said, 'All right! but the dipper hangs so high on the celestial pole that you will have to pay me a good deal to climb up to it.' And Taurus answered, 'All right!' And then the Bears set slyly to work to grease the pole, so that the dipper should slip down, and they get their pay without work; and Taurus he set to work to push the dipper higher up, so as to get more work than he had agreed to pay for; and, meantime, all the poor little stars languished, and grew dim. And then Orion got mad, and brought a lot of little dippers, and gave each of the little stars a full one. And the stars grew bright and glad. But the Bulls and Bears, finding that they were both beaten, didn't feel glad. The Bear began to bite his own paws, and the Bull went for Orion, and tried to toss him. But Orion laughed, and put up his shield, and called his dogs, and—"

"Upon my word, Carl," says Clara, "I think you put the stars to base uses when you set them to gambling in stocks. Have you told Captain Cary of our projected sail down the bay?"

"Poor Clara!" Melicent said, joining them. "We are planning some little pleasure-trip to distract her mind. You do not know, perhaps, that the Philistines are upon her?"

The sailor did not understand, but looked so inquiring and solicitous that Clara explained to him.

"I published a story ages ago," she said, "and the editor of the *Cosmic* has just become aware of it. He found it lately among the *débris* of his writing-table. The authoress, he says, has shaken up a few fancies in a kaleidoscope, and calls them life. They are about as much like life, he adds, as Watteau's shepherdesses are like real shepherdesses, or as Marie Antoinette's housekeeping at the Petit Trianon, with ribbons tied round the handles of silver saucepans, was like real kitchen-work. Still, he concludes, the story is amusing, in spite of its pinchbeck ideal, and, when the writer is older, she will, doubtless, do better. The musty old metaphysician!" exclaimed Miss Clara, warming with the subject. "I once read a paragraph in one of his articles, and found it comical. I had never seen any of the words before, except the articles and prepositions. My first impression was that he had made them up, for fun. I found them all out in the unabridged dictionary, though. They were real words, but I have forgotten what they mean."

"So much the better!" said Melicent. And then followed a controversy on the subject of learned women. Melicent denounced them as unwomanly; but Melicent was neither a student nor well read, and there might be a difference of opinion as to cause and effect in her case. Mr. Yorke mocked *les savantes;* but Mr. Yorke adored a wife whose literary acquirements were of the most modest kind, and he had once, in a never-forgotten argument, been worsted by a clever woman. Captain Cary was of opinion that clever and learned women were not fit wives for common men. At that, Clara took up the gauntlet with great spirit.

Clever women did not wish to marry common men, she said. And there were plenty of uncommon men

CHAPTER XX.

THREE SONGS.

CAPTAIN CARY had been three weeks in Seaton, and was to sail in two days for New York, where the *Halcyon* was sold, taking Dick Rowan with him. From New York, Dick was to sail immediately, on a three years' voyage, in the *Edith Yorke.* The captain did not say definitely what his own plans were, perhaps did not know them himself. "I did think of settling down on shore," he said to Mrs. Yorke. "But one person doesn't make a home, and all my people are dead. I'd half a mind to ask Rowan to take me as a passenger. He has a splendid ship."

They were all in the garden that last evening but one. Edith sat on a bench beside Melicent, and looked intently at Dick Rowan, who was talking with Clara and Mrs. Yorke. She was thinking over all his goodness, all his affection for her, studying his personal beauty, his frank, bright face and athletic form, and trying to excite in herself some enthusiasm regarding him. Carl stood near, listening to, but not joining in, the conversation. She compared the two young men. Their height, their form, were very nearly the same; but Carl had the proud and measured tread of one bred to the parlor and the promenade, Dick the free and springing step of the mountaineer. This was distinctive, yet each had moods like the other. On the deck of his own ship, the sailor trod like a king; and the man of the world could bound as lightly up a steep, or vault as lightly over an obstacle, as though his life had been spent in athletic sports. Dick Rowan's eyes sparkled like the ripples of his own blue sea, and looked ple, not through them; Carl's glance could become pierci keen as a two-edged blade. useless to compare them, the direct and transparent as a ch other noble, indeed, yet sul one aware of the world's wa guarded at every point.

"I must be very hard and Edith thought, finding hers moved, in spite of her efforts. perhaps, it may be because always known and been s him."

Looking her way, Dick m steady gaze, and flushed wit sure. If the expression was and regretful, what then? they not about to part? Mrs. Yorke to her, and the followed, to make arrangemen a sail they were to have th day."

"You had better wear dress wetting will not hurt," Dick "for you will be likely to get scud-water in your laps."

"And, pray, what is scud-w Mrs. Yorke asked.

Dick explained that it was blown off.

"How pretty!" exclaimed "You may fill my lap with it.'

They separated again, and was left with Edith.

"What shall I bring you Calcutta?" he asked.

"Bring me Dick Rowan sa again," was the answer.

Both were silent a little whil he spoke in a quiet voice: God to do that, Edith. H been so good to us, I think I refuse nothing."

effect on myself. In the society of such a man"—glancing to where Captain Cary stood—"I should be gentle and feminine. But with the wilted specimens of humanity I see ordinarily, I am in imminent danger of becoming a strong-minded woman. One must keep up a balance, mamma, and it is weak men make bold women."

Mrs. Yorke sank on to a bench. "What do you mean to do? What am I to think?" she exclaimed.

Clara laughed. "Don't be afraid, mamma. If this Neptune should offer himself to me—he will not!—I should refuse him, and then cry my eyes out afterward. But if he should take me by force, pirate-fashion, and run away with me, so that I could not help myself nor be responsible, I should be delighted. Now, don't say any more about it, please."

Mrs. Yorke threw off her fears with a shrug of the shoulders. It was a mere theory. It was one of Clara's enthusiasms. "Well, my dear," she concluded, rising, "all I have to add is that I hope your admiration of the rough diamond will not lead you to consume it in the blowpipe."

And so the subject dropped.

"There is a party of Indians camping out on the Point," Mr. Yorke said to them that evening. "You might find it interesting to visit them to-morrow. I met one in the woodland, this morning, cutting down a tree for basket-wood. I asked him who gave him permission to cut trees on my land. 'It was all ours once,' he growled out, and gave me a look that I shouldn't like to meet, unless I had friends near. I told him to take all he wanted."

The little sailing-party, only six with a sailor from the *Halcyon* as assistant, started early in the afternoon. The crew of the *Halcyon* gave them a hearty cheer as the down past the wharf where sh the fresh breeze, blowing off smoothed the waves, and, ove light clouds ran races with them of one cloud, that seemed sca hand's breadth, a shower of sun-lighted drops came cla down. In the midst of it they ed the Point, and stepped out the rocky shore. A clumsy c dian woman had just kindled and piled brush over it. Not a was visible, but thick white gushed out through the green, over into a shifting Corinthia tal, and rose into air, and in a instant it topped a shaft of The woman took no notice visitors standing near her, but tossing twigs into the fire. H was ugly, her dress careless, l small brown hands and mocc feet were models of beauty. or three men were lying about waiting for their dinner, and chievous little girl was wea basket. She alone noticed the gers, the others wore a look dainful unconsciousness. The talked with the child, and l baskets of her; the gentlemen themselves acquainted with th ers, and found them not ins to the charms of tobacco and Under these persuasive influ their taciturn hosts melted, a came almost friendly. Present other Indian appeared from the came straight toward them, and ped a long string of quivering bow-colored trout at the old wo feet. A whispered exclamation from the lips of the visitors a saw this dusky young Adonis. Greek outlines, with more tha cian richness of color, the p clustering hair, from which raindrops slid as from a bird's the eagle eyes, the fanciful

with its crown of braids. She leaned over the boat-side, and trailed her hand in the water, nor spoke a word, nor once lifted her eyes. As the water-lily, growing to maturity through unconscious sun and dew, when its appointed sunrise comes, shines through all its snowy petals, and opens to disclose another sun hidden within its folded whiteness, so her soul, now its time was come to know itself and be known, stirred through all its calm reserves and unconsciousness at the sound of that savage chant. She forgot, for the time, all that was cramping in her life, and had a new sense of freedom and joy.

The song ceased. They neared the Point, and a path of crimson trembled out from the camp-fire there and crossed the moonlight. Clara leaned, and whispered to Carl. He hesitated a moment, then, with a gesture that showed a sort of defiant resolution, acquiesced in her demand. Carl seldom sang, and, when he did, it was for the words rather than the music, and his style was that of an improvisator. He sang:

"The moon is climbing up the sky,
Back rolls the ether blue,
The folded roses stir and sigh,
With droppings of the dew;
The tide runs up to meet the stream,
And bear her to the sea:
Downward, as in a happy dream,
They're floating silently.

"The slumb'ring deeps of life upbreak,
Our childish play is o'er.
The footsteps of the future shake
The lintel of our door!
Awake, sweetheart! thou giv'st to-day
A soul, and not a toy:
Wake! lest the child's hand fling away
The woman's crowning joy.

"Cast off the dreams of childish days,
Take on thy woman's state.
Search thine own spirit's deeper ways,
Ere yet it be too late.
The time is come for thee to give—
The time for me to take:
Lift up thy lids, and bid me live!
O woman's soul, awake!"

Slowly Edith lifted her drooping head, her heavy eyelids, and looked at Carl, and he looked at her. The full moon shone in their faces, and they saw only each other, and were conscious only of each other. The lily had bloomed.

Some sharp sound, like breath drawn through teeth, was heard, and Melicent cried out, "Mr. Rowan!"

They looked just in time to see Dick's white face as he staggered backward. His eyes closed, and, before they could reach him, he fell over the boat-side, with a heavy splash, and sank.

Captain Cary threw off his coat, and was overboard in a second, and soon they saw him bearing up a pallid face on his arm. "Haul in sail, and row ashore!" he called out, and himself struck out for the Point, which they were close upon.

Philip Nicola met him there, and the other men came down, and, when the party had stepped on shore, Dick was in one of the tents. Captain Cary came out to meet them. "He has come to," he said, "and will soon be all right. But you had better go home. I will stay and take care of him. He doesn't wish to go up now."

"I must see him, I shall certainly see him," Edith said resolutely, stepping forward.

"I wouldn't to-night, Miss Edith," the sailor replied, standing in her way. "He doesn't feel like talking."

"I shall go in!" she said, and waved him aside, and went into the tent.

Dick Rowan lay on the low pallet, with his face turned away and hidden in his arms. Edith knelt beside him. "Dick!" she said, in an imploring voice.

He started slightly. "Don't speak to me! Please go home now," he said. "I don't want to talk."

mean to be true to you, Dick," ɔbbed, without rising. "I will see nor speak to any one vish me to avoid. I will go with you this time, if you say

; only reply was to bid her go. e me time to think," he said, 'ill tell you afterward." And there was no way for her but to go.

"I am going to walk home," Carl said, and started off through the woods.

When, the next morning early, they sent down to the village for news, the *Halcyon* had sailed, and Dick Rowan had sailed in her.

BETHLEHEM.

BETHLEHEM—House of bread: *
    Of the Bread that came down from heaven. †
  "For the life of the world 'tis given:
Eat of it," Jesus said.

"Father," he bade us pray,
    "Give us this heavenly bread."
    "Ours" we must call it, he said.
"Give us it day by day."

Knelt in the midnight cave
    The shepherds and sages three—
    Theirs (do we envy ?) to *see*
The Bread which the Father gave: ‡

We in the faith's broad day
    Kneeling—nor once, but at will—
    Take of that Bread our fill,
None "sent empty away."

How should we envy *them?*
    Yet as the grace the shame,
    If but in boast we claim
The goodlier Bethlehem.

ɔVENT, 1871.

* he literal signification of Bethlehem. † John vi. 33, 51, 58. ‡ Ibid. v. 32.

THE PROTESTANT RULE OF FAITH.*

Dr. Hodge is an Old School Presbyterian, and a sturdy opponent of what among Protestants is called the "New England theology." He is a man of learning and ability, and one of the most distinguished theologians in the Presbyterian Church. If he has failed to reduce Protestantism to a system, complete, uniform, and coherent in all its parts, it is not his fault, but undeniably the fault of Protestantism itself, which is not all of a piece, which consists of fragments only of truth, with no genetic relation one to another, or connecting links, and which no mortal man can mould into a systematic whole. What man can do with so untoward a subject Dr. Hodge has done, if we may judge from the volume before us, and, as far as our knowledge goes, his work is the least unsuccessful attempt to construct a complete and consistent system of Protestant theology that has as yet been made.

Neither our space nor our leisure permits us to review the entire volume, or to discuss the author's system in its several bearings; a better opportunity to do that will be presented when we have the completed work before us, of which only the first volume has as yet been published. We shall confine ourselves for the present to a single question, namely, the Protestant rule of faith. The author devotes the entire Chapter V. of his Introduction to the statement and refutation, as he understands it, of the

* *Systematic Theology.* By Charles Hodge, D.D., Professor in the Theological Seminary, Princeton, N. J. Vol. I. New York: Scribner & Co. 1872. 8vo, pp. 648.

Catholic, or, as he says, the R
ist rule of faith; but as his obje
to that rule and his supposed
tion of it presuppose the tru
Protestantism, and are of n
count if the Protestant rule o
is invalid or inadequate, we
not stop to defend it, but are
pass at once to the examinat
the Protestant rule which he o
to it. If that can be asserted and
tained as a rule of faith, or aut
for determining what is the fait
has revealed and commanded
believe, the Catholic rule is ind
ble, or at least unnecessary.

The author is not very cle
definite in his statement of th
testant rule of faith. He sa
150), "All Protestants ag
teaching that 'the Word of C
contained in the Scriptures
Old and New Testaments is th
infallible rule of faith and practi
but from his assertion of the ri
private judgment and several
objections to the Catholic ru
may, without danger of error
the Protestant rule of faith to
Scriptures of the Old and Ne
taments, or the Bible interpret
private judgment—that is, inter
without any public or cathol
thority—as the Protestant rule o
dard of faith. But this is rath
denial than the assertion of
because it presents no rule or
dard to which private jud
must conform in order to be
thing but naked opinion. The
even conceding its divine inspi
and sufficiency, cannot be the
or standard for private judgme

God, and not from the enemy of souls taking the guise of an angel of light in order to deceive. The learned professor, then, even with the restriction of private judgment to the regenerate, and the assumption of the interior assistance and guidance of the Spirit, though contradicting himself, gets no rule of faith, and has at best only the place of faith.

The learned author is aware that the Bible interpreted by private judgment is no rule, at least no adequate rule, of faith, and so he seeks to supply its deficiency by tradition. He says, "Protestants admit there has been a stream of traditionary teaching flowing through the Christian church from the day of Pentecost to the present time. This tradition is so far a rule of faith that nothing contrary to it can be true. Christians do not stand isolated, holding each his own creed. They constitute one body, having one creed. Protestants admit that there is a common faith of the church, which no man is *at liberty to reject, or can reject and be a Christian*" (pp. 113, 114). This would seem to make the Protestant rule not the Bible interpreted by private judgment and private illumination, but the Bible interpreted by the traditionary teaching of the church or the common faith of the Christian body. This, if it meant anything, would be fatal to Protestantism. The author says (*ubi supra*), "Christians constitute one body with a common creed. Rejecting this creed, or any of its parts, is the rejection of the fellowship of Christians, incompatible with the communion of saints or membership in [of] the body of Christ." It is undeniable that the Catholic Church included at the epoch of the Reformation the whole Christian body, except those cut off from that body as heretics and schismatics; and it is equally undeniable that the Refor-

[illegible]
[illegible]
or at least importa[illegible]
therefore, did reject[illegible]
[illegible]
liberty to reject, [illegible]
can reject and be a
Reformers, [illegible]
testants who hold [illegible]
and cannot be, Chr[illegible]

But the author [illegible]
clusion by making th[illegible]
cedes mean nothing[illegible]
ing tangible. When
of the common con[illegible]
he says (p. 115), "th[illegible]
Christians the true[illegible]
that is, "the truly
men, the temples of
They understand [illegible]
nal organic body,
and inorganic bo[illegible]
confined to no one [illegible]
nion, that is, men wh[illegible]
Catholic theologian[illegible]
of the church." Ye[illegible]
to Protestantism—[illegible]
whole body of Cath[illegible]
tholic Church, and
more firmly than [illegible]
creed, or the very p[illegible]
Protestants reject as
corruption. Even
restriction, the auth[illegible]
be able to avoid th[illegible]
Protestants do reje[illegible]
creed of the true pe[illegible]
these true people [illegible]
they might be, were
visible Catholic Chu[illegible]
faith. But let this p[illegible]
Protestant to [illegible]
people are? Or ho[illegible]
is their creed or con[illegible]
does not determine
publicly professed [illegible]
or visible church in
concealed?

Here is a grave dif[illegible]
graver than our Pro[illegible]

to regard it. The Scrip-
tected by unregenerate
ids, are no rule or crite-
n; it is only the private
f the regenerate, of those
by the Spirit, that is to
and the common faith of
true people of God, is
and the faith which no
ect in whole or in part
hristian. But we cannot
res of their traditionary
common consent as a
or for the interpretation
, unless we know who
But, as they are not an
ble public body, but an
rganic, and, so to speak,
dy, we cannot know who
out some rule or criterion
e can distinguish them
odly, or from those who,
St. Augustine, are *in*
but not *of* the church.
fficulty. We must have,
application of the Pro-
another rule, a catholic
h to determine and apply
not use the Protestant
re know what it is, and
now what it is without
for determining who are
ople of God, the elect,
their common creed, or
teaching from the day
down to our times. But
professor has neglected
is antecedent rule, with-
e one he gives us is no
He gives no mark or
h we can recognize the
ple of God, and we do
can; for we do not be-
ly know or will know
till the last judgment,
rets of all hearts will be

t do here to refer us to
r the rule by which to
m; for we must know
them and their common faith in order to obtain our guide to the sense of the Bible. We cannot take the sense of the Bible to determine them, and then take them to determine the sense of the Bible. It will not do, again, to say they are they who are led by the Spirit, for it is precisely those who are led by the Spirit that we wish to ascertain; nor will it do to appeal to religious experience, for it is only the religious experience of the true people of God that can avail, and that would be referring us to the people of God to tell us who are the people of God. It would be to reason like the poor Anglican, who makes orthodoxy the test of the church, and the church the test of orthodoxy. "Jack, where is the hoe?" "Wid de harrow, massa." "Where is the harrow?" "Wid de hoe, massa." The Protestant, in any case, gives no more satisfactory answer; for, with all his pretensions, he can only tell us that the true faith is the faith held and followed by the true people of God, and the true people of God are they who hold and follow the true faith.

The author, as we have seen, says: "When Protestants plead the common consent of Christians—the common faith of the Christian body—they mean by Christians the true people of God. Romanists, on the other hand," he continues, "mean the company of those who profess the true faith, and who are subject to the Pope of Rome. There is the greatest difference between the authority due to the common faith of truly regenerate, holy men, the temples of the Holy Ghost, and that due to what a society of nominal Christians profess to believe, the great majority of whom may be worldly, immoral, and irreligious." But where did the professor learn that the authority of the teaching depends on the personal

virtue of the teacher? How does he know that they who recognize the authority of the Pope are only nominal Christians? or that the Pope is not led and assisted by the Spirit in his office of teacher of the universal church? Nay, how does he know, or how can he prove to us or anybody else, that there are any of the true people of God among Protestants at all? He must prove his rule of faith before proceeding to apply it.

Dr. Hodge continues, on the same page (115): "The common consent for which Protestants plead concerns only essential doctrines; that is, doctrines which enter into the very nature of Christianity as a religion, and which are necessary to its *subjective* existence in the heart, or which, if they do not enter essentially into the religious experience of believers, are so connected with vital doctrines and precepts as not to admit a separation from them."

Here is the same difficulty again. What is the Protestant rule for distinguishing among revealed doctrines those which are essential and those which are not essential? Will the author tell us the essentials are those doctrines which all Protestants agree in teaching, and that those in which they do not agree in teaching are non-essentials? But who are Protestants? All those who agree in teaching the essentials? Where is the hoe? With the harrow. Where is the harrow? With the hoe. This would be only to adopt the principle of poor Jack's replies to the questions of his master.

But no. The essentials are " those doctrines which enter into the very nature of Christianity as a religion, and which are necessary to its *subjective* existence in the heart." But how determine what these are, unless we know the very nature of Christianity? And how can we know or

determine what is the very nat Christianity, unless we have a standard of faith? But the ess are those doctrines which "a cessary to its subjective existe the heart." What doctrines are Have Protestants any obj rule for determining them? professor gives none except the tures, which do not suffice, be as we have seen, the Scriptur the place, not the rule of fait what we are seeking is the r authority for determining what faith they contain. Among I tants there is a very great div of views as to what is necess the subjective existence of relig the heart. Schleiermacher, i *Discourses on Religion, addressed Cultivated among its Despisers,* tains that only the sense of c dence is necessary to the subj existence of religion; Tweste cited by the author, maintair same, and that in a subjective all religions are equally true, tl not equally pure; some Prote place the essence of religion in rence; Dr. Channing seemed to it in philanthropy, or in a sen the dignity of man; others in culture," in "self-worship"; and tinguished Protestant minister tained to us, some years ago, pantheist, like Spinoza, or an a like Shelley, might not only be religious, but a good Christian. are thousands and thousands Protestant denominations whc tually at least, regard the subj existence of religion in the he nearly, if not totally, independ all objective doctrines or faith. is at least the tendency of m Evangelicalism, Bushnellism, E erism, and from which even o thor himself is not always free. makes, indeed, a brave fight fo matic theology or objective fait

essions to Whitfieldian and notions of religious expe-ace him on the declivity religious subjectivism. All e the Scriptures, and profess hem for their rule of faith ice; but it is evident from have said that the Scriptures sufficient rule by which to what are essentials and not. What rule, then, have ts by which to make the dis-

odge says, in refutation of lic rule, which, by the way, not correctly state: "Our promising the Spirit to guide le into the knowledge of ecessary to their salvation, promise to preserve them r in subordinate matters, or hem a supernatural know- the organization of the e numher of the sacraments, ower of bishops" (pp. 115, hen, on these matters, the ion of the church, the num- sacraments, and the power s, Protestants have no pro- exemption from error, and is quite possible that they ecting the Catholic doctrine urch, of the hierarchy and nents. But the professor's of the promise of our Lord ranted by his own professed e promise, as recorded by gelists is unlimited: "But lete, the Holy Ghost, whom r will send in my name, he you *all* things, and bring to your mind *whatsoever* I e said to you" (St. John xiv. is is explicit enough. But, But he, the Spirit of truth, shall come, will teach you " (*ib.* xvi. 13). Therefore, said to his apostles, "Go ach all nations . . . . e all things whatsoever I have commanded you, and behold, I am with you all days, even unto the consummation of the world" (St. Matt. xxviii. 19, 20). This is a promise of guidance of the Spirit into all truth, and of exemption from error, in anything which our Lord has said or commanded.

If we were defending the Catholic rule, we should remind the author that this promise was made to the *ecclesia docens*, and only through that to the *ecclesia credens*; but, as we are not defending the Catholic rule, we suffer him to apply it to what he calls the true people of God. Yet, if he accepts the plain declaration of our Lord himself as recorded in the Gospels, he has no authority for distinguishing between essentials and non-essentials in the revelation of God, and none at all for restricting the promise of spiritual guidance and assistance to a promise of preservation from error only in certain fundamental truths of revelation. The author must either give us the rule or authority on which he makes the distinction and limitation, or concede that he makes it by no rule, and, therefore, on no authority.

Dr. Hodge tells us (p. 151) that "all Protestants agree in teaching that the word of God, as contained in the Old and New Testaments, is the infallible rule of faith." He should have said *some* Protestants; for many who claim to be Protestants do not agree in teaching that. Will the professor say that those who do not so agree are not Protestants? By what authority? By the authority of the Bible, interpreted by private judgment? But they have the Bible and private judgment as well as he, or those who agree with him. Will he appeal to tradition? But tradition taken as a whole condemns him as well as those who differ from him. Then he must discriminate in tradi-

themselves as to what books are or are not canonical. Some would exclude the Book of Ruth and the Canticle. As to the New Testament, Luther had doubts, if our reading or memory be not at fault, of the Epistle to the Hebrews, and that of St. Jude, and rejected the Epistle of St. James, which he called an epistle of straw, probably because it flatly contradicts his doctrine of justification by faith alone; others have doubted the canonicity of these, and, in addition, of the Apocalypse, the second Epistle of St. Peter, the second and third of St. John, and that of St. Paul to Philemon; others still reject the Gospel according to St. John, and indeed the whole New Testament, except the Synoptics—and these, while they admit them as authentic, they deny to be inspired. The Princeton professor may deny these to be Protestants, but they have as good a right to exclude from the canon such books as they judge proper as had Luther and Calvin; and there is no rule by which he can make out that he is a Protestant that will not equally serve to prove that they are Protestants. The only rule available is Catholic tradition, and that condemns him as well as them.

The professor does not rely on the authority of the Synagogue, though he adduces it, to settle the canon of the Old Testament, for that would be anti-Protestant; but attempts to settle it by the authority of the New Testament. Such books as he finds a text quoted from by our Lord or his apostles he assumes to be canonical and inspired; but such as he does not find thus quoted from, he rejects from the canon. But this is not conclusive, for the author concedes that our Lord and his apostles said many things that are not recorded in the New Testament, and how does he know that in those many

unrecorded . . . . which he rejects as . . . . . which Catholics hold . . . cal, were not quoted? The authority does . . . . tion of a text from . . . . book to be canonical or book to be inspired? S Athens, cites the Greek . . . and in his Epistle to the he manifestly adopts . . . a sentiment from Plato's must we therefore conclu . poems of Arrian and Plato are canonical, and Arrian to be included in the list inspired writers? Has th any assertion of our Lord writer in the New Testam Jewish or any other bool him or by his apostles is and divinely inspired? . not. St. Paul says in I Epistle to Timothy, "All divinely inspired is profita but he does not say what are or are not divinely insp

Then, again, as to the N ment, the author concedes ing the first century and canon of the New Tests uncertain. It, then, was i by our Lord or his apos selves. On what authos was it settled? Manifestl the authority of the churc of popes and councils. Princeton professor denies rity of popes and counci the infallibility of the chu he denies that the church or Protestant, has any te thority, fallible or infalli canon neither of the New nor of the Old is settled, th infallible rule or authorit then, can the professor ma Protestants have, in that an infallible rule of faith lible rule suffices for infa

testants are unable, without
rity of the church or tradi-
ttle the canon, so are they
ithout the same authority,
ine what books are or are
ely inspired. The author
that it suffices to prove that
rs were messengers from
commissioned to speak or
is name. But that cannot
d unless they accredited
as such by their miracles,
ven then, unless the mira-
attested to us by a compe-
credible witness of them.
hat, for Protestants, is that
The Record! But the re-
have been forged or inter-
and must, before it can be
as evidence, be authenti-
low can the Protestant au-
it, except by showing that
en carefully and vigilantly
rom the first till now by an
eper with whom it was de-
Deny the church as the
y of the record, as the Pro-
es, and there is no certain
authenticating the record,
none of authenticating the
then none of establishing
of the divine commission of
d writers, and consequently
proving the divine inspira-
e sacred writings, since in-
is a supernatural fact.
l it ever occur to our learn-
sor that he has, in order to
: inspiration of the Scrip-
only to take the authority
hurch for so much, but to
efore he can allege the
of the Scriptures, all the
has to prove, in order to
e divine authority and in-
of the church? He must
at our Lord and his apostles
d wrote by divine authority,
is all the Catholic has to
n either case, the authority,
whether of the church or of the Bible, turns on the fact of the divine commission, which the Protestant must prove in the very outset as well as the Catholic, and which he cannot prove if he rejects the testimony of the church as the contemporary and living witness of the facts. The church, having been founded by and grown out of that commission, and continuing without interruption from the apostles down to us, is herself the living witness of the facts which prove the commission. She authenticates the record; but the Protestant has, in addition to authenticating the record which proves the commission, to establish the genuineness, integrity, and authenticity of the sacred writings before he can infer their divine inspiration and infallible authority, or use them as a rule of faith, and not even then unless their writers expressly declare them to be inspired, for it is possible for divinely commissioned men to write at times on matters not covered by their commission.

But we are not yet through with the Protestant's difficulties, if he is to proceed independently of Catholic tradition. Supposing him to have proved all this, he still has to prove the completeness or sufficiency of the Scriptures. Dr. Hodge does not pretend that the Scriptures contain all the revelations made by our Lord to his apostles, but only what is now extant. "It is not denied," he says (pp. 182, 183), "that there may have been, and probably were, books written by inspired men which are no longer in existence. Much less is it denied that Christ and his apostles delivered many discourses which were not recorded, and which, could they now be known, would be of equal authority with the books now regarded as canonical." But how does he know that these discourses or the

instructions they contained are now lost, or that they are not preserved and as well-known and authenticated in the traditions of the church as the canonical books themselves? Furthermore, how does he know that it is not precisely in these discourses which were not recorded that is to be found the key to the sense of those which were recorded? The church has always so held and taught; indeed, the author himself concedes that, at the first, the whole revealed word, whether written or unwritten, went by the name of the tradition, and the written tradition was not distinguished from the unwritten. He says:

"In the early church, the word [tradition] was used in this wide sense. Appeal was constantly made to the traditions, that is, the instructions the churches had received. It was only certain churches at first that received any of the written instructions of the apostles. And it was not till the end of the first century that the writings of the Evangelists and apostles were collected and formed into a canon or rule of faith. And when the books of the New Testament had been collected, the fathers spoke of them as containing the 'traditions,' that is, the instructions derived from Christ and his apostles. . . . In that age of the church, the distinction between the written and unwritten word had not yet been distinctly made. But as controversies arose and disputants on both sides of all questions appealed to 'tradition,' that is, to what they had been taught; and when it was found that these traditions differed, one church saying their teachers always taught them one thing, and another that theirs had taught them its opposite, it was felt that there should be some authoritative standard. Hence the wisest and best of the fathers [who were they?] insisted on abiding by the written word, and receiving nothing as authoritative not contained therein. In this, however, it must be confessed, they [the wisest and the best of the fathers] were not always consistent. Whenever prescription, usage, or conviction founded on unwritten evidence was available against an adversary, they did not hesitate to make use of it. Durin
early centuries, therefore, the di
between Scripture and traditio
so sharply drawn as it has been
controversies between Roman
Protestants, and especially s
decisions of the Council of Tr
108, 109).

There are several inaccur
this passage. In the early
the church, when controversi
and contradictory traditions
leged, appeal was not made
written word, but to the c
founded by St. Peter, or by hi
diate authority, that is, to
Alexandria, or Rome, or to
cil, provincial, plenary, or œ
cal, as can hardly be unknow
learned a theological scholar
Hodge.* But two facts are c
in the passage: first, that the
for a hundred years or more h
unwritten tradition or the
structions of its pastors as its
faith; and, second, that the
and the unwritten traditions
word were deemed of equal a
by the wisest and best of the
and were not as to their a
distinguished, at least not
distinguished, before the rise
testantism. The professor, the
prove that the whole chur
wrong prior to Luther in rec
the authority of the unwritte

* If the written word had been re
the sufficient and only rule of faith, th
have been no occasion to appeal to
churches or to councils to ascertain
gelical or apostolical traditions. It w
been simpler to appeal to the written w
The reason of the council, as its pur
to collect by the testimony of the pas
several churches what was the traditio
handed over to each by its apostoli
and which it had preserved. By as
thus by the testimony of each the
common to them all, the controversy
tled. The frequency of councils in the
proves that during those ages, at least,
did not adopt the Protestant rule of
that they were by no means Protest
pretence of the Reformers that they
storing primitive Christianity, prim
and usage, is to be taken as a pretence

It is worthy of remark here that our Protestant professor is obliged throughout to adopt the principle of the Catholic rule of faith, only he applies it differently. The Catholic asserts the infallibility of the Pope in matters of faith and morals by virtue of the assistance or guidance of the Holy Spirit; the Protestant professor claims the same infallibility, by virtue of the same supernatural assistance, for each one of the people of God taken individually. But the Pope is a public personage, all the world knows or may know who he is, and can recur to him, and, supposing him to be assisted as claimed, all the world may know from him the true faith; but in the Protestant sense there is no public means of knowing who the people of God are, and, consequently, no public means of knowing what the Spirit teaches, or whom he guides or assists to a knowledge of the true faith, since he guides or assists only private individuals, not a public personage or a public body. It can be no public rule of faith, and, as we have shown, none for the individual himself, for he has no objective and independent rule for determining whether the spirit that leads him is the spirit of truth or the spirit of error. The professor has refuted his own doctrine in his refutation of the Quaker rule of faith. The interior illumination, he asserts, is private, and can be brought to no public or catholic test. Not the church, both because the church the Protestant recognizes is invisible, and recognizable by no external marks or notes, and because the church, according to him, has no teaching authority or faculty. Not to the Scriptures, because it is the test of the right understanding of them that is required, and to take them as the test of this is to reason in a vicious circle.

Protestants, his
ed, arrived at t
Protestantism, no
through the applic
and the fact is,
cally assert their
proved or obtained
testantism. They
prove their Protest
prove their rule, an
their rule in order
testantism. This i
nience. But, assur
that the Scriptures
and only rule of fa
against undeniabl
Bible is a plain boo
to the people, to ev
as it should be
divine Author to
and only rule of
their conclusion u
dify their statemen
their conclusion
necessary to sal
ing no agreement a
themselves who tak
sufficient and only
to what things are
tion, they divide.
more or less distinc
tive faith is necess
and another class, is
ed our author, as
taining the right of
the private illumina
Ghost as the rule fo
Scriptures, apparent
that they are in fl
tion with themselves

The professor ol
tradition as the rule
not adapted to that
of faith to the peop
thing they can appl
which they can jud
written tradition is
any one volume a
people and intelli
This were a valid

...to seek through all history and verify the tradition; objection at all, if we suppose an infallible teacher, always who preserves and applies how for the people. But Protestant escape his own by rejecting all unwritten and making the Bible alone of faith, which is at least as ble to the people as is unradition explained and apduly authorized preachers ord?

...e Bible ought, on Protestant, to be a plain book, interself to every person of ordie, or who has enough sense moral agent, we concede, stants should actually dedoctrines from it. But no...ws better than our author er is a fact. He knows that stant people, however much read and praise the Bible, m their own opinions from m their pastors or teachers, mmunity in which they are up. He knows, also, that e could never of themselves en the doctrines which he be essential and necessary om from reading the Bible Unitarians and Universalists t the Bible teaches them, people, as a matter of fact, from the tradition of their at best only find confirm them in the Scriptures; uch are the exigencies of sm that the ablest and most Protestant professors d in the face of these facts, with Chillingworth, "The Bible alone, is the religion ...ants."

...otestants should bear in t Catholics have the Bible d them-and it ages before ...ants ever heard of, and that it was from Catholics that they obtained it—strictly speaking, from the church *stole* it. How, then, can it be their religion any more than it is the religion of Catholics? Catholics, if they have not admitted it to contain the whole revealed word, have always held it, before Protestantism and since, to be divinely inspired, and, as far as it goes, the infallible word of God. They have always held that all Christians are bound to believe whatever it teaches, and forbidden to believe anything that contradicts it. This is all that Protestantism can really say. The church contends that in no respect does her doctrine conflict with the written word, and is in most respects, if not in all, positively sustained by it. Suppose her as fallible as Protestants confess themselves to be, what can Protestants have in the Bible that Catholics have not? or what have they from any source that can override the Catholic understanding of the Scriptures, or authorize them to say that it is a misunderstanding? Catholics may have more than Protestants, but in no case have they or can they have less. By what rule or standard, then, do Protestants judge the Catholic understanding of the Scriptures to be false and the Protestant understanding to be true? Private judgment is no rule, and, if it were, Catholics have private judgment as well as Protestants; they have, too, reason, Biblical, historical, and all other sorts of learning, as well as they, and, at least, in as eminent a degree. By what rule or standard of judgment, then, is Protestantism to be pronounced more Biblical than is Catholicity?

The professor says: "The people have the right of private judgment, and are bound to read and interpret the Bible for themselves." In matters left to private judgment,

hand, or into mysticism and cendentalism on the other. The is of both were in the original estant movement, and may be detected even in our Princeton ssor. Into one or the other he run, if he ever gets out of the vicious circle in which Protestantism, pretending to be Christian, necessarily gyrates, unless the grace of God relieves him and enables him to return to the bosom of the Catholic Church, where alone he will find true freedom and truth in its unity and integrity.

DANTE'S PURGATORIO.

CANTO SECOND.

is Canto of the *Purgatorio* is the one which contains that episode of the music-master, to which Milton alludes in his celebrated Sonnet to Henry Lawes, and perhaps all the more ated from this allusion to the passage in Dante.

sella was a dear friend of Dante's, and used to set his *canzoni* to music, and sing them with which it must have been delicious for Dante to have made immortal. Dante supposes in the hat Casella had gone to Rome in the year of the Jubilee, and, coming thence by sea, had d near the mouth of the Tiber.

r Canto I. of this translation, see CATHOLIC WORLD for November, 1870

Now that horizon whose meridian arch
  Hangs o'er Jerusalem its topmost height
The sun had reached: while opposite, her march
  Holding in countercourse, the circling Night
Walked forth from Ganges, bearing in her hand
  The Scales that she lets fall with her advance,
So that the morning's cheeks where I did stand
  From white and red grew orange to my glance.

Beside the sea we made a brief delay,
  Like lingering men, that on their journey dream,
Who go in spirit, but in body stay:
  And lo! as when, surprised by morning's beam,
Through the gross vapors Mars doth redly burn
  Down in the west upon the ocean floor;
A light appeared—oh! may that light return—
  So rapidly those waters travelling o'er,
That to its motion flying were but slow:
  Then, having momently withdrawn my gaze
To question of my Guide, I looked, and lo!
  Larger it burned, and seemed almost ablaze!
Soon from each side thereof, although I knew
  Naught what they were, something appeared of white,
And underneath another of like hue
  Little by little grew upon my sight.

My Master spake not: I meantime could spell
  Wings in those first white objects at the side:
Soon as he recognized the pilot well,
  "Behold God's Angel!—bend thy knees!" he cried:
"Lift up thy palms to him—now in thy ken
  See one of heaven's high ministers indeed!
Look, how he scorneth all device of men;
  He nor of oars nor any sail hath need
Save his own pinions (while he beats the air
  And heavenward stretches those eternal pens),
From shore to shore so distant—plumes that ne'er
  Moult like the changing tresses that are men's."

Then as more near and nearer to us drew
  That divine bird, so grew the splendor more
Till scarce the eye could bear a closer view:
  I bent mine down, and he arrived ashore
With a fleet skiff, so light upon the flood
  That without wake it skimmed the water's breast:
High on the stern the heavenly helmsman stood,
  In aspect such as Holy Writ calls Blest.
More than an hundred spirits in one band
  Within sat blending in one voice their strains,
"*In exitu Isràel*—From the land
  Of Egypt"—and what else that psalm contains.†

The sign of holy cross he made them then,
  Whereat they bounded all upon the strand,
And he, swift as he came, sped back again.
  The crowd that stayed looked wildly round, and scan
The place like strangers coming to things new.
  Now on all sides had Phœbus pierced the day
With his keen arrows, which so fiercely flew
  That Capricorn was chased from heaven's midway,
When the new-comers raised their brows to us,
  Saying: "Show us the pathway, if ye know,
Up to the mountain." Virgil answered thus:
  "Perchance you think us dwellers here? Not so.
We, like yourselves, are only pilgrims here:
  Just before you, and by another way,
We came, a road so rugged, so severe,
  That climbing this will seem thereto as play.
The spirits, by my breathing who could guess
  That I was living, wan with wonder grew;
And just as people round a herald press
  Who comes with olive wreaths, to hear what new

* "Blessed are the pure in heart: for they shall see God."
† Psalm cxiv.

Came crying: "How now, tardy spirits—why
  This negligence? why lingering do ye plod?
Run to the mountain, that from every eye
  The scales may fall that seal your sight from God."

As doves in barley, gathering grain or tares
  (Busy at pasture in a single flock,
Quiet, nor showing their accustomed airs),
  If aught approach the timid tribe to shock,
Fly from their food, assailed by greater care,
  So quit the song this new-come troop, and started
Hillward, like one who goes unknowing where:
  And with no less a pace we, too, departed.

THE LATE GENERAL CONVENTION OF THE PROTEST EPISCOPAL CHURCH.

THE doings of a body so large, and in a worldly point of view so respectable, as the Episcopal Church, ought to be of some consequence to the public. Unfortunately, however, the negative character of its legislation prevents it from reaching the wants of the day, or speaking to the heart of a restless age which is bent on physical progress. The gentlemen who form the convention meet together every three years, and spend three weeks in moving the interesting machinery of legislation, without doing anything whatever, and in disappointing every one who asks for a positive statement in matters of doctrine or discipline. Their body is formed after the plan of the United States Congress, and has no counterpart in any period of ecclesiastical history. The bishops form the upper house or senate, and the clerical and lay deputies constitute the lower or more popular house, one half of which is composed of ministers and one half of laymen. Each house acts as a restraint upon the oth no law can be passed witho agreement of the two branches. bishops might be disposed to the creed or make some new ar faith for their communion, bu cannot do so without the cons the deputies. The same thing of the ministers in the conv The laymen have a veto upo pastors, who in turn can tie legislation of their flock. A tive lay-vote in the lower hou nullify even the action of the b in council, as well as the wis the reverend clergy. If, for ex the Episcopal body should pro pass a law on ritual, and the mi were agreed to it, the lay d could defeat it by an adverse There is something very pecu this equalization of ecclesiastic rogatives between ministers an men, which strikes the unpr eye as unique and strange. Th stitution of the Protestant Epi Church was formed, as we hav

done. Although the convention did not pass any of the proposed canons against ritualism, it is yet true that an anti-ritualistic spirit was disclosed, which was entirely unexpected, and in the presence of which scarcely any one, in either house, dared to avow himself a ritualist. Although the convention did not repeal the restrictive and exclusive canons, still the evidence was most marked of the progress of liberal sentiments. If the questions involved in these canons had come fairly before the convention, we believe that the result would have surprised every one, and satisfied those who have been hopeless of favorable action.

"In our view, this convention has marked a transition period in the history of the Protestant Episcopal Church. The old ruts have been obliterated, and new paths of progress have been opened. It is our profound conviction that there has not been a convention for many years which has revealed a prospect so encouraging for truly liberal and evangelical principles."

The internal spirit of a legislative body is, however, hard to understand except from its public acts, and when there are no such satisfactory acts, honest observers may differ in their judgment. The High Churchmen felicitate themselves that their tenets were not pulled to pieces, while Low Churchmen see a *spirit* which accords with their sentiments, and so take courage for the future.

In spite of all these causes of happiness, the advanced ritualists find much to complain of, because the bishops, *though apostles*, did not realize their dignity, and the ministers, though *actually Catholic priests*, did not seem to know it. Besides their ignorance of "liturgies, ritual, canon law, and theology," they were not reverent in the house of God, nor did they seem to feel that they were, what the *Churchman* calls them, "apostles, occupied with the faith and practice of the apostolic age, and framing their conduct and teaching according to a model seventeen hundred years old [illegible] represented by Protestant [illegible] In church they seemed to [illegible] "real presence," and to [illegible] and sociable gentlemen, [illegible] meet their friends of the [illegible] century. So says the *Church*[illegible]

"Men and women seem too [illegible] excited for reverent devotion [illegible] merely was loud talking and [illegible] going on at one end of the [illegible] fore the blessed sacrament was [illegible] ed, but, within the very sanctu[illegible] bishops were seen exchanging [illegible] tesies of society with one han[illegible] with the other they were hol[illegible] Lord's body and blood. The[illegible] there cannot be proper reverence [illegible] building which is during one [illegible] scene of exciting debate and [illegible] of unrestrained conversation [illegible] the next, devoted to what ought [illegible] solemn worship of Almighty God[illegible] ly all the clergy and laity, ritua[illegible] cluded, seemed at times to fe[illegible] Emmanuel Church, though [illegible] convention hall, was a consecrat[illegible] of prayer. Constant introducti[illegible] sequent chattings, mild flirtati[illegible] ladies, and the frequent use [illegible] glasses, did a great deal toward[illegible] ing reverence for God's sanctuar[illegible] could not but feel the evil hab[illegible] dered there found its way into [illegible] the churches in which divine [illegible] was held on the following Sund[illegible]

As for the impression p[illegible] upon the world, we can [illegible] spirit of the press, which has [illegible] itself much in studying the [illegible] of using words, and saying [illegible] which the Protestant Episcop[illegible] cil possesses in the highest [illegible] Every one of the other [illegible] bodies has a distinctive c[illegible] and uses words according [illegible] received interpretation of [illegible] tionaries. The Episcopalian[illegible] ever, sit upon the [illegible] their faces now to the [illegible] now to the south, and [illegible] Sibyl, so as to be [illegible] with every one. No [illegible]

lian hierarchy we do not see; but this is none of our business. Our sympathies are with those who want it, and are unable to get it.

A joint committee of bishops and ministers has been appointed or continued on *religious reform* in Italy.

As far as we can learn, the labor of this committee will be very arduous. They are to watch for Catholics and infidels in Italy who turn Episcopalians. There are not many of these converts, but for this very reason they will be all the more difficult to find and provide for.

We would humbly suggest that a *branch* of their *branch* of the *one* church be established there, with a bishop whose travelling expenses should be prepaid, no matter what the cost may be. A committee in the United States can hardly be adequate to this critical work, for if there is no Episcopalian minister at hand when a man or woman is at the point of converting, he or she may be gathered in by a sect of Protestants who have no bishops. We should also have recommended that this committee have power to act in Bavaria, especially as there is no time to lose. Still, as our advice may not be understood, we do not press the subject. Old Dr. Döllinger has valid orders, and so has poor Father Hyacinthe, and might possibly be saved for the cause of Episcopacy.

Another thing which moves us very much is the magnitude of the work again thrown on the committee who are to seek for union with the Eastern heretical churches. So little has been accomplished beyond an exchange of courtesies that we fear the means are not adequate to the end.

Anglicans have already signified their willingness to throw the "Filioque" out of the creed, and to give up thus the doctrine of the Trinity,

but this does not
two or four bodi
ther. The Easter
the Anglicans her
have no orders, w
they prostrate the
walls of Constanti
burg, and ask for
of recognition. W
committee have d
as the prophet u
Baal, we beg t
These venerable p
sibly be asleep, o
ney. If they wo
the Episcopal m
certainly be a prie
American Branch
to adopt the Rus
is very like the R
could be translated
same doctrines a
in Russian or in C
in Latin, and the
Orthodox Church,
Catholic Church
in great error. T
Church, having
Thirty-nine Artic
ther severely the A
but our good frien
bear more than
discouraged. Be
reach the public,
copal Committee
opportunity to wa
Duke Alexis and
Church for his c
stay in New Yor
has been cut of
trunk can be can
tance to shade a
out of the ground
bility and from i
"How good and
is to see brethren
in unity!"

At the next c
to hear something
regular resolution

tee reported very plainly, and gave an opinion which can be understood. They recommended a canon which should forbid all the peculiar actions of the ritualists, such as "the use of incense, the placing or retaining a crucifix in any part of the church, the use of lights about the holy table, the elevation, of the *elements* in holy communion for the purpose of adoration, the mixing of water with the wine, the washing of the priest's hands, the ablution of the vessels, the celebration of holy communion when there is no one to receive, and using any prayers or services not contained in the *Book of Common Prayer*." This recommendation was referred to a joint committee, who, not being able to agree perfectly, brought forth as the result of their labors the draft of a law which makes the rule of ritual the *Prayer-Book* and "the canons of the Church of England in use in the American Provinces before 1789, and not subsequently superseded, altered, or repealed." Then, as few seemed to know about these canons, it was determined to appoint a new committee to find out about them, and inform the next General Convention. In the meantime, all mixed questions were to be settled by the bishops in their various dioceses, should it please them to interfere, or should any brother be offended by excess or defect of ritual. The evident result of all this legislation was to leave the whole matter just where it was before. This canon did not, however, seem to please. Some of the members wished to know what these "customs before 1789" were, before they could intelligently act, and on a division of the house the project was lost. Substitutes a little more decisive were offered, and they did not meet with favor. The bishops, anxious as it would seem to have some action taken on the su sent down to the deputies the f ing resolution, which they had ed, and for which they asked th currence of their brethren :

"*Resolved* (the House of Cleric Lay Deputies concurring), That t lowing canon be adopted and er to be entitled Canon ——:

"The elevation of the elements holy communion in such manner expose them to the view of the pe objects toward which adoration is made, in or after the prayer of cor tion, or in the act of administering or in carrying them to or from th municants, and any gesture, post act implying such adoration, an ceremony not prescribed as part order of the administration of the Supper or holy communion in th *of Common Prayer*, and the celeb or reception of the holy communi any bishop or priest when no pers ceives with him ; likewise, the u any administration of the holy cc nion, of any hymns, prayers, co epistles, or gospels other than appointed in the authorized form of the church or under § 14 of can title 1, of the Digest, are hereby f den."

This resolution was put to and lost by a small majority o clerical vote. The following p sition was then offered and ad unanimously, which, so far a know, was the end of the mat the convention :

"*Resolved*, That this convention l expresses its decided condemnati all ceremonies, observances, and ces which are fitted to express a dc foreign to that set forth in the auth standards of this church."

A slight review of this remar action on the subject of ritual show that the bishops were ar to pass a law against the pra peculiar to the few good peopl are called ritualists, but that were outvoted by the clerical

hat nothing has been done
ll have any weight. For
ws what the doctrine set
he authorized standards of
opal Church is? And who
nine when ceremonies con-
e doctrine about which no
ain? The Thirty-nine Ar-
k plainly enough when they
at "the sacrament of the

and do as they have done, interpreting the standards to suit themselves, and, above all, taking advantage of that blessed *Use of Sarum* which has been to them a source of so great consolation.

Appropriately of all this, we give an extract from the *Church Weekly*, regulating the order of service for the third week of November.

KALENDAR FOR THE WEEK.

Day of Week.	NOVEMBER.	Concordance.	Observance.	Altar Color.	
				Sarum.	Rom.
S.	24th after Trinity, . . .	..	Feast.	R.	G.
M.	[S. Edmund, K. M., . . .	A*	..	R.	R.
W.	[S. Cecilia, V. M., . . .	C*	..	R.	R.
Th.	[S. Clement, Bp. Rome, M., .	..	..	R.	R.
S.	[S. Katharine, V. M., . .	C*	..	R.	R.
S.	Sunday next before ADVENT,†	..	Feast.	..	G.

* Except in American Church. † Give notice of S. Andrew's Day.

ipper was not by Christ's
reserved, carried about,
or worshipped," and that
ifices of Masses were blas-
fables and dangerous de-
we are told that these words
ean anything which could
elevation and adoration
ly Eucharist, or the private
n of the sacrifice of the

moreover informed that
les are of no authority, al-
nfessedly they are the only
ch the Protestant Episco-
h possesses. So, when men
eriously argue, and quietly
other in the face, we de-
finding any words which
misinterpreted. So, as they
hanks to God for his great
r ritual friends will go on,

It must be observed that "Calendar" is spelt with a K, which is more ancient, and that the "authorized standards" of the Episcopal Rite have nothing about S. Edmund, S. Cecilia, S. Clement, nor S. Catharine (spelt with a K). The "altar color" is also very useful, especially as they give at the last column the Roman Rite. A friend of ours told us of a very solemn marriage which he witnessed in Trinity Church the other day. The Rev. Dr. Dix was the celebrant (as he thought), with a deacon and subdeacon, all beautifully vested, and the candidates were a young priest and a young lady, who in this most impressive manner was to become his wife. Oh! what will the Greeks say to this? We fear they will be scandalized, and that even the giving up of the "Filioque" will not

prevent them from staring with eyes wide open. The priest said the nuptial mass, and the other priest and his wife received the holy communion and the sacrament of matrimony. How does this compare with the services before 1789?

We cannot, however, pass over the action and language of the bishops in this matter. We suppose our Anglican friends will admit that neither priests nor laymen are by any rule of ecclesiastical antiquity allowed to judge in council on points of faith. This has generally been left to the episcopate, to which, in union with its head, Christ committed the government of his church. Now, for the advanced High Churchmen it is a sad fact that the bishops of their church have unqualifiedly condemned them. They have done this, first in the canon which they passed and sent down to the House of Deputies, and, secondly, in the language of their pastoral, which is the accurate expression of their doctrine. We know that their words can be explained away, but we respectfully submit that this time the attempt to do so will be dishonesty. If these reverend fathers in God can speak at all, then they have spoken. We give their words, and pray they may fall upon the open ears of their children who bow down before them as "apostles": "The doctrine which chiefly attempts to express itself by ritual, in questionable and dangerous ways, is connected with the Holy Eucharist. That doctrine is emphatically *a novelty in theology*. What is known as eucharistical adoration is undoubtedly inculcated and encouraged by that ritual of posture *lately* introduced among us, which finds no warrant in our 'Office for the Administration of Holy Communion.'" They then go on to say that whatever presence of Christ there may be is such as does not allow him to be there worshipped, and that to a elements is "an awful err give an extract from a write of our New York journals, w up to this time, to be hon understanding of his spiritua

"3. There are bishops : ops; there are doctors and Here is the Bishop of Arizo stance, who says that 'that (eucharistic adoration) is a *theology*.' But there is St. whilom Bishop of Milan, who adore the flesh of Christ in tl ies.' Here is the Bishop of Ce York, who declares that 'the and the practice which it implie certainly unauthorized by Holy and entirely aside from the pu which the holy sacrament was i But there is St. Gregory of N not recently, indeed, but most t op of Constantinople, who use pression, 'Calling upon him worshipped upon the altar.' H Bishop of Delaware, who unite Bishop of Connecticut in sa 'the doctrine and the practice implies are most dangerous in dencies.' But there is the poor Hippo, Augustine by name, w tunately for his reputation, c himself to the declaration that eateth that flesh till he have firs And how many other bishops, small, there are who have acted dictum of the misguided Afri only knows!"

His appeal is from bishop op, and from doctor to do cording to his own private ju We are pained more than we press at the malicious quibbl distort words so emphatical We submit that, if Jesus present in the Eucharist, he adored by all but infidels; ondly, that, if the bread is h as he said it was, it canno same time be bread, since stances cannot coexist in t space. All changes of wo the terms "spiritual and c are only the unfortunate soph

nor did they profess to say what regeneration means"; that in saying what it was not, they aimed to give no explanation whatever of the word. We give two short extracts, one from the *Churchman*, and the other from the *Church Weekly*, which for candor and sincerity certainly deserve the first premium:

"The object aimed at was 'the quieting of the consciences of sundry members of the church.' It was not to give an exhaustive definition of the word. Certain persons claimed that the term might be interpreted to signify a moral change in the subject of baptism. They knew that many would so understand it. And so the bishops, being asked, stated what no sound churchman ever denied, and no well-read theologian and respectable student of the meaning of language ever denied, namely, 'that the word is not so used' in that connection. The thing asked for was granted. The object aimed at was accomplished, and those who represented the unquiet consciences have acknowledged their grateful appreciation.

"We can illustrate this point by a single example. Some readers of the Bible may think that, whenever the word 'day' occurs in the first chapters of Genesis, it must mean a period of twenty-four hours. Common people have come to understand it in that sense. Now, suppose that the question has been raised in some Baptist or Congregational 'Sabbath-school.' The teachers think a declaration from their pastor or bishop—if they please to call him so—to the effect that the word does not of necessity imply a period of time limited to twice twelve hours, would quiet the consciences of some of their pupils who have studied geology. Suppose the thing asked for is granted: are we, therefore, to conclude that the pastor has pretended to give a definition of the word 'day,' and to state exactly 'what it does mean'? Shall we speak of him as having 'grappled with' the creation question, and yet 'failed to tell a waiting' Sabbath-school what the exact time indicated by that word 'day' was—whether ten thousand years, as some believe, or, as others think, ten million?"

"Alas! the House of Bishops have put forth a definition which is *no* definition! They pretend to define, and yet they do *not* define! [illegible] ever ignorant of [illegible] laugh in his sleeve at [illegible] tion, which will have [illegible] of making manifest [illegible] or the insincerity of "[illegible] vided that they remain [illegible] For, if the latter remain [illegible] it must be either because [illegible] a definition from an evasion of [illegible] or because they are in [illegible] excuse for not carrying out the [illegible] ous threats with which they [illegible] for some time past making [illegible] and night hideous to all peace[illegible] men."

The respect here shown [illegible] right reverend fathers in [illegible] nearly as great as their [illegible] Now, we insist that the new [illegible] water and the Holy Ghost [illegible] moral change of the most i[illegible] kind, and that even the fo[illegible] of original sin cannot ta[illegible] without such a change. [illegible] take the words of the [illegible] Catechism, and leave it to [illegible] mind if regeneration dete[illegible] *moral change*. There we a[illegible] that the inward grace, in[illegible] from baptism, else it is no s[illegible] is "a death unto sin and a [illegible] unto righteousness; for, b[illegible] nature born in sin, and the [illegible] of wrath, we are hereby [illegible] children of grace." To be [illegible] child of grace surely require[illegible] change, which the bisho[illegible] They will, therefore, have to [illegible] a new catechism or a new [illegible] ary. As for the quibbles [illegible] sense of the word "deter[illegible] if the venerable prelates [illegible] sport with the common [illegible] constituents, they are [illegible] deserve the notice of any [illegible] man. The plain fact is [illegible] pute, that the supreme [illegible] the Protestant Episcopal [illegible] formally denied the doctrine [illegible] tismal regeneration, which [illegible] tained in the Catechism and

bidden, as far as their words go, the *ordinary* practice of confession, and that they deprecate it as "an engine of oppression and a source of corruption." It remains now to be seen whether these counsels of the chief pastors of the Protestant Episcopal Church are to be followed by their children who think them to be successors of the apostles and fathers in God. Will the Right Rev. Dr. Potter, who once published, as we have been informed, a manual for the examination of conscience, to whom a prayer-book, with directions for confession, has been publicly dedicated, now interfere and put a stop to this great abuse? Will the handful of *ritual priests* in this city cease to sit in their pews or their libraries to hear and absolve penitents? To speak our honest opinion, the words of the bishops will have no influence whatever, and things will go on precisely as they did before. We only venture to wish, for the sake of propriety, that confessionals might be erected in all these churches, where at least the female penitents might be heard. We assure our friends that this advice comes from a good heart. If they cannot hear confessions in public, they would do well for themselves not to hear them at all.

The most reverend prelates go on to condemn "the tendency towards saint-worship, and especially its culmination in the worship of the Blessed Virgin." "The bare suggestion that the intercession of the Virgin Mary, or of any other saint, is in any way to be sought in our approaches to the throne of grace, is an *indignity* to the one only Mediator and Intercessor which we, his *apostolic* witnesses, cannot too strongly nor distinctly forbid in his holy and all-sufficient name." Is this language plain enough for our ritualistic friends? Do they think these words equivocal? They as *apostles* have forbidden any one to seek the prayers of the Mother of God or of any other saint. To do so is to offer indignity to Christ, according to their theology. On the same principle, Episcopalians must not ask the prayers of each other, unless they wish to insult the one Intercessor. The reason why the saints cannot intercede for us is that Jesus Christ alone may do it. We cannot, therefore, suppose that living men or women are in a different position in this respect from their departed brethren, especially from the great heroes of Christianity. We really blush at the stupidity of men who call themselves teachers and wear episcopal robes, but it is not our business to criticise their directions to their flock. We simply put before the world what they have so plainly said. All invocation of any one but Christ is to be stopped within their communion by their solemn decree, if, indeed, it was ever practised.

From this restriction of prayer, they pass on to condemn the devotional books which "have been insidiously multiplied of late years in England and America, and are alien in their character to the whole spirit of the Liturgy." We presume they here refer to the translations of Catholic books of devotion which have become for some time past the pious nourishment of all the advanced Episcopalians. We have seen many of these works ourselves, and have even seen the *Book of Common Prayer* bound up with parts of the Missal, and preparations for communion and confession taken from well-known Catholic authors. This, to say the least, is an acknowledgment that their own church does not feed their souls, and that they seek a life it can neither give nor support. This alone ought to be sufficient to send them where

find a religious system ac-
rth their wants. Certainly
do as they like in the mat-
y can put on all our vest-
d their bishops may wear
crosses, and bear mitres
ers, and they may cross
s with the left hand, and
before an altar which is
or stone. They may call
s the only Catholics in the
d out-herod Herod himself,
y put us Romanists in the
ut we think the bishops are
ll them that all this is in-
with Episcopalianism, and
ought to be either one thing
er. A man has a right *be-*
ne to play the Harlequin;
e a *moral* right to do so?
onest or fair thing to remain
ch and use devotions and
trines which it condemns?
aid of "that liberty where-
st has made us free." But
be a liberty to contradict
to profess to be what we
nd to carry private judg-
bsurdity? We are forced in
commend the advice of the
nd to say with them to our
ds, "Gentlemen and ladies,
h to use Catholic books, be
igh to go where they be-
lease do not attempt to
our people a spirituality
foreign to our Protestant
on." From our past know-
wever, we do not believe
ounsel of the reverend fa-
produce much effect. We
as ever have Catholic books
on luxuriously bound (the
oes a great ways), "and
o the use of the *American*
For our own part, we hope
will be the case, since the
of our prayers, and the
the masters of the spiritual
life, may do much to lead souls to the one true faith.

3. A few remarks will now suffice to show the position in which the Protestant Episcopal Church has placed herself by the action of this convention. If we regard the whole body, including the laymen as well as the clerical deputies, we can see how true to its birthmarks has been the legislation of a communion which glories in the non-committal character of its creed and profession. Two or three parties, with views diametrically opposite, are thus kept together, and in the diversity of opinions is the safety of the whole. When the Episcopal Church begins to have anything like a faith, then will it fall to pieces, and new sects will arise of its component parts. How long it will go on holding together High Church and Low Church, Broad Church and no church at all, we do not know. But this we think, its Protestant character is now well established to all mankind. Not one single link which could bind it to the doctrine or practice of the past has been left. If it will not baptize itself with the names of Luther, Calvin, or Zwingle, it can boast of no father or mother. In the words of its Bishop Lee, if it is not a *Protestant* church, it disowns its birth, and has no right to be called a church. Through the most solemn action of its supreme authority it has denied the real presence of Christ in the Holy Eucharist, the regeneration of children in baptism, the intercession of the saints, and the practice of confession. As for the ritualists, they have been handled without mercy, and their whole system of faith and worship summarily condemned. It will be of little avail to them to say that the bishops only have pronounced a decision, and that the division of the clerical and *lay*

vote in four or five dioceses saved them from a prohibitory canon of the whole convention. Are the presbyters and lay deputies the successors of the apostles, whom the Lord instituted to govern the church of God? Who made the sheep of the flock the judges in ecclesiastical causes?

We have no heart to believe that the condemnation of the bishops will do any good with the majority of them. A few earnest souls will come, one by one, into the true fold of the Good Shepherd, where a man has to *receive* and obey Christ, and not *make* a religion for himself. Yet we fear, and with sadness we say it, that no power whatever could open the eyes of many. If their church should deny the Holy Trinity or the incarnation of God the Son, they would explain away the denial. Blow after blow with a rough hand has been given to these so-called Catholics within the past few years. Many are not shaken, but in spite of all the decisions of their councils and the admonition of their pastors, they go on insisting on vanity, erecti idol which their own hands made, and blindly falling do worship it. Who shall reaso men who have histories an grammars and dictionaries o own? Who but God in his mercy can roll away the dark hearts which walk in a vain and disquiet themselves for calling evil good and good Here logic is wasted, and th with its lessons, ignored, as Word made flesh had never b earth, nor quickened with grace our fallen humanity. Catholics, let us to prayer, th souls may not die eternally their Father's house, strangers Bread of Life. In their grea the pitying heart of Jesus c will hear, and scales shall fal many eyes. Oh! how sad to long and far in this weary li then only to see from a dista promised land, but never to the tabernacles of the G Jacob.

CHATEAU REGNIER.

A CHRISTMAS STORY OF THE TWELFTH CENTURY.

A PROUD man was the Baron Regnier. In the old days of Charlemagne, the Château Regnier had risen, a modest mansion on the pleasant banks of the Garonne. That great monarch died; his empire fell to pieces; the lords became each one an independent sovereign in his own castle, making perpetual war on each other, and electing kin could enforce neither respe obedience. Then the Châtea nier was enlarged and fortif retainers and vassals became ous, and, as was the method o ing rich in those times, large of horsemen would sally fr gates, as suited their pleasure cessities, to plunder neighborin or defenceless travellers.

Regnier were brave
never was there a brilliant or
ous expedition wherein some
of the house did not distin-
nimself. When the first preach-
the Crusades stirred the soul
ope, there was bustle of pre-
n and burnishing of weapons
château; even in the motley
ny of Peter the Hermit went
the younger sons of the fami-
did his part of plundering in
ry and Dalmatia, and perish-
the shores of the Bosphorus;
the more orderly expedition
ollowed, the reigning baron
led a brave array under
nner of Raymond of Tou-

return of the crusaders
t more refined tastes into
, though not more peaceable
s. The Château Regnier was
d and beautified; troubadours
d there; feasts were continu-
read; still plunder and anar-
re the order of the day till
gn of Louis le Gros. That
ic king devoted his life to
hing law and order in France.
he house of Regnier, having
ed all that it conveniently
took part with the king to
all further plundering, so it
rong in its possessions.

such a line of ancestry to
ack on, no wonder that the
Regnier was proud. He him-
his youth had shared in the
s of a crusade. After his
ome, he had married a beau-
fe, whom he tenderly loved;
happiness had been of short
; in three years after their
he died, leaving him an image
lf—a frail and lovely little
he last flower on the rugged
that great house.

vely land is the south of
Two thousand years ago the old geographer of Pontus* called it the Beautiful, and its soft *langue d'or* is the very language of love. It was on the shores of the Garonne, in the twelfth century, that the troubadours sang their sweetest songs. Among them was found Pierre Rogiers, who wearied once of the cloister, and so wandered out into the world—to the court of the beautiful Ermengarde of Narbonne, to the palaces of Aragon, at last to the shores of the Garonne, and, finding everywhere only vanity of vanities, once more entered the gates of the monastery and lay down to die.

Here, too, lived Bernard de Ventadour, who loved and celebrated in his songs more than one royal princess. Here he dwelt in courtly splendor, till he too grew weary of all things earthly, and yearned for the quiet of the cloister, and, wrapping the monk's robe around him, he too died in peace.

No wonder if Clemence Regnier, growing up a beautiful girl in the midst of these influences, should yield her soul to the soft promptings of affection. She was the favorite companion of her father; no wish of hers was ungratified; her sweetness of temper endeared her to all around her. She was sought in marriage by many rich nobles of Toulouse; she refused them all, and gave her preference to the younger son of a neighboring baron—a penniless and landless knight.

When the old baron first discovered their mutual attachment, he was at first incredulous, then amazed, then angry. He persistently and peremptorily refused his consent. The De Regniers had for so long married, as they had done everything else, only to augment their power and wealth, that a marriage where

* Καλὴ δὲ καὶ ἡ τῶν Αβοκλων.—*Strabo.*

love and happiness only were considered, was an absurd idea to the baron.

"This comes of all these *jongleurs* and their trashy songs!" he exclaimed; "they have got nothing to do but wander about the world and turn girls' and boys' heads with their songs. I'll have no more of them here!"

So the baron turned all poets and musicians out of his château, but he could not turn love and romance out; the young heart of Clemence was their impregnable citadel, and there they held their ground against all the baron's assaults.

Four years went by; Clemence was pining away with grief, for she loved her father and she loved her lover; at last, her love for the latter prevailed, and, trusting to win the old baron's forgiveness afterwards, Clemence fled from the château with the young Count de Regnault.

Baron de Regnier was a man who, when moderately irritated, gave vent to his wrath in angry words, but when deeply wounded he was silent; and here both his pride and his affection had been wounded most deeply.

He signified to the guests at the castle that they might depart; he closed the grand halls, keeping near him a few old servants; dismissed his chaplain, whom he suspected, though falsely, of having married the runaway couple, and who had been their messenger to him, begging for his forgiveness and permission to come to him; closed his chapel doors; and shut himself up, gloomy and alone, in a suite of rooms in a wing of the château.

Many loving and penitent messages came to him from Clemence. At first he took no notice of them: at last, to one he returned an answer—"He would never see her again."

II.

The summer came and th
and many a summer and
passed, and the dreariest do
all France was the once mer
teau Regnier. Year after y
old man brooded alone. I
ship or chance brought gues
château, they were receiv
stately formality, which forba
stay; rarely did a stranger
night within its walls. The
ers kept their Christmas hol
best they might; no great
opened and lighted, no fe
spread. They wondered h
the baron would live such a l
what would become of the
should he die, for he had no
take it.

Ten years passed: the o
began to grow tired at last
solitude; he listened to the v
conscience—it reproached hi
ten long years of neglected
The first thing he did was t
the doors of his chapel. I
for artisans and ordered it
repaired and refitted, then he
messenger to the Bishop o
louse, asking him to send a c
to the Château Regnier.

The church was in thos
what she is now—the great
of the world; but at that ti
was the *only* republic, the
pregnable citadel where, t
all the centuries that we
middle ages, the liberties a
equality of men held their
against hereditary right and
despotism. In the monast
prior was often of lowly birt
among the humbler brethren
he ruled might be found r
patrician, even of royal
Virtue and talent were the on
acknowledged; the noble kn
confessed his sins, and receiv

from the hand of the serf.
side the princely-born Ber-
see the name of Fulbert,
strious Bishop of Chartres,
the episcopal throne from
nd obscurity—as he himself
icut de stercore pauper"; and
long friend and minister of
ne Sixth, Suger, the abbot of
s, and regent of France, was
of a bourgeois of St. Omer.

happened that when the
nt to the Bishop of Toulouse
aplain, a young priest, who
son of a vassal of Château
threw himself at the pre-
t, and begged that he might
The bishop looked on him
prise and displeasure.

seigneur," said the priest,
proach me in your heart for
pears to you my presump-
d boldness in making this
I have a most-earnest rea-
the love of God, in asking
a very brief time do I ask
in chaplain at the Château
but I do most earnestly ask
he was sent.

oung Père Rudal had been
hildhood a favorite with the
It was the baron who had
en notice of the bright boy,
had sent him away to the
hools of Lyons to be educat-
l now, when he saw his for-
orite return to him, the old
heart warmed again, and
to the young priest.

s with strange emotions that
Rudal stood once more in
e of his childhood. When a
boy there, with no very
plans for life, he had loved,
oy's romantic love, the beau-
mence. He was something
reamer and poet; she had
queen of his reveries. He
child of a vassal, and she of
th. This thought saddened
him, and many were the ditties wherein he bewailed, in true troubadour fashion, this mournful fact; but that he was a boy of twelve when she was a girl of seventeen did not at the time occur to him.

After he had gone to the university he heard of her departure from her father's castle, and the old man's unforgiving anger against her. The thought of her grief kept the remembrance of her in his heart, and now—though he could laugh at those old dreams of romance—he could love her with a nobler love. He knew the baron's former predilection for himself, and he prayed daily to heaven that he might once more see her restored to her father's halls.

At the château now he was the baron's constant companion. He led the old man little by little to interest himself once more in the duties of life—in plans for ameliorating the condition of some of the poor vassals—in some improvements in the château. Before two years had passed the old man seemed to love him like a son. Yet often a cloud passing over the weary face, a deep sigh, a sudden indifference to all earthly things, betrayed the lifelong grief of the baron's heart, and the thought still kept of her whom that heart so truly loved but would not pardon.

It was drawing near to the Christmas season, when one day Père Rudal said to the Baron:

"My lord, more than a year have I been with you, and although you have heaped many favors upon me, I have never yet solicited one; now I am going to ask one."

"My dear friend and companion," replied the baron, "whatever is in my power, you know you have only to ask."

"In the old days," continued the priest, "this château of yours saw many a gay feast, especially at the

Christmas-tide; then there were nobles and ladies here; now it has grown gloomy and silent. What I ask is, that this Christmas you will give an entertainment, but one of a novel kind; let the halls be opened and a banquet spread, and invite all your poor neighbors, your vassals, your retainers, their wives and children; let none be omitted: do this for the love of that little Child who was so poor and outcast for love of us. I myself will superintend the whole, and pledge myself for the good conduct and happiness of all; and moreover, you yourself will accompany and remain among your guests, at least for a little while. I know I am making a bold request in asking this, but I am sure you will not refuse it, and I promise you will not repent of it."

The baron acceded to the request. Had he been asked to entertain grand company at his castle, in his present mood he would have refused at once and haughtily; but he was too generous to refuse anything asked in the name of the poor; besides, he felt in his heart the truth of what the young priest had said to him: "There is no solace for grief like that of solacing the sorrows of others; and no happiness like that of adding to their happiness."

III.

Christmas Day came; and, after the Grand Mass was over, the great hall of the château was opened, and tables were spread with abundance of good cheer; there were presents for the little children too; and there were *jongleurs* who, instead of the customary love ditties, sang old Christmas carols in the soft Provençal dialect. Amidst the hilarity there was, what by no means was common in those days, order and decorum. Th[...] due in part to the restraint an[...] inspired by the old château—[...] for the first time in so many [...] but more to the presence i[...] midst of the baron and the pri[...] passed from one group to [...] with a kind word to each.

After a while the priest [...] hand on the baron's arm:

"Let us retire to yonder o[...] dow—there we may sit in q[...] contemplate this merry scene[...]"

The baron gladly escaped [...] crowd, but, as he seated hi[...] sigh of weariness escaped hir[...] cloud gathered on his brow.

"How happy you have [...] these good people," said th[...] "The merriment of child[...] something contagious in it[...] not?"

"What have I to do with [...] riment of other people's chil[...] a poor childless old man?"

The baron spoke bitterly [...] first time in his life had he [...] allusion to his griefs.

"But see these three pre[...] children coming towards [...] priest continued; "we did [...] them as we passed through t[...] And he beckoned them n[...] little girl about eight year[...] little boy some two or thr[...] younger, and the smallest j[...] to walk: beautiful children th[...] but dressed in the ordinary [...] peasant children.

"Do not refuse to kiss the[...] little ones for the love of t[...] Child who was born to-day," [...] the priest, as he raised on[...] own knee. "Now, my lo[...] were the poorest vassal in [...] mains, would he not be a ha[...] whom these pretty ones sh[...] grandpapa?"

The baron's face assumed [...] of displeasure. "I want no[...]

THE LIQUEFACTION OF THE BLOOD OF S[T]. JANUARIUS.

NO. V.

THE direct and positive arguments which we have presented in our last article, bearing on the miraculous character of the liquefaction, cover the ground so entirely that we might, indeed, rest our case on their presentation. We need, however, make no apology for going further, and examining also, and somewhat in detail, the difficulties and counter-statements which have been made, from time to time, by those who deny its miraculous character. Truth shrinks from no examination or proper test.

We are confident that, the more closely those objections are examined, the weaker they will be found to be; and their weakness is an additional argument for the truth of our conclusion.

The general charge is that this liquefaction is effected by some trick or other on the part of the priests. A vague charge by itself means nothing, and is of no value. To be worth anything, there must follow a "specification," some indication or explanation of the precise mode or trick by which the liquefaction is effected. HOW IS IT DONE? This is the first question to which a reply must be given, before the objectors can come into court.

The replies to it have been numerous, very numerous—in fact, so numerous as to lose all real value: they are so wonderfully discordant and so contradictory.

The liquefaction of the blood of St. Januarius has occurred, during the last two hundred and f —to go no further back just least four thousand times; i without any attempt at con under the eyes of believers a lievers alike, standing on e and within a few feet, it m immediate contact with th ing clergyman, and, theref sessing ample opportunity closest and most critical i of everything concerning it. such circumstances, it is i able that the precise trick, or secret, if there were an remain undiscovered. Yet, such discovery has been perfectly clear from this stril agreement among those wh that there is fraud, as soo undertake to state distinctl the fraud or trick consist one proposes is scouted by as so weak and so contra facts of the case, that it is v surrender of the cause. One it to be "one of the most tricks he ever saw"; but he ly silent as to the nature of so obvious to him. Anoth it to be a trick "of great in as well as of "long standin with equal prudence, he als as to its character. A third plain the manner in which A. it was done; and the very manner in which B. held th performed; while C. wit shrewdness proposed a thir The reader is considerately

facts demonstrated by experience or fully established by testimony.

We leave aside the chemistry involved in his supposition, since he candidly avowed that he never tried the experiment. It is a pity he did not make a similar candid avowal when speaking of the shape of the vial containing the blood. He should, for the sake of good faith, have warned his readers that he had never seen the vial itself, nor even an engraving of it; and should have let them understand that his whole explanation was based on his assumed ability to describe accurately and minutely the shape of a vial which, he must have been aware, and should have informed them, he was entirely ignorant of.

Any one who has seen the reliquary and the ampulla within it, or has even looked at the figure of it which we have given, or at engravings of it which are easily obtained in Naples and elsewhere, will see at a glance that the shape of the ampulla is just the reverse of an hourglass. In fact, in form it much more closely approaches a sphere. Not a single point set forth in the explanation is correct. There is no upper division in which the dry substance, compounded of *crocus martis* and *cochineal*, and perfectly resembling congealed blood, is or can be lodged; there is no lower division, unoccupied save by the few drops of aqua fortis, the color of which prevents its being discovered, even by keen, curious, prying eyes. There is in the liquefaction no sandlike fall, from an upper into a lower division, of a stream of particles of the dry substance, now separated or liquefied by the aqua fortis. The bishop has not only failed to hit the bull's eye, he has entirely missed the target, every shot.

And yet, with what delicious complacency he considers, and ‹ his readers to admit, that he, all others, has correctly expo: bungling trick, and has un the fraudulent dealings of the who can effect or prevent the as they please! It is a genui ple of the way in which a class of writers think they d anything Catholic. And how after reading this passage of t *terion*, may have closed the b perfect confidence that, after : exposure, so clear and detaile learned and so respectable an rity, it would be waste of read another word on the liqu of the blood of St. Januarius!

Need we go back to the t vious explanations he mentic which he will not adopt, unl forced by the failure of his planation? So many other urged them that we may n them entirely unnoticed.

The ordinary form of the t is this: The officiating prie holds in his hands the vial co the blood, rubs it with his h chief, and clasps it in his palm animal heat of his hands, ar heat as the friction may p suffices to bring about the l tion.

Let the reader cast an eye very correct figure of the r which we give. The priest l by the stem below; someti turning it, he may put one h the crown above. He does he cannot, touch the interic containing the blood. They side the case, held in position soldering above and below, : enclosed and protected by th metal rim, and the plates of front and rear. The heat hands, as he holds it, and the heat that can be produced friction—as occasionally, eve

tes, he may, if he thinks it , rub the plates of glass with handkerchief, in order to through them into the in- nnot possibly affect the con- e'ampulla in any apprecia- . As for causing them to uefy, one might as well ex- same animal heat of one's ight a wax candle by sim- ng and holding the candle- which it stands, or that bing the candlestick with a nief, every five or ten mi- keep it bright and dry, duce the same physical ef- candle placed in it as or- rtals obtain nowadays by lucifer match and apply- he wick.

who has ever witnessed ction can listen to this at- xplanation without a smile f contempt. Even in those hich the liquefactions take e the reliquary is in the the priest, it is equally in- nd absurd. It has no ap- hatever to the other many which the liquefaction oc- the reliquary stands on or is borne in procession. ther solutions we have ex- makes no attempt to ac- the reiterated hardenings factions which may occur day, nor for the variations and for the other phases presented. Yet we must nd that all these are strik- haracteristic points, which e strictly accounted for, th the simple fact of a so- ice becoming fluid.

the second mode of solu- oned by Bishop Douglas, attributes the liquefaction eral heat around the altar " vast number of wax tapers us size" burning on the altar, and also, not to omit what oth- ers have said, to the crowd closely packed around the officiating clergy- man—that attempted solution has already been disposed of. Thermo- metrical investigations by scientific professors, and the many times that the liquefaction takes place at the al- tar when there is little or no crowd, and also away from the altar and its "wax tapers of enormous size" dur- ing a procession in the streets, and while the reliquary is freely exposed to the open air of December—all alike combine to exclude this solu- tion. As for the convenient position in which the bishop places some of those wax tapers, and the practice of the priests to make use of this posi- tion and, "without any appearance of design," to "hold the glass so near to them as to make it hot, and con- sequently dispose the enclosed sub- stance to melt," we may ask, if he did not believe this to be true, why has he repeated the statement, and expressed his inclination "to sub- scribe to this opinion" even as a *pis aller?* If he did believe that the priest really so manipulated the vial in order to produce the liquefaction, ought not that to be sufficient? Why postpone the truth in favor of a pet theory about *crocus martis*, *cochineal*, *aqua fortis*, and the *hour-glass?* Evi- dently, his mind was rather cloudy on the subject. Seriously, the priest could not hold the reliquary so near to a lighted wax taper of enormous size, long enough to make it hot, without attracting the attention of hundreds each time he did it. Not to over- look the smallest point, we may re- mark that, on the six occasions when we were present at the lique- faction, on all of which it invariably occurred at the main altar of the *Tesoro* chapel, the lighted tapers on the altar were few. If our memory serves us right, they were just *six*,

three on each side of the crucifix over the centre of the altar, and all of them placed on tall and elevated altar candlesticks. The nearest blaze must have been, at least, seven feet away from and above the reliquary, as the chaplain held it in front of the altar. To achieve the feat which Bishop Douglas mentions, it would have been necessary to move back a portion of the crowd, near the altar, in order to get room, and then to bring in and make use of a good-sized step-ladder! The only burning light ever held in proximity to the reliquary is the single small taper, sometimes held by an assistant chaplain, and used on cloudy or hazy days, when the general light in the *Tesoro* chapel is not sufficiently strong to show through the glass plates of the reliquary and the sides of the ampulla, as distinctly as desired, the state of the blood in the interior of the ampulla. In such cases, this taper is now and then brought for half a minute or a minute within eight or ten inches of the reliquary, and is held a little downward, and behind it, in such position that its light may shine obliquely onward through the glasses, on the surface of the blood, and show, as we saw it show, the state of the interior with perfect distinctness. It is not applied to the reliquary in any way that can appreciably heat it. When the atmosphere is perfectly clear, the general light of the chapel is amply sufficient, and this taper is not needed nor brought forward.

What we have said of the modes thus examined is true of all attempted explanations based on some supposed feat of jugglery or legerdemain during the exposition. To one who has witnessed the liquefaction at Naples, and knows what is really done, they are simply ridiculous. We repeat: if nothing else can l the miracle must stand.

This has been felt, and quence we havę another proposed solutions, of a s higher character. Chemistry: into service. Some comp skilfully prepared, we are t inserted by the priests into pulla beforehand. It is c character that it appears mo hard and solid at the beginni exposition, and, during the e is made to melt or to appea Chemists, we are assured, c prepare such substances, thus reproduce the liquefa will. These experiments, it ed, settle the question. \ chemists do and acknowle priests do, and pass off as a

Let us analyze these exp and see whether in reality peat and renew the liquefac its characteristic and essen nomena, or in what resp how far they fail to do so.

The first of these of w have any account dates fror in 1734. On the 26th of in that year—so we are t letter dated a few days a published in Paris—Gasp mann, councillor of his court, doctor in medicine, fessor of chemistry, entert party consisting of fourteen friends, assembled to dine a tive board, with an imitatio liquefaction of the blood o nuarius. The letter was wr one of the party to his fr home. We carefully reproc facts which the letter states, the badinage and sneering with which it accompanies remarks quite characteristic school of Voltaire whenever or anything connected with

tion. In default of the origi-
nch, we quote from a transla-
blished in England.

professor, we are told, placed
his friends "a human skull."
produced from his labora-
hree vials of crystal or very
nd transparent glass, in each
:h was contained a matter in
small bulk, dry, black, and so
o produce a noise on the
f t the vial when shaken."
t vial being brought near to
d, the matter in it "became
eep-red color, liquefied, bub-
creased its bulk, and filled the
The second vial was also
near to the head, and the
of matter in it "bubbled but
But when the third vial
ilarly brought near the head,
le of its contents "remained
rd, and black."

writer evidently wished to
the impression—perhaps he
believed—that these vials,
e professor had carefully pre-
ı his laboratory and showed
riends after dinner, correctly
d the liquefaction in all its
hases. If the liquid in the
had also several times chang-
olor; if it had filled the vial,
adding bubbles to bubbles,
an actual increase of the vo-
the liquid within, independ-
f that frothing or bubbling;
d then similarly decreased in
if the liquid had solidified
any diminution of tempera-
d become fluid again without
of it, he would have pre-
a far stronger case than he
e.

hose points are absent. Per-
e writer did not know that
re necessary. The letter it-
ritten in a jocular and mock-
e, and evidently in a spirit
lished sharp epigrammatic
points, calculated to excite a laugh, far more than the humdrum reality of sober truth.

We find another account of this same experiment in a French work before us: *La Liquefaction du Sang de S. Janvier*, by Postel. This account is more calm and sober in style, and is based upon the *Bibliothèque Germanique*, a work to which we have not access. It varies considerably from the sportive account given in the letter. According to Postel, the contents of the first vial *liquefied entirely*; the contents of the second vial *liquefied only partially*; in the third vial there was *no change whatever*. The statement is distinctly made that neither in the first vial nor in the second was there any sign of ebullition. The variation is important.

As between the two accounts, we could scarcely hesitate a moment which to hold most worthy of credit on any point on which they differed. In neither account do we find any indication of the nature of the chemical compounds which Dr. Neumann had prepared in his laboratory and placed in the vials. But as the experiment was made known and repeated, especially in France, we may take it for granted that the material used in those repetitions is the same that he devised.

This material is a mixture of suet, or other similar fatty matter, and ether, the compound being brought to any desired tint—in this case, a deep or dark red—by a further admixture of any suitable pigment. The mixture or compound so prepared is solid at ordinary temperatures; but at about 92° F. it will melt. If a quantity of such a mixture be inserted in a small glass vial, and the vial be clasped in the palm of one's hand, it will soon receive from the hand sufficient heat to bring about a total

or a partial liquefaction, according to the greater or smaller proportion of the ether used in originally compounding it.

Neither would it be beyond the art of chemistry, in preparing this mixture, to introduce other ingredients, the particles of which would be brought into contact with each other when the liquefaction has been effected and the chemical combinations of which would then give rise to a greater or less amount of frothing or bubbles.

All this, however, is very far from being a reproduction of the liquefaction which is seen at Naples. The differences, or rather the failures to imitate and reproduce it, are essential and evident. We point out the chief ones:

I. This liquefaction of the laboratory *always and entirely* depends on the application of the proper degree of heat. So long as its temperature is below the melting point, the substance in the vial remains hard and unliquefied. When the temperature, from whatsoever cause, is raised above that degree, liquefaction ensues. If the temperature again sinks below it, the substance, if not meanwhile decomposed, returns to its previous solid condition. The operators themselves inform us frankly how the required degree of heat is usually communicated to it; by holding the vial, if small enough, in the palm of one hand, or tightly pressing it, if somewhat larger, between the palms of both hands. If the general heat of the room be raised high enough to reach the melting point of the substance in the vial, this circumstance alone would suffice to bring the compound to a fluid condition.

On the other hand, being from Naples and not from Brobdignag, the chaplain or canon has a hand only of the ordinary size, and is altogether unable to clasp in th[e] of one hand, or even wi[th] palms, an object so large as [the re]liquary. He is forced to hol[d] the stem; in which position, t[he] of his hand can have no app[reciable] effect on the contents of t[he] within the reliquary.

Moreover, the liquefaction takes place when the reliquar[y] held in his hands at all.

II. We repeat it again. T[he] liquefaction does not depend [on] It takes place at various te[mpera]tures. There is no fixed [melting] point for the substance in the [ampul]la. It will often solidify at a temperature than that at w[hich it] stood liquid; and will lique[fy] temperature notably below [that at] which it became or stood soli[d] is an essential difference, goin[g] root of the question.

III. The attempted imitati[on] at the utmost, present a bub[bling] frothing, produced in the w[ay] have indicated. This may e[xtend] to such an extent as to fill t[he] with froth or bubbles. But never cause the bulk or body liquid itself, free from those b[ubbles] and independently of them, t[o] and increase in actual visible so as to completely fill the via[l] amount of the liquid obtaine[d] at rest and in its tranquil sta[te] at the same temperature, will be the same. Precisely the happens in the liquefaction blood of St. Januarius. The blood may bubble and froth increasing its bulk, or it may i[ncrease] its volume with or without th[e froth]ing, or it may decrease its v[olume] again, with or without the f[roth]. And these changes of the bul[k] actual liquid in the ampulla depend on the temperature. are they points on which a is possible; for they reach,

ed, to the extent of twenty

ose two cardinal points, the
entirely fails. We need
ote the facts that the pre-
when solid, does not re-
agulated or hardened blood,
n liquid, could never be
for liquid blood, whether
r venous, nor does it pre-
changes of color so often
e real liquefaction.
her is an essential ingredient
ificial compound. Suet, or
other fatty substance is used
will dissolve in ether; while
t dissolve in water or in allow, ether is comparatively
discovery. Whether Pa-
it upon the discovery of it
a point mooted among
have studied his life and
ents in chemistry. But, if
e knowledge of it was lost
and it remained unknown
rld until Künkel discovered
overed it in 1681—early
or Neumann, but entirely
o be of any service in get-
compound for the lique-
Naples, which, for the
that, runs back far beyond
f Paracelsus himself.
xplanation, therefore, that
action of the blood of St.
is in reality the liquefac-
compound of ether and
ther fatty substance, must
le, because entirely insuffi-
eet the case, and because
a glaring anachronism.
too, in another point. The
in course of time, gradual-
though the pores of the
hen it is gone, the liquefac-
t an end. The fatty mat-
ill decompose in time. In
whole preparation would
frequently renewed. On
hand, as we shall see fur-
ther on, there is ample evidence that the ampulla remains unopened, and that the substance within it remains untouched and identically the same, from year to year, and from century to century.

These reasons were too patent to allow Dr. Neumann's attempted imitation to hold its own in the estimation of those who seriously examined the question. It was thrown aside for others. We find an account of one of them, written by La Condamine, and presented to no less a body than the Academy of Sciences in Paris, in 1757. His article may be found among the various articles published in the *Memoirs* for 1763.

La Condamine explains, with no little glee, and some detail, an experiment which he had lately witnessed in company with others, and which he was allowed afterward to repeat and study out in private and at his leisure, and with the assistance and explanations of the inventor himself. He does not give the inventor's name, but we know, from other sources, that it was San Severo.

There was a circular case of bronze or silver gilt. In front and rear, there were circular plates of glass. The whole stood on a richly ornamented foot, and was surmounted by a winged mercury. Within the case, between the plates of glass, was seen a vial. So far, the workman had prepared a vague imitation of the actual reliquary.

"The vial appeared half full of a stiff grayish paste, which, judging by its surface, seemed to be powdery or granulated. By inclining the case, alternately, from side to side, and shaking it for half a minute, more or less, the paste became liquid and flowing, sometimes only partially so; at other times, it grew hard again, and by shaking it anew it became liquid again. . . . I remarked beneath the vial two small cones, I do not know of what material, meeting by their points.

I was told (by the inventor) that there was a little passage through these points. He said, also, that the cones were hollow, and that, as the lower one was movable, it sometimes happened that its orifice exactly met the orifice of the upper cone, and sometimes did not; this was altogether a matter of chance. . . . As for the powder which I saw in the vial, I was told that it was an amalgam of mercury, lead, tin, and bismuth; that the bismuth, which amalgamated only imperfectly, hindered the mixture from becoming a pasty lump, and gave it rather the character of a powder too coarse to pass through the little opening which communicated with the cones. Finally, there was hidden, within the case, a circular tube communicating with the lower movable cone, and containing liquid mercury. In shaking the whole irregularly, whenever the openings of the two cones came together, more or less of this mercury made its way into the vial and liquefied the amalgam. It happened sometimes, in these various movements, that the mercury which had entered got out again, and then the amalgam returned to its previous condition and was fluid no longer."

This is the account which La Condamine has given, after a long and careful private examination, aided by the explanations of the inventor, and which, he tells us, he wrote down the same day. The inventor promised to give him in writing a fuller account, with minute drawings of all the parts; but up to the date of publication (five years later) he had, for some unknown reason, failed to keep the promise.

La Condamine acknowledges that he had never seen the real reliquary, and had never witnessed the true liquefaction at Naples. He thought this substitute just as good.

Had he witnessed the reality, and had he examined it with one-half the care he bestowed on the substitute, he never would have written his report.

I. He would have instantly seen the difference between a true liquefaction—where a substance prev
hard is unmistakably seen to b
gradually soft and then perfe
quid, as is often the case at Na
and this seeming liquefaction
experiment, which consists o
making the loosened grains or
cles of the amalgam swim in
the fluid mercury which has b
troduced, they themselves rem
hard and not at all liquefie
ready to be heaped together
in a hard mass of grains or p
whenever the liquid mercury
drawn. The difference betw
two processes is as clear as
and as great as the difference b
the melting of icebergs and a
ment of a fleet of ships on the
A child could not mistake it.
tunately, the icebergs melt and
pear as they are changed in
ter: with equal good fortu
ships do not melt, but float o
they reach their port.

II. He would see that this
amalgam, in its dry, powder
is totally unlike the hard, dar
of blood in the ampulla, and
pretended liquid state, it is
unlike the liquid blood. In
the mercury enters below an
meates the mass, its silvery
may somewhat enliven the du
ish hue of the amalgam, but
present nothing akin to the *ru*
the *bright vermilion*, or the *da*
of the liquid blood. Nor i
anything like the film which th
blood sometimes leaves on th
of the glass, nor like the fr
or the ebullition. On all these
the experiment failed.

III. After sufficient merc
been introduced to occupy th
stices in the granular mass, a
ditional supply will lift the pa
separate them, and allow th
tion which the inventor pass
for fluidity; and this seeming

which from the period of that visit, was manifested by that eminent scholar, and which led him to think seriously, at least, of entering her fold, even if he did not—as some thought he did—carry his purpose into effect before death.

And yet we are asked to believe that, "away back in the dark ages," those "ignorant monks and priests in Naples" possessed a knowledge of chemistry which enabled them to do this. And, more wonderful still, that they have secretly handed down that knowledge and power, within their own body, and that they continue to this day to effect the liquefaction in some strange way entirely unknown to the scientific world!

We pass on to other views of the question.

This charge of fraud implies that the ampulla is tampered with from time to time; and that those who have charge of it—clergy and laity alike—and especially those who hold it at the time of the liquefaction, are all playing a trick.

Is the ampulla or vial really tampered with? Is it regularly opened for the insertion of some duly prepared material?

The ampulla stands within a case or reliquary, as our figure shows it. The case or reliquary, of silver and of glass, is kept in an *Armoire*, or closet, wrought in the solid stone wall of the *Tesoro* chapel, as strong and secure as a bank-vault. This *Armoire* is closed by metal doors, each secured by two strong locks, with different keys, one set of which is always in the possession of the municipal authorities of the city, the other in that of the archbishop and clergy. They have been so kept for just two hundred and twenty-four years; for we need not take account just now of the previous centuries, when the relics were in the exclusive custody of

the archbishop and clergy, i
kept in the old *Tesoro*, c
room, still to be seen in th
story of the cathedral towe
ing all these two hundred a
ty-four years, the locks have
tampered with. The clergy
charged any one with doing
municipal authorities have n
pected it.

Moreover, the reliquar
brought out, remains expose
lic scrutiny for ten or twel
at a time, on eighteen day
year; and there is no man
or child in Naples, and no
in the city, who may not, if
ed, scrutinize it a score of
day, at less than twelve in
tance. Any opening or cl
the case, any taking out or p
of the vial, would leave so
of the fact, either in the si
or in the position of the via
or at least in the soldering a
and at top, which would h
disturbed, if not broken, ea
and then restored. Among
cial industries of Naples are
in jewelry and coral, retouc
repairing paintings, and—w
ry to say it—fabricating *Old*
The Neapolitans have eyes
and traces like these in qu
quick, sharp, and unerring a
dian on a trail. No change
of any tampering has ever b
by them. The vials are in
ly the same inclined posit
year to year—the same as r
ed in engravings a century
centuries old. The sold
which the bottoms and top
mersed, is hard, old, black,
age, and evidently untouche
outer case shows no sign
opening by which a side ca
screwed or lifted out, so as
the vials themselves to be
Probably, when originally m

and fifty, or seven hundred
, this could have been done.
screw or the joint has long
ted, and the whole thing is
mass of dingy and rusted
lding two glass plates.
year 1649, Cardinal Ascanio
ni was Archbishop of Na-
an of great culture and taste
ample private fortune, and
ven to the adornment of the
of his diocese.
new *Tesoro* had just been
d, and was shining in all the
splendor of newness. The
thought that the reliquary
in the vials of the blood, for
he *Tesoro* had been built,
correspond, as the bust did,
grandeur of the chapel itself.
dingy old silver reliquary,
they had been kept for so
nturies, did not do. He de-
to replace it by another of
excellent workmanship, and
with rich jewels. He had
le "regardless of expense,"
n all was ready, on Septem-
649, he came into the *Teso-*
some of his clergy and the
s from the city, and with
otaries, that proper legal re-
ght be made of everything,
chosen goldsmiths. Are
names of them all duly re-
The *Armoire* was opened,
uary was taken to the adjoin-
isty; and there, for several
presence of his eminence
clergy, and the honorable
s, "and of us, the undersign-
ies," the goldsmiths tried and
to open the reliquary. They
d gave it up. They could
e reliquary, if so directed;
could not open it. Accord-
e reliquary was locked up
it had been taken out. The
was a persevering man. He
er goldsmiths, and came a second time, on the 8th of September, with clergy, delegates, and notaries. For two hours again these goldsmiths tried to open the reliquary, and failed, as the first had done. They could break it, if required; but how could they open a case where all their trying could find neither joint nor screw? Again the reliquary was replaced in the *Armoire*. The cardinal's heart was set on using his new grand reliquary on the festival near at hand, the 19th of September. He thought over the matter, again summoned the delegates and the notaries, and on the 16th came, a third time, with his clergy and yet other goldsmiths. A third prolonged trial was made with the same ill-success. The reliquary might be broken, if they wished; it could not be opened. To break it was not to be thought of; that might endanger the precious vials within. So, the old silver reliquary was put up again, that evening, and his eminence was forced to use it on the festival of the 19th for the exposition that year. It has been used ever since. And now, two hundred and twenty-two years later, it was again brought out on the 19th of September in this present year, 1871. The cardinal, it is to be presumed, devoted his rich reliquary to some other pious purpose.

But if his eminence had lived to the age of the olden patriarchs, and had retained it in his possession, he might have at last found a more favorable opportunity for again trying to change that reliquary. On the afternoon of Tuesday, May 5, 1762, one of the glass plates, by dint, of course, of being rubbed for so many hundred years by white handkerchiefs, became somewhat loose in its groove or socket, and threatened to fall inward, endangering the precious vials. Accordingly, early next morning, an hour and a half before the

time for the regular exposition (for it was in the May octave), the archbishop of that day, Cardinal Sersale, came with clergy, city delegates, notaries-public, and goldsmiths. The reliquary was taken out of the *Armoire*, and the glass was fixed again firmly in its place, and the reliquary was returned to its *Armoire*, before the hour for the public exposition. It does not appear, from the very succinct account we have of the occurrence, whether or not, during the work, the vials or ampullæ were taken out of the reliquary, within which they are held in their places by the old soldering. Nothing is said of this having been done, nor of the soldering being touched and then repaired when they were put back in their places. On the whole, considering the nature of the repair to be done, and that it was done in a few moments at the door of the *Armoire*, back of the altar, we are inclined to think that they did not find it necessary to move them, and that they were accordingly left untouched in their places.

These are the only occasions on which the diaries say anything bearing on the feasibility of opening this reliquary, or of its being repaired. In the archives of the cathedral, another incident is mentioned, of an ancient date. In the year 1527, nearly a century and a half before the building of the new *Tesoro*, the relics were kept in the old *Tesoro* or strong room of the cathedral, a strong vaulted chamber of stone, in the second story of the tower, which rises at the northeast corner of the church. That *Tesoro* was then approached by a winding stairway. A very aged [illegible] was bringing down the reliquary from the *Tesoro* to the church for an exposition. At the very first step he tripped and fell; and the reliquary rolled down, from step to step, to the very bottoı present feared it was brok gave thanks when it was ta and found to be perfectly un Yet the alarm had been gre Maria Toleta, "the pious wi viceroy," who was present at and shared in the alarm, winding stairway taken dowr own expense, and replaced other one, straight, broad, a which is in use to this day.

We may take these facts evidence that the reliquary i and not very easily opened, they who know all about it believe that it is or can be r opened.

The same conclusion is als on us by considerations of an different character. We have drawn attention to the fa whatever the level at wh blood stands when the reli locked up at night, at the one exposition—whether *at it ry level*, or *somewhat increase much increased*, or *full*—it is bly found at the same lev taken out the next time for suing exposition, whether th be next morning or after the months. The level is one points specially noticed and r A variation would necessaril tected. Yet, if on each one or many of the four thousand o we have spoken of, the old had been privately taken out the expositions, and a fresh put in, would there not hav not unfrequently, some app inequality of level?

Again, sometimes the blo *hard* when put up. How hard substance be extracted narrow-necked vial of glass breaking it? According to bles, on three different occasi blood, after its usual liquefacti

n September, *filled* the am- was so locked up at the he novena. It was found *iard* in December following, liquefying at all, was again in the same condition. It l in precisely the same state reliquary was again taken May following. Here, on asions, the contents of the and completely filling it, remained unextracted from r to May, seven months. e May octaves that follow- quefactions went on as usu- freshly inserted compound ssary for the liquefaction. e reasoning applies in a to the numerous cases in h a fulness went over, four id a half, from May to Sep- r nearly three months, from r to December.

in quite a number of in- s the same tables show, the of the blood, when locked d as *liquid with a floating* , as was the case on the December, 1870. When ken out, the next day, or eral months, though often irely hardened, yet not un- —as on the 6th of May, was found in precisely the in which it had been put *with a floating hard lump.* se cases, the condition of its of the ampulla is a new erable objection to the sup- at a newly prepared amount had been inserted for the t liquefactions. Did other ices allow it, we might con- quid to be poured out of la, and a fresh liquid to be But how is the solid hard would not liquefy, to be And if got out, how is ard lump to be put in to ? Are the constituents of this new hard lump poured into the ampulla separately, as liquids or powders that can pass through the neck? Then their character must be such that, instead of uniting with the liquid already there, or the constituents of the liquid portion, they will, on the contrary, combine apart to form the hard mass. But if so antagonistic to the liquid portion, how is it that, when the lump does liquefy during the ensuing exposition, these constituents at once intimately unite with the liquid, the whole forming a homogeneous mass, which without the least indication of any antagonism between its component parts will henceforth solidify and liquefy as a single mass?

The more carefully the facts of the case are studied, the more imperatively do they exclude every hypothesis save the simple one which so many other facts corroborate, that no attempt has been made to change the contents of the ampulla. Everything about the ampulla excludes the idea that it is regularly tampered with privately between the expositions.

There is still another light in which we must view this charge of fraud. Ever since the opening of the new *Tesoro*, in 1646, there have been attached to that chapel twelve chaplains and a *custos*, with inferior attendants as needed. In the cathedral itself, at least from 1496, there have been twenty canons and beneficiaries, besides minor attendants. When the liquefaction takes place in the *Tesoro*, the reliquary is in the hands of the chaplains, who act in turn, or relieve each other as convenient. When it occurs in the procession or in the cathedral, or in some other church, the reliquary is in the charge of the canons, who similarly relieve each other. Hence, canons and chaplains, all alike, must

be cognizant of the fraud, if any there be, and must participate in it. Add to these the archbishops and their vicars-general in Naples since 1496. Add also those clergymen who, having been canons or chaplains, have passed to other dignities, or have retired from their office, but must of course still retain the knowledge of this fraud, if they once possessed it. We may say that there have been on an average, at all times, forty ecclesiastics, if not more, who had cognizance of the fraud, if there were any. The dignity of canon of the cathedral or chaplain of the *Tesoro* is ordinarily reached only after years of meritorious service in the lower grades of the ministry. Hence the canons and chaplains are usually men of mature and advanced age. We can scarcely give them more than fifteen years of average life. We have thus about a thousand clergymen since A.D. 1500, all charged with being cognizant of and participators in the fraud.

Now, what was the character of those men? Those among whom they lived, and who knew them, respected them as a body of men devoted to the service of God, pure and exemplary ecclesiastics, proved by years spent in the zealous works of the ministry. Some were men of honorable and noble families; others were men distinguished in the walks of literature and science; some had sacrificed all the world promised them, in order to spend their lives in the sanctuary. Some were revered in life, and remembered after death, as pre-eminently true servants of God, men of prayer, of strong faith, and of singularly pure and saintly lives. Of course, individuals here or there may indeed have been wicked or hypocritical. But this testimony of the people to their character must have been true of the great body.

Now, could such men ha
united in this fraud? On thei
principles and convictions, ac
cording to the doctrines they
and should themselves practise
could scarcely be a more heino
against God and his holy n
than to palm off a trick of
men as a miracle of God's w
Could they bring themselves t

Is it possible that no one of
ever repented, even in the p
of death, and sought to sa
soul, and to make reparation,
closing the fraud and arresti
evil? Could all have chosen
impenitent, with the certainty
lasting damnation before them
er than reveal the blasphemo
to them, henceforth useless
The thing is impossible.

Again, men, even though go
pious, may be garrulous. A
have their unguarded moments.
came it that the secret never
out from any one of them du
these years?

Again, among so many them
have been men wicked, ava
passionate, revengeful. How
it that no one sought to mal
ney by revealing the secret; t
one declared it through anger
no one did so in retaliation
he was punished by his eccles
superiors?

Nay, more, we fear that ins
might be found in which, tow
close of the last century, so
them were carried away by th
ligious mania then prevailing
became the companions of i
if not themselves infidels. A
less our memory is at fault,
two yielded to the blandishmen
the privileges of Protestantism.
comes it that, through suc
world has not learned how thi
quated trick is actually done?
viously, they had no disclos

'This is the only possible an-

is still more to be said on it. The civil authorities of are, and have been for two and twenty-four years, joint ns with the archbishop and f the *Tesoro* chapel and of es of St. Januarius. They e set of the keys of the *Ar*r closet, which can never be save in the presence of one members, whom they send as te, and whose sworn duty it to lose sight of the reliquary s placed in its closet, and he duly locking it up. During o hundred and twenty-four Naples has again and again masters. Austrians, Lom- paniards; and French—Bour- perial, and Republican—have the Piedmontese now hold, which in fact has oftener been strangers than by Neapo- These rulers have been men character, from the best to t; often rough, ruthless sol- ho brooked no opposition, ever ready with the sword; en, crafty civilians, ready to bribe, and to deceive, and ily practised to detect plots et out hidden things; some- ofessed infidels and avowed of all religion; oftener poli- mies of the Neapolitan cler- se hearts, of course, were eir own oppressed people. nes it that none of these ru- ny time have ever discovered e known the fraud?

e suppose that those rulers, ed as they often were to- clergy, could or would sac- ir own interests, their poli- jealousies, and their perso- g, in order to co-operate in the success of which would be less agreeable, perhaps far less profitable, to them, than its failure and exposure?

Would not the French infidels, in 1799, have gladly put this stigma on the odious cause of Christianity?

And, in these present years, would not Ratazzi, Garibaldi, and their party gladly do it if they could? What a triumph it would be for them if they could strike this blow at "clericalism"—a blow far more effective than fining, imprisoning, or exiling bishops and priests and religious! They would glory in doing it if it were possible. What holds them back? There are no limits to their hatred or to their powers of calumny. They are ever denouncing the ignorance and the blind superstition of priests and people. But the very gist and copiousness of their invectives prove that they themselves know and feel that the priests and people are alike sincere. It is the depth and earnestness of that sincerity which excites their rage.

Brought face to face, in Naples, with this manifestation of the supernatural, the civil government, whatever the political circumstances and whatever the private character of individual members of it, have always seemed struck with awe, and have never failed in respect. Nay, more, they have ever claimed and exercised their privilege of sending their delegate to intervene in the exposition.

And so, after all, on the 19th of this last September, as in times past, they did send a delegate, with his scarlet embroidered bag, and the two antique keys chained together; and the doors of the *Armoire* were opened; and the relics were reverently taken out and carried to the altar; and the blood was seen to be *hard;* and the clergy and the crowd prayed and waited for the miracle; "and, after eight minutes of prayer, the hard mass became entirely liquid."

There is an anecdote current in the world on this subject which we have heard cited as peremptory against much of what we have just said. The anecdote, in passing from mouth to mouth, has become so vague and so full of variations that we would scarcely know how to present it, had we not found a precise and *quasi* authoritative form of it in the columns of the *Coryphæus* of French infidelity, the *Siècle* of Paris of the date of October 11, 1856:

"The history of Championnet did some damage to the miracle of St. Januarius in the minds of a great many. In 1799, the French army was in Naples, where it had been well received at first. . . . . On the 6th of May, the crowd filled the chapel of the cathedral. . . . For more than half an hour the priest had been turning backward and foward, on his hands, the round silver lantern with two faces of glass within which is preserved the precious blood in a small vial. The little reddish mass would not quit its state of solidity. . . . The exasperated populace commenced to attribute the stubbornness of San Gennaro to the presence of the French. There was danger of a tumult, when an aid hastened to notify General Championnet of the suspicious conduct of the saint. In a few moments the aid returned, approached the priest politely, and said a few words in his ear. What he did say is not precisely known, but he had scarcely said it when the blood at once liquefied, to the great joy of the people, who at last had their miracle."

Alexandre Dumas, in one of his novels, narrates the same story much more dramatically. According to him, "General Championnet saw that it was important for his safety and the safety of the army that the miracle should not fail that year; and he made up his mind that, one way or another, it should positively occur." The first Sunday of May was near at hand. On the vigil (May 4, 1799), the procession marched, but between files of French grenadiers. That night the city was patrolled French and Italian soldiers jo All day Sunday the miracle wa tiently waited for; but in vain. the afternoon came—Champi with his staff, was in his el *loggia* or gallery. The people at length to lose patience and t ferate angrily. At 7 P.M. the brandishing knives and threa the general, who pretended not derstand or heed them. At 8 P streets around were filled with crowds equally threatening. grenadiers waited on a signa the general to charge bayonets. general continued unmoved.' half-past eight, as the tumult w increasing, "the general ben and whispered something to a de-camp." The aid left the and passed up to the altar an in the front rank, and waite five minutes the canon, beari reliquary, came round to him turn. He kissed the reliqu others did; but, while doi grasped the priest's hand in hi

"'Father, a word with you.'

"'What is it?' asked the priest.

"'I must say to you, on the par general commanding, that if in t utes the miracle is not accomplis fifteen minutes your reverence s shot.'

"The canon let the reliquary fa his hands. Fortunately, the you cer caught it before it reached the g and gave it back with every mark found respect. Then he arose turned to his place near the gener

"'Well?' said the general.

"'All right, general,' said the officer. 'In ten minutes the mira take place.'

"The aid-de-camp spoke the nevertheless he made a mistake minutes; for at the end of five m only, the canon raised the reliqua exclaiming, *Il miracolo è fatto.* blood was completely liquefied."

We suppose we may take th the best versions of the same

tract from a contemporary letter, published at the time in the official organ at Paris—the *Moniteur*, No. 259, of date 19 Prairial, Year VII. (June 10, 1799).

"Naples, 21 Floréal (May 13).—The festival of St. Januarius has just been celebrated with the customary solemnity. General Macdonald (successor to Championnet), Commissary Abrial, and all the staff, witnessed the renowned miracle. As it took place somewhat sooner than usual, the people think better of us Frenchmen, and do not look on us any more as atheists."

The writer little thought what a dramatic story a novelist's imagination would conjure up, and some credulous people would believe, instead of the simple matter-of-fact statement he gave *en passant* of the solemnity he had just witnessed. A more complete refutation of the whole story could not be desired than that afforded by the words and tone of this letter.

We have been diffuse on the charge of fraud. But when we consider the persistence with which it is made, and the variety of forms in which it is presented; and that, after all, for most minds, the alternative is between a suspicion of fraud, on one side, and the recognition of the miraculous character of the liquefaction, on the other—it was proper to treat this charge at length and in all its aspects.

We have seen that the publicity of everything about the exposition peremptorily forbids every form of leger demain during the ceremony. Equally inadmissible is the supposition of some chemical compound prepared beforehand. For no chemical compound which man can prepare will liquefy, as this does, independently of heat, and under such diverse circumstances, or will present the many varying phases which are here seen. The most artistic attempts have utterly failed, and must ever fail. For they are all subject to the laws of nature; while, in this liquefaction, the laws of nature are clearly set aside.

Again, all testimony goes to show that the ampulla is not opened from time to time to receive any chemical preparation.

Moreover, if there were any fraud, it would have been known to nearly a thousand clergymen, and no one can say to how many laymen. Yet pious men were never heard to denounce it; repentant men never disclosed it; high-minded and honorable men never repudiated it in scorn, vile and mercenary men were never moved by anger, revenge, desire of pecuniary gain, or other potent motives, to betray it. Even political enmities and fierce party strife, so prone to indulge in charges of fraud, have failed in Naples to stigmatize this as a fraud. Evidently, there was no fraud known or suspected there. In fine, were there a fraud, this universal silence would be a greater miracle than the liquefaction itself.

It has been asked, sometimes jeeringly, perhaps sometimes seriously, if the Neapolitans are in such perfect faith and so sure of the character of the substance which liquefies in the ampulla, why are they unwilling to submit that substance to the test of chemical analysis? Is not their omission, nay, their unwillingness to do this, a confession on their part of the weakness of their cause?

To one who knows them, or who even reflects for a moment on the subject, the answer is obvious. It is their perfect good faith itself, and their consequent veneration for what they look on as sacred and specially blessed of God, and not any fear or doubt, that would make them rise in

to avoid evil and to do good, and the good animated to greater fervor and earnestness in deeds of piety and virtue? And, after all, are not these the grand purposes of all God's dealings with men?

Nor is this miracle—for such we call it, although the church has never spoken authoritatively on the point—alien from doctrine. Wrought in honor of a sainted and martyred bishop, it is a perpetual testimony to the truth of the doctrines he preached, and of the church which glories in him as one of her exemplary and venerated ministers; it is a confirmation of the homage and veneration she pays to him because he chose rather to sacrifice his life than to deny the Saviour who had redeemed and illumined him. Wrought within her fold, it is a permanent evidence that she is in fact and in spirit the same now as in the early days of persecution—the ever true and faithful church of Christ.

It is a confirmation, likewise, of the doctrine of the resurrection of the dead — that special doctrine which the apostles put forth so prominently in the beginning of their preaching; which was ever present to the minds of the early Christians, cheering and strengthening them when this world was dark around them; which formed the frequent theme of their pastoral instructions and their mutual exhortations, and became the prevailing subject of their household and their sacred ornamentation in their homes and in their oratories, and over their tombs in the catacombs; which gave a special tone to their faith, their hope, and their charity and love of God, and was, as it were, the very life-blood of their Christianity.

Nowadays, outside the church, how faint, comparatively, has belief in this doctrine become, or, rather, has it not died out almost completely from the thoughts and the hearts of men? Within the church, the solemn rites of Christian sepulture, burying the dead in consecrated ground, tells us of it. The preservation and the veneration of the relics of saints and martyrs teach it still more strongly. Does not tangible evidence, as it were, come to it anew from heaven by this constant and perpetual miracle, showing that the bodies of the sainted dead are in the custody of him who made them, and who has promised that he will raise them up again in glory?

Finally, this miracle seems to us especially adapted to our own age, when over-much knowledge is making men mad. Men are so lifted up by their progress, especially in natural sciences, that they have come to feel that they can dispense with GOD and substitute NATURE in his stead, with her multifarious and unchangeable laws. They boast that, under the light of their newly-acquired knowledge, everything is already, or will soon be, susceptible of natural explanation. As for miracles—direct interventions of God in the affairs of the world, reversing or suspending in special cases, these ordinary laws of nature—they scout the idea. All past accounts of miracles, no matter when or by whom recorded, they hold to be either accounts of natural events warped and distorted by excited and unrestrained imaginations, or else the pure fictions of superstition and credulity. They are sure that, in the first case, had there been present witnesses of sufficient knowledge and caution—such knowledge and caution as they possess—the accounts of those events would have come down to us in a far simpler garb, and unclothed with this miraculous robing. They are equally sure that, in the other case, educa-

world imagine that men who concerned themselves with the destinies of states, behaved even in moments of relaxation like the men who buy and sell in the shops, and confine their cares to commonplace domestic matters. And yet what could be more absurd than to suppose that generals addressed their armies amid the heat of battle in a speech regularly compounded of exordium, argument, exhortation, and peroration; or that great men wore the grand manner to bed with them, and put on civic crowns before they washed their faces in the morning? It is not so very many years since Cato used to be represented on the English stage in a powdered wig and a dress-sword, which was not more incongruous than the spectacle presented by all the old statesmen and fighting characters of antiquity, mouthing orations, and posing themselves in the best of the classical histories. Perhaps it was something to be thankful for that, in the eclipse of learning during the disturbed middle ages, the art of writing history after the heroic manner was lost. The chroniclers of feudal times devoted infinite pains to the record of facts—as well as the record of many things that were not facts—but knew little of the graces of literary composition, and cared nothing for the dignity of history. They stripped off the heavy robes, and showed us the deformed and clumsy figures underneath. Lacking literary culture and the fine art of discrimination, they left us only the bare materials of history instead of the historical structure itself. Industrious but injudicious collectors, they were sometimes amusingly garrulous, sometimes provokingly uninteresting; but their labors were invaluable, and modern scholars owe them a debt which can never be repaid. It is only within a

hundred years th
have tried to
the ancient and th
discarding the
garments in whic
Livy used to wrap
and draping the
the annalists with
There was a port
most of the earlie
viving art, scarcely
Hume embodied hi
phy in a history of
infidel Gibbon thre
over the chronicle
empire. Both the
brought to their wo
style worthy of th
and a vigor of th
from the unreflecti
plodding predecess
hood underlying t
not readily percei
easily pardoned. .
and in Gibbon a s
interest to the char
story. But Hume
well as many of
guished contempo
der a radically wro
accommodated hi
to the illustration
principles, instead
principles from the
consequently, volu
argument, rather t
actual occurrences
actual society.

It was not until
in England, and
United States, th
school of historical
developed. Macau
own theory when
perfect historian
agination sufficien
make his narrativ
picturesque, yet
solutely as to conte
materials which

customs and ways of thought. The revolution, which not only exchanged one dynasty for another, but metamorphosed the very system of English government, merely followed in the path of a remarkable intellectual and social transformation, without which the political reversal would have been impossible. The events of the reign of James II. could not be explained under the old plan of writing history on stilts. They were incomprehensible except by one who could mingle familiarly with the English people, and learn by what steps they had reached their new departure. Only one period in the history of England showed changes of equal importance. That was the period which witnessed England's apostasy from the Catholic faith; and it is the period which one of the latest and most brilliant of English historians has chosen for the subject of a work planned (if not executed) after Macaulay's model.

Mr. James Anthony Froude attempted to trace the development of the English nation, from the day of Henry's formal separation from the communion of the Holy See to the final establishment of Protestant ascendency at the death of Elizabeth. This is by no means the task he has accomplished, but it is the task he set himself at the beginning of his work. He purposed to show the processes by which a people, devotedly and even heroically faithful to the Roman See, became first schismatic and then heretical; how their character under the change of faith took on a new color; how the foundations of the English supremacy over Ireland and Scotland were laid in blood and crime; and how the maritime ascendency which has lasted three hundred years was established by the daring and enterprise of English sailors during the latter half of Elizabeth's reign. Never had historian a more tempting theme. If Mr. Froude had been a man of philosophical spirit, acute insight, industry, and literary honesty, he might have produced a work that for brilliancy would have rivalled Macaulay's, and for dramatic interest would have been almost unequalled in our language. There was no lack of material. Since Hume and Lingard—one the most misleading, the other the driest of modern English historians—had treated the same period, an immense store of records and official documents had become accessible to scholars. The British State-Paper Office abounded with historic wealth which the earlier writers did not know. The archives of Simancas disclosed secrets long unsuspected, and unravelled mysteries that had long baffled investigators. And from a thousand sources new light had been thrown upon the social condition of England, new illustrations given of the tendency of English thought, new explanations offered of the development of English strength and English character.

In his first volume, Mr. Froude seemed to appreciate the nature of his task, and to go about it with something of the proper spirit. He set before us a lifelike picture of England in the early part of Henry's reign, and displayed admirable art in reproducing the manners, the conversation, and the tendencies of the common people, as well as the superficial characteristics of the chief actors in the historical drama. But even in the first volume he showed the glaring faults which vitiated all his later labors, and, increasing as the work went on, made his history at last one of the worst that the present generation has produced. Fired with the zeal of a blind partisan, he forgot all his earlier purposes and all his earlier pictorial art in the enthusiasm of a fierce religious bigotry. It be-

representation in making his authority convey a meaning diametrically opposed to the one intended. After this, Mr. Froude goes on with the story of the divorce as if Anne had no existence, and she does not appear again upon the scene until the stage has been nearly cleared for her.

This is a fair specimen of literary dishonesty or recklessness from the first volume. Later instalments of the work, especially those devoted to the Queen of Scots, have been dissected by an able hand in the pages of this magazine. The series of papers in which Mr. James F. Meline examined in our columns Froude's account of Mary Stuart, have now been incorporated with much additional matter in a volume entitled *Mary, Queen of Scots, and her Latest English Historian.** No more thorough scarification of a literary offender has been published within our recollection. Mr. Meline has traced the historian's authorities with admirable patience, disclosed his falsifications, his misconceptions, his suppressions, and his interpolations, and utterly demolished the case which Elizabeth's advocate made against the unfortunate Mary. It is common to meet with uneducated people who cannot tell a story correctly, or repeat the words of a conversation without grossly distorting their meaning. Partly from defects of memory, partly from an intellectual deficiency which prevents them from apprehending things exactly as they are, such persons invariably misreport what they have seen and heard. What such people are to society, Mr. Froude seems to be to history. The *Saturday Review* says that he has not "fully grasped the nature of inverted commas." If he quotes a state paper, he leaves out essential passages, and inserts statements which rest upon no authority but his own. He gives his conjectures as if they were recorded facts. He disingenuously combines unconnected facts so as to [illegible] his private conjectures.

These are serious charges to bring against a writer of history; but they are all proved by Mr. Meline's book. We do not purpose reviewing the whole story of the Queen of Scots, or reviving the endless controversy upon her innocence, so soon after the task has been performed in the pages of THE CATHOLIC WORLD by the author of the savage little volume now before us. But we shall select and arrange from this record a few specimens of Mr. Froude's sins, that our readers may judge for themselves how little claim this latest English history has to an honorable place on their library shelves.

1. Mr. Froude begins early to prepare our minds for Mary's imputed profligacy. "She was brought up," he says, "amidst the political iniquities of the court of Catharine de Medicis." The fact is that Mary never was at the court of Catharine de Medicis at all. Catharine had no court, no influence, no position in history, until after Mary had left France. And, besides, Mary and Catharine cordially detested each other.

2. On the authority of Knox's *History of the Reformation*, he relates that Knox had labored to save the Earl of Murray from the dangerous fascinations of his sister Mary, "but Murray had only been angry at his interference, and 'they spake not familiarly for more than a year and a half.'" But Knox gives an entirely different version of the quarrel. He writes that he had urged Murray to legalize by act of the parliament the confession of faith as the doctrine of the Church

* *Mary, Queen of Scots, and her Latest English Historian.* By James F. Meline. New York: The Catholic Publication Society.

nd, but Murray was more
pon his private interests—
dom of Murray needed con-
, and many things were to
d that concerned the help of
nd servants—and the matter
te betwixt the Erle of Mur-
John Knox, that familiarlie
t time they spack nott to-
ore than a year and a half."
nothing about Mary's in-
over her brother; the in-
vas all on the other side.
. Froude assumes to quote
dispatch of Randolph's to
lescription of Mary's luxuri-
ts. "Without illness or im-
of it, she would lounge for
bed, rising only at night for
or music; and there she re-
th some light delicate French
elessly draped about her,
ed by her ladies, her coun-
her courtiers, receiving am-
and transacting business of
t was in this condition that
h found her." (*Randolph to*
t. 4, 1563.) There is no such
on in the dispatch. On the
Mary is represented at this
oth by Randolph and by
thorities, as industrious, ac-
rgetic, and capable, but at
time in bad health.
Froude thus travesties Ran-
ccount of the return of Both-
65): "Suddenly, unlooked
uninvited, the evil spirit of
, the Earl of Bothwell, reap-
t Mary's court. She dis-
all share in his return; he
ttainted; yet there he stood
aring to lift a hand against
ud, insolent, and danger-
nd he adds that "the Earl
, at the expense of forfeiting
mains of his influence over
summoned Bothwell to an-
Edinburgh a charge of high
What Randolph really says is this: "The Queen misliketh Bothwell's coming home, and has summoned him to undergo the law or be proclaimed a rebel." It was the Queen therefore, and not Murray, who "summoned him to answer." Moreover, Bothwell did not appear at court, but sought refuge among his vassals in Liddesdale.

5. Mr. Froude speaks of Lennox having "gathered about him a knot of wild and desperate youths—Cassilis, Eglinton, Montgomery, and Bothwell." If he had read his authority (Randolph) with decent care, he would have seen that these were not the friends of Lennox, but, on the contrary, the strongest dependence of Murray and Argyle *against* Lennox. Moreover, Eglinton and Montgomery are one and the same person.

6. A blunder which has already excited some discussion is Mr Froude's statement, on the authority of a letter from Randolph to Cecil, October 5, 1565, that Mary, "deaf to advice as she had been to menace," said she would have no peace till she had Murray's or Chatelherault's head." There is no such letter. It appears, however, from a letter of Randolph's, dated October 4, that Mary was "not only uncertain as to what she should do, but inclined to clement measures, and so undecided as to hope that matters could be arranged." The document to which Mr. Froude refers is a letter from the Earl of Bedford, who was not at Mary's court, but at Alnwick, on the English side of the border, and who consequently had no such opportunities as Randolph for knowing the temper of the Scottish Queen. But even Bedford does not say what Mr. Froude reports. The earl merely relates the substance of information brought back from the rebel camp by one of his officers. According to this man, Murray and the other rebel

lords are dissatisfied with the little that England is doing to help them, and *they* say, "There is no talk of peace with that Queen, but that she will first have a head of the duke or of the Earl of Murray."

7. One instance of Mr. Froude's incorrigible propensity to blunder in that peculiar manner which is vulgarly called "going off at half-cock," deserves to be mentioned, not for its importance, but because it is amusing. He describes Mary on a furious night-ride of "twenty miles in two hours," at the end of which she wrote "with her own hand" a letter to Elizabeth, "fierce, dauntless, and haughty," "the strokes thick, and slightly uneven from excitement, but strong, firm, and without sign of trembling." It is a pity to spoil such a picturesque passage; but the very letter which Mr. Froude seems to have examined with such care contains the Queen's apology for *not* writing it with her own hand, because she was "so tired and ill at ease," and mentions, moreover, that the twenty-miles ride occupied five hours, not two.

8. In his account of the murder of Darnley, Mr. Froude pursues a singularly devious course, through which his reviewer follows him with inimitable pertinacity. The historian accepts without reserve the most notoriously untrustworthy authorities, distorts evidence, throws in a multitude of artful suggestions, and suppresses in a manner that is downright dishonest every circumstance that tells in Mary's favor. We have no space to recapitulate here the numberless blunders and perversions of which he is convicted by Mr. Meline; but some of them are too ludicrous to be passed over. For instance, Mr. Froude finds it suspicious that Mary should have "preferred to believe" that she herself was the object of the lords' conspiracy, though a dispatch from Paris had conve message to her from Cathar Medicis that ***her husband's l in danger.***" The message w from Catharine de Medicis, b the Spanish ambassador in] and wanted her to "take h herself," for there was "some r enterprise in hand against her.' a word is said of her husband.

9. It is again mentioned, a firmation of her guilt, that "s for none of the absent noble protect her," and that "Murr within reach, but she did not s desire his presence." Nov Froude's own authorities sho Mary *did* send for many of the noblemen, and in particular tl twice sent for Murray, who not come.

10. When Elizabeth sent K to Scotland to inquire into the c stances of the murder, *Murr* Killigrew himself relates) ente the English ambassador at and invited to meet him Hunt gyle, Bothwell, and Maitland- them among the murderers of ley. This was strong circum evidence of Murray's guilt. Froude accordingly (referri Killigrew as his authority) sup all mention of Murray, who ga dinner and presided at it, and that Killigrew "was entertai dinner by the clique who h tended her [Mary] to Seton" implying that Mary, instead o ray, was in league with Bothw the others to prevent his get the truth. The whole substa Killigrew's letter is most outrag misrepresented. Mr. Meline the original and the false versi by side.

But we must pause. We follow Mr. Meline in his adr discussion of the authenticity famous casket letters, or his ex

the hangings that tapestry the wall, bearing over their surface thick growths of the white fleur-de-lis; while above the simple benches of stained wood, at the back, rises a long, dark gallery. It was there I heard the first Midnight Mass I ever heard in my life.

Venite adoremus! It brings back visions of a mother's patient, doting love; of a gathering of friends; of pleasant, hushed talk of ghosts and spectres; of long, dark corridors, where the wind moaned like a soul in pain; of oriel windows, many-paned, through which came the distant sound of young owls hooting mournfully in the snow-covered plantations.

How kind a mother the church is! Are not all her feasts as many days of remembrances given to the past joys of home? Are they not a faultless calendar of our hopes and fears for years past? When the children, with earnest, unsuspicious gravity, debated upon the arrangements of the "crib," what excitement! what interest! When the parents and the old retainers closed one room in mysterious silence, and decorated the glittering Christmas-tree, what wonderment! what whisperings!—and on the revelation, what delight! When piles of blankets and warm clothing were distributed among the poor, what curiosity to see which child got the petticoat Eleanor hemmed, or the jacket Frances put together!

All this is in the voice of the *Venite adoremus* as it sounds faintly now through a half-opened door, a Sunday surprise in a house hardly given to much solemnity—a house far away from the old gabled homestead and the snow-veiled chapel-roof.

But it has other scenes to show, other memories to waken. It tells of a Southern church, gaudy and bedisened, full of frivolous worshippers, whose Christmas vigil has been kept

in the ball-room they
left to listen to the
preparing its
for the dread moment
tion. But pass we on
genial remembrance
simple, white-washed
son-ward in the Hol
reclaimed and forgive
worshipping the divi
has wrought their salv
them in their hour o
arms of his earthly ang
of Mercy; it tells of a
of the Vatican, leaving
nificence to come amo
sons, and spend with th
fying Christmas than
the public churches
humble devotion. *Ve*
It swells up in swee
from some recess of fa
but the halls throu
hymn was borne that
echo only to the heav
sentinel now, if not
blasphemies of the ung

It brings the medi
St. Mark's to the min
that unique basilica-
dream of the heave
with its curious barb
golden mosaics, its B
of victories that were
victories of civilizatio
but the triumphs of fa
stition. The glorious
dark masses of huma
about its broad-reach
here and there, like
heart-stars, shine the li
rope-like coils of w
resque forerunners of
and dream-dispelling
Mass in Venice is not
Mass, however, since
mission, it is celebrate
in the afternoon of t
sad to hear profane
this consecrated spi

beauty seems to inherit the
l solemn halo of the veiled
the Holy of Holies in the
Jerusalem; but corrupted
ainly does reign in the Ve-
silica, and a Mass full of
talian fioriture is annually
l in it at the festival of
s. Still, the mind sees be-
unhappy aberrations of the
Euterpe out into the long
oast centuries, when graver
er strains rang through the
ed temple, and the stern
heads of the state came in
to grace the triumph of
orn Saviour. From Ven-
neva there is a wide gulf,
'enite adoremus bridges over

again Christmas comes
nd the same world-wide
s in the now half-converted
d of Calvinism. It leads
ls the older town, far from
port hotels, into a winding
of steep, ill-paved streets,
rows of old houses, every
hich seems to have a history
n, and whose old-fashioned
and wide portals opening
t court-yards, remind one
vorn parchment bindings
ems for ever new. But is
ogy not a little true? for is
oem of the human heart as
s changeless as the ancient
of long-dead bards, and
e ever tire of its repetition,
e than we are weary of
and Shakespeare, of Homer
il?

adoremus! It lures us on
k church, dedicated to St.
where there is nothing
to strike the eye, nothing ar-
nake the heart beat. Plain
unsightly, tawdry and fad-
churches are whose histo-
tween the dreaded persecution of the sixteenth century and the Gothic revival of the nineteenth, St. Germain yet possesses that untold charm which the Italians so broadly but accurately describe by the word *simpatico.* Sympathy! yes, that is it. It breathes on us from every corner; it is the atmosphere of the little church; it softens every incongruity, and sweetly blinds us to every defect. After all, such churches, inartistic as they may be, are no unfit representatives of the church militant, while our glorious blossoms of stone, born of the Moses-like rod of Pugin, are types of the unfathomable beauty and jubilant repose of the church triumphant.

In this Midnight Mass at Geneva it was touching to see the crowds that flocked to the church through drifting snow and biting wind—real Christmas weather—and, without any attraction in the shape of noted preacher or imposing ceremonial, filled the church as full as the generous heart-blood does the bosom of the Christian martyr. Hundreds of silent worshippers were assembled there, and, when the last Gospel of the Mass had been said, the priests returned, in alb and stole, to give communion to the eager congregation. Hardly one present seemed to have left the church, and gradually the vast body of the faithful broke, like successive waves, at the foot of the altar. For one whole hour was this scene enacting, and no music was heard meanwhile, and, though few rules were enforced and little order reigned, yet the sight was as widely suggestive as any more carefully arranged demonstrations. Somehow these artless, unpremeditated outpourings of the heart of Christendom have a far higher power to interest, a far subtler charm to entrance, and leave a higher impression and a more healthful influence behind, than

those wonderful pageants which from year to year draw thousands of curious spectators to Rome. Here is everyday Christianity; here is the inner working of that silent, God-wielded mechanism whose outward robes and draperies only come to us in the shape of those glittering festas; here is the real work, the real core of things, the heart whose pulsation alone gives meaning to all that external magnificence, the sun of which those ceremonies are the radiance, the consuming fire of which that glorious ritual is but the outgoing heat and the coruscant light. And when we think of the darker and varied aspects, the inner complications of the lives of those who were crowding round the altar-rails of St. Germain, what a wonderful, manifold history, what a spiritual landscape of infinite shades of the most delicate pencillings, do we not see! Side by side kneel souls whose life-paths run in opposite channels: here is Martha, the busy household angel, whose faith is inwoven in her every daily movement, her every thought, though it be of toil and anxiety; there is the pensive Magdalen, whose sadness is her soul's beauty, whose memory brings before her even more tokens of merciful forgiveness and unwearied love than of her own little past, her sins and her hard-heartedness; there kneels the widow whose child has just been given back to her from the very portals of death, and whose only altar for many dreary months has been the darkened chamber and the curtained sick-bed. Close to her is a maiden whose life is one long act of pure preparation for the bridal feast, the marriage supper of the Lamb, and who, when next Christmas-chimes sound, will hear in them the glad knell that proclaims her death to the outside world, and her life-long vow of obedience to her Spouse. Here is a Monica, wrest in prayer for a wayward son wh hopeless lapse from the narrow of virtue is the heaviest cross Saviour could have chosen for burden; there again is the b kneeling by the side of the sin joyous, boyish bridegroom, whom she is just beginning a stage on the road to eternal bliss rough, so uniform, so common is the aspect of the crowd, that things are only visible to spi sight, to the eye of the soul; a visible even to our darkened o of spiritual understanding, how more clearly and far more touc ly to the eye of eternal Wi and fathomless Love! What a garden is a church full of hu communicants before the sigh God! How fragrant and varie blossoms to his illumined percep Men in every stage of conversi those who have just timidly set foot on the first round of Ja mystic ladder; those who have gled so far that they can dare to down one moment, and measur death from which God's love raised them, in order to 'gain tional grace to correspond wit future and more rapid calls he ward; those who have left al and danger so far behind that look upon them calmly, as one the rolling clouds far below fron crisp-breathing atmosphere of highest mountains; those whose versation is in heaven, and thoughts are silent angels wa ever with them as the living me gers of God. Such are the mi of grace that crowd the lowly ch the mysteries that we can only at beneath the crust of mate which we see; the wonders tha tle us in the swaying throng, a which we have so little knowl that we hardly even suspect

MR. CLARKE'S LIVES OF THE AMERICAN CATHO BISHOPS.*

"Like stars to their appointed heights they climb."—SHELLEY.

THE remark had become trite in the mouths of Europeans, that America has no history. Such was the inertness of our countrymen in the department of American history; such the want of works recounting the thrilling story of early adventure and colonization, the struggles of feeble colonies for existence and permanence, their long and steadfast preservation of free institutions inherited from the mother-country, and their gallantry in defending them against an unnatural mother; the birth and growth of a vast and mighty republic, maintaining at once order and liberty amid the convulsions and revolutions of European dynasties and empires, and eliciting from a European monarch, whose crown was afterwards torn from his head, the remark addressed to an American Catholic bishop, who told him of free and peaceful America, "Truly, that people at least understand liberty; when will it be understood among us?"—all these things remained so long an untold story, that it was believed but too generally that America was without a history to record. The subsequent works of Bancroft, Irving, Prescott, Parkman, and others have pretty effectually dispelled the delusion.

But it seems to have been equally thought, among the historians of the church, that her career in America was also devoid of historical i so few and meagre were our p ed records and histories. In neral histories of the church, that by Darras, commencing earliest ages, and coming d our own times, with but sligh ral allusions to America, n tion whatever is made of t and progress of the church United States. In the Ameri tion of Darras, there is an Ap written for the purpose by an can author, Rev. Charles I. D.D., giving a *Sketch of the and Progress of the Catholic Ch the United States of America*, tended to supply, in some m the omission.

In our article on Bishop in THE CATHOLIC WORLD o 1871, we remarked: "Sketc local church history, more complete, have occasionally ed—sketches, for instance, li *Catholic Church in the United* by De Courcy and Shea; and *History of the Catholic Missions* the Indian tribes of Americ Bishop Bayley's little volume history of the church in Ne But a work of a different kind, er in its design than some c excellent and useful publi more limited in scope than and costly general historie awaits the hand of a polish enthusiastic man of letters."

When we penned these lines, we knew of Mr. Clarke's lo tinued and unwearied labors

* *Lives of the Deceased Bishops of the Catholic Church in the United States, with an Appendix and an Analytical Index.* By Richard H. Clarke, A.M. In two vols. Vol. I. New York: P. O'Shea. 1871.

ent of American Catholic
t, had cheered at times his
nd faithful studies, and had,
ndness, been able to spread
ur readers some of his intend admirably prepared bio-
l papers, such as the *Life of*
Dongan of New York, in
THOLIC WORLD of Septem-
, and the *Memoir of Father*
S.J., in the July and August
, 1871, still we scarcely hop-
ve should see our desires so
lized, or that we should so
ve occasion to hail the ap-
of the splendid work now
s, the fruits of his accom-
en and energetic industry,
wo handsomely printed and
bound volumes, *The Lives*
eceased Bishops of the Catho-
h in the United States. The
on of such a work, prepared
he broken and fleeting mo-
leisure snatched from a life
to professional duties, and
tive participation in the Ca-
d public-spirited enterprises
usy metropolis, is something
a we, as a Catholic journalist
to literature, may be per-
o express our own thanks,
e of the Catholic communi-
t the same time to commend
nstance of successful literary
rich but uncultivated field,
what we hope and believe it
reward for long and pains-
esearches, careful collation,
literary study. There were
published works, as we have
, from which to draw the
d information necessary for
ook. Hence the author had
in a great measure, his ma-
om the archives of the vari-
eses, the unpublished corre-
ce and journals of the de-
relates, their pastoral letters
lresses, from the Catholic serial publications and newspapers of the last half-century (a task of great and protracted labor and fatigue), from the personal recollections of surviving friends, co-laborers, and colleagues of the bishops, from family records, from his own correspondence with numerous witnesses of the growth of the church and of the labors of our apostolic men, and even from the silent but sacred marble records of the tomb. The frequency with which the author cites, among his *authorities*, unpublished documents and original sources of information, which were in many cases the individual narratives of living witnesses, committed to writing at his request, and for this work, is a proof of the industry and labor with which this work has been prepared, and give us the means of appreciating the services thus rendered to our American Catholic literature, in securing and preserving from decay, oblivion, or total loss many valuable but perishable traditions and documentary materials. We will refer to two only, among many instances throughout these richly stored pages, of valuable documents thus given to the public; these are the royal charter of King James II., guaranteeing liberty of conscience to the Catholics of Virginia in 1686, and the beautiful and touching letter addressed by Archbishop Carroll, in 1791, to the Catholic Indians of Maine, the remnants of the pious and faithful flock of the illustrious and martyred Rale—for the publication of both of which we are indebted to Mr. Clarke.

Mr. Clarke has devoted many years to these valuable and excellent studies and compositions, and those who have read our Catholic periodical literature during the last fifteen years, will remember his *Memoirs* of Archbishops Carroll and Neale, of Bishops Cheverus and Flaget, of the

Rev. Prince Demetrius Augustine Gallitzin, of Fathers Andrew White and Nerinckx, of Governor Leonard Calvert, Charles Carroll of Carrollton, Commodore John Barry, the father of the American navy, and Judge Gaston; which were published in 1856 and 1857 in *The Metropolitan* of Baltimore. The favor with which these papers were received at the time, and the earnest recommendations of prelates, priests, and laymen, have, as we have learned, induced the author to enlarge his plans and undertake a series of works, which will give the American Church a complete biography of ecclesiastics and laymen, and, at the same time, literary monuments of classic taste and scholarship. The present book of the prelates will, as we rejoice to learn, be followed by the second work of the course, containing the lives of the missionaries of our country, such as White of Maryland, Marquette, Jogues, and Brébeuf of New York, Rale of Maine, the missionaries of the Mississippi Valley, of distinguished priests in later times, and of the founders of our religious houses, male and female. The remaining work of the series, more interesting probably than even the preceding ones, because not the least attempt has so far been made in that direction, will contain the lives of distinguished Catholic laymen, who have rendered signal services to our country, such as Calvert, Carroll, and Taney of Maryland, Iberville of Louisiana, Dongan of New York, La Salle and Tonty, explorers of the Mississippi River, Barry of Pennsylvania, Vincennes of Indiana, Gaston of North Carolina, and many others. The whole will form a complete series of Catholic biographical works, issued in the appropriate order of bishops first, priests and religious second, and finally of statesmen, captains, explorers, and

jurists. We cannot withhold pression of our pleasure at th pect of results such as these i partment of literature which ever been one of the objects CATHOLIC WORLD to encoura mote, and cherish.

That valuable materials e the country for all of these im works, we feel quite sure. W care will be taken of them, a they will be freely placed at vice of our Catholic historia authors. Their publication w the best means of preserving while rendering them useful present generation. We will incident in the experience Clarke, in preparing his *Live Bishops*, related by him to us evidence of the danger to wh luable historical matter is cor exposed of being lost and des He applied, in one instance, custodians of the papers rela the Catholic history of an im diocese and state, and was in that the diocesan papers and ments had been for many yea ed up in a strong chest or s fore and for some time aft death of the first bishop, and, ing opened and examined, the found to be in a state of co decay from the damp, fell to when handled, and that sca line of the writing was legible. er cases are related of valuab terials for American Catholic lost or sent out of the country observe, in the first volume bef a new and appropriate feat distinct and separate return of by the author to a long list lates, priests, and laymen who supplied him with materials or him in his labors. The app makes, in his preface, for the ance of such as possess ma has our cordial sympathy; a

appeal will not be made in

ook of prelates, whose ap-
we now hail with so much
is the most important and
contribution yet made to
rican Catholic biographical
. It covers the ground of
re Church history to the
ent times, possesses the pe-
terest which attaches to per-
d individual narrative, and is
re have said, from the dry-
e general history. Its pages
h an ardent love of country
our American institutions,
a devotion to true liberty,
ell accord with the traditions
ation of one of the descen-
the Catholic pilgrims of
d, who constitute the theme
ored chapter in our history,
g the magnanimity of a do-
Catholic majority in times
eration was not the fashion,
nony between Catholicity
ty, and an unflinching faith
generations of Protestant
on. Praise is freely bestow-
e praise was due, to our
nd to our countrymen; and
s administered in the spirit
ffection, whenever there are
abuses to be corrected, or
ere is conflict, in the civil
al order, with the sacred
religion and of conscience.
ntiquity of the Catholic
in America, her struggles
phs, are well worthy of the
all. Her struggles have
against vice and error, and
of liberty and virtue. Her
have been the conquest of
r heaven. No impartial
n study the career of the
Church in the United States
eing convinced of the puri-
motives, and the sacredness
s. Her conservatism, her sacraments, her defence of Christian marriage, her labors for religious education, her chastening influence over the consciences of her children, of which every day's record affords examples, her maintenance of law and order, have made her in the past, what they will prove in the future, the mainstay of society, of liberty, and of the republic. Her growth in our midst has been the work of Providence, not of man; a growth which, as our author shows, has proportionately far outstripped that of the republic. While the country has increased from thirteen states to thirty-seven states and eleven territories in ninety-five years, the church has increased from one bishopric to sixty-four bishoprics, six vicariates apostolic, and four mitred abbots in eighty-one years. The population of the country has increased from 2,803,000 to about 40,000,000, while the children of the Catholic Church have increased from 25,000 to 5,500,000. The increase of the general population of the country has been 1,433 per centum in ninety-five years, and that of the church has been 22,000 per centum in eighty-one years. The Catholic clergy have increased from twenty-one priests in 1790 to about four thousand eight hundred priests in 1871; they dispense the blessings of religion in 4,250 churches and 1,700 chapels.

After giving these statistics, the preface proceeds thus:

"To Rome, the capital of the Christian world, Eternal City, destined in our hopes and prayers and faith to be restored to us again as the free and undesecrated Mistress and Ruler of Churches, and to the Sovereign Pontiffs therein, Vicars of Christ on earth, we turn with love and gratitude for the care, solicitude, and support bestowed upon our churches, and for the exemplary prelates bestowed upon them by the Chief Bishop of the church. To our venerable hierarchy,

bishops and priests, and to the religious orders, both male and female, we render thanks for their labors, their sacrifices, their sufferings, and their suffrages.

"To our prelates, especially, is due under God the splendid result we have but faintly mentioned. They were the founders of our churches, the pioneers of the faith, and the chief pastors of our flocks. In poverty and suffering they commenced the work, and spent themselves for others. A diocese just erected upon the frontiers, in the midst of a new and swarming population, to anticipate and save the coming faithful, the hope of a future flock, an outpost upon the borders of Christianity and civilization—such was the frequent work and vigilant foresight of the Propaganda and of the Councils of Baltimore—such the charge confided to a newly consecrated bishop. To the religious enterprise and untiring providence of the Catholic Church, in her prompt and vigorous measures for the extension of the faith in this country, may well be applied the striking lines of Milton:

> 'Zeal and duty are not slow;
> But on occasion's forelock watchful wait.'
> —*Paradise Regained.*

"To assume the task of creating, as it were, building up, and governing the infant churches thus confided to their care, was the work that was faithfully and zealously performed by our bishops. It was no uncommon thing for a bishop to be sent to a diocese where there was scarcely a shrine or a priest; where he not only had no friends or organized flock to receive him, but where he had not even an acquaintance; where he would not meet a face that he had ever seen before. In some instances, he had to enter a diocese rent with disunion or schism among the people; in others, he was compelled to reside out of the episcopal city by reason of disaffection prevailing within. In other cases, such was their poverty that they had not the necessary means to procure an episcopal outfit, to provide a pectoral cross and crosier, or to pay their travelling expenses to their dioceses. In many cases the humble log-cabins of the West were their episcopal palaces and cathedrals; and frequently church, episcopal residence, parish school, and theological seminary were all under the same contracted roof. In the midst of such difficulties, we behold examples of humility, patience, cheerfulness, zeal, ch[arity,] love, poverty, and untiring labor. A[...] of such examples, and of lives so go[od and] heroic, has led us to undertake the [work] now presented to the public, in or[der to] repeat and continue their holy influ[ence,] to preserve the memory of such de[eds, to] render a tribute to those honored n[ames,] and to rescue, as far as we coul[d,] Catholic traditions from oblivion o[r] loss. We applied to ourself, and y[...] to the spirit of, the poet's appeal:

> 'Spread out earth's holiest records he[re]
> Of days and deeds to reverence dear[;]
> A zeal like this what pious legends t[ell?']

The two volumes contain th[e lives] of fifty-six American bishops, a[nd to] the second volume is affixed a[n ap]pendix containing the lives of [...] prelates of other countries, who [had] a special connection with the A[meri]can Church. The first volum[e, to] which we will confine our p[resent] writing, contains the lives of tw[enty-]nine prelates, a list of whom, [with] the dates of their consecrati[on or] appointment, and the religious [order] to which they belonged, where [such] was the case, will in itself prov[e in]teresting.

The antiquity of our chur[ch in] America is strikingly illustrat[ed in] this volume—an antiquity eq[ual to] that of the church in some [of the] old countries of Europe, exte[nding] back to the ages of faith, whe[n the] church was fighting her battle[s with] paganism, and before the time [when] altar was raised up against alt[ar by] the Protestantism of the sixt[eenth] century, and before the more m[odern] phases of infidelity and comm[unism] had declared war against all [order] and all religion. In the tent[h, ele]venth, and twelfth centuries [the] Northmen of Iceland, hardy a[dven]turers on the seas, pushed the[ir ex]ploits beyond the continent o[f Eu]rope, and landed colonies o[n the] shores of this continent. C[oming] from their ice-clad homes, o[n ex]treme north-eastern regions w[e ...]

untry of enchanting ver-
eceived the name of Green-
l, pushing their cruises
th, they entered our own
ett Bay, where, seeing the
tooned with vines teeming
s, they called it Vinland.
Longfellow, aptly quoted
arke, has celebrated some
oits of Vikings and North-
ea and shore. They were
oters and highwaymen of

ng the corsair's crew,
the dark sea I flew
ith the marauders;
was the life we led,
y the souls that sped,
y the hearts that bled,
r our stern orders."

time of which the poet
Iceland and Greenland
n. The mother-country
conversion to missionaries
nd, and she, in turn, sent
d priests, who converted
ts in Greenland and Vin-
e faith. Convents and
arose and resounded with
of God, chanted in Latin
e centuries and a half be-
mbus discovered America.
it among the Catholic
s was Eric, who, in the
of the twelfth century,
d his exalted labors at
, and afterwards particu-
the banks of Narragansett
site of the present city of
and its vicinity were the
ls of his apostolic labors.
tant did these Christian
become, that a bishopric
d at Garda, the episcopal
eenland, and Eric was con-
s first bishop by Lund, a
Scandinavia. He visited
cherished flock at Vinland,
e was devoted, and, rather
e them, he resigned his
crosier, went into the ranks
rgy, and gave his life for his flock—the first of American martyrs.

The colonies of the Northmen were swept away, and the record of them, even, faded from the histories and traditions of mankind.

"I was a Viking old:
My deeds, though manifold,
No skald in song has told,
No saga taught thee."

A glowing tribute is paid hy the author to the Catholic faith and genius of Columbus, the unrivalled discoverer of America. In the very generation in which Columbus lived, the church established a bishopric within the present limits of our republic. Among the ambitious and hardy captains of that day was Pamphilo de Narvaez, who, in attempting the conquest of Florida, aspired to add to the Spanish crown a realm equal in extent and wealth to Mexico, and to rival the fame of Cortéz by his own exploits. The Franciscans were at his side, seeking a holier conquest, fired by no earthly ambition, but by a heavenly zeal. A bishopric was erected for Florida as the expedition was about to sail from the ports of Spain, and Juan Juarez, who had already won the title of one of the Twelve Apostles of Mexico, was appointed, in 1526, Bishop of Rio de las Palmes. He spent his brief sojourn in Spain in securing ample provision for his future flock, and in obtaining royal guarantees for the liberty and kind treatment of the natives. No time was left for his consecration; he hastened on board the fleet, and rushed to the spiritual relief of his children, whom he knew and "loved only in Christ." After the disastrous termination of the expedition, he and his companions suffered shipwreck, and are believed to have perished of hunger—the second martyr of our church. Well has our author said of him, that he gave up

by God's help to overcome that
s and ingratitude of multitudes
ased from benumbing bondage,
ould clamor in the wilderness to
ack to the fleshpots of Egypt;
among the contemporaries and
followers of our Saviour, could
m to bear in solitude the agony
ross; and which in your case, we
nd, will yet manifest itself in
able expectations, extravagant
impetuous requirements, and in
ings that nothing has been earn-
ended, because everything has
already accomplished.
address of the Philadelphia
held January 10, 1848, contained
wing earnest words: 'May the
y grant you length of life,
of heart, and wisdom from on
order to bring to a happy con-
the beneficent reforms which
begun! May he inspire the
and people of Italy with the cour-
moderation necessary to second
rts! May he raise up to you
rs, who will continue to extend
ence of peace and justice on
nd the time will come when the
of God's poor will, if oppressed,
to summon the most powerful of
ressors to appear at the bar of
Christendom; and the nations
in judgment upon him, and the
or, blushing with shame, shall be
y their unanimous and indignant
render justice to the oppressed.'
ilar addresses were sent from
very city of any importance in
on to the Holy Father. But soon
hetic language of the New York
was realized; the clamor of the
inted populace was raised against
ather and best friend; Count
is secretary, is assassinated, and
ly Father himself is a fugitive
me. It was then that the devo-
Catholics manifested itself to-
he Supreme Pontiff, and many
artfelt were the testimonials of
and affection received by the
Gaeta from his children through-
world. The Catholics of the
States were not behind their
in these demonstrations, and the
as entertained that the Holy
would accept an asylum in our
... How vividly do the present
of that same Holy Father, and of
me holy church, recall the events
of his glorious pontificate! When, oh! when, will the Catholic peoples of the world demand of their governments the restoration of the capital of Christendom, and the liberty of the Vicar of Christ?"

As we were about to close our article, our eye fell upon the following fine passages in the *Life of Dr. England, First Bishop of Charleston*, and we yield to the temptation of transferring them to our columns, both as a tribute to that illustrious prelate and as specimens of Mr. Clarke's style:

"The great struggle of Bishop England's life in this country seems to have been to present the Catholic Church, her doctrines and practices, in their true light before the American people. In his effort to do this his labors were indefatigable. His means of accomplishing this end were various and well studied. He endeavored, from his arrival in the country, to identify himself thoroughly with its people, its institutions, its hopes, and its future. He was vigilant and spirited in maintaining and defending the honor and integrity of the country, as he was in upholding the doctrines and practices of the church. In his oration on the character of Washington, he so thoroughly enters into the sentiments of our people, and participates so unreservedly in the pride felt by the country in the *Pater Patriæ*, that his language would seem to be that of a native of the country. There was no movement for the public good in which he did not feel an interest, and which he did not, to the extent of his opportunities, endeavor to promote. His admiration for the institutions of the country was sincere and unaffected. Though no one encountered more prejudice and greater difficulties than he did, he, on all occasions, as he did in his address before Congress, endeavored to regard the prejudices and impressions entertained by Protestants against Catholics as errors, which had been impressed upon their minds by education and associations, for which they themselves were not responsible. In his writings and public sermons and addresses, he travelled over the wide range of history, theology, and the arts, in order to vindicate the spotless spouse of Christ against the calumnies of her enemies. If Catholic citizens and

voters were attacked on the score of their fidelity to their country and its institutions, Bishop England's ready pen defended them from the calumny and silenced their accusers. If a Catholic judge or public officer was accused of false swearing or mental reservation in taking the official oath, he found an irresistible and unanswerable champion in the Bishop of Charleston. He found the church in the United States comparatively defenceless on his accession to the See of Charleston, but he soon rendered it a dangerous task in her enemies to attack or vilify her; and many who ventured on this mode of warfare were glad to retreat from the field, before the crushing weapons of logic, erudition, and eloquence with which he battled for his church, his creed, and his people. . . . .

"Bishop England visited Europe four times during his episcopacy, for the interests and institutions of his diocese, visiting Rome, most of the European countries, and his native Ireland, which he never ceased to love. He was sent twice as apostolic delegate from the Holy See to Hayti. He obtained from Europe vast assistance for his diocese, both in priests, female religious, and funds. It was proposed to translate him to the bishopric of Ossory in Ireland, but he declined. The highest ecclesiastical dignity, with comfort, luxury, friends, and ease, in his native country, could not tempt him to desert his beloved church in America. He had become an American citizen and an American prelate, and he resolved to continue to be both as long as he lived. At Rome he was consulted on all matters relating to the ecclesiastical affairs of this country. The officials of the Eternal City were astounded at the great travels and labors of Bishop England. They heard him appoint from the Chambers of the Propaganda the very day on which he would administer confirmation in the interior of Georgia. The cardinals, in their wonder at all he accomplished, and the rapidity of his movements, used to call him '*il vescovo a vapore*,' or the 'steam bishop.' We have seen with what an insignificant force he commenced his episcopal labors. He increased the churches of his diocese to over sixteen, and lef behind him a well-organized and appointed clergy, and numerous ecclesiastical, religious, educational, and charitable institutions. The Catholic families of his diocese might have been counted, at the time of the erection of the See of Charleston, on one's fingers; at the bishop's death they were counted by thousands. But the good he accomplished was not confined to his own diocese. His elevating and encouraging influence was felt throughout the country, at Rome, and in many parts of the Catholic world."

His dying words to his clergy, and through them to his flock, were as follows:

"Tell my people that I love them; tell them how much I regret that circumstances have kept us at a distance from each other. My duties and my difficulties have prevented me from cultivating and strengthening those private ties which ought to bind us together; *your functions* require a closer, a more constant intercourse with them. Be with them—be of them—win them to God. Guide, govern, and instruct them. *Watch as having to render an account of their souls, that you may do it with joy, and not with grief.* There are among you several infant institutions which you are called on, in an especial manner, to sustain. It has cost me a great deal of thought and of labor to introduce them. They are calculated to be eminently serviceable to the cause of order, of education, of charity; they constitute the germ of what, I trust, shall hereafter grow and flourish in extensive usefulness. As yet they are feeble, support them—embarrassed, encourage them—they will be afflicted, console them. . . .

"*I commend my poor church to its patrons—especially to her to whom our Saviour confided his in the person of the beloved disciple: 'Woman, behold thy Son; Son, behold thy mother.'*"

The second volume contains the lives of thirty American bishops, and, in the Appendix, the lives of Right Rev. Charles Augustus de Forbin-Jansen, Bishop of Nancy, France, who visited this country in 1840, and rendered signal services to religion while here; of Right Rev. Edward Barron, who volunteered from this country for the African mission, was made Bishop of Africa in 1842, and died at Savannah, Georgia, in [illegible]

of men. It is the style, not of a mere essayist, but of a preacher. It is, therefore, far more pleasing and popular in its character than that of most books on the same topic. Every Catholic in the United States ought to read it, and we doubt if any book has been published on the Pope equally fitted for general circulation in England and Ireland. Neither is there any so well fitted to do good among non-Catholics. We hope no pains will be spared to give it a wide and universal circulation.

It is most important and necessary that all Catholics should be fully instructed in the sovereign supremacy and doctrinal infallibility of the Pope, and the strict obligation in conscience of supporting his temporal sovereignty.

Mr. Coddington has published this volume in a superior manner, with clear, open type, on very thick and white paper, and adorned it with an engraved portrait of the beloved and venerable Pius IX. Once more we wish success to this timely and valuable series of lectures, and thank the reverend author in the name of the whole Catholic public for his noble championship of the dearest and most sacred of all causes—that of the Vicar of Christ.

Antidote to "The Gates Ajar." By J. S. W. Tenth thousand. New York: G. W. Carleton & Co. 1872.

Mr. Carleton appears to be convinced that "*de gustibus non est disputandum*" by a bookseller, but rather that provision is to be made for all tastes. On the back of this little pious pamphlet we find advertised *The Debatable Land*, by Robert Dale Owen; *The Seventh Vial*, containing, we conjecture, a strong dose, by Rev. John Cumming; *Mother Goose with Music*, by an ancient, anonymous author; *At Last*, a new novel, by Marian Harland, etc. The *Antidote* is a rather weak and quite harmless dose, done up in pretty tinted paper. The writer naïvely asks, on p. 23: "Who would not like to fly away in the tail of a comet?"—a question which any little boy would answer in the affirmative, but cruelly dashes our hopes to the ground by telling us that "all this is mere conjecture." Again, on p. 26, he gravely reasons thus: "As to families in heaven living in houses together, as if they were on earth, that is simply impossible. When children marry here, they leave their parents, and have homes of their own; their children do likewise, and so on *ad infinitum*. Those who would live together in heaven would be only husbands and wives and the unmarried children. And as to the married who are not all happily united here, are they to be tied together for ever whether they like each other or not?" The little pamphlet is concluded by two pieces of poetry, one of which is pretty good, the other one of those cantering hymns which are such favorites at the week-evening prayer-meeting:

> "We sing of the realms of the blest,
> That country so bright and so fair,
> And oft are its glories confessed;
> But what must it be to be there?"

The doctrine of Miss Phelps's antagonist is more orthodox than hers, without doubt, so far as it goes, but it is presented in such a way as rather to provoke a smile than to convince or attract the mind of any one who is not already a pious Presbyterian. Our Presbyterian and other Evangelical friends contrive to make religion as sad and gloomy as a wet afternoon in the country. Even heaven itself has but small attractions for those who are not depressed in spirits, when described in the doleful strain which is supposed to be suitable to piety. Miss Phelps, as well as other members of the gifted and cultivated Stuart family, and many of similar character and education, revolted from the dismal system of Puritanism. She yearned after a brighter

could be preserved from future danger in an institution like the one proposed in the appendix to this volume. No place but a strictly religious house, in our opinion, could be a house of moral convalescence to these poor creatures. There is one way in which American Catholic women can lessen the number of these miserable outcasts. Watch over your servants, know where they spend their evenings, take them by the hand and give them loving, maternal advice as to their company, and endeavor to bring them often to confession and communion. The providence of God has committed these young girls to your care, and who knows but their souls may be required of you, negligent mistresses, in that day when we must all stand before the judgment-seat of Christ? With regard to the employments of women, should not women be allowed to do any honest business that they can do well? Many new openings have been made for her of late years in telegraphic and photographic offices and stores. But, after all, to touch the root of this matter, why should not woman be so trained that she could, in any emergency, have a resource and support herself? A great deal would be gained if children were brought up to feel that "it is working, and not having money, that makes people happy." "It is a noteworthy fact," says the author of *The Prisoners of St. Lazare*, "that three-quarters of the inmates are without knowledge of a trade or of any means of making a livelihood for themselves. The support of husband or father failing, then destitution followed, and then vice."

PROPHETIC IMPERIALISM; or, The Prophetic Entail of Imperial Power. By Joseph L. Lord, of the Boston Bar. New York: Hurd and Houghton. 1871.

Mr. Lord writes like a thorough gentleman, a point which we notice in this distinct and emphatic manner because it is a somewhat rare phenomenon in literature of this class. He writes, also, like a well-trained and cultivated scholar and thinker. It is, therefore, a pleasant task to read what he has written, more pleasant from the fact that his essay is a short one, and his thoughts are briefly as well as lucidly and elegantly set forth. Moreover, although a Boston lawyer, Mr. Lord really reverences the Holy Scriptures and believes the prophets. His spirit is pious and fervent, though sober, and he is alike free from cant and from unbelieving flippancy. The peculiar theory of Mr. Lord regarding the fulfilment of what we may call the imperial prophecies is not contrary to orthodox doctrine, and is in fact held by him in common with some Catholic writers, although diverse from the one held by the generality of sound interpreters. So far as all the empires preceding that of Christ are concerned, he agrees with the common interpretation. In respect to this last, he holds to a personal descent and earthly empire of our Lord. This is an hypothesis which, in our eyes, has no probability whatever. It is not wonderful, however, that a person who does not see the earthly empire of Christ in the reign and triumph of his Vicar and the Roman Church, should be driven to look for a personal descent and reign of the Lord in the latter times. In this respect, Mr. Lord agrees with a number of eminent Protestant writers, who, being disgusted with the fruits of the Reformation, and not so happy as to see the glories of the Catholic Church, fly for consolation to this brilliant but, as we think, baseless hypothesis.

Mr. Lord differs from most American Protestants in the very disrespectful esteem in which he holds democracy. It is curious to observe the very enthusiastic and adulatory language in which a number of divines express their conviction of the truth of his theory, imperialists

the vices, follies, and delinquencies of the rich and the otherwise highly placed in social rank, and whatever admonitions we may address to them respecting the duties and dangers of their position, must be taken as coming from a friend, not only to themselves as individuals, but to their class. With these preliminaries, we address ourselves to our task.

We have placed the title "In Reference to Communism" at the head of our first article for one special reason. Communism threatens the wealthy class with a war of extermination. It is obvious, therefore, that the rich have more need to reflect on the duties and dangers of their position, at the present time, than they have ever had before. So, then, we call their attention at the outset to the war which the fanatics of revolution are preparing for them, in order that our words may have more weight, and that they may give more serious thought to the subjects we intend to discuss with them. And here we will explain that we employ the single terms "rich," "rich people," etc., for convenience' sake, including under this designation other qualifications besides moneyed wealth, and other persons besides those who possess great fortunes; namely, all those who possess any species of privilege or power which gives them social dignity and influence.

We say, then, to the rich: your class, your privileges, your possessions, your lives, are threatened by an enemy whose character is disclosed by the bloody orgies of the Paris Commune. What application do we make of this grave and alarming fact? Simply this. The rich members of society ought to reflect seriously on all the questions which relate to their position in the commonwealth. They ought to think of their duties, to examine their own delin-

quencies, to consider the li
duct they ought to adop
their power and influence r
rationally, to educate their
carefully, and in every wa
vent and defeat the nefari
of the party of revolution.
earnestly and emphatically,
is now a special necessity
gation to use wealth, educ
tellectual power, social infl
litical power, moral and
force, to avert the dang
threaten society, and to pr
solid and firm establishm
right basis. Moreover, th
terest of the rich demand
them most imperatively.
private and personal interes
on the peace and good or
ciety. Their own safety d
them that they should wo
salvation of political and so
when they are in danger, ju
would bear a hand at the
board a leaking ship, or
batteries of their own be
city. Hostility between th
and the laborious classes
evil in society. When th
of the masses against the a
becomes violent, and tend
duce a revolution and an e
ing war of the former a
latter, there is a deadly s
the body politic which th
dissolution. This state of
ists at present in Christend
are not so deeply affected
this country; but we are
gether sound or safe from
tion, and there is reason
be on the alert to protect
from it. The rich have
ward society in general, a
its several classes and indi
particular. And they ha
present time and in prese
stances, a special obligatio
these duties careful attentio

time. The destruction of monasticism, therefore, resulted necessarily in a hostility of these two classes toward each other. So it has come about that the aristocracy, excited by kings against the church, turned next against the kings, the commercial and middle classes turned against the aristocracy, and now the masses are turning against the men of wealth, or, as their own leaders express it, against "the supremacy of cash." The condition of the laboring classes is, at best, in many respects a hard one. It is a great and an arduous thing which is required of them; to submit patiently to the supremacy of the higher classes. Religion alone makes their position tolerable; religion, binding together both the superior and the inferior classes in divine love. The hierarchy and the aristocracy must be recognized by the people as holding their high position for the common good of all, and as working with a self-denial equal or superior to their own; that is, as really *laborers* in another sphere of action, but with a common end in view, in order that they may contentedly acquiesce in the inequality of rank, wealth, and social privileges which prevails in society. So soon as the people are convinced, whether wrongly or rightly, that the privileges of their spiritual or temporal superiors are mere privileges of a caste, which despises, rules, and taxes the people for its own selfish aggrandizement and pleasure, they begin to hate them with a deadly hatred. The Catholic people are content that the Pope govern, rebuke, and punish them; that he possess the wealth and splendor of a spiritual and temporal sovereign; that he reign as the vicegerent of God on earth—because they believe that all this is for their own highest good. They are content that bishops and priests possess all the honors* and privile[...] their office, and willing to [...] them in these, for the same [...] Take away this belief, and it [...] long before they begin not [...] withhold their contributions, t[...] draw their allegiance, to refus[...] dience, to lose respect and l[...] their spiritual superiors, but [...] out for their overthrow an[...] clamor for their blood. It [...] same in respect to the secula[...] leged classes. And, at the [...] moment, since the greatest [...] of external and material pr[...] splendor, and worldly good i[...] ral has passed into the hands [...] wealthy class, it is this class w[...] most immediately exposed [...] brunt of the attack which is d[...] against caste and privilege. [...] quote the language of one of t[...] cial organs of the International[...] ty, the *Egalité* of Geneva, in [...] to show with the utmost cl[...] what is their spirit and aim:

"When the social revolutio[...] have dispossessed the *bourgeoisi*[...] interests of public utility, as the *[...]* *sie* dispossessed the nobles and th[...] what will become of them?

"We cannot answer with posit[...] tainty, but it is probable that [...] order of things will give them, to [...] an expression from one of our [...] an infinitely more precious weal[...] of labor, well paid, at their dis[...] so that they may be no longer ob[...] live by the labor of others, as th[...] hitherto lived. In case some [...] should be incapable of labor, wh[...] happen to a good many, seei[...] *hitherto they have never learned* [...] *of their ten fingers, what then?* then they will be given tickets fo[...]

"'But that is too little,' the *[...]* will howl.

"'Too little!' the workman will [...] 'too little to have work, at your [...] tion, well paid, and soup for the i[...] The deuce! You are hard to [...] We could have been well satisf[...] such terms formerly.'" *

* See the *Dublin Review*, Oct., p[...]

THE HOUSE OF YORKE.

CHAPTER XXI.

AMONG THE BREAKERS.

When the boat had slipped away from Indian Point, at one side, and Carl Yorke had strode off through the woods, at the other, Captain Cary lifted again the dingy canvas, and entered the wigwam that Edith had just quitted. In doing so, he was obliged to stoop very low, for the opening scarcely reached as high as his shoulders, and, had he stood erect inside, he would have taken the whole structure up by the roots.

Dick still lay with his arms thrown above his head, and his face hidden in them.

His friend bent over him, and spoke with an affectation of hearty cheerfulness which was far from his real mood. "Come! come! don't give up for a trifle, my boy. You're more scared than hurt. All you need is a little brandy and courage. Everything will turn out rightly, never fear!"

"Don't talk to me!" said Dick.

Captain Cary's heart sank at the sound of that moaning voice. When Dick Rowan's spirit broke, there was trouble indeed, and trouble which could neither be laughed nor reasoned away.

"Do take the brandy, at least," he urged; "and then I won't talk to you any more till the boat comes back. You must take it. You're in an ague-fit now."

Dick was, indeed, trembling violently. But, more to relieve himself from importunity, it would seem, than for any other reason, he lifted his head, swallowed the draught that was offered him, and sank back again.

His friend leaned over him one instant, his breast, strongly heaving, and full of pity, against Dick's shoulder, his rough, tender cheek laid to Dick's wet hair.

The poor boy turned at that, threw his arms around Captain Cary's neck, drew him down, and held him close, as a drowning man might hold a plank. "O captain, captain!" he whispered, "I've got an awful blow!"

When the sailor went out into the air again, all the Indians had retired into their wigwams, except Malie, and her father and mother. The child, wide awake, and full of excitement, was swinging herself by the bough of a tree, half her motion lost sight of in the dark pine shadow, half floating out into the light. Now and then, she stretched her foot, and struck the earth with it. When the stranger appeared and looked her way, she began to chatter like a squirrel, and, lifting her feet, scrambled into the tree, and disappeared among its branches.

Mr. and Mrs. Nicola crouched by the fire, and sulkily ignored the intruder. When he approached and stood by her side, the woman did not turn her head, but tossed a strip of

a-
ed,
sap-

ake to
stioned
I am go-
the ship,
n. It may
don't like to
than I must."
low-toned gut-
an nodded her
neither took any
ary.
ntrude," he add-
en a man is sick,
are of. Captain
oesn't half know
at he is about. I
as soon as I can.
for your trouble."
piece down be-
'When I come
e more," he said,
ack upon them,
woods.
wo elders stirred
sight; but Malie
ee, darted at the
ed it up. She
, when her father
money from her
into his pocket.
hen he let her go.
money, except to
around her neck,
ads was prettier.
her treasure—the
l given her that
herself on the
e, drew this book
ls of her blouse,
ves, reading here
age looked like
ngs written out.
and beasts had
do with making
Who would not
ssuwinoa was a

verse from a feathered songster? Malie would tell you that it means a "general." Probably the birds call their generals by that name. One looks with interest on a child who can read this chippering, gurgling, twittering, lisping, growling "to-whit, to-whoo!" of a thought-medium.

While she read, Captain Cary, tramping through the strip of woods between the encampment and South Street, recollected for the first time that his clothes were dripping wet. "What a queer, topsy-turvy time we are having!" he muttered, wringing the water from his cravat, as he hurried along. "The whole affair reminds me of that fairy play I saw last winter. There must be something unwholesome in this moonshine."

The play he meant was *Midsummer-Night's Dream*. But there was now no clamor of rustic clowns in a hawthorn brake, nor sight of Titania sleeping among her pensioners the cowslips. There were but his own steps, muffled in moss, and the lurking shadows creeping noiselessly away from the pursuing light.

By that short road across the Point, it was less than half a mile to the wharf where the *Halcyon* lay, and in ten minutes Captain Cary had reached his ship. His crew were all on board, and, as he walked down the wharf, he heard the refrain of one of their songs:

"And they sank him in the lowlands, low."

The verse ended in that mournful cadence that sailors learn from the ocean winds—those long-breathed, full-throated singers!

At sound of the captain's step, silence fell, and at his call a little imp of a Malay cabin-boy appeared, stood with twinkling eyes to take his orders, then shot away to execute them. When the sailor who had gone up to the bridge with the ladies

came back to the ship, the yawl was out, and Captain Cary sat in it waiting for him.

"Major Cleaveland wants to see you when you come up, sir," the sailor said, as they sped down the river. "He says you'd better bring Captain Rowan right up to his house. He will send the carriage down for you. He is obliged to leave town at four o'clock in the morning, in the Eastern stage, something about a trial of his in a court somewhere, so he can't see you in the morning."

"Did anybody else say anything?" the captain asked.

"Mr. Carl Yorke said that, as soon as he had gone home with the ladies, he would come back to see Captain Rowan. He got up to the bridge just as we did."

Captain Cary bent low over his oars, and muttered a word he did not choose to speak aloud. Plain men are almost always ready to have a jealous dislike of accomplished men, and a simple nature like Captain Cary's can never do justice to a complex one like Carl Yorke's. At that moment the sailor was thinking that, had Carl been the one to fall overboard, he would not have cared to wet his skin for the sake of saving him. And yet Carl had treated this man with friendly courtesy, and had admired and appreciated him thoroughly.

"Well, did any one else say anything?" he asked presently.

"Miss Edith felt pretty bad, sir. She leaned over the rail, and looked back to the Point, wringing her hands all the way, as we came up. She told me to say to you that she was sorry she had left Captain Rowan. I guess, sir, she is pretty fond of him, after all," the sailor said confidentially.

"What business have you guessing or thinking anything about it?" demanded his superior, with a h[illegible] sternness that would have del[illegible] Clara Yorke. "Keep your c[illegible] till I ask for it!"

"All right, sir!" respond[illegible] sailor, and shut his mouth. [illegible] was angry, he did not vent [illegible] show it.

"Well?" said the captain sl[illegible] after waiting a minute.

"Why, sir, there isn't mu[illegible] anything else," the man ans[illegible] "Miss Yorke said that they o[illegible] have taken Mr. Rowan up wit[illegible] and that she did not understan[illegible] they had allowed themselves [illegible] sent away in such a manner. [illegible] Miss Clara she said that you [illegible] there a boat ahead, sir?"

"No. What if there is? [illegible] on." He could not help bei[illegible] patient.

"Well, Miss Clara she sai[illegible] you knew best, and she wasn't [illegible] of leaving Mr. Rowan to [illegible] care."

The captain sat with his o[illegible] pended, and stared straight [illegible] The seaman hesitated, then re[illegible] good for evil. "Miss Clar[illegible] mightily taken with the way yo[illegible] overboard, sir. She thought th[illegible] did it in a very splendid fashi[illegible] told her I didn't know any oth[illegible] you could have done it, unles[illegible] had gone over back'ards, like [illegible] tain Rowan. She tossed up he[illegible] at that, and marched off, and g[illegible] the carriage."

The captain's oars flashed [illegible] into the water, and he gave [illegible] that made their boat skim the [illegible] like a bird.

When they reached the Poi[illegible] fire was out, and no person [illegible] sight. Captain Cary hastened [illegible] bank to the wigwam where h[illegible] left Dick Rowan, but as he la[illegible] hand on the fold of canvas a [illegible] voice inside challenged him.

subject; but Dick was inexora-
ıd the captain yielded. He
note of explanation and apo-
Mrs. Yorke; and so it hap-
that, when that lady's messen-
ıched the wharf in the morn-
ıe *Halcyon* was miles below,
ıg out through the Narrows,
blue, sunny sea stretching in
of her straight to the South
On the deck sat Dick Rowan,
on the rail, and watching the
oss and drop, toss and drop,
lulling motion, like the to-
of white, mesmerizing hands.
ıe face that watched that mo-
oked half-mesmerized, pale
eamy, with only a groping of
ıt in it.

ship went well, and within a
ıys they saw the rising sun
ın the masts and spires of New
The evening of that very day,
Fitzpatrick, of Boston—Father
his friends called him—coming
ıer late from a lecture, was
at a gentleman was waiting in
om to see him. He went in,
and Dick Rowan sitting there,
ot the Dick Rowan he had
ıd the year before, and wel-
home, and talked gayly with
a few short weeks. This man
have been Dick's elder broth-
a stern, pale man, too.

ıther," Dick said faintly, "I
you to keep me a little while.
come here for sanctuary. If
is any help in religion when
help fails, I want to know it
"

ıt what has happened? What
matter?" the priest exclaimed.
k sank back into the seat from
he had risen. "I've lost
sir, and my life has all gone to
"

she dead?" the priest asked.
o, sir; but she loves some one

Father John drew his chair close to the young man's side, and took his hand. "My dear son," he said, "are you going to despair because a woman has been false to you?"

Dick looked up as though not sure that he heard aright. What! any one call Edith false?

"No, sir, she was not false," he said. "It was something that she couldn't help. She would marry me now, if I would let her."

"Why, then, do you not marry her?" the father asked. "This is probably a fancy, which will pass away; and if she is good and true, she will do her duty by you."

Dick stared at the priest in an almost indignant astonishment. "What, sir!" he exclaimed, "do you think me mean enough to marry a woman who loves another man? I always feared this, at the bottom of my heart, though I would not own that I did. And it was always true, I suppose, only she did not know it. I made a great mistake. I thought that, if I tried to be good to God and to her, she would love me. But I have been thinking it all over during the last week, and I have found out that we choose by our hearts, not our heads, and that we do not really love a person when we can tell the reason why. I had no right to *buy* her. She belonged to some one else." He shivered, looked down a moment, then said huskily, "Yes, Edith was true!" and, dropping his face into his hands, burst into tears.

"My dear son!" Father John said, putting his arm around Dick's shoulder, "don't give up so! You have youth, and health, and friends, and a work to do in the world. Don't let this discourage you. She is only a woman."

"And I am only a man!" said Dick.

"What about your ship?" the priest asked, after a little while.

Dick raised his face, and controlled himself to speak. "Captain Cary is to take charge of her," he said. "I couldn't sail in the *Edith Yorke* again, sir. I would not trust myself off alone in her, with nothing else to think of, and no escape, unless I jumped into the ocean. It is haunted by her. Every plank, and spar, and rope of that ship is steeped in the thought of her. I have fancied her there, speaking, and laughing, and singing, just as I expected she would some day, and asking me the names of everything. When I used to walk up and down the deck, I'd imagine her beside me. I could see her dress fluttering, and the braid of hair, and two little feet keeping step. Why, sir, it was so real that I would sometimes shorten my steps for her sake. I never neglected my duty for her; but I looked at everything through a little rosy thought of her, and that made hard work pleasant. No, I can never again sail in the *Edith Yorke.* Have patience with me, father. Recollect, I have to overturn all that was my world, and have not a point to rest my lever on."

"You a Christian, and say that!" the priest exclaimed. "Where is your faith? Where is your reason?"

Dick started up fiercely, and began to walk the floor. "I cannot bear it! I will not bear it!" he exclaimed. "You preachers, with your reason, that tramples on all feeling, are as bad as the scientists, whose science tramples on all faith. God made the tide, sir, as well as the rock, and the storm as well as the calm, and it is for him to say whether either is a foolishness. People who are wise, when they sit in their safe homes, and hear the wind howling, pity the sailor, and tremble for him; but, when you see a soul among the breakers, you scorn it. I tell you, I will not bear such scorn! What do you this loss is to me?" he dem stopping before the priest, v looking steadfastly at him means that all the brightne sweetness of life, everything dear to human nature, are tor from me for ever. If I were lute man, I could find a mi substitute; if I were fickle, I fill her place; but I am neit stand here, twenty-eight yea and—I call God to witness!—less as when I was an infant mother's arms. It was Edit kept me so. 'Only a woma say; but that may mean mo an angel. She was my gu angel incarnate. 'Only a w but that woman's shape walke me through paths that migh led to perdition, and kept m If, in anger, an oath rose in my I felt her hand on my mouth, a not utter it. If I was tempte wine, I remembered her, and I the glass away. I can be thirsty, sir, if I am provoke many a sailor escaped the la irons for her sake. Once I h hand at a man's throat, with to wring his vile life out of him thought of her, and let him go. memory of this is not to be re away. Do you remember, time when you first thought o vocation, and sat down to cou costs? When you called u vision of your life before yo stripped from it, one after an wife, children, and home, and they mean, did you want any preach to you, in that hour, of mon sense and reason? Didn feel that you must let nature way a little while, and didn' find it go over you like a wave

While Dick Rowan, bold passionate feeling, poured fort torrent of words, the priest sa

toward the entry-door, her eldest daughter interposed, with an air of being in the charge of affairs. "I would not disturb Edith now, mamma."

"Melicent!" exclaimed her mother haughtily, and waved the young woman aside.

Edith was lying on her bed, dressed as on the day before, her face hidden in the pillow. She started when her aunt spoke to her, and turned a pale and tear-wet face. It did not need this to tell Mrs. Yorke that her niece's headache came from the heart.

"My head does ache, Aunt Amy," Edith said. "But I am distressed about Dick. He is displeased with me. I do not wish to speak of it to any one but him."

"I have sent Patrick down, my dear," her aunt said; "and you shall know as soon as he returns."

Mrs. Yorke and her two daughters sat together, pretending to read and sew, but all watching the avenue gate for the return of their messenger. When he had delivered his news, and gone, the mother spoke with authority.

"Girls, I insist on knowing, at once, the meaning of this!"

"You had better ask Carl, mamma; he is the one to explain," answered Melicent. "But I must say that Mr. Rowan has behaved ill. A young man whom one of our family has promised to marry should at least act like a gentleman."

"Send Carl to me," Mrs. Yorke said, rising. "And, Clara, say to Betsey that I shall see no one to-day, then go up and tell Edith."

Carl was pacing one of the garden paths, and, for the first time that day, his manner showed agitation. He had already heard Patrick's news, and his first thought was to echo Melicent's opinion that one who had been connected with their should at least act like a gen This sudden withdrawal nc gave occasion for gossip, bu rude to Edith. That it left the position of a culprit, Carl not allow himself to care.

"I thought the fellow ha spirit!" he muttered. "But it him to act like anything but tic."

As he said this, an inne made answer; not the voice science, for that acquitted h the voice which he expected from without: "Neither is it in speak or sing love to anothe promised wife, though silence break his heart."

"And what if it broke hers ed Carl, as though he ha spoken to.

He glanced up at the win Edith's chamber. The curt down, hanging in close, whi shutting her in.

Then came Melicent to cal

Carl found his mother in room, where she always to siesta in summer, and where s all her private conferences. a cosy, shady nook, with only and table, and chair in it, an ed intended as a place for c tial communion. In that roo nothing to save him from he eyes, Mr. Griffeth had sta out his apologies to Mrs. Y misleading her son; there, her ters came for advice and adm and there she herself retire she wished to be alone. I place where a rebel could be to submission, or a penitent c ed. It is almost impossible confidential in a large, well room.

"Have you had any quarr Mr. Rowan, Carl?" his moth ed, the moment he appeared

t, an unpleasant word has between us, mother," he an-

r

had been standing, but sank on the sofa as he spoke, and sed the door, and came and before her, doubting, at first, e tone of their interview would her question had been impe- and that he could not bear. are times in the life of the utiful when they feel that for them then no legitimate authority outside themselves. saw that her face was pale, the red curtain lowered over window behind her warmed light that entered; and her as entreating when she spoke

y son, have you nothing to tell

at down on the hassock at her d leaned on her lap; and she ll before he had uttered a

child," she whispered, lean- ing him, "your happiness is arest wish; but there is hon- ho . .

ook her trembling hands, and r look firmly. "Yes, mother, honor," he said. "But lis- me, before you conclude that ld be mentioned here in the ive sense. You know, mo- ould not speak of love to a I did not wish to. It was for me to see that Edith was though unconsciously, draw- ard me: If you had a rare with a single bud on it, would ank the one who would pluck d open before its time for ng? And what flower is so and sacred as a young girl's Besides, such a thought to a man also, when it comes ith a feeling of silence. To nd, it would have been rude and indelicate to speak hastily. There was time, and, meanwhile, I guarded myself and her. Of course I saw what Rowan wanted and meant, and he also understood me; I am sure of that. I never dreamed, though, that he would succeed. I was not prepared for that passion of pity and gratitude which Edith has shown for him. When I knew, last year, that he had proposed, it was all I could do to control my anger. I knew that he must have seen in her some instinctive recoil at first, and yet have appealed to her pity. He did not leave her free to choose. I do not say that he realized that. He is an honest, noble-souled fellow, and he loves her deeply; but he lacks a certain fineness which should have told him when urging was proper, and when it was coarsely selfish. I am willing to admit that it may have been only a mistake on his part; but people who make mistakes have to suffer by them, and, if they are not to blame, no one else is. I, too, made a mistake then, mother, and I have suffered for it. I had a thought of saying to Edith, 'Since you are to think of him as a suitor, think of me also, and choose between us.' Two motives prevented me. One was pride. I would not enter into competition with him; and there I was selfish. But the other was better. I saw that she was incredibly childish, and looked upon his proposal rather as a request that she should go and live with him and his mother, as she had lived with them before, than as a proposal that she should be his wife. I waited till she should perceive the difference, and this summer I thought that she was beginning to. The night before he came, I wanted to speak to her. I could hardly help it. I would have spoken but for him. But no, I thought. Let her answer him fairly first.' I supposed I knew

what that answer would be; and when she came down-stairs the next morning to meet him, I felt sure that it was to refuse him. I stood in the entry when she passed, and she knew that I was there, but would not look at me. She was very pale, I saw, and I thought it was for his sake. It seems it was for her own sake. No matter what I felt when I heard the words with which they met. I went away, you know; I did not choose to make a scene. When I came back, I had made up my mind to speak to him clearly, and as friendly as I could, and ask that he should give her back her promise, and leave her free to choose again. He would have done it, mother; I am sure he would. Had he been too loverlike, I should have made no delay; but, as it was, I thought best to wait till his visit was over. You could scarcely expect me to be perfectly cool and reasonable always. Under the circumstances, I think that I have shown as much fairness as any one has a right to require of me. I meant to see him last night, after the girls had come home—went to the sail with that intention. But he made me angry at starting. He stood there, and sang that ballad from *Le Misanthrope*,

'*Si le roi m'avoit donné*'

—sang it before *me*, and with such an air of triumph and certainty as made me feel anything but pitiful toward him for a little while. Edith was offended, too. I saw her color with resentment. '*Ma mie!*' It was too public a claiming. When we came back—you know what a night it was, mother." Carl stopped, his face growing very red. "There are some things not easy to tell," he said.

Mrs. Yorke put her arm around him, and drew his head to her bosom.

"Not even to your own dear?" she whispered, with resting on his hair. "It heart that taught yours to b

In that sweet confessiona on with his story. "It w scene as gives one that fain of the brain that just shows in our prudent resolutio moonlight, the music, th water, our very motion, we cating. And Edith was t so beautiful!—an Undine, over the boat-side, as th might any moment slip int ter, and disappear, if I did her. I sang what I would I called her, and she turne

Carl lifted his head, c mother's hands, and kissed fully, then stood up before an air as triumphant as I an's own. "The time h and she was mine!" he e "Edith belongs to me, moth

For the moment, everyt was forgotten; and the m got, too, till she saw his f over.

"Poor fellow!" said C knelt on the hassock agai heart aches for him. Whe Edith look at me, he fai seems cruel to be so happy cost. I went up to Hes night, to see him, but he there, and it was too late to ship. I would have born proach from him. I wou been patient, and have everything to him. I think that I could even have mad of him. He is generous. too late now."

"You must go away at on Mrs. Yorke said presently the only proper thing to family are pledged to Mr. and, till all is settled betw and Edith, you must have

e with her here. My position
e of great delicacy. I cannot
advise Edith."

ile they talked, Edith had risen,
written two letters, one to Dick
n, the other to Father Rasle.
were short, the former only a

'ou have no right to treat me
she wrote. "If you go away
ut seeing me, never call your-
y friend again!"

seemed hard; but she had said
self: "If he leaves me here with
I shall not be able to be true to

dressed herself to go out and
hese letters, and had just come
-stairs, when she met Carl in the
She stopped abruptly at sight
n, and a deep crimson mantled
ce as she waited for him to let

was a new blush for Edith, for
new why she blushed. But the
an spirit he had admired in the
was not dead, and she was her-
e next moment. She bade him
et "Good-morning, Carl!" and
assing on, when he asked to see
the parlor.

Certainly!" she said, too proud
rink.

rl smiled as he held the door
for her to pass, and closed it
them. He was pleased with
ignity.

have been talking with my mo-
' he said, "and she tells me that
ist go away immediately. Do
gree with her?"

ssibly she had seen, and misun-
ood his smile, for she chose to
ry high with him. "I do not
why you should go," she said
y.

hall I tell you why it seemed to
at I should?" he asked.

r look changed at the tone of
ice, which seemed reproachful. Why should she assume with him what was not true? When had he ever shown himself unworthy of her confidence?

"No, Carl," she said, "you need not tell me, and you must say nothing to me that you would not say to a married woman. I trust you, Carl. You have always been honorable. You are very dear to me, and I trust you perfectly. It is best that you should go."

The last words were spoken rather faintly, and she had turned from him, and opened the door.

"I shall go to Boston," he said, "and stay there. In a few weeks you will all come up, and I shall see you."

She stood in the door now, with her face half turned, and her forehead resting against the door-frame, so that he saw only her profile. And, so leaning, as though from faintness, she put her hand back, and held out her letters to him, and he took them.

"Read them both," she said, "and mail them for me. And, Carl, I shall not see you again before you go. And"—she stopped, as though her voice had failed her.

"I will not ask you to," he said.

"And, afterward," she went on, "I shall not see you in Boston. If you are at home, I shall go to stay with Dick's mother."

She did not look round again, but went up-stairs quickly, and shut herself into her room. It is not for us to intrude in that privacy wherein a young heart fought its first battle.

No one saw her that day; but the next morning she came out, and went about her usual employments, much in her usual manner. Whether, like that Russian empress, she was "too proud to be unhappy," or she had been soothed by that trust in God which makes every yoke easy

and every burden light, or the elasticity of youth made continued pain seem impossible, we do not pretend to say. Human motives are not always easy to be read by human eyes.

Everybody tried to act as though nothing were the matter, and there was enough for all to do. Many things had to be planned and arranged in preparation for their leaving Seaton, and Edith had her own business to attend to. There were the Pattens needing double care since they were so soon to lose her; and the Catholic school to visit, that being permitted now; and a great deal of shopping to be done for her little flock of pensioners.

Within a fortnight came a letter from Carl to his mother, taken up chiefly with business details. But he wrote: "I called yesterday on Mrs. Williams to ask for her son. He was not at home, and I have not seen him yet. He has given up his ship, for this voyage, to Captain Cary."

Carl could have added, but did not, that the call had not been a pleasant one. Mrs. Williams had just seen Captain Cary, and gleaned from him all that he had thought best to tell, which was, merely, that there seemed to be a slight misunderstanding between Dick and Edith. Her suspicions pointed at once to Carl, and she had not scrupled to express them to him when he came to her house.

"I am sorry not to see Mr. Rowan," he had said, when he got a chance, ignoring her accusations and reproaches; and, with that, had taken a ceremonious leave.

"A pretty mother-in-law for Edith!" was his conclusion.

A few days after came a letter from Mrs. Williams to Edith. It was what might have been expected from her. Dick had not been t mother; was stopping with and had refused to see he had Edith and those prou done to her son, that he everything and everybody, to hide himself in a Catholi house, instead of coming tc home?

Poor Dick! could he h seen that such a letter woul ten, he would have sacrifi self a good deal in order t it.

Edith dropped the lette feet after reading it, and for the first time since C away, "Oh! that Father Ra come!"

As she said it, and for a let slip the leash that held den feelings, one could however calm she might h outwardly, there had been a gnawing all the time. A bright words can mask a g When she dropped them, visible a whiteness about th shadows under the eyes, an thinning of the cheeks—the that short time.

Hearing her aunt's voic chamber-door asking ad Edith caught the letter up a her self-control with it.

Mrs. Yorke came in wit of quiet decision, and took her niece. "I saw the o your letter, my dear girl, a whom it was from," she said have no intention of allowir be killed by others, or to l self. I understand and r mother's feelings, Edith, a spect the obligation of a But there are common sens tice to be taken into accoun ings, and, especially, the fe a young person who has learned to know herself, ar

no one know that he is coming, he writes, but Miss Churchill, and Mr. and Mrs. Kent, at whose house he will stop. There will be time enough to notify the people when he has arrived. How glad they will be! That was a letter worth bringing, Uncle Charles!"

Looking up with her smile of thanks, she saw his face clouded. "Is there any trouble?" she asked anxiously.

"If he had come while Carl, and Rowan, and Captain Cary were here, I should have been better pleased," Mr. Yorke replied evasively. "He has, however, the right to come whenever he chooses. Answer his letter to-day, Edith, and invite him to stop with us."

"Dear Uncle Charles!" murmured Edith, and glanced enquiringly at her aunt.

"Tell him, for me, that we should all be very happy to have him as a guest," said Mrs. Yorke.

A smiling nod from Melicent and from Clara confirmed this assertion.

"Dear me!" Edith sighed out, wiping her eyes, "I do think that you are the most beautiful ever knew."

They all laughed at her saying it, and the little clou peared. Mr. Yorke did n it best to tell them that th Nothings had called a publ ing for the next evening. T been no such meeting for months, and this might not l consequence.

The invitation was writ sent, and on Saturday mor answer came, only a few hc ceding Father Rasle.

He thanked them for th ness, but found it necessar cline their invitation. He where all the Catholics cou to him, bringing their infan baptized, and going to c themselves. Besides the he could not think of subject house to such a visitation, w likely to continue till late in ning. His flock needed ev ment of his time.

But, meanwhile, between t and its answer, the public had taken place, and it had consequence.

TO BE CONTINUED.

THE NEW "OUTSPOKEN STYLE."

WE looked for dewy flower, and sunny fruit:—
He serves us up the dirt that feeds the root.

AUBREY DE V

and divine assistance. The prophets and apostles were divinely inspired to reveal truth; the Pope, according to Catholics, is divinely assisted to teach infallibly the truth revealed through the prophets and apostles, or as taught to the apostles by our Lord himself while he was yet with them. Now, if the inspiration which rendered the prophets and apostles infallible in revealing the truth which was hitherto hidden did not clothe them with the incommunicable attributes of God, how can you pretend that the assistance of the Spirit to teach infallibly what God revealed through them, which is far less, makes the Pope God, or clothes his nature with the attributes of God? If more did not do it in their case, how can less do it in his?

You say, "All men are fallible, and no man can teach infallibly." All men are fallible, it is true, in their own nature; but that no man by supernatural inspiration and assistance can teach infallibly, neither you nor I believe. We both hold, for instance, that St. Peter was a man, and yet that he was an infallible teacher of the word of God. We hold the same of St. Paul, of St. John, of St. Matthew, of St. Mark, and of St. Luke. Say you they were infallible not by their natural endowments, but only through the supernatural external assistance of the Holy Ghost? But Catholics, if I understand them, hold the Pope to be infallible not by nature or by his own natural powers, but only by the supernatural assistance of the Holy Ghost. Grant the supernatural assistance of the Holy Ghost, and there is no more difficulty in believing the Pope is infallible in his teachings than in believing, as you and I do, that St. Peter and St. Paul were infallible in teaching the revelation of God, whether by word or letter.

Do you not, my dear Ph
found, in the case of the Pope
bility with omniscience, and
that the Vatican Council, in
ing the Pope infallible in
pertaining to faith and mo
actually declared him to b
scient, and therefore God?
a mistake: first, because th
bility declared is not univers
second, because the infallib
clared is supernatural and b
assistance and protection. T
is declared to be infallible o
he is teaching the universa
faith and morals, and in con
the errors repugnant ther
even then only by superna
sistance and protection of
Ghost. The Pope, as a m
more infallible than other m
infallible only in exercising his
of universal doctor, or teach
whole church, and, as this
Holy Ghost, the infallibility,
niscience itself, pertains to
to him as a man, and is
to his function, not to his p
our Lord, who is perfect Go
as perfect man, has appoint
the office of universal teac
promised him the assistance
tection of the Spirit, there is
culty in believing him infall
if his personal knowledge sh
out to be no greater than
mine. The Pope is simpl
by the Spirit to the truth
revealed and deposited
church, and, for the most
least, contained in the Ho
tures, and is simply protec
error in declaring it.

Indeed, my dear Philo,
claim no more for the Pope
old Presbyterian parson cl
himself and for each and
dividual of the regenerat
people of God. He taug
you well know, that the r

guided by the Spirit into all
and protected from all error,
as to essentials. Some, per-
nost Protestants, go farther
is, and claim to have an in-
authority for their faith in the
nterpreted by private judgment,
erefore claim for private judg-
pretty much the same infalli-
hat the Council of the Vatican
for the Pope. Either, then,
enerate souls, nay, all men, if
ants are right, are each God,
the declaration of the Coun-
s not, actually or virtually, de-
he Pope to be God, or any-
more or less than a man
aturally assisted by the Holy
to perform the duties of the
which the Council holds he
naturally appointed by Him
as all power in heaven and
and is King of kings and
f lords.

say, "The supposition of an
le Pope is repugnant to the
and activity of the mind." I
see it. The human mind can
be said to have any rights in
e of its Creator. If any right
it is the right to be governed
word of God alone, and not
held subject to any human
ty or opinions of men. My
outraged when it is subjected
fallible opinions of men, and
to hold them as truth, when
no adequate authority for be-
that they are not erroneous.
nen its rights can be denied by
g furnished with an infallible
to the truth, to the word of
s supreme law, instead of the
of man, is what I do not ex-
comprehend, and I do not
you can comprehend any
han I. An infallible authority
the activity of the mind in
after truth, if you will; but
eing the element of the mind, that for which it was created, and without which it can neither live nor operate at all, cannot very well destroy its activity by being possessed. Does the possession of truth leave no scope for mental activity? If so, what is to constitute the beatitude of the blest in heaven? Your objection strikes me as absurd; for the real activity of the mind is in knowing, appropriating, and using the truth to fulfil the purpose of our existence and to gain the end for which God has made us.

You say, again, that "an infallible authority destroys man's free agency and takes away his moral responsibility." The intellect, you are aware, my dear Philo, if prescinded from the will, is not free. I am not free in regard to pure intellections. I cannot, if I would, believe that two concretes are five, or only three; and I am obliged to admit that the three angles of a triangle are equal to two right angles. I may refuse to turn my attention to one or another class of subjects, but I see and judge as I must, not as I will or choose. Free agency and moral responsibility, therefore, attach to the will, not to the intellect, and are enhanced in proportion to my knowledge or understanding of the truth. The authority teaching me infallibly the truth, I am bound by the law of God to accept and obey. So far from destroying free agency, it manifestly confirms it, and, instead of taking away moral responsibility, raises it to the highest possible pitch; for it leaves the mind without the shadow of an excuse for not believing. You forget, my dear Philo, that infallible authority presenting infallible truth is not only a command to the will, but the highest possible reason to the understanding. But at any rate, the objection is as valid against the infallibility of the Bible,

...of God as his vicar, infallible, he can declare and ...nly what is the law of God ...bound by the law of God. ...re wrong, then, old friend, in ...ng to the infallible authority; ... is what is needed to establish ...rine order in human affairs, ... make the church really the ...n of God on earth. Your ob... and your reasoning are misdi... and should be directed to ...hat Catholics assert infallibili... Pope who, in fact, is not in..., but fallible.

...and all Protestants claim infal...thority for the Bible read and ...eted by each individual for him..., rather, by each sect for itself. ... this interpretation is by an ...le authority, which it confess... not, you have in the Bible ...ally only a fallible authority, ...m to have an infallible author...d hence you claim and seek ...ree in the name of the Bible ...ur very fallible and contradic...pinions or theories. You are ... then, of precisely the offence ...arge against Catholics, that ...ming infallibility for a fallible ...ty, and of which it is possible ...ics are not guilty, and, if the ...e infallible, not only are not, ...not be guilty. You have, as ...said—even conceding, as I do, ...le in its true meaning to be ...e practically no infallible ...y. You have no infallible ...y to determine and declare ...w of God contained in the ... You have not the law itself, ...ly your view of it, which is ..., human view, and therefore ... To subject men to a mere ...view or to a mere human au...d not say, is intolerable ...; and hence your Protest...incompatible either with ...religious liberty, for all men are born equal, and no man or body of men has, except by divine appointment or delegation, any dominion over another.

Hence, as you and I both know, there is no solid basis or security for liberty under Protestantism. If Protestants grow indifferent and do not attempt to govern in the name of the Bible, there may be license, anarchy, a moral and political chaos; but if they are in earnest, and attempt to enforce the authority of the Bible as they understand it, they only enforce their own view of it, and, consequently, can establish only a spiritual despotism either in church or state. In Geneva, Scotland, in every state in Europe that became Protestant, in Virginia, in Massachusetts, in Connecticut, the dominant sect, you know, in early times established an odious tyranny, and would tolerate no opinion hostile to its own. Owing to certain reminiscences of principles inculcated in pre-Reformation times, and to the growing indifference of Protestants to their religion at the time our republic was instituted, and still more to the dissensions among Protestants themselves, civil and religious liberty were recognized here in the United States, but it had and has no basis and no guarantee, except in parchment constitutions, not worth the parchment on which they are engrossed, and which the people may alter at will; and even now the Evangelical sects are trying to unite their forces to abolish religious liberty, without which civil liberty is an empty name. The founder of Methodism was no friend to civil liberty, and he proved himself the bitter enemy of religious liberty by creating, or doing more than any other man to create, the shameful Gordon riots in England in 1780. Let the Methodists become, as they bid fair to become, the dominant sect

in the country, and able to command a majority of the votes of the American people, and both civil and spiritual despotism will be fastened on the country, for Methodism has only a human authority.

The sort of security Protestantism gives to religious liberty may be seen in the proceedings of the general government against the Mormons. It does not interfere with their religion: it pretends it only enforces against them the laws of the Union—laws, by the way, made expressly against them. All the government needs to suppress any religion or religious denomination it does not like is to pass laws prohibiting some of its practices on the plea that they are contrary to morality or the public good, and then take care to execute them. Queen Elizabeth held religious liberty sacred, and abhorred the very thought of persecuting Catholics. She only executed the laws against them. She enacted a law enjoining an oath of supremacy, and making it high treason to refuse to take it, and which she knew every Catholic was obliged in conscience to refuse to take; and then she could hang, draw, and quarter them, not as Catholics, but as traitors. Her judges only executed the laws of the realm against them. I have, as you well know, no sympathy with the Mormons, and I detest their peculiar doctrines and practices, but the principle on which the government proceeds against them would justify it, or any sect that could control it, in suppressing the church, and all Protestant sects even but itself.

Laws in favor of liberty amount to nothing, for all laws may be repealed. The Bible is no safeguard. Under it and by its supposed authority, Catholics have suffered the most cruel persecutions; even when not deprived of life, they have been deprived of the common rights of men by Protestant governments led on by Protestant ministers. Thus the Bible commands the extirpation of idolaters. But Protestants, by their private judgment, declared Catholics to be idolaters, and hence in the name of the Bible took from them their churches, their schools, colleges, and universities, confiscated their goods, and imprisoned them, exiled them, or cut their throats. The pretence of legislating only in regard to morality avails nothing for religious liberty; for morality depends on dogma, and is only the practical application of the great principles of religion to individual, domestic, social, and political life. You cannot touch a moral question without touching a religious question, for religion and morality are inseparable; your only possible security for liberty is in having a divinely instituted authority that is infallible in faith and morals, competent to tell the state as well as individuals how far it may go, and where it must stop.

You object, finally, my dear Philo, that the assertion of the infallibility of the Pope is incompatible with the assertion of the sovereignty of the people and the independence of secular government. The people and all secular governments, you have conceded, are subject to the law of God. Neither the people nor secular governments are independent of the divine law, and have only the authority it gives them, and the freedom and independence it allows them. How can they lose any right or authority they have or can have by having the divine law, under which they hold, infallibly declared and applied? It is singular, my old school-fellow, that so acute, subtle, and so able a lawyer as I know you to be, should have the misfortune, as a theologian, to object to the very thing

ally wish to maintain, and can alone save you from the u seek to avoid. Now, what ecessary to know in order to ine the rights and powers of ment, is to know precisely relation to government the God—including both the na- w and the revealed law, which lly only two parts of one and ne divine law—ordains, what it bes, and what it forbids. This dge can only in part be deriv- ough natural reason, because is in part supernatural, and known only by faith: it can- derived with certainty from iptures interpreted by our own judgment or by any human ty: it can be obtained infalli- m the teaching and decisions nfallible Pope, if really infalli- The infallible Pope will give to ople all the sovereignty they under the law of God, and in for civil government all the and powers, all the freedom dependence of action, the law l gives it. What more do you What more dare you assert il government or for popular gnty? Would you put the in the place of God, and e secular order above the spi- nan above God? Certainly not, t not avowedly either to your- to others. Then, how can you d the Papal infallibility is in- tible with the sovereignty of ople and the independence of vernment? Do you want the settled, and the law of God left undefined, and remitted, as you remit the Bible, to the private judgment of each people or each government, to be interpreted by each for itself, and as it sees proper? But that were to make the divine law practically of no effect, and to leave each people and each government without any law but what it chooses to be to itself. It practically emancipates the secular order from the law of God, and asserts complete civil absolutism.

The fact is, my dear Philo, you and many others in your own minds regard liberty and authority as mutually hostile powers. It is the error of the age, and hence we see the nations alternating between the mob and the despot, each hostile alike to liberty and authority. Both liberty and authority are founded in the divine order, and without recognizing and conforming to that order neither can be maintained. To restrain liberty by an authority that rests on a human basis alone is to destroy it; as to restrain authority by liberty not defined by the law of God, or by popular sovereignty to be defined by popular sovereignty, is to lose all authority, and to rush into anarchy and universal license. There is no true liberty and no legitimate government independent of the divine order; consequently, none without an infallible authority to present and maintain it. The question is, Has God, or has he not, established an infallible authority to declare his law? Yours affectionately,

DAMIAN.

THE FOXVILLES OF FOXVILLE.

A TALE OF THE PERIOD.

I.

AT a huge country-house, not many years ago, some few days after the close of the Christmas and New Year's festivities, the usual family circle, with one exception, met at the breakfast-table. A man on horseback had just pulled up at the house-door with the family letter-bag from the nearest town. The letters and papers were handed to the head of the family, who glanced over the addresses with the quick eye of a practised man of business, and placed one of the letters on an empty plate reserved for the absent member of the party.

"Oh! For Susy!" exclaimed a young lady, who seemed put to her wits' end to make herself still younger, for she was the elder daughter of the house, past twenty-six, and disengaged. "I should like to know whom that's from! A gentleman's hand, I declare!" And she eyed the characters with a searching scrutiny, but they would tell no more tales.

"Don't be so curious, Matilda. I shall recommend Susy to keep her letter a secret," said an obnoxious brother, by name Augustus, one year the junior of the first speaker.

"Yes! you would encourage her in every kind of deception, you would! She is quite artful enough," answered Matilda. "If I were papa, I would soon see who sends the What can make Susy late, this ing? She is invariably so regu

"No, child!" said a white-h old gentleman, Mr. Foxvill happy father of Matilda, Aug and Susan, his stock of dire scendants, and all told, "I meddle with other people's bu Susy is a good girl, and she w me have any news that may ir me."

"You are quite right; but sl a duty to her mamma," said Foxville, with a grand matron "Papa allows me to open all h ters, though he never opens and that's as it should be. If does not come down soon, as privileged, I will open the lette is a genteel hand, I perceive.

"Well, well," observed Mr. ville, "patience, patience! W wait."

"She is my child, Mr. Fox replied the matron.

"Shall I fetch Susy down?" Matilda, with curiosity ferme within her.

"Do, my dear," said Mrs. ville, laboring under the same plaint, but affecting more in ence.

With much nimbleness the sp ly Matilda dashed out of the having first made an attempt to off the letter.

!" cried Augustus, putting on it. "Suppose you bring he letter, and not the letter Fair is fair," he added, nothing like distrust in the -carrier.

w seconds Matilda and Susy he room, the arm of the el- tionately wound round the the younger sister.

you not well, Susy?" asked ville kindly.

ctly!" replied Susy, giving his morning kiss.

is a letter for you," said ble father.

k you," answered Susy, and the letter unopened into a s pocket, coloring and tre- she did so.

ld not wait like you for the y," said her mother frankly, tched her daughter closely. ld not be so rude as to read before others," answered

at all rude!" observed Mrs. with one of her grand airs. s nobody here but the fami- makes all the difference. I sh to make you sensible of child. Etiquette should not ed too far when we are *en*

t words were delivered with f self-importance, as if she solved a new problem of s and was vain of her dis-

ourse!" cried Matilda. "Do se, Susy. I should not. I take matters so coolly. The y be from some dear, dear

my advice, Susy," said that Augustus. "Breakfast first, ers afterwards."

st indeed! It may be some intelligence. So none of your interference, Gussy!" rejoined Matilda.

"Then I would not spoil my appetite; and my recommendation holds good," pursued that provoking brother.

"Ay! ay," said Foxville senior; "your breakfast first, girl." And this put an end to the dispute, for the old gentleman saw that Susy was pained at the discussion.

II.

It was true, as Miss Matilda Foxville had observed, that her sister Susy was the most regular in that exemplary household whenever there was a demand on her energies in domestic affairs, or on her good nature in diffusing happiness and cheerfulness around her. The fact that she had deviated from her usual course into the exceptional irregularity referred to, naturally called for comment such as any strange occurrence would provoke; and the uninitiated as naturally puzzled themselves with unsatisfactory conjectures. But the plain truth was this: Susy's absence was caused by nothing less than a consciousness that a particular letter would arrive for her that morning. She imagined that she should betray less concern about the letter, and keep her nerves more under control, by an apparently accidental absence of a few minutes from the breakfast-table, than if she ran the risk of being present at the opening of the post-bag, and of manifesting her expectation and her too probable excitement at its realization.

Susy had, as we have seen, only partially succeeded; but, under shelter of the timely command of her father, she managed to conceal a great deal of her uneasiness at the expense of a charge of indifference

toward her correspondents—a charge she was disposed to invite rather than disprove.

This little ruse, however, she was unable to carry very much further; for Matilda, more and more perplexed, and proportionably more curious, than ever, became, after the morning meal, more endearing in both manner and speech towards her sister than was customary with one who generally adopted the language of admonition or complaint. It was very clear that these famous time-honored weapons for eliciting obedience and respect would fail in the present instance; and Matilda had not spent twenty-six years of her valuable existence without acquiring an amount of knowledge that led her to that certain conclusion. But wheedling and an implied solicitude for her sister's welfare were more insidious and keener instruments to open the confidence-chest of the unsuspecting Susy.

"I hope you will have good news," began Matilda when the sisters were alone. Then she added, as if some sudden idea struck her, "But I forgot! I will leave you and come again presently, Susy dear; you would like to read and answer your letter?"

What it was that Miss Matilda professed to have forgotten would puzzle most men; but it was a phrase habitual to her, and coming from a person of her experience, it probably conveyed all she intended to those of her own sex who enjoyed her familiarity. Susy, whether she understood the form of expression or not, was attracted by her sister's winning ways and most unusual condescension, and was quite prepared to open her heart to her.

"Don't go, Till," she said, blushing. "I have something to say to you."

"To me!" exclaimed the deli
Matilda with well-feigned su
"Pray tell me what it is!"

"It is the letter," said Susy.

"Oh! that's quite private," p
Matilda, "if I might judge b
putting it aside unopened."

"But there is confidence b
sisters?"

"Most undoubtedly. Woul
unbosom myself to you?"

"You shall, then, be the
learn the news, but it must s
family property," said Susy, o
the letter, and reading it as M
looked over her shoulder. "I
perhaps, to show it to papa fir
added, as a glow diffused itse
her face and neck.

"Yes; it is indeed matter
pa's consideration: it is me
him. But whom is it from
Matilda, in a fever to see th
on the last page, which Susy h
yet turned to.

"Nathaniel Wodehouse!" s
sy, in trembling accents, as sh
down on a chair to support he
her novel situation.

"That trumpery fellow! f
exclaimed Matilda boldly. "I
soon settle his business. Let
you a reply, will you?"

"Matilda! sister Till!" crie
in amazement, and recalled
self. "How often have I hea
say what a charming, handsom
he is!"

"I! I!" said Matilda, asc
the gamut in her ejaculation
call him charming and hands
Then, with tremendous emph
spired by rage, she
"Never!"

"Well, then," followed
merciless witness, roused by h
ter's vain denial, "he *is* ch
and handsome! And you
it."

III.

Foxville was a retired butcher ad made a fortune, and still little business on 'Change to his hand in, and preserve his faculties from rusting. Be- he newspaper, which many will d was his "best public instruc- e had not many intellectual es; and as he allowed him- tle recreation, he devoted a eal of time to journal-reading he study of stocks and the et. Here was a fair amount rk for a busy mind; and sy was Mr. Foxville in keep- harp eye on his investments.

g fond of a country life, he several acres of land when he g business; and he had built f an unwieldy mansion, and ecting smaller houses and cot- at a respectful distance from n. This cluster of dwellings posed to call Foxville, while e big, special habitation he Foxville House. The name t adopted without reflection, ore than one debate between and wife.

ville's patronymic was simply That did very well for busi- at it was deemed unsuited for exigencies. Foxtown was in- and discussed, but it gave no tion. Was there anything dis- ed in Foxtown? Nothing! nd and wife were one on that

ngth, Mrs. Fox bethought her ench tutor to her girls, and excellent gentleman bore the of Portville. Monsieur Port- as a very agreeable man, to especially; and that circum- ssociated something pleasant ir name to the ear of Mrs. It was a habit with Mr. Fox, who could not remember names, to put the cart before the horse in endeavoring to call names to his recollection, and he always spoke of the Frenchman as Villeport. In facetious moments he would reduce this again to Vile Port, maintaining that this was the original name. Although it was by no means a complimentary cognomen, Mr. Fox had no intention of showing disrespect, for he had a rough kind of regard for the tutor, and only vented a poor joke at his expense, deriving his inspiration perhaps from the remembrance of a compound beverage familiar to Fox in his younger days in the country which had the honor of his birth. If Portville was euphonious, why not Foxville? Such was the argument of Mrs. Fox, and that settled the question.

Mrs. Foxville was the daughter of a grocer, who had so many daughters that all he could do for them was to make them a home and allow them a limited portion for their wardrobe—totally insufficient, according to their unanimous opinion, for their position! Mrs. Foxville was the oldest, and was the first to enter into wedlock. She would have scorned an alliance with a butcher, so superior did she think her father's calling, though on what grounds she never clearly stated; but the prosperity of young Fox proved a compensation strong enough to convert a woman's uprising negative into a positive affirmative.

The correctness of the lady's judgment could not be questioned in the days that lengthened Fox into Foxville. She continued, however, to regard herself as more than the equal of her husband; and she always spoke of my house, my family, my children Matilda, Augustus, and Susy, as if poor Foxville had no con-

cern or partnership in the property. Sometimes he would slip in 'our' in place of 'my,' and he always spoke in this manner himself, but both the correction or amendment and the example had no effect on the 'singular' appropriation, which seemed, it may be supposed, to convey higher origin and standing than if lowered by a joint ownership.

Miss Matilda Foxville's characteristics have sufficiently developed themselves, and Augustus, beyond being a plague to his elder sister, had no character at all. He was an existence, and little more; still, he was not without importance as the heir of a goodly estate.

Foxville House never failed to throw open its hospitable portals during Christmas week, and, not many days before the receipt of Susy's letter, a large number of guests had found a warm welcome within them. Nathaniel Wodehouse was invariably the life of these social gatherings, and in the estimation of the Misses Foxville evidently he possessed qualifications for the prominent part he took. He stood high in favor with Miss Matilda, there is no denying the fact. For him more than for any other male thing, she chignoned, and painted, and got herself up in the best style of fashion. She nearly succeeded in reducing twenty-six to twenty by other than arithmetical rules. But what, after all, are twenty-six summers? No great span in the life of a really handsome woman; yet, in Miss Matilda, so unpliable was her disposition, and so set was her general deportment, that candor must admit that the six years beyond twenty had produced a perceptible difference. She made the best of them, however, for Nathaniel Wodehouse.

Can it be wondered at, therefore, that she thought he had some appreciative taste? He w
good-looking most c
was very gallant, an
been, to Miss Foxvil
vited him with, an
than Matilda did to
House. Susy was
Matilda had outliv
safely pronounced N
company: so did
did Mr. Foxville.
settled conviction
Susy was silent.

Even when M
under sisterly secrec
epithets which
wished to revoke,
herself no further
mation of "Do
companied by a
acquiescence. Whe
tilda, repenting of
boldly denied it, Susy,
held her to it unflinc

It is sometimes go
others, and Scripture
good sense forbid ou
taking the best pla
joyed in this respe
which nature had
had all the benefit
years younger than h
was at once the you
est, and the most am
villes. Nathaniel w
blind indeed if he ha
discovery; and wha
led to, the intimated
has abundantly prov
however, he had n
that was the burning
cited in the bosom
ville, although he s
incur her displeasure

IV.

Foxville House al
motion when Matild

hen she was agitated, her agi-
ibrated in every part of that
s dwelling; and now she was
o madness in such a way by
taunt that she rushed about
maniac on fire. It was her
olicy, but she had lost the
of her discretion, and she cast
adrift on the surging waves of
a fury.

one apartment to another
in a whirlwind of passion in
of her mother, whom she
have found very near to Susy's
f she had not darted down-
with headlong precipitation.
rs she flew again, and at
flounced into the room in
Mrs. Foxville was eagerly
the issue of the consultation
her daughters.

at has happened, Matilda?"
Mrs. Foxville. "Your look
me."

u will be startled!" gasped

lm yourself, my child, and tell
leisure what is amiss," replied
ther, her words being at vari-
ith her feverish anxiety for the

at do you think, mamma?
iel Wodehouse has had the
ty to propose to Susy!"

athaniel Wodehouse! With-
ans! A beggar! I shall put
to that. No genteel poverty
or either of my girls!"

sure that you would save
! What is the use of his
with nothing to support

always were sensible, Ma-
and no doubt Susy is wise
to see the matter in the same

ere you mistake, mamma; Susy
a weak fool! The silly thing
head and ears in love with
him. She idolizes him! It is positively awful—wicked!"

"Oh! that's it, is it? And without asking my opinion? Deliberate disobedience! Let me see her this moment. I must talk to her!"

Forthwith the mother and elder daughter sought out the unfortunate Susy, and joined in giving her one of those 'talkings to,' as they termed them, which only ladies can inflict on one another. Susy let fall a tear or two, made very short replies, for she could scarcely squeeze a word in, and bore her rebukes with exemplary patience, contenting herself with asserting that she would comply with the request of the letter and lay it before her father.

"Let me catch you showing the letter to your father this day!" exclaimed Mrs. Foxville indignantly.

"To-morrow will do," replied Susy. "Papa must see it."

It was then agreed that Susy should reserve the letter for her father's perusal next day, on Mrs. Foxville consenting to take the blame for delay on her own shoulders; and it was finally stipulated that both the elder Foxville and Augustus should be kept in the dark for the next twenty-four hours.

Mrs. Foxville did not, however, consider herself bound by this contract, though not the least important of the high contracting parties. In fact, she intended to turn the interval to what she deemed the best account. Accordingly, she seized the opportunity which Mrs. Caudle, as depicted by Douglas Jerrold, devoted to curtain lectures, and plainly gave Mr. Foxville to understand that "she wouldn't have it," meaning the match in question, for she stated she knew that Wodehouse was as poor as a church mouse. "He was all outside show,"

she said—"all flimsy, with no backbone." She added that "that wouldn't do for her girls," and, having warned her husband at great length and with great force, she concluded her lecture by observing, "And now you know your duty to my child, and I shall expect you to perform it."

"Our child, my dear—our dear Susy is entitled to the best counsel I can give her."

"I knew you would take her part!" cried Mrs. Foxville. "Dear Susy, indeed! She is a very bad Susy. I would have you, Mr. Foxville, respect a mother's feelings!"

"Well, well; yes, yes, to be sure I will," replied the husband, who was as valiant as an ox and nearly as strong in muscle, but was now in dread of a second lecture. "I will, you may depend upon it."

With this promise on his lips he composed himself to sleep, after having first noticed its soothing effect—for which he took credit to himself—on his partner.

The next day, Mr. Foxville had some conversation alone with Susy. A little kindness soon reassured her, and, like a true-hearted daughter, she did not attempt to conceal her attachment to Nathaniel from her father. She opened her mind to him, and promised to abide by his advice; and on the question of questions—that of fortune—she professed her belief that Nathaniel Wodehouse would not be found in the forlorn condition in which her mamma and sister, in spite of her, had insisted. She acknowledged that she had no proof of this but her lover's word, which, she said, Matilda had derided. Her lover's word! that was all-sufficient for Susy! But she approved of her father's fully satisfying himself on this point, as a duty to his family and to her.

There are several ways of giving advice. It is a favorite plan with some to administer it as they would physic, and the more nauseous it is, the more they seem to like administering it; and they would quarrel with their best friend for not taking it. Even among the more considerate, not every one has the modesty not to have his equanimity disturbed by having his advice asked and then disregarded. Mr. Foxville was not one of either of these classes. He might allowably be a little more positive in counselling his own daughter, but practically he followed in her regard his usual method, heedless of all the admonitions of his better half. That method was to pile up all the pros and cons which occurred to him on both sides of a question, and leave his client very much to his own decision. In effect, this was to offer no advice at all, but the course of proceedings looked grave and offended no one, while it enabled him to remain true to his maxim of never meddling in other people's business. The only stumbling-block with Mr. Foxville, in the present instance, was a suitable position for his daughter, and that he would look into as a matter of imperative necessity. The rest he would leave to those most vitally interested, after his usual formal statement of all the disadvantages, which always came first, and then the advantages of the case under consideration. Susy was accordingly much comforted by her father's good sense and feeling, instead of being cowed and heart-broken as Mrs. Foxville and Matilda had expected to see her.

"You are a perfect fool!" said Mrs. Foxville to her husband on observing Susy's cheerful face after the *tête-à-tête*. "You have not the nerve to manage my child! I must take her

l, poor noodle that she is. is just like you. There's a r for you!"

oxville attached little importhese disparaging remarks, like of which he was famit he invariably did things his y, and left consequences to re of themselves. He re-, therefore, good-humoredly: too hasty, my dear! I shall thaniel Wodehouse, whether rove of it or not. That is all o say."

Foxville kept his word, for he y refrained from opening his enew the discussion. Not so xville. She had a very great say, but eventually wound up ollowing menace:

vare how you ruin my child! ll answer for it. I'll let you hether I am to be nobody in house!"

tremendous ferment which e Foxvilles at length began pon Augustus. That young his own view of Susy's con-

ll you what, Susy," said he, house is no gentleman. He ık. Didn't he get the better a an examination before old yfair, and when I challenged fight it out, and prove who better man, didn't he de-A pretty thing to marry a ce that. Marry him, Susy, what I will do!"

Susy was now regarded by amily, with the exception of er, who remained silent, as a te and outcast. When she n to her meals, she was treatshe were supported by charity. r times she was watched like al. Her fortitude and good ice, nevertheless, sustained er her unmerited wrongs.

In the meantime, the two gentlemen, Foxville and Wodehouse, conferred together. Mrs. Foxville at first insisted on being present; but it was to no purpose. Mr. Foxville's hardihood gave him the victory. He was declared to be the most obstinate of men; he bore the imputation and triumphed.

"What good have you done?" sneered Mrs. Foxville, when the meeting was over.

"Our Susy and Nathaniel will be man and wife!" replied the imperturbable Foxville.

"Oh!" was the sole response, in a tone that boded little harmony if the baffled Mrs. Foxville could have her way.

"Ay, ay," continued Foxville. "Nat's the richest man within a dozen miles of this place. I tell you, I have proof of it. Look, there's a *little* present, as he called it, for you!"

Foxville pulled out of his pocket a magnificent set of jewels in the neatest of morocco cases, and handed the gift to his wife.

What a transformation on the countenance and in the manner of Mrs. Foxville! Who could have suggested such a happy idea to Nathaniel as the magical present which turned out to be such a talisman of power? That secret was never known but to Susy and Nathaniel, and it cannot be divulged.

As Mrs. Foxville gazed with rapture on the jewels, her eyes vied in sparkling with the diamonds.

"Well, I cannot help forgiving him!" exclaimed the pacified lady. "Who would have thought this of Nathaniel Wodehouse? Twelvemonths ago I know he was scarcely worth a penny. But are you quite sure that you have not been taken in?"

"Trust old Foxville for that, eh?"

I have seen how he came by his money. Old Simpson, his uncle, died last March, and left him sole heir."

"Simpson his uncle! A good family! My father knew him well."

Mrs. Foxville's was not altogether a vain boast: the late Mr. Simpson had been the best customer at her father's grocery.

Augustus now joined his parents unexpectedly.

"Gussy, my boy," cried his father, "Nat is the happy man, after all! He could buy up all of Foxville if he chose. He wants you to dine with him at his club to-morrow. Do as you like. I meddle in no man's business!"

"Of course I will! He is a better fellow than I took him to be," said the sensible Augustus. "And here comes Susy," he added, seeing his sister approaching.

"Susy, we congratulate you," exclaimed the overjoyed father. "The course of true love runs smoothly a little too soon, eh?"

Susy blushed scarlet.

"Kiss me, my darling girl," said Mrs. Foxville.

"Bravo!" sang out Augustus. "But Till must hear the news me fetch Matilda!" And he with all speed, and soon return his sister.

"I told you I had somet show you," said he, addressi tilda. "Look at that pictur only want Nat to make us th ly jolly. You will make a bridesmaid, Till, though it!"

"Not I indeed!" replied M with a grand toss of her head

"You won't for Susy?" the Augustus went on. "That' of you; but I'll give you a So don't despair; it's often step to matrimony!"

Matilda bit her lip till it bled, but she suffered not a w escape her.

"For shame, Gussy!" crie as she flung herself, half-smilin crying, on her sister's neck.

With great adroitness Na eventually made his peace wi tilda, though it was rather than a peace; but sufficient h was in a little time restored t ville House to make Susy's w go off with *éclat*.

THE MARTYRS OF ARCUEIL.

following narrative of the im- ent and execution of certain cans, by the Paris Com- in May of last year, is trans- rom an account drawn up in , under the eyes and, in a e, at the dictation of witnesses sed the captivity of the mar- d survived their fate only by idential interposition which ittle less than miraculous. It een merely to preserve, in the s of the order, an authentic of the circumstances which it, morates; but it glows with ex- of Christian heroism and which ought not to be lost world at large. The branch Dominicans which gives this y of martyrs to the church nded by Father Lacordaire after the passing of the law of hich, by abridging the exclu- ivileges of the university of conferred upon the religious n France the right of opening and colleges, a right for Lacordaire and Montalembert tled for twenty years. Fa- ptier was one of the original y of four novices with whom Lacordaire founded, in 1852, order of Teaching Domini-

e spring of 1863, eighteen after the death of Father La- e, certain religious of the (Teaching) Order of Domini- ving as their head the Rev. Captier, were sent to establish, house formerly belonging to t, a college under the name Blessed Albertus Magnus. It was a difficult task, and from the outset was met by the government with an opposition equally obstinate and hypocritical. In order to prevent the virtual abrogation of the law of 1850, to which France is now indebted for such a gallant multitude of faithful instructors, the contest opened by Father Lacordaire, in 1831, in the matter of the free schools, had to be commenced anew. Deprived of their religious habit, and harassed by incessant and discreditable vexations, Father Captier and his companions nevertheless stood bravely at their post of honor. At last, after two years of labor and experiment, they were permitted to enjoy in peace the protection of the law, and to speak freely to their pupils according to the inspiration of their hearts and their faith.

The establishment at Arcueil, founded in trouble, thenceforward prospered without interruption, and grew apace under the watchful and affectionate care of Father Captier. He seemed to know every member of the community to his inmost heart. He cared for every one with a religious and at the same time manly tenderness. There was not one to whom he failed to do good. With the performance of these duties he combined an active interest in all questions relating to the education of youth, and opposed with all his might the encroachment of the system of godless schools which has since been so audaciously imposed upon Parisian families. Appointed a member of the Commission d'Enseignement Supérieur, as the most thorough

representative of the free schools, he brought to the service of that board the experience of twenty years, the devout aspirations of his holy community, and the enthusiasm of a spirit earnest in the cause of enlightenment and holy liberty. When he returned to his cell, he resumed the cares of a soul which aimed to be wholly and profoundly immersed in the religious life. He concerned himself about the progress of all his brethren and pupils in observing the rules of the community, well knowing that the best means of doing good to souls is to draw from God the courage and the light which one needs in order to serve them.

Such was the state of affairs at Arcueil when the war broke out. The school then contained nearly three hundred pupils. In an establishment where religion and patriotism were both so warmly cherished, the first thought of every one was to do his utmost to aid France in her struggle against the foreigner. The pupils raised a large contribution for the relief of the victims of the coming campaigns. The religious gave their persons. Three of them joined the ambulances and passed the winter on the fields of battle, while the others devoted themselves in the college premises to taking care of the wounded victims of the siege of Paris. About fifteen hundred sick and wounded soldiers were thus treated in the college ambulance; and it was a devotion all the more meritorious because Arcueil, situated on the French outposts, was constantly under the fire of the German artillery.

After the siege, the school of Arcueil reopened its doors to pupils, and in March resumed its classes and its regular life. Then came the civil war. Placed between Fort Montrouge, Fort Bicêtre, and the redoubt of Hautes Bruyères, the school found itself within the lines (Paris Commune. Instead of ab ing their house, the fathers re to continue their services t wounded. They displayed c front of the building the flag Geneva Convention, and, with of the assistant masters whc peace had collected around they began to traverse the fields on the south of Paris, ing up the wounded and buryi dead. Within the college, th soldiers, whether regulars or fe were tended by the charitable ha the Sisters of St. Martha. At t communists respected this sel -fice. The less violent of thei pleased to be so well cared for Dominicans of Arcueil. Many sitions, nevertheless, were mad the institution, and the hou ransacked from top to botto nothing was found in it exce evidence of a charity which buffs could discourage. Tl ligious continued with unre zeal to relieve the wounded field of battle, and awaited pa the triumph of justice and l A number of battalions of th tional Guard were thus brougl contact with the school. Sev them showed gratitude and sort of sympathy, but so far went everything depended up officers. Thus, the 101st Ba commanded by one Cerisier, vict "who had been three sentenced to death, and b neither in God nor in man," fa showing any good-will, seemec ly willing to forgive the religi their charitable labors in its be

On the 17th of May, events happened which grea cited and alarmed the insurger cartridge factory exploded Avenue Rapp, that is to say, the *enceinte* of Paris, and a

whose conduct in these trying days was above all praise.

When all the others were gone, the fathers, the professors, and the male servants were brought down into the first court, and surrounded by the men of the 101st and 120th Battalions. The door opened, and the sad cortége began its march towards the Fort of Bicêtre, situated three kilometres from the school. They first passed through the streets of Arcueil. The inhabitants looked on in silence, though their sympathies were all with the prisoners. "When they passed our door," said a poor woman, "and I saw Father Captier and all these messieurs, who had done us so much good, marching in the midst of the muskets, I imagined it was Jesus Christ with his disciples going to Jerusalem to be crucified." At Gentilly, which they were next obliged to traverse, the popular feeling was very different, and the most outrageous language was used towards the prisoners.

It was seven o'clock in the evening when the column arrived at the fort. The captives were first locked up in a small room where, insulted in the grossest manner, they were forced to wait their turn to appear before the governor of the fort, and go through the formality of registering on the books of the prison. These formalities lasted a long time, the number was so large. Each man was submitted to the pretence of an examination, though there was no question of any crime or misdemeanor, nor any indictment whatever. Then they were searched, and stripped of everything they carried (even the breviaries were taken away), and conducted to Casemate No. 10, which faces the entrance to the fort.* It

was nearly [illegible]
Captier and the other
were placed here. [illegible]
followed in small [illegible]
two o'clock the [illegible]
last of them. It was neve
for them again till they we
their death.

This first night was [illegible]
The casemate contained o
remnants of damp straw
spoiled and broken up by
varian soldiers, and each m
grope for a clean spot on
floor. When morning ca
sought for some alleviation
wretched condition. By di
est representation, they g
bundles of fresh straw, and a
days the breviaries were re
the religious. Father Cap
ceeded in obtaining paper a
and addressed a communi
the governor of the fort.
secured the liberation of
Emile Delaitre and Paul I
had been imprisoned with
servants of the school. He
difficulty in obtaining the f
serious examination, for th
twenty-five prisoners were a
ignorant of the cause of th
Something, at any rate, was
on Sunday afternoon, Fathe
and Cotrault were led befo
Lucy Pyat, who, after a long

* The following is a list of the prisoners: *In the Fort of Bicêtre.*—Father Captier, prior of the school of Arcueil; Bourard, chaplain; Delhorme, regent of studies; [illegible]
selin, censor; Chatagneret, [illegible]
fessed religious of the Third [illegible]
St. Dominic, except F. [illegible]
the Order of Preaching [illegible]
Gauquelin, L'Abbé Grancolas, [illegible]
Rézillot, Petit, and [illegible]
MM. Aimé Gros, Marce, [illegible]
nal, Dintroz, Simon [illegible]
pens, Delaitre (father and [illegible]
servants of the school. *In the* [illegible]
Lazare.—Mother Aloysia [illegible]
Sisters of St. Martha; [illegible]
Louise Marie [illegible]
Dorfin, and [illegible]
gèle Marce, [illegible]
and the widow [illegible]
Catherine Morvan, and [illegible]
years).

...informed them that they were to ...sidered neither as condemned ...accused, nor even prisoners, but ...were merely held as witnesses. ...was a prophet, though he did not ...r it; for God had chosen them ...ear witness, with their blood, to ...glory of his holy name.

...was hoped that the examinations ...d be resumed on the following ...(Monday), but this was not done. ...the contrary, the officers in com- ...d at the fort held no further com- ...ication with the prisoners. It is pro- ...e that in thus keeping away they ...ed to the wishes of their men; for, ...e the officers preserved an appear- ...of civility in the presence of the ...rs, their subordinates constantly ...bled their outrages, and took all ...e to render them more and more ...t. Drunken and infamous crea- ...showed themselves every few ...tes before the windows of the ...mate, jeering at the prisoners, ...ing them with unmentionable ...sts, or reading aloud, with infi- ...gusto, the most shameless arti- ...from the Communist newspapers. ...day, they saw the sub-governor ...e fort, cap in hand, ushering Fa- ...Captier into his prison after some ...of an examination. This mark ...spect so exasperated the federal ...ers that they raised a great dis- ...mce at the door of the casemate, ...thenceforth the provisions for the ...ners were regularly plundered or ...cepted on the way; for two days ...aptives were denied even a cup ...ter. On Wednesday, the 24th, ...cation took place in the court- ...of the fort, directly under their ... It was made the occasion of ...led menaces and heartless allu- ...s. The same day, the Abbé Fé- ...chaplain of the Hospital of Bicê- ...went in search of the governor of ...fort, and asked to be entrust- ...ith the custody of the members

of the Arcueil community, offering to answer for them with his life until they could be judged. This gener- ous effort was unavailing. The Com- mune had already settled everything. The school was to be pillaged and burned.* As for the prisoners, they belonged to the 101st Battalion and its commander, who would dispose of them according to circumstances.

What were the thoughts of the vic- tims during this long week of agony ? Their companions in captivity tell us that a gentle cheerfulness never ceased to prevail in that wretched dungeon. With the exception of some of the servants, married men and fathers of families, whose attitude and manner were somewhat gloomy and dejected, every one pursued his ordinary way of life—not that they forgot or despised death, but because they had offered to God the sacrifice of their lives for France. The reli- gious redoubled their usual devotion, encouraged each other and exhorted their companions. Every evening they said the rosary together, adding the usual mementos for their absent brethren. From time to time, Father Captier, though completely broken down by fatigue and privation, roused himself to give a pious reading, or to address the words of life and salvation to those who looked up to him as their chief. Outside, the federals gathered around to mock at their prayers. One morning, when the horizon was red with flames in the direction of Paris, Father Captier was pacing to and fro, saying his office, and some one cried to him through the window, " Oh, yes ! you had bet- ter pray God not to let the torpedoes that the city is full of explode !" " I am doing it," answered the good fa- ther sadly and quietly; and then,

* In point of fact, the school was plundered on the 25th of May. There was no time to burn it.

finishing his breviary, he asked his companions to pray with him.

On Thursday, the 25th, at daybreak, an extraordinary activity was observed inside the fortress. Guns were removed and spiked, and the bugles blew the assembly. At one time, the prisoners believed that the fort had been wholly evacuated, and they had only to wait the arrival of the Versailles troops to secure their liberty.

But this hope was of short duration. A body of armed men appeared at the door of the casemate in considerable confusion. As they had not the keys, they forced an entrance with blows from the butt-ends of their muskets, and ordered the captives to start immediately with the column, which was retiring into Paris. "You are free," said they, "only we must not leave you in the hands of the Versaillists. You must follow us to the *mairie* of the Gobelins, and then you will go to Paris, or wherever you like."

The march was long and painful. Every instant the prisoners were threatened with death. The women showed themselves especially furious, and eager to witness the death of these men who wore a sacred garb. They moved down towards the gate of Ivry, and on the road a few rifle-shots from Bicêtre caused a little disturbance, of which Father Rousselin took advantage to slip away and return to Arcueil. The others continued their journey towards Paris. Arriving at the *mairie* of the Gobelins, in the midst of cries of "death!" from the crowd maddened at the approach of the regular army, it was in vain that they reminded their guard of the liberty promised them. They were told, "The streets are not safe; you will be killed by the people; remain here." They were taken into the court of the *mairie*, and made to sit on the ground, exposed to the falling shells. Here the federals brought the corpses of their victims, to show "*ces canailles*" how the Commune served its enemies. At the end of half an hour an officer appeared, and took them to the *prison disciplinaire* of the 9th *secteur*, No. 38 Avenue d'Italie. As soon as they entered, the captives of Arcueil recognized the 101st Battalion and its chief, Citizen Cerisier, that is, the same who had made their arrest. It was then ten o'clock in the morning. About half-past two, a man in a red shirt threw open the door of the hall, and cried out, "Get up, *soutanes;* they are going to take you to the barricade." The fathers went out, and, with the Abbé Grancolas and the others, were conducted towards the barricade thrown up in front of the *mairie* of the Gobelins. There they were offered muskets to fight with. "We are priests," said they, "and, besides, we are non-combatants in virtue of our service in the ambulance. We shall not take arms. All that we can do is to relieve your wounded and bear away the dead." "Is this your fixed purpose?" asked the officer of the Commune. "It is." Then they were taken back to the prison, with an escort of federals and women armed with muskets. Once locked up, they thought of nothing but preparations for the last journey. They all knelt, made a final offering of the sacrifice of their lives, confessed and received absolution. They were not to have the dying Christian's last consolation, the divine viaticum. God did not judge this grace necessary for them; and, besides, from the prison to heaven the journey was to be so short!

About half-past four, a new order came from Citizen Cerisier. All the prisoners filed out into the lane which leads up to the prison, while the

Rousselin awaited them, with Jacques de La Perrière, and the pupils who had remained faithful to the house. But it would have been necessary to submit to long formalities, and the bodies were so dreadfully bruised that there was no time even to make them coffins. The hearse, followed by a great crowd of people deeply agitated with grief and anger, was driven to the common cemetery. There the martyrs lie side by side in one grave, with no shroud but their blood-stained vestments.

This undistinguished tomb ought not to be the last resting-place of the martyrs of Arcueil. Father Captier and his companions will sleep in the shadow of the school which their labor founded and their blood renders henceforth illustrious. Not only the religious who were the brethren of the victims, and the pupils who were their children, but all who care for religion and country, will come to pray at their sepulchre, and meditate upon the lessons of their death.

VEILED.

"Dilectus meus mihi, et ego illi." *—CANT. ii. 16.

No bridegroom mine of change and death :
  My orange-flowers shall never fade :
Immortal dews shall gem the wreath
  When crowns of earth have all decayed.

No bride am I that plights her troth
  With touch of doubt, or trust too fond ;
And risks the present, wisely loath
  To search too far the veiled beyond.

To me 'tis but the past is veiled :
  The world that mocks with joys that fleet ;
The " Egypt " that so long has failed
  To make its " troubled waters " † sweet :

The world with all its sins and cares,
  Its sorrows gained and graces lost ;
The garden of a thousand snares,
  The barren field of blight and frost.

But shines the future clear as truth :
  A few swift years of prayer and peace,
Where hearts may know perennial youth,
  And virtues evermore increase :

And then my Lord, my only love,
  Shall come, and lift the veil, and say :
" Arise, all fair, my spouse, my dove !
  The rain is over—haste, away ! ‡

"The rain is o'er, the winter gone,
  That sun and summer seemed to thee.
If sweet the toilsome journey done,
  How sweeter now thy rest shall be !"

* "My Beloved is mine, and I am his." † Jer. ii. 18. ‡ Cant. ii. 10, 11.

After riding a distance of three or four miles, the wildness of the scene is increased by huge formations of rocks; many streams murmur in the distance, and near the only house we approach on the route, a little maid, hurrying barefoot from the spring, presents a pail of water for the benefit of the thirsty stagers. There have been sundry flasks of *cau de vie* on top, and the gentlemen evince no desire for the milder fluid, quaffed by the ladies with such avidity.

The half-way point is a platform for shade built across the road, and here those who wish to explore Osceola, or Indian Cave, take a short walk down the hill. Not caring to receive any subterra impressions before the great cavern dawned upon us, we joined the ladies in picking wild flowers, which are of great beauty and variety in this region. The exploring party on their return reported Osceola to be mainly a dug-out cave, having some interest, but, like its illustrious namesake, very dirty! Nearly an hour having been devoted to resting the horses, we resume the stages, and, the road improving, proceed with accelerated speed, when a sudden halt causes us to look back—the second stage has broken down! What is to be done? Nothing but to squeeze two more ladies in our coach, while we gentlemen resign our places on top to the rest of the feminines, who really make the alarming ascent with grace; but after a short walk our gallantry oozes out at the very tips of our boots, and, one by one, we jump on the steps to talk, thence clamber to the roof to find seats as best we may.

After a nine miles' drive, we approach a long, low frame-building. An air of quiet and rustic simplicity pervades the spot! This is the "Cave House." The apartments to which we are conducted have lost n the rusticity of the exterior sur ings, but everything is scrup neat, and there are excellent servants in attendance—desiral tures in a hotel. Not less s vory broiled chicken, to whi were speedily introduced.

Being all impressed with th that about nine extra hours o were requisite to fit us for the of the morrow, we denied ou the pleasures of the large ball whence issued the strains, evol some black musicians, wooing giddy mazes of the dance! flannel suits are kept at the for those who come unprepa the cool climate and rough cli of the cave; but we found ou ball toggery to be the very thi wanted, and, arrayed therein, diately after an early breakfa sembled on the wide veranda, surrounds the house and m pleasant promenade.

The ladies look charming i picturesque costumes of brig lors. Being a modest ma merely mention that our st frame does credit to the unifo the "Yellow Garters," of whic rious nine we boast ourself a ber.

All in high spirits, we des thickly wooded ravine to the r the house: beautiful ferns and carpet the sides of the funnel-s opening surrounding the mo the cave, to the bottom of whi winding path is gradually l us, a descent of forty or fift Around and above, tall trees sentinel on the only approach secret underworld.

Our guide remarks that th ent is not the original mouth cave, which is distant a quart mile on the south bank of River. Many, many years a

must have given way, this opening into which we descending, and filling with ed stones that first part of the now called "Dickson's" and visited. The present entrance covered, in 1809, by a hunter a bear into it. So little was nt or value of the cave known, as soon afterward sold, with two acres of land, for forty dollars. sharp turn in the path brings g an archway of rock, over silver thread of water is fall- cold wind rushes from a dark , above which the condensed here floats like a veil. With f awe we descend some rough eps, and enter the cave. Al- larkness is becoming visible: y, numbering twenty-five, are d with lamps, and all with lgrim staves" set forth on the route."

ive some general idea of the of the cave, we cannot do than quote the simile of a c gentleman who, in writing subject, asks the reader to ne the channel of a large and river, with tributaries at in- some of them the size of the ream, emptying into the chief s, for instance, the Missouri hio joining the Mississippi; ibutaries also receiving their from creeks and rivulets, of them quite small and ex- but a short distance, while are much longer, larger, and eautiful. Now, it is easy to these rivers as being under or having a surface covering h and rocks, and that their channels and banks have eased from some cause to be with the waters which in ages ast flowed so freely along n fact, that they are quite dry, in a few of the avenues."

From this illustration it will be seen that we cannot "cut across country" from one point to another, but must explore each avenue, and then retrace our steps to the point where we left the main cave. Neces-sarily there are many avenues wel. known to the guides rarely seen by visitors, because too much time would be consumed in visiting any but the most interesting. To see the cave at all satisfactorily, one day should be devoted to the "Short," another to the "Long Route." And from our own experience, we would suggest that these two tramps should not be made one immediately after the other, but let an intervening day be devoted to some other of the many minor expeditions of this re-gion; then you are rested, and fresh for all the day in the cave of the "Long Route."

While indulging in these practical and retrospective reflections, we have left our party in the narrow archway, about seven feet high, which is just within the mouth, and called the Narrows. Here there was a slight detention caused by the lamps blow-ing out: Mat, our black guide, ex-plains this by saying, "The cave's breathin' out." To explain which still further means that, the atmo-sphere of the cave being at 59°, when the exterior air at the mouth is of a higher temperature, a strong current sets outward; in winter, of course, the current sets inward: thus the cave breathes once a year. This action is felt a short distance. Soon we leave behind everything reminding us of the upper world.

Before the eye has become accus-tomed to the darkness, a great sense of disappointment is felt in groping through scenes of such interest with in-sufficient light. This feeling, however, gradually wears off, and the guides burn oiled paper, blue-lights, etc.,

when we stop to inspect some special marvel.

After leaving the Narrows, we soon enter the Rotunda, the ceiling of which is one hundred feet high, and its greatest diameter seventy-five feet. This chamber is said to be immediately under the dining-room of the hotel. The floor is strewn with the remains of vats, water-pipes, etc., used by the saltpetre miners in 1812. From the entrance to this point, wheel-tracks and the impressions made by the feet of oxen used to cart the saltpetre more than fifty years ago may still be seen. At the time these indentations were made by the cleft foot of the ox and the cart-wheels, the earth was moist from the recent process of lixiviation in the saltpetre manufacture, and upon drying had attained the stony solidity of petrifaction; and the indentations aforesaid are yet distinct, though they have been walked over by thousands of visitors for many years. Leaving the Rotunda, we pass huge overhanging rocks, called Kentucky River Cliffs, and enter the Methodist Church, where services have been frequently held. The pulpit is formed by a ledge of rock twenty-five feet high: the logs used as benches were placed in the church fifty years ago, and are still in a good state of preservation. In this part of the cave, and in all the avenues near the entrance, millions of bats make their winter quarters. We saw only a few flitting about, but were told they returned in the autumn by hundreds. What wonderful instinct wakens these creatures from a winter's sleep, with tidings that the glorious summer is at hand? Various objects of minor interest are noted, and we pass on to Giant's Coffin, an immense rock, forty feet long, twenty wide, eight in depth—fit sarcophagus for one of the giants of old; but Kentucky has herself of late years produced an individual who will fill it. In many parts of the and more particularly in this some striking effects are produ the efflorescence of black g upon a surface of white lim On the ceiling and walls these figures thus produced stand bold relief. Quite startling i gantic family group—man, wi infant. Another is a very per presentation of an ant-eater.

Soon we notice several encl formerly occupied by invalids vainly imagined that this pur unchanging atmosphere would them to health.

Up to this point walking ha an easy matter, the way quite a path winding among loose of some size, and in many pl smooth, broad avenue offering struction; but when, one by o climb a steep ladder placed agai wall to the right of Giant's there is a realizing sense of ' ahead."

The Gothic Arcade, which w now entered, has a flat ceiling, s and white as if it had received of plaster, and leads to Gothi pel—a very beautiful room, y purely Gothic in its style of ar ture, the roof being quite fla ported by gigantic stalactites, e ing so nearly to the floor tha present the effect of fluted co and graceful arches. Here wa performed a marriage ceremo der romantic circumstances. A lady, having promised her that she would never marry "on the face of the earth," the letter of her contract by m the same in the bowels thereof. of the stalactites in this chape ed the Pillars of Hercules, a to be thirty feet in circumf These stalactites being pecu caves, it may interest the

to note their formation. If
holding bicarbonate of lime in
, drop slowly from the ceiling,
e to the air allows one part
nic acid gas to escape, the
then deposited in the form of
rbonate of lime, and the sta-
similar to an icicle, is slowly
; if the deposit accumulate
low upward, it is termed a
ite; sometimes, meeting in the
they become cemented and
solid column. An instance of
iven in the illustration of the
Arm-Chair. These forms are
ore interesting from their va-
f color: if the limestone is
e stalactite will be white, or
nsparent; if it contain oxide
the result will be a red or
color; black stalactites con-
a large proportion of oxide of
Many other things of interest,
numerous to mention, are
out before we reach Lake
a pool of shallow water, so
y transparent that stalactites
n at the bottom. Gothic
terminating a short distance
the lake, we retraced our
the ladder by which we had
this upper and older por-
he cave, and found ourselves
n the main cave near the
Coffin, passing behind which
r a narrow crevice, where, half
g and stooping, a descent is
Deserted Chamber. At this
he water, after it had ceased
out of the mouth into Green
ft the main cave to descend
ower regions and Echo Riv-
re we again leave the regular
o visit Gorin's Dome, to us
most beautiful of the many so-
lomes.

ng over a small bridge, and
ng a steep ladder, we are, one
assisted by the guide to a
here it is not easy to retain a foothold; but here is nothing to be seen—we seem to be against a black wall. "Why, Mat, what did you bring us here for?" But not so fast. Mat has been preparing blue-lights for an illumination, and now he directs us to grasp the rock, and, one at a time, peer through a small opening. What wondrous vision is this! A hundred feet above is the arched dome, from which depend stalactitic formations and shafts, of varying size and shape; facing us hangs a curtain-like mass, terminating abruptly in mid-air. In it you seem to trace the folds and involutions of drapery veiling this mysterious place from vision. Far below, more than two hundred feet, unfathomable depths are revealed by blue-lights thrown down, while shafts, curtain, and dome are frescoed in colors of pale blue, fawn, rose, and white. This dome is three hundred feet high, and sixty feet across its widest part; but, alas! the "lights departed, the vision fled," and we are forced to descend from our eyrie. Leaving this sublime spectacle, we return to the main cave, and, following it around Great Bend, are soon in the famous Star Chamber. This is an apartment sixty feet in height, seventy in width, and about five hundred in length, the ceiling composed of black gypsum, studded with numberless white points, caused by the efflorescence of Glauber's salts. This is what we learned of this remarkable spot after leaving the cave. We now will tell you what we saw. We were first seated on a narrow ledge of rock forming a bench on one side of the chamber, the guide taking away our lamps to a distant mass of rocks, behind which he leaves them, to shed a "dim, religious light" on the scene. As our eyes become accustomed to the change, we discover ourselves to be in a deep valley with gray, rugged sides, of

course outside of the cave, else why is the sky above so deeply, darkly blue? those countless stars shining? —shining, did we say? We vow they twinkled. The Milky Way is there; we will not vouch for the Dipper, but other constellations are visible, even a comet blazes across the heavens. The guide retires with his lamp to some mysterious lower region to produce shadows, and suddenly clouds sweep across the horizon, a storm is brewing, the stars are almost hidden, now they are out, utter darkness prevails, until we hear Mat stumbling about, a faint light is in the east, and a fine artificial sunrise, as he appears with his lamp. All this may read like child's play, yet so complete is the optical delusion that, when the lamps were all returned to us, the mystery dispelled, we drew a long breath of relief that we were not really shut up in that lonely defile, looking up longingly to the stars, but actually several miles underground, and merely under the influence of Glauber's salts! Beyond is Proctor's Arcade, a natural tunnel, nearly a mile long, a hundred feet wide, forty in height; the ceilings and sides are smooth and shining, chiselled out of the solid rock. This tunnel leads past several points not specially interesting, to Wright's Rotunda, which is four hundred feet in diameter. It is astonishing that the ceiling has strength to sustain itself, being only fifty feet below the surface of the earth; but no change need be anticipated, for at this point the cave is perfectly dry. A short distance beyond, several avenues branch off from the main cave, none worthy of note, except that which leads to Fairy Grotto, a marvellous collection of stalactites, resembling a grove of white coral; Here indeed might the fairies have held high revelry, with glow-worm lamps suspended from each pillar, and fire-flies flit branch to branch.

The Chief City or Temple in the main cave beyond th Pass, is rarely visited by now, yet, before the discove rivers and the wilderness c beyond, it was considered o great features. It is an chamber, excelling in size th Staffa. The floor at differen covered with piles of rocks ing the appearance of an an in ruins.

Three miles beyond Chief main cave is terminated ab rocks fallen from above, they could be removed, v doubt open communicatior cavern similar to the one been exploring. So many viewed in a few hours, l mind in a chaotic state, weary explorer is now ready to the creature comforts of there to ruminate, and, if arrange in some sort of orc "memory's mansion," sights sations so new and strange turning to the upper world pearance of the mouth is ve ful. To eyes so long ac to darkness, the light is a radiance, a fairy land in the until we emerge from t into the outer world, whi since we left it, to have bee millions of rainbow hues; ev the leaves, the trees, sh sparkled in the blessed lig —the air! the pure atmos have been breathing all the renders the senses painf scious of the decompositior table matter, causing such of oppression that fainting the consequence if issuing entrance is not made a i easy stages.

As a result of the wis

have been exhumed in one of the neighboring small caves, and sent to Cincinnati, where it was burnt in the museum many years ago.

If such discoveries were really made, it is a matter of profound regret that these relics of an unknown past should have been removed from their resting-places, where they were secure from the ravages of time, and would, at the present day, greatly enhance the interest of Mammoth Cave.

We descend the Steps of Time, which is an unpleasant reminder to those of us who already feel stiff in the joints, and enter Martha's Palace, not so palatial as its name implies, but near by is a spring of clear water, which all hail with pleasure. Side-Saddle Pit and Minerva's Dome are soon passed, and we reach Bottomless Pit. Do not shudder! there is no necessity of descending, and there is bottom at the distance of one hundred and seventy-five feet. It was not until the year 1838 that it was supposed possible to bridge this fearful chasm; it was then crossed by Stephen, the celebrated black guide, who is identified with most of the discoveries. We now cross on a substantial wooden structure, known as the Bridge of Sighs. This leads to the Revellers' Hall, and, judging from the number of empty and broken bottles on the floor of this wild-looking room, all visitors have done their part to perpetuate the name. A low archway, the Valley of Humility, leads to Scotchman's Trap, a circular opening, through which you descend a flight of stone steps. Directly over the opening hangs a huge flat rock, which would, should it fall, completely close the avenue to the river. The number of slight, slippery ladders we have descended gives a very realizing sense that we are getting down, down, deep into the bowels of the earth.

We now enter a narrow serpentining through the soli for fifty yards, varying in widt eighteen inches to three f height from four to eight feet. passage has evidently bee through by the mechanical of water. Any lady or gen weighing three hundred poun better not attempt Fat Man's for he may sigh in vain for "t solid flesh to melt," and this r ably solid rock will not yield a breadth to anything less than charged with carbonic acid. squeezing and groaning, backs, etc.! but these are for when we emerge in Great The avenue which leads the River Styx is River Hall, b leave this for the present, and right enter Bacon Chamber, may be seen a fine collection o stone *hams* depending from th ing. After walking three-four a mile in Sparks' Avenue, we Mammoth Dome, the largest cave; it is two hundred and fif in height. Climbing over im shelving rocks, whose jagged and yawning crevices offer foothold and a very unpleasant pect in case of a fall, we reac top of a terrace forty feet fro base, where the view is take grand, solemn spectacle it is the left extremity are five larg lars, called Corinthian Column vast, solitary waste stretche before the eye on every side; gl recesses and yawning abysses minated by the weird blue-l form a sublime picture. One ca fancy it to be the primal sta chaos. The descent from th race of rocks is even more pe than the ascent, but, once in th nue, we return quickly to River Our attention is now drawn body of water forty feet below,

ia, a gloomy spot, deserving
. Passing on, the distant
nvisible waterfalls strikes the
at the foot of the slope we
ending lies the River Styx:

he dark rock o'erhangs the infernal
ing streams eternal murmurs make."

er is one hundred and fifty
ng, from fifteen to forty in
nd in depth varies from thirty feet. It has a subterranean
ication with other rivers of
, and, when they rise to a
eight, an open communica-
all of them. The Natural
pans River Styx about thirty
ve it.

next body of water we ap-
is quite peaceful, and, the
being ninety feet above the
one loses the cavernous sen-
f the gloomy overhanging
Lake Lethe is one hundred
yards long, and, being cross-
ats not large enough to con-
of the party at once, some
umber embark, with Charon
at the helm. All are hushed
solemnity of the scene, the
ed a dim light upon the rip-
ter and phantom boat, which
glides outward and on
a projecting angle of rock,
is lost to vision. For those
it upon the shore the return
at, this is a solemn moment;
urself a ghost, doomed to
a hundred years ere Cha-
ld ferry us over Avernus!
brief interval of this musing,
ight appears from behind the
ich before intercepted our
Charon with his solitary lamp
row of the boat is returning;
also embark, but not before
drunk of the waters of Lethe,
experience of the upper
light be forgotten, for now
into dream life. Our friends who had preceded us formed a picturesque group waiting as we neared the shore. The bright dresses, the lights throwing fitful gleam and shadow into the darkness beyond, and our own gliding motion, form a picture not soon forgotten. Upon disembarking we enter Great Walk, extending from the Lake to Echo River, the floor of which is covered with yellow sand. Reaching the river, we all embark in a large boat, and soon find ourselves in a very contracted space, the rocks overhead being only three feet above the surface of the water. Stooping under the narrow archway for fifteen or twenty feet, we finally emerge into the open river, with the ceiling about fifteen feet above. At some points the river is two hundred feet wide, in depth it varies from ten to thirty feet. The water is now transparently clear, rocks can be seen twenty feet below, and the boat seems passing through the air. The illusion is heightened by the fact of our guide using no oars here, propelling the boat by a staff applied at intervals to the ceiling or side walls. We avoided looking at him, that we might still fancy ourself wafted over these mysterious waters by some invisible agency. Here is no feeling of danger, only a dreamy, delicious content to float on thus for ever into the "Silent Land."

An occasional song to wake the far-famed echoes is the only sound to disturb the stillness and the unutterable thoughts which fill the soul. Echo River is an idyl! Alas! that it should be so short—yet three-quarters of a mile of bliss should compensate poor human nature for many ills. Some of the gentlemen, in the adventurous spirit of youth, made their passage through a rugged avenue called Purgatory; from their description of which we prefer journeying to paradise by the river. Land-

ing on the farther banks, we enter Silliman's Avenue, extending a mile and a half to the Pass of El Ghor, the walls and ceilings of which, being of recent formation, are rugged and water-worn. Here is Cascade Hall, a circular chamber with vaulted ceiling, from which falls a stream of sparkling water, disappearing through a pit in the floor. The avenue leading to Roaring River takes its rise in this hall.

The Infernal Region is an irregular down-hill passage, the floor covered with wet clay. Such essentially and persistently sticky mud was probably never known above ground. The scrambling, slipping, miring, ejaculating crowd made an amusing scene. Our black guide, Mat, is a character, rarely relaxing into a smile, but displays a grim humor by saying "Sot her up," when some heavier slush than usual reveals the fact that somebody is down. Now, sotting her up is not nearly as easy as sotting her down. In some places the water is ankle-deep. Here the gentlemen pick up the ladies, and carry the fair creatures to dry ground. Several laughable incidents were the consequence of this manœuvre. One gentleman, feeling the mud slipping under his feet, fancied himself in a quicksand, and hurriedly set his wife down in the water to rescue himself. Another, a bashful young swain, felt a delicacy about the manner of picking up his young lady, so carried her under one arm, her heels on a line with her head. What a funny picture those little dangling boots presented! Alas! for the uncertainty of human events. When we started out fresh in the morning, we had observed the secret pride with which that young woman contemplated her jaunty tasselled boots, the neatest fit in the party, and amply displayed by her short dress.

We are now quite willing
the Hill of Fatigue, leading
ground. Among many na
objects of interest we shall o
tion Ole Bull's Concert-Roo
the great violinist performe
first tour through the Unite
The Pass of El Ghor, two
length, is one of the most pic
avenues in the cave, its
and lofty sides changing in
variety of uncouth, fantastic
again, the hanging rocks
suggest the idea of imminen
but we are assured by the g
no rocks have fallen during
a period of thirty years.*

This pass finally comm
with a large body of w
"Mystic River," which has
explored by visitors. Asc
very high, steep ladder, v
Martha's Vineyard, twenty f
the Pass of El Ghor. Here
mite, extending from the flo
ceiling, forms the stem of
vine, from which all over
and ceiling depend bunches
grapes—nodules of carbonat
colored with the black oxid
—and here the vintage ne
for is there not sulphur at h

An avenue directly over
Vineyard, which we did not
is said to contain a miniatu
of stalactites, in a dark roo
ing which, without ornamen
kind, is a grave hewn out o
This was considered so sug
a Catholic priest that he
the Holy Sepulchre.

The next place of great
ral interest is Washington H
were unpacked the hampe
by the extra guide, detaile

* "Old Mat" is now off duty, b
be seen about the hotel. He think
more about the cave than any ma
still better qualified than the youn
exhibit its wonders!

se. Keen appetites were brought
r upon the liberal luncheon
ed by the proprietor of the
Some of the party had added
agne, so we filled generous
ers to the genii of the cave.
an hour spent in rest and refresh-
we leave Washington Hall, and,
through Snow-Ball Room, cov-
with nodules of white gypsum,
Cleveland Cabinet, an avenue
iles in length, and so beautiful
e sight of it alone would fully
for the fatigue and time devot-
the cave.

s a perfect arch of fifty feet
averaging the height of ten feet
centre. Thus every part may be
l with ease. From summit to
a dazzling expanse of alabas-
loom—a grand conservatory
the Snow Flora moulds her
r ere she transports them to the
world and endows them with
l. Here are clusters of pale
roses sprinkled with diamond
waiting only the enchantress'
to convert them into a coro-
some fair bride; again, a per-
ross of flowers, which may yet
only companion of a rare soul
bed. Stately lilies, nodding
graceful fern shapes, are show-
in endless profusion on these
alls. Here and there are little
lined with flowers, a feathery
f rock bloom hanging over the
ce. We peep in curiously, but
ri is there. This seems truly
Enchanted Palace of Sleep,"
e princess is too deeply hidden
rtal eyes to discover.

gringly we leave this wondrous
At the very end is pointed out
rose of summer, resting against
ling; it is of snowy whiteness,
eight inches in diameter, and
lly the last to be seen in the
e. A short distance beyond is
Mountain, one hundred feet high, composed of large rocks which have evidently fallen from above. On top of the mountain is a stalagmite called Cleopatra's Needle—why a needle, and wherefore Cleopatra's, I am unable to explain. We are now nearing the end of the cave, and to the weary of our band the mountain seems an insurmountable obstacle, therefore only the more adventurous scale the heights, and, passing Dismal Hollow, a gorge seventy feet deep and one hundred wide, enter Crogan Hall, which constitutes the end of the "Long Route." It is covered with stalactites, very hard and white, fragments of which are worked into ornaments.

This part of the cave is evidently near the surface of the earth, and from the comparative abundance of animal life it is probable there is an open communication at some point not far distant. The rat found here differs from its Norway brother in that it is a size larger; the head and eyes, which are black and lustrous, resemble those of a rabbit, while its soft fur is of a bluish gray and white. Crickets and lizards are numerous; they are sluggish in their movements, and the cricket never chirps. Why should he, indeed, having neither hearth nor tea-kettle to inspire him? All these animals, although provided with large eyes, seem quite blind when first caught. The fish found in the various rivers are of the class known as viviparous; they have rudiments of eyes, but no optic nerve. There are also eyeless crawfish; both these and the eyeless fish are nearly white.

At certain seasons ordinary fish, crawfish, and frogs are washed into the rivers of the cave from Green River, the inference being that they also in due course of time lose the power of vision.

At the end of Crogan Hall we are said to be nine miles from the mouth

of the cave, and somewhere under ground near Cave City. Here is the Maelstrom, a frightful pit, one hundred and seventy-five feet deep, and twenty wide. It has been explored by two or three adventurous spirits, the first of whom was a son of the late George D. Prentice.

It is needless to describe our return, which was over the ground already explored; devoting less time, of course, to the examination of wonders, and not at all tired, for exercise in this exhilarating atmosphere is unlike that of the upper world. We finally reach the entrance, and emerge—into darkness again—for it is nine P.M, and only a few twinkling stars remind us that we are not still underground.

I shall not do more than mention Proctor and Diamond Caves, which we explored on the following day, but they excel in stalactitic formation and well repay a visit. They are on the direct route to Glasgow, a three miles nearer than that o City, and where there has be cently built a comfortable h the site of the ancient "Bell's T well known to Kentuckians in days. Those who have never Mammoth Cave will scarcely the assertion of the guides th hundred and fifty miles of tra necessary to see all of the avenues of the cave. When we this the statement that ne coveries are constantly being which reveal the fact that t still a wilderness of cave unt by the foot of man, spec passes all bounds.

None but a soul absolutely vious to the impressions of th lime and beautiful handiwork world's great Architect, can realize the highest expectation exploration of this greatest of now known.

OUR EPIPHANY.

WHAT though we cannot, with the star-led kings,
  Adore the swaddled Babe of Bethlehem!
Behold, as sweet a Benediction* brings
  A new Epiphany denied to them.
The Mary Mystical 'tis ours to see
  Still from his crib the little Jesus take,
And show him to us on her altar-knee,
  And sing to him to bless us for her sake.
Shall we the while be kneeling giftless there?
  In loving faith a richer gold shall please,
A costlier incense in the humblest prayer,
  Nor less the myrrh of penitence than these:
And there between us holy Priesthood stands,
Our own Saint Joseph, with the chosen hands.

* Benediction of the Blessed Sacrament.

object thought. The soul is appearance.

fore, by declaring the nal cannot be thought in itself without the Infinite ng that underlies it as its r reality, and then declaring mething to be unknowable, ble even, the new system that there is no knowable, sequently no science or ge at all. The new system phy, then, reconciles science gion only in a universal ne- that is, by really denying This can hardly satisfy either t or a Christian.

e second part, Mr. Spencer philosophy to us, as near as come at his sense, to be the on of the several religions and sciences in their respective generalizations in a gene- that comprehends them all. ation with him means the on of the *differentia*, or ab- . He therefore, in making hy a generalization, makes traction, and, so to speak, action of all particular ab- : But abstractions in them- nullities, and consequently hy is a nullity, and science ion are nullities. Mr. Spen- tains that we have "symbo- ceptions," in which nothing ived—symbols which sym- thing. Is his "new sys- philosophy" anything but alization and unification of symbolic conceptions"?

Spencer starts with the as- that all religions, including have a verity in common an error. The verity that in which they all agree; their differences, or in which they do not Eliminate the differences and at is common to them all, and you will have the universal verity which they all assert. But what verity is common to truth and falsehood, to theism and atheism? The verity common to religion and science, that the solution of the cosmic mystery is unknowable? But that is not a verity; it is a mere negation, and all truth is affirmative.

Atheism is not a religion, but the negation of all religion. Exclude that, take all religions from fetichism to Christianity inclusive; eliminate the *differentia*, and take what they all agree in asserting. Be it so. All religions, without a single exception, however rude or however polished, agree in asserting the supernatural, and that, if the cosmic mystery is inexplicable by human means, it is explicable by supernatural means. A true application of Mr. Spencer's rule, the *consensus hominum*, would assert as the common verity the supernatural, that is, the supercosmic, which is precisely what the cosmic philosophy denies and is invented to deny. Mr. Spencer does not appear to be master of his own tools.

All religions concede that the cosmic mystery is inexplicable by our unassisted powers, by secondary causes, or by physical laws; but none of them admits that it is absolutely inexplicable, for each religion professes to be its explanation. Mr. Spencer is wrong in asserting that all are seeking to solve the cosmic mystery; for each proposes itself as its solution, and it is only as such that it claims to be or can be called a religion. The question for the philosopher is, Do any of these religions give us a solution which reason, in the freest and fullest exercise of its powers, can accept, and, if so, which one is it?

Mr. Spencer tells us, p. 32: "Respecting the origin of the universe, three verbally intelligible suppositions may be made. We may assert that

it is self-existent, or that it is self-created, or that it is created by an external agency." The second supposition he rejects as the pantheistic hypothesis, which is a mistake, for no pantheist or anybody else asserts that the universe creates itself. The pantheist denies that it is created at all; and the philosopher denies that it creates itself; for, since to create is to act, self-creation would require the universe to act before it existed. The third supposition, which the author calls "the theistical hypothesis," he denies, because it explains nothing, and is useless. He explains it to mean that the universe is produced by an artificer, after the manner of a human artificer in producing a piece of furniture from materials furnished to his hand. "But whence come the materials?" The question might be pertinent if asked of Plato or Aristotle, neither of whom was a theist; but not when asked of a Christian theologian, who holds that God creates or created all things from nothing, that is, without pre-existing materials, by "the sole word of his power."

The first supposition, the self-existence of the universe, the author denies, not because the universe is manifestly contingent and must have had a beginning, and therefore a cause or creator; but because self-existence is absolutely inconceivable, an impossible idea. He says, p. 35: "The hypothesis of the creation of the universe by an external agency is quite useless; it commits us to an infinite series of such agencies, and then leaves us where it found us." "Those who cannot conceive of the self-existence of the universe, and therefore assume a creator as the source of the universe, take it for granted that they can conceive a self-existent creator. The mystery of the great fact surrounding them on every side they transfer to leged source of this great fac then suppose they have solv mystery. But they delude selves, as was proved in the of the argument. *Self-exist rigorously inconceivable*, and thi true whatever be the nature object [subject] of which it is cated. Whoever argues th atheistical hypothesis is unt because it involves the imp idea of self-existence, mus force admit that the theistical thesis is untenable if it contai same impossible idea." Bu ever argued that the atheistical thesis is untenable because it ir the idea of self-existence? A is denied because it asserts tl existence of that which cann and is known not to be, self-e

But it is evident that the rejects alike self-existence an tion; that the cosmos is self-e or that it is created by an in dent, self-existent, and super creator. How, then, can he the existence of the cosmos, phenomenal, at all? The either exists or it does not. does not, that ends the matt it does, it must be either cre self-existent; for the author an infinite series as absurd, a creation as only an absurd fo expressing self-existence. I the author denies self-existence ever the subject of which it dicated, and also the fact of cr it follows rigorously, if he is that the cosmos does not exist author cannot take refuge in vorite *nescio*, or say we do no the origin of the cosmos, for positively denied it every origin, and therefore has by i tion denied it all existence. ment ago, we showed that he by implication all science or

and now we see that, if held ly to his system as he ex-, he denies all existence, and, ication at least, asserts abso-lism. Surely there is no oc-o apply to his new system of phy the *reductio ad absurdum.* author is necessarily led to rtion that at least nothing is le by his doctrine, that all lge is relative. The Comtists in theory, all knowledge to things, their mutual relations, ncies, and the conditions and their development and pro-but they at least admit that ay be objects of science and y known. But our cosmic her denies this, and asserts tivity of all knowledge. We nd can know only the rela-hat is, only what is relative absolute, and relative to consciousness. In this he Sir William Hamilton, J. Mill, and the late Dr. Man-glican Dean of St. Paul's. ive knowledge is simply no ge; because in it nothing is The relative is not cognizable able in and by itself, be-in and by itself, or pre-from that to which it is rela-es not exist, and is simply What neither is nor exists gnizable nor cogitable. The y of all knowledge, then, is the denial of all knowledge. e, then, for Mr. Spencer to science. His science is only ous ignorance.

Spencer labors hard to prove tivity of all knowledge. He roves it or he does not. If not, he has no right to as-The does; he disproves it at the ne. If the proof is not abso-oes not prove it; if it is abso-en it is not true that all lge is relative; for the proof must be absolutely known, or it cannot be alleged. We either know that all knowledge is relative, or we do not. If we do not, no more need be said; if we do know it, then it is false, because the knowledge of the relativity of knowledge is itself not relative. The assertion of the relativity of all knowledge, therefore, contradicts and refutes itself. No man can doubt that he doubts, or that doubt is doubt, and therefore universal doubt or universal scepticism is impossible, and not even assertable. The same argument applies to the pretence that all knowledge is relative.

The relativists are misled by their dealing with the abstract and not the concrete. They regard all that is or exists either as relative or absolute. But both absolute and relative are abstract conceptions, and formed by abstraction from the concrete intuitively presented or apprehended. They exist, as St. Thomas tells us, only *in mente, cum fundamento in re.* There are no abstractions in nature or the cosmos, and there is and can be neither abstract science nor science of abstractions, for abstractions, prescinded from their concretes, are simply nullities. The absolute is, we grant, unknowable, and so also is the relative, for neither has any existence in nature, or *a parte rei.* They are both generalizations, and nature never generalizes. Whatever exists, exists *in concreto,* not *in genere.* Hence, the *ens in genere* of Rosmini is no *ens reale,* but simply *ens possibile,* like the *reine Seyn* of Hegel, which is the equivalent of *das Nichtseyn;* for the possible is only the ability of the real.

Now, because the abstract absolute is unknowable, unthinkable even, it by no means follows that the concrete, real and necessary being, cannot be both thought and known, or that

things cannot be both thought and known in their relations to it, without reducing it to the category of the relative. Sir William Hamilton says the absolute is the unconditioned, and is incogitable, because our thought necessarily conditions it. This would be true if the absolute is an abstraction or mental conception, but is false and absurd if applied to real, necessary, infinite, and self-existent being, which, as independent of us and all relation, is and must be the same whether we think it or not. The thought does not impose its own conditions and limitations on the object; certainly not when the object is real and necessary being, and in every respect independent of it. We cannot, of course, think infinite being infinitely or adequately, but it does not follow that we cannot think it, though finitely and inadequately. The human mind, being finite, cannot comprehend infinite being; but, nevertheless, it may and does apprehend it, or else Mr. Spencer could not assert the Infinite Something, which he says we are compelled to admit underlies the cosmic phenomena and is manifested in them. The human mind can apprehend more than it can comprehend, and nothing that is apprehensible, though incomprehensible, is unthinkable or unknowable, except in Mr. Spencer's *New System of Philosophy*.

Sir William Hamilton says, in defending the relativity of all knowledge: "Only relations are cogitable. Relation is cogitable only in correlation, and the relation between correlatives is reciprocal, each is relative to the other. Thought is dual, and embraces at once subject and object in their mutual opposition and limitation." This merely begs the question. Besides, it is not true. Relations are themselves cogitable only in the related; correlatives con-

note each other, so that the o
not be thought without thinki
other; but not therefore are
lations reciprocal, as the
between phenomenon and
non, cause and effect, creat
creation. Here are two ten
a relation between them, but
ciprocity. When we think
and effect, we do not think t
mutually opposing and limitii
other. The effect cannot op
limit the cause, or the creat
creator, for the creature c
on the creator and is nothin
out his creative act, and the
nothing without the cause
produces and sustains it. Th
ture depends on the creator,
the creator on the creature;
fect depends on the cause, l
the cause on the effect. Ther
then, be relation without reci

It is true, Mr. Spencer deni
tion, and relegates all causativ
er to the dark region of the u
able, and calls the origin of t
verse in the creative act of b
God "an hypothesis," and re
with ill-concealed scorn; yet c
is not "an hypothesis," but a
tific fact, and a necessary p
of all science. Without it t
mos would not be cognizabl
would have no dialectic const
It could not even be thoug
every thought is a judgment,
judgment is possible where t
no copula that joins the predi
the subject. Rejecting creat
author cannot assert the rela
cause and effect; rejecting
and effect, he cannot assert e
cosmic phenomena. They a
able to stand on their own l
and therefore not at all, unl
Something of which they are
says, manifestations, is a cau
ducing and sustaining them
submit, then, that Mr. Spence

the unknowable, and the re-
of all knowledge, estops him
erting anything as knowable,
ly denies all the knowable and
eal—*omne scibile et omne reale.*
econd part of Mr. Spencer's
"The Knowable" we might
t, but as it is that in which
as to be original, and in
e supposes he has made
luable contributions to the
hy of the cosmos, an omis-
examine it might seem un-
Besides, the inventors of
ems of philosophy must not
too rigidly to the logical
ences of their own doctrines,
a possumus. It is impossible
founder to foresee all that
rine involves, and it is but
e really has said anything
is true, that it should be
ed, and he receive due credit
en if it is an anomaly in his
system of philosophy. We
therefore, to consider Part

second part, the author pro-
treat the knowable, not in-
its several details, but in its
ciples, or ultimate generali-
The generalization of a
phenomena is science; the
ation of the several groups
mena observable in the cos-
stitutes the several special
and the combination of
cial sciences into one higher
comprehensive generaliza-
ich embraces them all, is
y. In constructing philo-
ie author, be it observed,
coral insect, begins below
ts upward, and bases the
on the particular.
eat point, or novelty, in this
art, however, is unquestion-
the author claims, the doc-
volution. By evolution, the
es not understand evolving
or unfolding, as do ordinary mortals; but the aggregation or contraction and diffusion, according to certain laws which he has determined, of matter, motion, and force. Evolution consists, therefore, of two processes, contraction and diffusion, and is either simple or compound. Simple evolution is where concentration and diffusion follow each other alternately; compound evolution is where the two processes go on simultaneously in the same subject, which may be said to be growing and decaying, or living and dying, at one and the same time.

Minerals, plants, and animals, including man, are all formed by the evolution of matter, motion, and force. The elimination or loss of motion, mechanical, chemical, or electrical, is followed by the concentration of matter and force, which may assume the form of a pebble, a diamond, a nettle, a rose, an oak, a jelly-fish, a tadpole, a monkey, a man. Life is simply the product of "the mechanical, chemical, and electrical arrangement of particles of matter." The concentration of motion is followed by a diffusion or dispersion of matter and force, and the disappearance of the several groups of phenomena we have just named; but as matter is indestructible, and as there is always the same quantity of motion and force, they disappear only to reappear in new groups or transformations. The diffusion of the mineral may be the birth of the plant; of the plant, the birth of the animal; of the ape, may be a new concentration which gives birth to man. Nothing is lost. The cosmos is a ceaseless evolution; is, so to speak, in a state of perpetual flux and reflux, in which diffusion of one group of phenomena is followed by the birth of another, in endless rotation, or life from death, and death

from life. Dissolution follows concentration "in eternal alternation," or both go on together. This is not a new doctrine, but substantially the doctrine of a school of Greek philosophers, warred against both by Plato and Aristotle, that all things are in a state of ceaseless motion, of growth and decay, in which corruption proceeds from generation, and generation from corruption, in which death is born of life, and life is born of death. Our cosmic philosophers only repeat the long since exploded errors of the old cosmists. But pass over this.

The author is treating of the knowable. We ask him, then, how he contrives to know that there is any such evolution as he asserts? He assumes that matter, motion, and force are the constituent elements of the cosmos; but he can neither know it nor prove it, since he maintains that what matter is, or what motion is, or what force is, is unknown and unknowable. He denies the relation of cause and effect, or at least that it is cognizable; how, then, can he assert the cosmic phenomena are only concentrations and diffusions of matter, motion, and force? A certain elimination of motion and a corresponding concentration of matter and force produces the rose, another produces an ape, another produces a man, says the author of this new system of philosophy. Does he know that he is only a certain concentration of matter and force, resulting from a certain diffusion or loss of motion? Can he not only think, but prove it? But all proof, all demonstration, as all reasoning, nay, sensible intuition itself, depends on the principle of cause and effect; for, unless we can assert that the sensation within is *caused* by some object without that affects the sensible organism, we can assert nothing outside of us, not even a phenomenon or external appearance. How does the author know, or can he know, that he differs from the ape only in the different combination of matter, motion, and force?

Mr. Spencer, in his work on *Biology*, asserts that life results from the mechanical, chemical, and electrical arrangement of the particles of matter. If this were so, it would, on the author's own principles, explain nothing. It would be only saying that a certain group of phenomena is accompanied by another group, which we call life, but not that there is any causal relation between them. That the supposed arrangement of the particles of matter originates the life Mr. Spencer cannot assert without the intuition of cause and causes he either denies or banishes to the unknowable. Analytical chemistry resolves, we are told, the diamond into certain gases; but is synthetic chemistry able to recombine the gases so as to produce a diamond? Professor Huxley finds, he thinks, the physical basis of life in protoplasm. Protoplasm is not itself life, according to him, but its basis. How does he know, since he denies causality, that life is or can be developed from protoplasm? Protoplasm, chemically analyzed, is resolved into certain well-known gases; but it is admitted that synthetic chemistry is unable to recombine them and reproduce protoplasm. Evidently, as in the case of the diamond, there is in the production of protoplasm some element which even analytic chemistry fails to detect. No synthetic chemistry can obtain the protoplasm from protein, and there is no instance in which life, feeling, thought and reason, are known, or can be proved, to result from dead matter, or from any possible combinations of matter, motion, and force. If it could so result, the fact could not be

prehending that persistence; but that persistence is not a fact of consciousness. How, then, can it be asserted, unless force is, and is apprehended as, a persistent substance? But substance is unknowable.

The author adopts the method of the physicists, the so-called inductive method, and proceeds from particular phenomena to induce by generalization their law; but no induction is valid that is not made by virtue of a general principle, which is not itself inferable from the phenomenal, and must be given and held by the mind before any induction is possible. This is the condemnation of the method of the physicists, for, from phenomena alone, only phenomena can be obtained. A method without principles is null, and leads only to nullity. The author does not understand that the reason why the cosmic phenomena are not cogitable without the assumption of the cosmic reality underlying them, is because the mind intuitively apprehends them as dependent on something which they are not, and at the same time, and in the same intellectual act, intuitively apprehends a reality beyond them, which by its causative act produces and sustains them. He is wrong in declaring that the something real is unknowable; it may be incomprehensible, but, as we have seen, it must be cognizable, or nothing is cognizable.

That the men who follow in the physical sciences the physical or, as they say, the inductive method, inducing general conclusions from particular facts or phenomena, have really advanced those sciences, and by their untiring labors and exhaustless patience achieved all but miracles in the application of science to the mechanical and productive arts from which trade and industry have so largely profited, we by no means deny; but they have done so because the mind, in their investigations and inductions, has all along had the intuition of the ideal principle which legitimates their generalizations, that of being or substance, and its creative or causative act, but of which they take no heed, or to which they do not advert; as St. Augustine says, the mind really has cognition of God in the idea of the perfect, but does not ordinarily advert to the fact. They suppose they obtain the law they assert by logical inference from the phenomena, because they do not observe that the mind has intuition of the causative or creative act, which is the ideal principle of the induction. The mind is superior to their philosophy, and they reason far better than they explain their reasoning. We may apply to them the advice Lord Mansfield gave to a man of good sense and sound judgment, but of little legal knowledge, who had been recently appointed a judge in one of the British colonies: "Give your decisions," said his lordship, "without fear or hesitation; but don't attempt to give your reasons." So long as they confine themselves to the proper field of scientific investigation, they are safe enough; but let them come out of that field and attempt to explain the philosophy or the principles of their physical science, and they are pretty sure to make sad work of it. *Ne sutor ultra crepidam.*

Mr. Spencer protests against being regarded as an atheist, for he denies the self-existence of the universe, and neither affirms nor denies the existence of God. But *atheist* means simply *no-theist*, and, if he does not assert that God is, he certainly is an atheist. It is not necessary, in order to be an atheist, to make a positive denial of God. His disciple, Professor John Fiske, who has been lecturing on the cosmic philosophy

before Harvard College, contends that the cosmic philosophy is not atheistical, because it asserts in the unknowable an infinite power, being, or reality, that underlies the cosmic phenomena, of which they are the sensible manifestations; yet this does not relieve it, because what is asserted is not God, and is not pretended to be the God of theism, but the reality or substance of the cosmos and indistinguishable from it. It is the real, as the phenomena are the apparent, cosmos.

The author denies that he is a pantheist, for he denies the hypothesis of self-creation; but, if he is not a pantheist, it is only because he does not call the unknowable infinite power or being he asserts as the reality of the cosmos, that is, the real cosmos, by the name of God, Deus, or Theos. But asserting that power as the reality or substance of the cosmic phenomena is precisely what is meant by pantheism. Pantheism, in its modern form, is the assertion of one only substance, which is the reality of the cosmic phenomena, and the denial of the creation of finite substances, which are the real subject of the cosmic manifestations. Pantheism denies the creation of substances or second causes, and asserts that all phenomena are simply the appearances of the one infinite and only substance; and this is precisely what Mr. Spencer undeniably does. The only difference between atheism and pantheism is purely verbal. The atheist calls the reality asserted cosmos or nature, and the pantheist calls it God, but both assert one and the same thing. The power Mr. Spencer asserts is simply the *natura naturans* of Spinoza, and that is nothing the atheist himself does not accept, and, indeed, assert. Neither atheists, nor does Mr. Spencer assert, any supercosmic being, or power on which the cosmos depends, and the power they do assert is as much cosmic as the phenomena themselves. Mr. Spencer's protest betrays rare theological and philosophical ignorance, or is a mere verbal quibble, unworthy a man who even pretends to be a philosopher.

Mr. Spencer hardly once refers to Christian theology, and, without ever having studied it, evidently would have us think that he considers it beneath his attention. Yet he, as evidently, has constructed his system for the purpose of undermining and disposing of it once for all. This may be seen in the fact that, when he refers to religion at all, it is always to some heathen superstition, which he assumes to be the type or germ of all religion, carefully ignoring the patriarchal, Hebrew, or Christian religion. He tells us "the earliest traditions represent rulers as gods or demigods." This is not true even of heathenism, which is in fact an apostasy from the patriarchal or primitive religion, or its corruption. The apotheosis of Romulus, according to tradition, took place only after his death, and it is only at a later period that the pagan emperors were held to be gods during their lifetime. Mr. Spencer's real or affected ignorance of the whole order of religious thought is marvellous, and we cannot forbear saying:

> "There are more things in heaven and earth, Horatio,
> Than are dreamt of in your philosophy."

There is no philosophy or science, if God and his creative act are excluded or ignored, because there is no cosmos left, and neither a subject to know nor an object to be known.

Mr. Spencer misapprehends the relations of religion and science, and consequently the conditions of their reconciliation. He says they are the two opposite poles of one and the

same globe. This is a mistake. Religion and science are indeed parts of one whole; but religion, while it includes science, supplements it by the analogical knowledge called faith. The truths of faith and of science are always in dialectic harmony, and between the Christian faith and real science there is no quarrel, and can be none; for religion only supplies the defect of science, and puts the mind in possession of the solution of the problem of man and the universe, not attainable by science.

There is a quarrel only when the scientists, in the name of science, deny or impugn the supplementary truths of revelation, and which are at least as certain as any scientific truths or facts are or can be; or when they reject the great principles of reason itself, which are the basis of all science. Let the scientists confine themselves, as we have said, to the study and classification of facts, or the development and application to them of the undoubted principles of the intuitive reason, and not attempt to go beyond their province or the proper field of scientific investigation, and there will be no quarrel between them and the theologians. The quarrel arises when men like Spencer, Darwin, Huxley, and others, profoundly ignorant both of philosophy and of theology, or the teachings of revelation, ignoring them, despising them, or regarding them with sovereign contempt, put forth baseless theories and hypotheses incompatible with the truths alike of reason and faith; and it will continue till they learn that an unproved and unprovable theory or hypothesis is not science, nor a scientific explanation of the facts either of the soul or of the cosmos, and is quite insufficient to warrant a denial of the belief of the great bulk of mankind from the first man down to our own

day. Then there may b
tween the theologians an
tists, but not till then.

We said, or intended to
philosopher is known by
ples. We add that he is
by his method. The physi
is unscientific and illogi
seeks through phenomen
at being, and from partic
tain general or universal c
Induction that is not base
versal principle can neve
anything but the particul
ralizations of particulars a
stractions, and abstraction
ed from their concretes, a
as the possible, without
actualize it, is nothing.
rising from particulars to th
unless we start with a univ
ciple intuitively given. It
ble to conclude, by logical
substance or being from p
The reality which Mr. Sp
we are compelled to ass
itself unknowable, as und
cosmic phenomena, is no
nor induction from these, l
intuitively as the ideal
ble in the very act in whi
nomena themselves are
ed. Mr. Spencer is wron
ing it, as we have said, to l
able, and still more so in
as the subject of the cosr
mena, which is simply
These phenomena are n
pearances or manifestati
Infinite Power or Being
Spencer asserts as unkno
of the finite and depende
ces which God, the Infi
creates and upholds as sec

The universal is not c
the particular, the infir
finite, the identical in t
the immutable in the m
persistent in the transitor
plurality, or the actual i

ıd therefore cannot be con- from it. The two categories ·t obtainable, either from the by any possible logical infer- and therefore must be given ·ely or neither is cognizable; ɔugh not reciprocal, they con- ıs all correlatives, each the since neither is knowable with- e other. This is the con- tion of the physical or induc- ıethod, when followed as a ɫ of obtaining the first princi- :her of the real or of the know- We say only what Bacon him- d. He said and proved that luctive method is inapplicable osophy, or out of the sphere of 'sical sciences. The great error en in attempting to follow it in ·phy, or the science of the ·s, where it is inapplicable, for ence can start without first les.

feel that some apology is due ıders for soliciting their atten- ı anything so absurd as Her- ıencer's *New System of Philo-* but they must bear in mind r. Spencer is a representative nd has only attempted to bring er and combine into a systema- ɔle the anti-Christian, anti-the- and anti-rational theories, hy- es, and unscientific specula- which, under the name and of science, govern the thought of the modern non-Catholic world. Mr. Spencer's book, which is a laborious effort to give the philosophy or science of nothing, and ends only in a system of "symbolic conceptions," in which nothing, according to the author, is conceived, has, after all, a certain value, as showing that there is no medium or middle ground between Catholicity and atheism, as there is none between atheism and nihilism. Mr. Spencer, we should think, is a man who has read comparatively little, and knows less of Christian theology or philosophy; he seems to us to be profoundly ignorant of his own ignorance, as well as of the knowledge other men have. He is only carrying out the system of Sir William Hamilton, Dr. Mansel, and providing a philosophy for the Darwins, the Huxleys, the Galtons, the Lubbocks, the Tyndalls, *et id omne genus*, and has succeeded in proving that no advance has been made by the non-Catholic world on the system of old Epicurus, which is rapidly becoming the philosophy of the whole world outside of the church, and against which the Bascoms, the Hodges, and the McCoshes, with honorable intentions and a few fragments of Catholic theology and philosophy, protest in vain. This is our apology for devoting so much space to Herbert Spencer's inanities.

ST. CECILIA'S DAY IN ROME.

St. Cecilia is one of the few figures among the representative throng of virgin-martyrs that strike us at once as the most familiar, the most lovable, and the most to be exalted. Every one knows the legend of her life, and the conversion of her husband and his brother, brought about by her prayers, as also by the miracles she obtained for their further confirmation in the faith. Her death, in itself a miracle, needs no retelling, neither does the history of her wondrously preserved remains, that are now laid in the shrine beneath the altar of *Santa Cecilia in Trastevere*, a church erected, by her own wish and behest, on the spot where her palace stood. This church is a basilica, and has its altar raised many steps above the level of the mosaic floor of the nave, and the front of the altar turned away from the people so that the celebrant at Mass stands facing the congregation, as in many other ancient Roman churches. Under the altar, on the lower level of the nave, is the shrine of the saint, and there lies her marble image, small and frail, though it is said to be life-sized, and reverently and truly copied from the sleeping body, whose form remained entire and uncorrupted, at least until the last time it was solemnly uncovered. To the right of the church is a dark side-chapel, floored with rare mosaic, once the bath-room of the young and wealthy patrician, and the consecrated spot where heathen cruelty twice endeavored to put an end to the sweet singer's life. The actual bath is said to be within the railings that divide a narrow portion of the chapel from the rest. There was the first miracle performed, of her preservation from the boiling water; there also the second, of the prolongation of her life after the three deadly yet ineffectual strokes of the unskilful executioner's sword. One can fancy the young matron, so childlike in years, so experienced in holiness, lying in meek and chaste expectation of the embraces of her heavenly Bridegroom, and of the purified reunion with her earthly and virgin spouse—while, all the time the wondrous, angel-sustained life lasted, the Christians, her brethren in the faith, her children through charity, would be coming and going, silently as to an altar, rejoicingly as to a saint, and learning, from lips on whom the kiss of peace of the glorified Jesus was already laid, lessons of fortitude and love most precious to their faithful souls. We are told, also, that Urban, the pope, visited her on her glorious death-bed, and, no doubt, he learnt from her entranced soul more than he could teach it in its passing hour; learnt, perhaps, things whose sweetness became strength to him in the hour of his own not far distant martyrdom.

Cecilia, in her short and heavenly life, seems a fitting model for all women, and especially for young maidens and wives. She was of those who know well how to put religion before men in its most beautiful garb and most enthralling form; purity with her was no ice-cold stream and repellent rocky fastness: it was beauty, it was reward, it was glory. Crowns of lilies and roses, heavenly perfume. [illegible] i- com-

men of all ages, all ranks, all nations, bearing in their hands the charity born of Cecilia's death-bed generosity, and in their hearts the faith of her death-bed professions.

And so, past the stately tomb worthy of Egypt's solemn magnificence, the road leads to a small door in a wall, which opens on to a field. A path fringed with red and purple flowers, the last-born children of a southern autumn, winds through the field, to the head of a steep but wide flight of stairs, at the foot of which is the entrance to St. Callixtus' Catacomb. The pure air, just mist-veiled in the morning coolness, shows the landscape around to its utmost advantage; the omnipresent dome of St. Peter's basilica clears the line of the blue horizon; the wide purple plain is crossed here and there by dust-whitened roads and arched aqueducts, as by the gigantic bones of a decayed and now powerless monster; the distant hills, darkened at their base by chestnut woods, and dotted with white villas, as with the loosened beads of a string of pearls, throw bluer shadows on the dusky, olive-spotted expanse: and we pause, and wonder whether, after all, things looked so very unlike this on the dawning day when the Christians bore the happy Cecilia to her first resting-place. Their hearts surely must have felt as ours do now, full of joy and thanksgiving, and, above all, full of peace. There would have been a silent throng, a quiet gradual gathering of the future martyrs around the narrow grave of their blessed forerunner; for in those days no one knew how soon he or she might be called from the altar to the stake, and summoned to carry the unconsumed sacrament within his bosom to the tribunal of an unjust and ignorant judge.

The avenues of the perplexing labyrinth of the catacomb are all guarded by the government on this day of St. Cecilia's, so that no one may stray from the one chapel where service is going on. Close to the entrance is the small recess where the saint was laid in her first sleep. It is low and reaches far back into the damp earth-wall; myrtle and bay-leaves are strewn over its floor, and flowers and little oil-lamps are spread about like stars. As each person leaves the chapel, he takes away a leaf or flower as a holy remembrance. Two altars are erected, one close to the martyr's grave, just beneath a Byzantine fresco head of our divine Lord, the other on the opposite side of the chapel. The space, small enough for a modern congregation, though large for a catacomb chapel, is so crowded that it is difficult for the priests to pass in and out from the altars to the temporary sacristy, and the worshippers almost lean upon them when they stand to say the "Judica me, Deus." No noise is heard, save the murmured words of the Mass and the tinkling of the elevation-bell. Foreigners are there with fair-haired boys serving the Mass of some favorite friend and accompanying chaplain; Romans are there with their intense, if not deep, southern devotion; rich and poor, prince and beggar, student and peasant, are alike crowding the virgin-martyr's shrine. A few hundred years ago, this was the church's cradle, and patrician and slave came to be baptized together and wear for one day the white robes that to-morrow twilight would see red with blood on the deserted sand of the gladiator's amphitheatre. The priest who said Mass in those days hardly knew, when he came to the consecration, whether the hand of the pagan soldiery might not be upon him be-

proud stone pyre, a mound of stones, each of which bears an imperial inscription, a rude shepherd's fence, or irregular stone wall, that is all you see. Not far from here, in a corn-field whose waves of brown and gold a few months ago kissed the foot of an ilex-crowned hillock, is the fountain of Egeria, a grotto, fern-clothed, with a broken goddess of mouldering stone. The water and the "maiden-hair" fern are there still, as beautiful as when the king of Rome is said to have wandered here in search of wisdom; the sage himself and the problematic nymph of tradition are dead and gone, forgotten by the owner of the corn-field, ignored by the peasant who drinks at the fountain, unknown to the brown, bare-footed child who gathers the feathery fern.

Of what use is it to say any more? Facts are more cruel commentaries on the past than any words.

Yet we have just seen children and peasants, women from northern lands, men from eastern climes, bearing away as a relic a leaf of bay or a starry flower from the once filled recess where Cecilia lay in peace-sealed slumber.

Where is the difference, and why?

A little child can tell, but the philosopher will not listen.

The feast of St. Cecilia, though to the writer of these pages it ended on the threshold of the catacomb, is not completed here.

At her church in the *Trastevere*, the church already mentioned, takes place the ceremony of solemn vespers, in which the artists of Rome assist and take part gratuitously, out of homage to the queen of music. The antiphon "Cantantibus Organis" is magnificent in art, but unresponsive in devotion. The phantom of the unhappy *Renaissance* breathes in these strains, religious only in so far as they are a fabric built on sacred words. The simple solemnity of the church's service dwells not in them, and the touching silence of the catacomb recalls the saint to our mind far more sweetly than these outbursts of paganized minstrelsy within the halls she once called her own. Still, if honor to God be meant by this concourse of the artist fraternity, let us be simple of intention, and see in it, as God does, the first-fruits of what they have offered to the God of all.

Reader, if you ever pray before the early shrine of the virgin-martyr in St. Callixtus' chapel, remember the writer of these few words, and let our prayers go up to God together, "as a morning sacrifice" and "as incense in his sight."

FLEURANGE.

FROM THE FRENCH OF MRS. CRAVEN, AUTHOR OF "A SISTER'S STORY."

PART FIRST.

THE OLD MANSION.

ıutiful, poor, and alone
will become of her ?"
ıird time Dr. Leblanc
ıese words in the pre-
ster, Mademoiselle Jo-
emained so mute that
e been thought deaf,
rregular click of her
s, and two or three in-
ıations as she paused
estified to a preoccu-
ual to that of her bro-
er at first manifested
triding up and down
in which they were,
sumed his usual place
y-corner opposite his
ınd shut his snuff-box
a useless profusion of
he forgot to convey
tion, and tapping the
oot in a manner that
t agitation or extreme

e Josephine continued
replying, and seemed
ed than her brother.
aid :
if she were not, as
oung and so beauti-

ɔor and alone in the
uld add. A sensible
! It is evident if she
rich, and surrounded
: situation would be

very different. I am indebted to you, Josephine, for the discovery."

"Do not be impatient, brother. I am only repeating what you have just said. To continue the subject: if she only had a different air—"

"Well, go on!"

"And another name—"

"Another name! Why so? What has her name to do with the matter?"

"A name which was not ridiculous."

"Ridiculous! The name of her father? Poor Gerard d'Yves' name was very respectable, and even noble, I believe. He committed a thousand extravagances and ruined himself. He then became an artist, and displayed talent enough to have repaired his fortunes had he been wise. Besides, he was of a good family, and his name—"

"I am not alluding to his name, but to his daughter's."

"Well?"

"Well, brother, do you think this young girl's name bears any resemblance to a Christian name?"

"Fleurange? I acknowledge it is perhaps an odd name. Her father had a taste for odd things, and hearing the name of Fior Angela in Italy, he translated it."

"Her mother should have had more sense."

"Her poor mother died when she

was born, so she had nothing to do with it."

"Did you not say her mother had a brother who was a professor in some city in Germany?"

"Yes, at Leipsic; but who knows where to find him now? Her whole family disapproved of her marriage, which was finally effected without her father's consent. Poor Margaret lived only a year, and Gerard, who remained a widower, declined all intercourse with his wife's relatives. He remained many years in Italy, and placed his daughter, as soon as she was five years old, in some convent near Perugia. He took her away only two months before he came here, already ill, to linger and die three days ago in this poor child's arms, leaving her entirely alone in the world."

"But was it not very injurious to his daughter's interests to withhold her thus from all intercourse with her maternal relatives?"

"He began to realize it himself, but only when it was too late. During his illness, finding his case daily growing more serious, he made some efforts to ascertain what had become of Ludwig Dornthal, of whom we have just spoken, who was Margaret's favorite brother, and never faltered in his affection for her. But he could ascertain nothing respecting him. Ludwig had married, and, long before, left Leipsic to settle in some other part of Germany, he could not find out what, and this fruitless effort was a source of pain, which was not the least he suffered during his last hours. He reproached himself, and not without reason, for the frightful loneliness in which he was about to leave his daughter. The poor, unhappy man bitterly expiated the imprudent and thoughtless act of alienating himself from those whose pardon he should rather have implored, or at least accepted. But it was th quence of his disposition, wh affectionate, enthusiastic, and ing, I imagine, when he was but weak, violent, and thou He was born neither to be himself, nor to make others and his daughter would hav almost as great an object had he lived, as she is now."

"Poor child!" said Made Josephine, raising her smal eyes, with an expression almo tial lighting up her pale and w face. After a moment's silen added: "God tempers the the shorn lamb! You will s ther, that some good luck wi her, or we shall have some f inspiration."

"Well, the sooner the bette have none. Your confidenc excites my admiration."

"I trust in God," simply Mademoiselle Josephine.

"Parbleu! and I too," said t tor. "I truly believe in his goo I hope in his mercy; but in this

"You would prefer to ha affair in your own hands?"

"Come, come, Josephine, stick to the point this time. eight o'clock, and we must po go for that poor child. She i lonely than ever to-day, for t ter who nursed her father, a mained with her after his dea this morning. She must not so sad a day, pass this first ni alone up there."

"Certainly not," said the ot

The doctor continued: "S not left that little room in the story for a fortnight, with the tion of this morning, when sh lowed her father to the grav since her return how do you i she has been occupied? Here at this."

Mademoiselle Josephine to

her brother held out, and
over it. It was a list of the
ist's debts.

whole amounts to five hun-
ancs, which are here. She
ie to settle the bills and pro-
receipts."

e that, according to her cal-
, one-fourth of this sum is
d for the physician who at-
ier father," said Mademoiselle
ie slowly.

o, in such a case, will not ac-
of course."

course not," said his sister.
this sum one hundred and
ive francs will be returned to
?"

sister, and that will be the
of her fortune."

ile we are talking, then, she
olutely nothing?"

hing at all."

conversation at this point
errupted by a low knock at
, and almost immediately the
whom they had been talking
d before them. She stopped
ned against the wall. The
prang toward her.

r child!" he exclaimed.
we were idly talking, she was
m exhaustion and fatigue."

ad, in truth, fallen into a
ainst the wall, and seemed
nsciousness. Mademoiselle
ie hastened to support her
d bathe her pale brow and
cheeks with cold water.
ovement of the doctor's el-
ter had become prompt and
At a sign from her brother,
ppeared an instant, but re-
almost immediately with a
a glass of water in her hand.
t is it," said the doctor. He
a few drops into the glass,
e then held to the young
s. Two or three swallows
to revive her.

"Excuse me," she said, raising her head, and forcing herself to rise "Excuse me, both of you. I did not think myself so weak, and did not intend to give you so much trouble when I came to see you."

"Do not talk now, but drink the remainder of this."

Fleurange put the glass to her lips, but returned it to the doctor without tasting it. "I cannot," she said, "I feel dizzy. I do not know what ails me—perhaps it is the surprise I have just had. Here, monsieur, read this. It was to show you this letter I came down."

The doctor took the letter, but, before reading it, led Fleurange to the fire, while the active Josephine, divining her brother's wishes, placed on the table a bowl of soup and some bread and wine.

Fleurange took Mademoiselle Josephine's hand between her own: "Thank you," she said in a low tone. "Yes, I think it was that: I am generally strong, but—but—"

"I dare say you have not eaten anything since yesterday?"

"No; and I am hungry."

The doctor briskly rubbed his spectacles, and abruptly opened his snuff-box, while the young girl hastily took the slight repast, which brought a lively and unusual color to her cheeks. Her face was generally very pale. Her large eyes, calm and mild, gray rather than blue, shaded by lashes black as her hair, gave her a peculiar and striking appearance. But, notwithstanding this peculiarity, notwithstanding her paleness, the delicacy of her features, and the pliancy of her form, which swayed like a reed at every movement, if obliged to characterize in two words the general impression produced by the appearance of Fleurange d'Yves, those words would be: simplicity and energy. Doctor Leblanc was doubtless

right in thinking that one so young, beautiful, and destitute needed protection, and yet it required only a glance to see that she, better than any else, could protect herself.

The doctor still held in his hand the letter she had given him. It was dated at Frankfort.

"My Dear Niece: It was only yesterday, and by the most unforeseen chance, we at last learned the state of your father's health and where he lives. None of us have seen him since his marriage with my poor sister Margaret twenty years ago. You know there was at that time a profound hatred against France throughout our country, and my father would never consent to receive a Frenchman as his son-in-law. Then my poor sister (God forgive her!) left the paternal roof to marry the man of her choice. My father was exceedingly grieved, very angry, and at first implacable, but before his death he forgave her. She was past knowing it. From that time we lost all trace of your father. We only learned he had left Pisa with his child, and, for a long time, had given up all hope of ever seeing him again, or knowing my poor sister's daughter, when yesterday a stranger, passing through this city, accidentally showed me a picture he had just purchased at Paris—the work, he said, of a dying artist. This painting represented Cordelia kneeling beside her father, and the canvas bore the name of Gerard d'Yves. The painter's address was given us by the owner of the picture, and I hasten to profit by it to tell you, my dear child, that your mother's relatives have not forgotten the tie that binds them to you. If you ever need a shelter, you can find one beneath our roof. My wife and children already regard poor Margaret's daughter with affection. The latter have thought of her fr fancy as an absent sister whose they awaited. If God restore father's health, bring him am If otherwise ordered, come y my dear child. The strange put us on your track told artist's daughter was the orig his Cordelia. If the resembl correct, it does not diminish sire to see you. Come soon, tl dear niece. At all events, this letter promptly, and be ass the affectionate regard of you

"Ludwig Dornte

"Josephine! Josephine!" exc the doctor. "Here, read thi first, embrace me. Yes, yo right. Your trust was bette my wisdom! Yes, yes, God t the wind to the shorn lamb. child, embrace me also."

Fleurange rose: "Oh! very ly," said she as she threw hers bing into the doctor's arms. tigue, grief, and the emotion by the unforeseen and unhoj offer of a refuge at the very m of extreme need, all combir agitate her mind, excite her and exhaust her strength. He swelled with the emotion she not repress, and tears unrest came to her eyes, rolled dow cheeks, and fell like rain o clasped and icy hands, while vulsive movement agitated her l and her trembling lips gave utt to a feeble cry.

The doctor allowed her to w long time in silence, not utte word to increase her agitation yet saying nothing to repress it length the paroxysm subsided Fleurange rose quite confused.

"Excuse me once more," sai "I am distressing you, inste showing my gratitude as I oug could not restrain myself, but I

safely promise it will not
n again. I seldom give way
s."

uttered these words in a firm
lrying her tears, and throwing
ier hair with her two hands as
ool her brow, then she rose.

here are you going, pray?"
Mademoiselle Josephine in an
tone of authority.

hy," stammered Fleurange, "I
ing up-stairs. I—"

rhaps you are thinking to
the night all alone in the cabi-
xt the chamber—the chamber
She stopped. Fleurange turned
and her lips trembled as she

hat can I do? It is sad, it is
l, I know well; but it must be
Besides, I am not afraid: I
am under your roof."

ell, for the present you shall
under the protection of our
nd key," said the kind Jose-
and, taking Fleurange by the
ie led her into a little chamber
er own, where a small bed sur-
d by white curtains was in
ss for the young girl. This
hamber, with its walls covered
ue paper, and lit up with a good
d a most cheering aspect.

ere, child, is your chamber and
ed," said she. "Come, come,
nks, and, above all, no tears!
bed at once without giving
lf the time to think, still less to
vord. You think you are not
to sleep, but you are mistaken.
ur knees? Well, I consent to
ut let it be a short prayer.
right. Now stop till I gather
ır thick hair. Is your head
that pillow? Well, I am glad.
od, and all good angels, watch
ou! Allow me to kiss your
d. Good-night!"

lemoiselle Josephine lowered
rtains of the bed, and softly left the chamber, while the poor orphan, in fact, lost all remembrance of the sorrows and joys of the day in a profound and beneficent sleep.

The chamber to which Mademoiselle Josephine had taken Fleurange rightfully belonged to the doctor's niece, now at school in one of the convents at Paris, but which she occupied during her vacation. However, it was far from being vacant the remainder of the year. Mademoiselle Leblanc was one of those persons who are devoted to the searching out of the unfortunate, and the alleviation of their woes. In such cases, he who seeks finds, and that without difficulty, consequently a week seldom passed without offering a good reason for opening the blue chamber for a few days' shelter to some poor girl out of work and destitute of a home, or to a poor abandoned child, or some one recovering from illness but too feeble to resume work. The doctor heartily approved of this. He would gladly have added to his dwelling a veritable *succursale* for the accommodation of his poor patients, and if he was not yet rich enough for that, though he reaped the benefit of his skill and celebrity, it was partly because he gave away with one hand what he received in the other, and that with a generosity not always in conformity with prudence. When there was a question of benevolence between the brother and sister, one was not more disposed than the other to count the cost. They had invented a proverb, worthy of the Gospel, which they made use of in reply to the remonstrances of their friends: "He who gives alms, grows rich," they said; and they continued to enrich themselves in this way by giving themselves up, both of them, to a noble excess of charity. Fortune, in fact, had not been unfavor-

able to them, and thus far had remained unfulfilled the sinister prophecies of those who take as a *devise* quite a different proverb, respecting charity, too well known and too often acted upon in the world. Doctor Leblanc and his sister knew nothing, it is true, of the luxury of elegant quarters and fine equipages. They still lived in a street of the Latin quarter where they were born; an old servant was the sole assistant of the cook; and Mademoiselle Josephine continued to preserve order and neatness around her with he hands. But at all times the magnificent in their own way; a artists they encouraged, the s befriended, and the sick grat attended and generously aided to the renown of the disting physician and gave to his r reputation he did not seek. and learned, healing the boo respecting the soul, he loved h fession as a mission from h and practised it as a sacred m with respect and with love.

II.

When Fleurange opened her eyes on the following morning, it was late, for it was broad daylight and in the month of December. She must have slept very profoundly, for she had not heard any one kindle the fire already blazing in the chimney. Her slumbers must have been such as in youth succeed great fatigue or prolonged efforts to endure anxiety and grief in silence. The fit of weeping the evening before and the long repose of the night had brought double refreshment to the exhausted strength of the young girl, and her first sensation was one of delicious comfort.

But her remembrances soon became more distinct, and the anguish of the first awakening after a great misfortune made her heart sink within her. She had, it is true, known her father but little. The convent where she had been reared was not even in the town where he dwelt, and she saw him but seldom during her childhood. But the days when he appeared at the convent were to both great festivals. It was difficult to understand how a father so glad to see his child could voluntarily have allowed her to grow up away from him. But the time of reunion came at last, a several weeks they rambled a Italy together. In unveiling wonders to a mind naturally c of appreciating them, the art all the enthusiasm of his you vive. But it was a flame only dled to be extinguished. Soon symptoms of illness, the sad ret Paris, the fluctuations of d which enfeeble the mind as w the body, and separated the from her father while he wa alive, and she night and day bedside. His look that gave no answering glance, the wor murmured in his ear without m him understand, convinced h her loss before the separatio death which soon followed.

" O father! father scarcely k and so soon lost!" Such was ange's cry, and perhaps an inv tary reproach mingled with h cents of grief. She did not s it was a sublime and paternal ir that had influenced the poor ar separating from his child. He ed her to be self-reliant; he w her to be pious and pure; he ed her rare mental gifts only developed when order, an imm

livine order, was established in
oul; finally, he desired her to
that he himself lacked, and
lessed this desire.

a beautiful spot near Perugia,
and at the head of a charity
one of those women whom
orld itself would honor and ve-
if it comprehended them. By
orld, I mean the mass of light
coffing people who are hostile
ery sentiment in which they
no share, and, above all others,
ligious sentiments. Yet this
is, on the whole, suspicious
than unjust, and incredulous
alse: if it sees the semblance
il, it immediately supposes it
f it sees the appearance of good-
t at once imagines this appear-
deceitful; but when virtue is
stionably manifest, irrecusable
simplicity and truth, and suc-
in being regarded in a true
the world—even the world of
we have been speaking—gene-
ows down before it. The thing
e, it is true, more so than it
be, because the most perfect
's aim not at displaying them-
, but at concealment; and the
to which I refer seeks not to
er, but to deny, their exist-

dre Maddalena was one of
great hidden souls. No one
poke of her, or of her little mo-
y, intended for the education of
children, but where a limited
er of girls of a more elevated
were also admitted. Like so
other monasteries in Italy, this
as in a poetic and charming
on, but not one of those visible
off on the lofty summits that
and views which ravish the
nd transport the soul—views
indle a desire in the most in-
nt heart to keel before them,
at have inspired Christians to perpetuate prayer amid them in permanent sanctuaries.

The Convent of Santa Maria al Prato was, on the contrary, in a deep valley, and surrounded by a landscape like those in which Perugino and Raphael placed their divine creations or their sacred representations. Afar off were mountains whose outlines were clearly defined on the horizon in soft and harmonious colors; a stream wound through olive groves, now and then encircling rustic dwellings—the evident handiwork of a people with an instinctive taste for the arts; the sombre verdure of a knot of pines or cypresses contrasted here and there with the azure of the morning sky or the purple tints of evening: such were the principal features of the landscape. The beauty of such a scene subdues and reposes, as that of sublime summits transports and exalts, and seems designed for meditation and labor, as the other for contemplation and ecstasy.

It was to this retreat Fleurange's father was providentially led—perhaps guided by the protective inspiration we love to attribute to mothers who are fond of their children. It was in the hands of Madre Maddalena that he left his daughter as soon as she was five years old, and, until the day she was eighteen, he only saw her twice a year. But from year to year he felt more sure of having realized the aim he had proposed respecting her. Fleurange had, nevertheless, no proof to give him of her progress under the form of prizes obtained or crowns conferred. The solemn occasions when such trophies are distributed were unknown at Santa Maria al Prato, as well as the examinations for which the memory is burdened for a day with facts that are often remembered no longer. In fact, they did not aim at giving her varied instruction, but they taught

her how to learn, and gave her a taste for study, work, and silence.

She was naturally sincere and courageous; she also became skilful and active. Madre Maddalena seemed to have foreseen that this young person, so sheltered in her early years, would one day be unusually exposed to the rough combat of life. She probably did not foresee that Fleurange would soon be left alone; but what she had read of her father's nature, what she knew of his history, made her comprehend that prudence and a certain premature experience would serve as a safeguard to his daughter. What would have been true had her father lived, was no less so now his death left her entirely to herself.

Fleurange resisted the temptation of remaining in bed absorbed in sad thoughts. She hastily rose, and was quite ready when Mademoiselle Josephine entered her chamber for the third time. A smile enlivened the features of the elderly maiden when she saw the effect of a good night's rest on the countenance of her *protégée*. The latter, affected and grateful, and retaining the Italian habits of her childhood, bent to kiss the hand of her benefactress.

"Do not kiss my old hand," said Mademoiselle Josephine, "but my cheek, if you like; now, let us not keep my brother waiting. It is nine o'clock, our breakfast-hour which never varies."

Fleurange followed her hostess to the breakfast-room, which was next the parlor. The furniture of these two rooms had not been renewed for more than fifty years, but nothing seemed dilapidated, thanks to the exquisite neatness that everywhere reigned.

The doctor was already seated at the table. His sister took her place opposite, giving Fleurange a seat between them.

"You have quite recovered," said the doctor, extending his hand to the young girl. "I am very glad to see it; but, for fear of relapse, you must remain under my eye for some days to come. Everything has been arranged, and from this time till your departure you will return no more to the fourth story."

"What can I say, monsieur? You are both so kind, and I love you so much that I accept alms from your hands without shame and almost without pain."

"I forbid you making use of so shocking a word," said Mademoiselle Josephine.

"Yet it is really alms," said Fleurange in a sad but firm tone, "for I have nothing of my own, and if in want of a piece of bread to-day, I should have to extend the hand of a beggar."

"Come, come! you are not reduced to that yet, thank God! But let us drop this, and speak of something more important. You must answer your uncle's letter without delay."

"Yes, indeed," said Fleurange. And after a short silence, she added: "I am going to ask him to be kind enough to receive me for a month."

"But from his letter, he seems disposed to offer you a much more extended hospitality than that."

"Perhaps so, but I am only willing to accept it till I have found the means of living without being a burden on him."

"What is your intention, then?"

"I do not know," said Fleurange; "but there are many means of gaining a livelihood, are there not? Well, I shall endeavor to find one not beyond my strength."

The doctor looked at her, and then said: "There are certainly many

ot beyond your strength, but
iitable for you."

y ?" asked Fleurange.

y would be unsuitable for
our age and condition."

y so ?" repeated she.

ill explain myself after you
what you think of doing."

ne !" said Mademoiselle Jo-
impatiently. "There is no
so much circumlocution in
ner that, when one is young
ty, caution is needful. If the
es not know that, the sooner
irned, the better it will be for

ng and pretty," repeated
ge quietly without the slight-
arrassment. "Yes, I know
be a great obstacle to me in
tion. It would be much bet-
e homely and ten years older.
lready thought of that. It is
fortunate; but what can be

doctor smiled. He had never
ny woman admit her own
with so little vanity. Fleur-
simplicity, the childlike can-
er large eyes, the expression
was yet grave and thought-
ck him, and he felt an in-
f the interest which up to this
had been excited by the
irl's destitute condition, rath-
herself. He resumed, still

o this misfortune, you must re-
rself to it, at least for twenty
come." But seeing that
ge did not smile in return,
the contrary, became more
e thoughtful, he continued:
, if you ever come to that,
find a means for surmounting
ulty."

nge's face expanded. "Oh!
ou, monsieur; if you could
now much courage I have.
n," she added, "I assure
you there are a great many things I know how to do."

"For instance ?" said the doctor.

"First, the instruction of children, to which I think myself adapted. I love them, and they are generally fond of me also, and readily obey me."

"What else ?"

"I know Italian and German (for I have made it a special point to understand my mother's native language thoroughly). My father thought me also a good reader, and preferred my voice and accent to those of any of the numerous readers and speakers he had heard. His fondness perhaps blinded him to my defects; yet he might have been right, and I could try."

"Hem!" said the doctor. "There is much to be said for and against that talent."

"Finally, monsieur, I can do all kinds of work. I know how to sew well—to wash, iron, and sweep. I could even cook a little."

The doctor again regarded the noble countenance of the young girl while she thus complacently enumerated the humble and laborious employments she thought herself capahle of. She was evidently sincere. Her ability and willingness to do all she said could not be doubted. He was affected, and remained silent.

But Mademoiselle Josephine exclaimed with enthusiasm: "That is what I call an education! And who, my dear child, taught you so many reasonable and useful things ?"

Tears of emotion filled Fleurange's eyes. "It was my dear Madre Maddalena," she replied.

This answer elicited fresh inquiries, to which Fleurange replied by minutely relating the way in which her childhood had passed. The doctor's satisfaction increased with every word of her account, which, nevertheless,

made a breach in two of his prejudices.

Without any antipathy to pretty faces, they inspired him with a kind of mistrust, or at least of solicitude, which his long experience had doubtless very often warranted. But in regarding this young girl, so self-reliant and so modest, so courageous and so delicate, and who seemed ready to struggle so bravely against the difficulties of life, how could he be angry with her for being beautiful, and how help overlooking it in one sense?

The doctor had also a singular and, considering his belief as a whole, an inconsistent prejudice against convents. He seemed to have retained this point of agreement with those whom he habitually opposed on every other subject. And here was an education which accorded not only with all his ideas, but with all his whims—a conventual education. He would be obliged to somewhat modify his opinions on this subject, as well as on some others, and he resigned himself to it with a good grace.

They finally resumed the subject of the letter to Frankfort. The doctor and his sister already began to look forward with sorrow to the departure of their young *protégée*, but they felt it was for her interest not to delay joining the relatives who had invited her at so opportune a moment. By their advice, Fleurange immediately began her letter. Short and to the point, it was soon completed, and she gave it to Mademoiselle Josephine. The latter began to read it with an air of satisfaction, but when she came to the signature, a cloud suddenly appeared on her face.

"What is it?" said Fleurange. "I have made some mistake or blunder?"

"No, you have not: the letter is very well, it could not be b but—"

"What, then? Tell me beg of you."

"Well, it is—indeed, I tell you."

"Pray tell me," said F "what has displeased you is nothing in the letter willing to correct accordin advice."

"It is—but you canno that."

But what is it, then, de moiselle? You really frighte sisted Fleurange with a dist

"You cannot change yo mal name," said the other,

"My baptismal name?" Fleurange with surprise. " name displease you to such I am sorry, for Madre M liked it so much! She sai fied *the flower of the a* fairest of all the angels— Gabriel, whom she consi patron. And she called r elle as often as Fleurange

"Gabrielle!" cried Ma Josephine eagerly. "Gabri that is a name everybody c stand. So that is the m Fleurange, according to yo Maddalena? Then I b conjure you, to assume t and give up the other!"

The doctor had for som been occupied in reperusing Dornthal's letter, which he evening before; he now eyes, and attended to the tion. While Fleurange hesitating what reply to Mademoiselle Josephine's request, he said:

"I do not understand persistency on this point. own opinion, it is oppose But it may be that the sim two names will be more in

: tastes of the good German
hat awaits you, and perhaps
e would have a better recep-
n Fleurange. Besides," he
d, smiling, "your young cou-
ond the Rhine would doubt-
nounce the name in a way to
its charm and deprive it of
ning according to the pious
tical interpretation you have
en it."

t might be," said Fleurange,
in return. "Anyhow, I will
ou advise respecting it."

will take it into considera-
id the doctor. Then, glancing
re over the professor's letter,
inued: "Do you know the
the stranger who, by buying
picture your father painted,
ittingly rendered you so great
?"

not. That picture was sold
remainder when, at the be-
of his fatal relapse, my father
finances diminishing, and lost
of ever repairing them. My
ther!" she continued with a
g voice, "he was very ill the
made me sit in order to fin-
picture—" Fleurange sud-
topped and blushed. The
look seemed to demand an
tion, and she continued art-
but not without confusion:
wner of the picture is perhaps
nger who visited the studio
y. At least, I acknowledge
has repeatedly occurred to

what reason?"

ause he was so delighted with
, and begged permission to
ter its completion. But my
rom that day, was obliged to
the use of the brush, and the
was sold as he left it, with the

"Was this amateur a German?"

"I do not know. He spoke French very well, but with a slight accent, I know not what."

"Was he some great lord?"

"I do not know—I have never seen a great lord."

"But what kind of an air had this visitor—God bless him!" interrupted Mademoiselle Josephine.

"A lofty and noble air, a remarkable physiognomy, and a grave and sonorous voice," replied Fleurange. "But, in spite of the gratitude I perhaps owe him, the remembrance of his visit always troubles and depresses me."

"Why so?" said Josephine.

"Because it was the cause of the last and fatal crisis of my father's malady, who at that time even could not bear the slightest agitation. I do not know the words the stranger murmured as he glanced at me, but they greatly excited my father, who requested me in a tremulous voice to leave the studio. As a general thing, he never allowed me to enter it at the hour for visitors. The evening of that day he spoke to me in an agitated manner of the lone condition in which I should soon be left, and gave me some incoherent counsels, which were his last words. He never recovered his full mind after that."

"Poor man!" said the doctor; but he did not pursue the subject that led to this account. Fleurange's fleeting blush disappeared, and she was again pale and calm as before, her pen in hand ready to correct her letter according to the doctor's advice. After a final deliberation between the young girl and her elderly friends, it was decided that the letter should be sent after it was signed *Gabrielle d'Yves.*

III.

The day Margaret married Gerard d'Yves, the aged Sigismund Dornthal blotted out his daughter's name from his will, and gave orders that it should never be uttered in his presence. Notwithstanding this, softened by illness, and urged by his second son Ludwig, Margaret's favorite brother, he soon consented to send her his forgiveness and blessing, but when they reached Pisa poor Margaret had just expired! In the fury of his despair, which increased the impetuosity and thoughtlessness of his character, Gerard tore up the letter containing the long-delayed pardon, and only replied in these two words: "Too late!"

It was thus the aged Dornthal was informed of his daughter's death. He himself died shortly after, ignorant of the existence of the child to whom she had given birth. His property was divided between his two sons, but Ludwig, devoted to study, and already in possession of a professor's chair at Leipsic, entirely abandoned to his elder brother the administration of their common fortune, and Heinrich Dornthal became the sole head of the commercial and banking houses founded by Sigismund. He thenceforth made use of his brother's capital as well as his own, paying him regularly his income, without any interference in his business on Ludwig's part. The latter was at the same time pursuing so brilliant a career as to attract the attention of all the learned men of Germany to his labors. One of these, a resident of Frankfort, invited him to pass at his house the annual vacations of the numerous students who attended his lectures. The result of these visits was that this professor's daughter became Ludwig Dornthal's wife, and, in the course of time, the mother of his five children. The professor, when he married, resigned his position at Leipsic to settle in his wife's native place. There, free from a professor's duties, he had leisure to write books that constantly added to his reputation and increased his income, which the flourishing business of the commercial house alone made sufficient.

Such was, in a few words, the condition of the new home that awaited Fleurange. A second letter came promptly in reply to hers. Her uncle expressed the liveliest joy at having found her, and invited her very particularly to arrive at Frankfort in time for Christmas, so dear to the Germans as the time of family reunions. To do this she would have to leave Paris, at the very latest, on the twenty-first of December, for at that time it took three days and nights for the journey to Frankfort. The doctor and his sister, though sorry to part with their young *protégée*, hastened the preparations for her departure. They were touched by the cordial tone of this unknown uncle's letters, and predicted a happy life for her in his family, which they did not wish to defer. But every day added to their attachment to Fleurange and to her tender gratitude to them.

"If this continued a week longer," said the doctor, "I could not part with that child."

"Then she must start soon," replied Mademoiselle Josephine; "it is for her good, and we should be wrong to keep her with us."

Fleurange said nothing, but her eyes turned sadly from one of her old friends to the other. At length came the last day she was to pass with them. She made an effort to repress her tears, that she might not

-s them, and quietly put up her -t packages, actively aided by -octor and his sister.

-n English proverb which I think -reasonable," said the doctor, -es the hospitality which speeds -rting guest on a level with that - welcomes his coming: it is -hich I am now showing you, -ar Fleurange."

-urange had just hastily finished -epast always so sad before a -ey. The doctor perceived her -ge failing. He was himself -y affected by her pale and -ful countenance, and in think- -f the long and lonely journey -as about to undertake, at the -f which she would be received -ople, perhaps kind, but wholly -wn. Nevertheless, he resum- -th an encouraging voice:

-ome, come, child, everything - favorable yonder; show your -ge, and do not allow yourself -cast down."

-ou are right," said Fleurange, -. "I feel I have reason to - God, and I only desire to be -ful. Be sure, at all events, that -ll be courageous."

-was eight o'clock in the even- -the fiacre was waiting at the -to take her to the diligence. -went out, accompanied by the -r and his sister, who entered -carriage with her. The night -dark, and the snow falling in - flakes, which the young girl, -d beneath the sky of Italy, now -for the first time in her life. The -icle excited curiosity mingled -ear. The new and the unknown -ed to surround her on every -and these two things, generally -ractive to those of her age, bore -an aspect more calculated to -ss her young heart than to ex- -it. She involuntarily shivered, -rew around her slender form the thick cloak that felt too thin to protect her from the severity of the weather, to which she was so unaccustomed. They all remained silent for some moments. Fleurange pressed Mademoiselle Josephine's hand, and carried it from time to time to her lips, in spite of the efforts of the latter to prevent it.

Mademoiselle Josephine, on her side, with a faltering voice renewed a multitude of counsels, which had already been repeated a thousand times—among others, to write to them often and regularly. Then she slipped on her arm a small basket which her provident kindness had filled with everything that could be useful to her on the way, as well as more than one souvenir which, when far distant, would recall her old friends.

They arrived too quickly at their destination. "I have bespoken a place for you in the coupé," said the doctor, getting out of the carriage. "You will be in company with one of my patients, still very feeble, but who will absolutely go to Germany to rejoin her husband. She has two children with her, and they will be your only travelling companions."

"Thank you," said Fleurange. "The prayers of the orphan are said to draw down blessings: may you both experience the effect of mine!" She could not utter another word. She threw her arms for the last time around Mademoiselle Josephine's neck, and the next instant, leaning on the doctor's arm, she was crossing with some difficulty the littered court at the end of which they found the diligence. The snow had delayed them on the way, and now rendered every step difficult. The other passengers had taken their places, and they were only waiting for Fleurange. The horses were harnessed, and to the noise of their stamping the driver added his impatient exclamations.

"Come, come! We are off!" he repeated in a rough voice. Fleurange, hurried, pushed about, stunned, and frightened, had only time to press the doctor's hand once more and spring into the coupé. The door was instantly shut. A fearful clashing of irons, mingled with cries, blows of the whip, and vociferations, above which could be heard: "Adieu! à revoir! à bientôt!" with other exclamations much less harmonious, and the heavy diligence was in motion. Fleurange, now free from the necessity of any restraint, allowed herself the solace of giving vent to her feelings and letting her tears flow freely and abundantly.

She continued to weep for a long time without the least attempt at repressing her emotion. Why should she? She was alone, entirely alone now. She had never been so to such a degree before. All the events of the past faded away in the distance, and the future offered nothing to replace them. She was separated from all whom she had loved from her infancy, either by death or indefinite absence. Would it be so always? Was that to be her lot on earth? Would she never be permitted to love with assurance, trust, and a sense of repose? Was she to be always thus torn from places and persons at the very moment her heart began to cling to them?—her heart, so tender and ardent, which she had so often felt beating with tenderness and joy, with admiration and enthusiasm? And while her eyes peered out through the darkness of night at objects that seemed in the obscurity like pale phantoms, her imagination set before her, as in a magic mirror, all the different scenes of her past life: the beautiful cloister of Santa Maria al Prato, with the terrace at the top, where the eye could wander so far, and the sweet and noble features of Madre Maddalena; then came the varied remembrances connected with her father; first, the angelic vision of Italy in all its splendor, then the terrible and dismal days at Paris, and finally, at the darkest hour of all, the beneficent forms of her old friends, whom she never wished to leave, but whom she had just bidden farewell—perhaps farewell for ever!

It was impossible for Fleurange, at this moment, to control her sad thoughts. But, now and then, her reason recalled those who awaited her, the welcome she had a right to expect, and the goodness of Divine Providence in opening such a refuge; but in vain—consolation seemed unable to find an entrance into her soul, and, in spite of her nature, despondency obtained the mastery.

"If they are kind, and I love them," she said to herself bitterly, "I shall soon have to leave them. If, on the contrary, they —" Here her imagination had free course and depicted the future in the darkest colors. But this new reverie had not the clearness of the first, and before long her anticipations began to mingle in vague confusion with her remembrances. Little by little, fatigue, the motion of the vehicle, and the influence of night lulled the young girl asleep, and transformed into uneasy and indistinct dreams all the thoughts that had successively assailed her.

Fifteen minutes after, she was suddenly awakened. Something quite heavy had fallen against her shoulder and thence into her lap. She sat up, and, groping in the obscurity, her hand came in contact with the long silky hair of a child. From the first, she had rather supposed than seen a pale, sick young woman in the opposite corner of the coupé, with her arm thrown around a child beside her, against whom slept

r still smaller. It was the lat-
o had just suddenly changed
ition. Fleurange began to com-
d the case, and bent down to
m softly to a more comfortable
her lap. Then she drew his
leepy head against her, and
his sweet face now near her
This trifling incident had the
and unforeseen effect of put-
flight all the phantoms her
ation had been conjuring up
ease her sorrows. She recalled
erior murmuring with remorse.
my God!" she cried, pressing
ld in her arms, "if I love this
ttle one, whose features I have not yet seen, if I am ready to watch the night long over his slumbers, what wilt not thou, who art *my Father*, do for thy child?" She raised her eyes a moment in prayer, not with her lips, but in her heart. The snow had ceased falling. The clouds passing away, the heavens appeared brilliant with stars. The cloud had also passed away from Fleurange's soul, and a mysterious light from on high was infused therein. She gazed at the starry sky with delight, then closed her eyes, and again slept sweetly, the child in her arms sleeping as profoundly as herself.

TO BE CONTINUED.

VERAL CALUMNIES REFUTED; OR, EXECUTIVE DOCUMENT No. 37.*

addition to the secular press,
seldom misses an opportunity
ng something ungracious of
tholic Church, we have pub-
in the United States over a
d so-called religious newspa-
e principal stock-in-trade of
seems to be unlimited abuse
ything Catholic, and unquali-
srepresentation of all who pro-
teach the doctrines of our faith.
gma or point of discipline of
city ever finds favor in the
the individuals who fill the
s of those publications, and
or woman who may see fit
ote his or her life to the dis-
ion of the Gospel is safe from
lice or scurrility of their pens. For the honor of the American character we are sorry to say that we have daily evidence of this blind prejudice and reckless disregard of truth on the part of this class of editors, many of whom arrogate to themselves the title of "reverend"; but we have some consolation in knowing that the more intelligent members of the sects are fast growing tired and ashamed of such senseless appeals to their passions and ill-founded traditions and that the time is not far distant when such efforts to sustain a sinking and indefensible cause will be encouraged only by the ignorant and wilfully blind.

These repeated and continuous attacks on the church are not the work of any one sect or confined to any particular locality, but are gene-

* Doc. No. 37, U. S. Senate, XLIst Cong., on. 1870-1.

ral with all Protestants, and extended over the whole country. As long as they are confined to newspapers, and afford employment and remuneration to a number of persons who probably could not gain a livelihood in any other manner, we scarcely consider them worthy of serious attention; but we have had recently placed before us an official document, printed at the public expense for the edification of the United States Senate—and no doubt widely circulated throughout the Union under the convenient frank of many pious members of Congress—in which are reproduced calumnies so gross, and falsehoods so glaring, that we consider it our duty not only to call public attention to it, but to demand from our rulers in Washington by what right and authority they print and circulate under official form a tissue of fabrications, misrepresentations, and even forgeries, against the religion, and the ministers of that religion, which is professed by five or six millions of free American citizens.

This document, known as *Executive Document No.* 37, XLI*st Congress*, III*d Session*, was furnished by Mr. Delano, Secretary of the Interior, in compliance with a resolution of the Senate, passed February 2, 1871, and is composed exclusively of information supplied by Rev. H. H. Spaulding to A. B. Meacham, Superintendent of Indian Affairs, who in his letter of transmittal says:

"I am respectfully requested by the Rev. H. H. Spaulding, the oldest living Protestant missionary in Oregon, to place on file in your department the accompanying documents, giving a history of the early missionary work and labors of Dr. Marcus Whitman, himself, and others; the progress and civilization of the Indians under their charge, without aid from the government; also, a history of the massacre of Dr. Whitman and others; also, resolutions of Christian associations in answer to *Executive D*[...] 38, *House of Representatives*, [...] riety of historical informatio[...] would seem proper to have placed in some more perman[...] future history."

It may be remarked th[...] ter from which the above [...] tract is dated on the 28th [...] ry, just five days before th[...] of the Senate resolution, an[...] ly in anticipation of such [...] the part of that body " [...] says a distinguished senato[...] the few in the secret, knew [...] of the matter until the doc[...] printed. All the previous [...] ings were as of course." '[...] ments that were thus to be [...] in a more permanent form [...] history," apart from their [...] infamous character, are pe[...] strangest in origin and co[...] that have ever been present[...] information of any delibera[...] much less one of the gravit[...] portance of the Senate of t[...] lic. They consist mainly o[...] from the religious press, [...] inflammatory letters from [...] disappointed preachers, [...] Rev. H. H. Spaulding hi[...] positions written out by th[...] tigable hater with his own h[...] changed in many essential [...] ter having been sworn to an[...] ed from the control of t[...] nents; false quotations from [...] *count of the Murder of Dr.* [...] by the Very Rev. J. B. A[...] V.G., and others' statemen[...] massacre; an address from [...] fessors of that advanced ed[...] institution called Oberlin [...] Ohio; answers to leading q[...] dressed to Oregon officials, [...] a false and supposititious [...] of facts; and, lastly, a repor[...] and endorsed by eight associ[...] cluding the Old School, Ne[...]

land, and United Presbyte-
Methodists, Baptists, Congre-
lists, and the "Christian
of Oregon," and claiming to
nt thirty thousand brother
rs, all of whom, though differ-
lically in other respects, are
usly unanimous in denouncing
esuits," and equally positive
ning a previous condition of
their knowledge of which
of necessity have depended
n the statements of the vera-
ev. H. H. Spaulding. In style,
uments are unique, and have
strong family resemblance.
judicious mixture of sanctimo-
ant seldom heard outside of a
eeting, with a dash here and
f Shakespeare and the mo-
ets, to give it variety, we sup-

t, whence this solemn assembly
byteries and conferences, this
affidavits and newspaper ex-
and the desire of the Senate to
ghtened as "to the early la-
the missionaries of the Ame-
Board of Commissioners for
n Missions in Oregon, com-
gin 1836"? Simply this. On
eek commencing on the 29th
ember, 1847, more than twen-
years ago, a certain missiona-
e Cayuse Indians, named Dr.
an, who had resided among
or several years, was, with his
nd twelve other Americans,
murdered by the savages;
is now attempted by Spauld-
o was his friend, and mission-
the Nez Perces, a neighbor-
e, to fix the guilt of this foul
c on the missionary priests
that year accompanied the
v. A. M. A. Blanchet, Bishop
qualy, to Oregon, and who, it is
, instigated the Indians to
the deed in order to get rid
Protestant missions. At the time of the slaughter, there was with others under Dr. Whitman's roof a young woman named Bewley, whom one of the chiefs desired to have for his wife; and it is also asserted that not only did the priests encourage her to yield to the Indian's wishes, but forced her from the shelter of their home and refused her any protection whatever. Other charges growing out of this sad calamity, such as baptizing children with the innocent blood of their victims on their hands, inhumanity to the prisoners left unharmed, attempting the precious life of Spaulding, supplying the Cayuses with guns and ammunition, etc., are likewise alleged, but the first two are the principal counts in this clerical indictment.

The slaughter of so many persons naturally created a great sensation in Oregon at the time, but for months after no one thought of attributing it to the interference of the Catholic missioners. However, Spaulding, whose mind had become disturbed by the contemplation of the dangers he had escaped, and having to abandon his mission among the Nez Perces, and finding himself unemployed, gradually began to give a new version of the affair, and in conversation, preaching, and writing at first hinted, and next broadly asserted, that the "Jesuits" were at the bottom of the whole matter. Considering that the shock to his nervous system was so great that he never entirely recovered from it, and that the repetition of the falsehoods was so persistent, it is charitable to suppose that he eventually came to believe them as truths; for no man in his right senses would persist in forcing on the world such a compilation of improbable statements and downright falsehoods as are contained in *Pub. Doc. No.* 37.

As there are always many persons, made credulous by ignorance or

prejudice, willing to credit any anti-Catholic slander, the Rev. Father Brouillet, the only priest near the scene of the crime, wrote and published, in 1853, a full and authentic account of the whole transaction, which was so clear and circumstantial that even the greatest opponents of the Catholic priesthood were silenced. In 1857, a special agent of the Treasury Department, J. Ross Browne, made a tour in the far West, and in reporting on the condition of the aborigines, and the potent causes of war between them and the white settlers, embodied in his statement Father Brouillet's pamphlet, which together formed *Pub. Doc. No.* 38, against which all the powers of the presbyteries and conferences of Oregon, under the fitting leadership of a crazy preacher, are now directed, after a silence of more than ten years. Is it any wonder that it is so often remarked that the only bond of union, the sole vitalizing principles, of the sects are their hatred to Catholicity?

A glance at the history of the early Indian mission in Oregon is necessary to a clear understanding of the subject. It is well known that for many years that portion of our common country was debatable ground, and, while our government claimed the sovereignty and appointed officials to administer its affairs, the Hudson Bay Company held possession and virtually controlled the inhabitants, nearly all of whom were Indians or half-breeds. Under the direction of the company, the natives were honest, peaceable, and well disposed. Captain Bonneville, who visited the Nez Perces in 1832, says of them:

"Simply to call these people religious would convey but a faint idea of the deep hue of piety and devotion which pervades their whole conduct. Their honesty is immaculate, and their purity of purpose, and the observance of the rites of their religion, are most uniform and remarkable. They are certainly more like a nation of saints than a horde of savages."

"This was a very enthusiastic view to take of the Nez Perces' character," says a Protestant authority, Mrs. Victor, "which appeared all the brighter to the captain by contrast with the savage life which he had witnessed in other places, and even by contrast with the conduct of the white trappers. But the Nez Perces were intellectually and morally an exception to all the Indian tribes west of the Missouri River. Lewis and Clarke found them different from any others; the fur-traders and the missionaries found them the same. To account for this superiority is indeed difficult. The only clue to the cause is the following statement of Bonneville. 'It would appear,' he says, 'that they had imbibed some notions of the Christian faith from Catholic missionaries and traders who have been among them. They even had a rude calendar of the fasts and festivals of the Romish Church, and some traces of its ceremonial. These have become blended with their own wild rites, and present a strange medley, civilized and barbarous.'"* It was in this happy and quiet condition that the first Protestant missionaries from the United States found the Indians. They were Methodist, and arrived in 1834, remaining for ten years. "No missionary undertaking," says Rev. Stephen Olin, himself one of the laborers, "has been prosecuted by the Methodist Episcopal Church with higher hopes and more ardent zeal. . . . This particular mission involved an expenditure of forty-two thousand dollars in a single year. At the end of six years, there

* Victor's *The River of the West*, p. 400.

sixty-eight persons connected his mission, men, women, and n, all supported by this socie- And the same writer adds: such a number of missionaries employment in such a field it is y to conjecture, especially as the body of the Indians never came the influence of their labors." E. White, Sub-Indian Agent, in 1843: "The Rev. Mr. Lee sociates are doing but little for dians. . . . With all that has xpended, without doubting the ness of the intention, it is most nt to every observer that the s of this lower country, as a have been very little bene-

two Methodist stations estab at Clatsop's Plains and Nes were speedily abandoned, and t the Dalles is described, in of *American Indian Life*, as in a most fearful condition. occurrence," the author says, g to a murder by a converted which he had witnessed, "is type of a thousand atrocities ccurring among these supposed ns." And we have the authority Gray for saying that "the of a few presents of any de- ns to them induces them to professions corresponding to the the donor." The success of sionaries at Willamette was, if s, still more disheartening. Mr. ys that of those who held rela- with them none remained in and Alexander Simpson, who the valley about the same ound the mission to consist of ur families, those of a clergy- surgeon, a schoolmaster, and ricultural overseer. It is not e, then, that two years afterwards the missions were entirely abandoned, and have never been attempted to be re-established. "Had they met vice with a spotless life," says Gray, "and an earnest determination to maintain their integrity as representatives of religion and a Christian people, the fruits of their labor would have been greater." We are forced, therefore, to conclude that the author of *The River of the West* is justified in saying on this and other indisputable authority, "so far from benefiting the Indians, the Methodist mission became an actual injury to them"—the Indians.

Thus ended the first chapter in the history of the progress and civilization of the Indians in Oregon, to which we desire to call the respectful attention of the United States Senate. We have the testimony of Captain Bonneville, endorsed by Mrs. Victor, regarding the honesty and piety of the natives in 1832, before the arrival of the Methodists. After nine years of missionary labor, we have the following grave statement from no less an authority than one of their own clergymen:

> "The Indians want pay for being whipped into compliance with Dr. White's laws, the same as they did for praying to please the missionaries during the great Indian revival of 1839" (p. 157).
>
> "As a matter of course, lying has much to do in their system of trade, and he is the best fellow who can tell the biggest lie—make men believe and practise the greatest deception" (p. 158).*

The Methodists having selected Lower Oregon as the field of their labors, the Presbyterians chose the upper or eastern portion of the territory. They arrived in 1836, three in number, afterwards increased to twelve, and backed up by the Board of Commissioners for Foreign Missions. Dr. Marius Whitman settled at Wail-

of Stephen Olin, vol. ii. pp. 427, 428.
Hist. of Oregon, pp. 231, 246.

* *History of Oregon.* By G. Hines.

atpu among the Cayuses and Walla Wallas, and Messrs. H. H. Spaulding and W. H. Gray at Lapwai, with the Nez Perces. In 1838, the Spokane mission was established by Messrs. Walker and Ellis. Their prospects of success were at first most brilliant. The savages received them kindly and listened to them attentively. "There was no want of ardor in the Presbyterian missionaries," says *The River of the West*. "They applied themselves in earnest to the work they had undertaken. They were diligent in their efforts to civilize and christianize their Indians." But they made a fatal mistake at the very beginning, which not only reflects on their personal honesty, but shows that they knew nothing of the character of the people they came to instruct. Mr. John Toupin, who was for many years interpreter at Fort Walla Walla, gave, in 1848, the following account of the establishment of those missions:

"I was there when Mr. Parker, in 1835, came to select places for Presbyterian missions among the Cayuses and Nez Perces, and to ask lands for these missions. He employed me as interpreter in his negotiations with the Indians on that occasion. Mr. Pombrun, the gentleman then in charge of the fort, accompanied him to the Cayuses and the Nez Perces. Mr. Parker, in company with Mr. Pombrun, an American, and myself, went first to the Cayuses upon the lands called Wailatpu, that belonged to the three chiefs—Splitted Lip, or Yomtipi; Red Cloak, or Waptachtakamal; and Tilankaikt. Having met them at that place, he told them that he was coming to select a place to build a preaching-house, to teach them how to live, and to teach school to their children; that he would not come himself to establish the mission, but a doctor or a medicine-man would come in his place; that the doctor would be the chief of the mission, and would come in the following spring. 'I come to select a place for a mission,' said he, 'but I do not intend to take your lands for nothing. After the doctor is come, there will come every year a big ship loaded with goods to be divided among the Indians. These goods will not be sold, but given to you. The missionaries will bring you ploughs and hoes to teach you how to cultivate the land, and they will not sell, but give them to you.'

"From the Cayuses Mr. Parker went to the Nez Perces, about one hundred and twenty-five miles distant, on the lands of Old Button, on a small creek which empties into the Clearwater, seven or eight miles from the actual mission, and there he made the same promises to the Indians as at Wailatpu. 'Next spring there will come a missionary to establish himself here and take a piece of land; but he will not take it for nothing; you shall be paid for it every year: this is the American fashion.' In the following year, 1836, Dr. Whitman arrived among the Cayuses and began to build. The Indians did not stop him, as they expected to be paid as they said.

"In the summer of the year 1837, Splitted Lip asked him where the goods which he had promised him were; whether he would pay him, or whether he wanted to steal his lands. He told him that, if he did not want to pay him, he had better go off immediately, for he did not want to give his lands for nothing."*

But the doctor and his co-laborers did not pay for the lands, nor indeed fulfil any of the promises of Mr. Parker, and thus the expected neophytes received their first lesson in duplicity, which eventually destroyed all confidence in the honesty and truthfulness of their teachers, and led directly to the massacre of Whitman and some of his companions, and to the total destruction of the Presbyterian missions. This latter event occurred late in 1847. Let us see what had been done in the eleven previous years by the agents of the Board of Commissioners for Foreign Missions. In 1842, they had but three stations. "At each of these," says *The River of the West*, "there was a small body of land under cultivation, a few cat-

* *Murder of Dr. Whitman*, pp. [illegible]

...hogs, a flouring and saw mill, • blacksmith's shop." In 1843, ...ing writes to Dr. White, ...b-Indian Agent: "But *two* ...have as yet been admitted in... ...church. Some ten or twelve ...give pleasing evidence of hav... ...born again." • It seems, then, ...took twelve missionaries seven ...to convert two savages, at an ...e of over forty thousand dol... ...one year at least! Can the ...h Protestant mission for con... ...; the Hebrews in Jerusalem ...any return more preposterous ...la?

...the years intervening between ...as and their entire discontinu... ...how no converts at all. Busi... ...was entirely suspended, as far ...itual affairs were concerned. ...Thomas McKay, an intimate ...of Whitman, under date Sep... ...11, 1848, says, "The doctor ...old me that for a couple of years ...ceased to teach the Indians, ...as they would not listen to him"; ...John Baptist Gervais about the ...time assures us that "Mr. Spaul... ...ding me himself, last fall, that for ...four years back he had ceas... ...ly to teach the Indians be... ...they refused to hear him"—a ...ich that unscrupulous apostle ...quoted in a conversation with ...preside, in the preceding Au... ...The Indians," he said, "are ...worse every day for two or 'cars back; they are threaten... turn us out of the missions. days ago, they tore down my and I do not know what the ...nary Board of New York to do. It is a fact that we are no good: when the emigra... ...asses, the Indians run off to and return worse than when me among them." † Even as

...ray's *History of Oregon*, p. 235. ...urder of Dr. Whitman, p. 69.

early as 1839, a missionary of the Spokanes, writing to Dr. Whitman, said that the failure of that mission was so strongly impressed on his mind, he felt it necessary "to have cane in hand, and as much as one shoe on, ready for a move." "I see," he adds, "nothing but the power of God that can save us." When we consider this condition of affairs in connection with the brutal massacre at Wailatpu by Dr. Whitman's immediate neighbors and even some members of his household and congregation, at a time of profound peace, we can form some adequate idea of the benefits of the "progress and civilization of the Indians under their [Presbyterian] charge." Will the United States Senate, in its laudable search after information, consult some of the authorities, who are with one exception Protestant, which we have quoted?

The Catholic missions may be said to have commenced in 1838. In that year, two Catholic priests pass-ed Walla Walla on their way from Canada to Fort Vancouver. In 1839 and 1840, one of them, Father Demers, occasionally visited Walla Walla, for a short time, to give instruction to the Indians, many of whom were in the habit of visiting him, particularly the Cayuses and Nez Perces at the fort. This presence excited the wrath of Dr. Whitman, and he presumed so far as to reprimand in severe language the gentleman in charge of the post. "From the time the Jesuits arrived," says Gray, "his own [H. H. Spaulding's] pet Indians had turned Catholics, and commenced a quarrel with him. These facts seemed to annoy him, and led him to adopt a course opposed by Smith, Gray, and Rodgers." The visits of the Catholic missionaries were, however, few and far between, till the 5th of September, 1847,

when the Rt. Rev. Bishop A. M. A. Blanchet arrived at Fort Walla Walla, accompanied by the Superior of the Oblates and two other clergymen, to establish permanent missions in Eastern Oregon. It was the design of the bishop to locate a mission on the lands of Towatowe (Young Chief), a Catholic Indian, who had offered him his own house for that purpose. The Young Chief, however, being absent hunting, Dr. Blanchet was delayed at the fort longer than he anticipated, and while there was visited by Protestant missionaries and Indian chiefs alike. The former treated him with great incivility and disrespect. Dr. Whitman, we are told by an eyewitness, "made a furious charge against the Catholics, accusing them of having persecuted Protestants, and even of having shed their blood wherever they had prevailed. He said he did not like Catholics; . . . that he should oppose the missionaries to the extent of his power. . . . He spoke against the *Catholic Ladder* (a picture explaining the principal points of Catholic faith), and said that he would cover it with blood to show the persecution of Protestants by Catholics. He refused to sell provisions to the bishop, and protested that he would not assist the missionaries unless he saw them in starvation."* The temper of the savages was milder than their would-be evangelizers. On the 26th of October, Young Chief came to the fort, and asked for a priest to be sent to teach his young people. He repeated the offer of his house, but suggested as a substitute the lands of his relative Tilokaikt, upon which Dr. Whitman was settled. On November 4, the four chiefs of the Cayuses assembled at Walla Walla, and after a long "talk" agreed to let the bishop

* *Murder of Dr. Whitman*, p. 46.

have a site fc
much ground
necessary to s
The bishop "to
Brouillet, "that
presents to the I
give them noth
asked; that in
him he would
work and no
just quoted was
uses to select a
finding one suit
Chief's offer, a
miles from Dr.
in the midst of a
er. As one of
Christian charit
the Catholic m
part of the worl
ed that, during
fort, one of the
Whitman in ver
ing him of dish
motives. Bisho
him instantly, st
the doctor was
he, the chief, h
so; and when
offered, by Tilo
mission for C
nothing, he po
torily declined
Doc. No. 37 wo
that the Catholi
Station, and we
at any cost. O
bishop, with his
Brouillet, procee
at Umatilla.
Sunday, they w
man, and on M
who remained f
gentleman, it se
their views duri
months' interco
aries. It was
tween two and
afternoon, that
companions w

nt of that horrible event, as re- by Father Brouillet, who was ground two days after, is still interesting. In a letter to el Gilliam, three months later, the facts were fresh in his ry, and every resident of the orhood was in a position to ve anything he might say that lse, he writes:

fore leaving Fort Walla Walla, it een decided that, after visiting the eople of my mission on the Uma- should go and visit those of Tilo- camp, for the purpose of baptiz- infants, and such dying adults as desire this favor; and the doctor r. Spaulding having informed me ere were many sick persons at missions, I was confirmed in the ion, and made preparations to go n as possible.

ter having finished in baptizing the and dying adults of my mission, n Tuesday, the 30th of November, the afternoon, for Tilokaikt's where I arrived between seven and 'clock in the evening. It is im- le to conceive my surprise and con- ion when, upon my arrival, I learn- t the Indians the day before had red the doctor and his wife, with ater part of the Americans at the n. I passed the night without ly closing my eyes. Early next g I baptized three sick children, whom died soon after, and then ed to the scene of death to offer widows and orphans all the assist- n my power. I found five or six and over thirty children in a con- deplorable beyond description. had lost their husbands, and others thers, whom they had seen massa- efore their eyes, and were expect- ry moment to share the same fate. ght of those persons caused me l tears, which, however, I was ob- to conceal, for I was, the greater f the day, in the presence of the rers, and closely watched by them, I had shown too marked an in- in behalf of the sufferers, it would ave endangered their lives and these, therefore, entreated me to my guard. After the first few words that could be exchanged under the circumstances, I inquired after the victims, and was told that they were yet unburied. Joseph Stainfield, a Frenchman, who was in the service of Dr. Whitman, and had been spared by the Indians, was engaged in washing the corpses, but, being alone, he was unable to bury them. I resolved to go and assist him, so as to render to those unfortunate victims the last service in my power to offer them."

The reverend father then goes on to relate how, after comforting the women and children as well as he could, and having been told by the chief "to say to them that they need fear nothing, they shall be taken care of and well treated," he set out toward his mission, in order to intercept Spaulding and warn him of his danger. He was accompanied by his interpreter, and closely followed by a son of the chief, who, it afterward appeared, was going to his uncle Camastilo to acquaint him of the slaughter. His meeting with Spaulding is graphic, and, if not for the hideous surroundings, would be amusing. He says:

"In a few minutes after, while they were thus engaged in smoking, I saw Mr. Spaulding coming toward me. In a moment he was at my side, taking me by the hand and asking for news. 'Have you been to the doctor's?' he inquired. 'Yes,' I replied. 'What news?' 'Sad news.' 'Is any person dead?' 'Yes, sir.' 'Who is dead—is it one of the doctor's children?' (He had left two of them very sick.) 'No,' I replied. 'Who, then, is dead?' I hesitated to tell. 'Wait a moment,' I said, 'I cannot tell you now.' While Mr. Spaulding was asking me those questions, I had spoken to my interpreter, telling him to entreat the Indian in my name not to kill Mr. Spaulding, which I begged of him as a special favor, and hoped that he would not refuse it to me. I was waiting for his answer, and did not wish to relate the disaster to Mr. Spaulding before getting it, for fear he might by his manner discover to the Indian what I had told him, for

the least motion like flight would have cost him his life, and probably exposed mine also. The son of Tilokaikt, after hesitating some moments, replied that he could not take it upon himself to save Mr. Spaulding, but that he would go back and consult the other Indians, and so he started back immediately to his camp. I then availed myself of this absence to satisfy the anxiety of Mr. Spaulding. I related to him what had passed. 'The doctor is dead,' said I; 'the Indians have killed him, together with his wife and eight other Americans, on Monday last, the 29th, and I have buried them before leaving to-day.' 'The Indians have killed the doctor—they will kill me also if I go to the camp?' 'I fear it very much,' said I. 'What, then, shall I do?' 'I know not. I have told you what has happened. Decide now for yourself what you had best do. I have no advice to give you in regard to that.' 'Why has that Indian started back?' he inquired. 'I begged him to spare your life,' said I, 'and he answered me that he could not take it upon himself to do so, but that he would go and take the advice of the other Indians about it; that is the reason why he started back.' Mr. Spaulding seemed frightened and discouraged. 'Is it possible! is it possible!' he exclaimed several times. 'They will certainly kill me.' And he was unable to come to any decision. 'But what could have prompted the Indians to this?' he inquired. 'I know not,' said I; 'but be quick and decide, you have no time to lose. If the Indians should resolve not to spare your life, they will be here very soon, as we are only about three miles from their camp.' 'But where shall I go?' 'I know not; you know the country better than I. All I know is that the Indians say the order to kill all Americans has been sent in all directions.' Mr. Spaulding then resolved to fly. He asked me if I were willing to take charge of some loose horses he was driving before him. I told him I could not, for fear of becoming suspicious to the Indians. I told him, however, that if the interpreter was willing to take them under his charge at his own risk, he was perfectly at liberty to do so. To this the interpreter agreed. I gave Mr. Spaulding what provisions I had left, and hastened to take leave of him, wishing him with all my heart a happy escape, and promising to pray for him. . . . The interpreter had not left Mr. Spaulding (after pointing out a by-road) more than twenty minutes, when he saw three armed Cayuses riding hastily toward him in pursuit of Mr. Spaulding. Upon coming up to the interpreter, they seemed much displeased that I had warned Mr. Spaulding of their intentions, and thereby furnished him an opportunity to escape. 'The priest ought to have minded his own business, and not to have interfered with ours,' they said in an angry tone, and started immediately in pursuit of him." *

This Spaulding escaped to tell the tale, and to traduce the character of the priest that saved his life at the risk of his own. At first, he was inclined to acknowledge the obligation, for in a letter to his "reverend and dear friend," as he styles Bishop Blanchet, eight days after, he writes: "The hand of the merciful God brought me to my family after six days and nights from the time *my dear friend* furnished me with provisions and I escaped from the Indians." This effort of gratitude was, however, too much for him to sustain, and, accordingly, we find published in *The Oregon American* (p. 13) the following choice specimen of bigotry and base ingratitude, "worse than the sin of witchcraft." He says:

"It has been said by some of my friends in this country that they were greatly mortified to see me in the dust at the bishop's feet begging for my life. . . This is not the first time that Protestants (that is, heretics) have lain prostrate at the feet of the Pope of Rome. I saw my life, under God, in the hands of the bishop and the priests. I had a right to ask it again. I seemed to see the hands of these priests wet with the blood of our associates. . . . I stopped not to ask whose hands placed the bishop's foot upon my neck, the lives of so many human beings were worth the struggle."

Can the force of prejudice and deception go further than this? Here is a man, who, if not an open enemy

* *Murder of Dr. Whitman*, pp. 32-33.

missionaries, was certainly a opponent, whose life was saved one of them at a most critical at imminent danger to his who was shown the pathway by he might escape the fury of savages whose hatred he had ned by long years of injustice, who was even supplied with food the poor priest's scrip, turning on his benefactors when he at- a place of safety, and vilifying church and religion to whose les- charity he owed his miserable nce. This is the man, too, upon authority the "Christian As- ions of Oregon" have under- to brand the heroic priests of ection as instigators of murder; who has undertaken to inform nate, and provide Mr. Delano matters for history "in a more nent form."

here it may be well to dispose e of the minor charges. *Pub.* No. 37, at page 30, says of the of the Whitman massacre:

> y [the Indian children] leaped amed for joy, throwing handfuls d around, drinking down the dy- onies of their victims as a pre- raught. These blood-stained little s were to receive the sacred ordi- of baptism a few hours after, at ds of the priest of God—the man- dies yet lying unburied around, d of dogs and wolves by night, hogs and vultures by day, seem- y down to the Indians for what done."

are not aware that in the whole of Protestant history there is und a more deliberate, cool, ocious tissue of fasehoods than bove. Two days, not a few after the murder, *three* sick en were baptized, of whom two so ill that they died the same Are those some of the children eaped and screamed for joy? The baptism took place two miles from Whitman's Station, so that the bodies of the slain could not well have been lying around. The dogs and wolves, hogs and vultures, are purely the creation of the Rev. H. H. Spaulding's imagination, and would, in vulgar parlance, be styled "piling on the agony." Before the arrival of Father Brouillet, Joseph Stainfield had already washed the corpses, and, with the assistance of the good priest, they were buried. The insinuation in the last line is worthy of Spaulding, and shows to what extremes a man will go whose sense of truth and even decency has become completely blunted.

Another charge against the missionaries is that they acted inhumanly with the captives, and that Father Brouillet, who promised to return to them, neglected to do so. It is true he did not do so, and the prisoners may thank Mr. Spaulding for his not returning. Had he not been as solicitous about saving that individual's life, and thereby enable him to go down to the grave at an old age with a load of falsehood and forgeries on his soul, he would never have incurred the ill-feeling of the Indians of Wailatpu, or be himself kept a prisoner in Young Chief's tent for two or three weeks. But his thoughts and those of his fellow-missionaries were with the unfortunates, and his every effort was used, and successfully too, for their liberation. While Spaulding, from his mission with the Nez Perces, was writing lying letters to his "reverend and dear friend," Bishop Blanchet, soliciting his good offices with the Indians with regard to the captives, amongst whom was his own daughter, that ecclesiastic was calling around him the chiefs of the Cayuses, admonishing them to treat their captives kindly, promising to write to the American governor for terms of peace, and attending a council at

Fort Walla Walla, at which the Indians consented and actually did liberate the prisoners, the ransom being paid by the agents of the much abused Hudson Bay Company. Spaulding himself was then virtually a prisoner among the Nez Perces, with whom he lived eleven years, and " was very much beloved," if we may believe his own statement.

We now come to what we may be permitted to call the first grand falsehood, as set forth in *Pub. Doc. No.* 37, for the information of the Senate and the benefit of history, namely, that the Whitman murderers were instigated by the "Jesuits." This calumny is repeated in several places and in many forms in this extraordinary public document, and may be supposed to be crystallized in the two following paragraphs :

" When the Jesuits and English had, by means of Indian runners, excited the surrounding tribes to butcher the Protestant missionaries and American emigrants at Wailatpu, and to exterminate the American settlements on the Pacific, the Nez Perces refused to join them, and rushed at once to the defence of their beloved teacher, Mrs. Spaulding, and rescued her and her infants from a band of forty of the murderers ; then, second, fled to the scene of the eight days' carnage, and by their influence stopped the bloody work of the Jesuits." (*Resolutions adopted by the Pleasant Butte Baptist Church of Linn Co., Oregon, Oct.* 22, 1869.)

"This Brouilette [Brouillet], it is proved in part by his own testimony, was present at the massacre, doing nothing to save the victims, but baptizing the children of the murdering Indians, and otherwise stimulating them to their work of death." (*Report of the Committee of the Presbytery of Steuben, adopted by the Christian Associations of Oregon,* 1869.)

Surely this is history run mad. In fact, so gross are the misstatements that we are inclined to think that Spaulding either forged the signatures or in-

terpolated the resolutions of the ciations—a proceeding which, appear further on, he was perfec pable of doing. Now, it is well k and stated even by Spaulding *Doc. No.* 37), that the so-called ' its," namely, Bishop Blanchet a priests, had only been in tha of the country a short time—l Brouillet says two months, but S; ing reduces it to six weeks ; th Catholic mission had been est; ed within hundreds of miles of man's Station till two days pr to the mission, when one was menced at Umatilla, twenty-five distant, among a tribe of the Ca who had no act or part in the c that there never was a Catholi sionary, Jesuit or otherwise, i camps of Tilokaikt, where Wh resided till two days after the n cre, but once, and that for a time when Father Brouillet was ed by the chief to go and pro site for a mission, in which he f and, finally, that the Indians wh the bloody deed were near neig of the doctor, the worst being a ber of his household ; and that *one of them were Protestants,* as S ding himself partly admits * *Doc. No.* 37). Even the Rev. Gus Hines, who is named as one c

* The five Cayuses who were hung in City, June 3, 1850, as accomplices in th sacre, were all Protestants, and remaine they received their death sentence. All ers who are known as murderers, among were Lumsuky, Tamahas, and the two Tilokaikt, were also Protestants. Josep field, Jo Davis, and the other half-breed, is said, plundered the dead, if anything, w tainly not Catholics. Three of the con on the morning of the execution solem clared that the Catholic missionaries had whatever to do with the murder. The fo letter to the Bishop of Walla Walla, fi Archbishop of Oregon City, will be fou resting :

OREGON CITY, June 2, 1

The supposed Cayuse murderers will cuted to-morrow. They have abando Whitman's religion and have become C I am preparing them for baptism and for
                              F. N. BLANCH
                              Archbishop of Oreg

ints in the compilation of this nent, says in his *History of Ore-* describing a council of chiefs 3: "Tilokaikt, a Cayuse chief, nd said, 'What do you read the or before we take them? We take the laws because Tanitan . He is a Catholic, and as a we do not follow his worship!" tory of Father Brouillet having on the scene of massacre stimu- the Indians in their work of is a poor fabrication, for the visited the bishop and his two at Umatilla, twenty-five miles t, late on Sunday, the 28th, and e 29th, the day of the slaugh- paulding himself supped with at the same place. The ridicu- eference to the Nez Perces, un- e supposition that they were stants, is simply absurd. The s that Spaulding says, in his to his "reverend and dear" the bishop, the Nez Perces promised to protect him and the can settlers if troops were not against the Cayuses, and that demanded and received from gden, of Walla Walla, clothing, nition, and tobacco before they release their "beloved teacher," isband and infants. The only erces who fled to the scene to 'the bloody work of the Je- were two messengers of that who bore his treacherous letter bishop, begging him to assure yuses that he would use every o prevent the troops from being ainst them, and which he after- declared was meant to deceive he bishop and the Indians.* oner, however, was he out of r than he used his best efforts ng on a war. "I recollect dis-," says Major Magone, "that not in favor of killing *all* the Cayuses, for he gave me the names of four or five that he knew to be friendly, and another whom I marked as questionable: the balance, if I am not very much mistaken, *he would have to share one fate*." Truly, this was strange advice from a minister of the Gospel of peace, and from one who wished the bishop to assure the Indians "that we do not wish Americans to come from below to avenge our wrongs," etc.

But apart from the credibility of the witness Spaulding, and the impossibility of the Catholic missionaries stirring up the Protestant Indians to the work of death, even if they so desired, not to speak of their early, continuous, and indignant denials of every statement and assertion put forth by the Oregon fanatics, we have the evidence of several persons, all Protestants we are inclined to believe, who were either in the neighborhood at the time, or arrived soon after. R. T. Lockwood, an old resident of Oregon and a prominent contributor to the press, relates the following conversation which he had in 1851 with one of the Indians who was a spectator of the murder:

"Q. Do the Indians generally want the Catholic priests among them, and, if so, why do they prefer them to such men as Dr. Whitman?

"A. No, not generally; yet a considerable number do, and prefer them because they do not try to get our land away from us.

"Q. Did the priests that came among you, a little before the massacre, encourage the killing of Dr. Whitman and the others?

"A. No. The killing of Dr. Whitman was resolved on before the priests came.

"Q. Are you a Catholic Indian?

"A. No, sir."

Some time after, Mr. Lockwood met a Mrs. Foster, one of the survivors. "I asked her," he says, "if she

* Oregon American.

thought the priest had anything to do with the massacre, and she said she did not think he did, as he appeared very much pained, and was very kind and tender towards the survivors. I asked her, also, if she thought that the priest did all he safely could, and she answered, 'I do.'" This impartial and well-informed gentleman winds up his letter thus: "Suffice it to say that, in all I ever heard said in regard to this lamentable massacre (and it has been much) *prior to the last two years*, there was not the slightest intimation of you or any other Catholic priest being implicated, or in any way responsible therefor."*

"Why is the Catholic exempt from danger? Why can the Hudson Bay Company employee remain amid these scenes of blood and Indian vengeance against the white race, at peace, undisturbed, and, what is more loathsome, neutral in such a conflict?" asks the Hon. Elwood Evans of Spaulding, in 1868. The answer is simple. Because the Catholic priests treat the Indians with uniform kindness and justice; because they neither deceive them with false promises nor appropriate their lands and labor without payment, and because, being ministers of peace, they are opposed to strife; all of which Whitman, Spaulding, and his missionary companions did not and were not. And this brings us to the real cause of the massacre. For the sake of the Senate which desires information, and for Mr. Delano's future history, we will give a few extracts from authorities which, if at all prejudiced, would be on the side of the Protestant view:

"'I came to select a place for a mission,' said he, 'but I do not intend to

*Letter of R. T. Lockwood to Very Rev. J. B. A. Brouillet, V.G., Sept. 29, 1871.

take your lands for nothing. Af doctor is come, there will come year a big ship, loaded with goods divided among the Indians. These will not be sold, but given to you missionaries will bring you ploug hoes, to teach you to cultivate the and they will not sell but give tl you.' . . . And there [among t Perces] he made the same prom the Indians as at Wailatpu." (*M Toupin's Statement, in 1848, of the l tion of the Presbyterian Missions l Parker, in* 1835.)

"Two years ago, 1846, a Cayus to my house in the Willamette settl and stopped with me over two During that time he often spoke Whitman, complaining that he pos the lands of the Indians, on wh was raising a great deal of wheat, he was selling to the Americans, w giving them anything; that he had upon their lands, and that they l pay him for grinding their wheat, horse for twenty sacks. He sai told him to leave, but that he woul listen to them." (*Ib.*)

"A man of easy, don't-care l that could become all things to all and yet a sincere and earnest man, ing his mind before he thought tl cond time, giving his views on al jects without much consideration recting them when good reasons presented, yet, when fixed in the p of an object, adhering to it with un ing tenacity. A stranger would co him *fickle* and *stubborn.*" (*Charac Dr. Whitman by a brother missionar W. H. Gray.*)

"The Americans had done them harm. Years before, had not one o missionaries suffered several of the ple, and the son of their chiefs, slain in his company, yet himself ed? Had not the son of another (Elijah), who had gone to Califo buy cattle, been killed by Americ no fault of his own? . . . So regarded the missionaries, Dr. Wl and his associates, they were d yet so many looked on the doctor agent in promoting the settlement country with whites, it was thougl to drive him from the country, to with all the missionaries, *several ye* fore. Dr. Whitman had known tl Indians were displeased with his ment among them. They had told

had treated him with violence, they tempted to outrage his wife, had his property, and had several warned him to leave their country, y should kill him." (*River of the* p. 400.)

e fulfilment of the laws which the recommended for their adoption, ccasioned suspicions in the minds Indians generally that the whites ed the ultimate subjugation of ribes. They saw in the laws they dopted a deep-laid scheme of the to destroy them and take posses- f their country. The arrival of a party of emigrants about this time, e sudden departure of Dr. Whit- the United States, with the avow- ention of bringing back with him y as he could enlist for Oregon, to hasten them to the above con- s. . . . The great complaint of dians was that the Boston people icans] designed to take away their and reduce them to slavery." (*Rev.* *us Hines, D.D., assistant of Spauld-* *Pub. Doc. No.* 37, *on the Nez Perces* ;. *History of Oregon*, p. 143.)

ey [the Indians] were demanding onable pay for their lands upon the stations were erected, and pay- t little or no attention to their can teachers." (*Gray's History of* , p. 365.)

e fact is also shown that, as far back 5, the Indians west of the Rocky ains protested against the taking of their lands by the white races, is was one of the alleged causes murder of Dr. Whitman." (*J.* *Browne, Special Agent of the Trea-* *eport to the Com. of Indian Affairs,* 1857.)

is we find that, whatever credit e claimed for Dr. Whitman as nist, his course toward the peo- hom he was sent to evangelize ything but just or Christian; not only did not pay for his and, but helped others to steal and he admits himself that for ears he had utterly neglected ritual and mental duties of his n. But there were other and s potent causes at work. Of steemed friend Dr. Whitman," Sir James Douglass, chief factor of the Hudson Bay Company, writes on December 9, ten days after the massacre:

"He hoped that time and instruction would produce a change of mind—a better state of feeling toward the mission, and he might have lived to have seen his hopes realized, had not the measles and dysentery, following in the train of immigrants from the United States, made frightful ravages this year in the upper country. Many Indians have been carried off through the violence of the disease, and others through their own imprudence. The Cayuse Indians of Wailatpu, being sufferers in this general calamity, were incensed against Dr. Whitman for not exerting his supposed supernatural power in saving their lives. They carried this absurdity beyond the point of folly. Their superstitious minds became possessed of the horrible suspicion that he was giving poison to the sick instead of wholesome medicine, with the view of working the destruction of the tribe, his former cruelty probably adding strength to their suspicions. Still, some of the reflecting had confidence in Dr. Whitman's integrity, and it was agreed to test the effects of the medicine he had furnished on three of their people, one of whom was said to be in perfect health. They unfortunately died, and from that moment it was resolved to destroy the mission. It was immediately after burying the remains of these three persons that they repaired to the mission and murdered every man found there."

Several other contemporary writers confirm this calm statement of events, which in themselves were enough to drive ignorant and desperate savages (for it must be borne in mind that Dr. Whitman had given up instructing them for some years to attend to his wheat and horses) to commit any act of murder or rapine. To show that the "horrible suspicion" of having been poisoned was not a mere groundless suspicion on the part of the Indians, we present the following testimony:

"I spent the winter of 1846 in Dr. Whitman's employment. I generally worked at the saw-mill. During the time I was there, I observed that Dr. Whitman was in the habit of poisoning wolves. I did not see him put the poison in the baits for the wolves; but two of his young men of the house, by his order, were poisoning pieces of meat, and distributing them in the places where the wolves were in the habit of coming, at a short distance around the establishment of the doctor. The doctor once gave me some arsenic to poison the wolves that were around the saw mill. . . . Some Indians who happened to pass there took the meat and ate it; three of them were very sick, and were near dying. . . . Mr. Gray, who was then [1840] living with the doctor, offered us as many melons to eat as we liked, but he warned us at the same time not to eat them indiscriminately, as some of them were poisoned. 'The Indians,' said he, 'are continually stealing our melons. To stop them, we have put a little poison on the bigger ones, *in order that the Indians who will eat them might be a little sick.*'" (*Statement of John Young, corroborated by Augustine Raymond.*)

In addition to these acts of imprudence, the doctor, it seems, had earned for himself an unenviable unpopularity. He was constantly extorting overpay in horses from them, and threatening them with soldiers and emigrants if they refused it. After having a quarrel with them on one occasion, "during which they insulted him, covered him with mud," and even attempted his life, "he started for the United States, telling the Indians that he was going to see the great chief of the Americans, and that when he would return he would bring with him many people to chastise them; the Indians had been looking to his return with great fear and anxiety." * At another time, in the fall of 1847, he said to the Indians at Walla Walla in the presence of several white men, "Since you are so wicked, such robbers, we shall send for troops to chastise you, and next fall we will see here five hundred dragoons, who will take care of you." But even Doctor Whitman, "fickle and obstinate" as he was, could not entirely overlook the dangers that beset him for so many years, and at the solicitation of his friend had been preparing to leave his station long before the arrival of the Catholic missionaries. Mr. Thomas McKay, whom the doctor had invited to stop the winter of 1847–8 with him for protection, says, "He told me repeatedly, during the last two years especially, that he wished to leave, as he knew the Indians were ill-disposed toward him, and that it was dangerous for him to stay there; but that he wished all the chiefs to tell him to go away, in order to *excuse himself to the Board of Foreign Missions.*" Dangerous and fatal mistake, which cost the lives of thirteen innocent people, and closed the unfortunate man's earthly career!

*Toupin's statement.

Now for the affair of the young woman Miss Bewley, who is described in *Pub. Doc. No.* 37, p. 35, indifferently as an "amiable young saint," a "dear girl," and "an angel." It is charged that, when Five Crows demanded her for his wife, and she refusing to go with him, the bishops and priests urged her to go, and even thrust her out-of-doors when she refused. So little credence was given this specific calumny, for many years after the alleged occurrence, that the only mention we find made of it in *The Murder of Dr. Whitman* is the following paragraph:

"Before taking leave of the chiefs, the bishop said to them all publicly, as he had also done several times privately, that those who had taken American girls should give them up immediately. And then all entreated Five Crows to give up the one he had taken, but to no purpose."

let us hear Father Brouillet's t of the affair in contradiction Bewley's deposition:

did," says the reverend gentle- ill that charity could claim, and re than prudence seemed to per- le kept her for seventeen days in se, provided for all her wants, ated her well, and if she had us, and heeded our advice and ns, she would never have been d to that Indian. When she e to our house, and told us that ows had sent for her to be his asked her what she wanted to d she want to go with him, or he said she did not want to go e. 'Stay with us, then, if you will do for you what we can,' offer. When the evening came, ian chief called for her. The hen requested his interpreter to that she did not want to be his d that, therefore, he did not want o with him. The interpreter, who Indian, allied by marriage to the , and knew the chief's disposi- l, would not provoke his anger, used to interpret. The writer, king use of a few Indian words picked up during the few days he n there, and with the aid of signs, o the Indian himself, and suc- in making him understand what nt. The Indian rose furious- without uttering a word went The young woman then got ed, and wanted to go for fear he me back and do us all an injury. ter tried to quiet her, and insist- she should remain at our house, no avail; she must go, and off it. The Indian, still in his fit of efused to receive her, and sent k. She remained with us three days undisturbed; until one , without any violence on the the Indian, or without advising she went with him to his lodge. e back the next morning, went r in the evening, and continued out being forced by the Indian, t of the time going by herself, ast she was told to select be- Indian's lodge and our house, e way of acting could not e any longer. That was the time that she offered any resistance to the will of the Indian; but, indeed, her resistance was very slight, if we can believe her own statement."

This is a very different account from that sworn to by Miss Bewley, but written by Spaulding, as he says himself, *Ex. Doc. No.* 37, p. 27: "I would go to an individual, and take down in writing what he or she knew, and then go before a magistrate, and the individual would make an oath to the statement, the officer certifying." There is no mention that the parties were permitted to read what their amanuensis took down, and all who are acquainted with such *ex-parte* depositions know how easily it would be to alter their sense and meaning by an unscrupulous person—which we are about to show Spaulding to be. In this very statement there are two interpolations, one of eight lines on page 35 of *Ex. Doc. No.* 37, beginning with the words "I arose," and one of six on the following page, at "The next day," which materially alter the whole meaning of the document. This alteration of a sworn statement by any but the affiant is at common law *forgery*, and ought to entitle the person who makes it to the delicate attention of the prosecuting attorney of his county. Whether the saint and angel, Miss Bewley, is now aware of the forgery connected with her name we know not, but we trust that the Senate will make a note of it for the benefit of future historians. But Spaulding, who is described by his co-missionary Gray as "quite impulsive and bitter in his denunciations of a real or supposed enemy," in endeavoring to make out a case, is not content with altering one affidavit. That of Mr. Osborne (*Ex. Doc. No.* 37, p. 32) is also materially changed in several places from the original, and the official reports of Mr. McLane (*Ex. Doc.* p. 33) and of Dr. White are

doctored in a manner that we venture to say would render it difficult for the writers themselves to recognize them. Even the plain statements of *The Murder of Dr. Whitman* are garbled in a most palpable and scandalous manner.

As to the other auxiliary charges against the Catholic missionaries, and the answers of Abernethy and a few others to questions propounded by Spaulding, we do not consider them worthy of serious attention. They are all directly or indirectly the creatures of Spaulding's fertile imagination, who, if not crazy as Colonel Gilliam said, has allowed his hatred of Catholicity to carry him down to fearful depths of crime, to calumny, falsehood, and forgery. His motives are apparent, the gratification of his lust for revenge, and his hatred of our faith; that of the associations who have signed his outrageous statements is the present flourishing existence of the Catholic missions in every part of Oregon; and the end proposed is to compass their destruction by appealing to the religious prejudices of the authorities at Washington. We have too much confidence in the wisdom and good sense of the Executive and Congress to suppose that they will be influenced by such inflammatory appeals—bearing on their face the palpable impress of dishonesty and prejudice—and attempts to disturb the good fathers in their labor of love, as well as of hardships and suffering; and we expect soon to hear of those fanatics receiving a fitting rebuke in our Senate for attempting to make that august body the vehicle of perpetuating the vilest sort of falsehoods and slanders against the Catholics of this country.

AFFIRMATIONS.

"Why does man go about organizing systems, when he himself must be reorganized?"

"The thing to be done will not unite the doers."

"When man forgets what he is, he soon is put into a state of uneasiness, and made to suffer in pain what was designed for him to be pleasure."

"We are always learning the way that heaven acts, but are very shy to invite it to act upon us, and are very unwilling to submit to the preparatory process."

"Self-improvement by the selfish spirit is the most deceitful of all deceits."

"While you persevere in washing a man's face with dirty water, it will never be clean; you must get pure water to wash with."

"A child is a religious being prior to its being an intellectual being; and must not be turned away from the divine order."

AN AFTERNOON AT ST. LAZARE.

ıaid a visit yesterday (Sunday) Lazare, and all that we saw ırd there struck us as so in- g, and so entirely different from conceived notions concern- t ill-famed centre of crime ıishment, that we cannot but ır readers will likewise be in- | in hearing a detailed and : account of it.

ad been told that the famous r, charged with the murder eigneur Surat, was still there, could not resist the opportu- red us by a friend of going :his extraordinary type of fe- ocity—the woman who put a !the prelate's head, and, when ly asked her what he had her that she should hate replied : "You are a priest!" t him on the spot. On arriv- ever, we found that she had Versailles the night before. 'ere still fourteen of her terri- ıpeers remaining out of the ndred and thirty that had ten on the barricades and in ral saturnalia of the Com- d locked up in St. Lazare.

ited the prison from begin- end. Nothing surprised us so the gentleness of the *régime*, absence of all mystery or restraint in the management risoners. The jail had no- the repulsive paraphernalia on about it, and but for its walls, its vast proportions, tain indescribable gloom in phere, inseparable, we sup- the mere presence of such tion, one might very well have mistaken it for an orphanage or any ordinary asylum conducted by a religious community.

The *salles* are magnificently spacious and lofty, with broad, high windows opening on courts; there are four courts—*préaux* they are called—one after another, within the precincts of the prison; the beds are like hospital beds; and there was nothing in the dress of the women, or the manner of the nuns toward them, to tell an uninitiated visitor that they were not patients rather than prisoners and malefactors of the worst kind. There was the same silence brooding over the place, the same quiet regularity in all the arrangements, the same supernatural sort of cleanliness that one never sees anywhere but in convents. The population of the prison varies from 1,200 to 1,800, and the government of these dangerous and desperate subjects is committed to the sole charge of a community of religious called *Sœurs de Marie-Joseph*. They are fifty in all. Their dress is black serge, with a black veil lined with a light-blue one. They were founded at the close of the last century by a Lyonnese lady, whose name the superioress told us, but we forgot it.

It was just two o'clock when we arrived, and the superioress and another nun gave up assisting at vespers in order to show us over the house, which from its immense size takes two hours to visit in detail. The prisoners are divided into several categories, and are kept distinctly separate from each other. There are first the *Prévenues*, who are put in

on an accusation which has not been investigated; then the *Détenues*, against whom proof is forthcoming, and who are awaiting their trial; then there are the *Jugées*, of whom the categories are various, as will be seen. These classes are never allowed to come in contact, even accidentally, with each other; they do not even meet at meals. Those who are condemned to one year's imprisonment remain at St. Lazare, but if the sentence extends to a year and a day, they are sent off to one of the *Succursales*. When their term is expired (those who are sentenced to a year only), they may continue at St. Lazare if they choose. Many of them, touched with grace, and sincerely converted from their evil courses, dread going back to old scenes and temptations that have proved so fatal to them, and beg to be kept as *filles de service* for the work of the house, or in the workshops, etc., and they are never refused. The superioress said they made very active official servants, and it is very seldom they fall away from their good resolves, and have to be expelled or punished. We were passing through one of the passages when a sudden noise of voices from the court made us go to the window and look out. We saw a troop of prisoners pouring out into the yard; they were running about, laughing and chatting, and apparently enjoying their momentary liberty with the zest of school-boys.

"Who are these, *ma mère?*" we inquired.

"*Hélas!*" The exclamation was accompanied by a sufficiently expressive gesture.

"They are generally a very numerous class here," she explained; "but just now there are but some two hundred of them; the *pétroleuses* were largely recruited from their ranks, and great numbers have been sent on to Versail

Some one asked if these nates were more refractory other prisoners, thieves, etc.

"As a rule, they are less plied the nun; "we hardly obliged to have recourse to *diens* with them, and we ha frequent conversions among than any other class of p There comes a time to many especially if they have had a of religious belief sowed minds in childhood, when th both of this world and the ne: on them with a sense of hor then grace has an easy ta them. I could tell you of wrought in the souls of the sinners that would sound li out of the lives of the saints, have had deathbeds among th short of saintly. But, again, often see all our efforts fail, a reject grace with a sort of de al obduracy, and go back to t lives without a moment's compunction: nothing seems t them or frighten them."

We asked if the nuns w afraid of them, if they never ened or insulted them.

"Oh! never!" replied the s ess emphatically; "the comm have over them, and the w yield obedience and respect t almost miraculous. You se poor outcasts down there; I there is nothing in the worl lost or degraded than they ar are the lowest specimens of t est stratum of vice and every of depravity. Well, the young in the community is as safe middle of them as if they v honest *mères de famille*. been a religious twenty-two ye out of that ten years at St. and I have never known th

...ension to any of us that call... reprimand."

...may add that she said the ...ajority of these offenders were ...om the provinces, young and ...rienced for the most part, and ...me to Paris expecting to make ...rtune, and unprepared for the ...tions awaiting them in this ...ap for souls.

...saw the words *Oratoire Israel-...itoire Protestant*, painted over ...oors, and the latter suggested ...uiry whether there were occa-... any English women amongst ...mates of St. Lazare.

...! yes, I am sorry to say we ...good many English," said the ...; and then, shaking her head ...iling, she added: "And I am ...o tell you that they are the ...manageable of all, for they are ...lly given to drink, and when ...the case they are like mad-... and we can do nothing with ... A little while ago we had one ...t into such a fearful fit of fury ...was necessary to put her in ...k-up; her shrieks were so loud ...ey were heard half over the ...and terrified the young *déte-*... toward evening she grew so ...ous that the *gardiens* were ... put her into the strait-waist-...hey are powerful men with ...hands and iron nerves, and ...to the work—but she baffled ...them for two hours; they were ...le to seize or hold her; at last ...ve it up in despair, and said: ...me, we must go for *les sœurs!* ...them came to fetch me, and ...to come or send some one to ...em. He was trembling in ...imb, and the perspiration was ...from his face as if he had ...estling with a wild animal. ...of the nuns with me, and ...nt down to the prison, where ...e obliged to spend the whole night with the prisoner, coaxing and caressing her, before we got her to calm down and cease shrieking."

We asked to what class in life the English culprits generally belonged—if they were exclusively of the lowest? The superioress said, on the contrary, they were often persons very *comme il faut* in their manners, and evidently had had an education far above the class of domestic servants—some of them were in fact quite like ladies; she believed they were mostly governesses, or teachers who come over to Paris in search of situations or lessons, and, not finding either, are driven by hunger and despair to steal, or do worse; but theft is generally the offence of the English prisoners.

"Sometimes, indeed," said the superioress, "it makes us laugh to hear the account of the thefts they commit, there is often something so comical in the way they do it, and the cunning and dexterity they display are beyond belief; the most accomplished French *filou* cannot hold a candle to them."

Sad as this testimony was, it could not be quite a surprise to any one living in Paris who had seen much of the class of English alluded to, but it will come probably as a new and terrible revelation to many in England; and if this paper should fall into the hands of any lone, friendless English girl hesitating about coming to Paris to earn her bread, the writer prays God she may ponder on the foregoing statement, and think twice before embarking on so perilous a venture.

Several *salles* are filled with a class of prisoners called *jeunes insoumises;* they are all very young, some merely children of the day; they are not always actual criminals, sometimes they are only subjects with dangerous propensities beyond the control of parents, and they are sent here to be trained to better ways;

ew a huge pair of scissors from
ckot—how she came by it we
discovered—and, holding it
and pointed at them with one
she beckoned them with the
to come on, yelling all the
like a raging lioness. The men
to terrify her, to dodge her, but
all useless, she baffled every
t to seize her. They gave it
hopeless, and came for me.
sooner saw me than she cried
'Send them away, and I will
h you; but I will never move a
ith these men!' I sent them
and told her to give me the
s; she gave it at once, and then
her by the hand and led her
hout a word.

n another occasion, one section
soners got up a scheme for
the *gardiens*. They were to
ir wooden *sabots* into clusters
ht together, and when the *gar-*
came to convey some refrac-
bject to the *cachot*, the others
o fling several batches of these
able missiles at their heads.
fect must have been fatal, but
ately there was some delay in
pearance of the *gardiens*, and
isoners, having all ready, grew
ent, and at last, losing all con-
ey began to yell and call out
m and brandish their *sabots*
ly. The nun who was in wait-
n down to warn the *gardiens*
come up, and then came to
what had happened, and to
about sending for the soldiers,
re always ready at the *poste*
the prison; the *gardiens* were
ned, and advised this being
I thought, however, the storm
subside without having re-
to such an extreme mea-
I was not the least afraid of
personally; I knew they
never lay a finger on one
whatever their fury might
be, so I walked into the midst of them.

"'What is this row about?' I said. 'I am ashamed of you; let me hear no more of it.' Then taking the ringleader—we always know the one to pitch upon—I told her I must put her in prison; she made no resistance, only stipulating that the *gardiens* were not to touch her.'"

"Are the *gardiens* cruel to them that they hate them so much?" I asked.

"No, never," she answered; "they have no opportunity for it if they felt so inclined; but they represent strength and justice, whereas the nuns represent only weakness and pity; the prisoners resent the one, but not the other."

Some one asked the superioress if she had ever known a conspiracy attempted to kill or hurt any of the sisters. She replied never, on which we related to her an episode of the Roman prisons, told us recently by the Papal Nuncio. The female prisons in Rome are, like St. Lazare, conducted entirely by nuns, without even the moral support of a *poste* at the gates to enforce their authority. One day a plot was organized for doing away with the nuns and making their own escape from the prison. The prisoners were sixty in number and the nuns twelve, so the scheme offered little serious difficulty. It was agreed that on a certain day when all the community were assembled with the prisoners in the workroom, the latter were to seize the nuns and fling them out of the windows into the yard. The signal agreed upon was the close of the work-hour, when the superioress clapped her hands for them to put aside their work. The secret was so well kept that not a hint transpired, but the superioress felt instinctively there was something abnormal brewing.

She had no apprehension at the moment, however, and gave the signal as usual when the clock struck the hour. No one moved. She repeated it. Still no one stirred. She gave it a third time more emphatically, and then the leader of the band walked straight up to her and struck her a blow on the face. The meek disciple of Jesus quietly knelt down, turned the other cheek, and said:

"If I have done you any harm, tell me so, but if not, why do you strike me?"

The woman fell upon her knees, burst into tears, and confessed everything. When the superioress had heard her to the end, she said:

"Now, my daughter, I must take you to the dungeon; you know this is my duty."

"Yes, mother, I know it is," and she gave her hand, and let herself be led away as meekly as a lamb.

How omnipotent is the power of love, and how lovely this world would be if love were allowed to rule over it everywhere!

Before we had finished our inspection of the house, we went to benediction in the prison chapel. There was a short sermon first on the gospel of the day. About eight hundred of the prisoners were present. Some were yawning, and evidently only there because they could not help themselves, others assisted with edifying devotion, but all were respectful in their attitude and demeanor. The organ was played by one of the nuns, and the choir was formed of prisoners from the class already alluded to. The singing was not very scientific, but it struck us all as peculiarly touching, the more so, no doubt, from the associations connected unconsciously with the choristers. The superioress said it was looked upon as a great privilege to sing in the choir, and it is held out as a reward for sustair and good conduct. As w little altar lighted up, and t rays of the monstrance shir upon the singular congreg could not but think what and beautiful manifestatic deeming love it was, this pı the God of holiness, a w soner in such a temple. T the Sisters of Marie-Josep of the purest, most unblemi: self-devoted victims to the died on Calvary for out sinners, kneeling side by si loathing sisterhood with offscourings of this great A sight wonderful beyond a understanding if the myst not explained to us by the v out the little crystal prisc "I came to seek sinners, an with them. . . . And w you do to the least of thes likewise to me. . . . An more joy in heaven for the one sinner than for ninety-n just."

And many are the joys him and his saints by the ir this great emporium of sinne All Saints' day five hundre prisoners approached the sa some in the most admirably spirit, but all of their own and for the moment at l hearts touched by grace an away from evil. They wer ed for the feast by a retreat days, preached by a Marist

After benediction we resu inspection, and came final *pétroleuses.* There was n the room where they were surroundings, to distinguish t the other prisoners, and if rioress had not whispered we were entering the dormi these were the women, w never have suspected the b

the government did not mean to carry out. It was like letting loose so many bloodhounds on France to set these women at large again.

"We have seen them *de près*," continued the superioress, "and we are one and all convinced that the next attempt will be worse than the first; we have terrible days in store—the *pétroleuses* have not said their last word."

Speaking of the Commune led to our asking about her own experiences under it. It appears that the employees at St. Lazare, the director, inspector-general, and their assistants, were among the first turned out, and agents of the Hôtel de Ville installed in their places. The first thing these guardians of public justice did was to set free one-half of the population, such as were available for the public services; and able servants they proved themselves on the barricades and as incendiaries. To account for and in some measure palliate the superhuman ferocity displayed by the women of the Commune, we may as well mention here a fact not generally known, and which was told to us by a distinguished medical man, who was here all through that terrible saturnalia, and by a Sister of Charity, who could also speak from personal knowledge. It would seem that the snuff dealt out to the people from the government manufactories was mixed in large proportions with gunpowder. The effect of this ingredient, taken in very small quantities, is to excite the brain abnormally, but taken in large ones it brings on a kind of savage delirium tremens. The wine distributed to the *pétroleuses* on the barricades and elsewhere was also heavily charged with some such element of madness. It seems to us that it is rather a consolation to hear this, for though it reveals a diabolical instinct of soul-hatred in the few, it

explains, on the other hand, l
was that occasionally we saw
and hitherto mild, inoffensive
suddenly transformed into den

The superioress said that f
first three weeks that the nu
duty for the Commune, n
could exceed the respect and
deration they received from th

"They were as docile as litt
to us," she said, "and never d
thing without coming to con
The *inspecteur-general* named
Commune happened to have
ly been a clerk at the prisor
surprise when I saw him in h
character, and with such cred
was great; but he seemed l
very much ashamed, and wher
ed him what had induced l
join the Commune, he repli
it was really devotion to the
he had accepted the office l
he knew we would want a pro
and he preferred being on th
to watch over us. It wa
laughing matter, or I could
laughed at his audacity. And
tually pleaded this argument
trial at Versailles, and was acc
on it! He had always been
conducted, honest man, and
not sure but in the bottom
heart this good intention tow
may not have been mixed up
great many other less worthy
During all the time he was i
stant communication with r
never had the courage once t
his eyes to my face. He tol
good deal about what was go
outside, and especially what t
men were doing. He spoke
thusiastic praise of their spi
courage. He said the fort of
rouge was lost one day but for a
seventeen, who, seeing the sold
moralized, and the gunners ab
ing their guns and turning to fl
ed up to one of them, and s

like that!—but I felt the same kind of internal voice saying to me: Now is your time; take the others and fly!

"We hurried down the stairs just as we were and went out. We turned to the left, and walked on as fast as we could, without running, toward the *Gare du Nord.* We could hardly have turned the corner of the street when the director was in pursuit of us. *Les Détenues,* who saw us leave the house and take to the left, called out to him: To the right, citoyen! They are not forty yards ahead! He followed the direction, and this saved us. We reached the station just as the train was about to move. The guards saw us coming, and cried out to us to make haste and jump in. 'But our tickets! We have not taken them!' I said.

"'Never mind, jump in! You will pay at the other end,' and they hustled us into the nearest carriage. We had not seated ourselves when the director appeared on the platform pistol in hand, and crying out frantically to the train to stop. But it moved on, and landed us safely at Argenteuil."

A few days after the *Sœurs Marie-Joseph* had cleared out from St. Lazare, the nuns of Picpus were taken there. This the superioress thought was one reason why the officials were anxious to get them out of their way; they meant to put the others there, and they did not want any inconvenient witnesses of their own proceedings.

When we had seen all that was to be seen in the vast building, the superioress took us to the private chapel of the community. It was formerly the cell of St. Vincent of Paul, that is to say, the space occupied by the sanctuary; the altar stands where his little bed used to be, and the window step is worn away by the pressure of his feet, when his increasing infirmities obliged him to have recou to the solace of a footstool. The son itself was formerly a Lazarist ı nastery; the refectory is exactly a was in the time of St. Vincent, changed in all except its occupaı and the great, sombre corridors ec ed for twenty years to the footsı of the sweet apostle of charity. memory is held in great venerat throughout the prison, and the po lation speak of him with a sort rough, filial affectionateness that, nuns told us, is often very touchi they seem to look on him as a fri who ought to stand by them.

I had nearly forgotten one incid in our visit that had a peculiar be ty of its own. We were passing the open door of what seemed an firmary; all the beds were occupi and there were several nuns sitting the room, when one of them ran and said:

"Oh! *ma mère,* you will not p without coming to say *bonjour* our old women. Ever since t heard you were showing the hoı they have been watching for you.

The superioress said it was l and she really had not time just n but the nuns begged harder, said that the old women knew was going into retreat that even so they would not see her for ei days, and the old women, seeing t were in danger of being refused. gan to cry out so piteously that mother, asking us if we would mind walking down the ward, yi ed, and we went in. These old men are all infirm and incurable. have been sent as such from one l pital or another to St. Lazare. T delight when the superioress cam and spoke a word to each was most rapturous. I stood to spea one old soul, but instead of deta her own aches and pains after usual manner of those dear, bl

THE INTERNATIONAL ASSOCIATION.*

THE Labor Question has become one of the most formidable questions—perhaps the most formidable question—of the day; and the worst feature of the question is that, though it has been looming up in the distance for nearly a century, and constantly coming nearer and nearer, and more and more pressing for a solution, the statesmen, reformers, and philanthropists of no country seem to know what answer to give it, or how to treat it. There is no lack of nostrums, and every petty politician is ready with his "Morrison pill"; but no one gives a satisfactory diagnosis of the case, and the remedies offered or applied have served thus far only to aggravate the symptoms of the disease.

There is a very general conviction among the workingmen themselves that, in the distribution of the joint products of capital and labor, capital gets the lion's share. Capitalists, or they who can command capital or its substitute, credit, grow rich, become millionaires, from the profits of the labor they employ, while the laborer himself, with the most rigid economy and frugality, can barely keep soul and body together, and not always even that. Yet, if we look at the millions deposited by the laboring classes in our savings-banks, and the large sums collected from them for eleemosynary and other purposes not necessarily included in the expenses of living, this statement seems exaggerated. Then, too, the majority of the millionaires with us, and, perhaps, in England and France, began life as workmen, or, at least, without capital and with very little credit.

It is not easy to say precisely what the special grievances of the workingmen are, at least in our country, since comparatively few of the wealthy or easy classes of to-day inherited their wealth, or had to start with any appreciable advantages, pecuniary, educational, or social, over their compeers who have remained in the proletarian class. The International Association of Workingmen do not tell us very distinctly what their special grievances are, nor can we gather them from the eloquent lecture of their mouthpiece, Mr. Wendell Phillips, the candidate of the labor unions of Massachusetts for governor of that state. The evils he complains of, if evils, grow out of what is called "modern civilization," and seem to us to be inseparable from it. This is also clearly his opinion, and *The Dublin Review* shows that it is the view taken by the Internationals in England and France. Mr. Phillips says:

"Modern civilization is grand in seeming large and generous in some of its results, but, at the same time, hidden within are ulcers that confront social science and leave it aghast. The students of social science, in every meeting that gathers itself, in every debate and discussion, confess themselves at their wits' end in dealing with the great social evils of the day. Nobody that looks into the subject but recognizes the fact that the disease is very grave and deep; the superficial observer does not know the

* 1. *The Dublin Review.* Article IX.: The International Society. London. October, 1871.
2. *The Labor Movement.* Lecture of Wendell Phillips. Steinway Hall. *New York Tribune*, Dec. 7, 1871.

is a vast organized revolt against this boasted civilization of this nineteenth century. And so far it is not wholly without excuse, and even much may be said in its defence, though their proposed substitute for it may be utterly indefensible.

Modern material civilization, dating from the Peace of Utrecht in 1713, and more especially from the accession of the House of Hanover to the English throne, and the accession to power in England of what in the time of Swift and Addison was called the Urban party — money-changers, bankers, traders, merchants, and manufacturers—has been based on capital employed in trade and industry, in opposition to capital invested in land and agriculture. It is a shopkeeping and manufacturing and maritime civilization, essentially and eminently a burgher civilization, and resulting especially in the burgher class, or, as the French say, the *bourgeoisie.* A civilization based on material interests, and proposing the multiplication and amassing of material goods, necessarily produces the state of things which excites the opposition of Mr. Phillips and the Internationals. It creates necessarily an antagonism between the interests of capital and labor, and therefore between the employers, as representatives of capital, and the employed, or workmen. The interest of capital is to get labor at as low a rate of wages as possible; the interest of labor is to get as high a rate of wages as possible. This antagonism is inevitable.

Employers in vain pretend that the interests of capital and labor are the same. They are not so under a civilization based on Mammon, or under a civilization that seeks only the advancement of material interests, and invests capital only for the sake of material profit. In the struggle, the stronger party, under a ma system, is always sure to suc And this is always the party of tal; for labor seeks employme live—capital, for profit or gain the capitalist can forego profit easily than labor can forego en ment, since to live is more than to gain. This secures th vantage always to the cap The inequality which necessari sults cannot be overcome by eq of suffrage, or the extension frage to the proletarian class, a ticians pretend; for, though nu may triumph at the polls, the s er interest, as our American e ence proves, is sure to carry th tory in the halls of legislation. stronger interest in a country,' Mr. Calhoun to the writer, "a in the long run wields the pow the country."

Universal suffrage, which w fended on the ground that it tend to protect labor against c has in fact a contrary tendency in practice almost invariably capital. The whole of our l tion—which so favors capital substitute, credit, or which mor the future for the present, and debt supply the place of c covers the towns with mon business corporations, and bui huge monopolies—has grow under a system of universal su In an age and country where rial interests predominate, wh people, capitalists or prolet ask of government is, laws that tate the acquisition of wealt when such laws are enacte more than one man in a hundr avail himself of the facilities th ford.

The great scientific discove which we boast, and which wrought such marvellous chan our modern industrial world, w

"Now look at it. [illegible] you that [illegible] with [illegible]. [illegible] some [illegible] and [illegible] with the coal of Pennsylvania. Why don't you have it here at [illegible] and [illegible] a ton? Why don't you have it here at an advance of [illegible] or [illegible] over what it is sold for at the mouth of the pit? Because of the gigantic corporations and vast organizations of wealth. The capitalists gather three or four millions of dollars in your city—sell it when they please, at such rates as they please, and the poor man struggling for his bread is the sufferer. A rich man is careful [illegible] his [illegible] any further than allows of its being pulled back. If he heard a groan coming from the people at something he did, he would withdraw his investment, for nothing is more timid than wealth. But let that man take [illegible] or so and put it in with nine others, and make a capital of [illegible]; then he is as bold as Julius Cæsar. He will starve out [illegible] coal miners. The London *Spectator* says that the colossal strength of Britain has reason to dread the jointure of [illegible] of railroad capital. How much more should America have reason to dread such combinations, when Britain has more than ten times our wealth?"

Yet is there not some compensation to the proletarian class in the very system which tends so fearfully to increase their numbers and dependence? Grant that coal might be delivered from the mines in Pennsylvania in this city at $3 a ton; but suppose there were no railroads and no railway monopolies, could or would coal from the same mines be delivered in this city as cheap as it now is? Suppose there were no railways between this city and the great West, would wheat, flour, beef, pork, and the other necessaries of life be cheaper for the laboring class in this city than they now are? Railway companies may charge exorbitant rates of freight, and yet the laboring classes get the chief necessaries of life cheaper than they would, other things being [illegible] managed, without them. [illegible] things might be cheaper in th[illegible] [illegible]es where they are produ[illegible] not elsewhere. The evil [illegible] monopolies and corporation[illegible] so much in the enhanced cost chargeable to them, as the [illegible]lication of the class deper[illegible] capital for employment; anc[illegible] power to shape the actior[illegible] government to their special i[illegible] It is far better for the worl[illegible] depend on a single wealtl[illegible] vidual who is likely to have than on a soulless corporatioi[illegible] combination of capital in corp[illegible] for industrial or trading [illegible] founds an aristocracy, or rulir[illegible] far more humiliating and crus[illegible] the class below them than arist[illegible] founded on land and birth, ed[illegible] and manners.

This is the view taken by [illegible]ternationals. They war [illegible] against the rule of the burgh[illegible] which is now supreme in soc[illegible] formerly were the church, kin[illegible] nobilities. In this oppositior[illegible] rule of the burgher class, su[illegible] the means and methods of th[illegible] fare just and honorable, we [illegible] we might sympathize with the nationals, as we have always [illegible] thized with the working-classe[illegible] never have been able to get u[illegible] liking for an aristocracy ba[illegible] Mammon, who, Milton tells [illegible] the meanest of all the ang[illegible] fell, and who, even in heave[illegible] about head down, and his ey[illegible] on the gold of heaven's pav[illegible] It is well for no country w[illegible] ruling class are the mone[illegible] business class. Yet it wo[illegible] difficult to say, as to our [illegible] at least, what class can be [illegible] trusted with the government, [illegible] class has more virtue, more [illegible] of sentiment, chivalric feeling,

private corporations, and which give for the time employment to large numbers of workmen, skilled and unskilled, we now offer any advantages to the laborer over those he has abroad—at any rate, if we do, those advantages are fast disappearing.

We are no more favorable to the system of corporations than is Mr. Phillips; and the writer of this for years opposed with whatever abilities he had their creation and multiplication. He did so till he saw opposition could avail nothing to check their growth. No opposition can avail anything now, since the abolition of slavery has, in a great measure, identified the great planting interests of the South with the burgher interests of the North, as it was intended to do. For this Mr. Phillips is himself in no small degree responsible, and as an International, or a leader in the labor movement, he is only trying to undo what he hoped to do as an abolitionist. Philanthropy is an excellent sentiment when directed by practical wisdom and knowledge; but, when blindly followed, it creates a hundredfold more evil than it can cure, even if successful in its special aims. Even Mr. Phillips doubts if the corporation system can be safely abolished. We tell him there is no power in the country that can abolish it, because it governs the general government and nearly all the state governments. Give Mr. Phillips the fifty thousand votes he asks for, and the party he wishes to organize, he would, no doubt, become a power in elections, and could command an important place in the government for himself, and places also for his friends; but, however important the place to which he might be elected or appointed, he would find himself impotent to effect anything against the system he opposes, or in favor of the syst approves.

Mr. Phillips tells us that hi reliance is on the "education masses." So do we, only we against calling the people wh rational souls "the masses." they were piles or heaps of matter. But education given burgher civilization as educa suffered to be freely given by tend to perpetuate that civili or the very system, social and trial, which Mr. Phillips and t ternationals war against, not place or reform it. Let the tion of all the children of th be entrusted to a society whos ciples were so admirably summ and approved by a former go of Massachusetts, namely, "L government take care of th and the rich will take care poor," how much would the tion given do to elevate or me that society? No order of ci tion or society ever does or ev educate in reference to a highe than its own. Hence the why the state or secular societ not be a fit educator of ch and youth, and why all edu can be safely entrusted only t spiritual society whose ideal God-man, perfect, and the h conceivable.

Purely secular education pr on the assumption that men ar tions always act as well as they or that all individuals and will act uniformly in reference t own interests so far as they kno —an assumption disproved by one's daily experience, as well the universal experience of m Mr. Phillips ought to know th who ought to know better ar carried away by their lusts, th sions, the force of events, and and other influences, to act ir

nobility, and resulted in the triumph of absolute monarchy in the sixteenth century and the seventeenth. The second phase was the union of the burghers, or the *tiers état*, and the people or a portion of them against monarchy and the church, which issued in establishing the supremacy of the burghers. The third phase is that in the midst of which we now are, and is—monarchy and the church gone or assumed to be gone—that of the proletaries against burghers. Neither of the preceding phases of the revolution effected the good hoped for, or satisfied the revolutionary appetite, but really aggravated the social evils it was sought to remedy. The friends of the revolution said it did not go far enough, and stopped short of the mark. It has now descended to the bottom, to the lowest stratum, or to the lowest deep, and proposes to wrest the power from the burgher class and rest it in the proletarian class. It is some consolation to know that we at length have reached the last phase of the revolution, and that after its failure, as fail it will, nothing worse is to be feared. "When things are at worst, they sometimes mend."

The principal objection to the Internationals is not that they oppose what is called modern civilization, or that they seek to remedy undeniable social evils; but that they seek to do it on false principles, by inadequate means, and unlawful and even horrible methods, and can only lose even by success.

The International has absorbed all the other labor unions, and may be said to represent the whole proletarian class in Europe and America, and its leaders are avowed atheists; they reject the entire supernatural order, disdain or contemn all forms of religion, and seek to redress the material by the material. This alone is sufficient in itself to condemn them. They reject not only religion, but also government, or the entire political and civil order. They will have no God, no king, no aristocracy, no democracy, no law, no court, no judges, but simply—we can hardly say what. Practically, they will fall under the authority of irresponsible and despotic leaders, governing in the name of nobody, and by their own passions or interests alone. They may aim at positive results, but at present their means are only adequate to the work of destruction. Thus an organized and secret, and, when practicable, open war on all religion, on God, on all authority, all law, and especially on capital or individual property. What positive result is to follow, Mr. Phillips confesses his inability to tell.

From Mr. Phillips we learn that they aim at the destruction of the whole modern industrial system, and propose that the workmen shall take possession of the establishments created by capitalists, incorporated or not, and run them on their own account, and share the profits among themselves, without any indemnification to the owners. As to land, no individual is to own it or any portion of it—it is to be made common, and open, as to the usufruct, to any one who chooses to occupy it. Mr. Phillips says:

"I have another proposition. I think when a man has passed five years in the service of a corporation, though he may not have bought a dollar of its stock, he is in a certain sense a stockholder. He has put his labor and persistency there, and I think every man who has been employed in a corporation for a year or two should have a voice in its financial management. In Japan, when a man dies, his land is left to the state. Do you not think that is a wiser plan than ours? The land becomes more valuable through the labor of the whole country, and not by that of the man who eats off of it.

M. Desmoulins' apology for the Commune; and it supplies, we submit, matter for reflection in its every line. The statesmen and the classes in society who delight in seeing the influence of religion weakened or destroyed, never seem to realize until it is too late that they are sure to be the especial victims of their own success. The great truths of life hang together and sustain each other:

> 'All is contained in each:
> Dodona's forest in an acorn's cup.'

The man who scorns to love God, how shall he continue to love his neighbor? The man who has said, 'There is no God,' is he not on the point of also saying, 'Lust is lawful,' 'Property is robbery'?"

We copy also from the same *Review* a letter from General Cluseret from this city to a member of the Society:

"NEW YORK, 17th February.

"MY DEAR VARLIN: I have just received your welcome letter of the 2d. It explains the delay in replying to my application. Need I say that I accept, and will set to work at once in endeavoring to be useful to my brethren in poverty and toil? The newspaper which I told you of is not yet established. I think it better not to renew my attempts in that direction, considering the late events in France, and the numerous letters I have received from my friends, who are unanimous in recalling me to Europe.

"In all probability, I shall be there next summer, but, in the interval, I shall have arranged international relations between the different French and American groups, and selected one person or several persons (at the discretion of the French committee) of proved zeal and capability, to replace me. As you say, we shall surely, infallibly triumph if we persist in demanding success from our organization. But we must remember that the aim of our Association is to associate (*solidariser*) the greatest number for action. Let us, then, be liberal; let us round off our angles; let us be really brethren, not in words, but in deeds; let not such mere terms as doctrine and individuality separate those whom common suffering, which means a common

interest, has united: we are all an
we must acknowledge that; if w
beaten, it is our own fault. I hav
been able to picture our people t
self during the late troubles. Wha
been the attitude of the workmen's
eties, and what are their present
sitions? Certainly, we must not
fice our ideas to politics, but we
not detach ourselves from them,
momentarily. In my mind, the me
of all that is going on is simply thi
the Orleans are slipping little by
close to power, and paring his nai
L. N., so that one fine morning the
merely have to substitute themselv
him.

"Now, we ought to be ready,
cally and morally, for that day. *C
day, we, or nothing.* Until then I
probably remain quiet, *but on that
affirm* — and you know my 'Nay'
means 'Yea' — *Paris shall be ou
Paris shall exist no longer.* This w
the decisive moment for the access
the people.—Yours ever, CLUSE

"You are mistaken in believing,
moment, that I am neglecting the s
ist in favor of the political move
No; it is only from a purely soci
point of view I am pursuing the r
tionary work; but you must thoro
know we can do nothing in the dir
of social reform if the old politica
tem be not annihilated. Let us no
get that at this moment the Empi
ists merely in name, and that g
ment consists in party abuse. If,
these grave circumstances, the so
party permits itself to be lulled to
by the abstract theory of sociol
science, *we may wake up one fine m
to find ourselves under new masters
dangerous for us than those we h
present, because they would be young
consequently more vigorous and more
ful.*"

We have personally known
ral (?) Cluseret, and we know h
be a man who acts from deliber
not impulse, who means wh
says, and who can be restrained
going straight to his end by n
gious principle, moral scrupl
sentiment of mercy, pity, or co
sion. His disposition is as ster

ıble as a physical law of na- When he threatened to burn rather than surrender it, he it, and he was the man to do o see that it was done if with- limits of the possible. Mr. s seems also to appear, at o threaten incendiarism as a of accomplishing his purpose. neans this, the closing sentence lecture: "The lesson taught icago is that wealth cannot to neglect poverty"? Does nean that the Internationals Chicago? or does it simply that other cities may be burnt l as Chicago, and will be, if continues to neglect poverty uses to yield to the demands : International Association of ıgmen? This gives the ques- startling aspect. Certain it is ıe Association holds itself free roduce its socialism or com- n by murder, assassination, rob- plunder, and conflagration at ıasure or dictation of its chiefs. the following letter, read and ed by Mr. Phillips before a York audience:

ore proceeding to speak of it, you ow me to read a notice which has laced in my hand, and in the ob- which I sympathize cordially, be- he great foreign movement can be morated by it. The French Com- ıas always seemed to me to de- he cordial respect of every lover progress of the masses throughout rld. I have no doubt that in due good name will be vindicated, ı leaders lifted to the unqualified of the civilized world. The no- old in my hand is as follows:

[illegible] Workingmen of New York, friends [illegible] enemies of bloodshed, and lovers [illegible] Citizens! The recent barbarous exe- [illegible] France, in cold blood, six months after [illegible] are over, and the ferocity with [illegible] pursue their victims, are a [illegible] shame to humanity. We must [illegible] human race to be stained by the [illegible] own blood without a protest. [illegible] would you let your friends the workingmen be murdered because they have defended our rights in any part of the world? No! certainly not without raising your voice and making it heard across the ocean. To give effect to these purposes, a grand funeral procession will take place in New York on Sunday, the 10th of December, at 1 o'clock, forming opposite the Cooper Institute. All men, without distinction of party, of race, of nationality, friends of justice and freedom, are invited to join. By order of the Committee of Arrangements of the Federal Council.'

"I hope every man who loves his fellow will show himself there. There was never nobler blood shed, never more high-minded and disinterested effort made in the long history of Freedom's struggle, than in Paris, when, in defiance of all the oligarchies of Europe, that city stood up for the individual and for liberty in the nineteenth century."

The impudence of the writers of this letter is sublime, and only surpassed by that of the lecturer in endorsing it. Why, these fellows would persuade us that they are "enemies of bloodshed and lovers of justice," meek as lambs, timid as sheep, and harmless as doves—they who, without a shadow of justice or excuse, made the streets of Paris run with the blood of the innocent, the noble, and the saintly. "Enemies of bloodshed"!—they whose hands are reeking with blood! Yes, to having their own blood shed, but not to the shedding of the blood of others. "Enemies of bloodshed and lovers of justice"! Good God! can hypocrisy or self-delusion go so far? Let the assassination of Generals Le Comte and Clement Thomas, the horrible murders, when it was known that the cause of the Commune was lost, of the holy and unoffending Archbishop of Paris, of Jesuit fathers, and a dozen Dominican friars and lay brothers, to say nothing of other murders hardly less horrible, reply to that false pretence. It would seem that these miscreants count for nothing the blood they shed without authority, in violation of law, religion, morality, and every principle of justice, and every sentiment of humanity; it

ngthen the burgher class and tions in towns by compelling ho are not favorable to these and interests to support them, only means left of saving society from lapsing into complete barbarism.

We shall probably return at an early day to this subject, for it is really the great question of the hour.

ON CATHOLIC LIBRARIES.

ust be confessed that the n of this country, in propor- their numerical strength and zeal for the interests of re- do not present that propor- large class of readers which among the Protestant sects. ertions in building churches, and charitable institutions en beyond all praise, and have tly elicited the admiration nishment of their opponents; yet very little organized effort made by the influential por- the laity to place within easy their humbler co-religionists ns of cheap and instructive The more intelligent and are too often content to pur- few standard Catholic works, ter perusing them with more ttention place them with their ooks on the shelves of their , there to remain secluded blic view, and of comparative value to any person but their The less favored class, who ous reasons are unable to in- n this luxury, are still practi- t off from one of the chief of knowledge and amuse- good books—and are neces- ompelled from uncontrollable ances to go through life ir minds and tastes undeve- nd their time dissipated in or wasted over the trashy terious contents of the many cheap story newspapers and novels which the American press is constantly scattering broadcast over the land.

This melancholy fact is most observable in the ranks of our adult immigrant population, who, coming from countries where education was almost unattainable, money scarce, and books dear, have not generally acquired either ability or taste for reading, though it has been remarked that even among them, when an opportunity is at all presented, the desire for information is excited in a remarkable degree, and only requires a reasonable impetus to develop it still more. Still, from the fact of their usually limited means and comparatively unsettled modes of life, they are as yet unable to purchase or retain any appreciable collection of desirable publications.

The remedy for this defect in our growing Catholic society lies, in our opinion, in the formation of local libraries, suitable in variety and extent to the wants and capacity of particular localities. There are at least twenty-five hundred centres of Catholic population in America where very respectable collections of books could be purchased and placed in some safe and accessible place, say in the school-rooms or church basements, and half as many more, particularly in our Western settlements, where at least a few good

books would be of great advantage to the hardy tillers of the soil, and where, even if there be no public place to deposit them, there is always some prominent settler who would willingly assume the honorary office of librarian. Experiments of both plans have been tried in many of our large city parishes, and in a few isolated instances in the country, with marked success.

The advantages of libraries conducted on this system are numerous, and ought to be apparent to every one, not the least of which would be *cheapness*. Let us suppose, for instance, that, in any given locality, fifty persons would each subscribe two dollars. This would create a capital of one hundred dollars, or sufficient to purchase, on an average, one hundred and fifty volumes, great and small, of readable books, from any of our large publishing-houses in Boston, New York, Philadelphia, or Baltimore. Thus, for two dollars, a subscriber would have, for reading or reference, the practical ownership of works at least fifty times the value of his contribution, and, by charging new members a small fee for the use of each volume, a fund might be created to purchase new books as they appeared from time to time. In this manner, and with proper attention, a library of dimension commensurate with the growing wants of the neighborhood would be brought into existence without much expense to any particular class of the community.

But the moral effect of the establishment of such small centres of intelligence would be incomparably greater. For the adults, it would at once be an attraction and a source of occupation, tending powerfully to withdraw them from those pursuits, not always edifying, in which unoccupied minds too often indulge, to the detriment of their health and morals. It would be the means of generating a taste for mental improvement, and of making them more confident among their companions, and more proficient and reflective in their various pursuits; for it is a well-recognized truth, that as a man, be he artisan, trader, or farmer, acquires those habits of thought which can only be derived from study, he becomes more skilful and methodical in his peculiar calling. The youth of both sexes, however, would reap the greatest advantages. There are hundreds of thousands of children of Catholic parents among us who can read, and, what is more, *will* read. The young American mind, no matter of what parentage, is a hungry and an investigating mind, and must have some sort of food, do or say what we will. If it cannot have good literary food, it will have what is poisonous, and in this lies the secret of the success of the sensational story papers, and the no less deleterious tales that, in a few years, have made fortunes for their publishers. It is well known that one of the former class, published in this city, boasts of a weekly circulation of three hundred thousand copies, and another of nearly as great a number. If we go into the large workshops of the principal cities, or the factories of New England, where so many young persons are engaged, at the hour allotted for dinner we will see every second boy and girl devouring with more eagerness than their food the contents of some flashy journal or specimen of what is generally known as "yellow-covered literature," in which vice is hidden under a thin veil of romance only to make it the more seductive. Now, the way to check this insidious and widespread evil is not by complaining of or railing at it, but by placing

easy reach, and in accessible sound and attractive Catho- rks. The impetuous mind of may be compared to a rapid ı, which, dammed up or check- its career, is sure sooner or lat- overflow its boundaries to the ction of its surroundings, but , if its course is directed by and experienced hands, not eases to be dangerous, but be- a source of usefulness and . To give this direction to the ıding intellect of the rising gen- ı, and to turn to good use night by neglect or repression ıe an evil and a curse, is one first and plainest duties of pa- for the proper performance of they will be held to a strict ntability. It is not enough em to see that their offspring l church on Sundays and holy- that they go to Sunday-school rly, and say their prayers and morning, if they allow ıfterwards to ponder from hour ıur over sickly romances; nor t serve to send their children ıool to learn to spell and read, knowledge thus gained be l to the enervation of their and the corruption of their s. Education is not in itself an is only the means to an end, and nd is the knowledge of God's nd the best way of conforming conduct to its requirements so secure our eternal salvation. is no excuse for a Catholic pa- or not putting into the hands s children entertaining and books, nor is there any pallia- ır any one professing our holy and who has arrived at the of discretion, for encouraging ading the thousand-and-one of fiction which we see every xposed on news-stands and in book-stores, and which are not only immoral in tone and spirit, but in effect positively anti-Christian. Besides books of a serious and practical character, we have numerous works of fiction, published in this country and easily obtained, of the highest order of talent united to rare dramatic force and interest, which are detrimental neither to morals nor religion. The writings of Griffin, Banim, Huntington, Julia Kavanagh, Mrs. Sadlier, Mrs. Anna Dorsey, Lady Fullerton, Lady Herbert, and many others that we could name, are of this character, and are worthy to be read by the highest as well as the lowest in society. Of works treating on history, science in its various departments, biography, travels, etc., Catholic in tone, and elaborate or elementary in arrangement, we have a large and varied supply; and new productions under these heads are constantly appearing, more fascinating to the cultivated taste than even the productions of our best novelists. But it has been objected that these publications are too dear; that poor people cannot afford to spend ten or fifteen dollars on a few books. Granted; but, if they can have the use of four or five score for a couple of dollars by subscribing to a parochial library, is not the objection removed? This is what local libraries, and they alone, can do.

Now, what would be the effect of this system of libraries on the general tone of public opinion? Decidedly most salutary. In addition to driving from circulation many of the demoralizing newspapers, periodicals, and books which even non-Catholics denounce as immoral, and for the suppression of some of which the aid of legislative action has been invoked, it would create and foster a pure literary taste among no inconsiderable portion of our diverse population, and, apart from its direct

moral effect, would render it more valuable and more reproductive in a material point of view. Many of the most important political, social, and commercial problems of the day, on the true solution of which depends the future welfare of our republic, can only be properly comprehended by reference to the history of the past, and to the biographies of the great statesmen who succeeded or failed in founding or destroying nations and empires. And even in the discussion of minor questions affecting our interests or liberties, some acquaintance with the antecedents of our country is absolutely necessary to enable us to form proper opinions of their merits. In individual cases, one of the compensations for declining years and one of the highest claims to respect is experience; but to the reader of history, no matter what his age, the accumulated experience of at least thirty centuries is accessible, and not only controls his judgment and enlarges his knowledge, but vastly enhances his social and political status. But this experience, to be of any value, must be based on truth and undoubted facts. It must arise from the just appreciation of unbiassed statements and philosophical deductions, stripped of all that false assertion and unlimited prejudice which have characterized so many European and American writers for the last three centuries. Hence the need of Catholic books and Catholic readers—for, in this as in commercial matters, the demand regulates the supply—and the creation of new facilities for the spread of reliable information.

Take the case of the *History of England* by Lingard. Before the appearance of that excellent work, we venture to say that seven-eighths of the reading population in every part of the world believed more or less in the falsehoods and forgeries with which the pages of the English historians of the post-Reformation period were crowded. Many more such instances of recent successful vindication of the truth of history might be cited, not the least valuable and complete being the production of our own countrymen, such as that very able and learned refutation of D'Aubigné's *History of the Reformation* * and the *Life of Mary, Queen of Scots*,† which has lately appeared, and in which the slanders and aspersions so repeatedly heaped on the memory and character of that beautiful but ill-starred sovereign are condemned, exposed, and, it is to be hoped, finally disposed of. The first of these works is the most elaborate and reliable book we have on that important epoch, when every throne in Europe was shaken to its base, and when men's passions, let loose by the preaching of the heresiarchs of England and the Continent, threatened to destroy every vestige of temporal and spiritual authority. There is no period in the history of Christendom about which so many falsehoods and such mendacious calumnies have been invented and circulated by prejudiced writers; and it was only on the appearance of the book in question that we have had, at least in English, any comprehensive and truthful account of the origin and progress of that rebellion against God's church and laws. This country, from its settlement to the present, the origin and growth of its institutions from their inception in the early part of the seventeenth century till their fruition in our present constitution, though full of incident and fraught with lessons of the highest political wisdom, is yet imperfectly known and

* *History of the Protestant Reformation.* By the Most Rev. M. J. Spalding, D.D. Baltimore

† *Mary, Queen of Scots.* By James F. Meline. New York. 1871.

papers. This is the poison that is carrying off so many of our juvenile co-religionists, more dangerous to their souls than the deadly upas would be to their bodies, and against which we must provide some antidote. If one of our boys is confronted with quotations from Hume or Macaulay, he must be prepared to answer them on the undoubted authority of Lingard; if he be taunted with the poverty or ignorance of the Catholics of Ireland, he can show whence came this penury and destitution by reference to McGee's, Cusack's, or any of the numerous histories of that country; he ought to be prepared to oppose Archbishop Spalding to D'Aubigné, Meline to Froude, the history of the Maryland settlers (the founders of religious liberty on this continent) to the eulogiums on the intolerant Puritans, the "Irish Settlers" to the Know-Nothing organs —in fact, truth and light wherever falsehood and darkness are to be found. The truth has nothing to lose, but everything to gain, by full and free discussion. It is only error that shrinks from thorough investigation. But we must take care that our sons and daughters are well supplied with plain and useful facts regarding their faith and religion before they are subjected to the ordeal through which all young Catholics must pass who mingle freely in Protestant society, lest through their ignorance the cause they espouse should be weakened by their imperfect advocacy.

Neither ought we to hesitate in learning lessons from our adversaries when it is possible to do so. If the children of darkness are wiser than the children of light in their generation, it is no reason why we should be guilty of folly. Apart from the falsity of their teachings, we have often had occasion to admire the systematic perseverance with which the Protestant sects have endeavored to disseminate their peculiar views throught the medium of cheap and attractive publications. All that art and skill can do has been done to render them pleasing to the eye and agreeable to the mind. The highest literary talent is employed and well rewarded, because the result of their labors is extensively circulated, and, even when persons are unable or unwilling to purchase, the purse of the wealthy is always open to enable them to obtain books free of cost, while our children are too often allowed to begin life but half-instructed, and to continue in it illiterate and untaught. Were our schools as efficient and as numerous as we wish and as we hope one day to see them, we might assure ourselves that all this might be taught in them; but they are not, nor can they be for some years, and we cannot ignore the fact or wait for the slow operation of time to perfect and extend their influence. We must endeavor by some means or other to supply the deficiency, so far, at least, as this generation is concerned. Besides, there will always be a large number of children of the working-classes who cannot remain long at any school, but must go into the world to earn their bread. With these the most critical period of their lives is from the time they pass from the control of the teacher till they reach manhood or womanhood, for then their characters for good or evil are formed. For this class of toilers, good books are not only a recreation and a solace, but an absolute necessity; but, being limited in means, we hold that it is only through the means of local libraries that they can gratify their wishes and find opportunities for mental improvement.

Literature itself would also gain much by the establishment of these libraries. How often has it been re-

d that, out of the large number holic young men of brains and ion which our colleges and nies turn out annually, there few writers. The explanation for them authorship is neither unerative nor an appreciated yment. The professions of law edicine and the attractions of erce and trade are constantly g into their vortices the best es and talent of our young tes, many of whom with encouragement and patron-ght, as authors, render incalcu-service to the cause of truth orality. What is required to this large amount of natural id acquired knowledge is sim-more extensive circulation of already published; the increase number of new books on sub-f general interest, in style and ent more in accordance with n forms than those published igo; but, above all, the cultiva-a correct standard of literary nce among the people, and the n of a widespread class of s and thinkers.

objection to the dearness of ic publications would also be ed by this means. It is well to those conversant with the ing business that, in proportion increase of the circulation of a book, the expense of its pro-n per copy is diminished in an ratio. A book of which three nd copies are sold at two dol-ch would be more remunera-both publisher and author at ne dollar if twenty thousand were disposed of. The pub-also, in his contract with the and in view of the uncertainty ales, naturally adds to the cost fection and to his fair percent-profit a certain amount for by losses by having a portion of his edition left on his shelves unsold. The establishment of local libraries would obviate the necessity of this additional cost. With, say, twenty-five hundred of these institutions, each ready and willing to subscribe for one or more copies of any really meritorious book that might appear, its success would be assured beyond doubt, the outlay of the publisher would be nearly reimbursed, and his risk, for which all book-buyers have now to pay, would be sensibly and materially diminished if not altogether done away with. Thus even individual purchasers as well as subscribers to libraries would be benefited in the reduction of price; and, while the bookseller would not suffer in the profits of his sales, the general public as well as the author would be sensibly the gainers.

As to what ought to constitute the necleus of a small library, some difficulty may be experienced in diverse tastes and opinions. In view of the multiplicity of good books constantly being imported or published in this country, it is nearly impossible to make a list of such as would be most desirable and useful without leaving out others perhaps as equally deserving of attention. Of works of fiction we have enough and more than enough in the productions of the authors above named and others of a less pretentious order, but, as this sort of reading is simply a matter of choice, each one must judge for himself in the selection.

Devotional and controversial works are numerous, and a few at least, such as the writings of St. Liguori, Father Faber, Dr. Manning, and Cardinal Wiseman, the *Guide for Catholic Young Women*, *Following of Christ*, *Catholic Christian Instructed*, *Lenten Monitor*, as well as several others, should be always found in Catholic libraries. In history, as far as the English lan-

guage is concerned, we are not so rich. We have, it is true, four or five histories of Ireland, possessing peculiar merits, and exhibiting more or less defects, but all full of useful information. Lingard's *England*, entire or abridged, is decidedly the best of that country. Shea's *History of the Catholic Missions in the United States*, McSherry's *Maryland*, Bishop Bayley's *Church in New York*, McGee's *Irish Letters* and *Catholic History*, De Courcey's and Shea's *Catholic Church in America*, go far to supply the defect, at least in part. Then there are the *Works of Archbishop Hughes*, one of the great prelates of the church in America, and the writings of Dr. O. A. Brownson, particularly his *Essays* and *American Republic*, than whom no man of our day, it is safe to say, writes with more vigor or with a clearer understanding of his subject. The works of Bishop England are, we regret to say, too little known, and, being for some time out of print, are now almost unattainable. Darras's *Church History*, the only complete history of the church yet published in our language, should, if possible, be read by every Catholic, and find a conspicuous place in all our libraries. *The Lives of Deceased Prelates of the United States*, by Clarke, which has just been published, is a very valuable book, containing a great deal of remote and contemporary history; and if Mr. Shea could be induced by proper encouragement to further develop the subjects he has selected for his books, as we feel certain of his ability to do so, a great deal of additional matter connected with the struggles and sufferings of the early pioneers of religion, now almost forgotten or unknown, would be placed before the public. In biography, which may be called history in detail, our resources are abundant. We have, besides numerous lives of Christ, a co *Lives of the Popes*, Butler's *L the Saints*, several of St. Patri *Vincent de Paul*, *Curé of Ar* some two hundred separate li the holy men and women who ir age of the church were conspicu their sanctity, wisdom, and de to the faith, a list of which n chosen from the catalogue of : our principal publishers; an though not least, is Montaler great work, *The Monks of the* an American edition of which published.

So far as materials are con we have a plenitude of th every variety and in all depar of literature, and we have end ed to show that very little m required to purchase them. is wanted is organization and For these we must depend to a extent on the local pastors, a the half a dozen leading l who are most generally to be in every congregation. Then homely proverb, but never true, that "what is everybody siness is nobody's business." one or two influential men i parish think seriously over th ter, call their associates togethe explain to them the advanta be derived by themselves an children from cheap and good ing, collect the subscription themselves in communication any of our Catholic book and the work is done. The fi most important step thus take future welfare of the library is ed. It is unnecessary to say tha a movement ought to and wo ceive the warmest encourag from their spiritual superiors. from the benefits arising fro reading of moral books to the of religion, the spirit of mutua course, interchange of though

and so successful that in a few years he was raised to the dignity of a prince of the church. Several times he was entrusted with important diplomatic missions by his sovereign, Charles II., and for many years occupied the position of grand almoner to Catharine of Braganza, the queen-consort. In addition to the biography of Cardinal Howard, we have a very full and interesting sketch of the history of the Dominican order, that glorious corporation of friar-preachers, whose labors extended to every part of the known world, and whose blood may be said to have been shed in the cause of Christ wherever the foot of man has trod. Father Palmer's treatment of the subject is in every way worthy of so great a theme. He does not, as too many biographers are apt to do, fall in love with his hero, and lose himself in senseless rhapsody and panegyric, but lets deeds and their results speak for themselves. Neither does he assume for the order, of which he himself is a worthy member, too much credit for its long-continued and extensive propagandism of the faith; but, keeping his praise within just bounds, makes the amplest acknowledgment to other missionaries when an opportunity offers. The author's style, also, is admirable. It is plain, bold, and exceedingly clear, and reminds us a good deal of the old days of classic English, which, we are sometimes tempted to fear, have departed for ever.

SERMONS BY THE FATHERS OF THE CONGREGATION OF ST. PAUL THE APOSTLE. New York: The Catholic Publication Society. 1872. 12mo, pp. 331.

This, the sixth volume of sermons, twenty-two in number, delivered by the Paulist Fathers of this city, has just been published, and in point of variety, ability, and adaptability to the everyday wants of Catholic congregations, may fairly be said to be equal, at least, to any of the preceding volumes from the same source. On first reading this valuable lection of sermons, the impres most likely to be produced on a man is surprise at the remark simplicity of style, earnestness argument, and, above all, the p tical application to the present dition of society, of the inspired t upon which the sermons are ba Men of the most ordinary com hension can understand them, we can imagine few minds so tracted or hearts so callous a be proof against their unado logic and impressive appeals. has sometimes been our good tune to have heard, as we have o read, exhortations of more brill cy, pathos, and even intellec power, but we are not aware t compressed within the limits o ordinary-sized book, there is to found in the English languag greater amount of wholesome tru well and clearly stated, or ter calculated to go directly to heart and conscience of the rea Of this character pre-emine are the sermons on "How to Pa Good Lent," "Humility in Pray and "The Sins and Miseries of Dram-Seller." In some respects latter differs from all others in collection—in its forcibleness rhetoric, and vividness, almost p ful, of description. Reading i the silence of our library, we aln shudder at the, alas! too trut picture drawn therein of the dru ard's fate in this world, and the less certain retribution wl awaits his mercenary temp here or hereafter. It is one of most powerful arguments aga the use and sale of intoxica liquors we have read since the of Father Mathew, and ought to in the hands of every advocate temperance, clerical and lay, in land. The three sermons trea of the temporal and spiritual au rity of the Sovereign Pontiff clear, distinct, and well-timed, besides being historically accu are replete with logical deducti one following and hinging on

other so harmoniously that conviction, even to a biassed mind, seems to follow as a matter of course.

But on a second and more critical perusal of this book, we are certain to discover new and equally commendable features. We feel as if we were in the presence of Catholic priests speaking to their spiritual children. There is an absence of all harshness or terrorism, and of that bitterness which too often accompanies the discussion of controversial subjects. While our errors are reproved and our sins denounced, hope and mercy are not denied us; the path of duty is plainly pointed out, but we are encouraged to tread its thorny ways, and we rise from the study of the *Sermons* conscious of our faults and weaknesses, without despairing, and with a renewed purpose of amendment. No one can read attentively the first and last of this series, on "Remembrance of Mercies" and "Fraternal Charity," without feeling softened and chastened in spirit. It is not, however, the mere contents of the sermons that we most admire. It is their suggestiveness. To a reflective mind there is matter enough in them to form the groundwork of a hundred discourses, and still the subjects would not be exhausted. This feature alone will extend their good influence far beyond the limits of one book or one pulpit. As we have come to a grand truth boldly stated, or a deduction logically and lucidly drawn, we have frequently found ourselves closing the book, and, following the drift of the reverend preacher's argument, preaching sermons to ourselves. If such be its effects on ordinary minds, how much more valuable will be the uses of this book to the younger members of the priesthood in the performance of the duties of their holy calling? And it is for them especially, we presume, it is intended.

Besides, as we are all aware, there are many persons with the best dispositions who, from family or other reasons, are frequently unable to hear a sermon on every Sunday and holyday of obligation, not only in country parishes, but even in our crowded cities. To this class the present volume ought to be of great value, affording them, as it does, an opportunity of reading in the seclusion of their homes, what they are debarred from hearing delivered orally. It is one of the rules of the faithful to consecrate a portion of each Sunday to hearing sermons, but, when this cannot be done, the reading of pious books is substituted, and we know of none recently published better calculated to edify and instruct a devout Catholic, or one so practical in its application to the wants and necessities of the present generation, as this collection of sermons; and it is for this reason that we heartily commend it to the laity of the United States.

MACARONIC POETRY. Collected, with an Introduction, by James Appleton Morgan, A.M. New York: Hurd & Houghton. 1872.

Of the many excellent specimens of the typography of the Riverside Press, the above-named work is one of the handsomest; and this merit is enhanced by the fact that the great variety of languages and characters, ancient and modern, used in its pages called for the best efforts of typographical skill and resources.

The title of the work gives but a modest idea of the wealth and diversity of its contents, which are creditable to the taste and industry of the author. We find in it not only all the most celebrated macaronic masterpieces, from the "Pugna Porcorum," of about three hundred lines, every word of which begins with the letter P, thus:

> "Plaudite, Porcelli, Porcorum pigra propago
> Progreditur, plures Porci pinguedine pleni.
> Pugnantes pergunt, pecudum pars prodigiosa," etc., etc.,

down to Dr. Maginn's "Second Ode to Horace," commencing.

"Blest man, who far from busy hum,
Ut prisca gens mortalium."

Then there are the literary trifles of the dipogrammatists and the pangrammatists, and curiosities in acrostics, telestics, anagrams, palindromes, sidonians, rhymed bagatelles, cento verses, chain verses, alliterative verses, and epitaphs. There are also some specimens of queer prescriptions, the whole family of which are but imitations of the celebrated recipe pasted on the door of the pharmacy in the Convent of the Capuchin Friars at Messina:

"Pro presenti corporis et æterna animæ salute.

RECIPE.

"Radicum fidei
Florum spei
Rosarum charitatis
Liliorum puritatis
Absynthé contritionis
Violarum humilitatis
Agarici satisfactionis
Ano quantum potes:
Misceatur omnia cum syrupe confessionis:
Terentur in mortario conscientiæ:
Solvantur in aqua lacrymarum;
Coquantur in igne tribulationis, et fiat potus.
Recipe de hoc mane et sera."

Any one may find much literary amusement in the volume, and to the Latin scholar in particular it affords material for many an hour of pleasant relaxation.

THE TAKING OF ROME BY THE ITALIAN ARMY, considered in its Causes and Effects. By C. M. Curci, S.J. Translated from the Italian by the Duke Della Torre. New York: D. Appleton & Co. 1871.

It is a matter of congratulation that we have among us at least one Italian gentleman of high rank, character, and education, who is a thoroughly loyal and devoted adherent of the Holy See. We are greatly indebted to the Duke Della Torre for translating F. Curci's *brochure*, prefixing to it a most sensible and excellent preface, and getting it published by our most eminent New York firm. The pamphlet itself is an able production of an able and celebrated writer. The only great fault in it is the discouraging tone it takes regarding the prospects of the temporal sovereignty of the Pope in the future—a point which has been strongly animadverted upon already in Europe. In so far as past facts are concerned, it is a thorough and unanswerable exposure of the fraud, violence, and perfidy of the Sub-Alpine government, and of the treachery and timidity of the policy of other European cabinets in their relations with the Pontifical States.

FLORENCE O'NEIL; or, The Siege of Limerick. By Agnes M. Stewart. Baltimore: Kelly, Piet & Co.

The eventful life and troublous times of James II. of England must always be a period of history mournfully interesting to every Catholic heart—those days of persecution, when throughout England a price was set upon the head of any priest who dared labor for the salvation of souls, all the penal laws against Catholics (some of them but lately repealed) being in full force.

The touching story of Florence O'Neil, who is represented as living in very constant intimacy with the royal exiles, carries us through those dark days, and gives us pictures of the court of the reprobate, hard-hearted daughter of James, where Florence was kept an unwilling captive for many months. Her journal during that time is written with charming simplicity, and the whole story has sufficient mingling of truth with the narrative to fill us with pity even for those crowned heads who lived harassed with anxious fears lest the sceptre so hastily and unjustly assumed should be as hastily snatched from their grasp; trusting nobody, never at rest from plottings and re-plottings even in their own household. In contrast with this, we have the devoted domestic life at the Château St. Germaine, sketched with a delicate and refined touch, giving us a lovely picture of wedded bliss in the union of James with his beautiful and tenderly attached wife—

ing none formally, endeavoring to possess at the same time the esteem of both Christians and pagans. The delineation of the vacillating spirit of many of the finest intellects among the Greeks, their proud, patronizing ways towards God's church, cannot but remind the careful reader of the position of many of the so-called *intellectual giants* of to-day.

The multiplicity of characters introduced, and the demand for mythological research which is necessary to make the story clear in all its parts, are rather detrimental to the unity of the tale; nevertheless, the story of Pelagia herself, and Nicephorus her lover, with their remarkable conversion and subsequent abandonment of the world, is very touching, and wrought out with simplicity and earnestness—the wonderful faith of Pelagia contrasting with the criticisms and doubts, and the ingenious hypotheses of Hypatia, whose strange life and fearful death have been the comment of historian and novelist.

The book contains many pages full of interest concerning Simon Stylites and the wonders of his life, besides several chapters devoted to charming descriptions of the monks who flocked in those times to monasteries in the deserts of Nitria and Tabenna, along the borders of the Nile, and even to Mount Sinai. One of the most attractive features of the volume will be found in the delightful conversations of these monks, enlivened with legends of those olden times, and pervaded throughout with a lovely, Christ-like spirit, which makes their religion an object of admiration even to the wise pagans around them.

JAPAN IN OUR DAY. Compiled and arranged by Bayard Taylor. New York: Charles Scribner & Co. 1872. 1 vol. 12mo.

This is the first volume of the *Illustrated Library of Travel, Exploration, and Adventure*, now in course of publication by Messrs. Scribner, & Co. and edited by Bayard Ta To those who take an intere Japanese affairs the volume prove interesting, as containin latest information with regar that country so long almost known.

SADLIERS' CATHOLIC DIRECTORY, NAC, AND ORDO FOR THE YEAR O LORD 1872. With full Report various Dioceses in the United and British North America, and of the Archbishops, Bishops, and F in Ireland. New York: D. & J lier & Co., 31 Barclay Street.

The *Almanac* for this year h peared. The sewing, type, an per are much better than in fo years. There are not so many takes in this as we noticed i previous volume. We are a there are many difficulties con ed with the publication of a s tical work which nothing bu utmost patience and persever will overcome, and are ther pleased to notice even slight provements.

THE AMERICAN HOME BOOK OF IN GAMES, AMUSEMENTS, AND OC TIONS. By Mrs. Caroline L. Smith (Carrie). Illustrated. Boston: L Shepard. New York: Lee, Shep Dillingham. 1872.

This book is one of the best o kind. The selection of games, am ments, etc., is very good, and directions given in regard to t are short, simple, and clear. It not fail to add to the happines any home it may enter.

THE WONDERS OF WATER. From French of Gaston Tissandier. Ed with numerous Additions, by S De Vere, D.D., LL.D. New Y Charles Scribner & Co. 1872. 1 12mo.

A most interesting and useful l volume, containing valuable i mation in regard to the use water, the history of artesian w ancient and modern water-w etc., etc. The book is elegantl up and well illustrated.

small army of literary and theological stragglers, bummers, and disgraced deserters hovering on the rear of these regular forces, always in the field with lectures, pamphlets, keys to Popery, horrible disclosures, and all the pestilent riff-raff of anti-Catholic literature. One would think the Protestant army of observation on such a footing sufficiently well-organized, active, and effective to guard the walls of the American Zion and sound a timely alarm.

But the publishing firm of Messrs. Harper & Brothers is not of that opinion, and they appear to have discovered that it is their duty to take under their special protection and keeping the public schools, the Bible, the Protestant religion, and the liberties of America;—thus demonstrating the wretched incapacity and utter failure of our civil authorities, our religious press, and the Protestant ministry to do their plainest duty. The gentlemen in question publish, here in New York, *Harper's Monthly Magazine*, and a hebdomadal called *Harper's Weekly: A Journal of Civilization.* These periodicals contain a variety of light literature, papers on current topics, poetry, anecdotes, and highly-flavored anti-Popery articles. Besides these last, the *Weekly* generally has one or more caricatures calculated to disseminate the worst falsehoods, and to excite hatred towards Catholics and contempt for their religion.

For years past, a constantly recurring subject of its most offensive form of caricature has been the person of the venerable Pontiff Pius IX. It is difficult to conceive how any man of even ordinary instincts of propriety —we care not what his religious prejudices might be—could have for this revered personage any feeling but one of profound respect. An aged bishop, fourscore years of age, whose purity of character is speck or stain, whose long l been one of labor and use piety and virtue, beginning hi dotal career as a missionar foreign land, then serving fa as the director of charitable tions and hospitals, whose first power were those of benevole universal amnesty, toward wh the part of the tens of thous Protestants who have seen and with him, no sentiments but t profound admiration and ver are ever expressed—such a ch as this is selected by the *Jou Civilization* as the favorite bu indecent ribaldry.

We here leave entirely out all consideration of the ques outrage upon the religious se ties of millions of Catholics United States, and place th ment of the offence upon the ground of civilized propriety men who perpetrate this seek to justify themselves on t that it is as king or tempor reign of Rome they caricatu Their offence is aggravated flimsy and paltry a pretext merits of the disputes among t narchs of Europe do not c us here in America to that and if they did, as a question narchical right and precede seniority, the kings and emper Europe are all new-comers a starts by the side of the Roma tiff.

While these caricatures are tially addressed to a sentim religious bigotry, their authors by the false association of so litical idea, not only to excus on that ground, but to reinfor bigotry with all the strength o tical hatred. Take, for instan filthy crocodile picture. Ther appeal whose falsity is only ex

shameful malversations of a religious Book Concern, to the gigantic thefts in our city administration, to the Drew complication of the Erie abomination, which shines by its absence in all the late *Harper* chronicles; and, having completed his catalogue, to present and denounce these crimes as the legitimate result of the teachings of the Methodist Church. It would be waste of words to point out the false reasoning, the injustice, the malice of such a performance. For, however Christian sects may differ on doctrinal points, and whatever may be alleged as to the extent of their theological errors, none of them deliberately teach immorality, and all inculcate the precepts of the decalogue.

What, then, shall be thought of a journal which, week after week, loudly and persistently, not only accuses the Catholic Church in the persons of her ministers of teaching the most flagrant immorality, but seeks—coupling with this grave charge the imputation of striving to create civil discord—by every artifice of rhetoric, by every device of exaggeration, by every appeal of gross caricature, to arouse the wildest passions and the fiercest bigotry? The journal in question labors to stir up, and it does stir up, bad blood and hot strife among hitherto peaceful neighbors.

The charge is a serious one, and we make it knowingly. Instances and illustrations in its support may be found in nearly all the numbers of the *Weekly* for years past.

For its anti-Catholic operations, the *Journal* is used as a sort of tender to the heavy transport, the *Monthly*, which frequently gives its readers long, elaborate, and malicious articles, made up mainly of exploded calumnies, threadbare anti-Popery rhetoric of the school of Brownlee and the early Know-Nothings, and the extraordinary lucubrations of a contributor whom we can only describe as Harper's comic historian. This singular writer undertakes to demonstrate, for instance, that the Apostle of Ireland was not a Catholic missionary at all, but in religious faith a sort of Old-School Presbyterian, who went about distributing Bibles among the "savage Irish," making strong "anti-Popery" speeches, and delivering lectures on popular education to the serfs of his day!

Absurd as these articles are from a literary point of view, they are yet full of inflammable material, and play as recklessly with fire as the more brutal incentives of the *Weekly*. For it must be borne in mind that most of these direct appeals to religious bigotry are intended not so much for home consumption as for their effect upon the general rural mind, and that their evident purpose is to arouse another Know-Nothing revival throughout the country.

There are, unfortunately, too many people thoughtless enough, or, perhaps, wicked enough, to respond to these incentives—people so far forgetting themselves as to imagine that their own religion, or something which they imagine stands for it, must be the state church in America, and that it is free to them to persecute and outlaw the professors of a faith which, in their ignorance, they despise and hate.

But we are satisfied that, on the other hand, there is too much intelligence, moderation, forbearance, and patriotism among American citizens to permit the success of schemes aimed at once against liberty of conscience, the peace of society, and the true freedom of our institutions.

And among these citizens we rank —by no means the last—the

perfect equality. The lady in the parlor and the servant in her kitchen abide by the same religious observances, the rich banker and his poorest clerk hold precisely the same faith, and the wealthy merchant and his drayman out there in the street, kneel at the same altar. We are aware that all this is "horridly ungenteel," but it is an old habit of our people. Eighteen hundred years ago and more, we were assured that the poor we have always. And we have them. They never leave us, and are not likely to. Poor-houses came in with the Reformation, and then poverty first became disgraceful. For poverty, and, yet more, for the shame of poverty, the needy and wretched cannot enter elegant Protestant conventicles.

And now that we have seen the nature and complexion of the attempted revival of Know-Nothing violence, it may be asked, Who are the men who promote it, creating prejudice, fostering bigotry, inflaming religious rancor, arraying neighbor against neighbor, and endangering the peace of the community? Have they a special mission from on high? Are their scribes inspired writers? Or, perchance, are the antecedents of those publishers and proprietors such as to have established a character for pure patriotism and disinterested virtue so pre-eminently superior as to authorize them to set themselves up the self-constituted guardians of American liberty and evangelical Christianity?

We propose to examine these questions in the light of the printed record of the responsible proprietors of the *Journal of Civilization.* To that printed record we shall strictly confine ourselves. And in taking the first step toward the fulfilment of our duty, we regret that circumstances will compel the revelation of some

AWFUL DISCLOSURE

The excitement and vio
nunciation of Catholicity
many years ago by the pu
of an infamous book said
been written by one Maria
still remembered among us
as the thorough exposure of
falsehood, made by Colonel
New York, and other P
gentlemen.

The book was entitled *Th*
Disclosures of Maria Monk,
its title-page purported to be
ed by *Howe and Bates.* H
Bates! Who were Howe an
There was none to mak
For neither to the book trac
the flesh were "Howe and
ever known of mortal man.

As to the character of the
question, we are further enl
by the author of a work entitl
testant Jesuitism, by a Pro
published by the Harpers
At page 34 of the book,
Monk's work is described
of the most arrant fictio
was ever palmed upon the
munity," and the author adds
people of this land—and it
common attribute of hum
ture—love excitement, and
tunately there are those wh
how to produce it, and profit
Unfortunate, indeed, it is tha
are those who stand ready t
by foul slander and malignan
hood concerning their n
Unfortunate, indeed, that m
be found who, for the sake o
dollars, could consent to
broadcast upon the world, pri
lification and outrage of nobl
minded women, who, solely
love of God and out of the
abundant charity, devote the
to alleviating the sufferings
needy, the afflicted, and th

: they who profited by it? If
obtain a satisfactory answer
question, we may probably be
the way toward solving the
which hovers over the exis-
"Howe and Bates."
. Monk's disclosures were not
e in the book published by
newhat nebulous firm. The
wful" of all her "awful dis-
" were made in the dignified
a bill in equity which she filed
her publishers, who, by their
nissions and declarations, turn
be not "Howe and Bates,"
m this moment for ever dis-
rom view, but Messrs. James,
seph W., and Fletcher Har-

bill filed for discovery and
against the defendants as
ers and publishers by Maria
a minor, through her next
hows that complainant was
s of a work which she had
ited and stereotyped, and
l stereotype plates were paid
her with money belonging
and that she was liable
balance unpaid; that after
yright had been so taken
said plates got into the pos-
of the defendants, and that
d published the work under
of "*Awful Disclosures of Ma-
k*, as exhibited in a narrative
sufferings during a residence
years as a novice, and two
s a black nun, in the Hôtel
t Montreal." Further, that
a minor, was entirely unac-
l with the modes of doing
, that she believed that per-
fessing to be her friends had
ome bargains for her in rela-
said work, that this was
to the defendants, and yet
tended to take out another
it of the same work in the
of Massachusetts, and published a large number of impressions from the plates, and issued the book; and that they had large profits in their hands which belonged to the complainant.

Prayer that the said James, John, Joseph W., and Fletcher Harper make full statement, etc., and deliver over all sums of money and property, with account of sales and amount received for same.

We have had occasion to see that the proprietors of the *Journal of Civilisation* are fiercely patriotic. And they were so, long before that civilizing journal was founded. Their first impulse on receiving a copy of this latest "awful disclosure" by Maria Monk was an impulse of patriotism, of indignation that a foreigner should presume to expect copyright protection in the United States. Thrice is he armed who has statutory law, patriotism, and an act of Congress upon which to fall back, and the defendants, in such panoply as that, straightway filed a demurrer.* Maria Monk's copyright was first issued and had precedence of seniority, but respondents demurred, first and principally, on the ground that "the complainant did not show herself to be a citizen entitled to take out a copyright." The demurrer also set up other matters in avoidance.

In deciding the case, the Vice-Chancellor closed the delivery of his opinion by saying: "It [the bill] does not show any privity of contract or dealing between the parties; no agreement expressed or implied by which the defendants can be held to account to the complainant for the profits of the work. It rather shows

* Demurrer is thus defined; "A stop or pause by a party to an action for the judgment of the court on the question, whether, assuming the truth of the matter alleged by the opposite party, it is sufficient in law to sustain the action, and hence whether the party resting is bound to answer or proceed further."

that, by fraud or wrong, the defendants obtained possession of the stereotype plates, and, altering the title of the book to that of *Awful Disclosures*, etc., published it in defiance of her rights. If she has sustained loss by such conduct of the defendants, she must persuade a jury to give her compensation in a verdict of damages against them, when, perhaps, the merits of her *Awful Disclosures* and *Nunnery Unveiled, and the motives of those who have promoted and prompted the publication, will duly be considered.*"

Demurrer sustained, and bill dismissed at costs of complainant.

All of which, and more, may be found in *Edwards's Chancery Reports*, vol. iii., p. 109.

PAST AND PRESENT.

Within the past twelve years, a new generation of readers has grown up in the United States—a generation far outnumbering its predecessor, and the circulation of the journal published by the Harper Brothers has increased immensely. The great body of its readers of to-day are profoundly impressed with a sense of its unvarying and undying patriotism, and it probably never occurs to the soldier who, when a mere boy, shouldered his musket in defence of the Union, that his now furiously patriotic *Harper's Weekly* was originally, and as long as it was found to pay, the advocate of secession and the apologist of slavery. How sadly true this is, we propose to show by presenting the results of our examination into

THE JOURNAL IN THE HOUR OF TRIAL.

On opening the volume of the *Weekly* for the year 1861, we felt quite confident of finding an admirably executed full-length picture of the then President-elect of the United States, and confess to some disappointment when, instead thereof, occupying the entire first page, we discover portraits of "The Georgia Delegation in Congress," followed by sketches highly laudatory of the seven gentlemen composing the delegation. The same number makes calm and commentless record of "The South Carolina Proclamation of Independence," and the spread of secession through the South.

January 12, 1861.—Under the heading "The Great Southern Movement," the publishers "beg to draw attention to the following list of illustrations of the *Pending Revolution*," such unseemly words as rebellion and treachery being left to the unprincipled Abolition papers of that day. In the same number we have "The Revolution at Charleston" in cuts of "Anderson at Sumter" and "The Charleston Militia taking Fort Pickens"—thus making a nice balance. Doubtless the Lincoln portrait will come in our next number.

Why, what are these? Portraits and laudatory notices of Governor Pickens, Honorable Judge McGrath, and "Rev. Dr. Bachman, who asked a blessing on the Secession Ordinance," the signing of which, according to the fervid account cited from a Charleston paper, was a scene "profoundly grand and impressive"; there were "patriarchs in age—the dignitaries of the land—the high-priests of the church of Christ—reverend statesmen—and wise judges of the law"—in the midst of whom "the President advanced with the consecrated parchment"—which holy document was the ordinance of secession. We continue turning leaf after leaf with but slight edification—Skating Park—Old Fashions—Humors of the Day—Rarey the Horse

illustrate, those topics upon which he addresses the House."

Naturally enough follows, on page 88, a View of the City of Montgomery, showing the state-house where "THE CONGRESS OF THE SOUTHERN CONFEDERACY MEETS."

February 16, 1861.— Concerning so-called stay-laws passed in the South, which were at the time generally understood to mean practical repudiation of mercantile debts due to the North, hark how sweetly sings the Northern secession siren with elaborate Harp accompaniment: "We trust that our Southern friends will believe that we have no partisan purpose in view if we direct their attention to the fatal consequences of the stay-laws, etc., etc. For many years our Southern States have enjoyed first-rate credit, both at the North and abroad. Southern obligations have always been preferred in New York to obligations from the East or West. . . . Southern men have been considered here as good under all circumstances. Their honor has been relied on to any extent. *Houses which would not trust Western or Eastern dealers a hundred dollars have been delighted to give credits of thousands to Southerners.* The simple reason was that people have had an undying faith in the honor of the Southern people—a firm conviction that under no circumstances would they seek to evade payment of their debts." And here the siren's song is broken by a gush of tears— "Is this faith, is this conviction to be demolished now by the passage of stay-laws?" Then follow the perennial "View of Sumter," double-page Paris fashions, etc., until we reach (p. 109) Views of the "Mint and the New Custom House," New Orleans, "of which the United States have had only a brief occupancy"— "both of which have been seized by the state authorities." There is no comment on this "seizure" by the state authorities, but more than three months afterward we shall find "civilization" waking up in wrath and fulminating thus: "All that the rebels of New Orleans wanted when they stole the mint was to be let alone." In this same number (p. 112) we have the sneering caricature of the calamity of the country which at the time afforded the enemies of the American Union exquisite delight and "prolonged shouts of laughter." It is entitled "*The Crippled American Eagle, the Cock, and the Lion.*" To the eagle, dilapidated, lame, and on crutches: "LION.—Why, Brother Jonathan, you don't look so fierce as you used. How about the Monroe Doctrine now? COCK.—Yes, my good Jonathan, what you tink of PRIVATEERING under de present circumstance?"

At last, in the number of February 23, we reach portraits of "President and Vice-President"—what? surely we must be mistaken! No—the print is very clear in its large capitals—"Of the Southern Confederacy." And very good portraits they are, too, but not of the President and Vice-President we were expecting to see. The number of March 2 gives us a full-page woodcut of "The President-elect Addressing the People." The "people" are represented by twenty-six hats and the scanty outlines of eleven men, but in compensation we have a thrilling view of two gigantic lamp-posts, and, in exaggerated disproportion, the pillars of the balcony over the centre of whose summit appears the upper half of a small, lean figure supposed to be that of A. Lincoln. This is somewhat disappointing, but, by way of consolation, the next page enlightens us on the subject of patriotism:

e subject of patriotism is in a
way of being more thoroughly
lated than it ever was before.
ybody appears to admit that
otism is a virtue, and that a
should love his country. But
uestion arises at every corner,
t is our country?" The topic
strated by watery hypotheses
Smith, Jones, and Thomson,
he editor adds some strong milk
water with—"Can he claim the
of patriot if he loves his state
and confesses no obligation to
st of the confederacy?"
r men who have progressed far
gh in constitutional law and pa-
m to call the Union a confedera-
e have strong hopes. Further
under heading, "The Southern
federacy," we are advised that
President has nominated"—
d so—"to his cabinet." Then
ws "President Davis's Inaugu-
—not the President we are look-
or. Then come "Snake Stories,"
nt Maria," "The Mazed Fid-
" "Romance by Lever"—plea-
reading for perilous times—un-
last, our search is ended, our
nce rewarded, and at page 144,
e number of March 2, 1861,
ave a full-length portrait of
ham Lincoln, President-elect of
nited States. It is

A REMARKABLE PICTURE.

Indeed a picture so remarkable
we would advise every Ameri-
who voted for Mr. Lincoln, eve-
merican who, whether he voted
r against him, yet credited him
the reputation of being at
a decent person, and every man,
hatever nationality, who consid-
him not positively a degraded
r—we would advise all such, if
can find a copy of *Harper's*
ly *Journal of Civilization*, of March 2, 1861, to contemplate and study that picture, and then form their opinion of the Christianity and the patriotism of the men who, at that crisis of the country's fate, and in that dangerous hour of feverish excitement and political passion, could, in cold blood, spread such a firebrand sketch broadcast through the land. We further commend this counsel more especially to those present readers and approvers of the *Journal of Civilization* who cherish the memory of a murdered President whom they remember as at least blameless in life, pure in character, kind of heart, charitable in impulse, and noble in patriotism.

We will endeavor to describe the drawing. Mr. Lincoln is represented, in a room at the Astor House, standing, or rather staggering, under the influence of liquor, with a just emptied glass in his hand. He is surrounded by four boon companions, two of them with drunken leer and Bardolphian noses; a third in the background looks vacantly on with expression of maudlin stupidity; while the fourth, like the rest, glass in hand, stands at the open window, and—partially sobered by the shock—gazes at a passing funeral procession. On the moving hearse, accompanied by mourners and decked with solemn black plumes, are inscribed the words:

UNION,

CONSTITUTION.

Under this work of art—a wretched, scratchy woodcut—we read:

OUR PRESIDENTIAL MERRY-MAN.

"The Presidential party was engaged in a lively exchange of wit and humor. The President-elect was the merriest among the merry, and kept those around him in a continual roar."
—*Daily Paper*.

Now, let it be borne in mind that this very suggestive piece of malice was published just on the eve of Mr. Lincoln's inauguration at Washington, whose atmosphere was black with lowering clouds of rebellion, where threats were rife that he would never take his seat in the Presidential chair, and where men's minds were already warped and inflamed by misrepresentations and falsehoods concerning him, the belief in which by a large portion of the community would seriously blunt any sharp opprobrium of murder, and soften down assassination to the meritorious taking off of an unworthy drunken demagogue. If the conductors of this organ of "civilization" are capable of giving the greatest publicity to a horrible caricature on such a subject, and at a moment fraught with such dreadful contingencies, need there be any room for surprise that they do not stickle at far worse when the subjects of their defamation are "only Catholics"?

ANOTHER PICTURE.

But we have not yet done with this number of March 2. It was the strongest bid of the journal for Southern favor and patronage. On the same page with the cut we have described is another, a more elaborate, more artistic, and better executed picture. Scene: Interior of a church—pews full of worshippers—minister officiating — administration of the sacrament. At the chancel railing kneels George Washington. With one hand, the clergyman standing in the sanctuary holds away the cup from the would-be communicant, and with the other contemptuously waves him off. The Father of his Country makes a gesture of indignant remonstrance, while the minister's assistant with a long stick points to a tablet in the wall, on which are engraved the words:

THE HIGHER LAW.

NO COMMUNION
WITH
SLAVEHOLDERS.

Is the reader edified? There is more to come. The officiating minister is Henry Ward Beecher—an unmistakable portrait. His assistant is John Brown—an excellent likeness—and the pointer he uses is one of the well-known "Harper's Ferry Pikes." Under the engraving we read:

NO COMMUNION WITH SLAVEHOLDERS.

"Stand aside, you Old Sinner! We are holier than thou."

Will the members of Plymouth Church in Brooklyn, who now see the efforts of the journal to misrepresent Catholics in doctrine and in morals, please read these efforts by the light of this George Washington picture?

We also commend careful examination of this picture to the friends and admirers of Mr. Beecher. Let them ask themselves this question: Would the men who, for the sake of a little larger circulation, do not hesitate to caricature their own Protestant co-religionists—would these men, we say, be reasonably expected to be very scrupulous in the vilification of those whose Catholic faith they detest?

And for similar reasons, we commend consideration of both these pictures to all readers of a *Journal of Civilization* which, week after week, by innuendo, assertion, falsehood, and caricature, strives to awaken the lowest prejudices of religious

the inauguration is described as "solemn and impressive."

At page 160 (March 9) we have a cartoon of four vulgar caricatures, entitled collectively "The Flight of Abraham" (as reported by a Modern Daily Paper), and separately: (1.) THE ALARM.—A gaunt figure sits upright in bed with night-cap on. A lantern is held in at the open door, from which come the words: "Run, Abe, for your life, the Blood Tubs are after you!!!" (2.) THE COUNCIL. — General Sumner, with a pair of large cavalry boots in one hand, and in the other a handkerchief which he holds to his eyes, weeping vociferously — boo - o - o, stands near "Abe"; on the other side is Mrs. Lincoln in dowdy dishabille, crying bitterly, "Do go!" (3.) THE SPECIAL TRAIN.—"He wore a Scotch plaid cap and a very long military cloak, so that he was entirely unrecognizable" — an ignoble picture. (4.) THE OLD COMPLAINT.—Lincoln presents himself to the astonished Buchanan dissolved with fright, while Seward whispers to Buchanan, "Only a little attack of ager, your excellency."

Editorial correspondence at page 162 gives us the valuable information that "Senator Wigfall is a finished orator—probably the most charming in the senate," and that he is "the exact opposite of Chandler and Wilkinson"—"very unpleasant speakers to listen to." Senator Mason, we are told, "with all his faults is perhaps the nearest approach in the present senate to the beau ideal of a senator." At page 168 (March 16) we have a large cut representing "The Inauguration of Abraham Lincoln *as* President of the United States," and we cannot help contrasting the phraseology of this announcement with a previous one: "Inauguration of President Jefferson Davis of the Southern Confederacy."

And so we progress to April 27, 1861, page 258, where we find President Lincoln's Proclamation of April 15 thus announced: "War is declared. President Lincoln's proclamation, which we publish above, is an absolute proclamation of war against the Gulf States." Better late than never, we at last, after long, weary waiting, find in this number, page 268, the long-looked-for "Portrait of the President," accompanied by a biographical sketch of Mr. Lincoln. It was really high time that the readers of the *Civilization* should be told something of their President nearly two months after he had assumed the reins of government. To make everything pleasant and impartial, however, the opposite page gives us the copy of a full-length photograph of General Beauregard. Having paid your money, choice is optional.

We have thus seen with what persistence and industry the *Journal*, during the long, critical months of the beginning of that eventful year 1861, was the ardent panegyrist of everything Southern, the stern rebuker and enemy of anti-slavery, the mocker and caricaturist of Northern Union sentiment, and the contemptuous sneerer at Abraham Lincoln. But all this fine talk about principle and lofty assumption of stern virtue was a mere question of circulation, and the sympathy of the *Journal* went with its pecuniary benefit, so far and no farther.

The immutability of its principles was subject to be disturbed by just such considerations as those which carried conviction to the understanding of Hans Breitman, and which he so admirably explained in his great political speech:

"Dese ish de brinciples I holts,
 And dose in vitch I run:
Dey ish fixed firm and immutaple
 Ash te course of de 'ternal sun:

—ut if you tink [illegible] of dem—
[illegible] vot I say—
shall only be too happy
To alder dem right avay."*

n an editorial leader of May e hear that the *Weekly* is in of abusive and threatening from various persons in the rn States, the cause assigned ch rude conduct is "the statem *our editorial of March* 4, to ct that civil war between the *tates on one side and the Slave on the other* will inevitably, or later, become a war of pation," etc., etc. The readnotice here that the expres-Free States on one side and ve States on the other," just rly and forcibly puts forth the e of state sovereignty and the f secession, as does the title nander Stephens's late work, in the smallest of nut-shells, he same doctrine in the few *The War between the States.* at is of as great importance the contingent danger of pation was not presented by rnal at so early a date as 4. There is no such editorial rch 4, there is no editorial of al of March 4, and, moreover, was no number of *Harper's* published on that date. The l referred to appeared *May* nd here we would frankly t we are quite willing to acis March 4 for May 4 as the f mistake, oversight, or careoof-reading.

i the abusive and threatening came advices that "In Tennessee vigilance committees forbid its (*Harper's*) being sold." "In Louisiana, the governor prohibits its distribution through the post-office." And now, the Harpers, like Macbeth, have heard enough, and, seized with the frenzy of patriotism, thunder after this fashion:

"As for *Harper's Weekly*, it will continue, *as heretofore*, to support the government of the United States,* the stars and stripes,† and the indivisible union ‡ of thirty-four states.

"We know no other course § consistent with the duty of citizens, Christians, and honest men. If any subscriber to this journal expects us to give our aid or countenance to rebellion ‖ against the government, he will be disappointed. If any man buys this journal expecting to find us apologize for treason,¶ robbery, rebellion, piracy, or murder, he will be disappointed. That is not our line of business. The proprietors of *Harper's Weekly* would rather stop this journal to-morrow than publish a line in it which would hereafter cause their children to blush for the patriotism or the manhood of their parents."

* give this passage not only because we [illegible], but also to vindicate the witty [illegible] the [illegible] aspersions of the *Harper's* [illegible] deliberately reaches the solemn opin-"in Hans Breitman there is nothing it the grotesque dress. Translate his nto English, and it is, with here and solitary exception, the baldest of all laces."

* "Wanted, a Capital."

† "The Crippled American Eagle."

‡ "There can be no question but the enterprise of holding the Union together by force would ultimately prove futile. *It would be in violation of the principle of our institutions.*"—*Harper's Weekly, editorial leader of March* 9, 1861.

"If the Union is really injurious to them (our Southern friends), heaven forbid that we should insist on preserving it."—*Harper's Weekly*, 1861, p. 146.

§ "Most of them" ("alterations in the Constitution *effected by the Congress at Montgomery*") "would receive the hearty support of the people of the North."—*Harper's Weekly, March* 30, 1861.

"Some practical people, viewing the dissolution of the Union as a fixed fact."—*Weekly, Jan.* 26, 1861.

‖ "Is it wise, is it prudent, is it possible to punish it?"—*Harper's Weekly*, p. 146, 1861.

¶ "He [Jeff. Davis] is emphatically one of those 'born to command,' and is doubtless destined to occupy a high position, either in the Southern Confederacy or in the United States."—*Weekly, Feb.* 2, 1861.

This sharp change of sentiment, this sudden right-about face, may be best illustrated by the notes we have appended and by the utterances of the *Journal* before and after certain occurrences.

BEFORE.

Editorial (leader) March 30, 1861, *entitled "The Two Constitutions."*

"The Const'tution of the Southern Confederacy has been published. It is a copy of the original Constitution of the United States, with some variations. The principal variations are" — nineteen of these are then described, and the article concludes: "We have thus enumerated the principal alterations in the Constitution effected by the Congress at Montgomery. *Most of them would receive the hearty support of the people of the North. But comment is superfluous.*"

Editorial (leader) April 20, 1861.

It begins by stating that Virginia affirms "the right of a state to secede from the Union at will," and that Missouri and Kentucky "declare that, in the event of forcible measures by the general government to resist the dismemberment of the Union, they will take sides with the seceded states."

"It seems questionable," continues the *Weekly*, "whether the continued alliance of these states, on these conditions, is an unmixed gain. If this Union of ours is a confederacy of states which is liable to be dissolved at the will of any of the states, and if no power rests with the general government to enforce its laws, it would seem that we have been laboring under a delusion these eighty years in supposing that we were a nation, and the fact would appear to be that," etc., etc., etc.

Editorial "Better than Dollars," April 20, 1861.

Portrait of the typical Northern man in contrast with the typical Southern man, in which the first is described as mean, avaricious, and unprincipled. "Cotton Pork is a Northern man, mostly from New England, though often transplanted to New York, and doing well in our climate. Some varieties of his genius have been tried at the South, but they don't

AFTER.

Editorial (leader) May 18, 1861.

"Mr. Jefferson Davis, Ex-Senator from Mississippi, has transmitted to the sel council of rebels at Montgomery a docu ment which he calls 'A Message.' It is most ingenious and plausible statemen of their case. Mr. Jefferson Davis is renowned for having made the most specious argument on record in justificatioa of Mississippi repudiation. He has not forgotten his cunning. His 'M essage' would almost persuade us—if we would forget facts and law—that rebellion is right, and the maintenance of government and the enforcement of law a barefaced usurpation."

Editorial (leader) June 8, 1861.

"The rebellion in this country has not half the excuse that the Sepoys had. The Indian soldiers were at least standing upon their own soil and opposing a foreign race which had vanquished them by arms. It was a blind stroke for the independence of their nationality. But the Davis rebellion is the resistance of a faction of citizens against the government of all; and the liberty for which they claim that they are fighting means baldly and only the liberty of holding other people in slavery."*

Editorial May 18, 1861, *headed "In Memoriam."*

"They have led us by the nose, and kicked us, and laughed at us, and scorned us in their very souls as cravens and tuppeny tinkers. They have swelled, and swaggered, and sworn, and lorded it in Washington and at the North, as if they

* "Stand aside, you Old Sinner! We are holier than thou!"—OUR COMMENT.

ne. They can't stand so much

e South—an odd region—dol-
well thought of, to be sure, but
don't govern. . . . It seems
e, but people talk and think
re about honor at the South than
llars."

Pork, we are told, "is *for his
f dollars are on his country's side,
he crawls on his belly to lick the
e enemy who offers him dollars.*"

ge how differently they talk
uth! They spend no energy in
ng civil war. They do not want
They seek peace. But if it comes,
make no wry faces. It will cost
h, but they utter no such phil-
shrieks as proceed from the
Cotton Pork. They seem to
t there are things worse than
in this world, and better than
An odd people, surely."

were peculiarly *gentlemen*,* because they have lived by the labor of wretched men and women whom they did not pay—whom they sell to pay their debts, and whipped and maimed savagely at their pleasure. They have snorted superciliously about their rights, while they deprived four millions of human beings of all rights whatsoever, and have sought to gain such control of the general government that they might override altogether the state laws which protect the equal rights of men. They have aimed to destroy the beneficent, popular system which peacefully and patiently and lawfully was working out the great problem of civilization; and while they have been digging about the foundations of the temple to make sure of its downfall, they have loftily replied to our inquiries, 'We only want to be let alone.'"

ust that the Southern gentle-
l Cotton Pork, Esq., "a Nor-
an," are pleased with their
e portraits.

ave long and patiently borne
insults and aspersions upon
h and conduct as Catholics
in for years by *Harper's*
Trusting that better coun-
ld prevail, and unwilling to
controversy a single spark to
already kindled, we have
from day to day, and from
to month, saying what we
any time have said.

aware of the by no means
e "anti-Popery" antecedents
oprietors, of their palpably
g motive, and of the specu-
ey saw at the bottom of the
nt, we might, so far as we
onally concerned, have look-
the malicious movement as
ing serious attention.

e are also aware to how
extent the prestige of the
nd commercial standing of
publishing-house, the wide-
culation of their periodi-
those especially their noisy
and incessant proclamation of a patriotism claimed as at once unvarying, inflexible, unselfish, and devoted, had misled or blinded the general public, ignorant of their real precedents, and we have, therefore, found it our duty to enlighten as well our own readers as those of the *Weekly* as to the real state of the case.

In so doing, we wish to call attention to the fact that we have here confined ourselves to the information furnished by public judicial decisions, and to their own record as published by themselves.

Finally, we most earnestly, and in the spirit of charity, urge these gentlemen to devote themselves to their plain, and what they may make their noble, duty as journalists. Let them be advised for their own good to cease fanning the flame of a hateful bigotry, and to pursue in the future such a course as may induce right-minded men to look upon their title-page illustration as indeed the flambeau of civilization, and not the torch of the incendiary.

* So italicized in the article.

THE HOUSE OF YORKE.

CHAPTER XXIII.

THE TOWN-MEETING.

BEFORE allowing her husband to go to the town-meeting, Mrs. Yorke had given him a word of admonition, not the usual wifely charge to keep himself out of danger, but an exhortation to justice and reason.

"Justice and reason!" he exclaimed. "Why, for what else have I been contending, Mrs. Yorke?"

"True!" she answered gently. "But may it not be possible that there is more cause than you will allow for this upheaval, and that it is not a superficial excitement which can be easily soothed or beaten down? These sailor friends of ours have told me that, when the water is dimpled and green, it has a sand bottom, and, when it is black and easily fretted into foam, there are rocks underneath. Now, this anti-Catholic excitement is dark and bitter enough to show that there is some fixed obstacle, which breath, though it be ever so wisely syllabled, will not remove."

"So there is," Mr. Yorke replied promptly. "The devil is there."

"Charles, the devil, or human weakness, lurks under the surface of every side of every question," his wife said with earnestness. "Good men are not entirely good, nor bad men utterly bad. There are men, and not ignorant ones, either, who have engaged in this movement from an honest conviction that there is need of it. They may be prejudiced and short-sighted, but they are worthy of a patient, if not a respectful, hearing. My wish is th[a] night you would be in no ha[ste to] speak, and that, when you do [speak,] you would address the real me[aning] of the trouble, and not the mis[...] froth on the surface."

What man likes to be told th[at he] is not reason personified, espe[cially] by his wife? Not Mr. C[harles] Yorke, certainly. But the littl[e ...] was not one to be scouted, ev[en by] her liege lord, and he heard h[er re-]spectfully to the end. Ma[...] must be asserted, however, an[d he] compensated himself for the m[orti]cation after a manner that is [often] adopted by both men and wo[men:] he first absurdly exaggerated [the] charge made against him, and answered to that exaggeration.

"I am much obliged to yo[u, my] dear, for explaining the matt[er to] me," he said with an air of meel[ness.] "I am afraid that I cannot st[ay to] hear more, for it is time to go. I will remember your warning, [and] try not to make a fool of myself."

Nine women out of ten [would] have made the reply which su[ch a] pretence is calculated to call for[th:] shocked and distressed denia[l of] having had any such meanin[g,] senseless begging pardon for h[aving] been so misunderstood, and a [...] giving up of the point, and te[mpo]rary utter humiliation and [...] followed later, on thinking the [mat]ter over, by a mental recurren[ce to] their abandoned position, and [...]

ing conviction that men are
ies artful creatures, after all,
y to be pleased by flattery.
Yorke was not to be so en-
. She accepted her husband's
ion with perfect tranquillity,
gh she believed it both pro-
sincere, and laughed a lithe went away. "My poor
l" she said, looking after him
der indulgence.
e little faults are so endear-

hall where the meeting was
s filled in every part; a dense
people struggled up or down
flights of stairs leading to it,
hrong of men obstructed the
utside. Edith Yorke had
the lane to see a sick woman,
aring that Miss Churchill also
the neighborhood, had lin-
onger than was prudent, hop-
her company home. Starting
e, at last, she soon found her-
he midst of this crowd. They
about her, muttering insults
aledictions on "that Catholic
girl," and seemed every mo-
n the point of stopping her.
ar in advance was Miss
ill. An enthusiastic boy threw
at her, and the teacher wiped
er cheek a stain of blood
it struck. Edith held her
p, and walked straight on,
, neither to the right nor left,
hatever ruffianly intention any
y have had, those who looked
face stood aside, and kept si-
hile she passed. If the spirit
rdened her brow to the like-
marble, shone in her eyes,
rved her red lips with a still
was less Christian humility
tural loftiness, it was at least
y pride, and it needed but the
of actual personal danger to
it to supernatural lowliness.
conviction, "They dare not touch me!" prevented the advent of that martyr-spirit which brings with it every virtue.

Humility is a flower that grows on the mountain-tops of the soul, and is reached only by striving and endeavor. That is not true humility which the mean heart plucks in the lowlands, calling on God 'twixt swamp and slough; nor does the child's hand bear it, nor yet does it shadow the untried maiden's brow, over her lowered eyelids. We must come out above the belt of pines and the gentian meadows, we must scale the dizzy track where to look down is destruction, and face the bitter cold of the glacier. and, over all, we shall find that exquisite blossom, its pure blue drooped earthward under the infinite blue of heaven.

Therefore we claim not humility for Edith, for she was not wise enough for that, and she was too true and brave for its counterfeit; but she had that scorn for meanness and tyranny which is one of the first milestones on the road to humility.

While his niece was walking unprotected through the crowd without, Mr. Yorke was in the hall, seated near the platform, on which were all the ministers, and the prominent Know-Nothings, several of the latter town-officers. One after another spoke, and was loudly applauded. The excitement and enthusiasm were immense. Mindful of his wife's charge, Mr. Yorke restrained his indignation, and listened attentively, sifting out what was essential in this commotion and common to all its participants. As he listened, the vision of a possible future of his country appeared before him, and made the hair rise on his head. He saw the anarchy and bloodshed of a religious war more terrible than any war the world had seen—a massacre of innocents, a war of extermination.

[illegible]

... the Bible ... for the larger ... never read it at home, many quoted it only in mockery, and every one denied the truth of one of its most plainly uttered ... In short, the rock on which this ... rose and dashed was ... and hatred, not of the Catholic Church, but of the Catholic clergy. The only question which interested these men in connection with any Catholic dogma was, How much temporal influence will it give to the priest? The supernatural side they cared not a fig for. To their minds it was impossible that a Catholic priest should be a truthful, plain dealing, straightfor-

[illegible]

"... mistake, gentlemen," he ... that the doctrines of the Catholic Church are either ridiculous or bad. Such an opinion would show you ill-informed or incapable of comprehension. On the contrary, they are glorious. But they are such as can be safely preached and enforced only by saints and angels, or by men of such exalted holiness as the world seldom sees. In the hands of weak men, they may be, and have been, perverted to base uses. The dogma of the Infallibility of the church is a crown of living gold on the head of the mystical Spouse, and a mantle of cloth of gold

manner been quite unlike what he had shown on former occasions of this sort, they might have refused to hear him. As it was, a reluctant and impatient silence was accorded. Some listened, doubtless because they wished to be exasperated, and hoped for another pretext for outbreak. But he looked like one who fully appreciates the strength of his opponent, and does not hope for a speedy victory.

"Gentlemen," he said, with a certain grim emphasis on the word, "after Mr. Griffeth's pyrotechnic display of eloquence, I cannot hope that my words will not fall with a dull sound on your ears. He has gone up like the rocket, and I must come down like the stick. I promise, however, to be brief, and to speak to the point. 'First, I thank him for having spoken like a gentleman, and left the subject clear enough for a gentleman to touch. On all that preceded him, I have but two comments to make. Concerning the attacks on the personal character of the Catholic clergy, I will only say, 'Set a thief to catch a thief!' To the misrepresentations of their creed, I would say, theologians should be better educated than to make them sincerely, and honest men should not fear to tell the truth, even of a foe.

"I come, then, to Mr. Griffeth's argument: that these men, simply from human weakness, not from personal depravity, have always abused their power, and, being men, always will abuse it, and that, therefore, we must, in self-defence, either banish them from the country, or deny them the rights of citizenship; their doctrines all the time being perfect, or, at least, tolerable.

"I am not here to defend the character of the Catholic clergy. I know well that your deep-rooted prejudice will not yield to any w mine or theirs. They must live your enmity with what patienc may; and the day will come, b me! when the still, small voi those lives that have been con ted to God will silence and p shame the blatant accusation pseudo-patriotism which now whelm it. Whatever may have proved against some, the world knows that that clergy has for its admiration many a mod Christian behavior, and that a its missionaries have been, and men worthy to stand beside and Paul, and John—men enan of the things of God, and de the attractions of earth. If it b that you can find Judases in company, it is equally true that tolical laborers are not found o of their fold. It may still be apostolical church, though on twelve were a Judas.

"This part of the question is, ever, irrelevant. We stand her we are worthy to speak, for prin and not for men. If the fault partisans are to be used as an a ment against an institution, no tution on earth can stand, and testantism and freedom must s to their foundations.

"Assuming, though, that his a tion is true, and that the clergy always been the enemies of fre and enlightenment, though would be strong circumstantial dence against their future trust thiness, still the conviction whic invokes is too grave and arbi for so just and enlightened a j as our country promises to be. I deny the truth of his premises, since proof is out of the questic this place, set my bare denial ag his bare assertion.

"But if his assumption and clusion were both true, if these

untrustworthy, and if we had
fore the right to refuse them
ity, we are still bound to give
efusal, not with the howling of
beasts, not with mobs and
tenings, but decently, and ac-
ng to law, or we are ourselves
to be trusted with that freedom
we deny to them.

Io, I a· not here to prove that
lergy ot the Catholic Church
l saints, or even all good men;
am here to say that, hate them
u may, you cannot, in these
d States, under the constitution,
annot with impunity persecute
nor deprive them of any of the
eges which that constitution
ntees to them as rights. 'Work
cret,' do they? 'Undermine,'
ey? And from whom does
ccusation come? What of that
y in which this movement
its rise?—that society which
dominates the land, stirring up
from Maine to Louisiana, mak-
ws and changing laws, and set-
the off-scouring of the earth in
igh places? What of those
s where men assemble to con-
measures for governing the
ry, yet where no citizen can
without the pass-word and oath
crecy? Josiah Quincy, Senior,
ston, a man whose name car-
much weight as any name here
is hall, has said of these same
ies, '*The liberties of a people are more certain in the path of destruc- han when they trust themselves to idance of secret societies. Birds night are never birds of wisdom. They are for the most part birds y. The fate of a republic is when the bats take the lead of gles.*' Our atmosphere is black these same bats!

'o Mr. Griffeth's parting anathe-
respond, ay and amen! Palsied
e hand that would quench one letter of that sacred legend! But whose is the hand that threatens it in this town? Is it Father Rasle, who asked a right of you, and, when you refused it, asked it of the law—in a neighboring town, mark, there being no law here!—and when the law refused it, submitted in silence? Is it the few hundreds of harmless Catholics among you, not one of whom has raised a hand in violence? Or is it your brutal mobs, who have insulted both priest and people, destroyed their property, and threatened their lives? Think of this, citizens! If the laws are dear to you, keep them! If you love freedom, do not practise tyranny! If you claim to be an intelligent people, think for yourselves, and do not let demagogues do it for you! Who is he who truly loves and honors his country? Not that man who holds its constitution to be a pretty myth, fine to quote, but impossible to act upon; but he who demands that its most generous promise shall be fulfilled, and is not afraid that in sincerity will be its destruction.

"Mr. Griffeth has uttered his war-cry, 'Down with the church!' and you have applauded it with enthusiasm. While I have listened to-night, there has risen before my vision the possible demolition of another edifice —a demolition which is inevitable, if such counsels are to prevail. Our fathers raised in this land a temple to civil and religious liberty, and pledged to its support their lives, their fortunes, and their sacred honor. That was no empty pledge, for the structure was cemented with their blood from corner-stone to pinnacle. And the genius whom they enthroned in the centre was no idol of wood and stone, to be used as a puppet by the designing, but a living creature. She was strong, and pure, and generous, and she had eagle's eyes. She

opened her arms to the world. She feared no alien foe, for her strength could be shorn and her limbs manacled only by her own renegade children. It is you are her foes. These narrow and violent counsels which pretend to protect, do contradict her; the manacles which you forge for others, will fetter her; with the violence which you do to others, will her strength be shorn; and the spirit which you obey under her name will dethrone her. But do not fancy that you can blind and make sport of her with impunity. The time may come when that insulted spirit will take in her mighty arms the pillars of the nation, and pull it down in ruin on your heads. No, the foe is not the orphan she has cherished, nor the stranger within her gates, but the children she has nourished at her bosom.

"Who is here so vile that will not love his country? If any, speak: for him have I offended."

When Mr. Yorke went home that night, though it was late, he found his wife and Betsey waiting for him at a turn of the road. He expressed no surprise nor disapprobation, but walked slowly homeward with them.

"What have they done?" Mrs. Yorke asked. She perceived that her husband's arm trembled.

"Nothing can stop them but themselves," he [illegible] "They must fall by th[illegible] speed."

"They listened to yo[illegible] asked.

"Yes, they were civil, [illegible] applauded a little. But [illegible] that? In spite of all that [illegible] do, they have passed a [illegible] passed it unanimously, that [illegible] Rasle comes here again, [illegible] give him a suit that is n[illegible] bought at the tailor's."

"What does that mea[illegible] Mrs. Yorke's wondering que[illegible]

"You little goose! it mea[illegible] feathers! Well, don't let us [illegible] more about it. I am d[illegible] words."

"Edith got [illegible] the [illegible] night," Mrs. Yorke said. [illegible] were impudent. She [illegible] quietly then. I think [illegible] got home she was [illegible] I thought the child would [illegible] self to death."

"She had no business [illegible] her uncle exclaimed. "N[illegible] you and Betsey. How [illegible] what they may do?"

"You are right, dear," [illegible] soothingly. "In future we [illegible] in the house, and who will [illegible] us."

CHAPTER XX[illegible]

[illegible]

Mr. Yorke was in the Senate House [illegible] mail-coach came [illegible] morning, but Fa[illegible]ther Rasle was not a passenger. The mail brought [illegible] [illegible]

[illegible]

sense of relief on learning
y had escaped the danger
'ould have threatened them
priest been their guest, they
express that feeling. They
te ready, in spite of the dan-
:epeat the invitation. Mr.
lone sincerely regretted Fa-
sle's decision. Even Edith,
:w nothing of the action of
ı-meeting, perceived that the
)lace was with his own peo-

.ve seen the sheriff and Dr.
ıis morning," Mr. Yorke said,
; niece had left the room,
ıey both agree in thinking
her Rasle will not be molest-
>ming here to stay over one
They are probably right.
at objection is to his settling
Besides, he comes so quietly,
g here will not be widely
Half of his own people do
v that he is coming."

wo gentlemen named by Mr.
'ere among the few who se-
ındemned the conduct of the
ıt did not publicly avow their
ıts, possibly because they
ıt such a proclamation would
.emselves without doing any
Catholics. Aside from the
ioience to person or proper-
physician would be accused
ring his principles for an in-
ıf practice, the politician of
ıg for the Irish vote. That
could speak a good word for
rch or the Irish from a dis-
'd motive, was not for a mo-
.mitted.

lay was overcast, threatening
ut to Edith Yorke it was as
spring and sunshine were at
r; for Mother Church, long
bent once more toward her
d children.

at I do not tell him volunta-
will ask," she said to herself, thinking of Father Rasle. "He will point out what has been wrong in me, and reprove me once for all, and have done with it; and the fault that is not mine, he will lift off my shoulders. It is very heavy!" she whispered tremulously, and for a little while could say no more.

Edith was not breaking under her burden, but she was bending wearily, and the constant weight of it had taken away all her elasticity, not of spirits alone, but of body. While making her last examen of conscience, she felt too weak to kneel, and sank into an arm-chair instead, dropping her head back against the cushion, and closing her eyes. So seen, the change in her face was startlingly evident. Her manner was always so fresh, and her eyes and teeth lighted up her smile so brilliantly, whether she spoke or listened, or only looked, that one could not see that she was pale and thin. But the face that lay against the chair-back was very pallid, and even the hands stretched out on the arms of the chair looked sick.

"There are six sins that I am sure of, besides all the doubtful ones," she said presently, sitting up. "That takes all my right hand, and the forefinger of my left hand. And now it is time to go."

The shortest way to the house where Father Rasle was to stop led through the wood-path that Edith and Dick had taken when he left her after his first visit to Seaton. She recollected that walk as she passed again through the forest, and murmured a tearful "Poor Dick! where are you now?"

The trees were not, as then, bright with a prodigal splendor of color, and steeped in mellow sunshine. The gold was tarnished, the reds looked dark and angry, and the lowering sky seemed to press on the

branches. That silence which, in the glory of autumn, expresses contentment with finished work and wishes fulfilled, seemed now to mean only suspense or endurance. No leaf came floating trustfully down to give its earth to earth, and free the imprisoned gold into its native air; no gray squirrel was discovered gathering its store of beech-nuts for the coming winter; no bird flitted about to take one more look at its summer haunts. All was silent and deserted.

"You poor old woods! I know just how to pity you," Edith said, looking about. "But cheer up! These are the days in which Nature tells over the sorrowful mysteries in her long rosary. Your garments are rent away, and the thorns are on your head; but after all is ended, then comes the glorious mystery of the spring resurrection. There! now I have exhorted you, you may exhort me. If you have anything to say, please to say it!"

And then the woods answered: "Child, I know my rosary all by heart, for I have said it six thousand times—six thousand times, child, and yet man will not listen. I tell of resignation and hope, and still his ears are dull. I tell him that in obedience is wisdom, and in wisdom contentment, and he does not cease to rebel. That is a sorrowful mystery over which I grew sad many a time before the cross became the sign of salvation. My very birds are wiser than the children of men; my beasts less cruel. Do not blush, little one! It was your ignorance that spoke, and not presumption. No fairer flower has bloomed in my shadow than your loving thought. Cheer up! Hearts will find the way when heads cannot; for when true love is blind, then an angel leads it."

"I thank you!" Edith said after having listened. "It is very true our teachers have a hard time w[ith] us. There is you, Mother Nat[ure], with your book full of pictures, [to] catch our eyes; and the chur[ch] speaking our own language, to ca[tch] our ears; and conscience, with its t[wo] words only, yes and no, to catch o[ur] thoughts, and we fight against yo[u] all. I am very, very blind! Will some good angel lead me?"

She came out into East Street, and stood a moment on the spot where she and Dick had stood to look at that exquisite bit of meadow. The violet mist that had hung over it, like a parting soul over its body, had long since dissolved, and the little incarnate song that had floated there, yellow-winged and feathered, had been loosed into the heavenly orchestra. Half-way down the hill, a footpath led off to the left of the street, passed a few back-doors of houses on High Street, and ended at the door of the house where Father Rasle was. She knew by the buggy standing in the yard that he had come. If it had not been there, the smiling face of the woman who stood in the door would have told the story.

The woman stepped out to make way, and Edith ran in through the narrow entry to the square room that was both kitchen and parlor.

"O father, father! A hundred thousand welcomes!" And then, between grief and gladness, her voice was stopped.

"Dear child!" he said affectionately. "So you needed me very much?"

Several women were in the room. Some of them had arrived before the priest came, nearly all of them had made their confession, but not one could persuade herself to go away while she was allowed to remain. They meant to stay till he should bid them go, and even then wait for a second telling. To see their be-

pastor, to hear him speak, to t over and over their demon-ive welcome, was a happiness h they would fain prolong.

e host and hostess were in their attire. They had given up all occupation to the supreme one tertaining their priest. Their shone with a proud delight, poor house was scrupulously , and, though Father Rasle was n to be abstemious, they had to the extent of their means for ntertainment.

e priest talked jestingly to the n to cheer them. "What is t you cry about? But you not tell me, for I know. It is use you have had nothing but words and the absence of your to bear. You cry because you not blown up in the school-e, or did not have your heads n in the church. Or perhaps were in hopes that I should , and find you all strung up to ranches of trees. That is the fruit that a tree can bear—a r. The Bread of Life grew on ree of the cross. Courage! have not done with you yet. s a good communion to-morrow, afterward keep yourselves free sin, and then, when I come , I may have the happiness of g all your bodies hung to trees, ll your souls in Paradise.

Now, you two who have not been nfession will confess at once. I want every one of you to go . I have to talk to that little

That little girl" seated herself in idst of these poor women, who gly made room for her—they not jealous of her—and all their faces away from Father , and sat silently looking into re while the confessions were ed. And at last Edith found herself free to tell all her story to the priest.

The Catholics of Seaton could not, if they would, have concealed from their enemies that Father Rasle had come. Their joyful faces would have betrayed the secret if their lips had remained silent. All who could do so laid their work aside, and gathered in knots in the lane, or visited each other's houses, to talk the matter over. They smiled and nodded to each other in the street with a significance which every one understood. Poor souls! to the cruel eyes that watched them their pathetic and sacred delight was a crime, their silence, treachery.

Toward evening the scattering visitors who had taken their way during the day to the house under the hill became a steady stream. It looked as though every Catholic in Seaton was going to confession. It looked, too, as though every Protestant in Seaton was willing that they should, for no one molested them, and the town was perfectly quiet. Those who had been anxious ascribed this quietude to the weather, and congratulated themselves that the threatening rain prevented any gathering of their persecutors.

At nine o'clock the crowd around the house where the priest was began to thin off. The road by which they sought their homes that night was a *via sacra;* for, newly shriven, and moved to the depths of their hearts, they carried with them, every one, the memory of an earnest exhortation to humility and forgiveness, and resignation to the will of God. At half-past ten only three or four women were left in the house, and the rain was beginning to fall outside. The confessions were over, Mrs. Kent had set out a late supper for Father Rasle, since he would have to fast till noon of the next

day, and he was standing to say good-night to the last of his visitors, who even now seemed unwilling to leave him. While he spoke to them, some one was heard running toward the house, and the next minute a man burst into the room, breathless, and bespattered with mud.

"They are coming!" he gasped out. "Run for your life, father!"

In the midst of the outcry that rose from those present, Father Rasle stood fixed and silent. Perhaps he was startled at the sudden and unexpected announcement; perhaps his color had changed; but there was no other sign of excitement. He calmly questioned the man, and learned that a mob of fifty or more masked men were rapidly approaching the house.

"And they will kill you, father," the messenger concluded. "They don't put on masks and come at night to break windows. They can do that in broad daylight. For God's sake, save yourself!"

"They shall take me where I am," the priest said firmly. "It is the will of God. I will not resist, and I have nowhere to fly to."

"Here is hot water. Put on more!" cried one of the women. "We'll scald them!" And instantly they took the boiling tea-kettle from the fire, and put cold water to heat.

"Run over to the lane, and rouse the people!" cried another. "They'll kill everybody in the town in your defence, father, if you say the word."

"My children, I command you to use no violence, and make no resistance," the priest said with authority. "If the people rise, it will be to their own destruction. Pray! It is all that you can do."

They fell on their knees, weeping loudly as they heard the muffled tramp of many feet outside. But one said, "The cellar! the cellar!" and Mr. Kent, catching the priest's arm, almost forced him toward the cellar-door. It was a pitiful hiding-place; but Father Rasle had no time for any thought except that, if there were a chance of escape, it was his duty to take advantage of it.

Scarcely had he disappeared, before the outer door was thrust open, and the room was filled with men wearing crape masks. They came in silently and swiftly, and as swiftly their companions outside surrounded the house, and stationed themselves at each window to bar all egress.

It was not in the hearts of these poor people to utter no word of reproach to the perpetrators of such an outrage, even though the priest had commanded their silence. Mrs. Kent pointed to one man after another, calling him by name. "I know you under your mask!" she cried. "And the Almighty would find you if I didn't."

No one replied to her. The only one of the mob who spoke was he who seemed to be their leader. "Where is the priest?" he asked.

Of course no one told him.

The lower rooms and the attic were searched, and there remained but one place. The hearts of the Christians died within them as the leader of the mob took a candle from the table, and went toward the cellar-door. A girl who was near the door caught up a chair to defend the passage, but another took it from her, and pulled her down to her knees. The next moment Father Rasle was led out amid the sobs and prayers of his children. He was very pale, but perfectly calm, and, like his divine Master, he uttered not a word. But as the mob surrounded and led him away, he cast one glance on those who knelt and stretched their clasped hands toward him, and raised his hand in silent benediction. That he

ɔeing led to death, neither he ιey doubted. And they had no ı to doubt it. What violence, of murder, had these men any ı to fear to do in open daylight? night they not well believe that the murderer could escape if d only the law against him? was not true only of Seaton. a Catholic priest in the United , at that time, owed the preion of his life, not to a fear of .w, but to a fear of Catholic ance.

:y did not take their victim ;h the lane which Edith had ed, but through a shorter one g to High Street. The family in the house at the corner of ;treet were well-bred people, though Protestants, friends to r Rasle. He had been receiv- that house as a guest; and seeing a light in one of the , the instinct of preservation and forced a cry from him. : me!" he cried out, calling the ɔy name.

ɔse nearest immediately silencm with threats. If he spoke they said, they would kill him : spot.

; voice had not been heard, and int hope faded as quickly as it sen.

:y avoided the thickly-settled ıf the town, and took their way one of the back streets leading : river. Half-way down they ι man on horseback, carrying ιtern. He held the light up, sked whom they had there.

'o one," they replied, making to conceal their prisoner. "We no one with us."

t till too late did Father Rasle that he had missed another e of escape, and that it was ιeriff who had met them.

: mob, feeling now secure of their prey, could indulge in revilings. "So they persecuted Jesus of old," said one, with a laugh.

"Will the Virgin save you?" asked another.

But enough. One does not repeat the talk of those through whose lips the arch-fiend speaks without disguise. They reviling, and he praying, disappeared in the darkness and the storm.

Edith Yorke had passed that evening in her own room. It had been her custom to keep the eve of her communions in retirement, and tonight she had more than ordinary food for reflection. It was almost eleven o'clock when she began to prepare herself for bed, but she still heard her aunt and Clara up downstairs. Mrs. Yorke had not been well, and, unwilling that her husband should lose his rest, had sent him upstairs to sleep, and kept Clara with her. Edith was just thinking that she had a mind to go down and see how her aunt was, when she heard the small gate of the avenue open, and shut again instantly, as if some one had run through.

Her window was partly raised. She threw it up, and stepped out on to the top of the portico. Her heart divined the danger at once. Already the messenger was half-way up the avenue, and, before she could see that it was a woman, she heard her panting breath and half-exhausted voice: "Help! They are killing Father Rasle!"

A faintness as of death swept over Edith. She would have spoken, but could only sink on her knees and lean over the railing. Mrs. Yorke, too, had heard the click of the gate, and had opened the sitting-room window, and Edith heard her voice and Clara's. To them the woman told her story.

"Do not speak loudly," Mrs.

Yorke said. "Mr. Yorke and Edith must not know. They can do no good, and would only make trouble. Clara, go and wake Patrick, and do it quietly. I tell you, my poor woman, my husband could do nothing, and I shall not allow him to be called."

Edith grew strong the moment she knew the truth. The woman had left the house before Father Rasle did, and a rescue might still be possible. She opened her door noiselessly, stepped out, and closed it after her; then fled down the back-stairs, out through the back-door, and down the avenue to the upper gate. Reaching the road, she flew over it with winged feet. At North Street, instead of going down toward the centre of the town, she crossed to a lumber-road leading to the river. The bridge was far below, but one who dared could go over here on the boom that kept the logs. Edith dared, considering the peril not worth a thought. When some bugle-toned reveille of the soul wakes up our slumbering faith, then miracles become possible.

The bank was high on the eastern side, and the descent was by two immense timbers, or masts, chained together and chained to the shore at the upper end, and to the boom at the lower. The inclination was steep, and those who walked through the air on that slippery bridge stepped warily even by day, timing their steps to the heavy vibrations of the timber. But Edith ran fleetly down, and sprang on to the swaying boom ankle-deep in water. Lumber-mills above and below sent out their long lines of red light through the misty darkness, and the noise of their saws was like the grinding of teeth. The logs knocked against each other with a dull thump as the river flowed, and here and there little spaces of water glistened. To slip into one of those black holes was death. You miss the boom, and step on a log instead, and, unless you are a practised log-walker—possibly, too, if you are—the log rolls, you go under, and there is an end of you. You cannot scream when you are under water; you cannot rise to the surface, for the logs keep you down, or close together and crush you, and no one can see you.

The boom did not reach straight but zigzagged across the river, the lengths chained together, but not closely, and hidden under water. In those spaces, the logs, trying to get through, pushed their bobbing ends up, and tempted the foot. More than once Edith's foot was in that trap, but she did not sink till just as she reached the western bank. Then, as she went down, she caught an overhanging sapling, and drew herself to land, wet to the waist.

Irish Lane did not reach so far up, by about a quarter of a mile, and there was no road, the way being pasture and ledge. As Edith reached the upper end of the lane, some one else came into it from the lower end, next the bridge, and she heard a woman's voice lamenting. She did not stop for lamentation, but ran from house to house, bidding them come out and save Father Rasle.

They gathered immediately, asking questions all in confusion, knowing not which way to go, but ready to follow her lead. Had they no rifles nor pistols? No; why should they have them? An Irishman's weapon was his fist and a cudgel, and whatever he could catch by the way.

An Irishman, indeed, usually goes into battle first, and arms himself afterward.

But the enthusiasm which Edith's words had kindled the other messenger soon quenched. It was too late

him, she said. He had been away, they knew not whith- course he must be dead long that time. And he had bid rewell, and commanded them no violence—to do nothing y.

heard no more. The hand her earnestness, she had laid e one's arm, slipped off, and pped to the ground without a

s more than half-past eleven and raining quite hard, and d had begun to rise. Broken spirited, the Catholics went eir houses again, but not to In one of these houses Edith her eyes, and saw about persons gathered, some bend- r her, others praying, others about and wringing their She got up. "I wish that uld all kneel down, and say ny of our Lord Jesus," she "I am going to find Father

eeded only that something be proposed for them to do. n of the house took his pray- , and they all knelt. Others n and filled the room, fright- ildren cowering close to their and watching the door, as if pected to see a foe enter.

i went slowly out. One of men had kindly put a shawl r shoulders, but she was quite cious of the storm. The town as striking twelve, and as she l to count its strokes, the cho- praying voices reached her the open door:

"King of Glory, have mercy on us!
the Sun of Justice, have mercy on us!"

Sun of Justice!" she repeat- l lifted her clasped hands.

went on, but heard again, in a of the storm:

"Jesus, most patient, have mercy on us!
Jesus, most obedient, have mercy on us!"

"Ah! yes, patience! It is not for us to invoke justice," she thought. "'Enter not into judgment with thy servant, O Lord! for in thy sight shall no man living be justified.'"

The road was heavy with mud, and in the darkness she scarcely could find her way. Only the occasional twinkle of a lighted window told where it did not lie. She went wearily, for the spirit that had sustained her while there was hope failed now, and the storm grew every minute worse. In another lull there came again, more faintly:

"Jesus, the good Shepherd, have mercy on us!
Jesus, the true Light, have mercy on us!"

At that tender petition the tears started forth, and she walked on weeping. They were indeed as sheep among wolves. The blast almost swept her off her feet, and in some sudden current snatched the sound of prayer, and brought it to her once more, clearly as if it had been cried in her very ears:

"Jesus, the Strength of martyrs, have mercy on us!"

The wind went sighing off to right and left, and opened a pathway of calm before her, in which she walked firmly, wiping her tears away, and taking courage again.

At the entrance to the lane, near the bridge, she paused and looked back. All was darkness there, but out of the dakness came faintly, "Lamb of God—" It was all she heard, and it was all! It meant patience, humility, immolation, and final triumph.

The cottage where Father Rasle had been was all alight when Edith came in sight of it, and as she approached the door a man came out and almost ran against her.

"Where is he?" she asked.

"Why, Miss Edith!" exclaimed Patrick Chester.

She only repeated her question.

"He has come back," Patrick answered, "and Dr. Willis is with him."

"Will he die?" she whispered.

"No, Miss Edith; but he has been vilely used. He was out two hours in this storm. He found his way back more dead than alive. He has been tarred and feathered."

She cried out in disgust: "The brutes! They were, then, too base for murder!"

"You may say that," Patrick answered. "But now come home. You can't see him, you know."

But she would not go till she had heard his voice, and Patrick was obliged to go back to the entry with her. The entry was filled with men and women, all listening for any news that might reach them. The door was ajar into the kitchen, where two or three men were admitted. The priest was with the doctor in an inner room.

"You had better drink this," they heard Dr. Willis say; and Father Rasle's voice replied: "No, doctor. It is after twelve o'clock, and I must say Mass to-morrow."

"But, if you do not take it, you may be very sick," the doctor persisted.

"I cannot take it," Father Rasle said again. "My people must be disappointed."

"Thank God, it is really he," Edith exclaimed. "Come, Patrick, we will go home now."

Mrs. Yorke, fearing to alarm her husband, had put out the lights, and Edith, seeing the house all dark, took no precaution to conceal herself in approaching it. The first notice she had, therefore, that any of the family were awake, was her aunt's frightened voice calling from the open window of the sitting-room, "Is it Edith? Has Edith been out?"

"Yes, but I am safe back, auntie," she made haste to say; "and everything is right."

Clara, Melicent, and Betsey were there. No one in the house slept but Mr. Yorke and the two Pattens, and, since the worst was probably over, it was not so much matter now if they waked. So a large fire was kindled, and Edith's dripping garments taken off, while Patrick told his story. Then she also told where she had been, and smiled at their terror.

"But to cross the river on the logs and boom!" her aunt cried. "Why, child, your escape is a miracle! If you had fallen in, you would surely have been drowned."

"I could not have drowned to-night," Edith answered. "If I had fallen in, I should have set the river on fire."

TO BE CONTINUED.

for itself, as in England, for instance, a place in the real aristocracy. In our own country, where hereditary rank does not exist, it has a clear field. It has no special rights in the political order, and is not, therefore, strictly and completely the successor of the noble class in our ancestral British constitution. Yet, by the very fact of being a wealthy class, it does possess, and ought to possess, a certain pre-eminence, influence, and real though indirect power in public affairs. Men of superior intellectual ability, men of learning and letters, those who fill the higher professional positions, and office-holders, belong to the same class; partly because their position in many instances gives them at least a moderate share of wealth, but chiefly because they have power by their very position, and are able to influence and direct the disposition of wealth even when they do not personally possess it. By this very fact, they have duties to the commonwealth—they are not mere private persons, but public persons. They are important and distinguished members of the community, and, as such, have a greater responsibility to society and the state than others. This will not be disputed as a general statement. We do not intend to go into a minute and detailed exposition of all the particulars which it includes and comprehends. We confine ourselves, for the present, to certain specific duties of those who are rich in the literal and technical sense. And what we have to say of them is, that they ought to fulfil the duties which were annexed to the privileges of the class to which they succeeded, in so far as they have inherited those privileges.

However grossly feudal barons may have in a multitude of instances abused their privileges and their powers, the Christian idea of their state was always that their privileges and were entrusted to them for th mon good. Sound political p phy and common sense acco the higher teaching of Chris It would be, therefore, a change for the worse, a miser gression in civilization, if moneyed aristocracy, possessin leges without corresponding took the place of an aristoc birth, obliged by its nobility to the most important services state. A mere *caste* existing self, having no end but the sel altation and enjoyment of its bers, with no purpose except in fine houses, wear fine drink choice wines, drive ab sumptuous equipages, and fin buried in great pomp under monuments, would be the mo Christian, the most despicab most odious of constitution would be *succeeded by Commun*

The rich have political they are bound to be a bulwa a tower of strength to the st ornament to the commonwea only bright, but useful; as a epitaph of the seventeenth designates a certain eminent "*of Hartford Town the Silve ment.*" We presuppose in men of wealth of whom we as a matter of course, hones probity. Swindlers, gambler honest speculators, bribe-take the whole set of vampires with the blood of the state individuals, are excluded. It i who have inherited or acquire wealth honestly who are able t the state. It is not necessar more into detail regarding th and methods in which they can We are content merely to i their ability and obligation to in general terms, and pass other topics.

of these other topics relates ty of Catholic citizens which erly classed under the head their duties, but which we do inate precisely as a duty to to as such, but as one which es owe to themselves, to their natural rights of conscience, religion. We call it, never- a political duty, because it be performed by them as citi- d in the exercise of their po- ights. This is the duty of g and defending their liberty science against any encroach- which may be attempted by tical party, or any legislation to the letter or spirit of our ital law. This duty, which f all Catholic citizens indis- tely, devolves especially on those wealth, education, in- al power, or social and politi- ition gives them a special op- y and ability to fulfil it. ersons are the natural chiefs ders of the Catholic laity; in the front rank; and they ed to give the example, en- ment, and direction to the body which they need and ok for.

can be more base and cow- him for those who have a place in society than their fel- who have ordinarily risen e ranks of the poor, laboring our Catholic people, to de- regard with apathy that sa- se for which their ancestors and died, and for the sake they have sought an asylum is country, where they have dom and prosperity? Here so found that inestimable liberty of conscience, freedom p and practise their religion, provide for their posterity the ing the same. They are to use all the power and influence which God has given them to preserve and perpetuate these rights, and to protect the more helpless classes of their fellow-Catholics, the poor, the orphans, the sick, the outcasts of society, in the enjoyment of their religious rights. This includes a great deal. First and foremost at the present moment is liberty of education. Besides this, there are the rights of religious instruction and sacraments for those who are in the army and navy, in hospitals, asylums, and prisons, and in those institutions where children are justly or unjustly placed by the civil authority as vagrants. In short, everywhere, where the state takes hold of the individual, or exercises a right of control over any lesser corporation which takes hold of him, in such a way that there is a chance for tyranny over his conscience, and the violation or abridgment of his religious rights and liberty in the interest of sectarianism or secularism, it is the duty of the most eminent Catholic laymen to become, together with their bishops and priests, the champions of the oppressed.

Does any one say that there is no need of vigilance or action, because there is no danger that our rights will be disregarded or infringed? We think he is in error. "Eternal vigilance is the price of liberty." And as one proof that Catholics in this republic have need to exercise this vigilance, we will cite an example of the disastrous consequences which have followed from the neglect of it in another republic.

The Confederation of the Swiss Cantons established and guaranteed in the most solemn and explicit manner the liberty of religion for Catholics and Protestants alike. Nevertheless, the liberty of the Catholic Church has been taken away in the most flagrant manner, even in the Catholic Cantons, by tyrannical fed-

eral and cantonal legislation. Fifty religious establishments were suppressed at one blow. Since that time,—that is, since 1848—religious houses and schools have been forcibly suppressed at Ascona, Lugano, Mendrisio, and Bellinzona, and the diocesan seminaries at Pollegio and Aargau. Nearly all the Catholic schools in most of the mixed cantons have been changed into mixed schools, and in Thurgau they have been all suppressed. No priest can be admitted to the exercise of his functions who has studied at any Jesuit college. The catechism of the bishop in whose diocese Aargau is situated, the Bible History of Schuster, and the Moral Theologies of Gury and Kenrick, have been interdicted by the civil authority. Prohibitions have been issued against missions, retreats, the publication of the Jubilee, and the devotions of the Month of Mary. In Aargau, no youth can embrace the ecclesiastical state without the leave of the cantonal assembly, before which august and holy tribunal he must pass two examinations. In the Catholic canton of Ticino, the cantonal assembly arrogates to itself the right of changing the destination of religious foundations, fixing and regulating the election, installation in benefices, and official functions of beneficiaries, erecting new parishes and abolishing existing ones. The *placet* of the civil authority is requisite for all ecclesiastical decrees of the bishops and the Pope under penalty of fines varying from five to five thousand francs. In several cantons civil marriage is obligatory. In short, the Catholics of Switzerland are in an enslaved and insupportable condition, as is proved by a memorial of the whole body of the Swiss Episcopate, in which these and many other particulars are given.*

* See *Dublin Review* for October, 1871.

The profession of liberalism affords no guarantee to Catholics against the most flagrant and cruel oppression. Neither is there any security in the mere fact that the form of government is democratic or republican. Everywhere, as well in countries called Catholic as in those which are not, under republican as well as under monarchical constitutions, the price of liberty is unceasing vigilance and activity. Catholics must rely entirely on themselves, and not delegate the office of protecting them to any party or ruling power. This is necessary in the United States as well as in Switzerland. We do not ascribe to the majority of the non-Catholic citizens of our federal republic or of any state a disposition to abridge our liberty. But it is not the majority which really governs. Principles, maxims, arguments, watch-words, measures, are initiated by a few persons. Majorities are carried along by leaders, orators, writers for the press, they know not why, how, or toward what end. There is danger, therefore, though not from the American people, from the masters of state-craft, but from restless, revolutionary spirits, from violent sectarian leaders, from ambitious demagogues, from parties which may start up and be violently impelled by sudden excitements.

The conclusion of all this is, that the *élite* of the Catholic laity are bound to understand the sound Catholic principles of public law and right which are involved in the relation of liberty of conscience and religion to the sovereignty of the state, under our American republican institutions. They are bound to instruct those who are uneducated in their rights and obligations as citizens. They are bound to set before the public the grounds and reasons

ıtholic rights, as based on the al and divine law, and the ican constitution. And they ›ound to exclude unprincipled, ınt demagogues from the lead- › of the Catholic people by tak- themselves, and in that position ıing with all their might every political scheme for giving the state a usurped power over conscience and religion. Those who are incapable of doing anything else in this direction can at least aid by their wealth the Catholic press in diffusing true and just ideas, and advocating Catholic rights.

TRAVELS IN THE AIR.

ɔUT ninety years ago, on the ›rable 21st of November, 1783, 'arisian world had a sensation ı can never be repeated. On lay, men for the first time dared st themselves in a balloon, which o be freed entirely from the and take, as we may say, its :e as to the time and manner in ı it was to return to it. One 'asily imagine the intense ex- ent and admiration which must filled the hearts of the specta- and the feelings of triumph, h mingled, it must needs have with some apprehension, on ırt of the occupànts of the car, 1arquis d'Arlandes and M. Pi- de Rozier, when they for the ime, trusting themselves to the ›f their new machine, invented a few months previously, were d by it into the unknown region : clouds. Fortunately, this first ıscent was a success; if it had ɜen, who knows how long further iments in aeronautics might have postponed by prohibitory laws the fears of men, both of which l certainly have been quite jus- e? As it was, this first excur- erved as a stimulus to other at- :s, and the number which have been made since then is beyond all estimate. It is certain, however, that the immense majority of them have been every way as successful as this first one was, and many, of course, very much more so. The danger of balloon ascents is really very trifling; accidents occur hardly once in a hundred times, and very seldom, when they do occur, involve the loss of life. It is hardly more dangerous to travel by balloon than by railway or steamer, and certainly very much more agreeable.

If our reader desires a most convincing proof of this last statement, we cannot do better than to refer him to a book bearing the title which stands at the head of this article, and imported by Lippincott & Co. We must confess to having become somewhat enthusiastic on the subject of balloons since reading this book, and hardly think any one else who even looks at it can fail to have something of the same feeling. By a mere glance at it one is introduced to quite a new world, and to read it is the next best thing to going up above the clouds one's self. It is illustrated by six beautiful chromo-lithographs, and has a hundred and twenty other illustrations.

Mr. Glaisher, the editor, is a thoroughly scientific man, possessed of remarkable steadiness and coolness, as his name would imply, and as the accounts of his voyages sufficiently demonstrate. He is one of the best meteorologists in the world, and it is in the interests of science that his ascents have been made. But, together with the accounts of his own excursions, he gives others by three French gentlemen, also accomplished aeronauts, and whose enthusiasm on the subject almost equals our own, and practically perhaps surpasses it, for we find that M. Tissandier seems to have had no objection to starting from Calais when the wind was blowing straight out toward the German Ocean. These gentlemen, MM. Flammarion, De Fonvielle, and Tissandier, just named, often made long journeys, landing at a point quite remote from that of starting—a thing almost out of the question for Mr. Glaisher, for, as he pathetically remarks, "whatever part of England we start from, in one hour we may be over the sea." His endeavor rather was, in the short time allotted him, to rush for the upper regions of the atmosphere, in order that he might there, as well as on the way up and down, make observations on temperature, electricity, magnetism, sound, solar radiation, the spectrum, ozone, direction of wind (for this, as before remarked, his opportunity was limited), actinic effects of the sun, density of the clouds, etc., and he consequently went up quite beleaguered with instruments, as the illustration "Mr. Glaisher in the car" clearly shows. The effects of great elevation on the human constitution naturally did not escape his attention, nor that of his companion and aeronaut, Mr. Coxwell; he says that, on one occasion, "at the height of three miles and a half, Mr. Coxwell said my face was of a glowing purple, and higher still, both our faces were blue. Truly a pleasing state of things!"

But three miles and a half was a small elevation for Mr. Glaisher. In several of his ascents, he rose to the height of about five miles, on one occasion meeting with dense clouds all the way up. Certainly such clouds are not common, except in "our old home"; but such a day as that must have been even an Englishman could hardly have called "fine." His third ascent, on September 5, 1862, was the most interesting of all; in this he rose to the astonishing height of *seven miles*, or 37,000 feet. Probably our readers have generally been accustomed to see in their atlases, by the side of the enormous congeries of mountains which usually forms the frontispiece, a small picture of a balloon, with "highest point ever reached by man," or words to that effect, appended to it, at the elevation of 23,000 feet; with a reference to the name of Gay-Lussac. But this ascent, made on September 15, 1804, is entirely insignificant now, compared with this stupendous one, to a point a mile and a half above the summit of the Himalaya Mountains, into regions where only one-quarter of the atmosphere lay above the aeronauts, and where it was rarefied about in the same proportion. If their faces were blue at four miles, what were they now?

The account of this ascent is very exciting, and at the same time places Mr. Glaisher's qualities as an observer in the most favorable light. In company with Mr. Coxwell, who was his pilot as usual, he left Wolverhampton at about one o'clock, and attained the height of five miles in about fifty minutes. Think of that, compared with the trouble of ascending an Alpine peak, where, after

...of most exhausting la-
... can only get three miles
... the earth ! And Mr. Glaisher,
...d of having to strain every
...e in his body, was able to sit
... and calmly observe the baro-
..., thermometer, etc. The bal-
... was, however, revolving so
...y that he failed in taking pho-
...hic views. Mr. Coxwell had
... exhausting work in the man-
...nt of the balloon, and was
...g for breath when they were
... miles high. For two miles
... however, Mr. Glaisher "took
...ations with comfort." But,
...t 1h. 52m., or later," he made
... reading ; after this he could
...e the divisions of the instru-
..., and asked Mr. Coxwell to
... read them. They probably
... beginning to think it was time
... about coming down ; but in
... to do so, the valve-rope had
... pulled, and it was caught in
...gging above, owing to the ro-
... motion of the balloon. The
...ometer was about ten degrees
... zero ; Mr. Glaisher was fast
...ing insensible, and Mr. Cox-
... hands were almost useless
...numbness. Still, something had
... done, for they were rising a
...and feet every minute ; and ac-
...ngly, Mr. Coxwell climbed into
...ng of the balloon, and pulled
...pe with his teeth. He has the
... distinction of having been five
... feet higher above the earth
... any other man, for of course
... immediately began to descend.
...ning back to the car, he found
...mpanion quite insensible ; after
... minutes, Mr. Glaisher came to
...lf, as they sank from that terri-
...evation, to which it is probably
...sible for man safely to ascend.
...ke a thoroughly scientific man,
...is, he had observed his sensa-
... the last. First, his arms and legs gave out ; and his neck became weak, so that his head fell over to one side ; he shook himself, and noticed that he "had power over the muscles of his back, and considerably so over those of the neck." This suddenly left him, however, and the sense of sight immediately afterward ; as for hearing, he could not tell, as there was probably nothing to hear at that height. He fell back helpless, resting his shoulder on the edge of the car. The next words he heard were "temperature" and "observation" ; it can hardly be supposed that these were the first words Mr. Coxwell employed to rouse him, though they were probably the best. Then "the instruments became dimly visible." Immediately on recovering, he says : "I drew up my legs, which had been extended, and *took a pencil in my hand to begin observations.*" Is not this characteristic ?

Perhaps it may not be clear how it can be proved that the height of seven miles was attained on this occasion. It is, of course, well known that the elevation of a balloon is determined, as that of a mountain-peak usually is, by the barometer ; and this method is very accurate, though, if there be a rapid motion upward or downward, the barometer may lag a little. Still, it gives the absolute height, and also the rate of ascent or descent, with sufficient accuracy for all practical purposes. By this instrument Mr. Glaisher had found that, just before he became insensible, they were 29,000 feet high, and ascending at the rate of 1,000 feet a minute ; when he recovered after the lapse of thirteen minutes, they were 26,000 feet high, and descending 2,000 feet a minute. These data are sufficient to determine the greatest height attained ; but Mr. Coxwell also, on coming down from the ring, happened to glance at the aneroid

barometer, and afterward remembered pretty nearly the direction of its hand; its reading confirms the conclusion got by the other method. A minimum thermometer agreed in the same result. They landed safely at about twenty minutes to three, the whole excursion having taken only a little over an hour and a half. The illustration called "Mr. Glaisher insensible at the height of seven miles" is one of the most remarkable in the book, and most readers will probable turn to it repeatedly. It represents the supreme and critical moment; Mr. Coxwell is in the ring, and is just loosening the valve-rope. His hands, his companion tells us, were black when he came down; and Mr. Glaisher generally means what he says.

It is not every one who will care to compete with these gentlemen in making lofty ascents; and it is not probable that they had any merely ambitious motives in undertaking to soar so high. Mr. Glaisher's enthusiasm for and interest in science are perfectly genuine; and his results, which are of course only hinted at in these popular accounts which he gives of his excursions, are very valuable. It is not likely that any one else could have accomplished so much as he did. Still, though they were not led on by ambition, their achievement on the occasion just mentioned is one which must discourage others who may be; for it would be very difficult and dangerous to attempt to do purposely what they did only as it were accidentally, and which they would not have done had they known its peril. There are, it is true, some remarkable effects, such as the blackening of the sky (as well as of the hands of the aeronauts), which cannot be so well attained at lower altitudes; but still, substantially the same can be enjoyed at heights of four or five miles, and really the most beautiful ones are presented as soon as we rise above the clouds. The effect seems to us, judging from the illustrations, to be especially magical when the canopy (or carpet, as it may more properly be called from our new point of view) is complete, so as to reach to the horizon, and shut out all view or idea of the earth completely. Many of the pictures illustrate this well. One would seem to lose all sense of height or of being in a dangerous position; the quiet sea of clouds beneath can never seem very distant, owing to the impossibility of judging of the real dimensions of its rolling waves; and these waves seem, by their apparent solidity yet softness, almost to invite a fall. And one seems to be entirely in a new state of existence; the change is more complete than could be obtained by travelling to the other side of the globe; and yet it can be realized in the space of five or ten minutes on any ordinary cloudy day. There above, with the dark-blue sky overhead, with the glorious bright sun in it lighting up the masses of white vapor below, far from all the dust, noise, and confusion of the lower sphere, what an exhilaration must the aeronaut feel, if indeed his eye is not entirely employed on the divisions of his barometer and the pages of his note-book! The idea of such a vision is almost enough to make one's enthusiasm for ballooning equal that of M. de Fonvielle, who, however, was willing to put up even with lower elevations; for he says that in his younger days he "was ready to be shut up in a sky-rocket, provided that its projectile power were carefully calculated, and that it were provided with a parachute"! If the sky-rocket could only be sent above the clouds—but, on the whole, one would probably be calmer, enjoy the view

horoughly, and take in its va-
eatures better, in the car of
esent beautiful and majestic,
somewhat unmanageable, ve-

yet in all respects the balloon
unmanageable. Its rise and
a be regulated with great ex-
; and by means of the pretty
ion of the guide-rope, due to
ebrated English aeronaut, Mr.
its final fall to the earth, if a
wind is not blowing, can be
very easy. This rope hangs
three or four hundred feet be-
e car, and as it touches the
l, and then coils up upon it,
ight and the descending power
balloon are continually and gra-
lessened. And by parting
as or ballast, the ascent and
t can always be most carefully
ed; so much so, indeed, that
as to be somewhat careful.
M. Tissandier, on making a
l ascent with no more ascend-
wer at his disposal, was oblig-
regret that he had not gone
t his breakfast; the least little
ion of weight affects the equi-
a so much that the loss of
cken-bone which he thought-
once threw out, he says, "cer-
caused us to rise from twenty
ty yards." One can certainly
r fall without much difficulty;
ly, danger is that too much
ay escape after the ballast is
sted, or when there is only a
supply on hand, and that the
nt may be too rapid. Mr. Glai-
wice at least came down so hard
break nearly all his instru-
; but once this was in a man-
ntentional, for the wind had
drifting him out toward the sea,
n discovering through an open-
the clouds that it was almost
ly under him, he had only the
ative of coming down with a rush or being drowned. On another occasion, M. de Fonvielle descended with a party in the *Giant* balloon in a rapid and inevitable manner, owing to the escape of gas; but records, besides the breaking of the instruments, only that "one of the travellers had his face covered with blood, another was wounded by a thermometer, and a third complained of a pain in his leg." One curious danger there is, however, about even a quiet descent which is worth noticing. The last-named gentleman had just made a very successful excursion without an aeronaut; and, on coming down, his grapnel had caught in a tree near the edge of a forest. The sequel shall be in his own words:

"At this moment, I was deceived by an optical illusion which might have had dangerous results, and I call the attention of my readers to it in case they may ever be tempted to undertake the management of an aerostat. Let them never get out of the car till it is fairly landed upon the soil. Let them be perfectly sure that no solution of continuity exists between the car and the earth before they think of stepping out of it, for their eyes, accustomed to the immense proportions of things above the clouds, have lost their power of appreciating dimensions. Objects appear so small on the earth's surface during a descent that great trees look like mere blades of grass. At this moment I believed we had descended upon heath bushes, and we were at the top of the high trees. I had actually got one leg out of the car, and was preparing to leap down!"

If a strong wind is blowing, it is not so easy to descend. The horizontal motion of the balloon is beyond the control of gas or ballast. MM. de Fonvielle and Tissandier set out once in a high wind; they came down on a plain, were dragged across it, and over the tops of some trees, which broke and crashed as they passed; again they rushed over some plough-

ed ground, where they were finally rescued by some peasants. What was their velocity during this remarkable trip? On consulting maps and watches, they found they had come forty-eight miles from Paris in thirty-five minutes, or the rate of eighty miles an hour; in the air, however, they probably travelled faster, and in the last five minutes of "dragging" not so fast.

But "dragging" is not the worst thing that can happen when there is a high wind. Let aeronauts beware how they attempt to anchor in such circumstances before coming tolerably near to the ground. The grapnel was once let out at the height of about sixty yards when they were skimming along with great velocity, and at first took no hold, but finally caught in the edge of a small pond. The wind, however, took revenge on the balloon, which now suddenly refused to obey its impulse:

"I was busily engaged," says M. Tissandier, "in stowing away the loose bottles, that might have injured us seriously in case of bumping, when I heard a sharp cracking sound, and Duruof [their pilot] immediately cried out, '*The balloon has burst!*' It was too true; the *Neptune's* side was torn open, and transformed suddenly into a bundle of shreds, flattening down upon the opposite half. Its appearance was now that of a disc surrounded with a fringe. We came to the ground immediately. The shock was awful. Duruof disappeared, I leaped into the hoop, which at that instant fell upon me, together with the remains of the balloon and all the contents of the car. All was darkness; I felt myself rolled along the ground, and wondered if I had lost my sight, or if we were buried in some hole or cavern. An instant of quiet ensued, and then the loud voice of Duruof was heard exclaiming: 'Now come from under there, you fellows!' We hastened to obey the voice of the commander, and found that the car had turned over upon us, and shut us up like mice in a trap!"

What next? They had fallen from a height of about two hundred feet, and yet were not much bruised: but the very wind that had caused their disaster helped them out of it; in fact, their balloon was transformed into a kind of gigantic kite, and let them down pretty easily.

But let us get up above the clouds again. That is the place really to enjoy life. Once there, one hardly thinks about coming down or its difficulties; the earth is out of sight, and almost out of mind. We are sailing along, perhaps at a quicker rate than that of an express train; but the motion is as imperceptible as that immensely more rapid one of the magnificent planetary projectile on which we are whirling through space. For the clouds are moving with us, and, though they are breaking up and changing their forms, we cannot see that they move as a mass. Occasionally, through a break, we may see the earth, or be saluted from it, as M. Flammarion once was to his great surprise, by cries of "A balloon! a balloon!" when he was quite unaware of there being any hole through which the balloon could be seen. Sounds, by the way, will go up much better than they will come down; the reason of this is the lesser density of the air above. Of course we feel no wind, for the wind is taking us with it: so that even the cold at any ordinary height and at any season usual for ballooning is not troublesome. Sometimes, indeed, it is warmer aloft than below; on the occasion of the eighty-mile-per-hour voyage, just mentioned, the thermometer was actually at eighty-two degrees at the height of a little over half a mile, while below it stood at fifty-five. The balloon is as steady as the Rock of Gibraltar; M. Flammarion assures us that he once filled a tumbler with water till it was brimming over, so that not another drop could be

"The Rhine flows along with its silver ripple in the distance. . . . All nature is silent, save from time to time the timid chirping of some little bird; when, suddenly, a vast golden streak of light breaks forth from the east, and caresses the highest clouds of the atmosphere, clothing them in rosy and golden tints."

The illustration representing this sunrise is magnificent, as the sight must have been in the highest degree. What could be more inspiring than to be borne along amid the glorious clouds of morning toward the rising sun—the cheering influence of whose beams the balloon itself seems to feel, as, dried and expanded by their heat, it rises proudly into the sky—with the Rhine glistening before us, and the green plains and forests of Germany inviting us to continue our voyage?

They hear the sound of church-bells, and, soon after, that of cannon.

"From minute to minute the voice of this gracious apparatus of civilization and progress growled among the clouds. It was the artillery of Mülheim preparing itself for the next war.

"The ancient city of Cologne forms beneath us a regular semicircle soldered to the left bank of the Rhine. Unless one examined it attentively, it might be taken for a moderate-sized snail sticking to the thin branch of a tree."

Poor M. Flammarion thought he was going to enjoy his sail some time longer, perhaps all day. But his inexorable aeronaut thought differently. There was very little ballast and no breakfast; it was probable that the wind would rise, and that they would come to grief. His word was law; so the valve-rope was pulled, the French flag run up, and down they came at Solingen, near Düsseldorf, 330 miles from Paris, which distance had been accomplished in twelve hours and a half. The good-natured Germans rushed up to help them; the greatest difficulty was to prevent them from smoking near the balloon.

This journey is a fair example of what balloon travelling may be in skilful hands. Of course it has its disadvantages. The principal one is obvious; that you can only go just where the wind will take you; but there is an advantage corresponding to this in the quietness and steadiness of the motion, and it is not at all improbable that, with the rapid advances which are being made continually in the science of meteorology, the laws of winds will be ascertained sufficiently to enable the aeronaut to find one which will carry him in the general direction in which he wants to go, on most occasions, by choosing a proper elevation. Certainly this can often be done, as in the case of M. Tissandier's trip from Calais over the German Ocean. A lower breeze brought them back to land. The difficulty remaining is that of changing our elevation. On the present system, this requires a loss of gas or ballast, which cannot be kept up indefinitely. An ingenious plan has been proposed by Gen. Meusnier—to have a double balloon, one outside the other: the inner one is filled with gas, the space between the two with air; into the outer one more air is forced by an air-pump when we wish to descend, and allowed to escape when we wish to rise. The compressed air is itself heavier than the air surrounding, and the compressed gas in the inner balloon is also less buoyant than before. This is applying the principle of the bladder of the fish to aerostatics. The *Giant* was constructed on this plan, but it does not appear that the practicability of using it in this way was ever tested.

Still, notwithstanding the great utility and advantages of the balloon

make scientific observations: but if attached to a moving body, it is a very pleasant vehicle to ride in, or could easily be made so. Our French aeronauts were once pulled in this way through the streets of a town, and at another time were towed for some distance at the height of five hundred feet by a number of their excitable countrymen. But it must be acknowledged that on the whole a captive is not so pleasant to ride in as a free balloon. Besides the feeling of exultation accompanying a free ascent, it also has the advantage of being really a great deal more comfortable. The captive, being restrained by the rope, feels the full force of whatever wind there is, and is moreover apt to be tipped over considerably when the breeze is strong. Nevertheless, going up in one is a tolerably popular amusement when the opportunity is offered, though hardly enough so to make it profitable for the proprietors. This is one of the miserable difficulties about the pursuit of science, that experiments cost something, and often it is very troublesome to raise the necessary funds. Free ascensions have, however, been common enough for a good deal more to have been accomplished in the way of experiment and observation than has usually been the case, and Mr. Glaisher's example deserves to be generally followed. The balloon itself may do a good deal towards the investigation of the laws of the atmospheric currents, the knowledge of which would be so useful for its own guidance, as well as in answering questions concerning storms and climate. Mr. Glaisher, on January 12, 1864, met with a warm current of air from the southwest, more than half a mile in depth; and he considers that this may, perhaps, be an aerial Gulf Stream, and increase the warming effect which that celebrated current no doubt produces on the western and northern coasts of Europe.

But we must not dwell longer on his scientific results, or those of his friends on the other side of the Channel. In fact, it is time that we should come down from the clouds, and occupy ourselves with the affairs of this base and grovelling lower world. We should like to do it gradually, but, as is the case with the balloon itself, our descent must needs be accompanied by something of a shock. It is with difficulty that we can persuade ourselves to quit, even in imagination, those magnificent regions so near to us and yet practically so far away; which all of us could see even now in ten minutes if our balloon was ready—would that it were!—and which, if the art of flying progresses with due rapidity, we may yet see some time before we die.

by no means wishes to disturb you."

"Do not come any nearer," replied the inmate of the tower, motioning him back with his hand. "Come no nearer: you are in the presence of an unfortunate being afflicted with leprosy."

"Whatever may be your misfortune," replied the traveller, "I shall not go away. I have never shunned the unfortunate. But, if my presence annoys you, I am ready to withdraw."

"You are welcome," replied the leper, suddenly turning around. "Remain, if you have the courage after looking at me."

The officer remained for some time motionless with astonishment at the frightful aspect of the unfortunate man so completely disfigured by leprosy.

"I willingly remain," said he, "if you will accept the visit of a man led here by chance, but detained by a lively interest."

"Interest!—I have never excited anything but pity."

"I should be happy to offer you any consolation."

"It is a great one to behold a human face and hear the sound of a human voice, for every one flies from me."

"Allow me, then, to converse with you awhile and to visit your house."

"Very willingly, if it can afford you any pleasure." Saying which, the leper put on a large felt hat, the flattened brim of which covered his face. "Go to the south," added he. "The few flowers I cultivate may please you. There are some rather rare. I have procured the seeds of every kind that grow among the Alps, and try to make them grow double and more beautiful by cultivation."

"You have flowers which are indeed entirely new to me."

"Look at this little rose-bush. It is a rose without thorns, which only grows on the higher Alps, but it is already losing its peculiarity, and putting forth thorns in proportion to its cultivation and growth."

"It should be considered the emblem of ingratitude."

"If any of these flowers please you, you can take them without any fear: you will incur no danger by gathering them. I sowed the seed. I take pleasure in watering them and looking at them, but I never touch them."

"Why not?"

"I fear I might infect them, and should no longer dare give them to any one."

"For whom do you raise them?"

"The people who bring me food from the hospital are not afraid to gather them. And sometimes children from the city stop before my garden-gate. I immediately ascend the tower, for fear of frightening or infecting them. They look up as they go away, and say with a smile: 'Good-by, Leper,' and that gives me a little pleasure."

"You have succeeded in collecting quite a variety of plants; and you have vines yonder, and several kinds of fruit-trees."

"The trees are still young. I set them out myself, as well as that grape-vine, which I have trained to the top of the old wall, you see: it is thick enough for me to walk on, and is my favorite resort.—Go up on these stones. I am the architect of this staircase. Hold on to the wall."

"A charming nook! the very place for a hermit to meditate in!"

"It suits me, too. I can see the country around, the laborers in the fields, and all that is going on in the

come attached to the very rocks and trees, and it seems to me that all created things are friends whom God has given me."

"You encourage me to explain, in my turn, what passes within me. I have a genuine affection for the objects that are, so to speak, my daily companions, and every night, before going to my tower, I come here to take leave of the glaciers of Ruitorts, the dense woods of Mont St. Bernard, and the fantastic peaks that overlook the valley of the Rhine. Though the power of God is as evident in the creation of an ant as in that of the whole universe, the grand spectacle of yonder mountains fills me with greater awe. I cannot look at those lofty elevations, covered with eternal glaciers, without being filled with solemn wonder. But in the vast landscape spread out before me, I have favorite views to which I turn with special pleasure. Among these is the hermitage you see yonder on the top of Mount Charvensod. Alone in the woods, near a deserted pasture, it catches the last rays of the setting sun. Though I have never been there, I feel a peculiar pleasure in looking at it. When the daylight is fading away, seated in my garden, I turn my eyes toward that lonely hermitage, to seek rest for my imagination. I have learned to look upon it as a kind of property. It seems as if I had some confused reminiscence of once living there in happier days which I cannot fully recall. I love especially to gaze at the distant mountains, which look like a cloud on the horizon. Distance, like the future, inspires me with hope. My overburdened heart imagines there may be a far-off land where, at some future time, I may at length taste the happiness for which I sigh, and which a secret instinct is constantly assuring me is possible."

"With such an ardent sou
yours, you must have passed thr
many struggles in resigning you
to your lot, instead of yielding t
spair."

"I should deceive you in allc
you to think I have always bee
signed to my lot. I have not a
ed that self-abnegation to v
some anchorites have arrived.
entire sacrifice of all human affe
has not yet been accomplished.
life has been one continual co
and the powerful influences of
gion itself are not always able
press the flights of my imagin
It often draws me, in spite of m
into a whirlpool of vain desires, v
tend toward a world I have no k
ledge of, but strange visions of v
are ever present to torment me."

"If you could read my soul
learn my opinion of the worl
your desires and your regrets w
instantly vanish."

"Books have vainly taught
the perversity of mankind, and
misfortunes inseparable from hu
ty: my heart refuses to believe t
I am continually representing
myself circles of sincere and v
ous friends; suitable marriages fu
the happiness resulting from he
youth, and fortune. I imagine t
wandering together through gr
greener and fresher than the
above me, with a sun more daz
than that which brightens my w
and their lot seems worthy of
in proportion to the misery of n
At the beginning of spring, whe
wind from Piedmont blows thr
our valley, I feel its vivifying wa
penetrating me, and a thrill p
over me in spite of myself. I
an inexplicable desire, and a
fused notion of a boundless h
ness that I am capable of enjo
but which is denied me. Then
from my cell, and wander in the fi

conceal myself beneath the vines, so we can talk without seeing each other."

"Why so? No, you shall not leave me. Come nearer." In saying these words the traveller involuntarily put out his hand to take the Leper's, but the latter hastily withdrew his.

"Imprudent man! You were going to take hold of my hand!"

"Well, I would have pressed it heartily."

"It would have been the first time such a happiness was granted me: my hand was never pressed by any one."

"What! Have you never formed any ties, except the sister of whom you have spoken—never been loved by any of your own condition?"

"Happily for the human race, there is not another in my condition on the earth."

"You make me shudder."

"Pardon me, compassionate stranger! You know the unhappy love to speak of their misfortunes."

"Go on, go on: you interest me. You said your sister lived with you, and aided you in bearing your sufferings."

"She was the only tie that bound me to the rest of mankind! It pleased God to break it, and thus leave me isolated and alone in the midst of the world. Her soul was ripe for the heaven where she now is, and her example sustained me under the discouragement which has often overwhelmed me since her death. But we did not live in that delightful intimacy which I so often imagine, and which should bind together the unfortunate. The nature of our disease deprived us of this consolation. When we came together to pray, we avoided looking at one another, for fear the sad spectacle might disturb our meditations: our souls alone were united before God. After prayer, my sister generally retired to her cell or beneath the nut-trees at the end of the garden, and we lived almost constantly apart."

"But why did you impose so cruel a restraint upon yourselves?"

"When my sister was attacked with the contagious disease to which all our family were victims, and came to share my asylum, we had never seen one another. Her fright was extreme when she beheld me for the first time. The fear of afflicting her, and still more of increasing her malady by approaching her, made me resolve on this sad kind of a life. The leprosy had only attacked her breast, and I had still some hopes of her being cured. You see the remains of a neglected trellis: it was then covered with a hop-vine that I trained with care, and divided the garden into two parts. On each side of this, I made a little path where we could walk and converse together without seeing or coming too near each other."

"It would almost seem as if heaven wished to embitter the sad pleasures it still left you."

"But at least I was not then alone. My sister's presence gave some cheerfulness to my asylum. I could hear the sounds of her steps. When I returned, at dawn, to pray beneath these trees, the door of the tower would softly open, and my sister's voice would imperceptibly mingle with mine. In the evening, when I watered my garden, she sometimes walked here at sunset, in the same place where we now are, and I could see her shadow pass and repass over my flowers. Even when I did not see her, there were everywhere traces of her presence. Sometimes it was only a withered flower in the path, or some branch of a shrub she had dropped, but now I am alone, there

and dragged him away. I could not help looking at him once more as he was going out of the gate; his eyes were turned towards me, as if to beg the assistance which it was not in my power to give. They wished to drown him in the Doire, but the crowd waiting on the outside stoned him to death. I heard his cries, and took refuge in my tower more dead than alive; my trembling knees refused to support me: I threw myself on my bed in a state impossible to describe. My grief made me regard the just though severe order only as a cruelty as atrocious as it was needless, and, though I am now ashamed of the feeling that then excited me, I cannot yet think of it with coolness. I passed the whole day in the greatest agitation. I had been deprived of the only living thing I had, and this new blow reopened all the wounds of my heart.

"Such was my condition when, that same day, towards sunset, I came here, and seated myself on the very rock where you are now sitting. I had been meditating awhile on my sad lot, when I saw a newly-married couple appear yonder, near the two birches at the end of the hedge. They came along the foot-path through the meadow, and passed by me. The sweet peace that an assured happiness confers was imprinted on their handsome faces. They were walking slowly arm-in-arm. All at once they stopped; the young woman leaned her head upon her husband's breast, who clasped her in his arms with joy. Shall I confess it? Envy for the first time penetrated my heart. Such a picture of happiness had never struck me before. I followed them with my eyes to the end of the meadow. They were nearly hidden by the trees when I heard a joyful cry. It came from the united families who were coming to meet them. Old men, women, and children surrounded them. I heard a confused murmur of joy. I saw among the trees the bright colors of their dresses, and the whole group seemed enveloped in a cloud of happiness. I could not endure the sight: the torments of hell seized hold of my heart. I turned away my eyes, and fled to my cell. O God! how frightfully lonely and gloomy it seemed. 'It is here, then,' I said to myself—'I am to live for ever here. After dragging out a wretched existence, I must await the long-delayed end of my life! The Almighty has diffused happiness, and in torrents, among all living creatures, and I—I alone!—am without support, without friends, without a companion.—What a terrible destiny!'

"Full of these sad thoughts, I forgot there is one Being who is the Comforter. I was beside myself. 'Why,' I said to myself, 'was I permitted to behold the light? Why has Nature been so cruel a step-mother to me?' Like a disinherited child, I saw before me the rich patrimony of the human race, of my share of which heaven had defrauded me. 'No, no,' I cried in my fury, 'there is no happiness for thee on earth. Cease, then, to live, poor wretch! Thou hast disgraced the earth long enough with thy presence: would it might swallow thee up and leave no trace of thy miserable existence!' My fury continuing to increase, a m desire to destroy myself took session of my mind. I resolved last to set fire to my dwelling, allow myself to be burned up in with everything else that might my memory. Excited and enra I went forth into the fields. I dered for some time in the dark around my dwelling. I gave ven my overburdened heart in invol tary shrieks, and frightened m

silence of the night. I se-
d full of rage, crying: 'Woe
ce, Leper! Woe to thee!'
as if everything conspired for
estruction, I heard the echo
the ruins of the Château de
ıfan repeating distinctly: 'Woe
ee!' I stopped, seized with
, at the door of the tower, and
echo from the mountains re-
l a long time after, 'Woe to

took a lamp, and, resolved to set
o my dwelling, went into the
room, carrying with me some
and dry branches. It was the
my sister occupied, and I had
tered it since her death. Her
ıair was in the same spot where
ed it for the last time. I shiv-
with fear at the sight of her veil
ome of her clothing scattered
d. The last words she uttered
her departure came back to
nind: 'I shall not forsake you
I die: remember, I shall
s be with you in your suffer-
Placing the lamp on the
I perceived the cord which
he cross she wore on her neck.
ad placed it herself within her
I drew back, filled with awe
e sight. The depths of the
into which I was about to
were at once revealed to my
led eyes. Trembling, I ap-
hed the sacred volume. 'Here,
I cried, 'is the aid she prom-
ma!' Drawing the cross from
ok, I found a sealed note
my dear sister had left for me.
tears, which grief had not
allowed me to shed, now
d in torrents: all my detest-
rojects vanished at once. I
the precious letter to my
long time before I could read
n, falling on my knees to im-
the divine mercy, I sobbingly
ıe words that will be for ever
graven on my heart: 'Brother, I shall soon leave you, but not forsake you. From heaven, which I hope to enter, I will watch over you, praying God to give you the courage to endure life with resignation till it pleases him to reunite us in another world. Then I shall be able to show you how much I loved you. Nothing will prevent me any longer from approaching you: nothing can separate us. I leave you the little cross I have worn all my life. It has often consoled me in my sorrows and been the only witness of my tears. Remember, when you look upon it, that my last prayer was that you might live and die a good Christian.'

"Cherished letter! it shall never leave me. I will carry it with me to the grave. It will open to me the gates of heaven which my crime would have closed for ever. When I had finished reading it, I felt faint, exhausted by all I had undergone. My sight grew dim, and, for some time, I lost both the remembrance of my misfortunes and the consciousness of existence. When I came to myself, the night was far advanced. In proportion to the clearness of my mind, I experienced a feeling of profound peace. All that had taken place the evening before seemed like a dream. My first impulse was to raise my eyes heavenward in thanksgiving for having been preserved from the greatest of misfortunes. The heavens had never appeared so serene and glorious: one star before my window outshone the rest. I gazed at it a long time with inexpressible delight, thanking God for granting me the pleasure of beholding it, and felt interiorly consoled at the thought that some of its rays were permitted to cheer the gloomy home of the Leper.

"I went up to my cell in a calmer frame. I spent the remainder of the

night in reading the Book of Job, and the sublimity of his thoughts at length entirely dispelled the gloomy ideas that had beset me. I never experienced such fearful moments during my sister's life. To feel her near me made me at once calmer, and the very thought of the affection she had for me afforded me consolation, and inspired me with courage.

"Compassionate stranger! may God preserve you from ever being obliged to live alone! My sister and my companion is no more. But heaven will grant me the strength to endure life courageously; it will grant it, I trust, for I pray for it with all the earnestness of my heart."

"How old was your sister when she died?"

"She was barely twenty-five, but her sufferings made her look much older. In spite of her fatal disease, which changed her features, she would have been handsome, had it not been for her frightful pallor, the result of a living death which made me groan whenever I looked at her."

"She died quite young?"

"Her delicate and feeble constitution could not resist so many sufferings combined: for some time I had perceived her loss inevitable. Her lot was so sad that I could not desire her to live. Seeing her daily languishing and wasting away, I felt, with a fearful kind of joy, that the end of her sufferings was approaching. For a month she had been growing weaker; frequent swoons were constantly threatening her life. One evening (it was about the first of August) I saw her so weak that I was unwilling to leave her. She was in her arm-chair, not having been able to lie down for several days. I seated myself near her, and in the profound darkness we held our last conversation. I could not restrain my tears. A sad presentiment agitated me. 'Why do you weep?' she said. 'Why distress yourself? I shall not forsake you when I die. I shall always be with you in your sufferings.'

"A few moments after, she expressed a desire to be carried out of the tower, that she might offer her prayers in the grove of nut-trees where she passed the greater part of the pleasant season. 'I wish,' she said, 'to die looking at the heavens.' But I did not imagine her end so near. I was about to take her in my arms, when she said, 'Only support me. I am, perhaps, strong enough to walk.' I led her slowly to the nut-trees. I made a cushion of the dry leaves she herself had gathered together, and, covering her head with a veil to screen her from the dampness of the night, I seated myself near her. But she desired to be left alone during her last meditation, and I went to a distance, but without losing sight of her. From time to time, I could see the flutter of her veil and her white hands raised to heaven. When I drew near the grove, she asked for some water. I carried her some in a cup. She wet her lips, but could not swallow. 'I feel the end has come,' said she, turning her head. 'My thirst will soon be assuaged for ever. Support me, brother: aid me in crossing this gulf—so long desired, but so terrible. Support me, and say the prayers for the dying.' These were her last words. I drew her head against my breast, and said the prayer for the departing soul: 'Go forth from this world, my beloved sister, and leave thy mortal remains in my arms.' I held her in this way for three hours, during the last throes of nature. At length, she quietly passed away, and her soul left the earth without a struggle."

At the end of this account, the

overed his face with his hands. hy deprived the traveller of wer of speaking. After a .'s silence, the Leper rose. er," said he, "when grief or n comes over you, think of er of the city of Aosta, and it will not have been a use-."

walked towards the garden-. As the officer was about to go put his glove on his right 'You have never pressed any nd," said he. "Do me the press mine. It is the hand end who is deeply interested lot."

Leper drew back some steps ind of terror, and, raising his d hands towards heaven, he 'O God of goodness! pour down thy blessings on this compassionate man!"

"Grant me another favor, then," resumed the traveller. "I am going away. We may not see each other again for a long time. Can we not write one another sometimes, with the necessary precautions? Such a correspondence might divert you, and it would afford me great pleasure."

The Leper reflected for some time. At length he said, "Why should I cherish any delusion? I ought to have no other society but myself, no friend but God. We shall meet in his presence. Farewell, kind stranger, may you be happy! Farewell for ever!" The traveller went out—the Leper closed the door and drew the bolts.

'HE PRESENT CONDITION OF THE HOLY FATHER.

FROM LA CIVILTA CATTOLICA.

fourteen months ago, a was made in the *Porta Pia*, entry effected into Rome in e of Italy.

achinations of those who ef- at entry in order to subvert ority of the Pope are still at d most assiduously, in en- g to convey the impression act of theirs now stands be- world simply as *an accom- fact*, and as such is, if not ap- at least tolerated by those terested in contesting it. ey endeavor to delude the d lull to sleep the misgiv- Catholics; for in order to and strengthen this impression there is scarcely a stratagem or subterfuge to which the government (itself the author of the fact) does not resort, through the journalism notoriously in its pay, not only throughout the Peninsula, but elsewhere.

This government, which sprang from *accomplished facts* and *falsehoods*, hopes by means of these same *accomplished facts* and *falsehoods* to place on a firm foundation its sway in the *Campidoglio*, which now rests on a very insecure footing; therefore it endeavors to persuade the world, and especially Catholics, that the Supreme Pontiff, while in its hands and under the law of its Guarantees, is

actually more at liberty, more independent in action, and more useful to the church, than he was when he reigned as a sovereign prince and was *bona-fide* ruler in his own state.

The absurdity of this claim is manifest; but what absurdity is there of which the government of the Subalpinists in Italy does not avail itself, in order to attach credit to itself, by means of the arts learned in the school of its great father and master, Bonaparte?

It is important, therefore, or rather we should say it is absolutely necessary, that an honest and Christian journalism should perseveringly oppose manifest truths to this interminable repetition of falsehoods, paid for by the Subalpine rulers, respecting the present condition of the Holy Father; and thus, by ventilating fraud, undeceive simple and credulous minds.

With this intention, we shall in few but veracious strokes of the pen describe the undisguised reality of the state in which the head of the church, the Supreme Pontiff, Pius IX., finds himself at the present moment in Rome, six months after the solemn publication of the laws of the *Guarantees.*

II.

We assert, then, that the Pope endures imprisonment in Rome at the hands of the Subalpinists, and that his captivity, instead of being mitigated, is every day aggravated. This is proved by the following facts:

1. He is in the hands of an *inimical power*, or, as he himself has defined it, he is *sub hostili dominatione constitutus.* Now, he who is in the hands of an enemy, however much that enemy may affect humanity and regard towards him, is beyond all contradiction his prisoner.

2. The Holy Father fell into the hands of this inimical power through sheer force. This is rendered evident by the formal declaration made by the Subalpine ministers before taking up arms against him, in which they affirmed that to invade or take Rome with bomb-shells and cannons would be an act contrary to the rights of nations, an act so iniquitous that it would be unworthy even of a barbarian government: yet in the very face of these declarations they did take Rome with the argument of bomb-shells and cannons, and with the same argument they continue to occupy it.

3. The Holy Father, being in the hands of an inimical power, which has dispossessed him by violence of all sovereignty, and substituted its own in lieu of his, is now by this same power subjected to every kind of ridicule in his double majesty as pontiff and as king: burlesque honors are proposed to him, which would by preference be offered to him publicly, in order to induce the idea that the Holy Father, by accepting them, is reconciled to the government, and has basely ceded to it the inalienable rights of God, of the church, and of the Catholic world. Moreover, the obligation resting on the Sovereign Pontiff of preserving his own dignity keeps him shut up in the Vatican: the outer doors of which are guarded *by a guard of honor* formed of the self-same wretched soldiery who, led on by Subalpine leaders, made the breach in the *Porta Pia*, and struck to the earth his own sovereign banner in Rome.

4. Finally: The inimical power in whose hands the Holy Father now finds himself is, either from weakness or malice, incapable of protecting his august person from any kind of insult. So that, supposing it to be *morally* possible for him without com

sing the dignity to leave the -rs of the Vatican, yet would a *al* obstacle present itself in the es and dangers, threatening life to which he would be exposed the crowds of cut-throats, athe- nd the lowest rabble of every ry, which this power has con- ted together and maintains in , to represent in that city the of the plébiscite; that is, a e hostile to the Papacy and re- us to its throne.

ese are the principal facts which clearly demonstrate the state of sonment into which the Sov- Pontiff was thrown, by the of the 20th September, 1870, wn city of Rome: and we defy sophistry of all the journalists, cians, and diplomatists of the nment, seated as it is in the polis of the Catholic world, ny it, without denying the light sun at mid-day.

ides this, that the captivity of Holy Father has been aggrava- uring these fourteen months is and felt by every one who is not the influence of the Subal- s, those men who have carried affrontery to the length of plac- e centre of their government in ty of Rome itself, and with one eir laws of *guaranty* for the in- dence of the Pope have arro- to themselves the right of im- g the future conditions of his nce in the Vatican, as if they the rulers of the Holy See. ever considers the forces of mor- d material hostility that these pinists have accumulated in against his prerogatives, can- ail to perceive that the rights in this city are most readily n under foot, are, after those d, those of the Pope: and the who is the most insulted n is, after that of Christ, precisely the person of the Sovereign Pontiff, Pius IX., *decreed sovereign and inviolable*, by the law, as the person of the king himself.

From this it follows that the Holy Father is at the present moment the legal prisoner, in Rome, of the Subalpine government, since by the aforenamed laws, termed those of the Guarantees, not only has that government confirmed the violent spoliation of himself, but, in spite of the opinion of the world, has dared to justify the act by defining in those laws the limits of the liberty it intends to concede to him. This is neither more nor less than the usage commonly observed towards a prisoner of state or of war.

By this means, the present condition of the Pontiff in his own Rome is in truth that of the strictest imprisonment by the anti-Christian sect, headed by the government of the Subalpinists now lording it over Italy.

III.

Neither is the Holy Father, Pius IX., the prisoner of an inimical power solely on account of his civil prerogatives: it is his ecclesiastical jurisdiction that is aimed at more than anything else: while usurping the regal crown, it seeks equally to abolish the Papal tiara; and, if, after having barbarously dispossessed him of his kingdom, it does not also make a barbarous assault on the majesty of his Pontificate, this reserve arises only from the hindrance occasioned by very strong and extrinsic causes, and not from good-will or any other than a reprobate sentiment.

This profound enmity of the Subalpine rulers to the Pope as the supreme pastor of the Catholic Church is so well-known as to need no demonstration. Yet for superabundance

of proof, we will say that it is shown:

1. By all that has been previously done against Catholicity for twenty-two years past in Piedmont, and for half that time throughout the rest of Italy, by the faction to which these rulers belong—a faction whose politics are expressed by an obstinate war, sometimes of a Julianistic character, sometimes of that of a Nero—a war which attacks directly or indirectly the church itself, and all connected with it, and this in such a manner as to render it palpable that not even the Unity of Italy is desired for its own sake, but rather as a means by which to work the destruction of Catholicity and the overthrow of the Papacy.

2. It is shown by the special mandate which the Subalpine faction superintending the Masonic government of the Peninsula have received from the General Masonic Order—a mandate bidding them become the immediate (because proximate) instruments of the downfall of Papal Rome, the centre of the Catholic Church; and which then bids them proceed to the utter spoliation of the Sovereign Pontiff himself—two events which it hopes will lead (if that were possible) to the annihilation of Catholicity, that being the ultimate end of all the conspiracies of the order.

3. It is shown by the open confessions made in Rome, throughout Italy, and in all Europe, by journalists united by the bonds of faction to our Subalpine patrons; and even more by the discovery, lately made, that persecution is already well established in Rome against everything ecclesiastical or Catholic—whether in things or persons.

From these facts, it is demonstrated that the Holy Father is now the prisoner in Rome of a government which in his person hates above everything, and as far as it dare makes war against, his prerogatives as Pontiff, and as Head of the Catholic Apostolic and Roman religion. Pius IX. is in the hands of Turks embittered to the last degree. Against him and his tiara every tool is made use of, and with equal skill—whether it be cannons or sophistry, buffoonery or the judgment-hall, the pick-axe or calumny.

IV.

The war of Nero carried on against the Holy Father and the church is at the present moment tempered by the war of Julian. It was for this purpose that our Subalpinists devised the law of the Guarantees, behind which they know how to mask the ugliness of their rascalities, at least for a time. "Do you see?" they exclaim in every tone, and have had written in every language: "We have surrounded the Pope with so many *privileges* that the like was never seen. Of what do you complain, O you insatiable Catholics? Have we not constituted the Pope *inviolable* as is the king? What more would you have?"

We would have—simply that the Pope should be inviolable, because he is a king in earnest truth, and not a mere semblance of one. But to this question of to-day concerning the sovereign and personal inviolability of the Pope, facts are the best reply. These show that *practically* he is as inviolable as the first article of the statute, and has been inviolable throughout the kingdom.

This privilege of inviolability implies that the person sovereignly inviolable can, in no manner whatsoever, be publicly insulted without the offenders being repressed by force and punished according to law.

[illegible] to perform a sacred function, without exposing himself to contumely and insult by the very side of St. Peter's tomb, and even on the altar itself. The occurrences of the 8th December, 1870, in the vestibule of the Pontifical residence; of the 10th March, 1871, within the Gesù; and of the 23d, 24th, 25th August, close to the Lateran and the Church of Maria soprà Minerva, confirm what we assert.

This, then, in its veritable reality, is the present condition of Pope Pius IX. in Rome, after the oft-repeated promulgation of the law declaring him an inviolable sovereign like to the king.

Nor may the salaried apologists of our patrons treat these matters as a jest in order to exculpate themselves from so horrible an abomination. Facts are facts, while words are but breath. The most irrefutable facts prove that if our Holy Father were to show himself publicly in the Rome of to-day, uncivilized as it is by these Subalpine rulers, the treatment he would receive would be no other than such as is given alike to the clergy as to the most holy things, nay, to Christ himself, in the blessed sacrament of the altar.

Now, it cannot be denied, for the Roman journals attest it, citing days, time, places, names and surnames, that every day priests or religious, bishops or prelates, are attacked or abused in the most populous districts of Rome; that almost every day sacred images are stoned or profaned at the corners of the streets; and not unfrequently the adorable eucharist, when borne as a viaticum to the sick, is exposed to mockery in the public square, even by those who wear military badges; and all this occurs with the tacit consent of the officers charged with keeping order in the city, no one of whom has ever imprisoned a single person guilty of such misdeeds. And after that they would have us believe that Pope Pius IX. would be safe either in the city or in the Vatican from the outrages or even from the blow of these most civilized gentlemen who form the new Roman people!

Be silent, as long as we live, O whited sepulchres!—race fit only to patronize assassins!

V.

Moreover, the Holy Father, by the noble munificence of his jailers, is reduced to that degree of poverty that, were it not for the oblations of the faithful, he must either pine in misery or suffer the degradation of his majesty. The glorious conquerors of Rome have taken everything from him, excepting the Vatican. And if, up to this time, they have refrained from sacking this edifice, it is owing to that *veto* of potentates which, as yet, has forbidden them access to it. Jugglers are in possession of the Quirinal; and they drew near to the public treasury of the Pontificate with the sword of guardianship. In one flash of lightning, the Pope saw himself deprived of everything. With a simple substitution of voters, the Pontifical estate is become the Subalpine estate—a magnificent example! since then magnificently imitated by the Commune of Paris!

Is is true that, in their law of the Guarantees, they have deigned to assign to him a species of civil list amounting to several millions of lire. But this was done for the sake of appearance alone; for well they knew that, in practice, this article would have precisely the same effect as that other article prescribing the famous inviolability. How in fact could these persons, who for five-and

y years have known the magna-
na firmness of character of Pius
persuade themselves that he
l lower his dignity to accept an
n from their criminal and sacri-
s hands, in compensation for
ingdom they have taken from
They understood beforehand
this would be impossible, be-
, even admitting that the Holy
r had been willing to admit
civil list, under the title of res-
n, a thing not unlawful in itself
ne without prejudice to his
, they perceived only too clear-
t he could not have done so in
of the malignant interpreta-
which would have followed the
ccasioning an immense scandal
lamor; as if the Pope by receiv-
modicum of that property the
of which belongs to him by
had conceded the rest, over
he has immemorial claims.
e matter, however, took such a
that these brave gentlemen
n ample field in which to dis-
large figures, and even to ac-
the name of prodigality in of-
round numbers to their vic-
Yes, indeed, they were prodi-
like unto those who offered
r to the crucified Saviour.
d, ever adorable in his provi-
, has so disposed events that
earts of Catholics throughout
orld have been moved to com-
nate their father in chains, and
old of their filial charity has
ded so wonderfully in his hands,
e has been able to succor most
fully those of his faithful ser-
who have fallen into straits for
ence' sake, together with many
nt persons who have no oth-
source for a livelihood than the
of the imprisoned Pontiff.
c glory of this munificence is
o God alone, and the merit of
to be ascribed to the faith of good Christians. On the other hand, the infamy of having embittered the captivity of the Holy Father, by reducing him, with the Sacred College and his whole court, to a state of absolute want, if he would not wear the appearance of dishonor, this belongs exclusively to the Subalpine rulers, who at the foot of the Campidoglio are enjoying the spoils of the Pontificate, as the crucifiers on Mount Calvary enjoyed the spoils obtained by rending the garments of Christ.

VI.

The jailers, and the friends and servants of the jailers of the Holy Father, boast very much of the ample liberty he enjoys, which he can use during his imprisonment for the regulation of the church and for performing his office as Pope.

Let us examine a little in what this charming liberty consists. This at the very first glance resolves itself into the following very clear formula: The Pope is at liberty to do that—and that alone—which the inimical power whose prisoner he is permits him to do.

And, in point of fact, the Holy Father is under this power, which holds him in its hands, being *sub hostilem potestatem redactus*, as he himself lately expressed it again in the Encyclical of May 15, 1871, in which he formally repudiates the *Guarantees* offered him in exchange for his principality. He who is under is *dependent*, and can do only that to which he who is above consents. Thus the liberty of the Pope is subject to the limits which the inimical power, his oppressor, pleases to impose on him. And this same law of the Guarantees is the proof of the fact, inasmuch as it contains only a concession of hypothetical privileges. But he who

concedes accounts himself superior to him to whom the concession is granted. Whence the true measure of the liberty of Pius IX. as Pope, is now simply the arbitrary will of Italian Masonry, governed by the Subalpinists. This is a certain fact as to matters in general.

With regard to particulars, the Holy Father uses such liberty as he owes to his own courage and diligence, and the inimical power, his jailer, cannot hinder him, though it would willingly do so, because a power stronger than itself, or certain human respects, forbid such opposition. As, for example, the Subalpine patrons would gladly hinder his Holiness from publishing bulls or encyclicals, in condemnation of their lofty enterprises against God, religion, and the Apostolic See. His Holiness, not being at liberty to publish them in Rome under their very nose, sends them out of Italy to be printed, and in this way publishes them.

Now, what can these very liberal gentlemen do in a case like this? Drag the Pope before the courts, and imprison him in the Castle of St. Angelo? Most willingly would they do this; but the rulers of Europe would oppose it. There is, then, no course left to them except to interdict the publication of them within the state by sequestrating the papers which reprint these acts of the Pope; and this they did with the Encyclical of November 1, 1870. If for others of later appearance they have shut their eyes and left them to their course, it has been because they have at last been obliged to pay some regard to public opinion, and have found their account in putting on a semblance of toleration.

In a similar manner, the Holy Father, finding that the Subalpine masters trumpeted forth loudly to the world that he was left at h in the creation of bishops througho Italy, embraced the opportunity exercise his right and to fulfil h duty. With prudence certainly, b yet with boldness, he addressed him self to the work. The matter was displeasing to our gentlemen. how were they to hinder it? 'I wanted to give the Christian worl to understand that they are honora ble men, not only in the mod sense of the word, but also som what in the ancient sense: they want ed to prove that they knew how keep their word without being co pelled by cannons so to do. So *this time* it does not appear that th will refuse entrance into their dioc es to the new pastors.

But thieves and loyalists as t are, they have taken advantage this act of the Holy Father, turnin it to their own interest by cowardl proclaiming in every direction th the Holy Father, by thus using privileges comprised in the law the Guarantees respecting the indu tion of bishops into their sees, h *ipso facto*, *accepted* their law, thus retracted his refusal of the 1 of May, 1871, and thus (according them) the conciliation between th selves and the Holy See is in progress; and it will not be long be fore the august Pontiff will give his kingly crown into the hands John Lanza: and in this manner Italy of the Subalpinists will enj the distinguished honor of hav the supreme head of the church the court-chaplain, and most hum servant of his ministers: an ho certainly due to their merits as aga faith, morality, and Catholic ship.

This attempt at imposition is more senseless in that it sup that the Holy Father had no right to nominate the bishops

tate privilege; while the con-
s the case: the insertion of the
n these nominations is merely
lege granted by the Pope: and
:t that the Pope has not thus
ized the Subalpine gentlemen
· of their own territory proves
e, far from accepting their
ntees, does not even recognize
as juridically masters of the
in which they compiled the

the senselessness of the at-
·d imposition serves to prove
etermined they are to prevent
oly Father from exercising any
berty.

VII.

epting the above-named use of
erty, which the Holy Father
'eously exercises in spite of the
repugnance of his jailers, he
rything else remains in all the
and perplexities with which
iink fit to surround him. And

'ius IX. is not at liberty to
journal in Rome, in which
y contradict the infinite num-
falsities which the inimical
through its officious and offi-
acles, utters against his person,
t his acts, those of his court,
le of the ministers of the Holy

ild he do so, the executive
subject him to all those rigor-
ieasures and sequestrations to
all the Catholics sheets of
have been subjected which
ndeavored to defend his honor
cause.

ius IX., as we have already
out, is no longer at liberty
olish his bulls, encyclicals, or
ions in Rome: the fact being
e inimical power, in this same
the Guarantees, has reserved to itself the faculty of judging them; and hence, either by way of legal or illegal confiscations, has full and absolute power to suppress their publication by main force. This obliges the head of the church to make public his acts regarding the universal government of Catholicism, by despatching them to be divulged outside the dominion of his jailers; as he has done up to this date, and will continue to do *donec transeat iniquitas.*

3. Pius IX. in Rome is not at liberty to contradict publicly by telegraph the inventions concerning himself and his Pontifical acts which the inimical power, his jailer, diffuses through the world by this said telegraph; because the telegraph is under the express authority of said power, and the use of it can be denied or rendered difficult at its pleasure. Thus, last March the world received through the telegraph fabulous accounts of a consistory held by the Pope, of an allocution and other particular acts, all invented on the spur of the moment; and before the world can detect the disgraceful imposture, it may expect that for many days the falsehoods will be printed even in Catholic journals, because our Subalpine gentlemen have it in their power to mislead by means of the telegraph the Catholic community with any kind of misrepresentation concerning the words and deeds of the Pope, without the possibility of the Pope's being able immediately to undeceive them. Whence the necessity that *no reliance at all* should be placed on any telegram that the agency of the Subalpine government transmits from Rome respecting the words or affairs of the Supreme Pontiff.

4. Pius IX. in Rome is not at liberty to carry on a private corre-

spondence securely with the bishops and faithful of the world by means of letters or telegrams; because both mails and telegraphs belong to the inimical power which holds him captive. As an inimical power, precisely because it is inimical, believes itself licensed to take every precaution regarding its imprisoned *enemy*, so no one can ever feel certain that the secrecy of the letters interchanged has not been violated, or that the telegrams have not been altered or refused. All this is *a question of trust.* But meanwhile, setting aside the case of telegrams directed to the Pope, and refused by the telegraph officials, it is a fact that the Holy Father is obliged to keep his missives away from the mail-bags of Italy when he has any important correspondence to carry on, as also other persons are obliged to do when they wish to communicate with the Holy See. We repeat it: *it is a question of trust:* and how much those who now command in Rome may be trusted is attested by the honesty they have thus far exhibited.

5. Pius IX. in Rome and in the Vatican is not at liberty to receive every one who wishes to visit him, or whom it may be necessary he should see. All the approaches to the Pontifical palace are guarded by bailiffs of the inimical power. And these men, though they may often allow the goers and comers to be insulted by the rabble, never, however, omit to play the spy. This office they perform so well that certain journals written by those who are doubly linked with the police of the Subalpine gentry would be able to furnish, if needed, the daily list of all those admitted to the vestibule of the apostolic residence. It is clear from these circumstances that it depends solely on the arbitrary will of the inimical power to forbid an the power of ingress, or, if it pre expel the individual from the and thus save him the trouble journey to the Vatican.

In addition to these fact stonings, menaces, hootings, an ilar acts of urbanity practised streets of Rome and in the nei hood of St. Peter's toward th merous Catholic deputations came this year to pay their h to the august prisoner, by the introduced through the breach *Porta Pia*—these attest how gr that beautiful liberty enjoyed t Pope in receiving visitors, w they come of their own acc that he sends for them.

6. Pius IX. in Rome wi long be at liberty to regulate t ligious institutions, and to e them in the service of the chu as is right and proper he shoul because the inimical power is al on the alert to deprive the Hol of this strong spiritual garrison abolishing the orders, and dep them of their property. The riors-general of these orders, are immediately subject to the tiff, will in a short time have no to eat, no room to shelter them will wander homeless over the and lose their subjects on all In this way, one of the instru of the Pontiff, most useful to h the administration of the churc be, as it were, broken in his han in the city in which the Head Catholic Church has his sea profession of the evangelical will be prohibited; and the will not be even able to give s to the various missionaries wh toiling in the cause of Christ among the heathen of Asia America, when they come to r an account of their newly fo missions; for in all Rome he w

have a religious house of hos- at his disposal.

will not lengthen details in to enumerate the various other lar modes of liberty which the Father can no longer exercise fulfilment of his supreme office. position we have already given to prove that he has no lib- ave such as the author of his permits, either from his own ity or from other causes; the sion being compulsory on the the enemy, and most unwill- given. And this is the marvel- berty now enjoyed by the Sov- Pontiff, thanks to the Subal- who have dethroned him and sed him in Rome itself, out of as they say, for the holy !

VIII.

us be just. Our Holy Father be in a much worse condition he present one. His jailers as not do him all the wrong they wish, but are not able to do This is true enough. They ot as yet assailed the Vatican, agged Pius IX. to the Fortress cona, as they have done to ustrious Cardinal Morichini, of Jesi; or to a convent of as they have done to the im- table Cardinal de Angelis. We it: they would like to do this, not able; they would like to do nd worse, but the governments rope have absolutely forbidden o set foot in the Vatican, or to nds on the Sovereign Pontiff. ut nothing else restrains them frenzy of their hatred from be- g him at once. This and no- lse constrains them to mode- e impetuosity of their hatred rying on their persecutions the Papacy. Fear compels ittle Neros to don the mantle of Julian; for, while under the eyes of two diplomatic bodies in Rome, they dare not carry their outrages on the Pope and his dignity beyond a certain limit.

From this we may infer that the only and *ultimate* safeguard remaining at the present moment to the Holy Father in the Vatican is not the law called the law of the Guarantees, nor is it trust in the governors, but the corps of diplomatists who have received from their various governments instructions to maintain inviolate the asylum of the octogenarian Pontiff, and to protect his august person.

Were it not for this only and ultimate safeguard, Catholics throughout the world would now be weeping over their Father exiled from Rome, and perhaps as having already expired from the bullets or sword of the enemy.

IX.

But how long will this only and ultimate safeguard endure?—this protection which renders the life and person of the Holy Father secure in Rome?

As long as the Subalpinists hold the reins of government in Italy, there seems no reason to fear that the security will become less. These men know too well that, were they to lose Rome, they would lose everything; and the only mode of keeping possession of Rome a little longer is not to violate the Vatican. But on that day on which the Italian faction shall get tired of being led by these ten or twelve Piedmontese who form the perpetual Zodiac of the ministry; on that day when this faction is weary of seeing all the master-machinery of the state, the army, finance, bureaucracy, and diplomacy regulated by Piedmontese; on that day when it takes it into its head to render the

government of this factious Italy *Italian* in its manner of rebellion, rather than provincial—on that day the danger will arise that even this said only and ultimate safeguard may lose its force. For in such a case, the mobocracy would come to the surface, and a scene of destruction would be inaugurated varying little from that carried out by the Commune of Paris.

The dilemma is this: either the Subalpinists or the Socialists must prove fatal to our poor Italy, prepared as it is for revolution. God alone knows what is to happen in the proximate future. But it is certain that the present condition of the Holy Father in Rome cannot endure much longer: it is certain that any agreement between him and his spoilers is utterly out of the question. It is also certain that Europe could not tolerate for a series of years that the Head of the Catholic Church should be held as a prisoner by the men who at the present day hold dominion throughout the Peninsula; and, finally, it is certain that in his own time God will interfere, and his intervention will not be to reward the persecutors of his Vicar on earth. These four certainties keep the world in suspense, and the authors and approvers of the transitory triumph of the *Porta Pia* in uneasiness.

But in this extremity of affairs and in this intense trepidation of mind, what is the duty of Catholics?

Is it to wish for an agreement between the Pope and the inimical power which oppresses him?

This is but to assume the office of members of the faction, under the disguise of zealous Catholics. He only who hath his part in the leaven of the Pharisees can believe it possible for the successor of St. Peter to sacrifice the eternal rights of Christ to the interests of Belial.

Is it to recommend the H
ther to abandon his own st
seek compensation in some C
country outside of Italy?
the advice of the impruden
Holy Father has received fr
the grace of office to de
what is the best for the Apost
and for the church. No on
trouble himself to give advice
ed. He has his natural cou
and above all he has the S
the Lord, with whom he is i
and fervent communion. If I
remains in Rome, notwiths
the satanic tempest which h
wildly and so furiously agair
it is a sign that he knows su
the will of God, and therefore
it his duty to remain. In th
of events, we shall see that, if t
has remained in Rome, it is
it was best that he should
there.

The real duty of Catholic
the other hand (besides as
prayer, conformably to the e
of the primitive Christians w
Peter was *in vinculis*), to unite
work as to hasten the libera
our common Father.

The Italian factionists re
us Catholics of Italy with bei
ricides because we implore fro
and men this sighed-for lib
But it seems to us that it is th
commit parricide who, havi
prisoned the Pope after officia
claring such an act to be cont
the laws of nations and mor
barbarous, have brought inju
evil upon the country which
ever praying God to diminis
for the rest, we Italian Catho
not understand how the ind
ence, glory, and prosperity o
country can be made prop
consist in the spoliation and c
of the Supreme Pontiff, and in
trod under foot by the Subalpi

nploring the liberation of
r Father, have not the re-
ea that that liberation will
part of Italy its independ-
he honor of calling foreign-
taly, to subject it to personal
e, and to pay for such pow-
resenting these foreigners
an provinces, nay, with the
Italy itself—we Catholics
s to the idol of the Sub-
to their Cavour, and to their
every color.

alian Catholics, we say it
not desire that the domin-
our Father should bring with
eign domination, not even
nd's-breadth of Italian ter-
The shameful traffic in peo-
n Italian territory could not
a means of liberating the
for the Subalpinists it has
eans of the so-called liber-
Italy. In this we are all
we wish for the independ-
justice, because justice
sures the happiness of na-

Italian Catholics can of
do little, because the dom-
imical power, being the
the Pope, is naturally our
so, although we are the immense national majority. We are the deplorable victims of modern liberty, which wholly consists in the oppression of the many, who are honest but weak, beneath the feet of the few, who are crafty and strong. Besides this, very serious and insuperable difficulties of conscience oblige us to abstain from using the most powerful of legal arms which liberalism says it has left in the hands of that majority which is trodden under foot by the minority. So that, if we may from this take occasion to cherish more solid hopes that God will at length assist us in effecting means of safety, yet in actual combat we now find ourselves unequal to the contest.

This is not the case with the Catholics of the other countries of Europe. It is their peculiar privilege so to address themselves to the work that their governments may not only preserve and strengthen the only and ultimate safeguard of the life and person of the Holy Father in Rome; but that they may use their power for his liberation; that thus with his full liberty the true liberty of the people may again flourish—that liberty which is now enchained with Pius IX. in the Vatican.

ELINOR'S TRIAL.

"I DO think John Lloyd is very weak in giving in to his wife so much! To think now of his letting her send Elinor to a convent school! Such a risk for a Protestant! Ten chances to one that Elinor comes back a Papist. And then her *reasons* are so absurd, that Protestant boarding-schools cultivate too much of folly and fashion, etc.! I have no patience with Elizabeth. If she were a Catholic herself, there might be some excuse for her wanting her daughter educated among them, but as she is a Protestant, I think Protestant schools might serve her purpose."

Thus speaks Mrs. Robert Lennox of her husband's sister. She is talking to her husband while they are going home from a fashionable church in New York. She is a stately, handsome lady, to whom her rich attire seems well adapted. Just now she appears displeased and somewhat more haughty than usual, but the face is refined and the bearing polished.

More gentle than his wife in the treatment of the question in hand is Mr. Lennox.

"Well, I cannot say Elizabeth is so very far out of the way. You know John's means are very limited, and these convent schools are cheaper than ours. Besides, Elizabeth knows Elly cannot compete in dress and all the furbelows, as our Lizzie does. So she prefers not to have her exposed to the uncomfortableness of being the subject of derogatory comparisons. You know young folks are keenly sensitive on such points."

"But, Robert, must such reasons weigh against the risk of perverting the girl's faith, the undermining of her religion? Would you trust those sly, insinuating sisters with our daughter?"

Mr. Lennox smiles significantly as he replies: "I would not object to Lizzie's receiving some of that peculiar, modest, quiet air which those sisters have and so often impart to their pupils. There is some nameless charm, I cannot describe it better than by saying it is the opposite of that which the young ladies of the present day cultivate for their deportment, and which seems to belong almost exclusively to this training."

"Pshaw! Mere affectation of meekness. The girls are all the same at heart. Why should not they be? I tell you it isn't worth the risk! Mark my words, you'll see the effect on Elly's religion."

"Well, you know Elizabeth said that even that change of religion was better than the irreligion or isms of the day."

"Now, Robert, it is just to oppose me that you so persistently uphold Elizabeth in this. Is it to be supposed that girls of sixteen are going to take to isms in Protestant schools or irreligion either? Why, they don't know enough for that, at their age."

"I do not dispute you. I only think that Elizabeth has preferred for Elly this risk rather than have her of John's state of mind. And that is why John is so easy in the matter. Being of no faith himself, he prides himself on being also of no prejudice. 'The greater the faith, the greater the bigotry,' he says."

id I think you are just about as John," says the lady. "I believe you listened to the ser- t all to-day."

last charge passes unanswer- cause they have arrived at their oor, where we leave them.

II.

·years after this, the cousins, Lennox and Elinor Lloyd, have ed from their respective schools: from her fashionable seminary, she has received every advan- 1at money could purchase, and she has associated with the ters of the wealthiest, if not the efined, families in the land. And lth will not purchase the means pen the way for refinement, what will? Does it not free ath from the thorns of toil, me and means for culture and vel, and to surround ourselves he ennobling influences of art? bove all, does it not grant us ee indulgence of generous im- ? Do not all the mortal ills h which bear upon the rich lso on the poor, with more to stand in the way of their nent? It would seem so.

ie Lennox has all these advan- of wealth in her case, but her Elinor Lloyd is the daughter poor man. Poorer now than s two years ago, when he let ident wife have her way in the of a convent school for her ter. Elinor has been very with the sisters, to whom she become sincerely attached. good example has not been pon her, but she denies indig- that any under-handed means een used to warp her religious s. They have simply and ly acted out the dictates of own faith, exacting from her only such general compliance as would be required in the schools of any denomination among Protestants. If her affections have been won, and her young heart drawn toward the religion of these gentle teachers, that was the risk her mother took when she sent her willingly among the Sisters of Charity.

The cousins are nearly of an age. Lizzie is named after her father's sister, Mrs. Lloyd, and Elinor after her aunt, Mrs. Lennox.

These cousins are strikingly alike, and yet singularly unlike in their appearance. Their faces seem to have been cast in almost the same mould, so exactly does every feature correspond, but the coloring is so different that they present opposite types of beauty. For they are very beautiful. Lizzie is exceedingly fair, with light auburn hair and hazel eyes; the same reddish tint seeming to lurk in the eyes and lashes as in the hair, which peculiarity any close observer of faces may often see in this type. But Elinor's eyes are a dark brown, and her hair is very dark. She is too fair and pale for a brunette, and her eyes are not black enough. Despite this difference in color, they are very like her cousin Lizzie's light orbs in expression. It is as if a painter should take two sketches of the same face, and simply change his colors for the touching of them. Indeed, a cast of each might pass for the same person, so like are they, even to the carriage of the head, the turn of the throat, the curve of the shoulders. I am thus exact in my description, because out of this wonderful likeness and difference of face and form came Elinor's trial. But now, at eighteen, Elinor's face is softer and sweeter than that of her blonde cousin. This difference is seen as they are listening or talking, more than while their faces are in

repose. Shall we say that it is the result of training and education that Elinor seems the more refined and modest? Or is it only a matter of inheritance, or a trick of manner betokening nothing? I present them thus to the reader, who may guess somewhat of their respective characters, as they sit chatting their cousinly talk in Lizzie's room. Lizzie is dressing to go out with Elinor, and talking while she proceeds with her toilet.

"But, Elly, where is the harm of flirting a little, so long as you do nothing serious, and never commit yourself?"

"I think you do commit yourself, Lizzie, when you put pen to paper to answer a stranger's letter, and when you cannot tell whether he is true or false. More likely he is the latter, from the very fact of his trying to draw you on. How do you know how he may use your letter?"

"But I haven't signed my name, only my own initials. I use E. L., not L. L. And you know I am known rather as Lizzie Lennox than Elizabeth Lennox. No one ever thinks of me as Elizabeth—I don't seem to be that to myself. Now, you are either Elinor or Elly, but I am just Lizzie. So you see I can hide under my own honest initials."

"Ah Lizzie! why hide at all? Give it up. I don't like this kind of thing. I don't believe the men who write to girls in this way care one bit for them, except to make them contribute to their own amusement, and feed their conceit. What good does it do when you don't even see each other?"

"But we may, after, if we want to, you know."

"I shouldn't want to see him, Lizzie; I hope you will never meet."

"Now, Elly, it is just being with those sisters that makes you talk so. Why, all the girls do so. It is only for fun, and the young men know we don't mean wrong. I could say 'Evil he who evil thinks,' only I know you are not evil, only sistenfied in this matter."

"But, Lizzie, sisterified or not, you know I like fun as much as other girls, only I don't think this *is* fun: I think it isn't just right. It is making yourself too cheap. I don't like men well enough to do so much for their amusement. I may be peculiar, but I certainly hate a covert thing, and personals in the newspapers are very covert and very cowardly. Mamma says a respectable paper will not publish them. Besides, you dare not let your father and mother know this, dare you?"

"Oh! of course they would get a great scare, and think I was going to do something much worse than I mean. But that doesn't prove I would do wrong."

"No; but, Lizzie, don't you hate to deceive them when they trust you so freely? Is this stranger to be trusted and they not?"

"Well, I don't want to give pain to either papa or mamma; and so if they don't know it, they will be spared all pain and fuss in the matter, and nobody hurt. Now I'm ready. Let's go." And the two leaving the house, the subject is dropped for the time

Only one month has passed since the cousins have had this morning's talk together, but it has brought a great change in their feelings and relations to each other.

First, Elinor has quietly but courageously avowed herself a Catholic. Alone and unsupported she has made the great step—alone she goes to Mass and Vespers—and without sympathy from her family she practises faithfully all the observances of her

h. In all this, she has shown
unt Lennox a wise prophet,
the lady is no less indignant on
account. She enlarges upon
avorite text, and congratulates
f that she has taken no such
or her own daughter's falling
popish pitfalls, and traps set for
young and innocent. Lizzie
es to consider herself called
to give up the intimacy and
all intercourse with her cousin.
she is secretly governed by a
of annoyance at Elinor's per-
, discountenancing of her clan-
e correspondences, but she
a show of setting herself against
ish influences."

parents of Elinor have taken
atter with seeming indifference.
ses none of their love in conse-
e of the change in her faith,
hey are sure she is quite as
a daughter as ever. But a
r trouble, if this is a trouble,
absorbs their minds. John
has failed in business and fail-
health. He is a broken-down
In this emergency, Elinor has
mined to accept a situation as
al governess in a wealthy fami-
he has felt the tug at her heart-
, no less from her wounded
in the matter of her changed
position, than in the hard ne-
to leave her home and pa-
She is no saint, only a good,
minded girl, who is scrupulous-
scientious in all things. She
s against a bitter feeling of al-
envy toward the better luck
asier life of her cousin. She
not really wish Lizzie to be as
as herself, and she is sure she
rather be herself than Lizzie,
he does wish her father and
r were in the same comfortable
hat her uncle and aunt enjoy.
ncle is disposed to be very kind
r, but he is hampered by his
wife and daughter in their bitter opposition to her. He has sent her a check to defray all necessary expenses in her wardrobe. So she goes to her new home so nicely clad that at least no air of shabbiness clings to her. Brave as she may be, this feminine sensitiveness to her appearance is very acute in her. Foolish vanity concerning dress she may not have, but, being young, she is only natural in liking to look well, to pass criticism which she cannot ignore at least creditably. If a young woman has not this much of feeling concerning her toilet, she is probably slovenly, or else she affects an eccentricity which is more disagreeable than a love for finery. Elinor is refined in her nature, and she is not strong-minded, so she likes the good opinion of others.

Elinor soon settles into the new and changed relations of her life, the more easily because her employer proves exceedingly kind. As her forte is music, she is of course, in the exercise of that accomplishment, brought into more constant contact and intercourse with the guests at the house than the mere instruction and supervision of her pupils would demand. Her seat at the piano calls to her the attention and brings upon her the criticism of many who otherwise might never notice her. And so it has happened that young Mr. Schuyler, the brother of her hostess, has more frequently than any other turned the leaves of her music, sang to her accompaniment, and gazed admiringly upon the pretty hands moving over the keys and upon the charming face turned to the pages before it. Mr. Schuyler is an agreeable young gentleman, good-looking enough, graceful enough, and flattering enough in his address to ladies to win their pleased recognition of his attentions. But buzzing

in his admiration around each sweet flower like the veriest male coquette of a bee, he is just unstable enough also to tantalize the fair recipients of his attentions. Elinor likes him, but with a little reserve. She is not of a distrustful nature, but she does not quite like Mr. Schuyler's manner to her. He has been very unreserved in his admiration. He has attempted some sentimental love-making, but there has always been a sort of holding back—a non-committal manner, which has not seemed to her straightforward and manly. It has appeared to her that he has been attempting to gain her regard without making any actual avowal himself, and that he is trying to amuse himself or feed his own vanity at her expense. Yet she is so afraid of being unjust to him, knowing that her position in the family may make her unduly sensitive, that she strives against this feeling. He really is very kind in a great many little ways which she would be ashamed not to acknowledge, and she thinks, if she were not a governess for his sister, she might receive his attentions in a less cavilling spirit.

In the meantime, Mr. Schuyler studies Elinor from quite a different point of view from any she imagines. He has found by repeated experiment that he cannot make her understand or respond to various little devices which he has been in the habit of using to flirt with certain school-girls whom he has met often in his daily walks and rides. All these signals pass unnoticed upon the convent girl. But in fluttering thus around this innocent, cold light, the gay moth has got his wings singed. He does really love Elinor as much as such a nature is capable of loving. Just because she has *not* responded to any of his advances, he has become more seriously interested in her. But just when an honorable feeling of choosing her from all others is dawning as a possibility on his mind, a wonderful discovery bursts upon him.

He has been amusing himself by conducting a correspondence with some unknown lady who has signed herself "E. L." This incognita has at last yielded to an oft-urged request to send her picture, and a fine photograph of a beautiful girl has come to him. Whose face does he see? "By all that is astounding," he says, "Miss Lloyd!" He cannot be mistaken. The very same. It is a Rembrandt shadow picture, by which he studies every line of the profile, while it shows also the contour of the full face. There is the dark hair waving from the same fair forehead. The eyes are the same dark orbs with the long lashes, only he has never seen just this bright, coquettish, laughing look in them before. It is wonderfully charming in the picture, but he really does not like it as well as the other thoughtful, intent gaze he has lately come to love so well.

"The demure little cheat!" he says. "Well, she is very versatile, it must be confessed. Who would have thought it? But stop. This may be a cheat. The whole thing is so unlike her. I do believe the writer has sent Miss Lloyd's picture instead of her own. 'E. L.' L for Lloyd certainly, and I saw Elinor Lloyd written on her music, and, by Jove! I think it was the very writing. I'll look again"—which he does, and finds it to be just the very same E and L; and no wonder, for Lizzie Lennox wrote it in other days, when she gave that music to her cousin.

Then he observes, what careless Lizzie has never once thought of, the name of the photographer, to whom he goes at once, and by no very

means discovers the name of original. And here he is again bed. He finds he has the graph of Miss Lizzie Lennox. ," he says to himself, "and L., after all," and in his bewil- it is actually some days be- occurs to him that Lizzie is name for Elizabeth.

, having arrived thus far in his of information under difficul- is unable to decide whether Miss Lennox or Miss Lloyd. dilemma he questions his sis- s. Wood, and determines that n scarcely be any other than ss Lloyd she professes herself. false name has been given the grapher, he thinks; and he up his mind that Miss Lloyd, unquestionably very charm- about as profound a coquette s ever likely to meet.

so believing, his manner to- Elinor takes on a new phase, pleases her so little that it has ect of making her more re- than heretofore. She now him as much as possible, and e is conscious of a sharp pain being driven to an attitude of e. She is young and frank, ould be light-hearted if in her osition. She has really liked rick Schuyler because she found mpanionable in a house where either older or younger than except him. Their tastes are in many things, and of late d seemed to her more honest. ow he treats her with a certain arity of look and tone which of- , her nice sense of propriety. nnot guess at the false position hich she is placed. She has very reticent concerning herself her relatives. True pride and y have made her forbear to to her wealthy relations, the oxes, now that she is supporting herself. She does not wish to seem to make any claim for consideration outside of her own individual merits. This is not vanity, but proper self-respect; and this feeling is increased by the utter silence which Lizzie has preserved toward her. But as she withdraws from even the slight friendship which she had allowed to spring up between herself and Mr. Schuyler, she feels more lonely. Her religion separates her also from a closer confidence with Mrs. Wood, who goes to a fashionable Unitarian church.

But Frederick Schuyler does not give up his interest in this baffling coquette, for so he firmly believes Elinor to be. Does he not hold the proof? He has sent his own picture to E. L. at the usual address, and he firmly believes that Elinor Lloyd has that picture in her possession. He waits until he receives an acknowledgment from E. L.; and then he watches Elinor. He is prepared to see her betray her overwhelming confusion at discovering who her unknown correspondent is. What, then, is his amazement, his disappointment, at seeing no ripple of disturbance in her composed demeanor! He is exasperated at this assurance. He determines to shake her composure by direct means. The opportunity offers only too soon.

As the last music lesson for the day is finished and the pupil bounds from the room, Mr. Frederick Schuyler presents himself with a peculiar and, to Elinor, an offensive smile on his face.

"Miss Lloyd," he says blandly, "do you not think it is time to drop this masking?"

Elinor looks at him with wondering and offended eyes. They are not the eyes of either the picture, or the soft brown ones he has known hitherto as hers. They flash up to

him in angry brilliancy as she replies:

"I do not understand you, sir!" So sure is he, and so amazed at this stubbornness, that he almost as indignantly replies:

"And I am sure I cannot understand you!"

"I do not desire that you should," she retorts: "but I think it due to myself to demand why you presume to thus address me, Mr. Schuyler."

The offended tone remains, but blended with it is a little faint touch of grieved feeling, which his nice ear detects.

"Can you pretend to still treat me as if you did not recognize me? Is my picture so unlike me that you do not know the original?"

"Your picture!" and such a world of wonderment is expressed in her voice that he thinks she ought to be on the stage for consummate acting.

"Perhaps you do not recognize this," and he holds before her a picture so like herself that she is confounded. For the moment, she really does not see her cousin Lizzie as plainly as herself. The photograph, like one of those libellous stories which are true in detail, but false in implication, has given the reddish tint in Lizzie's hair, brows, and lashes dark as her own, and there is the blonde cousin presented, the very counterpart of the brunette, one. The light hazel eyes are in the photograph, dark as Elinor's own.

Elinor gazes speechless for a moment. Then she recognizes the dress of her cousin, and the expression *not* her own which she knows so well. It all rushes upon her perception at once—the cruel mistake—Lizzie's clandestine correspondence, of which she disapproved so much—the well-known resemblance between them—the picture more like herself than Lizzie—she sees it all, and she sees Mr. Schuyler's triumph in her discomfiture. Guilty Lizzie would not look so guilty as innocent Elinor looks now.

"Checkmate!" says Mr. Schuyler. His tone stings her.

"Mr. Schuyler, this is not my picture. I never sat for it."

"Miss Lloyd!"

"I repeat, sir! This is not my picture, and I wear no mask."

"But you are 'E. L.,'" he says, showing her his last missive with that signature, "and you acknowledge receiving one like this," and he confronts her with a duplicate of his own picture.

"My name is Elinor Lloyd, and I have never written to you, and this is the first time I have seen either of these pictures," she replies, glancing disdainfully at each of them.

"Do you know whose this is?" he asks.

At this point-blank question, Elinor bursts into tears. The cruelty of the position in which she finds herself is too much for her. She will not betray her cousin, and she knows that on her own denial alone, against overwhelming evidence, rests her defence of herself. And in tears, distressed beyond measure, she rushes from the room. Mr. Schuyler gives a long, low whistle. He is inclined to believe she has told him the truth, in spite of all he knows and has seen. For why does she wish to deny it? What girl who could do this thing would so spurn the accusation? Her proud assertion, "My name is Elinor Lloyd, and I have never written to you," rings in his ears. He believes it, as we will all of us sometimes believe, apparently against reason. He knows that he wishes to believe in her truth, despite his vanity.

A little book lies near a roll of music on the piano, with her gloves

ıat. He takes up this book xamines it, for no reason exıat it appears to belong to her. y of Dickens' *Barnaby Rudge*, mark at the description of the ieorge Gordon Riots, and pen-:ks on the margin. He turns the fly-leaf, and sees written, beth Lennox, from her brother ." O cruel evidence! "Cirnce, that unspiritual god and ıtor," again shows Elinor as a Vhat can he do now but doubt rd? Elinor meanwhile is pacr room in a tumult of agita-Her first impulse is to abanr engagement with Mrs. Wood ·, and go to her parents. But · among other hard imposiorbids us acting on the dicf pride, be it ever so honora-Elinor shrinks from staying, o shrinks from giving her rear leaving to her parents or to Wood. To give false ones, g her real one, never for one it occurs to her. She feels the cruelty, the injustice of ne position in which Lizzie's s placed her. Yet she, is too s at heart to betray Lizzie her mother. She knows that izzie told her of this "bit of was in confidence, and troue as the trust has proved, she eep it until she is released. feels how hard it is to know act rightly, unaided, uncoun-One refuge, however, she has counsellor who never betrays t, and who does not require ain's name or identity. O privilege of a Catholic! The re refuge of the confessional or's. What better human nd comforter than her pastor seek? No fears of a betray-t is here. So to him she goes, n him she receives the needgth to bear her heavy trial—for heavy trial it is on such a young heart, all the more so because she cannot suppose her silence has put a stop to this disgraceful affair. She has written to Lizzie explaining what has happened, and begging her to lift this weight from her, and at least free her from this blame. And Lizzie has indignantly replied that she will not interfere, and that she believes Elinor to be the betrayer of her name to Fred Schuyler, and moreover hints that it has been done to win him to herself.

This rouses Elinor to such a degree that she nearly forgets her counsel to "return good for evil." Prayer and meditation, however, those best of medicines for disturbed souls, work their good effect for her, and she is able still to bear in silence, trusting that time will lift the stigma off her. So she shuns as best she can all intercourse with Mr. Schuyler.

And thus about three unhappy weeks pass. Mr. Schuyler gives up trying to enlist Elinor's attention, and he leaves the last communication of E. L. unanswered. He receives no more of those interesting missives. Lizzie, thoroughly frightened, stops this amusement for herself.

But at last the Nemesis, circumstance, overtakes her—the circumstance of meeting Mr. Frederick Schuyler at a party. A very small circumstance apparently, but pregnant with much for three individuals. He sees her standing not far off from him, in all the blaze of gas-light and full dress. He has never seen Elinor at this advantage, but the perfect profile and the proud carriage of the head impress him at once. Yet those blonde locks and the light laughing eyes—these are neither like Elinor's nor the picture. Lovely this face certainly is, but he remembers the darker one as pleasing him more.

The remarkable resemblance, however, has so startled him, that he actually trembles as he asks a friend who has been talking with her to tell him her name.

"Miss Lennox."

"Do you know her first name?" he says, with forced composure.

"Oh! yes. Lizzie Lennox and I are old friends; let me introduce you." And in the brief interval before he is presented, he only remembers that it is L. L. and not E. L., the lady of the photograph but not of the correspondence.

Lizzie passes this ordeal with a frightened, throbbing heart, but a polite, calm exterior, thankful to be very soon claimed for the next dance, and to leave Mr. Schuylèr for the present at least. She is a foolish coquette, but not an evil-minded girl. Weak, vain, selfish, but not bad-hearted—she has really felt troubled by the mean way in which she has refused to clear her cousin of the suspicion which she has brought upon her, but her selfishness has prevailed in the matter. To protect herself has seemed to her of more consequence than to clear Elinor. And the possible consequence of her parents knowing all about this little escapade has not seemed to her at all pleasant to contemplate. And so she has been vacillating between the desire to do right and the fear of exposure ever since she has received Elinor's letter. She is equally ignorant of how much she may be known to Mr. Schuyler, or how far she may be protected by her cousin's magnanimity. She moreover finds Mr. Schuyler better than his photograph on inspection, as a handsome face generally is better than a photograph of it. Meanwhile, that gentleman has recollected that Elizabeth and Lizzie are the same name. He has been watching this airy, graceful dancer, and he has seen that she has been observing him. Elinor is absolved from all blame in his mind. The only shred of mystery left is the name in that book of hers. Lizzie, resting after her last round dance, sees him approach with both dread and pleasure. He wastes no time in prefatory remarks, but says, "Miss Lennox, are you related to a Miss Elinor Lloyd?"

Lizzie has the command of this situation better than Mr. Schuyler. She knows the full purport of the question, but being asked by Elinor in a letter to speak the truth while she can yet hide it, and by handsome Fred Schuyler looking into her eyes, and knowing her for the girl he has been flirting with, are two very different matters. Here she may make a virtue of necessity, and perhaps a conquest at the same time. Ah! if our good deeds are viewed by the light of our motives, how very much the virtue in them seems to pale.

Lizzie says with charming candor, "Oh! yes, she is my cousin; do you know her?"

"Yes, Miss Lennox, and I saw your name in a book she had—*Barnaby Rudge*—and it appeared to have been quite attentively read, from the marginal notes I saw."

Lizzie shows a momentary astonishment. "Why, Mr. Schuyler, the only copy of Dickens' *Barnaby Rudge* I have is at home in the New Riverside set papa gave me only lately—since"—she pauses a little confused—"since I have seen Elly last. Besides, I don't make notes on the margins of my books, and I am quite sure Elly would not in mine. I think it could not have been my name you saw."

"Indeed, I saw it, 'Elizabeth Lennox,' and from your 'brother Robert.'"

Lizzie laughs merrily, and she looks

ay image of innocent fun as
sponds to this triumphant as-
n.

h! that's a good joke! My
r Robert! Why, that's papa!
he name is his sister's. She is
s mother. Why didn't she
ou! I hate such mysteries."
she shoots such a glance as
once have been a challenge
tible. He keeps up the badi-
but he is answering that ques-
Why did she not tell you?"
manner not flattering to Miss
x, but very much so to Miss
. The former young lady is
ite pleased with his abstracted
r. True, he dances with her,
with her, compliments her, but
not satisfied. She is wishing
his was the first intercourse she
d with Mr. Schuyler, and that
d nothing to remember of Liz-
ennox, and no previous know-
of her—she has an intuitive
that she does not stand as well
cousin in his estimation, and
er chance would have been
if she had never written to
He, however, generously makes
lusion to that correspondence.
ashamed of it for her, and
y wishes it had never been.
thinking how he can make his
with her cousin, of whom he
lad to think so well, when he
led by the words.

linor and I are not friends now
were once—before she became
holic."

iss Lloyd a Catholic!"

s, Mr. Schuyler, did you not
that? All of the family are
tants except her. Her mother
very liberal as to allow her to
ucated at a convent of those
of Charity, and this is the re-
I have never been intimate
r since."

Schuyler is very uncomforta-bly astonished by this information. He has had pleasant thoughts of the possible consequence of his reconciliation with Elinor. She has so much risen in his estimation by this solution of the picture mystery and her generous, honorable forbearance toward Lizzie, that he is thinking how very pleasant it would be to pass his life with such a companion. She certainly has proved herself very trustworthy. But a Catholic! That changes the aspect of affairs. Does he want a wife of that faith? Would not the coquettish blonde beauty be more desirable? And yet he cannot say that the ways of Miss Lennox altogether please him. He has been willing to amuse himself by a clandestine correspondence with the unknown beauty, but the known writer of those entertaining epistles does not seem to him just the one to trust with his life's chance of domestic bliss. The trust is not for just such as she. He really believes no harm of Lizzie, but he knows a worse man might think worse of her than she deserves. He wishes she were the Catholic and Elinor the Protestant. Why now, for the upholding of all his cherished beliefs and prejudices, could not the result of the two different systems of education have been reversed? Surely, he thinks, "Popery would, as a rule, have made such a girl as Lizzie rather than one like Elinor. After all," he concludes, "the difference is in their own natures, and would have shown itself had they both had the same training," and in this we cannot dispute him. But possibly, although Elinor might never have condescended to such a course, Lizzie might with better teaching have been saved from it also. The girl is not evil, only young, weak, vain, and she has needed just that which Elinor has had to sustain and strengthen her. Lizzie relies on

herself, on her own crude knowledge of the world, and on just as much advice as she chooses to accept. She never bares her conscience and her soul, as Elinor does, to any one. Therefore, she not only robs herself of the counsel of wiser heads, but she never brings upon herself that searching self-examination necessary to the seeing of herself rightly. Had she done that, had she been forced to look with this introverted gaze upon herself, she would have shrunk from placing herself in this doubtful position. She will remember this in after years with a sense of annoyance, if not of any deeper sentiment. And yet her present feeling toward Elinor is one of irritation. She knows that Elinor was right in her advice to her, and that she can look down upon her from a more exalted height. The fact that she has not taken airs of superiority on herself has not lessened Lizzie's resentment. The feeling that she is on a lower moral plane than that of her Catholic, convent-educated cousin, is a sufficient grievance of itself, and admits to her unregulated mind of no extenuation in Elinor's behalf.

It is not very easy for Mr. Schuyler to find an opportunity to explain to Elinor his enlightenment and change of views. She shuns him so sedulously that he begins to think he will have to tell her at the table, in the presence of the family, that he has met her cousin. True, he could do this without any indelicacy, but he has planned a little programme of a *tête-à-tête*, which he thinks more pleasant, to himself at least, than leaving her to draw her own conclusions from such meagre information as he can give her in the presence of others. Moreover, he does not wish to startle her before others by mentioning Lizzie's name—a sore subject to her, he suspects. So he bides his time, although impatiently. If Elinor were like her cousin, he thinks he would not wait so long for opportunity to speak. His man's nature is aroused by the necessity of pursuing.

But Mr. Schuyler has not made up his mind that he is willing to take a Catholic wife. He is at present only desirous of establishing the old pleasant, friendly footing between Elinor and himself—possibly a more tender one; but he will not yet commit himself. Not until he has seen how deeply rooted is her Catholicism—only an ism, it seems to him. He is getting impatient, however, at her continued indifference toward him. He sees that he must make his opportunity; and, being a young gentleman fertile in expedients, he resorts to waylaying her at the hour when her last music lesson is ended for the day.

Elinor's face flushes and her brow contracts—a little indignant flash is in her brown eyes as he confronts her. She remembers the last scene between them at that hour by the piano, and it does not tend to soften her manner. Evidently he has got all the work to do, unhelped by her. So he starts off, as is his usual manner, with an abrupt introduction of the subject.

"Miss Lloyd, I owe you an apology for declaring that I had your picture in my possession. I know now whose picture it is."

"You should have known it was not mine, sir, when I told you so," and she blushes again at the thought of Lizzie's being known. Even when the blame is lifted from herself, she does not rejoice in her cousin's exposure.

"I did know it, Miss Lloyd; I did believe you, on my soul, against all the wonderful evidence of the remarkable likeness to you. I did be-

that picture was not yours, or t least you did not send me it, w of my having it. But how I know that it was your r's name in your book?"

stops confused. Elinor has yet known of that added testi- against her. Had she known would at once have told him her mother's name. There reason for any mystery con- that, it being no part of Liz- onfidences to her. If he had at clue, perhaps he might have to some imperfect glimpse of th. In answer to her won- inquiry, "What book?" he w humbly:

u left a book you appeared to the piano. I took the liber- oking at it, and read a name hich I knew belonged to her picture I mistook for yours. ousin, Miss Lloyd, is very like ry unlike yourself. I met her t time since at a party; and eeing her before me, the ori- f that picture, I could scarcely it was those fair locks which made so dark in her picture. certainly be excused for not bering this trick of photo- , especially when you two are ires so very similar." He says t pleadingly, because the dis- l look is not gone from her face.

. Schuyler," she says, "your concerning that picture was natural and more excusable our supposing me the writer letter, or the giver of that pic- I think, whatever the evidence ay have supposed yourself to , my uniform bearing and r toward you should have ne from any such supposition ir part. I could not tell you picture you had, but I was tell you whose name was in ok."

"But, Miss Lloyd, even if you had given me the chance to ask you, I could scarcely take upon myself the liberty of seeming to make you accountable to myself for any name written in your book. The very asking of that would have seemed an accusation."

Elinor's quick sense of justice sees this readily, and her brow clears. Hard as it has been against herself, she admits that it was an entanglement for him. So she says more graciously: "We will let it pass, Mr. Schuyler. I wish the whole matter for all parties could be disposed of as easily as I can pass out of it." And she endeavors to leave him, with a provoking air of taking no further interest in him or his changed footing toward herself. He gently makes a motion of barring her way. She stands waiting to hear what he has further to say to her, but there is no evidence of any desire to remain.

"It is so long since we have spoken together in this friendly fashion, that I think you need not be in such haste to shorten our conversation."

He says this in such a flattering way, implying that to talk with her is the one great delight for him, that her girl's sense of pleasing and being pleased is quickened, but she only toys with the tassel of the curtain near which she is standing, and says nothing.

Again Mr. Frederick finds he has all the advances to make toward conversation, unaided by her.

"Miss Lennox tells me you were educated at a convent. Is that the reason you are so shy of me, or is it because I am a Protestant, Miss Lloyd?"

"My parents are Protestants, and all my relatives. It would be strange for me to be afraid of a Protestant."

"And yet you can be of so very different a faith. May I ask, is it a matter of conscience with you, or only one of taste?"

"I do not understand religion being a matter of only taste, Mr. Schuyler," she says simply.

"Why, don't you think it is taste, preference only for the gorgeous and ceremonial, which makes the Ritualists of St. Alban's and St. Mary's do as they do?"

"I cannot decide upon their motives, Mr. Schuyler. I only know that if my conscience were not in this, I should not separate myself in my faith from that of my family." She says this with a firm bearing and a lofty look at him which abashes him. He begins to suspect that this young convert *will not* swerve from her path from any regard for him. He has a full share of conceit, fed by his success with the girls of his acquaintance. He has won their smiles so readily heretofore, and he has pleased and flattered them so easily, that he is piqued at making no better impression now when he really tries.

Again Elinor moves to the door. He lets her pass with the words, "We are friends now, are we not?"

"Friends, oh! certainly," she says, but her tone does not seem so delighted at this change in their relations as he thinks it should be.

The truth is, Elinor has thought much over Mr. Schuyler's little flirtation with her cousin, and he has not come out from that inspection of his conduct with any great credit, in her way of looking at it. She thinks that although he may pass unscathed by such indulgence, it is not honorable in him to tempt one younger and weaker than himself into such practices. She thinks if Lizzie could find no one like him to entice her into this folly, she must perforce amuse herself in some other way. It seems to her that his motives were bad. And she suspects that if she would have lent herself to this sort of thing, he would have been just as ready to conduct an affair of the kind with herself. Her native good sense shows her this, and she is thankful for the different example and teaching which has hedged her in from ever giving a chance for such a thing. The amount of all this is, that the little inclination to like Mr. Fred Schuyler which she had once is now gone. she has no trust in him, and without trust there can be no abiding love.

Therefore, when, some days after that gentleman overcomes his dislike of her religion so far as to absolutely offer his heart, hand, and fortune to her, this disdainful Catholic astonishes him with these words:

"I think, Mr. Schuyler, that these protestations are more due to my cousin Lizzie than to me. If you speak truth to me, you have spoken false to her. If it is truth to her, what am I to believe? Mr. Schuyler, 'I must trust all in all,' or not at all."

OWEN ON SPIRITISM.*

OWEN, though he has since member of Congress, and an :an minister at Naples, was ly well known in this city as ted with Frances Wright in the *Free Enquirer*, as the of an infamous work on moral ogy, and as an avowed athe- [e now claims to be a believer existence of God, and in the of the Christian religion; but d has no freedom of action, hedged in and bound hand and y the laws of nature, and his anity is a Christianity without and indistinguishable from gated heathenism. How much s gained by his conversion, h the intervention of the spi- om atheism to demonism and superstition, it is not easy to ough it is better to believe in :vil, if one does not mistake r God, than it is to believe in g.

Owen makes, as do hundreds :rs, a mistake in using the word *ılism* for *spiritism*, and spiritual :ital or spiritalistic. Spiritualism opriated to designate a system losophy opposed to sensism or alism, and spiritual stands op- to sensual or carnal, and is ly a term to be applied to spi- ping, table-tipping, and other of the spirits. Mr. Owen is py in naming his books. He holds that the universe is governed by inflexible, immutable, and imperishable physical laws; that all events or manifestations take place by the agency of these laws; that the future is only the continuation and development of the present; and that death is only the throwing off of one's overcoat, and the life after death is the identical life, without any interruption, that we now live. We see not well how he can assert another world, or a debatable land between this world and the next. If all things and all events are produced by the agency of natural laws, and those laws are universal and unchangeable, we are unable to conceive any world above or beyond nature, or any world in any sense distinguishable from the present natural world. His books are therefore decidedly misnamed, and so named as to imply the existence of another world and a world after this, which cannot on his principles be true.

Mr. Owen's first book was mainly intended to establish the fact and to show the character of the spirit-manifestations; in his last work, his design is to show that these manifestations take place by virtue of the physical law of the universe, that they are of the same nature and origin with the Christian miracles, inspiration, and revelation, and are simply supplementary to them, or designed to continue, augment, and develop them; and to show, especially to Protestants, that, if they mean to make theology a progressive science, and the victory over their enemy the Catholic Church, they must call

* *he Debatable Land between this World Next.* With Illustrative Narratives. ert Dale Owen. New York: Carleton 1872. 16mo, pp. 542.
otfalls on the Boundary of Another With Narrative Illustrations. By Role Owen. Philadelphia: Lippincott & Co. 16mo, pp. 528

in the spirits to their aid, and accept and profit by their inspirations and revelations.

This shows that the author leans to Protestantism, and seeks its triumph over Catholicity; or that he regards Protestantism as offering a more congenial soil for the seed he would sow than the old church with her hierarchy and infallibility. Certainly, he holds that, as it is, Protestantism is losing ground. In 1580 it held the vast majority of the people of Europe, but is now only a feeble minority. Even in this country, he says, if Catholics continue to increase for a third of a century to come in the same ratio that they have for the last three-fourths of a century, they will have a decided majority. As things now go, the whole world will become Catholic, and the only way to prevent it, he thinks, is to accept the aid of the spirits. We are not so sure that this aid would suffice, for Satan, their chief, has been the fast friend of Protestants ever since he persuaded Luther to give up private Masses, and has done his best for them, and it is difficult to see what more he can do for them than he has hitherto done.

Mr. Owen, since he holds the spirit-manifestations take place by a natural law, always operative, and always producing the same effects in the same or like favorable circumstances, of course cannot recognize in them anything miraculous or supernatural; and, as he holds the alleged Christian miracles, the wonderful things recorded in the Old and New Testaments, are of the same order, and produced by the same agency, he, while freely admitting them as facts, denies their miraculous or supernatural character. He thinks that the circumstances when these extraordinary events occurred were favorable to spirit-manifestations; the age was exceedingly ignorant, superstitious, and semi-barbarous, and needed new accessions of light and truth, and the spirits, through our Lord and his apostles as medium—God forgive us for repeating the blasphemy—made such revelations as that age most needed or could bear or assimilate. This age also needs further revelations of truth, especially to enable it to throw off the incubus of a fixed, permanent, non-progressive, infallible church, and secure an open field, and a final victory for the rational religion and progressive theology implied in the Protestant Reformation. So the spirits once more kindly come to our assistance, and reveal to us such further portions of truth as man is prepared for and especially needs. Very generous in them.

This is the doctrine, briefly and faithfully stated, of Mr. Owen's *Debatable Land*, which he sets forth with a charming *naïveté*, and a self-complacency little short of the sublime. There is this to be said in his favor—the devil speaks better English through him than through the majority of the mediums he seems compelled to use; yet not much better sense. But what new light have the spirits shed over the great problems of life and death, time and eternity, good and evil, or what new revelations of truth have they made? Here is the author's summary of their teaching:

"1. This is a world governed by a God of love and mercy, in which all things work together for good to those who reverently conform to his eternal laws.

"2. In strictness there is no death. Life continues from the life which now is into that which is to come, even as it continues from one day to another; the sleep which goes by the name of death being but a brief transition-slumber, from which, for the good, the awakening is immeasurably more glorious than is the

earthly morning, the brightest shone. In all cases in which ll-spent, the change which men to call death is God's last and to his creatures here.

e earth-phase of life is an es-eparation for the life which is to s appropriate duties and callings e neglected without injury to elfare and development, both in d and in the next. Even its ats, temperately accepted, are fit te the happiness of a higher

ie phase of life which follows the nge is, in strictest sense, the nt of that which precedes it. e same variety of avocations, joyments, corresponding, in a to those of earth, but far more , and its denizens have the same character and of intelligence; too, as men do here, in a state ss. Released from bodily earth-r periscope is wider, their per-more acute, their spiritual ge much greater, their judgment heir progress more rapid, than astly wiser and more dispas-han we, they are still, however, and they are governed by the neral laws of being, modified orporal *disenthralment*, to which *subjected* here.

r state here determines our ini-there. The habitual prompt-pervading impulses, the life-rnings, in a word the moving what Swedenborg calls the oves' of man—these decide his on entering the next world: vritten articles of his creed, nor cidental errors of his life.

a do not, either by faith or *rn* heaven, nor are we sentenc-ry day of wrath, to hell. In the rld we simply gravitate to the for which, by life on earth, we ed ourselves; and we occupy tion *because* we are fitted for it.

iere is no instantaneous change ter when we pass from the pre-e of life. Our virtues, our vices; ligence, our ignorance; our as-, our grovellings; our habits, ties, prejudices even—all pass i us; modified, doubtless (*but to nt we know not*), when the spiri-emerges, divested of its fleshly ance; yet essentially the same as when the death slumber came over us.

"8. The sufferings there, natural se-quents of evil-doing and evil-thinking here, are as various in character and in degree as the enjoyments; but they are mental, not bodily. There is no escape from them, except only, as on earth, by the door of repentance. There as here, sorrow for sin committed and desire for an amended life are the in dispensable conditions-precedent of ad vancement to a better state of being.

"9. In the next world love ranks high-er than what we call wisdom; being it-self the highest wisdom. There deeds of benevolence far outweigh professions of faith. There simple goodness rates above intellectual power. There the humble are exalted. There the meek find their heritage. There the merciful obtain mercy. The better denizens of that world are charitable to frailty, and compassionate to sin far beyond the dwellers in this: they forgive the erring brethren they have left behind them, even to seventy times seven. There, is no respect of persons. There, too, self-righteousness is rebuked and pride brought low.

"10. A trustful, childlike spirit is the state of mind in which men are most re-ceptive of beneficent spiritual impres-sions; and such a spirit is the best pre-paration for entrance into the next world.

"11. There have always existed in-termundane laws, according to which men may occasionally obtain, under cer-tain conditions, revealings from those who have passed to the next world be-fore them. A certain proportion of hu-man beings are more sensitive to spirit-ual perceptions and influences than their fellows; and it is usually in the presence, or through the medium, of one or more of these, that ultramundane intercourse occurs.

"12. When the conditions are favor-able, and the sensitive through whom the manifestations come is highly gifted, these may supply important materials for thought and valuable rules of con-duct. But spiritual phenomena some-times do much more than this. In their highest phases they furnish proof, strong as that which Christ's disciples enjoyed —proof addressed to the reason and tan-gible to the senses—of the reality of an-other life, better and happier than this, and of which our earthly pilgrimage is

but the novitiate. They bring immortality to light under a blaze of evidence which outshines, as the sun the stars, all traditional or historical testimonies. For surmise they give us conviction, and assured knowledge for wavering belief.

"13. The chief motives which induce spirits to communicate with men appear to be—a benevolent desire to convince us, past doubt or denial, that there *is* a world to come; now and then, the attraction of unpleasant memories, such as murder or suicide; sometimes (in the worldly-minded) the earth-binding influence of cumber and trouble: but, far more frequently, the divine impulse of human affections, seeking the good of the loved ones it has left behind, and, at times, drawn down, perhaps, by their yearning cries.

"14. Under unfavorable or imperfect conditions, spiritual communications, how honestly reported soever, often prove vapid and valueless; and this chiefly happens when communications are too assiduously sought or continuously persisted in: brief volunteered messages being the most trustworthy. Imprudence, inexperience, supineness, or the idiosyncrasy of the recipient may occasionally result in arbitrary control by spirits of a low order; as men here sometimes yield to the infatuation exerted by evil associates. Or, again, there may be exerted by the inquirer, especially if dogmatic and self-willed, a dominating influence over the medium, so strong as to produce effects that might be readily mistaken for what has been called possession. As a general rule, however, any person of common intelligence and ordinary will can, in either case, cast off such mischievous control: or, if the weak or incautious give way, one who may not improperly be called an exorcist—if possessed of strong magnetic will, moved by benevolence, and it may be aided by prayer, can usually rid, or at least assist to rid, the sensitive from such abnormal influence."—(*Debatable Land*, pp. 171-176.)

We have no intention of criticising this creed of the spirits as set forth by their learned medium. It is heathen, not Christian, and we have discovered in it nothing new, true or false. It denies the essential points of the Christian faith, and what few things it affirms that Christianity denies are affirmed on no trustworthy or sufficient authority. A man must have little knowledge of human nature, and have felt little of the needs, desires, and aspirations of the human soul, who can be satisfied with this spirits-creed. In it all is vague, indefinite, and as empty as the shades the heathen imagined to be wandering up and down on this side the Styx. But in it we find a statement that dispenses us from the necessity of examining and refuting it. In Article 4 we find it said: "Vastly wiser and more dispassionate than we, they [the spirits] are still, however, *fallible*."

Whether the spirits are wiser and more dispassionate than we or not may be questioned; they do not seem to be so in the author's illustrative narrations, and the fact that they have undergone no essential change by throwing off their overcoat of flesh, and living the same life they lived here, and are in the sphere for which they were fitted before entering the spirit-land, renders the matter somewhat doubtful, to say the least. But it is conceded that they are *fallible*. Who or what, then, vouches for the fact that they are not themselves deceived, or that they do not seek to deceive us? By acknowledging the fallibility of the spirits, Mr. Owen acknowledges that their testimony, in all cases, when we can have nothing else on which to rely, is perfectly worthless. We can bring it to no crucial test, and we have no vouchers either for their knowledge or their honesty. Even supposing them to be what they profess to be, which we by no means concede, it were sheer credulity to take their word for anything not otherwise verifiable.

Mr. Owen and all the spiritists tell us that the spirit-manifestations prove undeniably the immortality of

ing frequent communications with them, assured us that he held them to be evil spirits, and knew them to be lying spirits. "I asked them," he said, "at an interview with them, if they could tell me where my sister then was. 'Your sister,' I was answered, 'has some time since entered the spirit-world, and is now in the third circle.' It was false: my sister was alive and well, and I knew it. I told them so, and that they lied; and they laughed at me: and then I asked whose spirit was speaking with me. I was answered, 'Voltaire.' 'That is a lie, too, is it not?' Another laugh, or chuckle rather. I assure you," said our friend, "one can place no confidence in what they say. In my intercourse with them, I have found them a pack of liars."

This pretension of the spiritists that the spirits that manifest themselves through nervous, sickly, half-crazy mediums, or mediums confessedly in an abnormal or exceptional state, are really spirits who once lived in the flesh, is not sustainable; for they cannot be relied on, and nothing hinders us from holding them to be devils or evil demons, personating the spirits of deceased persons, as the church has always taught us. This, certainly, is very possible, and the character of the manifestations themselves favors such an interpretation; for only devils, and very silly devils too, dealing with very ignorant, superstitious, and credulous people, would mingle so much of the ludicrous and ridiculous in their manifestations, as the thumping, knocking, rollicking spirits, tipping over chairs and tables, and creating a sort of universal hubbub wherever they come. The spirits of the dead, if permitted at all to communicate with the living for any good purpose, we may well believe, would be permitted to do it more quietly, more gravely, and in a more open and direct way; it is only the devil or his subjects that would turn all their grave communications into ridicule by their antics or comic accompaniments. These considerations, added to the fact that the spirits communicate nothing not otherwise known or knowable, that is not demonstrably false, and that they tell us nothing very clear or definite about the condition of departed souls, nothing but what their consultors are predisposed to believe, convince us that, if they prove the existence of powers in some sense superhuman, they prove nothing for or against the reality of a life after this life. They leave the question of life and immortality, of good and evil, rewards and punishments, heaven and hell, where they were.

Mr. Owen places the spirit manifestations, and the Biblical miracles, and Christian inspiration and revelation, in the same category, attributes them all alike to the agency of the spirits, and thinks he has discovered a way in which one may accept the extraordinary events and doings recorded in the Old and New Testaments as historical facts, without being obliged to recognize them as miracles. This is absurd. The resemblance between the two classes of facts is far less than honest Fluellen's resemblance of Harry of Monmouth to Alexander of Macedon. "There is a river in Macedon, so is there a river also in Wales." The man who can detect any relation between the two classes of facts, but that of dissimilarity and contrast, is the very man to believe in the spirit-revelations, to mistake evil for good, darkness for light, and the devil for God. We find both classes of facts in the New Testament. The Christian miracles are all marked by an air of quiet power. There is no bluster, no rage, no foaming at the mouth,

tasy, and shows us how easily men who break from the unity of divine tradition, and set up for themselves, can lose sight of God, and come step by step to worship the devil in his place. The thing seemed incredible, and we had some difficulty in taking the assertion of the Holy Scriptures literally, "All the gods of the gentiles are devils"; but since we see apostasy from the church running the same career, and actually inaugurating the worship of demons, actually exalting the devil above our Lord, the Mystery of Iniquity is explained, and the matter becomes plain and credible.

It is curious to see what has been the course of thought in the Protestant apostasy in regard to the class of facts in question. Having lost the power of exorcism with their loss of the true faith, the Protestant nations had no resource against the invasions of the spirits but to carry out the injunction of the Mosaic law, "Thou shalt not suffer a witch"—that is, a medium—"to live." Hence we find their annals in the sixteenth and seventeenth centuries blackened with accounts of the trials and cruel punishments of persons suspected of witchcraft, sorcery, or dealings with the devil, especially in England, Scotland, and the Anglo-American colonies. Having no well-defined and certain criteria, as the church has, by which to determine the presence of Satan, many persons, no doubt, were put to death who were innocent of the offences of which they were accused. This produced a reaction in the public mind against the laws and against the execution of persons for witchcraft or dealing with the devil. This reaction was followed by a denial of witchcraft, or that the devil had anything to do with matters and things on earth, and a shower of ridicule fell on all who believed in anything of the sort. Then came the general doubt, and then the denial of the existence of the devil and all infernal spirits, save in human nature itself. Finally came the spirit-manifestations, in which Satan is no longer regarded as Satan, but is held to be divine, and worshipped as God, by thousands and millions.

We must be excused from entering into any elaborate refutation of Mr. Owen's blasphemous attempt to bring the Christian miracles under the general law, as he regards it, of spirit-manifestations. He has proved the reality of no such law, and if he had, the spirit-manifestations themselves would prove nothing more than a gale of wind, a shower of rain, a flash of lightning, or the growth of a spire of grass. Could we prove the Christian miracles to be facts in the order of nature, or show them as taking place by a general law, and not by the immediate act of God, and therefore no miracles at all, we should deprive them of all their importance. The value of the facts is not in their being facts, but in their being miraculous facts, which none but God can work. The author does not underderstand this, but supposes that he has won a victory for Christianity when he has proved the miracles as facts, but at the same time that they are no miracles.

It is clear from his pages that the author does not know what Christians understand by a miracle. He cites St. Augustine to prove that a miracle is something that may take place by some law of nature to us unknown, but St. Augustine, in the passage he cites, is not speaking of miracles at all; he is speaking of portents, prodigies, or extraordinary events, which the ignorant, and the superstitious ascribe to a supernatural agency; but which may, after all, however

·rful, be produced by a natural as in our days not a few believe the case with the spirit-manions themselves, and no doubt is se with most of the wonders iritists relate. The devil may portents or prodigies, but not es, because he has no creative , and can work only with macreated to his hand.

s necessary also to distinguish n what is simply superhuman hat is supernatural. Whatever ature is in the order of nature. e embraces the entire creation tever exists that is not God or uishable from him. Whether eated powers are above man low him in the scale of existhey are equally natural, and whatever they are capable, as causes, of doing. The angels aven, the very highest as the , are God's creatures, distinble from him, and therefore in- in nature. The same must id of the devils in hell, or the , if the spirits of the departed, ence whatever they do is with- natural order. The devil is or, if you will, by nature to -for man is made little lower he angels, and the devil is an anllen; he may know many things d human intelligence, and do things beyond the power of but what the devil does, is, if suman, not in any sense supernatuit as natural as what man himes. We agree with Mr. Owen, h not for the same reason, that is nothing miraculous in the manifestations, even supposing to be facts, and therefore are value in relation to the truth sehood of Christianity as a reon of and by the supernatural. I alone, and what he does imtely by his direct act and imte act, is supernatural. God alone can work a miracle, which is a supernatural effect wrought without any natural medium, law, or agency, in or on nature, and is, as far as it goes, a manifestation of creative power.

Miracles do what portents, prodigies, spirit-rappings, etc., do not—they manifest the supernatural, or the existence of a real order above nature. They do not indeed directly prove the truth of the Christian mysteries, but they do accredit our Lord as a teacher sent from God. As Nicodemus said when he came by night to Jesus, "Rabbi, we know that thou art come a teacher from God, for no man can do the miracles thou doest, unless God were with him," God in the miracles accredits the teacher, and vouches for the truth of what he in whose favor they are wrought teaches. What our Lord teaches, then, is true. If he teaches that he is perfect God and perfect man in hypostatic union, then he is so, and then is to be believed, on his own word, whatever he teaches, for "it is impossible for God to lie." The facts, then, are of no importance if not miracles. Hence the "natural-supernaturalism" of the *Sartor Resartus* is not only a contradiction in terms, but utterly worthless, as are most of the admired utterances of its author, and aid us not in solving a single problem for which revelation is needed.

Deprive us of the prophecies under the Old Law and the miracles under the New, and we should be deprived of all means of proving Christianity as a supernatural religion, as supernaturally inspired and revealed, and should be reduced, as Mr. Owen is, to naked rationalism, or downright demonism. The prodigies of the devil do not carry us above nature. They are indeed Satan's efforts to counterfeit genuine miracles, but at

best they only give us the superhuman for the supernatural. If the author could prove the Christian miracles are not miracles, though credible as facts, or if he could bring them into the category of the spirit-manifestations, he would in effect divest Christianity of its supernatural character, and render it all as worthless as any man-constructed system of ethics or philosophy. His Christianity, as set forth in his pages, has not a trace of the Christianity of Christ, and is as little worthy of being called Christian as the bald Unitarianism of Channing, or the Deism of Rousseau, Tom Paine, or Voltaire, or the Free Religion of Emerson, Higginson, and Julia Ward Howe.

What Mr. Owen regards as a highly important fact, and which he urges Protestants to accept as the means of triumphing over the Catholic Church, namely, that the Christian miracles and the spirit-manifestations are worthy of precisely the same respect and confidence in a Christian point of view, is far less important than he in his profound ignorance of Christianity imagines. How far he will be successful with Protestants we know not; but his success, we imagine, will be greatest among people of his own class, who, having no settled belief in any religion, who know little of the principles of Christianity, are, as all such people are, exceedingly credulous and superstitious. These people hover on the borders of Protestantism, have certain sympathies with the Reformation, but it would be hardly just to call them in the ordinary sense of the term Protestants. Yet Protestantism, being substantially a revival in principle of the ancient Gentile apostasy which led to the worship of the devil in the place of God before our Lord's advent, there can be no doubt that Protestants are peculiarly exposed to Satanic invasions, and there is no certainty that they may not follow Mr. Owen back to the devil-worship from which Christianity rescued the nations that embraced it. But we have said enough for the present. Perhaps we may say more hereafter.

THE ANNUNCIATION.

MARCH 27TH.

SHE kneels in prayer—a childlike, virgin form;
What purity is mirrored in her eyes!
Her dove-like glances, with devotion warm,
Are raised in worship to the midnight skies—
But look! a heavenly radiance bright has shone
Around the virgin chosen of the Lord;
In her rapt prayer she hears the angel's tone,
"Hail! full of grace! for lo! upon the word
Of thy consent waits now the heavenly dove,
Whose wings o'ershadowing thee shall lightly rest
One moment on thy pure and humble breast,
And make thee by that awful seal of love
The mother of thy God!" She bows her head,
While *fiat mihi* in meek tones is said.

FLEURANGE.

BY MRS. CRAVEN, AUTHOR OF "A SISTER'S STORY."

TRANSLATED FROM THE FRENCH, WITH PERMISSION.

PART FIRST.

THE OLD MANSION.

IV.

.N daylight appeared, Fleur-
ıwoke first, but in a few
ȝ, while she was admiring the
till sleeping in her arms, his
eyes opened in their turn.
ırst expression was one of ex-
surprise, somewhat mingled
ar, but Fleurange's look and
oon had a reassuring effect.
·es grew smiling, his mouth
ened, his little arms stretched
; her and were soon clasped
her neck, and the acquaint-
·as made. During this time
e and languid young mother
deavoring to shake off a heavi-
ɔre difficult to overcome than
She slightly blushed and mur-
some words of excuse when
·ceived her child in the arms
ɔeautiful stranger. But Fleur-
ırotested with an accent of in-
ɔle truth that the child did not
her in the least. She soon
·ed she could be of some ser-
the poor convalescent. The
n, aroused from a long night's
were now wholly awake.
one knows that children
and, confined within a narrow
soon arrive at a degree of tur-
: whose only advantage is to produce lassitude and then sleep. During the first of these two phases, the poor mother made a vain and feeble effort to restrain them. After a few minutes she fell back, not only exhausted, but faint. Fleurange drew near, and began to improvise a pillow for her head out of the shawls scattered around. Then she opened the small basket Mademoiselle Josephine had given her, and took out a flask, the contents of which, poured on a handkerchief and applied to the sick woman's pale face and temples, soon revived her.

"Thank you," she said; "you have done me a great deal of good. I am feeble, that is all, but I did not suppose myself so much so."

"Do not exert yourself," replied Fleurange. "I will take care of the children."

The mother smiled, and touched her head, showing by this gesture how fatiguing she found the noise she had not succeeded in quieting. At that very moment, the younger of the two children was standing on the seat, trying to reach the net, of painful memory, suspended like the sword of Damocles over the travellers' heads, and which served as a recepta-

cie for everything that could not be stowed away elsewhere. The child was not climbing without a motive. His brother had already successfully preceded him, and found means of seizing, through the meshes of the net, a small hunting-horn, on which he was now executing a flourish. Why could not he also get his drum, almost within reach? If he could only stretch a little farther—and he looked at Fleurange with a supplicating air; but the latter, instead of heeding his mute appeal, laughingly laid hold of him and drew him on her lap; then skilfully bearing off the hunting-horn from the other, she promised to relate them the most charming of stories if they would be quiet. In an instant they were both leaning beside her, and then, in a low tone, she related one story after another, keeping them silent and attentive till the hour of sleep returned.

By the end of the second day the travellers had made great progress in their acquaintance. "How can I thank you sufficiently?" said the young mother. "How fortunate I was to meet you!"

"Do not thank me: your children have done me more good than I can return."

This reply, of course, did not at all diminish the gratitude mingled with admiration with which she had inspired her companion, and as there is only a step from attraction to confidence, the latter soon related the whole story of her uneventful life to Fleurange. She had met with a severe fall three months before, and her life was despaired of; then her husband took her to Paris to consult Dr. Leblanc, who effected a cure. Fleurange's eyes brightened. It was such a gratification to be able to talk about her dear old friends!

"He is so skilful and kind," she said.

"Oh! yes, indeed! he is more than a physician: he is a benefactor, and yet I disobeyed him in starting so soon! He said I was still too feeble, which I denied; but I see he was right."

"Why did you do so?"

"Because my poor Wilhelm is alone and impatiently awaiting me."

"Your husband?"

"Yes."

"Could he not have come for you?"

"No; he is M. Dornthal's head clerk, and it is very difficult for him to leave his post."

Fleurange's heart gave a leap at this name. "Are you alluding to M. Ludwig Dornthal?" said she.

"No; to his brother, the rich banker."

"And the other—the professor—do you know him?"

"I have never seen him, but Wilhelm is well acquainted with him, and is sometimes invited to the soirées he gives. They are not balls—they are not fond of dancing there—but réunions for conversation, reading, music, and looking at engravings. Wilhelm says they are all learned, the girls as well as the boys, and madame as much so as her husband."

Fleurange slightly shuddered at this brief communication respecting her uncle's family. She was very fond of study, still more so of the arts; she had a taste for reading she was often obliged to repress, but this word "learned" she did not find attractive.

"Learned!" she said to herself. "That means pedantic, grave, and tiresome. Well, I must make the best of it. Perhaps that does not prevent them from being good, which is the essential point, and I certainly should not aim at amusement in this short life."

Another night—another long day

The only reply she received was an affirmative nod of the head; a moment after, a concise order, promptly obeyed, brought down from the heights of the imperial the modest luggage belonging to Fleurange. In an instant it was fastened behind the light carriage which he afterward assisted her in entering, then, carefully and silently wrapping around her a large fur cloak which he had brought, he took his seat, and the horse set off, as he came, at a fast trot.

Fleurange at first felt giddy with the rapid motion of the carriage, but it soon became agreeable, contrasted with the heavy movements and violent jolting of the diligence. The weather was sharp, but the warm cloak that covered her prevented her from feeling it, and, thus protected, the keen air, so far from being unpleasant, gave her, on the contrary, an unaccustomed animation which was like a fresh infusion of youth and life. The sky above was sparkling with stars. It was one of those brilliant winter nights which we love to imagine like that which witnessed the coming of Christ, and saw angels hovering over the heights that surround Bethlehem, to convey the glad tidings to the shepherds, and sing on earth their divine hymn.

In about twenty minutes the horse slackened his pace a little, and the young coachman turned around and seemed to make some attempt at an explanation which Fleurange tried her best to comprehend, but the rattling over the pavements rendered this nearly impossible, and she only seized the words "My father" and "*Christ Kindchen!*" after which his head, turned around for an instant, resumed its former position, and the horse his usual pace.

But Fleurange gathered from this that the youth was one of M. Dornthal's sons, and her uncle had not been able to meet her for some reason connected with the festival of the following day. Her first impression was that her cousin's manners were rather abrupt, and his face somewhat peculiar, but on the whole he had shown himself very efficient and attentive. As for his skill in driving it was unrivalled, the reins could not have been in better hands.

After this short interruption, they kept on their way without slackening an instant, notwithstanding more than one turn through the winding streets, and at length arrived at a place planted with trees, where the carriage stopped before a flight of steps leading to an oaken door adorned with a massive brass knocker.

Some one was evidently watching for them, for the door instantly flew open. Fleurange caught the glimpse of a bright light and many forms. Her cousin hastened to aid her in alighting. Confused voices were audible, all having a cordial accent of welcome. A strong hand supported Fleurange as she ascended the six stone steps and entered the passage. A tall woman dressed in gray, and wearing a cap trimmed with flowers, approached and embraced her. "It is my turn now!" said a deep and sonorous voice, "for I am her uncle." Fleurange raised her eyes toward a noble countenance which had too young a look to be crowned with such white hair, and her uncle embraced her, murmuring in a softened tone the name of Margaret. Beside him stood a lovely young girl, grave and blonde, while another, fair as her sister but younger, divested Fleurange of the heavy fur cloak and untied her bonnet. A boy of seven years ran out into the street to aid his brother, and a little girl of four or five clung to her mother's skirts, looking curiously, but with delight, at the strange visitor.

You are at home, you must understand: remember that. No thanks are necessary. You are one of our children. We had five: now we have six. It was Clement, my oldest son, who went to meet you, because his father could not leave the children this evening. You saw Hilda and Clara at your arrival, as well as the two little ones, Fritz and Frida, who were also there to receive you. There is Gabrielle besides: that is all. Your uncle has mourned so much for his poor sister Margaret! Now he has found her again, it is a happy day for us all!"

Fleurange quietly wiped away her tears without replying. Just then some one knocked at the door.

"Who is there?"

"It is I."

It was Clement with a cup of coffee, which, at her aunt's injunction, Fleurange drank with docility.

"Will you now go up to your room for the night, or will you return to the drawing-room among the others?"

Fleurange replied without any hesitation: "I prefer to go back to the drawing-room and see them all, at once."

A pleasant smile lighted up Madame Dornthal's face. "I like you very much, Gabrielle, not because you are handsome, that has nothing to do with it; I should love you quite as much were it otherwise; but because there is so much simplicity about you—which is quite to my taste. Now, let me see: it is eleven o'clock, our friends are going to take their children home, and our youngest are going to bed. As to the rest of us, we shall presently go to the Midnight Mass, and not sup till our return. Make your own choice—to follow the children's example, or go with us."

"Oh! with you, with you!" cried Fleurange. "Pray, take me to church; I am neither feeble nor fatigued."

"And yet you are fatigued," replied Madame Dornthal, "only you do not yet feel it. But as it will do you no harm, you shall do as you wish. So save your strength, and do not return now to the drawing-room. You can remain here and wait for me."

She left the room, and Fleurange remained where she was, happy to obey such kind orders without any resistance. Five minutes after, the door opened. It was Clement again, holding his little brother by the hand, and carrying his young sister in his arms.

"Fritz and Frida wish to bid you good-night," he said. The little boy timidly approached. Fleurange immediately spoke to him in that language which all children understand, and which can only be learned and spoken by those who love them: he was speedily reassured. She then took Frida, and kissed her blue eyes, which, while looking at her with surprise, began to close. When she gave the child back to her brother, she was asleep, and he bore her away without awakening her, holding her with an ease that showed how accustomed he was to the care. His little brother followed him out of the room.

Half an hour of silent repose succeeded this interruption. It was more beneficial to Fleurange than sleep, which strong excitement kept her from feeling the need of. At the end of that time, Madame Dornthal reappeared with her two daughters. Clement and his father were waiting for them in the passage. They set off by starlight on foot, for the church was near. They were all silent and thoughtful, for the children's festival had not made them forgetful of the solemnity of this great night.

hour before, bearing a basket which contained garments similar to their own.

"Why not?" said Fleurange, somewhat astonished.

"Do you not know that, in Germany, mourning is laid aside on great festivals?" replied Clara, the younger of the two. "You must dress like us to-day, as you will always do when the time for this sad mourning is over."

The elder of the two sisters noticed that her cousin made no reply: she approached her and said affectionately:

"Excuse Clara if she has distressed you. She is so gay and happy herself, that she cannot comprehend misfortune and sadness."

"I do not wish to remind her of them to-day," said Fleurange, "and will do as she requests. But you, dear Hilda," continued she—looking with admiration at her cousin's golden locks and grave brow, which a queen's diadem would have suited, or the aureola of a saint—"are you not as gay and happy as your sister?"

"Yes, as happy," said Hilda, "but not as gay."

After some explanations, Fleurange conformed to her cousins' wishes. But when, before dinner, the beautiful Hilda, clothed in white, brought a garland like that she wore herself and wished to place it on her head, she objected: "As to this garland, Hilda, you must excuse me from wearing it."

"Why so?"

"Because I have never worn any ornament of the kind: because, after all, I cannot and do not wish to forget I am a poor orphan, who should not dream of adorning herself, or mingling in the world."

"But, Gabrielle, you must know we only adorn ourselves to celebrate at home the great annual f and we never mingle in the w

"Never? But then, wh flowers without any reason?'

"It is not without a reaso father likes us to wear the of the season at every feast poor wreath you have refu brielle, look at it: it is, like holly, reflecting the bright Christmas, with its shining lea berries red as coral. There, is not becoming in your rave As she spoke, Hilda held the over her cousin's head: at stant Clara appeared, and h was no longer possible. She ly took her sister's place: th leaves and red berries were like a crown on Fleurange who laughed and only made resistance, while the mirror the forms of the three young as graceful a picture as ever an artist's dreams.

"There," cried Clara, " both beautiful—one fair as and the other brilliant as nig I," continued she, arrang long curls, among which hol were also twined—"let me I resemble myself."

"A flower, a star, dear Cl rything that is best worth g by day or night," said Fleur fectionately.

She preferred the elder of sisters, but there was an in grace about the other, wh could not help caressing w eyes and tones, as if she child.

"Ah! that is charming, and very applicable! Tha Cousin Gabrielle. I will p ask our poet to divine my e We shall see if he agrees wit

"If our poet is in a fit of tion, you must ask some c who certainly will not be," sai

When Fleurange entered the drawing-room, she perceived her Uncle Ludwig was rather impatiently awaiting her, for the moment she appeared he advanced, and, taking her by the hand, led her to the other end of the apartment, where stood a gentleman whose features bore some resemblance to his own, but with so different an expression, that the likeness, which at first was apparent, grew less and less as the two brothers were better known.

"This is our sister Margaret's daughter," said Ludwig to the banker. "She is doubly your niece now, for I have adopted her as my child."

M. Heinrich Dornthal bowed and cordially embraced the young girl, but he could not resist saying: "Another daughter, when you have three already, is a great addition."

This cool and unpleasant remark disconcerted Fleurange, and she had not recovered from her painful sensation of embarrassment when a young man of rather a fine figure approached and offered her his arm. Fleurange looked at him with an air of astonishment. She had never been to a large dinner-party, and knew nothing of the usages common to all countries on such an occasion. She slightly retreated, and, opening her large eyes, said: "Who are you, monsieur, and where do you wish to conduct me?"

This question and movement caused a general smile around her, in which she saw her Uncle Ludwig join, and with that simplicity which was her greatest charm she began to laugh herself, and so innocently, that he who had involuntarily caused this little scene exclaimed half aloud: "This is truly the most charming piece of rusticity I ever met with;" and then, bowing to her with mock gravity, and an air at once gallant and bantering, he said:

"Mademoiselle, my name is Felix Dornthal: I have the honor of being your cousin, and I offer you my arm to conduct you to the dining-room; but I acknowledge there would have been more propriety in first making us acquainted with each other."

Fleurange, blushing and smiling, accepted the arm offered her, and, once seated at table beside this new cousin, and freed from the embarrassment of this little incident, she looked around and began to enjoy her novel position.

Was it really her own self, who recently felt so isolated? She who had stood face to face with want and abandonment? Could she be the same person now, surrounded by numerous relatives, a member of a large family, feeling herself beloved by all, and loving all in return—yes, all, excepting the cousin seated beside her, who caused her involuntary confusion; and yet he had just said some words to her in Italian, pronounced with so pure an accent that she experienced a lively sensation of surprise and joy, for Italy was her native land—her own country almost, left only a few months previous for the first time. But her cousin's words embodied a compliment to which she did not know how to reply, and when she raised her eyes toward him she met a look that disconcerted her still more. She therefore only uttered a few words in return, and then silently resumed her examination of the company, beginning with her Uncle Ludwig. As to him, she thought she had never seen a nobler and sweeter face. It was impossible not to be struck by the contrast in this respect between him and his wife, which must have been even more striking in their youth than now. While she was dwelling on this thought, she met her aunt's eye resting on her for a moment, and

can deny that he is a poet whose name is familiar to every one, and whose songs are in every memory."

"As for me," replied Felix Dornthal, "I am not fond of rhymsters; this one is particularly disagreeable to me; and his approaching departure does not at all afflict me."

"Is he going away?" said Fleurange.

"Yes, it seems he has been offered a place at the court of ——, I hardly know what position, but one that will allow him to fully gratify his taste for old books, and at the same time—a thing by no means to be disdained, even by a poet—give him ample means of livelihood. He has suffered sweet violence, and in a short time we shall be deprived of the honor of receiving him within our walls—for ever deprived, it seems, for the kind prince, who is taking him away, insists on his not quitting his post."

Fleurange made no reply: her glance had just fallen on her cousin Hilda, who was sufficiently near to hear the conversation, but not enough so to be able to take any part in it. She saw her suddenly stoop down to pick up a flower just fallen from her hand, and when she rose up there was a lively color in her face. This was a natural consequence of the movement she had just made, but what was less so was the paleness which gradually succeeded, and the trembling of her hand when she endeavored to raise a glass of water to her lips. Fleurange was observing this with a vague uneasiness, when her attention was suddenly called away by a question her Uncle Ludwig addressed to a young man seated at Clara's side.

This question led to a reply which momentarily deprived Fleurange of the power of thinking of anything else.

"Steinberg," the professor said, "look at my niece, and tell me if you can see the resemblance spoken of."

The young artist turned toward Fleurange, and looked at her with an attention that, till now, had been exclusively absorbed by his fair neighbor. All at once he exclaimed: "Yes, certainly; I remember, and I see Count George was right. That is truly *Cordelia* herself before us!"

Every eye was turned toward Fleurange, and it was her turn to blush. But why did she thus tremble from head to foot? What were the mingled remembrances, sweet and poignant, that were suddenly recalled by the name of *Cordelia?* Of course it was natural that she should be affected by hearing her father's last work mentioned—that picture connected with so many painful associations. On the other hand, it was that same picture which enabled her uncle to find her, and now, appreciating more than ever the extent of this happiness, it was perhaps natural that the name of her unknown benefactor, suddenly pronounced in her presence, should inspire this lively and inexpressible emotion—but was this all?

However that might be, she remained the rest of the evening troubled and absorbed in the same thought. She had not, then, been deceived. It was really the stranger she had seen in the studio who now owned the picture, for he not only knew she served her father as a model, but said the likeness was perfect. And his name was Count George! Count? Then he was a man of high rank? What was his other name? Where did he reside? And was he still in this city?

Fleurange wished to give utterance to these questions, but an invincible

enced without always knowing the cause, and sometimes, later, they are transformed and modified to such a degree as to efface the first impulse they inspired. Perhaps it would not be impossible to prove that upright souls are less rarely deceived in this respect than others. However it may be, and independent of this instinctive repulsion, the antipathy Fleurange felt was owing, among other good reasons, to the constant irony which was so strong an ingredient in Felix's nature, as to wither every feeling of kindly impulse or flow of reason around him. Goodness found no attraction in his nature, and those who conversed with him almost ceased to believe in it themselves. He had not discernment enough to see that Fleurange was one of those persons who may be wounded by a compliment as well as by an insult, and more than one flash of her large eyes was necessary to make him comprehend it. And when he suddenly stopped, his silence excited anxiety to know the cause of his sudden preoccupation and what sombre cloud enwrapped him. Some insinuated with a nod of the head that M. Heinrich Dornthal's only son should yield with more reserve to his love for play, and his father had repeatedly remonstrated with him on this point. But as, apart from his whims and irregularities, Felix had a remarkable capacity for commercial affairs, the banker was blindly indulgent to him, and often remarked that being "perfectly satisfied, and sure of his son in matters of *serious* import (meaning thereby his aptitude for business), he did not trouble himself much about the rest, and only patiently awaited the epoch when the marriage of his choice would lead him back to a more regular life."

It should be added that, for several months, the health of the head of the Dornthal family had, without his acknowledging it, been seriously declining. The greater part of the business formerly done by himself was now transacted by his son, and his confidence, or his weakness, in this respect, increased to a degree unsuspected by any but him who was its object. The banker occasionally felt, with a return of his former cautiousness, some anxiety on this point, but Felix knew how to reassure him by a few words, and he now felt only one desire, which grew stronger and stronger—to see his son married, and settled down to a life of greater conformity with the importance of the affairs he could transact so skilfully, and to which he had only to give his undivided attention. He could have wished him to choose one of his two cousins, but Felix did not find them to his taste, and often declared that it would not be within the walls of the Old Mansion he should find her to whom he would sacrifice his independence. But after Fleurange entered them he suddenly changed his tone, and his ill-concealed admiration now directed toward her all the banker's matrimonial hopes respecting his son.

We left Felix beneath his cousin's balcony, his riding-whip in hand: "Away with poetry, which is not in my line," he soon said, "and deign to listen, fair cousin, to the petition I am about to address you in humble prose."

Fleurange, still leaning on the balcony, replied: "I am listening."

"See what a lovely spring day! My horse stands yonder: will you not have yours saddled, and allow me to ride in your company?"

Fleurange drew herself up with an air of surprise, and shook her head without otherwise answering.

"No?" said Felix.

"No, certainly not. How could

scholar? You are not generally so fluent. Indeed, if you were only a few years older, I should imagine the large gray eyes of our fair, disdainful cousin had fascinated you in your turn."

Clement did not look up; he neither blushed nor was vexed.

"Felix," said he, "I am only nineteen years old, it is true, and you are ten years older; but I have one advantage which the younger does not generally possess: you do not know me. But I," continued he, looking him full in the face, "as you are aware, I know you well."

At these words a black look came over Felix's face, he bit his lips, and would perhaps have made some angry reply had not the three girls appeared at the end of the alley. At the sight of them Felix abruptly turned around, and, leaping on his horse, galloped off, slightly waving his hand to Julian Steinberg, whom he met at the garden gate.

Fleurange and her two cousins approached to meet Clara's betrothed. "I am late," said he to Clara, "but you must not think it is my fault. I have been detained by an unexpected meeting. Count George is here."

"Count George de Walden?" said Clement, "the same one who visited the gallery about a year ago?"

"The very one," replied Julian; "and it was he who showed us the beautiful Cordelia that resembles you so much, mademoiselle," he added, turning to Fleurange.

"And the source of our good luck in finding her," said Hilda.

"But, since he has seen you, Gabrielle," said Clara, "you must know him."

Fleurange, strangely surprised, moved, and confused, nevertheless replied in a tolerably calm tone: "I did not know who purchased the picture until I came here."

"But," persisted Clara, "you saw him, however?"

"Yes, once, but without speaking to him.

"In that case, you must remember him, for Julian pretends his face is the most remarkable one he ever saw."

"Yes, his features are not only fine," said Julian, "but there is in his physiognomy and his whole appearance something—something—"

"Striking and noble," said Clement.

"Yes, that is true."

"Assuredly," replied Julian; "but that is not all. There is something extraordinary about him—how shall I express it? heroic—yes, that is the word, he looks like a hero."

"Of romance?" said Clara.

"No, of history: if I had to paint a celebrated soldier, or the leader of some famous exploit, I should choose him for the original."

"And then, he is a great lover of art," said Clement.

"Yes," responded Julian, "he seems, indeed, gifted in every way."

"And is he going to remain here?" said Clara.

"Unfortunately he will not, for in that case he would be at our wedding, but he is obliged to go to St. Petersburg without any delay."

"What! is he a Russian?" said Clara.

"No, not wholly."

"What do you mean by that?"

"I mean he is a Livonian or a native of Courland, I do not know exactly which. But he is one of the emperor's subjects, and cannot trifle with his orders, which obliged him to leave Florence suddenly, where he was, and now forces him to keep swiftly on his way."

The conversation took another turn, of which Fleurange did not hear a word. As soon as she had an excuse for leaving her cousins, she returned to her chamber, where she took a small note-book from her pocket, and carefully inscribed therein the name of Count George de Walden.

THE MARTYRDOM OF ST. AGNES.

"Sancta Agnes! ora pro nobis."

Calm she stood,
An ivory statue, yet instinct with life,
So stately was that gently breathing form,
Of grace and dignity so perfect, yet
With all youth's pliant softness.
On her brow,
White as the ocean pearl when first the waves
Complaining cast their treasure on the shore,
Was stamped the seal of that creating hand
Whose spirit dwelt within that temple rare,
Her holy virgin heart; and from her eyes,
Soul-lit, beamed forth the splendor and the depth
Of that informing mind whose lights they were,
Until you heeded not their violet hues.

CATHOLICITY AND PANTHEISM.

NO. XIII.

THE COSMOS IN TIME AND SPACE—CONTINUED.

In the preceding article, we have seen that, in consequence of the sacramental extension of the Theanthropos in time and space, substantial creation in its highest and noblest element, which is personality, has received its last initial and inchoative perfection of being, by the union of human persons with the Theanthropos by means of his substantial and sacramental presence, and through that union the elevation to a higher similitude of and communication with the three persons of the infinite. Now, this last complement of the cosmos, this union of the Theanthropos, with human persons, through his sacramental extension in time and space, constitutes the Catholic Church, which may be defined to be:

The Theanthropos present in the cosmos through the sacraments, and through them incorporating into himself human persons in time and space, raising them to a higher similitude of and communication with the three personalities of the infinite, and thus not only realizing the highest initial perfection of the cosmos, but also unfolding and developing that initial perfection, and bringing it to its ultimate completion in palingenesia.

The Theanthropos, therefore, has placed himself in the very centre of the cosmos by his sacramental and substantial presence, as became his great office and prerogative of mediator. By those moments of his sacramental presence to which he has only attached his infinite energy and power, he disposes and fits human persons for the real incorporation into himself in the following manner: By the sacramental moment of order, through the moral instrument in whom this moment is realized, he propounds and explains his doctrine, the *gnosis* respecting God, and the cosmos which he came to reveal to men. By the sacramental moment of regeneration, he infuses into human persons the term of the supernatural order in its essence and faculties, and thus raises them to a higher state of being, and to a closer communication with the Trinity, but all this in an initial and inchoative state. By the sacramental moment, called confirmation, he brings that essence and its faculties to a definite and determinate growth. When human persons are thus fitted and prepared, he by his substantial presence incorporates them into himself, and enables their supernatural being to live and develop itself by being put in real, actual communication with all the proper objects of its faculties. Thus, the cosmos of personalities, perfected in its initial supernatural state, can act and develop itself—the Theanthropos himself, through his moral agents, organically constituted, governing and directing its action to the safest and speediest acquirement of its last perfection.

From this metaphysical idea of

iurch, derived and resulting very essence, it follows:

;, That, next to the Theanthro- e Catholic Church is the end the exterior works of the infi- The supreme end of the exte- orks was the highest possible mication of the infinite to the This was primarily realized hypostatic union which bound ited natures to the infinite, and sed next in the union of all ilities with the Theanthropos, rough him with the Trinity. he very essence of the Catho- urch consists in this union. uently, as such it is the *last r. imperative* law of the cos- The last, because with it clos- cycle of the creative act, and the cycle of the return of rms to their principle and Supreme, because no higher perfection of the cosmos can ized after supposing its exis- Imperative, because it is ssary complement of the plan cosmos.

ce, without the Catholic i the cosmos of personalities have no aim or object. It stand alone, and unconnected ie other parts of the cosmos, ticular end of each personali- d never be attained, and the vould present a confused mass nents. without order, harmony, pletion.

llows, in the second place, that tholic Church is fashioned after postatic moment, and is its ively representation. For as oment implies the bringing to- of a human and divine ele- finite and infinite, absolute lative, necessary and contin- dependent and subject, visible visible, in the unity of one personality, so the Catholic is the result of a double element, one human, the other divine; one visible, the other invisible; one finite, the other infinite; one necessary, the other contingent; one immutable, the other variable; the one independent and authoritative, the other subject and dependent, in the union of the Theanthropos with the sacramental element. This union of the Theanthropos with the sacramental element, both moral and physical, is, as we have said, the very essence of the Catholic Church, and which endows it with that double series of attributes and perfections, one belonging to God, the other essentially belonging to the finite, but which are brought together in one being in force of that union; and all the difficulties brought against the church hinge upon that very thing—the sacramental union of all the divine attributes of the Theanthropos with the finite attributes of the sacramental element. All those who object to all or some of the Theanthropic attributes of the church object to the possibility and existence of that union.

But that union, as the last supreme imperative law of the cosmos, is such a strict consequence of the plan, is so connected and linked with all the other moments of God's action *ad extra*, depends so entirely upon the identical principle which originates the others, that once we deny it we are obliged to yield up all the other truths, and take refuge in nihilism, and proclaim the death of our intelligence. For once we admit the impossibility of the union of the attributes or substance of the Theanthropos with the sacramental element, on the plea that the attributes of each are opposite and contradictory, for the self-same reason we must admit the impossibility of the union of the Word of God with the human nature, and sweep the hypostatic moment clean away; because, if it

is impossible to bring together opposite attributes in one sacramental being, it is much more impossible, so to speak, to bring not only attributes but two natures quite opposite together, into one subsistence and personality, and entirely exchange attribution and names, and call man God, and God man, and attribute exclusively divine acts to human nature, and *vice versa*. But, having denied the hypostatic moment in consequence of that pretended impossibility, we cannot logically stop here. We must generalize the question, and deny all possible union between the finite and the infinite. For what can there be more opposite and more contradictory than these terms, absolute and relative, necessary and contingent, immense and limited, eternal and successive, immutable and changeable, universal and particular, self-existing and made, infinite and finite? And could they possibly be brought together into any kind of union? Nay, we must go further, and deny the very coexistence of both terms, because one certainly seems to exclude the other—the universal being, for instance, including all possible being, must necessarily imply the impossibility of the coexistence of any particular, circumscribed, limited being. Arrived at this, we must conclude that all finite things which come under our observation, not being able to coexist with the universal being, must be only modifications and developments of that same, and throw ourselves into pantheism. But once pantheism is admitted, we must, to be logical, suppose the existence of a universal something impelled by an interior instinct of nature to unfold and develop itself by a succession of efforts, one more distinct, marked, and perfect than the other. Now, taking this substance at one determinate stage of development, and backward, from a more perfe velopment to one less perfec from this to one still less perf must necessarily arrive at th indeterminate, indefinite, al *something*, at the idea-being of —that is, at nihilism.

Nihilism is consequently th cal product of the denial of th of the infinite attributes of th anthropos with the sacrament ment, the very essence of the lic Church. *The Catholic C therefore—or nihilism.*

And we beg the reader to c that this logical conclusion wh have drawn is simply the hist the errors of the last three hu years, and consequently our c sions receive all the support the gradual unfolding of err three hundred years is able to

The impossibility of the un the infinite attributes and subs presence of the Theanthropos sacramental element was proc in the sixteenth century by P antism, when on one side it the authority and infallibility church, and consequently den union of these Theanthropic butes with the moral instrume hierarchy, and on the other s nied the real presence, and th fused to allow a union of the sul of the Theanthropos with the mental elements of bread and It did not then see the full m of its denial, but yet establish principle of the impossibility union of the Theanthropos in or substance with the sacra elements. Deism followed, an ing the Protestant principle i added a logical application to asked: How can the uncreate nite, and absolute being be ur a nature created, finite, and re or, in other words: How cou

from that essence, yet, for the sake of those who cannot see all the consequences included in a general principle, we shall dilate at some length upon all the essential attributes of the church, and those characteristic marks which constitute her what she is, and point her out from any other body pretending to the same name.

The first attribute, which evidently emanates from the essence of the church, is its externation, and capacity of coming under the observation of men. For, if the essence of the church consists in being the Theanthropos, incorporating his power, as well as his substantial presence, in physical as well as personal instruments, and through them incorporating all human persons unto himself, who can fail to perceive that church must be visible, outward, able to come under the observation of men, in that double relation of sacramental extension of Christ and of having men as objects of incorporation with him?

An invisible church would imply a denial of any sacramental agency, and would be absolutely unfit for men, who are *incarnate* spirits. Hence, those sects which hold that the saints alone belong to the church have not the least idea of its essence. Holiness being altogether a spiritual and invisible quality, the saints could not know each other, nor, consequently, hold any communication with each other; the sinners could not find out where the saints are to be heard of; and therefore there could not be any possibility of discovering the church or any moral obligation of joining it.

The next attribute essentially belonging to the church is its *permanence*, in theological language called indefectibility, which implies not only duration in time and space, but also *immutability* in all its essential elements, attributes, and rights. The church must continue to be, as long as the cosmos lasts, whole and entire in all time and space, in the perfect enjoyment of all its attributes, characteristic marks, and rights.

The reason of this attribute is so evident and palpable that we are at a loss to understand how it could enter men's minds that the church could and did fail or change in its essential elements. When Protestantism, to cloak over its rebellion in breaking loose from allegiance to the church of the living God, alleged as reason that it had failed and changed in its essential elements—when Protestantism repeats daily the same assertion, it exposed and exposes itself to an absurdity at which the merest tyro in logic would laugh. It is one of the first axioms of ontology that the essences of things are immutable and eternal: immutable, inasmuch as they can never change: eternal, inasmuch as they must be conceived as possible from eternity, whether they have any subjective existence or not. Essences are like number. Add to it, or subtract from it, and you can never have the same number; likewise add to the essence of a thing, or subtract from it, and you may have another thing, but never the same essence.

Now, what is the essence of the church? It consists in the Theanthropos incorporating his infinite power and his substantial presence in physical and personal instruments, and through them uniting to himself human persons, elevating them to a supernatural state, and enabling them to develop and unfold their supernatural faculties until they arrive at their ultimate perfection, and all this in time and space.

Now, how can we suppose the church to fail when its very essence is founded on the union of the The-

anthropos with the sacraments? The only possible failure we can suppose is if the presence of the Theanthropos were to be withdrawn from the sacraments; and this could happen either because the Theanthropos may be supposed powerless to continue that presence or unwilling; in both cases, the divinity of the Theanthropos is denied; because the first would argue want of power, the second a senseless change. Protestantism would do much better to deny at once the divinity of its founder, instead of admitting the failure of the church he founded. It would be by far more honest and logical. We can respect error when it is logical and consistent, but we must despise obstinate nonsense and absurdity. The same attribute is claimed by the end of the church—which is, to communicate to human persons in time and space the term of the supernatural moment. As long, then, as there are men on earth, so long must the church continue to possess invariable and unchangeable those elements with which it was endowed by its divine founder. Should it fail or change, how could men after the failure be incorporated into the Theanthropos? Should it fail or change, how could men believe in the possibility of their attaining their end? Should it fail once and at one period only, men would no longer possess any means of knowing when, and how, and where it might not fail again, and therefore they could not but look upon the whole thing with utter contempt.

The next attribute is infallibility.

Certainty objectively considered is the impossibility of error in a given case. Infallibility also, considered in itself, is the impossibility of error in every case within the sphere to which that infallibility extends. This attribute is essentially necessary to the church, but before we enter upon its vindication we will say a word about its nature, the subject in whom it resides, the object it embraces, and the mode of exercising it. The nature of the infallibility claimed by the church does not consist in a new inspiration: because inspiration implies an interior revelation of an idea not previously revealed or known. Now, this does not occur, and is not necessary, in order that the church may fulfil its office. The revelation of the whole *gnosis* respecting God, the cosmos, and their mutual relations in time and in eternity, was made by the Theanthropos in the beginning. The church carries it in her mind, heart, and life, as she traverses centuries and generations. But as all the particular principles constituting that *gnosis* are not all distinctly and explicitly formulated and set in human language, so it becomes the office of the church from time to time to formulate one of those principles. In this she is assisted by the Theanthropos in such a manner that she may infallibly express her mind in the new formula she utters. Again, an error may arise against the revealed gnosis she carries in her mind. Then it is her office to proclaim what her mind is upon the subject, and condemn whatever may be contrary to it. Again, she is assisted by the Theanthropos in such a manner as to effect both these things infallibly. Infallibility in the present case, therefore, may be defined a permanent assistance of the Theanthropos preserving the church from falling into error in the exercise of her office.

The object of this attribute is limited to these three:

1. She is infallible in teaching and defining all theoretical doctrines contained in the revelation, be it written or not, but handed down socially from the beginning.

2. In all doctrines having reference to morality.

3. In the choice and determination of the external means of embodying that doctrine, theoretical or practical; whether the external means which embodies the doctrine be used by the church, or, used by others, must be judged by the church.

This last object of infallibility is so absolutely necessary that without it the other two would become nugatory and fictitious. If, in propounding a doctrine, the church could err in fixing upon such objective expressions of language as would infallibly exhibit her mind, men could never be assured whether the church had expressed herself correctly or not, and could never, consequently, be certain of her meaning. Likewise, if the church could err in teaching whether such and such expression of language, intended to embody a doctrine, contains an error or a truth, men would be left in doubt whether to embrace or reject it, and could never, in embracing it, be absolutely certain whether they were holding a revealed doctrine or a falsehood.

From this it follows that: First, the church is not infallible in things belonging exclusively to natural sciences, and in no way connected with revelation; second, she is not infallible in reference to historical facts, and much less in reference to personal facts, unless these are connected with dogma. The subjects in whom this attribute resides are the following:

1. The Supreme Pontiff, the head of the hierarchy, who, independent of the rest, enjoys this attribute, in reference to all the objects above explained. Because, by the interior organism of the church, as we shall see, he is made the source of all authority in teaching and governing.

2. The hierarchy, together with the Supreme Pontiff, eitner assembled in council or agreeing through other means of communication.

We almost blush to have to remark that this infallibility, centred in the Pope or bishops, does not render them personally impeccable. The two things are as distant as the poles, and can only be brought togeth and confounded in minds who, a cording to the expression of Dan have lost the light of the in and live in a darkness which is li short of death.

The modes of exercising this attribute are three:

She is infallible as teacher, as witness, and as judge.

As teacher: when she proclaims and expounds to the faithful the revelation of the Theanthropos.

As witness: when she affirms what belongs or does not belong to that revelation.

As judge: when she pronounces final judgment on controversies and disputes which arise in relation to revealed doctrines.

Having thus given a brief idea of all that belongs to the subject of infallibility, it seems to us that no one who has understood the nature and essence of the church, and the object for which it was established, can fail to perceive not only the entire reasonableness, but also the absolut necessity of such a doctrine.

We have said that the church its active element is nothing than the Theanthropos himself, municating the term of the sup tural moment, which includes t ing, through the agency of agents, both physical and The church, therefore, under the pect, from which we are now regard ing her, is the Theanthropos teachin his revelation, expounding his revel tion, affirming and witnessing to revelation, declaring what

with it, and what is contradictory to it, through the agency of the Supreme Pontiff, or of the Pontiff and the rest of the hierarchy. And can anything be more reasonable than the assertion that she is infallible? Protestantism has boasted, and boasts yet, of having emancipated reason, of having brought it to the highest possible degree of culture and development. But when will Protestantism begin to exercise its vaunted reason?

Is it reasonable to suppose that the Theanthropos, the God made man, the infallible wisdom of God, the very intelligibility of the Father, who established the church, that is, united himself, either as to action or substance, with a sacramental element, be it material or personal, in order, among other things, to teach all men in time and space what was absolutely necessary for them to know to attain their ultimate perfection—is it reasonable to suppose, we say, that the Theanthropos should, through his personal agents, teach anything but absolute truth?

Deny the divinity of the Theanthropos, deny that the Theanthropos ever did or could unite his activity with personal agents, deny the essence of the church, and then you would be logical, then you would be consistent, then we could understand you. But to admit that the Theanthropos *is* God, to admit that he *did* unite his infinite and divine activity to the sacramental element, to admit that he did so on purpose to teach all men in time and space, and then to affirm that the church is not and cannot be infallible—that is, that the Theanthropos cannot teach infallibly through his personal agents—is such a logic as only the highly cultivated reason of Protestantism can understand. It is above the reach of that reason which is satisfied with a moderate share of culture and refinement, and cannot claim to soar so high.

We beg the reader to reflect for an instant on this single question: Is it the Theanthropos, or is it not, who teaches through the agency of his personal instruments? To this simple question, a simple answer should be given. Say you answer, It is not. Then you deny that the Theanthropos united his infinite energy to a sacramental element. Then you deny the essence of the church, and, in denying that, you must deny every other union between the infinite and the finite, as we have demonstrated. If you say it *is* the Theanthropos who teaches through the agency of his personal instruments, then what can be more logical or more consistent than to say that he teaches infallibly? What is there more reasonable than to say that a God-man should know what is truth, and should express his mind so, should embody it in an external means so, as to represent that mind infallibly?

Then, why so much opposition against this plainest attribute of the church? Why so much obloquy, so much sneering, except that the so boasted Protestant reason is nothing but a vile, unmanly prejudice, except that those who boast so much of exercising their reason resemble those innocent and unconscious animals of which Dante speaks:

> "As *sheep*, that step forth from their fold, by one
> Or pairs, or three, at once; meanwhile, the rest
> Stand fearfully, bending the eye and nose
> To ground, *and what the foremost does that do
> The others, gathering round her if she stops,
> Simple and quiet, nor the cause discern*"?
> —*Cary's Translation.*

The next attribute of the church is authority. This, like the rest, flows from her very essence. That essence consists in being the sacramental ex-

tension of Christ incorporating unto himself all human persons in time and space, communicating to them the term of the supernatural moment in its essence and faculties, and aiding them to develop those faculties, and to bring them to their ultimate completion. The church, therefore, as sacramental—that is, outward and sensible extension of the Theanthropos intended for men—is a visible, outward society of human persons with the Theanthropos. Now, what does a visible society require? That the external relations of the associates should be determined and governed by the authority legitimately constituted in the society. For, if those relations were not determined and directed by proper authority in a visible society, it is evident that no order could be expected, and that all the members could not form one moral body, by a proper external communication. The church, therefore, as a visible society, must have authority to determine all the external relations of the members, and to govern and direct them.

This authority or power of establishing the external polity in the church is, of course, essentially residing in the Theanthropos, who communicates it whole and entire to the Supreme Pontiff, and through him to the whole hierarchy and the rest of the active church.

Having vindicated the essential attributes of the church, we think it necessary to dilate at some length upon the interior constitution, the internal organism of the same, in order to exhibit a fuller and more adequate idea of this masterpiece of the infinite. And in order to do it thoroughly, we must give a cursory glance at its eternal type, the supreme exemplar of everything—the Trinity. The reader will remember that the genesis of God's life takes place as follows: There is in the infinite essence and nature a first subsistence, unborn, unbegotten, which terminates in the first person. This is the supreme, active principle of the second, and both are the active principle of the third. In this third termination closes the cycle of infinite life. The production of the second person is brought about by intellectual generation. For the primary unbegotten activity, being infinitely intelligent, can scan with his glance the whole depth, breadth, height, and length of his infinite nature. Now, to intelligence means to produce an intellectual image of the object which is understood. Consequently, the primary unbegotten principle, by intelligencing himself, produces an intellectual image, absolutely equal to himself, the act of intelligencing being infinite, and also distinct from him, inasmuch as they are opposed as principle and term. The first contemplates himself in his substantial image, and is attracted toward himself and his image. The second contemplates himself in his principle, and is attracted toward himself and his principle. This common, mutual attraction or love, being also infinite, is consequently substantial, and results in a third termination of the infinite essence.

From this brief explanation of the genesis of God's life, it follows:

1st. That the infinite, though one in nature, has three distinct terminations or persons.

2d. That, though these three persons are absolutely equal, because possessed of the same identical nature, we find in them a necessary subjection of order founded on the law of origin and production, the second being originated by the first, and being in this respect subject to him; the third being originated by both, and under this respect being subject to both.

The three persons, possessing ame identical nature and sub-, possess, consequently, all the tions and attributes flowing the substance in the same idenmanner. Hence they possess nmon all the metaphysical ates of the substance, such as in- eternity, immensity, immuta; all the intellectual attributes, as truth, wisdom, etc.; all the attributes of the substance, as goodness, etc.

As nature is the radical prinof action and life, it follows as the three persons possess the nature, they possess one idenction and life. But as the terion is the immediate principle ion, and the three persons have inct termination, their one idenaction receives the impress of stinct termination of each.

Finally, the essence being cal in all the three persons, and cond and third being originatan immanent action, and all essentially relative to each it follows that they all live in other by a common indwell-

w, the interior constitution, the al organism, of the church must odelled, both in its active and e moments, after this supreme of everything; always granting ecessary distance of proportion ening between the infinite and ite. For, if the whole cosmos must be fashioned after that ne pattern, how much more the church, which is the inchoad initial perfection of the whole s, the cosmos of personalities! quently, we must find in its r organism all the laws of the s of God's life—laws which in hole cosmos are reflected in of *unity*, *variety*, *hierarchy*, *com-n.*

And, first, as to the active moment of the church. As in the infinite we find one nature and essence, the abyss of all perfections, the *Being*, so in the active church we must find one nature and essence, the reflex of the essence of God. And that one nature consists in the fulness of the priesthood of the Theanthropos, communicated to the whole active church in the sacrament of order, and in the fulness of his authority.

As in the infinite the divine nature is possessed in common by a multiplicity of persons, the three terminations constituting the Trinity, so in the active church the priesthood of Christ and his authority must be possessed in common by a multiplicity of persons, some possessing it in its fulness, some partially, because distinction in the finite is by gradation, and cannot be by perfect equality, but all having the same identical priesthood as to its nature.

As in the Trinity, we find the law of hierarchy absolutely necessary in organic and living beings, which hierarchy consists in this, that the three divine persons, though absolutely equal as to nature, are distinct as to personality—a distinction which arises from opposition of origin. Now, this opposition of origin necessarily gives rise to a hierarchical superiority of order; the Father as such being necessarily superior in order to the Son, and the Son as such inferior to him; both as the aspirants of the third person necessarily superior to him, and *vice versa*.

Now, this hierarchical law must be found also in the church, and we must find a superiority of one over the other, not merely of order, but of gradation; the finite, as we have said, not being distinct except by gradation of being. Hence, we find the Theanthropos to have establish-

ed three distinct elements constituting the hierarchy, and organically brought together. The first, a primary principle of authority from whom all receive, and he receives from none—the Supreme Pontiff, his own vicar on earth, the visible head of the church. The second, who receive from the first in measure and limit—the episcopate, who receive from the Supreme Pontiff their authority and its extent. The third, also, receive from both in a more limited manner—the priesthood.*

As in the Trinity the divine nature, being the radical principle of action and life, and the termination, the proximate principle, there is one common action and life, but the same bearing the impress of the constituent of each person; so in the church the authority being the same as to nature, the Pontiff, the episcopate, and the priesthood have one common life and action radically, but each one displaying it according to the degree resulting from his dignity—the Pontiff in its fulness, the episcopate within the range of their dioceses, the priesthood within the limits appointed by the episcopate—the second as holding it from the first, the third from both.

The reader can see by the theory we have just explained, and which cannot be gainsaid, how the late definition of the infallibility of the Supreme Pontiff is in accordance with and flows from the principles we have laid down. The Pontiff in the church of Christ is the first and primary visible principle of all authority, as in the interior of infinite life the eternal Father is the first primary principle of authority over the Son and the Spirit, as we have explained above.

From the Pontiff all must receive authority, and he can receive from none, as the Father in the internal organism of the infinite communicates and receives from none. Consequently, the Supreme Pontiff being the first, primary, supreme, visible principle of authority in the church of Christ, is the first, primary, supreme, visible teacher—the office of teaching being essentially included in the fulness of authority communicated to him by Christ.

And as the office of teaching in the church of Christ would be of no avail except it were endowed with the attribute of infallibility, it follows that the Supreme Pontiff is the first, primary, supreme, *infallible* teacher in the church of Christ. He must teach all, and can be taught by none. He teaches by himself the whole universal church, and none has and can have any authority for disputing, objecting to, and gainsaying his teaching.

We cannot perceive how any persons holding the supremacy and independence of his authority could ever have reconciled with their logic the dependence of his authority with reference to teaching.

We come to the interior organism of the passive church, to which the active church also belongs in different relation, and we find in it also a reflex of the Trinity.

For as in the infinite there is one nature common to all, communicated by the first person to the second and by both to the third, so in the passive church we find the same nature, the term of the supernatural moment, consisting in a higher similitude of and communication with the Trinity; this term communicated by the active church; primarily by

* We have said *authority* and not sacerdotal character, because as to that there is no difference between the Supreme Pontiff and the episcopate, but only between the episcopate and the priesthood.

episcopate, and secondarily by priesthood.

s in the Trinity, the nature being same, the three persons partake ll the attributes flowing from the re, likewise, and with due pro- ion in the church, the nature of supernatural moment being the , all the members partake of the attributes and faculties flowing that nature; hence they have common supernatural intelli- ce, one common supernatural

s the Trinity, the nature being radical principle of action, and personality the proximate, all the same action, but each acts rding to the constituent of his onality; so in the church, the of the supernatural moment, tituting its nature, being the , all have the same supernatural n and life; but personally, some bers belonging to the active ch, and some to the passive, it fol- that those who belong to the first ay that life in that relation, and who belong to the second dis- it in the second relation.

s in the Trinity we find an in- ling of all the persons in each r, and a living perpetual commu- tion founded on the identity of re and on the relation of person- s; so in the church of Christ ind a perpetual communication its members with each other, ded on the identity of nature, erm of the supernatural moment, pon the relation of personalities, members of the passive church municating with and living, as it , in the active church, because eeding from it.

e see, therefore, what is the in- r organism of the church. As to active church, the fulness of the thood of the Theanthropos is to the whole active church. The organism is constituted and es- tablished by authority. The fulness of his authority is communicated to one, the Supreme Pontiff, the visible head of the church. From him, and from him alone, all others must receive authority. And hence the unity of the whole active church, unity of authori- ty, of action and life, and the proper hierarchical order. The passive church is established upon the bestowal of the supernatural nature and faculties and acts. The two are brought to- gether by the community of the same supernatural nature, faculties, and acts; and, by the dependence of origin, the second proceeding and being originated by the first. Both have one common life and action, but hierarchically exercised, the pas- sive being governed and directed by the one which originates it, and thus exhibiting a most perfect image of the Trinity.

We have only been commenting upon those words of the Theanthro- pos: "Holy Father, keep these in thy name whom thou hast given me, that they may be one, as we also are." Here we have the necessity of the church being modelled after the Trinity, the archetype of every- thing.

"As thou hast sent me into the world, I also have sent them into the world." The common nature of the active church, the mission and au- thority of the Theanthropos.

"And not for these only do I pray, but for all those who, through their words, shall believe in me." The continuation of that authority.

"Sanctify them in truth." The common nature of the passive church, the term of the supernatural moment.

"That they may be one, as thou Father in me and I in thee, that they may be one in us." The com- pletion of the inchoative society, brought about by the supernatural

element of union, and by the incorporation with the Theanthropos.

To complete the theory of the church, we have now to point out the characteristic marks which distinguish it from any counterfeit institution of men. These marks are four: unity, holiness, catholicity, and apostolicity.

Unity. What is the church, viewed in its essence, attributes, and interior organism? It is the Theanthropos annexing his infinite energy and his substantial presence to a sacramental element, both physical and personal, and through them first elevating human persons to a supernatural being, with its essence and faculties of supernatural intelligence and supernatural will in an incipient and inchoative state; secondly, through his sacramental, personal element proposing and expounding his *gnosis* to their supernatural intelligence; by a second sacramental moment elevating this supernatural essence and faculties to a determinate and definite growth: by the sacramental moment of his presence incorporating all elevated persons unto himself, and thus putting them in immediate contact with himself, and through him with the Trinity on one side and with all the cosmos in nature and personality on the other side, and thus affording their supernatural faculties proper objects on which they may feed, expand, be developed, and arrive at their ultimate perfection. Finally, by the personal sacramental element governing and directing all their exterior relations and communication to one social final end; and all this not in any particular spot or period of time, but in all space and in all time. From this it is evident that the church of Christ is *one* in force of the unity of the Theanthropos with the sacramental element; *one* in consequence of the interior unity of organism, both of the active and passive church; *one* in consequence of the unity of the supernatural being and faculties, the end of the church; *one* in force of the unity of the object of the supernatural intelligence; *one* in consequence of the unity of the object of the supernatural will—God and his cosmos, in their relations to each other; *one* in consequence of the real communion and intercourse between the members of the church; *one*, finally, in consequence of the oneness of the visible government of the church, all emanating from one invisible and one visible head.

The second distinctive mark of the church must be holiness. For the end of the church is to impart to human persons in time and space the term of the supernatural moment, together with its faculties, and especially the faculty and habit of supernatural intelligence and supernatural will or charity, in which, as we have demonstrated in the tenth article, the very essence of holiness consists. If the church, therefore, were deprived of this distinctive mark, she would fail in that very object for which she was instituted.

But it is to be remarked that not any degree of holiness would be sufficient to constitute a distinctive mark of the church, but a certain fulness of it is required in some of its members, for a twofold reason.

Like every moment of God's exterior action, she is subject to the law of variety by hierarchy. This involves the necessity of the church ranging between the lowest degree of sanctity to the very pinnacle of sublimest and loftiest exhibition of it; otherwise, those two laws could not be realized.

Secondly, an ordinary degree of holiness can easily be counterfeited. But none could for any length of time or any extension of space as-

sume a sanctity which soars far above the ordinary and common level, and which exhibits itself as such. *Nemo personam diu fert* could be applied in this case more than in any other.

The next distinctive mark is *catholicity* or *universality*. She is such not only because she contains all truth; not only because she embraces all the moments of God's action, as the finishing stroke of them all; but because she is intended for all time and all space.

Finally, the last mark is *apostolicity*. The first members of the hierarchy chosen by the Theanthropos to communicate as moral instruments the term of the sublimative moment, with the power and authority to transmit to others that very same dignity of being moral instruments, were the *apostles*. Therefore, that church alone can be the church of the Theanthropos which to this day and for ever can show that her own hierarchy are the legitimate successors of the apostles, by an uninterrupted communication. For we have said that the essence of the church is to be the Theanthropos acting in time and space, through the agency of the hierarchy and other sacraments. Now, suppose a hierarchy who cannot claim or make good their claim to be the legitimate successors of the first ones who composed it, who could not claim any communication or union with them, how could we suppose them to be those very instruments in whom and through whom the Theanthropos lives and acts?

Before we draw the consequence which follows from all we have said concerning the church, it is necessary to recapitulate in a few words all we have written in these articles.

We set out with the question of the infinite, and after refuting the pantheistic idea of the infinite, and showing that pantheism in its solution of the problem destroys it, we gave the Catholic idea of the infinite. Here another problem sprang up—multiplicity in the infinite. No being can be conceived endowed with pure, unalloyed unity. It must be multiple, under pain of being inconceivable. What is the multiplicity which can be admitted in the infinite? We demonstrated that the pantheistic solution which says that infinite becomes multiple by a necessary interior development, destroys both terms, the unity and the multiplicity. We proceeded to lay down the Catholic answer to the problem, and explained, as far as lay in our power, the mystery of the ever-blessed Trinity. The question next in order was the finite. And we showed the finite to be the effect of an absolutely free act of infinite power, free both to its creation at all and also with regard to the amount of perfection to be created; though we admitted and proved that it was befitting on the part of the Creator to effect the best possible manifestation of himself. Here we found ourselves in face of a duality which claimed reconciliation. How could the finite and the infinite be united together, so as to preserve whole and entire the two respective natures, and at the same time to effect the best possible manifestation of the infinite? We answered by laying down the Catholic dogma of the hypostatic union, which raised the finite to a hypostatic or personal union with the infinite, and elevated finite natures to the highest possible dignity. But as the hypostatic moment raised to a personal union only nature, and left out personality, another duality arose: how to unite human persons with the Theanthropos, and through him with God, and make them par-

takers as far as possible of the dignity and elevation of the nature hypostatically united to the *Word.* The sublimative moment answered the question. This moment, medium between the Theanthropos and substantial creation, by bestowing upon human persons a higher nature and faculties, enabled them to unite in close contact with the Theanthropos and through him with the Trinity. But what was the medium chosen to transmit the term of the sublimative moment to human persons in time and space? The Theanthropos himself, the essential mediator between God and the cosmos; and to that effect he united his infinite energy and his substantial presence to personal and physical instruments, and through them imparted to human persons in time and space the term of the sublimative moment; and thus the cycle of the procession of the cosmos from the infinite was perfected in its being and faculties, to begin a movement of return to the same infinite as its supreme end. The sacramental extension of the Theanthropos in time and space we have demonstrated to be the Catholic Church, and from its essence we have drawn her essential attributes of visibility, indefectibility, infallibility, and authority, and also its intrinsic marks of unity, holiness, catholicity, and apostolicity.

After this necessarily imperfect sketch of all our articles, we submit to the reader this necessary consequence—*the Roman Catholic Church is the only true church of God.*

First, because it is in the teaching of the Roman Catholic Church alone that the life of the intelligence is possible. We have shown throughout our articles that in every question which the human mind raises, there is no possible alternative—either embrace the Catholic solution, so coherent with reason; or the pantheistic solution, and the death of the intelligence. Now, when we speak of the Catholic solution, we mean of the solution which is given by the church whose head is the Bishop of Rome, for no other pretended Catholic Church gives all the true solutions.

Second, because it is the Roman Catholic Church alone which knows her own essence and attributes. All others are more or less ignorant of the essence and attributes necessary to the church of the Theanthropos.

Thirdly, it is to the Roman Catholic Church alone to which the essence, attributes, and marks which we have shown *à priori* to belong necessarily to the Church of Christ apply. Consequently, the Roman Catholic Church is the real cosmos of God in its perfection of being and faculties, and men have no possible alternative but to join it, to submit to its authority, under pain of the death of the intelligence, of being a creature out of joint with the whole system of God's works, of being in the impossibility of attaining their last end in palingenesia. The Roman Catholic Church or pantheism—all truth or no truth—death or life here and hereafter.

"Oisin, in heaven the praises swell
To God alone from Soul and Saint:—"
"Then, Patrick, I their deeds will tell
In a little whisper faint!

"Who says that Fionn his sentence waits
In some dark realm, the thrall of sin?
Fionn would have burst that kingdom's gates,
Or ruled himself therein!"

"Old man, for once thy chiefs forget"
(Thus oft the Saint his rage beguiled):
"Sing us thine own bright youth, while yet
A stripling, or a child."

"O Patrick, glad that time and dear!
It wrought no greatness, gained no gain,
Not less those things that thou wouldst hear
Thou shalt not seek in vain.

"My mother was a princess, turned
By magic to a milk-white doe:—
Such tale, a wondering child, I learned:
True was it? Who can know?'

"I know but this, that, yet a boy,
I raced beside her like the wind:
We heard the hunter's horn with joy
And left the pack behind.

"A strength was mine that knew no bound,
A witless strength that nothing planned:
When came the destined hour, I found
Some great deed in my hand.

"Forth from a cave I stept at Beigh:
O'er ivied cliffs the loose clouds rushed:-
With them I raced, and reached ere they
The loud seas sandhill-hushed.

"By Brandon's cliff an eagle brown
O'erhung our wave-borne coracle:
I hurled at him my lance, and down
Like falling stars he fell.

"On that green shore of Ardrakese
An untamed horse I made my slave,
And forced him far o'er heaving seas,
And reinless rode the wave.

"Methinks my brow I might have laid
Against a bull's, and there and then
Backward have pushed him up the glade,
And down the rocky glen!

"So ran my youth through dark and bright,
In deeds half jest. Their time is gone:
The glorious works of thoughtful might
For Oscar were, and Fionn.

"When met the hosts in mirth I fought:
My war-fields still with revel rang:
My sword with such a god was fraught
That, while it smote, it sang.

"My spear, unbidden, to my hand
Leaped, hawk-wise, for the battle's sake:
Forth launched, it flashed along the land
With music in its wake.

"A shield I bore so charged and stored
With rage and yearnings for the fight,
When foes drew near it shook, and roared
Like breakers in the night:

"Then only when the iron feast
Of war its hungry heart had stilled,
It murmured, like a whispering priest
Or frothing pail new-filled."

"Say, knew'st thou never fear or awe?"
Thus Patrick, and the Bard replied:
"Yea, once: for once a man I saw
Who—not in battle—died.

"I sang the things I loved—the fight—
The chance inspired that all decides—
That pause of death, when Fate and Flight
Drag back the battle tides;

The swords that blent their lightnings blue—
The midnight march—the city's sack—
The advancing ridge of spears that threw
The levelled sunrise back.

"And yet my harp could still the storm,
Redeem the babe from magic blight,
Restore to human heart and form
The unhappy spell-bound knight.

"And some could hear a sobbing hind
Among my chords; and some would swear
They heard that kiss of branch and wind
That lulled the wild-deer's lair!

"I sang not lies: where base men thronged,
I sat not, neither harped for gold:
My song no generous foeman wronged,
No woman's secret told.

"I sang among the sea-side flocks
When sunset flushed the bowery spray,
Or when the white moon scaled the rocks
And glared upon the bay.

"My stately music I rehearsed
On shadowing cliffs, when, far below,
In rolled the moon-necked wave, and burst,
And changed black shores to snow.

"But now I tread a darker brink:
Far down, unfriendlier waters moan:
And now of vanished times I think;
Now of that bourn unknown.

"I strike my harp; I make good cheer;
Yet scarce myself can catch its sound:
I see but shadows bending near
When feasters press around.

"Say, Patrick of the mystic lore,
Shall I, when this old head lies low,
My Oscar see, and Fionn, once more,
And run beside that Doe?"

expressions, *policy of labor*, *idea of justice*, are in daily use by the *Internationale*, and not in a sense particularly intended to tranquillize society. But let us go on.

But this form of government, this policy, how is its establishment to be brought about? Why, by universal suffrage, that foremost of rights, that sole and sovereign tribunal, that army of peace. And how is universal suffrage to be persuaded and drawn to the desired end? By giving to public opinion, through *democratic intermingling*, proofs of the *morality*, the *political value*, and the *adaptation* for *business* of the republican party; by demonstrating that the *republican government is the most liberal of all forms of government*, etc.

Really, sir, all this must have appeared admirable to your audience, and, if your republic is of that sort, many of our most upright conservatives will tell you: Let us clasp hands, for that is the very republic which the National Assembly, acting with and through M. Thiers, is endeavoring to realize at the cost of so much self-denial, disinterestedness, and honesty.

But let us be frank.

You have no right to claim that your republic answers this description. Your sweetness is purely oratorical and Platonic; for two sentences of your address reveal you and show who you are.

"No one," you say, "must ever give his opinion except as a means of adding to the general good; and each one must convert his mind into, as it were, a memorandum tablet for himself, in which he puts down, with a view of obtaining them, the institutions which the people have a right to expect from the democratic republic."

If a priest had uttered these words, which seem more befitting the lips of an Italian than of a Frenchman, he would be charged with hypocrisy and mental reservation. It would be said that he is playing saint; that he is concealing his game by not revealing his innermost thoughts. But everything is forbidden to the cleric, while to the radical any and everything is allowed. This everybody knows. I confine myself to merely quoting this first sentence, without further dwelling on its merits; and I pass on to a second one, which gives me a right, not only to suspect you, as in the case of the former one, but to make a direct attack on you; its tenor is as follows:

"What I have done in the past is the true pledge of what I will do in the future, toward definitively establishing the republic."

It is here, sir, that I must challenge you.

In the first place, I have to express my amazement that, having to account to your country, under so grave a responsibility, and for misdeeds for which you might have been rendered far more seriously liable, you can be so ready to accuse others and to glorify yourself, that you go so far as to dare to say. "What I have done in the past is the true pledge of what I will do in the future."

What have you done in the past?

You were a young lawyer, and were turned all of a sudden, and in consequence of a tumultuous lawsuit, into a political character. The audacity of your revolutionary opinions enabled you to become a candidate for the Corps Législatif, and in the next place to take your seat as a deputy by the side of your friends Blanqui, Raspail, and Rochefort.

On the 4th September, you seized upon the governing power, and, without consulting with your colleagues, you assigned to yourself the Ministry

of the Interior. Did you, as soon as you got into the ministry, extend to all good citizens those arms which you seem now to be opening so widely? Not at all. In the Hôtel de Ville,* you installed such men as Etienne Arago, Ferry, and Rochefort; in the *mairie*, such characters as Delescluze, Mottu, Bonvalet, Clémenceau; in the *préfectures*, such as Duportal, Engelhard, and Jacobins of all sorts. You filled these places with your friends—your friends only, and these of the most excitable kind. Afterward, when your colleagues, in order to get rid of you, were so signally weak as to give you the entire realm to operate upon, when, through a fortunate contingency, you had suddenly entrusted to you that magnificent part which, to a heroic and truly patriotic heart, would have been unsurpassable, what did you do? You sought rather to force the republic—your republic—on the country than to save France. It is well for you to talk about universal suffrage. You have treated it as naught. By a first decree, you broke up the *conseils-généraux*, and did not re-establish them. By a second decree, you adjourned the elections. By a third decree, you abridged the legal qualifications for election. What have you, sole ruler everywhere obeyed, done with the treasure, the men, and the blood of her children which the nation lavished upon you? Was it not a republican who called your fatal rule the *dictatorship of incompetency!*

Though only three months in power, you had become almost a greater burden upon us than the late Imperial Government; and when you assert that the National Assembly has completed its work, which was to put an end to the war, you forget that the Assembly had received from France not one mandate only, but three. The Assembly had, and has still, given it the charge to rid our country of the Prussians, of demagoguism, and of yourself.

After the dreadful catastrophes in which the Empire sank to ruin, do you know, sir, what proved to be France's greatest misfortune?

It was that just then, in that so terrible a crisis, you stood the absolute master of France. I make no reference to the two aged men who were at Tours with you. It was from you, a lawyer, that our generals received their orders; it was you who dictated plans for campaigns; it was you who scattered our forces, and blindly hurled our armies right and left, multiplying your lying bulletins, and at the same time and to the same extent as our reverses.—But I must turn away my thoughts from those disasters, as also from the remembrance of those poor soldiers, without clothes, without shoes, without food, without ammunition! How great an organizer, my dear sir, you proved yourself to be! How fortunate you turned out to have been in the selection of your contractors for supplies!

Nevertheless, the nation, ever generous, might have measurably accepted, as an offset to this, your personal activity, and your efforts, although unsuccessful; it had given you credit for having withdrawn yourself momentarily; but you reappeared too quickly, only a short time before the day when the Commune of Paris was putting forward your friends, your lieutenants, your teachers, or your disciples, such as Delescluze and Millière, Rigault and Ranc, Cavalier and Mottu, all those fellows who have made themselves as

* The Hôtel de Ville is the seat of head municipal authority for the city of Paris; the *mairies* are the subordinate seats of local authority for the arrondissements into which Paris is divided.
TRANSLATOR.

ignominious and ridiculous as possible, some of whom are still around you; in fine, all that party which you have never, even to the extent of a single word, disavowed, and the members of which you called upon to give evidence of their morality, their political worth, and their aptitude for the business of government! That evidence has been given, and really, sir, you rely too much on the frivolity, the folly, or the credulity of the public. You preach to it about a debonair republic, but that public has not forgotten the grotesque, ruinous republic, accompanied with bloodshed, which during six months was fastened on France.

You have avoided with prudent care to call your republic *social* as well as *democratic;* and why? In order to enjoy the happiness of a fleeting hour of dictatorship, I suppose it is worth your while to run the risk of more calamities. Alas! unfortunate land, fated to be thus perpetually the dupe and the victim of most guilty ambition!

No, in spite of all that you may say or leave unsaid, your promises are contradicted by our memories. We need, in order to be persuaded, something else than sonorous words. It is true that, in one point only, you depart from the vague style of your programme. You declare that you seek, above all things, to lay the foundation of the future of democracy on a reform, to wit, in education; and with this idea, you proclaim that you and your friends are alone capable, alone worthy, to bring up youth. You seek to turn out *just*, *free*, strong-minded and able men. This is very fine. But how? By means of a national education given after a *truly modern* and *truly democratic* manner.

And here you dare to affirm that the church and preceding governments have done nothing for public instruction, that they view every person who knows how to read as an enemy, and you claim to reform the world with your schools.

Allow me to reply that in this matter you are taking advantage of ignorance instead of combating it. For it argues a singular reliance on the ignorance of an audience to attempt to make it swallow at one and the same time, and in the same sentence, calumny and nonsense.

The governments that have ruled France for the past sixty years have in that period established more than 50,000 schools, and have trebled the appropriations for primary instruction.

As to the church, she is founded on two things: a book, the Gospel, and a divine command, to wit: *Ite et docete*, Go and teach. This sentence, which has become commonplace, "*Ignorance is the source of all evils*," was uttered by a pope, and he added besides, "*particularly among the working-classes.*" These were the words of Benedict XIV., uttered more than a century before you were born.

The calumny is consequently shown to be dull-witted, and the nonsense still more so. It would seem that you also, M. Gambetta, hope, by means of schools, to stamp your effigy on future generations, just as if they were coin. But men versed in the subject know, and experience shows, that such a design is absurd, and may become a horrid tyranny. The instruction, whether primary or secondary, even with as much as you can add to it of the higher sciences, such as algebra, chemistry, etc., will not produce morals; and the parties who flatter the teachers expect, after all, much more from their influence on voters than from their action on their scholars.

buld you like to know what, e all things, exerts an influon the family and on socie- It is education, whether it loral or immoral, religious or stic. And do you know why I ust your reform? Because it e neither a moral nor a religious

sober truth, what sort of tuiis a *really modern*, a *really de-tic*, one? Is there such a thing odern geometry? a democraammar? moral teachings of regrowth, and a geography not ablished? All these big words but windy oratory, empty and re, which affords no meaning mind when it attempts to ana-

vertheless, after having thrown ese sentences to your hearers, o on and recite the mottoes of rty, the watchword of the day. a pity that you left out tithes rced service under feudal law. ay tuition is to be *free of cost*— s equivalent to adding thirty ns to our budget of expendibut what does that signify? You managed to spend a large sum s. The poor will pay for the but the lower classes will dehemselves with the belief that re not paying at all, and that re indebted to you for the beon. Tuition is besides to be *sory*. Well, let it be so, if you vise some adequate sanction for ntemplated enactments, a reprotection for the liberty of s, and, in particular, a reliable tee for the teachers, so that n feel sure enough of them to e, without practising the most able of all tyranny, to compel s to entrust to them, what they nost in this world, their chil-But then, minor details do op you. To conclude, the tuition is to be by *laymen*—and now the cat is let out of the bag.

It is an easy matter to attack and calumniate absent priests, religious who make no defence. To do so is neither fair nor generous, but much popularity is to be got in that way in your party, and the hard flings at the church will offset the sweetness displayed toward other persons. So let us strike hard on this spot. The church is henceforward to be separated from the state—that is not enough, the church is besides to be separated from the school, and the school from all religion.

You have said, sir, that your republic would be a liberal one. If you accordingly begin by excluding from the common right to teach an entire class of citizens and of women, solely because their religious belief is not the same as yours, do not call yourself liberal, and do not charge the church with being intolerant, or else be logically consistent, and separate the *state from the school*. For the state, in this connection, means the budget; that is to say, the moneys which are got of all of us by taxation. You cannot, without being tyrannical, compel families to send their children to the school of the state. Lay aside these high-sounding phrases, and call things by their right names. By the church you mean *us*. By the state you mean yourself. To deprive us and our doctrines of our money, in order to bestow it on yourself and your doctrines—that is what is called separating the church from the state. But I feel pretty easy as to the choice families will make when I learn from you what the programme of this teaching is to be.

The programme is this: "It is an extensive and varied one, so that, instead of mutilated learning, man will have dealt out to him *entire truth*,

so that *nothing which the human mind can grasp* will be concealed from him." *De omni re scibili!* Well, that is wonderful indeed! No doubt you will have the power to create minds capable of taking in this encyclopædia! You are equal to so many undertakings! So that which you have in view, gratuitous, compulsory, lay tuition, integral besides for every one and complete to an impossible degree—this is the formula of socialism, and is also the formula of absurdity.

"In the schools," you add, "children will be taught scientific *truth* in its rigor and *its majestic simplicity*," and by this process "you will have reared citizens *whose principles will rest on the same bases on which our entire society is founded.*"

What do you mean by these big words? What are these *principles?* what are these *bases?* Whether it be that *those principles rest on these bases*, or that these bases are fast to those principles, how much of this will you teach to children from the ages of seven to eleven years? I call upon you to give me plainly the text of the *programme of science* which our worthy village teachers, who are to seek to instil into children of from seven to eleven years the sense of duty and sacrifice, will have to substitute for the Ten Commandments of God, and for the sublime and popular Gospel of our Lord Jesus Christ.

What is it, pray, sir, that renders you so ungrateful towards the voters of Paris or of Lyons, who nearly all have been educated by the Brothers, so severe on the priests, who perhaps have done something for your early education, and so unjust towards the church?

It is my duty to insist on this point, and to protest against your calumnies.

What! though the clergy of France have devoted themselves, as they have done, to the service of our soldiers and our prisoners, and though when, only four months ago, our chaplains and our Brothers of the Christian Schools had served and died on the battle-fields, and though all our female religious have devoted themselves to the care of our ambulances, you have the heart to come and tell us that we are no longer French! And it is immediately after the massacre of the hostages that you repeat these calumnies, and represent us as constituting for modern society "the greatest peril." Such are your very words, and you hold us up anew to the blind fury of our enemies.

And you direct your calumnies not against us alone, but, besides, against the Pope. Ah! I admit, the horrors, treachery, meanness, and falsehood by which he has been surrounded during the past twenty-five years have not brought him to look with favor on the charms of that sham liberty which you promise him, and he may well fail to admire that Garibaldi for whose sake you, perhaps, sacrificed our army of the East. But in the Encyclical which your hearers have never read, the Pope has not condemned the various forms of government as they exist in the laws of various nations. He has condemned liberty unrestrained, rights without countervailing duties, and societies that know not God. As to the family and property, sir, is it becoming *your* friends to style themselves their virtuous defenders?

But what is singular in this pell-mell gathering of confused and incoherent ideas, is your alleged motive for denying to French priests the right to teach which belongs to them in common with all their fellow-countrymen: "When you have appealed to the energies of men reared

:h teachers, when you seek to
: in them ideas of sacrifice, of
edness, of patriotism, you will
hat you have to deal with an
:ulated, debilitated class of
And the reason you assign
e emasculation and debilitation
s class reared under our care is
ıore singular: it is because *we*
them to believe in Providence,
ecause teachers that believe in
lence *are only fit to emasculate*
'ebilitate the human race. At
oint, sir, you set "the doctrine
accustoms the mind to the
f a Providence" in opposition
:volution, which teaches the au-
y and responsibility of the will
ın and free agency." But, sir,
things are not incompatible
ne another. Both are taught by
ian doctrine, and, by setting
in opposition as you do, you
that you neither understand
:lf nor the matters of which
re treating.

: you, who do not believe in
lence, and who are consequent-
ther emasculated nor debilitat-
ı you know of any other belief
can better teach mankind to
with life and brave death?
ıave this year ordered many
o rush to destruction. Would
ave dared to recommend our
rs to go forth to meet death,
ng God? And do you believe
the souls of the Pontifical
'es, and of the Breton *francs-*
r, were enervated by their faith
ovidence?

be cautious. In order that your
ıing be consistent, a belief in
lence appertains not to priests
but to whoever professes the
ian faith; consequently, if
; are to be banished from the
ls because they teach that emas-
ng dogma, then all Christians
be kept out as well, and hence-forward you must exact from every teacher and every professor not to believe in Providence.

Avow, sir, that seldom have calumnies and absurdities been mixed up together with greater facility than you have done in these words of yours.

Nevertheless, you manage to go on still further, and you attempt to create a division between the *higher clergy*, whom you traduce, and those whom you call the lower clergy, whom you flatter, by endeavoring to excite them to envy. You labor in vain, sir; and, besides, I do not recognize any lower clergy as such. The rank of the priesthood is the highest to which we can attain; no bishop, not even the Pope himself, has a sacerdotal character different from that of the most humble priest. All ecclesiastical dignities are, in one sense, beneath the title of priest, which leads to the highest offices and dignities of the church. So that, in this regard, it may be said that no institution is so democratic as the church. Sprung from the people as we nearly all of us are, educated together and fed together on the words of him who died for the people, we will suffer ourselves to be neither divided nor deceived.

Our fraternity is of the right sort. Our God is the true God, and you are without any. Be sincere, sir: come out of this mere talk, and answer me plainly and without oratorical precaution, whether, yes or no, *the free thought* in which you are a believer, and *human science, which, according to you, has nothing to equal it,* recognize the existence of a personal and living God? Candor leaves you no alternative but to reply. Either dare to declare to your friends that you do believe, or dare to proclaim to our land that you do not believe, in God.

If indeed your sham science de-

nies God, I pity you, sir; but you must admit that it hardly becomes you to talk about religion, and to endeavor to beguile and divide priests who have consecrated their lives to him. You assert that, if they dared to disclose their convictions, they would own themselves democrats. Do you know what our village priests would tell you if they were to make disclosures to you? They would inform you that in every hamlet is to be found a handful of petty rhetoricians, tavern orators, fellows who lead municipal councils, who drive away the Christian Brothers and Sisters of Charity, and do their best to deprive the curate of the small pittance without which he cannot subsist, who forbid teachers to take children to Mass, refuse to have churches repaired that need it most, recommend mutual-guarantee-association marriages and burials, and know no better way of serving a republic than by hating priests and by persevering in a low and silly infidelity. Now, in every village these very rhetoricians are your friends.

It is with their assistance that you contemplate establishing that education, "national and truly modern," in which, in order to teach children "their duties as citizens, to excite in them ideas of sacrifice, of devotion to country, to make out of them an unemasculated race," you will have not only to avoid speaking to them of God and of *Providence*, but besides to combat and root out of their minds the idea of *Providence*, and, in fine, to force upon French youth a *teaching without religion*, and a moral instruction without God.

Well, would you have me tell you what such education will turn out for you? Instead of rearing men, it will give us monsters, and a learned barbarism, armed with abundant means of destruction, barbarism in the heart and in manner—in a word, ju what we have witnessed during t reign of the Commune; young m and girls from eighteen to twent three years old ruling Paris and d stroying it by incendiarism; and, it is after having witnessed su scenes of horror and the lessons wh they teach, that you have nevertl less ventured to deliver the addr to which I am replying, and your au ence went so far as to applaud yo words!

In my view, this latter fact is indication of the disorder in which this very moment we still are. I the end of France's afflictions is n yet!

But I have said enough, sir. I h sought, as the only reply to your rangue, to put facts in opposition words. I have sought, while reply to you, to defend the church; an think I have at the same time fended public peace. In theory against this or that governm neither my faith, my reason, nor patriotism would raise great ob tions, were it not that I have s your party at work, and that sight is still filled with those som scenes, and my memory with recollection of your deeds. In v do you try to cover them over v clever words and honeyed insinuati My knowledge of the preacher sp the effect of the sermon on And my recollection of the whi dictator puts me on my guard aga the impressiveness of the candid who is aspiring not to establish li ty, as he pretends, but to destroy ligion and to get into power. are not an apostle, you are a pre der. *The republic is I!*—that is y programme and the sole object of y discourse. Well! depend upon France has a republican governm now, the need of a change to anot even though accompanied with

ntage of having you for its dent, is not at all felt.
ease accept, sir, with the expres- of my regret to be compelled to combat you, that of the senti- ments of respect which, as your colleague, I have the honor to offer you.

✠ FELIX, Bishop of Orleans,
Deputy at the National Assembly for the Department of Loiret.

NEW PUBLICATIONS.

ARIANS OF THE FOURTH CENTURY. John Henry Newman, formerly Fel- of Oriel College. Third Edition. ndon: E. Lumley. For sale by The holic Publication Society, New rk.

is work was written in 1832, saw the light in the following The author had already made nark in Oxford as a keen and thinker, as a scholar of wide accurate erudition, and as a and vigorous writer. He was minent leader in the Oxford or yite movement, and was, as we from his *Apologia*, a stanch ican. The work, looked for at ime with interest, was received ly equal to the high reputation e author. Its singularly lucid ment of a subject involving the abstruse questions of ancient ogical controversy, as well as tricate and shifting phases of y eventful period of ecclesias- history, was a valuable addi- to English theological litera- The author had evidently n his soul into the work. history he was treating seemed m to present many points of lelism to their own living strug- n the Anglican Church. The ceans and kindred Arian sects representatives of the Socini- which had reached even the st dignities, and the rational- and humanitarianism which beginning to spread among lergy and the laity of its fold. Semiarians with their compromises and varying phrases and formulas of faith, which might mean much or little, as each one chose to understand them, were equally good representatives of the modern Broad Church compromisers. The Eusebians, ever seeking to bask in the imperial favor, and to guide or to wield the civil power for their own interests, were the type of the modern Erastians, who look for nothing higher than an act of parliament or an exercise of the royal supremacy. And the continual assumption of ecclesiastical authority by the Arian and Semiarian emperors in the fourth century, and their often tyrannical action towards faithful bishops and clergy, who would not give to Cæsar the things that are God's, made the Puseyites think of the enthralled condition of their "own branch," in which the sovereign claims and exercises the exclusive right of appointing the archbishops and bishops, and of deciding finally all questions of doctrine, discipline, or church law, and without whose sanction convocations cannot meet, nor synods be held or pass decrees. In the fourth century, the church, though long and sorely pressed, ever struggled on, and finally succeeded in vindicating her own liberty, and casting the heresy out of her fold. It was hoped that the example might teach them how their English Church might similarly struggle and eventually triumph.

A few years sufficed to convince

Dr. Newman that such hopes were futile, and that his position was false. He and others sought refuge in the fold of the true church. Meanwhile, within the Anglican Church, the successive decisions in the Gorham case and in several other cases that have since come before the Privy Council, show that the evils he lamented and feared have increased in strength, while the power of opposing them has grown gradually weaker.

The present is a third edition of the work under the care of the author; we can scarcely say, revised by him. German professors, in publishing successive editions of their works on any subject to which they devote continuous study, have no scruple in retracting, cancelling, or directly confuting what they had previously published, as often as they may be led to change their opinions on material points, so much so that you must be sure you have the right edition before you can quote it. We turned to this edition to see if Dr. Newman had followed such a course. He has not. With him, *litera scripta manet*. The book is the same now as when it first appeared. In a few instances he changes the structure of a sentence, that his thought may stand out more clearly. He has added a few more references in the foot-notes, scrupulously indicating such additions by enclosing them in brackets. He has enlarged the table of contents at the beginning and the chronological table at the end of the volume. No change has been made affecting the opinions, sentiments, or speculations of the original edition. There are expressions which now, of course, displease him as a Catholic; but he lets them hold their place. He has cast out only two sentences, as needlessly put in originally, and even these he has, in signal humility, pilloried, as it were, in a page by themselves at the end of the appendix. This appendix, at the close of the volume, is mostly made up of extracts from subsequent works of his own, and are intended to throw further light on several points touched on in the original work.

The volume presents an admirable critical, theological, and historical summary of the whole Arian controversy in the fourth century, and was a turning-point in English Protestant literature on the subject. Dr. Newman was the first to establish what has since been generally accepted, that Arianism was connected, historically and intellectually, with the Judaic Aristotelic schools of thought prevailing at Antioch and through Asia Minor, and not, as had been previously held by many, with the Platonic schools of Alexandria.

The work deserves and will amply reward a careful study. The Catholic reader will, of course, find himself in something of a Protestant atmosphere. The authority and action of the Roman Pontiffs is scarcely glanced at. Twice or thrice reference is made to the important support which the Roman See gave to St. Athanasius, and to the determined resistance which honorably distinguishes the primitive Roman Church in its dealing with heresy, and the ground is taken that the acute and sophistical training of the Eastern intellects led them to indulge in abstruse distinctions and discussions which the calmer and more practical minds of the Western Church entered into with difficulty, and could scarcely express in their Latin tongue, so much less pliable than the Greek. Theologically speaking, as well as historically, the controversy in the fourth century was Eastern, rather than Latin. Still, we are sure that, were Dr. Newman to write afresh this history, now that he is a Catholic, the important part acted by the Roman Pontiffs would be more strongly set forth. Writing as a Protestant, he was sufficiently emphatic on the case of Liberius—so much so that he has added a foot-note to say that there is a differ-

ence among writers which was the Sirmian formula that Liberius subscribed; and the appendix further shows that there is also a discrepancy as to the number and the chronological order of the various formulas, and that in some cases alterations and additions were subsequently made in the original text. It might also be added that there are grave reasons for doubting the fact of any such subscription by Liberius, inasmuch as the charge seems to have been first put forth by heated controversialists long after his death, and is scarcely reconcilable with the undoubted facts of his life after the date of the alleged subscription.

Here and there the Catholic will meet phrases implying or stating some special Anglican view or Protestant principle. To all these Dr. Newman's present position is a practical and sufficient refutation. In the clear and lucid arrangement of the topics, in accurate and subtile tracing of the various and varying forms of the Arian heresy, and in the vivid portraying of that greatest and most earnest battle in the early life of the church, the work is worthy of Dr. Newman, and claims a place in every theological library.

MEMOIR OF ULRIC DAHLGREN. By his Father, Rear-Admiral Dahlgren. Philadelphia: J. B. Lippincott & Co. 1872.

Though war, in whatever light we may view it, cannot but be considered a national calamity, it must be admitted that it has a tendency to generate certain mental and social qualities which are unknown or of slow growth in civil life. Personal courage, disinterested friendship, and patient self-sacrifice, no mean qualities in themselves, are doubly valuable when enlisted in the cause of one's country on the side of law and justice, and hence we consider the soldier, no matter what may be his rank, who bravely and intelligently risks and loses his life in defence of his nation's integrity, deserving of a high meed of praise. Young Dahlgren, the subject of this memoir, was one of this character, and though he had scarcely attained the years of manhood at the time of his death, in his attempt to liberate the Union prisoners in Richmond, in 1864, he had risen from civil life to the rank of colonel, and had repeatedly distinguished himself for his skill, tact, and heroism. The account of his short but eventful career was written by his father, the late Admiral Dahlgren, and is now published under the auspices of his stepmother, the gifted widow of that naval hero. It is very minute in details, and composed with a richness of coloring and a warmth of affection such as might be anticipated of a fond and gallant father in describing the deeds of a son in every way worthy of him. During his short military career, Colonel Dahlgren made many friends, some of whom survive him, who will be glad to be put in possession of the particulars of his brilliant and edifying career.

THE INTERNATIONALE—COMMUNISM. A Lecture by Rev. F. P. Garesche, S.J., of St. Louis University. St. Louis: P. Fox. 1872.

This is a lecture both logical and eloquent. The learned Jesuit traces Communism to Protestantism through materialism and false civilization. He shows its horrid and dangerous nature, and administers a well-merited castigation to that arch-agitator and firebrand of mischief, Wendell Phillips, who has made himself its apologist. All persons ought to read this, and especially those who pretend to call themselves Catholics, and yet, by joining Masonic or other condemned societies, have renounced their allegiance to the church and become accomplices in the conspiracy against religion and society. Every good Catholic who reads it will have his horror deepened against this conspiracy in all its forms, and will learn what estimate is to be placed on those who seek to palliate and extenuate doc-

trines and acts which have been condemned by the Holy See.

LENTEN SERMONS. By Paul Segneri, of the Society of Jesus. Vol. I. 12mo, pp. 361. New York: The Catholic Publication House, 9 Warren St.

This is a translation of a portion of the celebrated *Quaresimale*, or course of forty sermons for Lent, of Father Paul Segneri, S.J., who was one of the most remarkable missionaries that the church has produced, and also a man of great sanctity and austerity of life. These discourses are models of eloquence, and lose but little of their original force by the translation, which is a very good one. They are fourteen in number; but it is intended that the remaining ones shall be published, should the present volume meet with sufficient encouragement. They are admirable examples of what sermons for Lent, or for a mission, should be, and will be of great assistance to clergymen. They are now for the first time made easily accessible to the American public. The volume is of a convenient size, and well printed, and such as we can in every way commend to the attention of our readers.

THE SPOUSE OF CHRIST: Her Privileges and Her Duties. Vol. I. By the author of *St. Francis and the Franciscans*, etc., etc. Boston: Patrick Donahoe. 1872.

This is a volume of spiritual conferences or reading, specially intended for female religious. The piety and talent of its authoress are well known to the Catholic world. The present work has the *imprimatur* of the Bishop of Kerry, accompanied by a handsome tribute to the writer.

THE VESSELS OF THE SANCTUARY: A Tale of Normandy.—THE INHERITANCE. New York: D. & J. Sadlier & Co. 1872.

Two charming little stories, translated from the French. We can heartily recommend them as affording pleasant and instructive reading for children.

"The Catholic Publication So ty" has just published in *Tract f* the *Pastoral Letter* of the Archb ops and Bishops of Ireland on School Question. The price of document is $3 00 per 100 cop The same Society will also pub in pamphlet form *Several Calum Refuted, or Executive Document* 37. This will also be sold at $3 00 100. No less than 100 copies either of these pamphlets will sold at any one time.

"The Catholic Publication So ty" has just issued a list of r books to be published by the So ty this spring. It comprises teen books altogether. These a *Lenten Lectures*, by Father Segne *The Liquefaction of the Blood of Januarius; Sermons on Ecclesiasti Subjects*, Vols. II. and III., by Arch shop Manning; *French Eggs in English Basket; Little Pierre, Pedlar of Alsace*, illustrated by twe ty-seven first class woodcuts; *Ma gie's Rosary; Constance Sherwood*, Lady Fullerton, illustrated; *T House of Yorke*, with illustration *The Eighth Series of Sunday-Sch Libraries*, illustrated; *The Life a Letters of St. Francis Xavier*, by Re H. J. Coleridge, S.J.; *Madame Chantal and Her Family; St. Je and his Correspondents; Biblio Catholica Americana*, by Rev. J. Finotti—this book is published subscription; and *The Men and W men of the Protestant Reformatio England*. All these books, as so as ready, will be announced in *Literary Bulletin*, as well as all ot new Catholic books published this country or in England.

Mr. P. O'Shea, New York, nounces as in press, *Lectures on Church*, by Rev. D. W. Merrick, of St. Francis Xavier's Church, N York.

Received: *Landreth's Rural R ter and Almanac*—1872. Publis for gratuitious distribution. D Landreth & Son, 21 South Sixth Philadelphia, Pa.

Lightning Source UK Ltd.
Milton Keynes UK
UKHW021109160119
335572UK00008B/279/P

9 780267 002481